INTERNATIONAL ACCLAIM FOR THE BERLITZ COMPLETE
GUIDE TO CRUISING AND CRUISE SHIPS

"One way to find the right cruise is to get a copy of Berlitz...which rates all the cruise ships in the world, the facilities they offer and the kind of passengers you can expect to meet."

International Herald Tribune

"...helps you pick a ship that most closely meets your needs."

The Travel Agent, New York

"...indispensable for choosing a ship the first time, or for experienced cruisers wanting to try a new ship."

Tourist Echo, Paris

"...a variety of knowledgeable advice and opinion."

Chicago Sun-Times

"Only once in many years does one find a book so very well done."

The Travel Store, Los Gatos, CA

"...informative about all aspects of cruising...sensible and comprehensive."

Sunday Telegraph, London

"...required reading when selecting a cruise ship."

Travel & Enjoyment, Hamburg

"...the do's and don'ts of taking a cruise."

The Houston Post

"...includes simply everything you ever wanted to know about...cruise ships."

Knight-Ridder Newspapers

"...extensively describes ships in a chart format and evaluates oceangoing vessels, giving star ratings and numerical scores to each."

Chicago Tribune

STOP PRESS

The very nature of a book such as this, which contains so much factual information, is always subject to change, just as the cruise industry changes constantly. It was up to date and as accurate as possible up to July 1995, when this book was completed, but last minute changes received up to the end of August 1995 are noted below.

◤ The ship shown as *Regent Calypso* is known to the German-speaking market as simply *Calypso*. Although shown in the Regency Cruises brochure, this is only for selected sailings. The ship is under a five-year charter to Transocean Tours of Bremen, Germany.

◤ Dolphin Cruise Lines' *Dolphin* will operate two-day Bahamas cruises year-round, from Port Canaveral, starting January 1, 1996 (the ship has been sold to the Kosmas Group, but is still operated by Dolphin Cruise Lines). Additionally, the company's *OceanBreeze* will operate three- and four-day Bahamas cruises from Miami, starting May 3, 1996.

◤ Epirotiki Cruise Line and Sun Line Cruises merged in August 1995. Sun Line Cruises' ships now include *Odysseus*, *Stella Oceanis* and *Stella Solaris*. Epirotiki Cruise Line's ships now include *Olympic*, *Orpheus* and *Triton*. Royal Olympic Cruises' ships include *Argonaut*, *Jason*, *Neptune* and *Stella Maris*. The *World Renaissance* has been sold to interests in Asia.

◤ Swan Hellenic Cruises will change ships in 1996, from *Orpheus*, which the company has used for 21 years, to *Minerva*, a slightly larger ex-Russian former reconnaissance vessel with an ice-hardened hull.

◤ Louis Cruise Lines purchased *Sea Prince* (ex-*Ocean Princess*) from Sunshine Cruise Line in August 1995. The ship has been renamed *Princesa Oceanica*, and will operate short cruises to Egypt and Israel from Cyprus, commencing April 1996.

◤ Please note that correspondence with the author is *no longer possible* due to his constant world-wide travel, inspection, evaluation and consultation schedule. The author travels aboard the world's cruise ships for more than nine months of each year. Further, note that absolutely *no* correspondence will be entered into regarding the ship ratings and evaluations. Anyone wishing to inform the author of any serious mistakes or major errors not caught before press time (please remember this book was completed in July, 1995), should do so in writing, to the author, at Berlitz Publishing Company Ltd., Berlitz House, Peterley Road, Oxford OX4 2TX, England.

THE NEXT EDITION OF THIS BOOK WILL BE PUBLISHED IN SEPTEMBER 1996

All evaluations of cruise ships in this book were made without bias, partiality, or prejudice. In almost all instances the ship has been visited recently by the author in order to update earlier ratings or assess current status. Much of the information contained in the profiles in Part Three was supplied and checked by the cruise lines and shipowners themselves. Any errors should be addressed directly to:

Douglas Ward, c/o Berlitz Publishing Co. Ltd., Berlitz House, Peterley Road, Oxford OX4 2TX, U.K.

BERLITZ®

1996 Complete Guide to

CRUISING

and Cruise Ships

by

DOUGLAS WARD

President
The Maritime Evaluations Group (MEG)

Berlitz Publishing Company Inc.
New York, New York

Berlitz Publishing Company Ltd
Oxford, England

ACKNOWLEDGEMENTS

The ship silhouettes and cabin layouts were drawn
by Oxford Illustrators.

The black and white photographs were kindly
supplied by the cruise lines concerned.

Photograph on p. 213 supplied by the author.

1996 Edition

PUBLISHER'S NOTE

The Maritime Evaluations Group (MEG) has
evaluated cruise ships since 1980, issuing
annual reports on the world's cruise fleet.
All professional opinions and ratings are
strictly those of the author and not of the
publisher, Berlitz, which makes this survey
available in bookstores.

ISBN 2-8315-5080-7

Printed in the United States of America

Contents

Contents

Who Goes Where?

With over 500 destinations to choose from, today's cruise ships do indeed roam all over the world. For the sake of simplicity, some of the major cruise areas are grouped together on the following pages, together with the names of the companies and, in most cases, the ships that will take you there.

Note that large cruise lines that operate several ships tend to switch ships to operate certain itineraries from year to year, and the names of the ships used may not be those listed here. When compiled, the list was as accurate as it was possible to make it, given that many companies had not released their 1996 itineraries and ships.

Note also that occasionally a ship will appear under different operating companies in the same section. This is because the ship is under different charters for periods during the same year or season. As this book is sold on a global scale, I have tried to list the more obscure ships and the operating companies that are known in several countries rather than in one localized market only.

BAHAMAS: YEAR-ROUND SHIPS (3/4 DAYS)

Carnival Cruise Lines	*Ecstasy* (a)
Dolphin Cruise Line	*Dolphin IV* (a)
Majesty Cruise Line (*)	*Royal Majesty* (a)
Norwegian Cruise Line	*Leeward* (a)
Premier Cruise Lines	*Star/Ship Atlantic* (b)
Royal Caribbean Cruises	*Nordic Empress* (a)
Royal Venture Cruise Line	*Sea Venture* (c)

Key
(*) winter season only
(a) sails from Miami
(b) sails from Port Canaveral
(c) sails from Ft. Lauderdale

BERMUDA (SUMMER)

Only the five ships that have long-term Bermuda government contracts for weekly summer season cruises to Bermuda are listed here, although many other ships operate cruises that include Bermuda infrequently.

Celebrity Cruises	*Meridian* (c) *Zenith* (a)
Majesty Cruise Line	*Royal Majesty* (b)
Norwegian Cruise Line	*Dreamward* (a)
Royal Caribbean Cruises	*Song of America* (a)

Key
(a) sails from New York
(b) sails from Boston
(c) sails from several U.S. east coast ports

EASTERN CANADA/NEW ENGLAND

CTC Cruise Lines	*Southern Cross*
Clipper Cruise Line	*Nantucket Clipper*
Cunard Royal Viking	*Royal Viking Sun* *Vistafjord*
Hapag-Lloyd Cruises	*Europa*
Princess Cruises	*Royal Princess*
Regency Cruises	*Regent Sun*
Royal Cruise Line	*Royal Odyssey*
Seabourn Cruise Line	*Seabourn Spirit*

CARIBBEAN

Note that there are several more ships than those listed here that visit the Caribbean infrequently, but their schedules are seldom known far enough in advance to be included here.

Carnival Cruise Lines	*Carnival Destiny** *Celebration** *Fascination** *Festivale** *Holiday** *Imagination** *Inspiration** *Sensation**
Celebrity Cruises	*Century**
Club Med Cruises	*Club Med I*
Compagnie des Isles du Ponant	*Le Ponant*
Costa Cruises	*CostaAllegra* *CostaClassica* *CostaRomantica* *CostaVictoria*
Cunard Crown Cruises	*Cunard Countess** *Cunard Crown Dynasty*
Cunard Royal Viking	*Sea Goddess I*
Deilmann Reederei	*Lili Marleen*
Dolphin Cruise Line	*OceanBreeze** *SeaBreeze**
Fred Olsen Cruise Lines	*Black Prince*
Holland America Line	*Maasdam* *Nieuw Amsterdam* *Noordam* *Rotterdam* *Ryndam* *Statendam* *Westerdam*
New Commodore Cruise Line	*Enchanted Isle** *Enchanted Seas**
Nina Cruise Line	*Italia Prima*
Norwegian Cruise Line	*Norway** *Seaward**

P&O Cruises	*Victoria*
Paquet Cruises	*Mermoz*
Phoenix Seereisen	*Maxim Gorki*
Premier Cruise Lines	*Star/Ship Oceanic*
Radisson Seven Seas Cruises	*Radisson Diamond*
Regal Cruise Line	*Regal Empress*
Regency Cruises	*Regent Isle* *Regent Sea* *Regent Spirit* *Regent Star* *Regent Sun*
Royal Caribbean Cruises	*Majesty of the Seas** *Monarch of the Seas** *Sovereign of the Seas**
Royal Cruise Line	*Queen Odyssey* *Royal Odyssey*
Royal Venture Cruise Line	*Royal Venture**
Sea Cloud Cruises	*Sea Cloud*
Seawind Cruise Line	*Seawind Crown**
Silversea Cruises	*Silver Cloud*
Star Clippers	*Star Clipper** *Star Flyer*
StarLauro Cruises	*Monterey*
Tall Ship Adventures	*Sir Francis Drake*
Windstar Cruises	*Wind Star* *Wind Spirit*

Key
* = Year-Round ships (7-day cruises)

ALASKA (SUMMER)

Alaska Sightseeing	*Spirit of '98* *Spirit of Alaska* *Spirit of Discovery*
Carnival Cruise Lines	*Tropicale*
Celebrity Cruises	*Horizon*

Crystal Cruises	*Crystal Symphony*
Cunard Crown Cruises	*Crown Dynasty*
Cunard Royal Viking	*Sagafjord*
Hapag-Lloyd Cruises	*Europa*
Holland America Line	*Maasdam*
	Nieuw Amsterdam
	Noordam
	Rotterdam
	Ryndam
	Statendam
Norwegian Cruise Line	*Windward*
Phoenix Seereisen	*Maxim Gorki*
Princess Cruises	*Crown Princess*
	Regal Princess
	Royal Princess
Regency Cruises	*Regent Isle*
	Regent Rainbow
	Regent Sea
	Regent Star
Renaissance Cruises	*Renaissance*
Royal Caribbean Cruises	*Legend of the Seas*
Royal Cruise Line	*Royal Odyssey*
Society Expeditions	*World Discoverer*
Special Expeditions	*Sea Bird*
	Sea Lion
World Explorer Cruises	*Universe*

MEXICAN RIVIERA: YEAR-ROUND (3/4/7 DAYS)

Base: U.S. West Coast

Carnival Cruise Line	*Jubilee*
Royal Caribbean Cruises	*Viking Serenade*

11

HAWAII: YEAR-ROUND (7 DAYS)

Note: A number of cruise lines have ships that call on Hawaii, but none on a regular basis, owing to the Jones Act (U.S. cabotage laws).

American Hawaii Cruises	Constitution
	Independence

MEDITERRANEAN (INCLUDING BLACK SEA/GREEK ISLES)

Airtours Cruises	Carousel
	Seawing
AquaMarin Cruises	Astor
CTC Cruise Lines	Southern Cross
Club Med Cruises	Club Med I
Compagnie des Isles du Ponant	Le Ponant
Costa Cruises	CostaAllegra
	CostaClassica
	CostaMarina
	CostaRiviera
	CostaRomantica
	CostaVictoria
	Daphne
	EugenioCosta
Crystal Cruises	Crystal Harmony
Cunard Royal Viking	Royal Viking Sun
	Sea Goddess I
	Sea Goddess II
	Vistafjord
Deilmann Seerederei	Berlin
Delphin Seereisen	Kazakhstan II
Deutsche Seetouristik	Arkona
Dolphin Hellas Cruises	Aegean Dolphin
Epirotiki Cruise Line	Odysseus
	Olympic
	Orpheus
	Triton
	World Renaissance

Fantasy Cruises	*Amerikanis*
Festival Cruises	*Bolero*
	The Azur
Fred Olsen Cruise Lines	*Black Prince*
Holland America Line	*Maasdam*
Louis Cruise Lines	*Princesa Amorosa*
	Princesa Cypria
	Princesa Marissa
	Princesa Victoria
Majestic International Cruises	*Ocean Majesty*
Mar Line	*Vistamar*
Mediterranean Queen Lines	*Atalante*
Neckermann Seereisen	*Astra*
	Italia Prima
Nina Cruise Line	*Italia Prima*
Orient Lines	*Marco Polo*
P&O Cruises	*Canberra*
	Oriana
	Victoria
Paquet Cruises	*Mermoz*
Phoenix Seereisen	*Albatros*
	Maxim Gorki
Primexpress Cruises	*Taras Shevchenko*
Princess Cruises	*Island Princess*
	Pacific Princess
	Royal Princess
Radisson Seven Seas Cruises	*Radisson Diamond*
	Song of Flower
Regency Cruises	*Regent Calypso*
	Regent Spirit
Renaissance Cruises	*Renaissance*
Royal Caribbean Cruises	*Song of Norway*
Royal Cruise Line	*Crown Odyssey*
	Queen Odyssey
	Star Odyssey
Royal Hispania Cruises	*Don Juan*

Seabourn Cruise Line	Seabourn Pride
	Seabourn Spirit
Silversea Cruises	Silver Cloud
	Silver Wind
Soviet Danube Shipping	Ayvasovskiy
StarLauro Cruises	Monterey
	Rhapsody
	Symphony
Sun Line Cruises	Stella Maris
	Stella Oceanis
	Stella Solaris
SunFest Cruises	Sapphire Seas
Sunshine Cruise Line	Sea Prince
Transocean Tours	Columbus Caravelle
	Lev Tolstoi
Travelwise Cruises	Romantica
Windstar Cruises	Wind Spirit
	Wind Star

NORTH CAPE & BALTIC

AquaMarin Cruises	Astor
Baltic Line	Baltica
CTC Cruise Lines	Azerbaydzhan
	Kareliya
	Southern Cross
Costa Cruises	CostaAllegra
	CostaMarina
Crystal Cruises	Crystal Harmony
	Crystal Symphony
Cunard Line	Queen Elizabeth 2
Cunard Royal Viking	Royal Viking Sun
	Vistafjord
Deilmann Reederei	Berlin
Deutsche Seetouristik	Arkona
Fantasy Cruises	Amerikanis

Festival Cruises	*Bolero*
	The Azur
Fred Olsen Cruise Lines	*Black Prince*
Fritidskryss	*Funchal*
Hanseatic Tours	*Hanseatic*
Hapag-Lloyd Cruises	*Europa*
Holland America Line	*Maasdam*
Noble Caledonia	*Caledonian Star*
P&O Cruises	*Oriana*
	Victoria
Paquet Cruises	*Mermoz*
Phoenix Seereisen	*Albatros*
	Maxim Gorki
Primexpress Cruises	*Taras Shevchenko*
Princess Cruises	*Royal Princess*
Radisson Seven Seas Cruises	*Song of Flower*
Regency Cruises	*Regent Calypso*
Renaissance Cruises	*Renaissance*
Royal Caribbean Cruises	*Song of Norway*
Royal Cruise Line	*Crown Odyssey*
Seabourn Cruise Line	*Seabourn Pride*
	Seabourn Spirit
Silversea Cruises	*Silver Cloud*
	Silver Wind
StarLauro Cruises	*Monterey*
Sunshine Cruise Line	*Sea Prince*

ATLANTIC ISLES (CANARY ISLES/MADEIRA)

Airtours Cruises	*Carousel*
	Southern Cross
Club Med Cruises	*Club Med I*
Costa Cruises	*CostaRiviera*
	EugenioCosta
Crystal Cruises	*Crystal Harmony*

Cunard Line	Queen Elizabeth 2
Deilmann Reederei	Berlin
	Lili Marleen
Festival Cruises	The Azur
Fred Olsen Cruise Lines	Black Prince
Grimaldi Cruises	Ausonia
Holland America Line	Maasdam
P&O Cruises	Canberra
Phoenix Seereisen	Albatros
	Maxim Gorki
Radisson Seven Seas Cruises	Radisson Diamond
Renaissance Cruises	Renaissance
Royal Hispania Cruises	Don Juan
Silversea Cruises	Silver Cloud
Star Clippers	Star Flyer
Transocean Tours	Columbus Caravelle

ARABIAN GULF

Epirotiki Cruise Line	Odysseus
Noble Caledonia	Caledonian Star
P&O Cruises	Victoria
Renaissance Cruises	Renaissance

INDIAN OCEAN

CTC Cruise Lines	Azerbaydzhan
	Kareliya
	Southern Cross
Crystal Cruises	Crystal Symphony
Cunard Line	Queen Elizabeth 2
Cunard Royal Viking	Royal Viking Sun
	Sea Goddess II
Hanseatic Tours/Hapag-Lloyd	Bremen

NYK Cruises	*Asuka*
Noble Caledonia	*Caledonian Star*
Orient Lines	*Marco Polo*
P&O Cruises	*Canberra* *Oriana* *Victoria*
Primexpress Cruises	*Taras Shevchenko*
Princess Cruises	*Island Princess* *Pacific Princess*
Radisson Seven Seas Cruises	*Song of Flower*
Renaissance Cruises	*Renaissance*
Royal Cruise Line	*Royal Odyssey* *Star Odyssey*
Seabourn Cruise Line	*Seabourn Spirit*
Silversea Cruises	*Silver Wind*
Star Line Cruises	*Royal Star*
Transocean Tours	*Lev Tolstoi*

SOUTHEAST ASIA

CTC Cruise Lines	*Azerbaydzhan* *Kareliya*
Club Med Cruises	*Club Med II*
Crystal Cruises	*Crystal Symphony*
Cunard Royal Viking	*Royal Viking Sun*
Far East Shipping	*Antonina Nezhdanova* *Mikhail Sholokhov*
Lines International	*Nautica* (*)
Mitsui OSK Passenger Line	*Fuji Maru* (*) *Nippon Maru*
NYK Cruise Line	*Asuka*
New Century Tours	*Leisure World*
Noble Caledonia	*Caledonian Star*
Orient Lines	*Marco Polo*
P&O Spice Island Cruises	*Bali Sea Dancer* (*)

Pearl Cruises	*Pearl* (*)
Princess Cruises	*Island Princess*
	Pacific Princess
Renaissance Cruises	*Renaissance*
Royal Caribbean Cruises	*Sun Viking* (*)
Royal Cruise Line	*Royal Odyssey*
	Star Odyssey
Seabourn Cruise Line	*Seabourn Pride*
	Seabourn Spirit
Siam Cruise Line	*Andaman Princess* (*)
Show Line	*Oceanic Grace*
Star Cruise	*Langkapuri Star Aquarius* (*)
	Megastar Aries (*)
	Megastar Taurus (*)
	Star Pisces (*)
Transocean Tours	*Lev Tolstoi*
Venus Cruise Line	*Orient Venus* (*)
Windstar Cruises	*Wind Song* (*)

Key
(*) = Year-Round

AUSTRALIA/NEW ZEALAND/SOUTH PACIFIC

CTC Cruise Lines	*Azerbaydzhan*
	Kareliya
	Southern Cross
Club Med	*Club Med II*
Crystal Cruises	*Crystal Symphony*
Cunard Line	*Queen Elizabeth 2*
Far East Shipping	*Mikhail Sholokhov*
Hanseatic Tours/Hapag-Lloyd	*Bremen*
NYK Cruises	*Asuka*
Orient Lines	*Marco Polo*
P&O Holidays	*Fairstar* (*)

P&O Cruises	Canberra
	Oriana
Princess Cruises	Golden Princess
	Island Princess
	Pacific Princess
Royal Cruise Line	Royal Odyssey
Seabourn Cruise Line	Seabourn Spirit
Windstar Cruises	Wind Song

Key
(*) = Year-Round

ANTARCTICA

Abercrombie & Kent	Explorer
Clipper Cruise Line	World Discoverer
Hanseatic Tours/Hapag-Lloyd	Bremen
Hanseatic Tours	Hanseatic
Orient Lines	Marco Polo
Quark Expeditions (Noble Caledonia)	Kapitan Dranitsyn
	Yamal
Society Expeditions	World Discoverer

AROUND BRITAIN

Cunard Line	Queen Elizabeth 2
Cunard Royal Viking	Royal Viking Sun
Deilmann Reederei	Berlin
Deutsche Seetouristik	Arkona
Hapag-Lloyd Cruises	Europa
Noble Caledonia	Alla Tarasova
	Caledonian Star
Princess Cruises	Royal Princess
Regency Cruises	Regent Calypso
Royal Caribbean Cruises	Song of Norway

Silversea Cruises	*Silver Cloud/Silver Wind*
Transocean Tours	*Columbus Caravelle*

AROUND AFRICA

Phoenix Seereisen	*Albatros*

AROUND SOUTH AMERICA

Cunard Royal Viking	*Royal Viking Sun* *Vistafjord*
Hanseatic Tours	*Hanseatic*
Holland America Line	*Rotterdam*
Phoenix Seereisen	*Maxim Gorki*
Regency Cruises	*Regent Sea*

AROUND THE WORLD CRUISES

Crystal Cruises	*Crystal Symphony*
Cunard Line	*Queen Elizabeth 2*
Cunard Royal Viking	*Royal Viking Sun* *Sagafjord*
Delphin Seereisen	*Kazakhstan II*
Hapag-Lloyd Cruises	*Europa*
NYK Cruises	*Asuka*
P&O Cruises	*Oriana*
Phoenix Seereisen	*Albatros* *Maxim Gorki*
Regency Cruises	*Regent Sea*
Royal Cruise Line	*Royal Odyssey*
Transocean Cruise Lines	*Odessa*

ROAMING SHIPS

You are just as likely to see the following ships in Nosy-Be (Madagascar) as in the Amazon, in Greenland, Barcelona, Oslo, Singapore, the Maldives or Seychelles. In fact, all they seem to do all year long is roam the oceans of the world, on mostly non-repeating itineraries of varying cruise lengths.

Abercrombie & Kent	*Explorer*
AquaMarin Cruises	*Astor*
Cunard Royal Viking	*Royal Viking Sun*
	Sagafjord
	Vistafjord
Delphin Seereisen	*Kazakhstan II*
Deutsche Seetouristik	*Arkona*
Hapag-Lloyd Cruises	*Europa*
Phoenix Seereisen	*Albatros*
	Maxim Gorki
Society Expeditions	*World Discoverer*
Transocean Tours	*Odessa*

Foreword

by Robert H. Duffet, Director
Passenger Shipping Association, London

There is no doubt that the fastest expanding element of the travel and tourism industry over the last decade has been cruising. If we look at the current number of new ships being built for delivery to the cruise operators over the next three to four years, it is obvious that this will continue far into the future.

A Truly Fully Inclusive Vacation

Why is it that cruising is so very popular and seems to attract more and more holidaymakers every year? Without doubt one of the main reasons is the fully inclusive nature of the vacation—all your food, all your entertainment, and, in some cases, even shore excursions and gratuities are included in the price of the holiday. This is tremendously important when one considers family vacations. Just think how many times one is opening the purse or the wallet for children's ice-creams, hamburgers, hot dogs, etc., whereas on most cruise ships it's all included. This is of enormous advantage to those of us who have to plan our holiday expenditure carefully and like to budget well before departure from home on just how much the entire vacation is likely to cost.

The Most Pampered Vacation

I suppose the next most important point that attracts us to cruising is the pampering that we receive from the crew of our chosen ship. Whilst I do not agree with the attitude that every cruise ship is a luxurious vessel, I certainly would accept that, no matter what particular style or rating of cruise ship is chosen or selected, the pampering that the vacationers receive will be vastly superior to most land-based holidays.

Of Equal Attraction to the Very Active or the Laid-Back

There is no doubt that a cruise vacation can be of immense attraction to the very active, that is, people who seem to be wanting to do something every moment of every day whilst on vacation, but it's equally attractive to the people who, like myself, can best be described as downright lazy when it comes to vacations. All some of us want to do is curl up in a shady spot with an interesting book. No matter what our particular interest may be, the cruise ship in all its wonderful diversity can meet our individual requirements. If you are one of those people who would like to do a hundred and one different things every day, then that is

possible, but if, on the other hand, it's purely a relaxing vacation that you are looking for, with plenty of opportunities for basking in the sun, then the cruise can equally meet your needs and expectations.

One of the new trends that has occurred over recent years in cruising has been the dramatic expansion of the family market. Numerous cruise lines now go out of their way to provide special facilities for children of all ages. Indeed, there are ships with separate discos for teenagers. There are cruise lines that will arrange separate shore excursions for young people, and there is, of course, the constant availability of snacks and refreshments and this is of special appeal to children. It is equally true, of course, that there are some cruise lines that do not particularly welcome children, because the majority of their passengers will be of a slightly older generation, people whose children have now left home, and who are beginning to cherish a new-found affection for their partner, with perhaps only occasional visits from the grandchildren.

A Fine Dining Experience

For many cruise passengers the main attraction continues to be the dining experience. In addition to food being available virtually 24 hours a day, and all being included in the price of the holiday, there is the extremely wide choice available, particularly at the main meal times. The only menu that isn't changed every day of the cruise is the breakfast menu. The reason for this lack of change is simply that the passengers themselves make the changes throughout the duration of the vacation simply by their various selections from the enormous number of items contained on those breakfast menus.

For many people the highlight of the day is the evening meal. The numerous varying tastes and dietary requirements are all taken into consideration. Many ships now have extensive vegetarian menus. The "lean meals" that have been specially designed for the calorie-conscious passenger are available at every meal time.

A cruise vacation can be truly described as a hassle-free holiday, and the only really serious decisions that cruise passengers need to take are their selections of dishes from the dining room menu.

Seek the Advice of the Experts

In view of the multiplicity of products that are offered by the cruise industry today, it is, of course, vitally important that the intending cruise passenger gets expert advice. This book will, I know, be enormously helpful to those people who perhaps have never cruised before. It will also appeal to those who like to learn more about their chosen cruise ship prior to commencing their vacation. In the final outcome, I strongly urge readers to seek advice from qualified and professional travel agents. In North America, these will be agents who are members of CLIA (Cruise Lines International Association). In the United Kingdom, the

agents best qualified to talk about cruising are members of PSARA (Passenger Shipping Association Retail Agent Scheme). Both these organizations provide their travel agency members with highly professional training, extremely detailed manuals and an up-to-date information service so they are able to match the ship to the passenger, which is so important in having a satisfactory cruise vacation. May I bid you welcome aboard your chosen cruise ship for what I know will prove to be the holiday of a lifetime.

Robert Duffett is director of the London-based Passenger Shipping Association, and has been in the travel industry for 50 years.

Why Take a Cruise?

Why is a cruise vacation so popular?

Cruising has become a popular vacation today because it takes one away from the pressures and strains of contemporary life ashore, and offers a means of escape from reality. Cruise ships are really self-contained floating resort cities, but without the crime, and can take you to many destinations in the space of just a few days. The sea has always been a source of adventure, excitement, romance and wonder. It is beneficial and therapeutic, and, because you pay in advance, you know what you will spend on your vacation without any hidden surprises. There's no traffic to deal with, no pollution, no telephone to answer. And the hassles of ordinary travel are almost completely eliminated in one pleasant little package. It's no wonder that 85% of cruisegoers want to go again. And again.

Just who takes a cruise?

Singles, couples, families, honeymooners, second or third honeymooners, groups of friends, are all cruisegoers. Some are probably your next door neighbors.

But isn't cruising for wrinkly old people?

Nothing could be further from the truth. Indeed, the average age of cruise passengers becomes younger each year. Although those of silver years have found cruising to be a very safe way to travel the world, the average age of first-time cruisegoers is now *well under 40*. But do remember that even wrinkly old people can have a lot of fun, too, and many of them have more get up and go than many people under the age of 40!

Won't I get bored?

Usually it's the men that ask this. But get them aboard, and it's almost guaranteed that there won't be enough time in the day to do all the things they want to do (as long as you choose the right ship, for the right reasons). So, whether you want to lie back and be pampered, or go non-stop, you can do it on a cruise vacation, and you'll only have to pack and unpack once.

Is cruising for singles?

Yes indeed. A cruise vacation is ideal for people traveling alone, because it is easy to meet other people in a non-competitive environment. Many ships also have

special cabins for singles as well as special add-on rates for single occupancy of double cabins. Some cruise lines will even find a cabin-mate to share with, if you so desire.

Are cruises for honeymooners?

Couldn't be better. In fact, cruising's the ideal setting for romance, for shipboard receptions, and honeymoons. Most decisions are already made for you, so all you have to do is show up. Most ships have accommodations in double, queen, or king sizes, too. And for those on a second honeymoon, many ships now perform a "renewal of vows" ceremony.

Are cruises for children, too?

Absolutely. In fact, a cruise provides families with more quality time than any other type of vacation. Events on board are tailored to various age groups. In addition, a cruise is very educational, and allows children to interact in a safe, crime-free environment, and takes them to destinations in comfortable and familiar surroundings. In fact, you'll have difficulty getting them off the ship at the end of the cruise, if you choose the right ship. And you, as parents (or as a single parent), will be able to get time to enjoy life too. Again, choosing the right ship is most important.

Can I find a quiet, serene cruise, away from children and noise?

Yes, indeed. If you don't like crowds, noise, scheduled activities or long lines, there are some beautiful small ships that are only too ready to cater to your every whim. Perhaps a river or barge cruise would provide the right antidote. There are so many choices.

Are there different classes aboard ship?

Not any more. Gone are the class distinctions and the pretentions of formality of the past. Differences can be found, however, in the type of accommodations chosen, in the price you may be expected to pay for a larger cabin (or suite), and the location of your cabin (or suite).

Can I go shopping in ports of call?

Yes you can. In fact, many passengers engage in "retail therapy" when visiting ports of call such as Hong Kong, Singapore, St. Maarten and St. Thomas, among so many others. Just remember, though, that you'll have to carry all those purchases home at the end of your cruise, as the luggage companies know well enough.

Aren't all ships and cruises quite similar?

Indeed no, far from it. Look through this book and you'll see that ships range from under 200 feet to over 1,000 feet in length. They carry from under 100 to over 3,000 passengers, and facilities vary, quite naturally, according to the size of the ship. The ambiance ranges from ultra-casual to formal. Entertainment, likewise, ranges from amateur dramatics to full-fledged high-tech production shows, from corner cabaret to world-famous headliner, and everything in between.

Isn't cruising expensive?

Cruising can be an all-inclusive vacation, or an almost all-inclusive vacation. If you compare what it would cost on land to have all your meals and entertainment provided, as well as your transportation costs, fitness and sports facilities, and social activities, educational talks, parties and other functions, you'll soon realize the incredible *value* of a cruise vacation. And, remember, a ship is a destination in itself, which moves to other destinations. No land-based resort could ever do that! Ask anyone who has been on a cruise recently, and you'll see. Finally, give yourself a vacation budget, and go to your professional travel agent with it. The rest, as they say, will be taken care of.

Where can I go on a cruise?

Pick any one of 500 destinations in the world, and you'll find a ship and cruise to take you there. A cruise can also take you to places inaccessible by any other means, such as Antarctica, the North Cape, South Sea islands, and so on.

How to Use this Guide

Ever since my first transatlantic crossing, in July 1965, on the largest passenger ship ever constructed, Cunard's giant 83,673-grt RMS *Queen Elizabeth*, I have been captivated by passenger ships and the sea. More than 730 cruises, 130 transatlantic crossings and countless Panama Canal transits, shipyard visits, maiden voyages and ships later, I am even more fascinated by and absorbed in every aspect of cruising and passenger-ship travel.

For the discerning vacationer, there is simply no better way to get away from it all than on a cruise. Those who have cruised before will be unstinting in their praise of it. They may talk about a specific ship, line or cruise, but always with enthusiasm. So will you—that is, if you choose the "right" ship for the "right" reasons.

That brings me to the purpose of this book: it is intended to be a primary and comprehensive source of information about cruising and the ships and companies that offer to take you away from the pressures, stresses and confines of daily life ashore. When you first start looking into the possibilities of taking a cruise you will be confronted by an enormous and bewildering choice. Don't panic. Simply read through this book carefully. At the end you will be nearer to making the right choice and will leave for your cruise as well informed as most specialists in the industry! In fact, cruise consultants, travel agents and personnel connected with the industry will also find this book a valuable reference source on ships and cruising.

The book is divided into three distinct sections. Parts One and Two comprise 21 chapters and various charts and diagrams; introduce you to the world of cruising; help you define what you are looking for in a cruise; tell you how and where to book and what kind of accommodations to choose; and provide valuable advice on what you should know before you go. There is a complete picture of life aboard ship and how to get the best from it: the world-famous cuisine, the evolution of cruising, nautical terminology, amusing anecdotes, who's who on board, and advice about going ashore. If you are looking for the cruise with a difference—along a river or an adventurous expedition—there is a survey of these aspects, too, culminating with that ultimate travel experience: the world cruise, and other grand voyages.

Part Three contains profiles of 220 oceangoing cruise ships of the world (including expedition, "soft" expedition cruise vessels and sail-cruise vessels). From large to small, from unabashed luxury to moderate and economy, old and new, they're all here. The ratings are a painstaking documentation of my personal work, much of it undertaken in strict secrecy. To keep this book up-to-date and accurate, I travel throughout the world constantly (this translates to approximately one million air miles every year) and inspect hundreds of ships (including

areas that passengers don't normally see, but which are a necessary part of the total evaluation), and this involves, quite naturally, much on-board cruising as well.

The ratings are best used selectively—according to your personal tastes and preferences. If cuisine is important to you, or your concern is for entertainment, then these aspects of the ratings will obviously be more significant for you than the overall score or number of stars awarded. The attraction of cruising is in the variety of opportunities available. This book is intended to help you make an informed choice, given the differences between ships today.

As soon as new ships enter service, a survey is undertaken for the next edition of this book. This edition covers the state of the cruise industry through the end of 1994 with a look at 1995 and beyond.

This book is a tribute to everyone who has made my seafaring experiences possible, and to everyone who helped make this book a reality. In addition, I would like to give a brief mention to my mother and father, without whom I would never have gone cruising. With my love.

Douglas Ward
July 1995

During the early part of his sea-going career, starting in 1965, Douglas Ward worked on some 15 well-known liners (some of which are no longer in service) as follows:

Andes, 25,689 grt; scrapped in 1971

Black Watch, 11,209 grt; withdrawn

Blenheim, 10,420 grt; now *Discovery I*

Calypso, 20,204 grt; now *OceanBreeze*

Cunard Countess, 17,593 grt

Cunard Princess, 17,495 grt

Franconia, 22,637 grt; now *Fedor Shalyapin*

Kenya Castle, 19,904 grt; now *Amerikanis*

Ocean Monarch, 22,552 grt; withdrawn in 1966, scrapped at Kaohsiung in 1975

Oronsay, 27,632 grt; withdrawn in 1973, scrapped at Kaohsiung in 1974

Queen Elizabeth, 83,673 grt; withdrawn 1968; caught fire in Hong Kong under suspicious circumstances Feb. 9, 1972

Queen Elizabeth 2, 66,451 grt

Queen Mary, 81,237 grt; withdrawn in 1967, moored at Long Beach, California

Reina del Mar, 21,501 grt; withdrawn in 1975, scrapped at Kaohsiung in 1975

Southern Cross, 20,204 grt; still in service as *OceanBreeze*

PART ONE

What's New for 1996 and Beyond

The cruise ship industry is truly alive, vibrant, and is still growing at a fairly healthy rate. In 1996 and beyond, the introduction of new ships will continue at a dizzying rate (with some 26 new ones due to be delivered in the three years between January 1996 and December 1998 alone), partly fueled by the knowledge that subsidies to all European shipyards will be phased out by 1998, and by the expected increase in demand for the high-value cruise vacation product.

These new ships will incorporate the latest high-tech electronic equipment and the best in advanced ship design and construction, and will offer passengers an unprecedented number of options, choice of facilities, dining and entertainment experiences.

Here are some of the things to look forward to with the incoming generation of cruise ships.

First, speed. Several new ships are being provided with diesel-electric propulsion systems which will propel them at speeds of about 25 knots (few ships can go faster, except for *Queen Elizabeth 2*, which has a service speed of 30 knots). This in turn will better equip these ships for attractive long-distance itineraries, and will give them the capacity of having reserve speed when crossing vast stretches of ocean, such as those of the Atlantic, Indian and Pacific. Among the newest ships capable of speeds of 25 knots or more are *Grandeur of the Seas*, *Legend of the Seas*, *Oriana*, *Splendour of the Seas*,

Vision of the Seas. Their shape will also be sleeker from an aerodynamic viewpoint. Diesel-electric power systems are the power philosophy of choice because of their varied service profile and the tough requirements placed on power used by the various departments of the floating hotel.

EXTERIORS

On the subject of exteriors, the curved, indented and tiered after-decks of the P&O Cruises' *Oriana* are quite stunning, and very practical, overlooking, as they do, the aft pool area (more dramatic, but no less practical, than the terraces on Norwegian Cruise Line's well-designed *Dreamward* and *Windward*). Other cruise ships have the "block" approach, and fill in their aft areas with cabins that have an aft-facing view (*Carnival Destiny*, *Century*, *Galaxy*), or multi-level dining rooms with a huge expanse of glass windows, or other public rooms and facilities. Also, there will be more and more glass areas created, the purpose being to provide the "connection" between passenger and sea. The *Legend of the Seas* and *Splendour of the Seas* have more glass than any other ships afloat, although ships such as *Dawn Princess* and the *Sun Princess* also have huge expanses of glass (the race between ships used to be for the greatest number and size of a ship's funnels; now it's for the greatest glass areas!).

As for the outdoors, golfers will like the 6,000 sq. ft., 18-hole miniature golf courses on board the *Legend of the Seas* and on the *Splendour of the Seas*. The courses are complete with the foliage, grass, sand traps, bridges, water hazards and other "trappings" of a traditional miniature golf course (but there is no room for caddies!). Holes range from 155 to 230 sq. ft. in length. The courses were designed by the same firm that designed the one for the world's largest shopping center, the Mall of America in Bloomington, Minnesota, which provides an insight into the type of passengers who will be expected to cruise in these ships.

Obviously serious golfers will find these greatly downsized courses somewhat beneath them (no pun intended), but looking at it positively, at least they'll enjoy the fresh air.

INTERIORS

On the subject of interiors, consider such things as a 10-deck-high atrium (*Legend of the Seas*, *Splendour of the Seas*) theaters with revolving stages and hydraulic orchestra pits (*Carnival Destiny*, *Century*, *Oriana*); interactive television in cabins; nightclubs located 15 decks above the sea, and accessed by moving stairways (*Dawn Princess/Sun Princess*). Indeed, the *Oriana*'s show lounge even has individually air-conditioned seats, while the grand atriums on *Legend of the Seas* and *Splendour of the Seas* connect with a Viking Crown Lounge at the base of the funnel, a first on any ship.

As for interior decor, well, the sky's the limit. Actually, some of the most stunning, bold and graphic interiors will continue to be found on the latest

P&O Cruises' brand new Oriana, *introduced in April 1995, was built specifically for the growing British cruise market.*

35

ships being built for Carnival Cruise Lines. The *Imagination* has ancient mythological figures such as sphinxes, Medusas, cherubs and winged Mercury figures to reflect the refinement of civilizations past. Somehow, lilac neon, mosaics and multi-colored carpeting all go together here while they never would in any other setting. It's all a feast for the eyes and mind, but for many (especially for European passengers), it could be sensory overkill, though a wonderful advertisement for the fiber optic and lighting industries.

Ships are now being built to include two atrium lobbies (*Carnival Destiny, Dawn Princess, Galaxy, Sun Princess*), and one new ship will have a forward observation lounge complete with a waterfall, spanning some four decks (*CostaVictoria*). On the *Century*, the atrium contains a waterfall with rock background (even moving rocks were considered), and the different levels of the atrium appear to "float" with the use of glass covered perimeters.

On *Dawn Princess* and *Sun Princess*, the aft swimming pool is "layered" over two decks. Several new ships will have magrodomes, those glass enclosed structures that are used to cover swimming pools just in case of inclement weather (the *Carnival Destiny, Galaxy, Legend of the Seas, Splendour of the Seas*). These may not be new facilities (*Europa* has one, and *QE2* had one until removed in her latest refit), but they do make it possible for cruise passengers to enjoy all-weather swimming. Unlike the sliding multi-fold magrodomes that are on various other ships, the glass structures used on both the *Legend of the Seas* and the *Splendour of the Seas* are one-piece affairs.

Several of the cruise ships already have two-deck-high dining rooms (for example, the *Maasdam, Ryndam, Statendam* and the *Veendam*), and several more ships will feature this expansion of the massive dining hall experience (these include *Century, Dawn Princess, Galaxy, Legend of the Seas, Splendour of the Seas, Sun Princess*). And the days of grand staircases will return to the seas with a vengeance. The *Century* has a majestic staircase that connects the two levels of its dining rooms (the *Nordic Empress* is an excellent example of a ship with fine staircases).

Staying on the dining theme, more ships are now providing alternative dining spots. At the moment *Crystal Harmony, Crystal Symphony, Langkapuri Star Aquarius, Star Pisces,* and *Vistafjord*) already have them, but several brand new ships will include more choices. *Sun Princess* will eventually have five dining spots (*Langkapuri Star Aquarius*, placed into service in 1993, has seven!). Some ships also have special theme bars/lounges, serving delicacies such as caviar and champagne, cheese, dessert and pastry items.

The physically challenged will be pleased to know that as many as 19 cabins catering for them are being fitted out on board *Dawn Princess* and *Sun Princess* (the largest number on any passenger ship) to the Americans with Disabilities Act (ADA) standards, while those on *QE2* have push-button electric sliding doors to the bathroom.

Health and fitness spas are now one of the hottest passenger facilities on the latest cruise ships, with more space than ever being devoted to them. It is one area where the larger, newer ships differ from older, smaller ships.

DID YOU KNOW ...?

...that Verdi wrote an opera to commemorate the opening of the Suez Canal? Its name is Aida.

...that the average time for a ship to pass through the Panama Canal is 8 hours? The fastest transit time was set by the uss *Manley*, at 4 hours and 38 minutes.

...that the first passenger ship to be fitted with stabilizers was the 24,215 grt, 1949-built *Chusan* of the Peninsular & Oriental Steam Navigation Company (P&O)?

...that the first passenger ship to exceed 10,000 grt was the *City of New York* of 1888 (British)?

In recent years the basic sauna and massage facility has given way to specially designed marine spas that provide the latest in high-tech muscle exercising, aerobic and weight-training machines and relaxation treatments in a completely "themed" environment. Close by will be the ship's swimming pools and whirlpools.

The latest shipboard spas contain a combination of all or several of the following: reception desk, changing area, aerobics exercise room, gymnasium, sauna, steam room, massage and other treatment rooms. Facilities will include all or some of these: a hydrotherapy and thalassotherapy ("thalasso," from *thalassa*, the Greek word for the sea) center, jet blitz, and other treatment rooms (for treatments such as phytomer, exfoliating treatment, herbal wraps, etc.).

On some ships, the beauty salon is adjacent to the spa complex, or contained within it, rather than being a separate entity on a different deck. The latest spas, with their "feel better" personal treatments and affiliated beauty salon have become major revenue producing areas for both cruise line and concession.

The most common (and popular) location for spas on the latest ships is on an upper deck area with windows that provide ocean views, particularly for exercise areas. The ambiance created must be in harmony with the objective of spa programs. Treatment rooms must be flexible so that they can be adapted to incorporate the latest trends (and gimmicks). The best spas combine the above with a relaxed atmosphere. Look out for the innovative 9,340 sq. ft. AquaSpa that is positioned forward and high in the *Century*. Traditional Japanese design elements, including a rock garden and shoji screens, provide a cool, serene environment for passengers.

What else? Telescopes for stargazing will also be incorporated on the *Century*, positioned in its forward-facing "Hemispheres" discotheque and nightclub atop the ship, set in three tiers. Carnival Cruise Lines was the first, in the spring of 1995, to introduce cash-dispensing ATMs (automated teller machines) aboard some of its largest ships. I expect other cruise lines to follow suit.

How about cabins? Well, standard cabins *are* getting a little larger, thank goodness. For example, at 170 sq. ft. the cabins on *Legend of the Seas* and *Splendour of the Seas* will be larger than on any other cruise ships in the Royal Caribbean Cruises ships to date. Those two ships will also have huge suites measuring some 1,148 sq. ft. But the *largest* living quarters aboard any cruise ship will be found on the Celebrity Cruises' *Century*, where two penthouse suites can be expanded to an outstanding 1,515 sq. ft. by using the adjacent mini-suite and its lockable inter-connecting door. The penthouse suites will also have built-in teleconferencing capabilities. On many of the ships, more cabins will have private balconies than ever before. On the *Sun Princess*, for example, there are 750 outside cabins (70%) with balconies.

Non-smokers will be pleased to note that many ships (particularly those cruising in the Caribbean and Alaska areas) now feature totally non-smoking dining rooms. While on the subject of smoking, Holland America Line has now discontinued the cigar humidor service for which they had been known for many years (it performed best on the *Rotterdam*). Cigar smokers will be pleased to learn, however, that Celebrity Cruises will introduce it on the *Century* with all attendant ceremony, to be performed by Filipino specialists in Michale's Club, a particularly lovely room specially created for smokers.

Hot destinations? Well, apart from the usual run-of-the-mill Caribbean and Mediterranean ship cruising areas, there's Europe, with the Baltic and Russia, the Black Sea and the eastern Mediterranean. But the hottest "new" area to be discovered, particularly for European passengers, is perhaps the Arabian Gulf, with ships now calling at Dhahran (Saudi Arabia), Kuwait City (Kuwait), Manama (Bahrain), Abu Dhabi and Sharjah (United Arab Emirates), and Muscat (Oman), not to mention the Red Sea ports of Aqaba in Jordan, Aden and Hodeidah in Yemen. And then there is the mystical area of South-East Asia, including China, Japan, Thailand, Malaysia and Singapore. Who said cruising was boring!

Speaking of destinations, in another cruise industry first, Royal Caribbean Cruises has established a "Crown and Anchor Club" in St. Thomas. This is to Royal Caribbean Cruises passengers what private airport lounges are to business people who fly a lot. There's no charge for the use of the "club," located in Hibiscus Alley in Charlotte Amalie, where passengers can enjoy complimentary tea and coffee, rest in comfortable seating, be able to check their shopping purchases, pick up brochures, purchase spirits, and discuss any shopping and tourism questions with the Royal Caribbean Cruises staff who are in attendance. The company, which has a reputation as an innovator, is expected to expand the program to

other ports of call on its cruises. A fine, practical idea.

FOOD AND SERVICE

Generally, cruise ship food and service has suffered somewhat in the past two years, after deep discounting took a firm foothold in the North American marketplace. As a result, standards of food quality, presentation, delivery, and service has fallen little by little. Also, because of the acute shortage of waiters who speak good English (the majority of cruise passengers being North American), many cruise lines have had to train personnel from Caribbean basin and Central American countries, whose command of the English language is less than desirable. Finding quality personnel to work on board the ships that operate standard seven-day cruises on the same itineraries is becoming increasingly difficult.

I am pleased to say, however, that most of the major lines have realized their mistakes and have made great advances in upgrading the food and service aspect of the cruise experience.

Let's look at the current four major cruise ship companies (arranged here in alphabetical order). These are: Carnival Cruise Lines, Norwegian Cruise Line, P&O/Princess Cruises and Royal Caribbean Cruises:

- Carnival Cruise Lines has increased the quality of its food, although service remains fast and robotic, and communication (in English) with waiters is frustrating.
- Norwegian Cruise Line has also been sprucing up its menus, food

quality and presentation. The company has also introduced lighter fare in informal surroundings with its fleetwide "bistro" concept, at no extra charge.

- P&O Cruises now offers Anton Mosimann-designed menus on the *Oriana*, while its Princess Cruises division has introduced on to its ships new, lighter-fare menus and spruced up service aspects.
- Upgraded menus offering a wider choice for non-meat eaters have also proved popular on the ships of the Royal Caribbean Cruises. New uniforms for waiters and assistant waiters (no longer called bus boys), much improved food presentation and the addition of new complete vegetarian menus have been introduced. Royal Caribbean Cruises, however, does not have fish knives in the dining rooms of its ships (except for *Legend of the Seas* and *Splendour of the Seas*, where they are available on request).

Still on the dining theme, some 2,000 Methuselah-sized bottles (the equivalent of 8 bottles) of Cristal champagne will be specially made for Crystal Cruises' passengers to purchase for the eve of the year 2000. The cost, of course, will be $2,000 each!

WHAT'S NOT SO HOT

Sadly, the cruise industry seems to insist on creating floating resort hotels that travel at night, and are usually in port during the day. There is thus little connection with the sea and nature. Unfortunately, this floating hotel concept has really spoiled the nature of the

39

latest cruise ship designs. As a result, almost everything is designed to keep passengers *inside* the ship (hopefully to spend money and thus increase on-board revenue).

Keeping passengers inside the ship creates another, worsening, problem; that of so-called "cruise directors" who insist on interposing themselves into every part of your cruise, both day and night. Public address systems are consistently overused by these aggressive, bouncy youngsters, and are often far too loud, which hardly makes for a restful cruise experience. Some of them have learned well from past masters, but many of today's cruise directors, who may make good cheerleaders, are unable to communicate with anyone over the age of 30!

Another problem with the homogeneous new ships are the cabins. As cookie-cutter standard cabins are all the same basic size (good for incentive planners, but not for individual cruisegoers), they also tend to be the same basic color, monotonous monochromatic white, eggshell white, off-white, or computer-colored light beige! While such colors are welcome after days in the sun, for example, they are tedious on voyages over long stretches of water. Only the bold bedspreads or the occasional color prints that adorn a spare wall bring relief. Close to useless are the wall-mounted hairdryers in the bathrooms (they seldom have enough directed pressure).

Ships in the standard cruise market now charge for all sorts of things they never used to, such as bottled mineral water (few cruise lines make this clear in their brochures), cups of cappuccino and espresso coffees (even in the dining room) and postcards. But prices just seem to keep rising for such things as photographs and medical services (these are free only aboard Russian or Ukrainian-owned ships).

Non-U.S. cruise passengers sailing on ships catering to Americans should be aware that the air-conditioning tends to be powerful, and makes you feel rather like you are sailing in a floating refrigerator. Take a couple of sweaters, or some thermal underwear!

Calling passengers "guests" is really confusing, and nautically incorrect. A guest in one's house is someone that doesn't pay. Passengers on ships pay to be there. On land, hotels have paying guests, but "guest" should be changed to "client" as in "clientele." Ships, however, are different (and they should always remain so). They provide a nautical experience, and move across the water; passengers have cabins and suites; and ships have decks, not floors. That's how it should remain, but some cruise lines think they are in the hotel business, being run as they are by hoteliers and accountants, not by shippers.

One thing that's almost gone by the wayside are the streamers and the free champagne provided at bon voyage parties on deck on sailing day (with the exception of world cruises). Now it's a case of waiters hustling for you to buy a "bon voyage" cocktail. Shame!

Finally, in the 7-day cruise market, particularly from U.S. ports, the disembarkation process leaves much to be desired, with passengers on large ships complaining that after the cruise they are unceremoniously dumped ashore with no help after the trying procedure of locating their luggage and customs inspection, and no representation once

they get to their respective airport for check-in. Of particular concern is that the same procedure applies to all passengers, whether in the finest penthouse suites, or the smallest inside cabins. Last impressions of these 7-day cruises, therefore, are poor. Comment forms should also be sent to passengers two weeks after their cruise has ended to get a better feedback about this matter rather than asking passengers to complete their forms and hand them in just before they disembark. Worst offenders are: Ft. Lauderdale, Miami and San Juan, with Los Angeles and San Francisco only marginally better.

YOUR FIRST CRUISE: WHAT TO EXPECT

If you've never been on a cruise before, allow me to take you through a typical initial embarkation process.

Let's assume that you have arrived at the airport closest to your ship's embarkation point, and retrieved your luggage. It's probable that there will be a representative from the cruise line waiting, holding up a sign that says "Condor Cruise Lines" or similar. You will be asked to place your luggage in a cluster together with other passengers on the same flight as you, or perhaps with passengers on other flights of the same airline, arriving at roughly the same time as yours.

Alternatively, you could have perhaps driven to the port of embarkation, in which case you will hand over your luggage to a representative of the cruise line, or to a baggage handler (who will probably expect a tip, even for moving it a few feet).

In any case (no pun intended), the next time you see your luggage should be aboard ship, where it will be delivered to your cabin). Now, let's proceed to the check-in point.

Head to the registration (check-in) area in the terminal building. For large ships, several desks will be set up (with the alphabet split into several parts), probably with long lines of people at each of them. Go to the desk which displays the letter of your surname, wait in line (having filled out all the embarkation, registration and immigration forms), and then check in.

If you are cruising from a U.S. port and you are a non-U.S. citizen or "Resident Alien", you will go to a separate desk to check in. You will be asked for your passport, which you leave with the check-in personnel, but remember to ask for a receipt for it (it is, after all, a valuable document).

If you are cruising from any other port in the world that is not a U.S. port, be advised that each country has its own check-in requirements, set-ups and procedures (passport control and inspection, for example). In any event, once you've checked in, you'll be only a few steps away from your ship and the start of your cruise.

Documents in hand, you'll probably go through a security screening device, for both your person and hand luggage. Next, you'll walk a few paces towards the gangway (this may be a covered, airport-type gangway, or an open gangway (hopefully with a net underneath it in case you drop something over the side). It could be flat, or you may have to walk up a steep gangway, depending on the location of the gangway, the tide, etc. When you

41

get to the gangway, you'll probably be greeted by the ship's photographers, a snap-happy team ready to take your photograph, bedraggled as you may appear after possibly having flown or otherwise traveled for hours. If you don't want your photograph taken, just say "no" firmly, and then proceed to the gangway.

Once on the gangway, you'll feel a heightened sense of anticipation. At the ship side of the gangway, you'll find a decorated (hopefully) entrance, and the comfortable feel of cool air-conditioning if the weather is hot. You should also be greeted by well-dressed young men and women of the cruise staff, probably accompanied by an officer or security personnel who will ask for your boarding pass, and your cabin number. Show them your cabin number and a steward should magically appear to take your carry-on luggage (or perhaps the winter coat you are carrying) from you, and take you to your cabin. At last you've arrived.

The door to your cabin should be unlocked and open. If it is locked, ask the steward to obtain the key to open the door. On the newest ships, you'll probably be handed an electronically coded key card, which you insert into the door lock. Once inside the cabin, put down your personal effects and take a good look. Is it clean? Is it tidy? Are the beds properly made? Check under them to make sure the floor is clean (on one cruise I found a pair of red ladies shoes, but, alas, no one to go with them!). Make sure there is ice in the ice container. Check the bathroom, bath (if there is one), or shower. Make sure there are towels and soap. If all is clean and shipshape, fine.

If there are problems, bring them to the attention of your cabin steward immediately. Or call the purser's office (or reception desk) and explain the problem, then quietly, but quite firmly request that someone in a supervisory position see you to resolve it.

The housekeeping on cruise ships is generally very good, but sometimes when "turnaround" time is tight, when passengers disembark in the morning, and the new passengers embark in the afternoon, little things get overlooked. They shouldn't, but they do (just as in any hotel ashore).

One thing you should do immediately is to learn the telephone number for the ship's hospital, doctor, or for medical emergencies, just so you know how to call for help should any medical emergency arise.

Your luggage probably won't have arrived yet (if it's a ship carrying more than 500 passengers), so don't sit in the cabin waiting for it. Once you've oriented yourself with the cabin and its features, put your hand luggage away somewhere, and, deck plan in hand, take a walk round.

Familiarize yourself with the layout of the ship. Learn which way is forward, which way is aft, and how to reach your cabin from the main stairways. This is also a good time to learn how to get from your cabin to the outside decks, in case of an emergency. It is more than likely that a Passenger Lifeboat Drill will be held *before* the ship sails. This is good, in that the drill will not disturb your cruise (or your sleep) should it be held next morning. In any case, the drill *must* take place within 24 hours after the ship sails from the port of embarkation.

Cruising: A Backgrounder

In 1835 a curious sample advertisement appeared in the first issue of the *Shetland Journal*. Under the heading "To Tourists," it proposed an imaginary cruise from Stromness in Scotland, round Iceland and the Faroe Islands, and went on to suggest the pleasures of cruising under the Spanish sun in winter. So it is said that the journal's founder, Arthur Anderson, invented the concept of cruising. Just two years later, Anderson, along with his partner Brodie Wilcox, founded the great Peninsular Steam Navigation Company (later to become P&O).

Sailing for leisure soon caught on. Even writers such as William Makepeace Thackeray and Charles Dickens boarded ships for the excitement of the voyage, and not just to reach a destination. The Victorians had discovered tourism, and they promoted the idea widely. Indeed, Thackeray's account of his legendary voyage in 1844, from Cornhill to Grand Cairo by means of the P&O ships of the day, makes fascinating reading, as does the account by Dickens of his transatlantic crossing in a Cunarder in 1842. The P&O's *Tagus*, which journeyed from London to the Black Sea in 1843, was the subject of Mark Twain's *The Innocents Abroad*, which was published in 1869.

In 1881 P&O's 2,376-ton *Ceylon* was sold to the newly formed Oceanic Yachting Company for conversion into

The Royal Viking Sun *(Cunard Royal Viking), presently the highest rated cruise ship in the world.* **Rating ★★★★★+**

a commercial pleasure yacht capable of sailing round the world—the first passenger ship to do so. The ship continued its cruising career after it had been sold to the Polytechnic Touring Association.

Cruising in its more modern sense eventually got underway on March 12, 1889, when the 33,847-ton Orient liners *Chimborazo* and *Garrone* were taken from their normal services to Australia and employed for seasonal cruises to the Norwegian fjords. By 1893 seasonal cruises were also being offered to the Mediterranean, and in 1895 a third vessel, the *Lusitania*, was sent on a 60-day cruise around the West Indies, Madeira, Tenerife and the Azores. From then on, both the Orient Line and the Royal Mail Steam Packet Company featured regular cruises for the wealthy. In 1912 the former Orient Line's *Ortona* emerged after refit, operating under Royal Mail as the 8,939-ton *Arcadian* (ex-*Asturias*). With beds for 320 first-class passengers (there was no other class), facilities included a 35-foot-long swimming pool and a three-deck-high dining room.

The first vessel built exclusively for cruising was the Hamburg America Line's two-funnel yacht, the 4,409-ton *Prinzessin Victoria Luise*. This luxury vessel even included a private suite for the German Kaiser.

Following World War I there was a shortage of ship tonnage, and cruising activities were curtailed, but with one notable exception—Royal Mail's *Arcadian*, which built up an enviable reputation as a British cruise vessel. Among her facilities were a tiled swimming pool and hot and cold running water supplied to every cabin.

The first *official* round-the-world cruise was made in 1922-3 by the Cunard Line's *Laconia* (19,680 grt)—a three-class ship that sailed from New York. The itinerary included many of the ports of call that are still popular with world-cruise travelers today. The vessel accommodated 350 persons in each of its first two classes, and 1,500 in third class, giving a total capacity of 2,200 passengers—more than most of the ships of today.

In the 1920s, cruising became the thing to do for the world's well-to-do. Being pampered in such grand style was "in," and is still the underlying concept of cruising. The ship took you and your belongings anywhere, and fed you, accommodated you, relaxed you, and entertained you. At the same time, it even catered for your servants who, of course, accompanied you.

The cruise idyll was helped greatly by Prohibition in the 1930s. After all, just a few miles out at sea you were free to consume as much liquor as you wanted. And cheap three- and four-day weekend "booze cruises" out of New York were preferable to "bathtub gin." Then came short cruises, with destinations as well as booze. In time, the short cruise was to become one of the principal sources of profit for the steamship companies of the day.

During the late 1920s and well into the 1930s ships became floating luxury palaces, offering every amenity imaginable in this era of social elegance. One of the most beautiful flowing staircases ever built was on board the French liner *Paris* (35,469 grt), constructed in 1921. It is reported that seagulls made this ship their five-star favorite because of its *haute cuisine* garbage.

In the 1930s a battle raged between the giant cruising companies of the world, with Britain, France, Germany and the United States building liners of unprecedented luxury, elegance, glamor, and comfort. Each country was competing to produce the biggest and best afloat. For a time, quality was somehow related to smokestacks: the more a ship had, the better. Although speed had always been a factor, particularly on the transatlantic run, it now became a matter of national ambition.

The first ship designed specifically for cruising from the United States after World War II was the *Ocean Monarch* (Furness Withy & Company Ltd.), which was awarded a gold medal by the U.S. Academy of Designing for the "outstanding beauty and unusual design features of a cruise ship." Her maiden voyage was from New York to Bermuda on May 3, 1951. I worked aboard her for a short time.

One of the most renowned cruise liners of all time was Cunard's lovely *Caronia* (34,183 grt), which was conceived in 1948. She was designed and built to offer a transatlantic service in the peak summer months only and then spend the rest of the year doing long, expensive cruises. One of her outstanding features was a single giant mast and one smokestack—the largest of her time—and her hull was painted four shades of green, supposedly for the purposes of heat resistance and easy identification. Known for making extensive world cruises, she was one of the first ships to provide a private adjoining bathroom for every cabin—a true luxury. Lovingly known as the "Green Goddess," she was sometimes called the "millionaires' ship."

In June 1958 the first commercial jet aircraft flew across the Atlantic and completely altered the economics of transatlantic travel. It was the last year in which more passengers crossed the North Atlantic by sea than by air. In the early 1960s the passenger shipping directories listed more than 100 ocean-going passenger ship lines, with more than 30 ships featuring transatlantic crossings for the better part of each year. Up until the mid-1960s, it was cheaper to cross the Atlantic by ship than by plane, but the appearance of the jet aircraft changed that rapidly, particularly with the introduction of jumbo jets in the early 1970s.

Today, one major superliner alone is still offering a regular transatlantic service—Cunard Line's elegant, modern *Queen Elizabeth 2* (70,267 grt). Built in 1969, then re-engined and extensively refurbished in 1987, and with a major interior refit in 1994, the *QE2* offers more than two dozen crossings each year between the ports of New York and Southampton, with some occasional calls at other U.S. east coast ports, as well as Cherbourg in France. Besides the *QE2*, there are another two dozen or so cruise ships that offer occasional transatlantic crossings, usually twice a year when relocating between cruise areas, such as the Caribbean and the Mediterranean.

The success of the jumbo jets created a fleet of unprofitable and out-of-work passenger liners that appeared doomed for the scrap heap. Even the famous big "Queens," which were noted for their regular weekly transatlantic service, found themselves at risk. The *Queen Mary* was withdrawn in September 1967. Her sister ship, the

Queen Elizabeth, at 83,673 grt the largest passenger liner ever built, made her final crossing in October 1968. I was aboard for the last few voyages of this great ship.

The transatlantic shipping companies searched desperately for new ways to employ their aging vessels, but few survived the ever-successful growth of the jet aircraft. Ships were sold for a fraction of their value, and many lines simply went out of business.

Those that survived attempted to mix transatlantic crossings with voyages south to the sun. The Caribbean was so appealing. Cruising became an alternative, and an entire new industry was born, with new lines being formed exclusively for cruising.

Then came smaller, highly specialized ships, which were capable of getting into the tiny ports of developing Caribbean islands (there were no commercial airlines taking vacationers to the Caribbean then), and which were built to carry a sufficient number of passengers in one single-class arrangement to make money.

Instead of cruising long distances south from northerly ports such as New York, the new lines established their headquarters in Florida. Having their ships based in Florida not only avoided the cold weather and rough seas of the northern ports, it also enabled the lines to save on fuel costs with the shorter runs to the Caribbean. So, cruising was reborn. California became the base for ship cruises to the Mexican Riviera, and Vancouver on Canada's west coast became the focus for the summer cruises to Alaska.

Flying passengers to embarkation ports was the next logical step, and there soon emerged a working relationship between the cruise lines and the airlines. The air/sea package therefore came into being, with the cruise lines using the jumbo jets for their own purposes. The concept of fly-cruising was introduced in 1960 by Chandris Cruises in the Mediterranean cruise area; these days passengers are flown to almost anywhere in the world to join up with cruises.

Next came the "sail 'n' stay" packages, which are joint cruise and hotel vacations that were all included in the cruise fare. Cruising had become an integrated part of tourism, with ships and hotels offering comfort and relaxation and the airlines providing quick access. Some of the old liners came out of mothballs—purchased by emerging cruise lines. These ships have been refurbished for warm-weather cruising operations, often with their interiors being almost entirely redesigned and refitted.

One of the finest examples of the refurbishment of a famous transatlantic liner is the *Norway* (which is operated by the Norwegian Cruise Line), formerly known as the *France* (when it was owned by Compagnie Générale Transatlantique). This ship has been successfully converted into a Caribbean cruise liner, and is a striking sight in all its attendant bold redesigns and vibrant colors.

During the late 1970s the cruise industry was growing at a rapid rate. It is still expanding today and is, in fact, the fastest-growing segment of the travel industry. Several brand new cruise ships enter service each year, and the growth in new ships being built will continue well into the late 1990s.

CRUISING TODAY

Today's cruise concept hasn't changed a great deal from that of earlier days, although it has been improved, refined and expanded. Cruises now place more emphasis on destinations and feature more ports. Modern ships are larger, on the whole, than their counterparts of yesteryear, and yet cabin size has decreased in order to provide more space for ship entertainment and other public facilities.

Today's ships boast air-conditioning to keep heat and humidity out, stabilizers to keep the ship on an even keel, an excellent high level of maintenance, safety and hygiene, and more emphasis on health and fitness facilities.

Cruise ship design has moved from the traditional, classic, rounded profiles of the past to extremely boxy shapes with square sterns and towering superstructures. Although ship lovers lament the changes in design, many changes were brought about by a need to fit as much as possible in the space provided—you can squeeze more in a square box than you can in a round one, although it may be less aesthetically appealing. Form follows function, and ships have changed in function from ocean transportation to floating vacation resorts.

With new ships being introduced at the rate of one every few months to cater for the increase in demand for cruises, and old tonnage in the process of being converted, reconstructed or upgraded in order to comply with the latest international safety and hygiene regulations, the choice for cruise vacations has never been more comprehensive, nor more bewildering.

Whatever you enjoy doing, you'll find it on a cruise. Although ships have long been devoted to eating and relaxation in comfort (promulgating the maxim "Traveling slowly unwinds you faster"), cruise lines now offer so much more in the way of activities as well as learning and life-enriching experiences than were available years ago. Also, there are now so many more places you can visit on a cruise: from Antarctica to Acapulco, Bermuda to Bergen, Dakar to Dominica, Shanghai to St. Thomas, or if you wish, even *nowhere at all*. All told, more than 500 ports are visited by the world's cruise fleet (including 115 in the Aegean/Mediterranean area and 145 in Northern Europe alone).

Although small when compared to the figures for tourism in general, the cruise industry is a $12 billion business worldwide, with over $7 billion in the United States alone and growing at a rate of around 8 per cent each year. Clearly, cruising is in the mainstream of the vacation industry.

With well over 5 million gross registered tons of ships, the global cruise industry provides employment to an increasing number of personnel, both directly (there are over 50,000 shipboard officers, staff and crew, as well as about 15,000 employees in the cruise company head offices) and indirectly (as in the case of the suppliers of foodstuffs and mechanical and electrical parts, the port agents, transport companies, and also a wide variety of other peripheral workers).

The spin-off effect on tourism in those areas that are adjacent, or close to, the world's principal ports for the embarkation and disembarkation of cruise passengers is tremendous, with

direct and indirect benefits to both mainland and island destinations, airlines, railways, bus firms, other transportation systems, hotels, car rental companies, and so on.

In 1995 more than 6 million people worldwide took a cruise, packaged and sold by cruise lines through tour operators and travel agents or cruise consultants. By far the greatest number of passengers were Americans, followed by the British, Germans and Canadians. Most of the cruising took place from the North American ports. While four times as many Americans still prefer to visit Europe on vacation than go for a cruise, the latter is now clearly emerging as a highly attractive value-for-money escape.

The most recent (1995) breakdown of passengers by nationality choosing to take cruise vacations is provided below (taken from figures that have been supplied by the Maritime Evaluations Group):

United States	5,000,000
U.K.*	300,000
Germany	235,000
Canada	200,000
Asia	200,000
Rest of Europe	200,000
France	125,000
Italy	115,000
Australia	100,000
Cyprus**	75,000
Japan	75,000
Total	6,625,000 *

*This figure does not include the 130,000 British passengers that take 2- to 7-day cruises from Cyprus in conjunction with a resort/hotel stay.
**Local Cyprus market (non-British).

In terms of popularity, the Caribbean (including the Bahamas and Bermuda) is still at the forefront of warm-weather cruising, followed closely by Europe (including the Aegean, Mediterranean and Baltic, all of which offer not only sunshine but also historical, cultural and archeological interest). Following this comes Alaska, then comes South-East Asia. And there are several short cruises leaving from Florida, California and San Juan—excellent for a short break and for introducing people to the idea of a longer cruise. As more and more ships are built, it is likely that some will have to move out of the Caribbean and develop new ports of call or home bases. This promises to make a wider range of cruises available to cruisegoers everywhere.

Ship cruising has come of age. No longer the domain of affluent, retired people, the industry today is vibrant and alive with passengers of every age and socio-economic background. Also, cruising is no longer the shipping business, it is the *hospitality* industry.

CONSTRUCTING A MODERN CRUISE SHIP

More than any other type of vessel, a cruise ship has to fulfill fantasies and satisfy exotic imaginations. It is the job of the shipyard to take those fantasies and transform them into a steel ship—without unduly straining the laws of naval architecture and safety regulations, not to mention budgets.

While no perfect cruise ship exists, turning ship owners' dreams and concepts into ships that embody those ideals is the job of specialized marine

architects and shipyards, as well as consultants, interior designers, and a mass of specialist suppliers. Computers have simplified this complex process, which seems to be mostly successful, though shipboard management and operations personnel very often become frustrated with shoreside designers who are more idealist than they are practical.

At one time ships were constructed in huge building docks by being put together from the keel (backbone) up. Today's ships are built in huge sections, then joined together in an assembly area (as many as 45 sections for one of the current ships). The sections may not even be constructed in the shipyard, but they will be assembled there.

Cost is the predominant factor in all ship design and size today. The larger the ship, the more cabins can be incorporated, hence the greater the potential in earnings, both in bookings and on-board revenue. It is said that a 2 per cent increase in cabin capacity on a 1,400-passenger ship could mean an increase of $1–$1.5 million in annual income. But adding more facilities and cabins does increase the weight and cost of a ship.

Ships today represent a compromise between ideals and restrictions of space and finance; the solution, according to some experts, is to design ships for specific conditions of service. That means making a ship to fit a specific operating niche and cruise area, rather than for general use.

Traditionally, passenger spaces have been slotted in wherever there was space within a given hull. Today, however, computers provide the possibility

Building a cruise ship. This view shows the keel of the 72,000-grt Galaxy *being laid. Behind this is the 70,000-grt* Century *nearing completion in the massive building hall at the Meyer Werft shipyard in Papenburg, Germany. (Celebrity Cruises)*

of highly targeted ship design. CAD (computer-aided design) is standard, and enables a new ship to be built within a two-year period instead of within four or five years in the 1950s.

The maximum noise and vibration levels in the accommodations spaces and recreational areas are stipulated in any owner's contract with the shipyard. Global vibration tests are carried out once the ship is built and launched, using what is termed a finite method element of evaluation, which embraces analyses of prime sources of noise and excitation: the ship's propellers and main engines.

In the outfitting of a large cruise ship today, prefabricated cabin modules, including *in situ* bathrooms with toilets, are used. When the steel structure of the relevant deck is ready, with the main lines and insulation already installed, a specific cabin module is then affixed to the deck, and power lines and sanitary plumbing are swiftly connected. All the waste and power connections, together with hot/cold water mixing valves, are arranged in the service area of the bathroom, and can often be reached from outside the cabin module from the passageway.

While accommodations modules in ships can be successfully systemized, the public spaces cannot. Areas such as food preparation galleys and pantries can, however, be supplied on a turnkey arrangement by outside contractors. They install these highly specialized areas during the fitting out period. Electrical wiring is another area that is normally subcontracted today. In the building of the ss *France* (now known as the ss *Norway*), some 18,000 miles of electrical cabling had to be installed.

Numerous contractors and subcontractors are involved during the fitting

Two views of Carnival Cruise Lines' Celebration, seen here in the open air building dock of Kockums, Sweden, with large sections about to be added by an overhead gantry crane.

out period of one of today's cruise vessels, the whole being a massive effort of coordination and timing. If just one or two contractors or subcontractors fall behind schedule, it can put the entire shipbuilding process behind, causing as many problems as, for example, a fire or strike would.

CRUISING TOMORROW

A report by the Maritime Evaluations Group (MEG) states that less than 10 per cent of any national population has discovered cruising, but more ships are being constructed every year because of the expected, and growing, increase in popularity. This has led to an over-capacity of (or rather, less demand for) berths in some cruising areas during certain "soft" periods each year, which has kept prices modest and extremely competitive in favor of passengers (in 1995 several cruise lines offered two for one discounts). Since 85 per cent of people who take cruises are eager to go again, the overcapacity should decline as the margin increases.

The average age of all cruisegoers is decreasing, with almost 40 per cent of new passengers under the age of 35. Clearly, this has meant a revamping of on-board facilities and activities for many ships, the provision of more and better health and fitness facilities and programs, and a higher, more international standard of entertainment.

There is a definite trend toward "specialty" cruising, on smaller ships which are equipped to cater to young, active passengers pursuing their hobbies or special interests, such as watersports. Cruise areas are developing for the islands of the South Pacific, the Far East, South America, and around East and West Africa.

As for ship design, current thinking in the industry follows two distinct avenues, both based on the "economy of scale" and on market forces. The economy of scale helps the operator to keep down the cost per passenger. This is the reason for the move toward either large ships that can carry 2,000 passengers or more (*Carnival Destiny, CostaVictoria, Ecstasy, Fantasy, Imagination, Inspiration, Legend of the Seas, Majesty of the Seas, Monarch of the Seas, Oriana, Sensation,* and *Splendour of the Seas,* for example), or smaller luxury vessels that do not accommodate more than 250 passengers (*Oceanic Grace, Queen Odyssey, Radisson Diamond, Renaissance 1-8, Sea Goddess I, Sea Goddess II, Seabourn Pride, Seabourn Spirit, Song of Flower,* for example).

This presumes that some passengers will think "bigger is better," whereas others will think "small and exclusive." Somehow, it is difficult to make a profit out of mid-sized ships in an economically variable environment as in the U.S. (Caribbean) market (but they are ideal for the small ports of the Aegean and the Mediterranean cruise areas); ships that have been delivered during the past few years are either large-capacity mega-ships or small-capacity yacht-like vessels, with only a sprinkling of mid-sized ships.

True, large ships can offer more facilities than small ships, but they can't get into so many ports; and a metropolis at sea, while it might be good for large conventions and meetings, poses a challenge for the individual cruise passenger who simply

51

SAFETY

Safeguards for cruise passengers include lifeboats and life rafts. Since the introduction of the 1983 amendments to Chapter III of the *Safety of Life at Sea* (SOLAS) *Convention 1974* (which actually came into effect in 1980), much attention has been given to safety, particularly to ships' lifeboats, their design and effectiveness. All cruise ships built since July 1, 1986 have either totally enclosed or partially enclosed lifeboats. The totally enclosed lifeboats have diesel engines that will still operate when inverted.

The latest life rafts, called Hydrostatic Release Units (HRU), were designed in Britain and approved by the Royal Navy, and are now compulsory on all British-registered ships. Briefly, an HRU is capable of automatically releasing a life raft from its mountings when a ship sinks (even *after* it sinks), but can also be operated manually at the installation point, saving precious time in an emergency.

The 1990 SOLAS standards on stability and fire protection (mandating the installation of sprinkler systems) for new ship construction are taking effect in 1994. Existing ships have another five years to comply (the retro-fitting of sprinkler systems is an expensive measure that may not be considered viable by owners of older ships).

A lifeboat drill must be conducted on board within 24 hours of leaving port. You will hear an announcement from the bridge, which goes something like this:

"Ladies and Gentlemen, may I have your attention, please. This is the captain speaking to you from the bridge. In fifteen minutes time, the ship's alarm bells will signal emergency lifeboat drill for all passengers. This is a mandatory drill, conducted in accordance with the requirements of the Safety of Life at Sea Convention. There are no exceptions.

"The emergency signal is a succession of seven or more short blasts followed by one long blast of the ship's whistle, supplemented by the ringing of the electric gongs throughout the ship. On hearing this signal, you should make your way quickly but quietly to your cabin, put on some warm clothing and your lifejacket, then follow the signs to your emergency boat station, where you will be kept fully informed over the loudspeakers through which I am speaking to you now."

wants to have a quiet, restful vacation. However, with two cruise companies, Carnival Cruise Lines and Princess Cruises, launching three ships between them that measure over 100,000 grt, the "bigger is better" principle is being pursued for all it's worth, even though these ships might be limited to the Caribbean as they are too wide to transit the Panama Canal.

The "small is exclusive" concept, on the other hand, has now gained a strong foothold, particularly in the luxury category. New specialist lines offer very high quality ships of low capacity. A small-draft vessel can enter ports larger ships can't even approach, and it can provide a highly personalized range of quality services. However, small ships aren't as stable in bad weather, which is why they tend to follow itineraries close to shore.

Some cruise lines have expanded by "stretching" their ships. This is accomplished by taking a ship into dry dock, literally cutting it in half, and inserting a newly constructed midsection. This instantly increases the vessel's capacity, enabling it to add more accommodations space and enlarge public room facilities, with the advantage of maintaining the same draft.

One interesting example of such a ship stretch can clearly be seen in Holland America Line's *Westerdam* (ex-*Homeric*), where the midsection that was built and inserted has larger windows than the fore and aft sections which formed the original ship. The *Westerdam* was, in fact, the first ship ever to be stretched in dry dock (in the world's largest covered building dock at Papenburg, Germany). Other examples of ships that have been stretched

(all of them done in "wet" dock with the ship in the water and the new midsection floated into place and then welded together) are: *Golden Princess* (ex-*Royal Viking Sky*), *Royal Odyssey* (ex-*Royal Viking Sea*), *Song of Norway*, and *Star Odyssey* (ex-*Royal Viking Star*).

Besides the traditional monohull construction of all but one cruise vessel up to now, a switch to multihull and "swath" (small water area twin hull) is most unlikely. Although multihull vessels provide a sound, wide base on which a platform can be constructed, with both accommodations and public areas lying well above the water line, one such example being the twin semi-submersible-hulled *Radisson Diamond*, there has as yet been little attempt to extend this idea.

Whatever direction the design of cruise vessels takes in future, ships, and the companies that operate them, will have to become increasingly environmentally friendly, and passengers will need to be taught to behave accordingly. With growing concern about the environment, particularly in eco-sensitive areas such as Alaska and the South Pacific, better safeguards against environmental pollution will have to be built into the vessels themselves.

The cruise industry is quickly heading toward "zero discharge," whereby nothing is discharged into the world's oceans at all, at any time. This is, naturally, an easier objective to attain for the latest batch of ships (in particular for small vessels). Older ships will have a more difficult time of achieving zero discharge owing to now outdated equipment. The future, however, is in total environment protection through zero discharge.

Choosing Your Ship and Cruise

So, you've decided your next vacation will be a cruise. Good choice! But the decisions don't stop there. Bombarded with glossy cruise literature tempting you with every imaginable lure, and the overly prolific use of the word "luxury," you may find choosing the right cruise for you difficult.

Whether you are traveling alone, or with your loved one or family, there are different ships to fit different people and their personal needs. Despite company claims that theirs has been named the "Best Cruise Line" or "Best Cruise Ship," there is no best cruise line or best cruise ship, only what's best, and *right*, for you.

WHAT A CRUISE IS

A cruise is a vacation, that is, a complete change of scenery, environment and people. It is an *antidote* to the stresses and strains of contemporary life ashore. It offers you a chance to relax and unwind in comfortable surroundings, with attentive service, good food, and a ship that changes the scenery for you as you go—and you don't even have to drive. It is virtually a hassle-free, and, more importantly, a crime-free vacation (which is a major consideration that cruise lines don't advertise, but it applies especially to families with children). On a cruise, you never have to make blind choices. Everything's close at hand, and there are always polite people to help you.

WHAT A CRUISE IS NOT

Some cruises simply aren't relaxing, despite cruise brochures proclaiming "that you can do as much or as little as you want to." Watch out for the high-density ships—mega-ships that carry 2,000 or more passengers—or older ships with limited public room space; they tend to cram lots of passengers into small cabins and provide non-stop activities that do little but insult the intelligence and taste buds, and assault the pocket.

How do you begin to select the right cruise for the right price? Price is, of course, the key factor for most people. The cost of a cruise provides a useful guideline to the ambiance, passengers and degree of luxury, food and service that you'll likely find on board.

The amount you are prepared to spend on a cruise will be a determining factor in the size, location and style of the shipboard accommodations you will be assigned. You should be wary of cruise lines that seem to offer huge discounts, for it either means that the product was unrealistically priced at source, or that there will be a reduction in quality somewhere. Remember, discount the price, and you end up with discounted quality. Aside from cost, ships are as individual as fingerprints: no two are the same and each one of them can change its "personality" from cruise to cruise, very much depending on the make-up and character of the passengers on the ship.

WHERE TO?

With approximately 500 destinations available to cruise ships, it's almost certain that there's a ship to take you wherever you want to go. Because itineraries vary widely, depending on each ship and cruise, it is wise to make as many comparisons as you possibly can by reading the cruise brochures for descriptions of the ports of call. If, for example, you would like a Caribbean or a Mediterranean cruise, it is possible to choose from over 100 itineraries.

Several ships may offer the same, or similar itineraries, simply because these have been successfully tried and tested. You can then narrow the choice further by noting the time spent at each port, and whether the ship actually docks in port or lies at anchor. Then compare the size of each vessel and its facilities.

Caribbean and Mediterranean Cruises

If you want to take a cruise around the Caribbean or the Mediterranean, what you will notice when making your choice of cruise is the trend and marketing strategy of some companies to offer more ports in a week than their competitors. Indeed, there are several ships that feature seven or more ports in a week, which means you will be visiting at least one port a day on some of the Greek Isle cruises.

This kind of intensive "island hopping" leaves little time to explore a destination to the full before you have to be back on board for a quick sail to the next port. While you see a lot of places in a week, by the end of the cruise you may need another week to unwind. Ultimately, this is not the best way to cruise, unless you really wish to cover a lot of ground in a short space of time.

Private Islands

Several cruise lines with Caribbean itineraries have their own "private island" (often called an "out-island")— a small island in the Bahamas close to Nassau (or in the Turks and Caicos Islands) that is outfitted with all the ingredients to make an all-day beach party a memorable occasion. These are

Celebrity Cruises' 1,354-passenger Horizon, *seen here arriving in New York*
Rating ★★★★

55

extremely popular with passengers as it's like having a full day in paradise, with watersports, scuba, snorkeling, crystal-clear waters, warm sands, even a hammock or two. And there are no reservations to be made, no tickets to purchase, no hassle with taxis. Norwegian Cruise Line was the first to use an out-island, way back in 1977.

Cruise lines have their own inventive names for these islands, such as Blue Lagoon Island (Dolphin Cruise Line), Great Stirrup Cay (Norwegian Cruise Line), Princess Cays (Princess Cruises), Royal Isle (Majesty Cruise Line). Some of the out-islands may change names, depending on what day of the week it is, and what ship is in. Note that the beaches, while idyllic for 200 passengers, can prove extremely noisy and crowded when filled with 2,000 (or possibly more) passengers from one of the large ships, anchored for a "Beach Barbecue Day." The good thing is that the "private island" will not be cluttered with hawkers, as are so many beaches in the Caribbean today.

European Cruises

If you are planning to go to Europe (including the Baltic and the Mediterranean areas), then think about traveling there by cruise ship. So many of Europe's greatest cities—among them Amsterdam, Barcelona, Copenhagen, Genoa, Helsinki, Lisbon, London, Monte Carlo, Nice, Oslo, St. Petersburg, Stockholm and Venice—are situated on the water, and it is much less expensive to take a cruise than to fly and pay enormously high rates to stay in decent hotels. Another advantage of the cruise is that you won't have to contend with trying to speak or understand different languages when you are aboard ship as you would ashore.

You should be aware that small- or medium-sized ships are better than large ships, as they will be able to get berthing space (large ships may have to anchor). On some of the itineraries, one company may give you more time ashore than another, so it pays to compare cruise brochures. On ships that cater to passengers of different nationalities, you should be aware that daily programs, and announcements, will be in as many as six different languages.

Alaska Cruises

For a real cold rush, try an Alaska cruise. You should know, however, that some ships must anchor rather than dock in several ports of call, because of the limited amount of docking space. Some lines also may pay more in fees so that their ships can dock alongside, making it easier for passengers to go ashore; this is particularly useful when the weather is poor. Unfortunately, most cruise brochures don't indicate which ports are known to be anchor (tender) ports (European, and particularly German, brochures are much better at providing this information).

Holland America Line and Princess Cruises both have such comprehensive shoreside facilities—hotels, tour buses, and even trains—that they are totally committed to Alaska for many years. Holland America Line-Westours and Princess Tours (a division of Princess Cruises), for example, have invested as much as $170 million and $75 million in Alaska respectively. Other lines have to depend on what's left of the various forms of local transportation for their shoreside tours.

Holland America Line's 1,212-passenger Noordam, *seen here in Glacier Bay, Alaska.*
Rating ★★★★

Sadly, there is now so much congestion in the tiny Alaskan ports, where there can be several ships in port on any one day, that avoiding crowded streets becomes an unpleasant part of the cruise experience. Even nature is retreating; with more humans around, wildlife is becoming harder to spot. Mass tourism is having its effect.

Transcanal Cruises
Transcanal cruises take you through the wonders of the Panama Canal, which was started in 1880 by Ferdinand de Lesseps (who also built the Suez Canal in 1860-9) and which was finally opened in 1914. The canal traverses from north to south (not east to west as many believe), and the best way to experience this feat of engineering is from the privileged position of a cruise ship. Cruising from the Caribbean to the Pacific, your ship will be raised by almost 80 feet by three canal locks (at Gatun), negotiate the narrow Gaillard Cut, a series of six reaches cut through

a range of green hills, and then will be lowered again by two more locks (located at Miraflores), just by the sheer forces of nature. What is known as mechanical "mules" are attached to pull your ship through the locks. Most ship journeys start in Fort Lauderdale or San Juan and end in Acapulco or Los Angeles, and vice versa.

Australasia and Orient Cruises
If you like the idea of Australasia, South-East Asia and the Orient, and you live in Europe or North America, be aware that the flying time to get to your port of embarkation and ship will be long. It is advisable to arrive at least two days before the cruise, as the time changes and jet lag can be quite severe to those not used to long distances. The whole area has so much to offer, however, that it's worth taking a cruise of a minimum of 14 days in order to make the most of it.

Choose an itinerary that appeals to you, and then read about the proposed

destinations and their attractions. The public library or your local bookstore are usually valuable sources of information, and your cruise or travel agent will also be able to provide some of the essential background on destinations and help you select an itinerary.

HOW LONG?

On many ship cruises, the standard of luxury and comfort is generally in direct proportion to the length of the cruise. Naturally, in order to operate long, low-density voyages, cruise lines must charge high rates to cover the extensive preparations, high food and transportation costs, port operations, fuel and whatever other expenditures. The length of cruise you choose will depend on the time and money at your disposal and the degree of comfort you are seeking.

The popular standard length of cruise is seven days, although trips vary from a one-day gambling jamboree to a slow exotic voyage around the world lasting over 120 days. If you are new to cruising and want to "get your feet wet," you might try a short cruise of three or four days first. This will give you a good idea of what is involved, the kind of facilities and the lifestyle on board. While a three- or four-day cruise from a Japanese port should be quite relaxing, you should be advised that a three- or four-day cruise from an American port such as Miami, Fort Lauderdale or Los Angeles, or from the Greek port of Piraeus, could end up as more of an endurance test. It's fine if you like non-stop activities, noise and razzle-dazzle stimulation, but it is

hardly what you need if all you want to do is to relax.

Some of the spectacular modern ships, such as Majesty Cruise Line's *Royal Majesty*, Norwegian Cruise Line's *Leeward* and Royal Caribbean Cruises' *Nordic Empress*, operate in the Miami-to-Bahamas marketplace, while Carnival Cruise Lines' *Fantasy* cruises to the Bahamas from Port Canaveral in Florida. Then there are the three- and four-day cruises operated by Premier Cruise Lines, particularly for families and children, where out-island beaches provide an attraction.

WHICH SHIP?

Because cruise ships (particularly the larger variety) are self-sufficient resorts, there really is a cruise line, cruise and ship to suit virtually everyone, so it is important to take into account your own personality when selecting a ship.

Ships are measured (not weighed) in gross registered tons (grt) and come in a variety of sizes, from intimate (up to 10,000 grt), small (10,000–20,000 grt), medium (20,000–30,000 grt) to large (30,000–60,000 grt) and mega-ship size (60,000–100,000+ grt). But whatever the dimensions, all the ships provide the same basic ingredients: accommodations, activities, entertainment, food, good service, and ports of call, although some of them tend to do it better than others.

There are a few "all-inclusive" ships where there really are no bar bills to pay, nothing to sign for, no gratuities to give, and no standing in line to sign up for shore excursions, but these tend to be the smaller "luxury" cruise ships

that cost upwards of $500 per person, per day (although there are suites on larger "standard" market cruise ships that can easily cost that). Once you're on board, you may never have to say "how much?" Most of the larger cruise ships, however, will entice you in many ways to spend money on board, which is one way that cruise lines manage to support their low fares.

If you like or need a lot of space around you, it is of little use booking a cruise on a small, intimate ship where you knock elbows almost every time you move. If you like intimacy, close contact with people and a homey ambiance, you may feel lost and lonely on a large ship, which inevitably will have a more impersonal atmosphere. If you are about to enter the world of cruising for the first time, do choose a ship that's in the small or medium-size range. To get an idea of the amount of space you'll have around you on the ship, look closely at the Passenger Space Ratio given in the evaluation of each ship in Part Three of this book. A Passenger Space Ratio of 40 and above is the ultimate in terms of space per passenger; 30 and above can be considered extremely spacious; between 20 and 30, is moderately so; between 10 and 20 would be high density; and below 10, extremely cramped, as in "sardine-style."

A ship's country of registration or parent company location can be a clue to the atmosphere on board, although there are many ships that are registered, for financial reasons, under a flag of convenience, such as Liberia or Panama. The nationality of the officers or management often sets the style and ambiance of a ship and the cruise.

You can estimate the standard of service by looking at the crew to passenger ratio. You will find a better service on those ships that have a ratio of one crew member to every two passengers, or higher.

Except for those ships with a single-nationality crew (as in the case of the Greek Epirotiki Cruise Line and Sun Line Cruises or the German-speaking Hapag-Lloyd Cruises), the crew mixture can give the impression of the ship being like a miniature United Nations. On a ship carrying a multi-nationality crew, you can expect to find the language proportions something like the following: 38% will be European, 36% North/South American, and 26% will be Asian (Celebrity Cruises).

If the crew is a happy one, the ship will be happy too, and passengers will certainly be able to sense it. The best way for any cruise ship to have a happy crew is for the cruise line to provide good accommodations, food and relaxation facilities for them. The best ships in the world, from the point of view of the crew's living and working conditions, are the *Europa* (Hapag-Lloyd Cruises) *Crystal Harmony* and *Crystal Symphony* (Crystal Cruises), *Asuka* (NYK Cruises), *Queen Odyssey* (the Royal Cruise Line), *Royal Viking Sun* (Cunard Royal Viking), and *Seabourn Pride/Seabourn Spirit* (the Seabourn Cruise Line). At present, there are few other ships that come close to these. Indeed, Hapag-Lloyd Cruises even has a pension plan for its crews. Holland America Line has a school for its service personnel in Jakarta, but few seem able to speak English well even when they've been to the school (maybe due to lack of time learning the language).

59

SHIPS UNDER 10,000 GRT

Andaman Princess
Antonina Nezhdanova
Astra
Ayvasovskiy
Berlin
Bremen
Caledonian Star
Columbus Caravelle
Daphne
Explorer
Funchal
Hanseatic
Hebridean Princess
Klaudia Yelanskaya
Konstantin Simonov
Le Ponant
Megastar Aries
Megastar Taurus
Mikhail Sholokhov
Nantucket Clipper

Oceanic Grace
Orient Star
Orpheus
Polaris
Princesa Amorosa
Princesa Cypria
Princesa Marissa
Queen Elini
Queen Odyssey
Regent Calypso
Renaissance One
Renaissance Two
Renaissance Three
Renaissance Four
Renaissance Five
Renaissance Six
Renaissance Seven
Renaissance Eight
Romantica
Royal Star

St. Helena
Sea Cloud
Sea Goddess I
Sea Goddess II
Seabourn Pride
Seabourn Spirit
SeaSpirit
Sir Francis Drake
Song of Flower
Star Clipper
Star Flyer
Stella Maris
Stella Oceanis
Vistamar
Yorktown Clipper
Wind Song
Wind Spirit
Wind Star
World Discoverer

SHIPS OF 10,000–20,000 GRT

Aegean Dolphin
Americana
Amerikanis
Arkona
Atalante
Ausonia
Azerbaydzhan
Bali Sea Dancer
Black Prince
Bolero
Club Med I
Club Med II
CostaPlaya
Crown Dynasty
Cunard Countess
Dimitri Shostakovich
Dolphin IV

Gruziya
Ilich
Island Princess
Italia Prima
Kareliya
Kazakhstan II
La Palma
Leisure World
Lev Tolstoi
Mermoz
Nautican
Ocean Majesty
Odessa
Odysseus
Princesa Victoria
Radisson Diamond
Rhapsody

Regent Spirit
Sea Prince
Seawing
Silver Cloud
Silver Wind
Song of Norway
Southern Cross
Stella Solaris
Sun Viking
Superstar Gemini
Symphony
The Azur
Triton
Ukraine
Universe
World Renaissance

SHIPS OF 20,000–30,000 GRT

Albatros
Asuka
Carousel
CostaAllegra
CostaMarina
Enchanted Isle
Enchanted Seas
Fairstar
Fedor Dostoyevsky
Fedor Shalyapin
Fuji Maru
Golden Princess
Ivan Franko
Kapitan Dranitsyn

Kapitan Khlebnikov
Leonid Sobinov
Marco Polo
Maxim Gorki
Monterey
Nippon Maru
OceanBreeze
Olympic
Orient Venus
Pacific Princess
Regal Empress
Regent Isle
Regent Rainbow
Regent Sea

Regent Star
Regent Sun
Royal Odyssey
Sagafjord
SeaBreeze I
Seawind Crown
Shota Rustaveli
Sovetskiy Soyuz
Star Odyssey
Taras Shevchenko
Victoria
Vistafjord
Yamal

SHIPS OF 30,000–60,000 GRT

Aida
Canberra
Celebration
Constitution
CostaClassica
CostaRiviera
CostaRomantica
Crown Odyssey
Crystal Harmony
Crystal Symphony
Dreamward
EugenioCosta
Europa
Festivale

Holiday
Horizon
Independence
Jubilee
Langkapuri Star Aquarius
Maasdam
Meridian
Nieuw Amsterdam
Noordam
Nordic Empress
Rotterdam
Royal Majesty
Royal Princess
Royal Viking Sun

Ryndam
Seaward
Sky Princess
Song of America
Star/Ship Atlantic
Star/Ship Oceanic
Statendam
Tropicale
Viking Serenade
Westerdam
Windward
Zenith

SHIPS OVER 60,000 GRT

Carnival Destiny
Century
Crown Princess
Ecstasy
Fantasy
Fascination
Grandeur of the Seas

Imagination
Inspiration
Legend of the Seas
Majesty of the Seas
Monarch of the Seas
Norway
Oriana

Queen Elizabeth 2
Regal Princess
Sensation
Sovereign of the Seas
Splendour of the Seas
Star Princess
Sun Princess

NEW VS OLD SHIPS

Some executives in the cruise industry, whose fleets comprise new tonnage, are often quoted as saying that all pre-1960 tonnage should be scrapped. Yet there are many passengers who like the older-style ships. While it is inevitable that some older tonnage cannot match up to the latest in high-tech section-built ships, it should also be noted that ships today are simply not constructed to the same high standards, or with the same loving care, as in the past. Below are some advantages and disadvantages of both.

New Ships—Advantages:

- They meet the latest safety and operating standards, as laid down by the international maritime conventions.
- They offer passengers more public room space, with public rooms and lounges built out to the sides of the hull, as open and closed promenade decks are no longer regarded as an essential requirement.
- They have public room spaces that are easier to convert if necessary.
- They offer more standardized cabin layouts and fewer categories.
- They are more fuel efficient.
- They manage to incorporate the latest advances in technology, as well as the latest in passenger and crew facilities and amenities.
- They do have a shallower draft, which makes it easier for them to enter and leave ports.
- They have bow and stern thrusters, so they seldom require tug assistance in many ports, in this way cutting operating costs.

- They have plumbing and air-conditioning systems that are new—and that work.
- They have diesel engines mounted on rubber to minimize vibration.
- They are usually fitted with the latest submersible lifeboats.

New Ships—Disadvantages:

- They do not "take the weather" as well as older ships (the experience of sailing across the North Atlantic in November on one of the new mega-ships can be unforgettable). Because of their shallow draft, these ships roll—even when there is the slightest puff of wind.
- They tend to have smaller standard cabins, which can mean narrow—and very often short—beds.
- They have thin hulls and therefore do not withstand the bangs and dents as well as older, more heavily plated vessels.
- They have decor made mostly from synthetic materials (due to stringent fire regulations), and therefore could cause problems for those passengers who are sensitive to such materials.
- They are powered by diesel engines, which inevitably cause some vibration; although on the latest vessels, the engines are mounted on pliable, floating rubber cushions and are therefore virtually vibration-free.
- They have cabin windows that are completely sealed instead of portholes that can be opened.

Older Ships (pre-1970)—Advantages:

- They have very strong, plated hulls (often riveted) that can withstand

Costa Cruises' 810-passenger CostaAllegra *cruises the Mediterranean, and offers a dramatic wall of glass in the restaurant at the stern of the ship.*
Rating ★★★+

tremendously hard wear and tear. They can "take the weather" well.

- They have large cabins with long, wide beds/berths, due to the fact that passengers of yesteryear needed more space, given that voyages were much longer.
- They have a wide range of cabin sizes, shapes and grades which are more suited to those families traveling with children.
- They are powered by steam turbines, which are virtually free of vibration or noise and are considerably quieter and smoother in operation than modern vessels.
- They have portholes that, in many instances, actually open.
- Their interiors are built from more traditional materials such as wood and brass, with less use of synthetic fibers (and are therefore less likely to affect anyone who is allergic to synthetics).
- They have deep drafts which help them to achieve a smooth ride in the open seas.

Older Ships (pre-1970)— Disadvantages:

- They are not so fuel efficient, and therefore they are more expensive to operate than the new ships.
- They need a larger crew, because of the more awkward labor-intensive layouts of the ships.
- They have a deep draft (necessary for a smooth ride), but need tugs to negotiate ports and tight berths.
- They have increasing difficulty in complying with the current international fire, safety and environmental regulations.
- They are usually fitted with older-type open lifeboats.
- Any vessel 10 years old or more is likely to have plumbing and air-conditioning problems in cabins and public areas.

The International Maritime Organization (IMO), which is a United Nations agency, was formed in the late 1940s to vote in legislation among its 130-plus member nations regulating the safety

63

of life at sea. The IMO Safety Committee has voted to bring older ships up to date by making various safety features—such as smoke detectors—mandatory in all cruise vessels. From 1994, and covering an 11-year period, all vessels are required to fit sprinkler systems (this is an expensive retrofit for many older ships).

MAIDEN/INAUGURAL VOYAGES

There is an element of excitement in taking the plunge on a maiden voyage of a new cruise ship, or in joining the inaugural voyage of a recently refurbished, or reconstructed, or stretched vessel, or in exploring a new cruising area. But although it can be exciting, there is usually an element or two of uncertainty in any first voyage, as with, for example, Orient Lines' *Marco Polo*, whose maiden voyage was postponed until its programmed second voyage, due to the ship not quite being finished. Of course there are many things that can, and invariably do, go badly awry. Then again there are maiden voyages that have no major problems, but, on most, Murphy's Law prevails: "if anything can go wrong, it will."

If you are a repeat cruiser who has a degree of tolerance, and isn't phased by some inconvenience, or perhaps slow or non-existent service in the dining room, fine; otherwise, it is best to wait until the ship has been in service for at least two or three months. Then again, if you book a cruise on the third or fourth voyage, and there is a delay in the ship's introduction, you could find yourself on the maiden voyage! One

thing is certain—any maiden voyage is a collector's item. Bon Voyage!

So, what exactly can go wrong?

- A strike, or fire, or even a bankruptcy at a shipyard are possible causes of delay to a new ship or a completely new cruise line about to embark on its first venture. Ship introductions such as *Club Med I*, *Crown Monarch*, *Crown Dynasty*, *Ecstasy*, *Fantasy*, *Marco Polo*, *Nieuw Amsterdam* as well as the eight small Renaissance vessels were all delayed by shipyard strikes and bankruptcies, while the *Astor* (which is now called *Arkona*), *Crown Dynasty* and *Monarch of the Seas* were delayed as a result of extensive fires while still being fitted out.

- Service on new or recently refurbished ships or a new cruise line is likely to be uncertain at best, and could be a complete disaster. An existing cruise line may well use experienced crew from its other vessels to help "bring out" a new ship, but they may be unfamiliar with the ship's layout and have problems training other staff.

- Plumbing and electrical items tend to cause the most problems, particularly on reconstructed and refurbished vessels. For example: there could be toilets that don't flush, or don't stop flushing; faucets incorrectly marked, where "hot" really means "cold" and vice versa; room thermostats that have been mistakenly fitted with reverse wiring; televisions, audio channels, lights and electronic card key locks that don't work; electrical outlets incorrectly indicated; "automatic" telephones

that simply refuse to function; and so on it goes.

- The galley (kitchen) of a new ship causes perhaps the most consternation. Even if everything does work, and the executive chef has ordered all the right ingredients and supplies, they could be anywhere other than where they should be. Imagine if they forgot to load the seasoning, or if the eggs arrived shell-shocked!

- "Software" items such as menus, postcards, writing paper, or remote control units for television and/or video systems, door keys, towels, pillowcases, glassware, and perhaps even toilet paper, may be missing—lost in the bowels of the ship, or simply not ordered.

- In the entertainment department, some item, such as spare spotlight bulbs, may not be in stock, or there may be no hooks on which to hang the costumes backstage—if such an area is provided, for many ships don't even have dressing rooms. Or what if the pianos arrived damaged, or the charts for the lectures didn't show up? If the ship has been supplied with German-made sound and light equipment, the operating manuals might be in German, so what does the American stage technician do? So, in the ship's entertainment department there are many things that can go wrong.

At the real luxury end of the market, where the best in luxury and personal service corresponds to a per day cost of over $500 per person, the choice is between either the large ships, which, because of their size, have more facilities and entertainment for passengers, or the small ships, which can provide a greater degree of personal service.

LARGE LUXURY SHIPS VS SMALL LUXURY SHIPS

Large ships (those which measure over 30,000 grt) have the widest range of public rooms and facilities—but no large ship has yet been constructed with a watersports platform/marina at its stern. The finest in personal butler service is featured in the top penthouse suites on ships such as *Crystal Harmony*, *Crystal Symphony*, *Queen Elizabeth 2* and *Royal Viking Sun*.

Small (country club) ships (those measuring under 10,000 grt) may lack space and some of the facilities that larger ships offer, but they usually have a hydraulic marina watersports platform located in the stern. They also carry equipment such as jet skis, windsurfers, a waterski power boat, scuba and snorkeling gear, and, in the case of two ships in particular, a swimming enclosure for use in areas where waters may be unsafe. Small ships can also truly cater to the highest degree of culinary excellence. On *Sea Goddess I* and *Sea Goddess II*, those seeking the ultimate in decadence can revel in Beluga caviar, champagne and a variety of fine wines whenever they want—and all at no extra cost.

THEME CRUISES

If you still think that all cruises are the same, the following list will give you an idea of what is available in the way of special theme cruise:

65

Adventure	Fashion
Archeological	Food and Wine
Art Lovers	Holistic Health
Backgammon	Jazz Festival
Big Band Bridge	Maiden Voyage
Chess Tournament	Movie Buffs
Chocoholics	Murder Mystery
Classical Music	Naturalist
Computer Science	Photographic
Cosmetology	Singles
Country and Western	Square Dancing
Diet and Nutrition	Steamboat Race
Educational	Theatrical
Exploration	

Perhaps the most successful theme cruise is the annual Classical Music Cruise aboard the *Mermoz* (Paquet French Cruises), which is organized by André Borocz, who is himself an accomplished musician. Famous classical musicians who have been engaged to perform (or sing) on the cruise have included Annie Fisher, Isaac Stern, James Galway, Jean-Pierre Rampal, Mystislav Rostropovich, Tamas Vasary, Maurice André and Vladimir Ashkenazy. Shore excursions consist of concerts in some of the world's most beautiful settings.

For enthusiasts of jazz, the most comprehensive cruise is the Annual Floating Jazz Festival in October each year aboard the *Norway* (Norwegian Cruise Lines), in which performers of such standing as Clark Terry, Gary Burton, Joe Williams, Jimmy McGriff, Lee Konitz, Lou Donaldson, Jimmy Giuffre, Stanley Turrentine and Dick Hyman can be found.

Other music styles that are gaining popularity at sea include Country and Western, Rhythm 'n' Blues, and '50s and '60s music cruises.

25 SIGNS YOU'VE CHOSEN THE WRONG SHIP

- When, after you've embarked, a waiter hands you a drink in a tall plastic glass from a whole tray of ones of identical color and froth, then gives you a bill to sign and doesn't even have the courtesy to say "Welcome Aboard."
- When the so-called "luxury" cabin you booked has walls so thin you can hear your neighbor combing his hair.
- When what the brochure describes as a "Full Bathtub" actually means "a large sink" located at floor level.
- When you wanted a quiet, restful cruise, but your travel agent has put you on a ship with 300 baseball fans and provided them all with signed baseball bats and ghetto blasters for their use (solution: read this book thoroughly first)!
- When you packed your tuxedo, but the ship's passengers take "formal" attire to mean clean cut-off jeans and a less stained T-shirt. Check the brochure carefully.
- When the "medical facility" is in fact located in the purser's office and consists of a box of plasters with directions for their use in a foreign language only.
- When the gymnasium equipment is kept in the maître d's office.
- When you have a cabin with an "obstructed view" (this will usually mean there's a lifeboat hanging outside it!), and it is next to or below the disco. Or laundry.
- When the "Fresh Selected Greens" on the menu means a sprig of parsley on the entree plate, at every

lunch and dinner sitting (boring even on a three-day cruise).

- When the cruise director tries to sell the passengers a watch, or a piece of art, over the ship's public address system.

- When you have to buy shin pads to prevent injury just in case 600 children try to run you over in the passageways.

- When the cruise brochure shows your cabin with flowers and champagne, but you don't get either. If you want them, you get a bill, and in any case the flowers are never watered anyway.

- When the Evian water bottle on your dining room table comes with a bill ever so quickly if you dare open the bottle.

- When "Fresh Catch of the Day" on the menu means the fish is so old that it would be best used as a door wedge.

- When the brochure says "Butler Service" but you have to clean your own shoes, get your own ice and still tip him double the amount you would for a cabin steward.

- When the Beer Drinking Contest, the Hog Calling Contest, Knobbly Knees Contest, and Pajama Bingo are listed as "enrichment lectures."

- When the "fresh squeezed orange juice" you just ordered means fresh-squeezed, but last week, or the week before that, on land, and then poured into industrial size containers, before transfer to your styrofoam cup on deck.

- When the brochure says tipping is not required, but your waiter and cabin steward tell you otherwise, and threaten they'll break your

kneecaps if you don't hand them something that approaches what to you is a large sum of money.

- When the cruise director thoughtfully telephones you at 2:30 a.m. to tell you that the bingo jackpot is up to $1,000!

- When, on the final day the words "early breakfast" means 5:00 a.m., and "vacate your cabin by 7:30 a.m." means you spend about three hours sitting in the showlounge waiting for disembarkation, with 500 available seats, your hand luggage and 2,000 other passengers.

•. When the Lifeboat Drill consists of some crew member handing you a lifejacket and asking *you* to teach *him* how to wear it, and then asking you what the whistle's for.

- When you're out on deck, you look up and notice a big hole in the bottom of one or more of the ship's lifeboats.

- When the cabin steward tries to sell you a time-share in his uncle's coal mine in wherever he's from, at a greatly reduced price, or go without soap and towels for a week.

- When the proclaimed "five-course gourmet meal" in the dining room turns out to be five courses of salty chicken soup.

•. When the "Deck Buffet" literally means that there are no tables and chairs, only the deck, to eat off.

- When the brochure shows photos of smiling young couples, but you and your spouse/partner are the only ones under 80.

- When the library is located in the engine room.

- When the captain tells you he isn't licensed to sail the ship.

Comparing the
Small Luxury Cruise Ships

Big ships are like big resorts, with more impersonal "you're one of a number" service; for the best in personal attention, food and service, try one of the small cruise ships. Almost every ship owner wants to be a "luxury" cruise operator, and most passengers want to sail on one of the top-rated "luxury" ships. But not everyone can, and very few operators can really deliver a five-stars-plus product. It is therefore refreshing to find that there are ships to cater to more discerning travelers.

Fifteen "boutique" cruise ships, more like small inns than mega-resorts, are more specialized; the latest breed of small luxury vessels—under 10,000 grt—carry less than 250 passengers in great comfort, providing an unstructured lifestyle. They offer a level of service not found on most larger ships, and which is superior to that of many five-star hotels on land.

COMPARING THE SHIPS*

CUNARD SEA GODDESS CRUISES

Sea Goddess I (4,260-grt; 116 passengers; PSR: 36.7)
Sea Goddess II (4,260-grt; 116 passengers; PSR: 36.7)

These two ships started the luxury ball rolling in the early 1980s, by featuring "yacht-harbor" destinations that were not accessible to larger cruise ships.

While the cabins are quite small, each of the ships offers a setting of fine luxury and a standard of culinary excellence and creativity unmatched by any other. There's an exclusive country club atmosphere, and all drinks are included. The highly personal service is practiced as an art, and most staff remember passengers' names—which is no mean achievement.

RADISSON SEVEN SEAS CRUISES

Song of Flower (8,282-grt; 214 passengers; PSR: 38.7)

This ship, while not exactly handsome externally, features destination-intensive cruises in relatively luxurious surroundings, with a fine level of warm, personal service. The staff—many have been with the ship since her maiden voyage—learn passengers' names and favorite drinks. The cabins are not as finely appointed as the Sea Goddesses' or Seabourns' (though the price is much lower), and there's no in-cabin dining. In the dining room, creative excellence and presentation prevail.

RENAISSANCE CRUISES

Renaissance 1/2/3/4 (3,990-grt; 100 passengers; PSR: 39.9)
Renaissance 5/6/7/8 (4,280-grt; 114 passengers; PSR: 37.5)

These eight ships offer in-depth, destination-intensive cruises. Itineraries are

*in company alphabetical order

planned in order to avoid crossing large stretches of open ocean, where the ship size and hull configuration could make them vulnerable in poor weather conditions. The company frequently charters ships to tour operators, alumni and other groups, so check with your travel agent to see which ships are operating on which itinerary. The cabins are beautifully appointed, but, with a limited galley size, the variety and choice of foods is not up to the standards achieved by the other cruise line ships compared here.

ROYAL CRUISE LINE
Queen Odyssey (9,975-grt; 212 passengers; PSR: 47.0)

The smallest ship in the Royal Cruise Line fleet is almost identical in size and features to the two Seabourn ship, with which it vies for exclusivity. The *Queen Odyssey* places greater emphasis on entertainment, however, giving passengers a scaled-down big-ship feeling while carrying them in luxury—with the latest high-tech features—to well-programmed destinations. Transferred from the Royal Viking Line fleet in early 1995, she has lost some finesse in service standards and food levels, and with Greek officers instead of Norwegians, has a more casual air. Gratuities are no longer included.

SEABOURN CRUISE LINE
Seabourn Pride (9,975-grt; 204 passengers; PSR: 48.8)
Seabourn Spirit (9,975-grt; 204 passengers; PSR: 48.8)

These two ships have carried the *Sea Goddess* theme further; they are larger

ships, with more facilities and some entertainment, but no drinks included (the company believes that passengers who don't drink shouldn't subsidize those who do). Fares are higher than those on the Sea Goddess cruises (but the cabins are larger). Seabourn Cruise Line has achieved an impressive level of service and style, notably with fine food, but the level of personal service is just below that of the Sea Goddesses.

SHOWA LINE
Oceanic Grace (5,218-grt; 120 passengers; PSR: 43.4)

Showa Line's only ship features cruises around the coast of Japan, calling in at places such as Abaratsu, Abashiri, Funukawa, Hiroshima, Hofu, Ishigaki Island, Kobe, Kochi, Miyako, Nagasaki, Oki Islands, Rishiri Island, Sendai, Uwajima, Yokohama and Yoron Island, as well as many others. Whale-watching cruises around Ogasawara Island are also offered. The majority of passengers are Japanese. The standard is almost comparable to that delivered by the Sea Goddesses. Cuisine in particular is outstanding.

OTHER COMPARABLE FEATURES

All the above ships have similar facilities and features, including an "open bridge" policy—which means you can visit the bridge at almost any time. They have almost totally unstructured environments, which means you are not asked to participate in any scheduled activities. Instead, you can have total privacy, should you so wish.

Sea Goddess I, *the world's highest-rated small luxury ship (together with sister ship* Sea Goddess II*), seen here going through London's Tower Bridge.*
(Cunard Royal Viking)
Rating ★★★★★+

All ships feature outside cabins only (usually but incorrectly called "suites" by most "upscale" cruise companies, as they are really well-equipped luxury cabins), with two beds, which, when placed together, can form a queen-sized bed. The cabin accessories, which include fluffy cotton bathrobes, hairdryer, color television, VCRs, and flowers and fruit (replenished daily), are also common to all. On most of these small ships, you can go from your cabin to other parts of the ship (particularly to the health spa and outside decks, but not the restaurant) in your bathrobe. But after 6 p.m., the passengers become more formal.

In the case of cabins on the *Oceanic Grace, Queen Odyssey, Renaissance 1-8, Seabourn Pride* and *Seabourn Spirit*, the cabin lounge area is adjacent to a large picture window. On *Sea Goddess I* and *Sea Goddess II* the bedroom is adjacent to the window and the lounge area is adjacent to the picture window.

Bathrooms on the *Song of Flower* are smaller—and more difficult to manoeuvre in than on the other ships. The "half-tubs" are also more difficult to get into and out of. Bathrooms on *Seabourn Pride* and *Seabourn Spirit* are fitted with two washbasins. Those on *Oceanic Grace, Queen Odyssey, Renaissance 1-8, Sea Goddess I, Sea Goddess II* and *Song of Flower* have one. *Sea Goddess I, Sea Goddess II, Seabourn Pride* and *Seabourn Spirit* have towels of 100% cotton, but on *Renaissance 1-8* the content of the towels is a mix of 86% cotton/14% polyester. The *Song of Flower* has both kinds of towels.

The cabin windows on *Seabourn Pride/Seabourn Spirit* have electrically operated blinds, while those on *Queen Odyssey, Sea Goddess I/Sea Goddess II* are manually operated. *Oceanic Grace, Renaissance 1-8* and the *Song of Flower* have no blinds.

On *Sea Goddess I, Sea Goddess II* and *Song of Flower* all liquor, champagnes, wines, as well as soft drinks, are included in the cruise fare. On the *Queen Odyssey*, only wines, spirits and soft drinks that are for in-cabin use are included when you first embark. Soft drinks are provided free afterwards, while everything else that is consumed in public rooms is charged for (at fair prices). The Sea Goddesses aim to deliver an all-inclusive product—which they do—although port taxes and insurance are, strangely, extra.

Afternoon tea on *Sea Goddess I* and *Sea Goddess II* is superior to that on all the other small luxury ships, notably due to the choice of many different teas, including herbal teas. Most, however, serve tea in a silver pot (quite incorrect, as tea should be served only from a bone china/porcelain teapot). On *Queen Odyssey* and *Seabourn Pride/Seabourn Spirit*, individual bone china pots are used in the casual dining area, while in the more formal dining room, and for afternoon tea, the silver pots (fine for coffee, never for tea) are used.

In some ports of call, newspapers, when available, are delivered to each cabin aboard *Sea Goddess I, Sea Goddess II, Seabourn Pride, Seabourn Spirit* and *Song of Flower*, but not on *Oceanic Grace*, on *Queen Odyssey*, or on *Renaissance 1-8*.

The health spa/sauna/steam room complex is open 24 hours a day on *Sea Goddess I* and *Sea Goddess II*; it is open from 7:00 a.m. to 7:00 p.m. on board the *Queen Odyssey*, and from 8:00 a.m. to 8:00 p.m. on *Seabourn Pride* and *Seabourn Spirit*.

Queen Odyssey offers entertainment, including full mini-production shows, classical concerts and cabaret acts, while *Seabourn Pride, Seabourn Spirit* and the *Song of Flower* offer cabaret. *Oceanic Grace, Renaissance 1-8, Sea Goddess I* and *Sea Goddess II* offer only a small live band for dancing.

All have watersports facilities, but only *Queen Odyssey, Seabourn Pride* and *Seabourn Spirit* feature a floating, enclosed aft marina pool, and air-conditioned mahogany shore tenders (the two tenders on *Oceanic Grace* have a shower as well!). However, the marinas are frequently impractical as they are used only in flat calm sea conditions.

In the dining room, tableside flambeaus are featured on *Queen Odyssey, Seabourn Pride, Seabourn Spirit, Sea Goddess I* and *Sea Goddess II*, but not on *Oceanic Grace, Renaissance 1-8* or *Song of Flower*. All the ships usually offer full room-service breakfast, even on the day of disembarkation. This is not usually the case on large ships.

If you are thinking about a long cruise on one of these smaller vessels, do remember that they are really like a small village rather than a large town. But if you like people, they can be the epitome of fine living at sea.

The 212-passenger Seabourn Pride, one of two sister ships in the Seabourn Cruise Line fleet, offers a superbly elegant environment for refined living at sea.
Rating ★★★★★+

71

PRODUCT COMPARISON CHART (Small Luxury Ships)

What's Included	A.	B.	C.	D.	E.	F.
Leather ticket wallet:	No	No	No	Yes	Yes	Yes
All beverages:	No	No	No	Yes	No	Yes
Wines with dinner:	No	No	No	Yes	No	Yes
Shore excursions:*	No	No	Yes	Yes	No	No
Gratuities:	No	No	Yes	Yes	Yes	Yes
Port taxes:**	No	No	Yes	No	No	No
Insurance:	No	No	No	No	No	No
In-cabin dining:	No	Yes	No	Yes	Yes	Yes
Open-eating dining:	Yes	Yes	Yes	Yes	Yes	No
Tableside flambeaus:	No	Yes	No	Yes	Yes	No

Product Comparison	A.	B.	C.	D.	E.	F.
Food quality:	7	9	8	10	10	8
Menu choice:	6	9	7	10	10	8
Special orders:	6	9	6	10	9	9
Food service:	7	8	8	10	10	8
Activities:	6	8	6	5	9	7
Lecturers:	3	8	4	6	9	9
Entertainment:	5	9	5	6	8	8
Officers:	4	7	8	10	9	8
Tender operation:	4	7	7	10	9	8
Watersports:	6	8	9	10	10	8
Accommodations:	7	10	7	9	8	10
Staff friendliness:	6	7	8	10	10	8

KEY

A. *Renaissance 1-8*
B. *Queen Odyssey*
C. *Oceanic Grace*
D. *Sea Goddess I/Sea Goddess II*
E. *Seabourn Pride/Seabourn Spirit*
F. *Song of Flower*

Sea Goddess I, *Sea Goddess II*, *Seabourn Pride*, and *Seabourn Spirit* include some shore excursions on selected itineraries. *Sea Goddess II*, for example, includes all shore excursions (except any overnight stays) on all South East Asia cruises, but not on either *Sea Goddess I* or *Sea Goddess II* in Europe.

* Most shore excursions are included, but those in Northern Europe are not.

** Port taxes must be included in all brochure prices for passengers who are resident in any country of the European Union (E.U.) which is participating in the European Travel Directive.

Booking Your Cruise

TRAVEL AGENTS

Many people think that travel agents charge for their services. They don't (perhaps they will, soon), but they do earn commission from cruise lines for booking their clients on a cruise.

Can I do my own booking direct with the cruise line? Yes and no. Yes, you can book your cruise direct with a small number of cruise lines (mostly in Europe/Asia/Japan), and no, because most of the cruise lines do not generally accept personal checks, thus in effect requiring you to book through a travel agent; in the United States, 95 per cent of cruise bookings are made by travel agents.

A good travel agent will probably ask you to complete a profile questionnaire. When this is done, the agent will go through it with you, perhaps asking you some additional questions before making suggestions about the ships and cruises that seem to match your requirements.

Your travel agent will handle all matters relevant to your booking, and off you go. You may even find a nice flower arrangement in your cabin on arrival, or a bottle of wine or champagne for dinner one night, courtesy of the agency.

Consider your travel agent as your business adviser, not merely as a ticket agent. As a business adviser, a travel agent should have the latest information on matters such as changes of itinerary, the cruise fares, fuel surcharges,

discounts, and any other related items, and should also be able to arrange insurance (most important) just in case you have to cancel prior to sailing. Some cruise lines now have a totally automated booking system by computer. Some are linked into the computer systems of major airlines and allow agents access to almost all shipboard information, and even displays details such as cabin dimensions and if there is a porthole or window.

10 Questions to ask your travel agent

1. Is air transportation included in the cabin rate quoted? If not, what will be the extra cost?
2. What extra costs will be involved? (These can include port charges, insurance, gratuities, shore excursions, laundry, drinks).
3. What is the cruise line's cancellation policy?
4. If I want to make changes to my air arrangements, routing, dates, etc., will the insurance policy cover me for everything in case of missed or canceled flights?
5. Does your agency deal with only one, or several different insurance companies?
6. Does the cruise line offer advance booking discounts or other incentives?
7. Do you have preferred suppliers, or do you book any cruise on any cruise ship?

8. Have you sailed on the ship I want to book, or that you are recommending?
9. Is your travel agency bonded and insured? If so, by whom?
10. If you book the shore excursions offered and recommended by the cruise line, what insurance cover is provided?

CRUISE CONSULTANTS

Remember, there is *no* "Best Cruise Line in the World," or "Best Cruise Ship," only the ship and cruise that's right for *you*. It's the job of your cruise agent or travel agent to find exactly the right ship for your needs. They're all out there, but there's a more bewildering choice than ever before.

A number of cruise-only agencies—often called "cruise consultants"—have sprung up in the last few years. While most are reputable, some sell only a limited number of cruises. These are "preferred suppliers" because they may be receiving special "overrides" on top of their normal commission. If you have chosen a ship and cruise, be firm and book exactly what you want, or change agencies. In the U.K., go to a member of the Guild of Professional Cruise Agents. PSARA (the Passenger Shipping Association of Retail Agents) provides in-depth agent training in the U.K., as well as a complete "bonding" scheme to protect passengers from failed agencies or cruise lines. In the United States, look for a member of NACOA—the National Association of Cruise Only Agents (note that in the U.S. most agencies are not "bonded" in case of failure).

Many traditional travel agencies now have a special cruise section, with a knowledgeable consultant in charge. A good agent will help you solve the problem of cabin choice, but be firm in the amount you want to pay, or you may end up with a larger and more costly cabin than you had intended.

In the United States, CLIA (Cruise Lines International Association) is a marketing organization with about three dozen member lines, which does an admirable job providing training seminars for cruise/travel agents in North America. Agencies approved by CLIA (there are about 25,000) identify themselves through a blue, white, and gold circular emblem on their door, and can gain one of two levels of certification status for their training.

In the U.K., a similar scheme is run by the Passenger Shipping Association, via PSARA. In the U.K., passengers should also note that cruise and tour packagers registered under the Passenger Shipping Association's bonding scheme are fully protected against the risk that a cruise line goes into bankruptcy (there is no similar scheme in the United States).

CRUISE BROKERS

Cruise brokers are useful for making last-minute bookings. They often have unsold cabins at substantially discounted rates. Most brokers have low overheads, being equipped with only a phone and automated message services. British cruisegoers can look at Teletext, on television channels 3 and 4, for information on travel companies offering discounts (Note: this is *not* an

DID YOU KNOW ...?

...that the first "en suite" rooms (with private bathroom in cabin) were on board Cunard Line's *Campania* of 1893?

...that the first ship-to-shore wireless telegraphy took place on an American passenger ship, the *St. Paul*, in 1899?

...that the last three-funnel passenger ship was the Cunard/White Line's *Queen Mary* (1939–1967)?

endorsement of those companies that are offering discounts).

If you're looking for full service, and help in choosing a cruise, then a cruise broker isn't for you; but if you *can* book at the last minute, a cruise broker may save you a substantial amount of money. But what advantage you gain in price you may lose in choice—of dinner sittings, cabin category and location, and other arrangements. You may also have to pay your airfare to join the cruise.

If you do book through a large consolidator or packager, you should find out exactly who is responsible for getting you where you are supposed to be at the right time. Read the fine print.

The cruise line/operator/packager may seem, initially, to be responsible, but there is no set standard within the industry at present. Standards and legal requirements also vary from country to country. The best advice is to make sure you read the fine print when booking. If you have complicated travel arrangements, you must make sure the cruise line provides you with a list of contacts for every stage of your journey.

RESERVATIONS

Rule number one: do plan ahead and book early. After you choose a ship, cruise, date, and cabin, the agency will ask for a deposit—roughly 10 per cent for long cruises, 20 per cent for short cruises (most cruise lines ask for a set amount, such as $250).

When you make your initial reservation you should also make any special dining request known, such as your seating preference, whether you want the smoking or non-smoking sections or any special dietary requirements. The prices quoted in cruise brochures are based on tariffs current at the time the brochures are printed. All the cruise lines reserve the right to change these prices in the event of tariff increases, fluctuating rates of exchange, fuel surcharges, or other costs beyond their control.

Confirmation of your reservation and cruise fare will be sent to you by your travel agent. The balance is normally requested 45 to 60 days prior to departure, depending on individual

line policy. For a late reservation, you have to make payment in full as soon as space is confirmed. Shortly after full payment has been received by the line, your cruise ticket (if applicable) will be issued, along with baggage tags and other items.

When it arrives, check your ticket. In these days of automation, it is prudent to make sure that the ship, date, and cruise details you paid for are correctly recorded. Also do verify that any connecting flight times are okay.

EXTRA COSTS

You will read brochures boldly proclaiming that "everything's included," but in most cases you'll find that this isn't strictly true.

Your fare covers things such as ship transportation, landing and embarkation charges, cabin accommodations, all meals, entertainment, and service on board. With very few exceptions, it does not include alcoholic beverages, laundry, dry cleaning or valet services, shore excursions, meals ashore, gratuities, port charges, cancellation insurance (this covers you only if the cruise itself is canceled by the cruise line or the tour operator), optional on-board activities such as skeet shooting, bingo or horse-racing and casino gambling, or special features or conveniences that were not mentioned in the cruise line's brochure.

On most cruise ships, you should expect to spend about $25 per day per person on extras, plus another $10-$12 per day per person in gratuities. This can add up to as much as $500 per couple on a seven-day cruise. Gen-

uine exceptions are *Sea Goddess I* and *Sea Goddess II* (Cunard), where everything *is* included, and *Seabourn Pride* and *Seabourn Spirit* (Seabourn Cruise Line), where everything *except* the bar drinks and wine is included.

Here are some examples of the extra costs:

Dry-Clean Dress	$3.00-$7.50
Dry-Clean 2-Piece Suit	$4.50-$7.50
Hair Wash/Set	$17.00-$28.00
Haircut (men)	$20.00
Ice Cream	$1.00-$2.50
Massage	$1.00 per minute (plus tip)
Satellite Phone/Fax	$6.95-$15.50 per minute
Souvenir Photo	$5.00-$8.00
Trapshooting (3 or 5 shots)	$5.00, $8.00
Wine with Dinner	$7.00-$500
Bottled Water	$2.50-$4.50

In order to calculate the total cost of the cruise you've chosen, not including any of the extra-cost services you might decide you want once on board, read the brochure and, with the help of your travel agent, make up a list of the costs that might be involved. Below are the approximate prices per person for a typical seven-day cruise on a well-rated medium or large cruise ship. This estimate is based on an outside two-bedded cabin:

Cruise fares	$1,500
Port charges	$100 (if not included)
Gratuities	$50
Total per person	$1,650

Divide this by seven and you get a rough cost of $235 per person per day For this price, you wouldn't even get a decent hotel room in New York City!

DISCOUNTS AND INCENTIVES

Looking at the fares listed in current cruise line brochures is only just the starting point. Because of overcapacity in certain cruise markets at specified times of the year (such as at the beginning and at the end of the summer) cruise discounts and special incentives are widespread. It is wise to enlist the eyes and ears of a good travel agent and check out current discounts.

One way of saving any money is to book well ahead, so that you can profit from one of many variations on the "super savers" theme. Some cruise lines are now offering larger discounts for those that book the farthest ahead, with discounts decreasing as the date of the cruise comes closer. Another method is to reserve a cabin grade, but not a specific cabin—booked as "tba" (to be assigned). Some lines will accept this arrangement and they may even upgrade (or possibly have to downgrade) you on embarkation day if all the cabins in your grade have been sold. It is useful to know that the first cabins to be sold out are usually those at minimum and maximum rates.

Another way of economizing is to wait for a "stand-by" cabin on sailing day or shortly earlier. Some lines offer stand-by fares 30 days before sailing (60 days for transatlantic crossings). They may confirm a cabin (some lines even assign the ship) on the day of embarkation.

Those who can go suitcase-in-hand to the dockside might be lucky enough to get on at a minimum rate (or less) and be assigned a last-minute cancellation of a high-grade cabin.

For cruises to areas where there is year-round sunshine, there is an "on" and an "off" season. Naturally, the best cruise buys are in the off season, while the on season commands the highest prices. Some lines offer a "shoulder" season, which is somewhere between the on and off seasons. Peak season is during the Christmas and New Year vacation. Check with your travel agent to get the best rate for the time you wish to go.

Many of the cruise lines offer highly reduced rates for third and fourth persons sharing a cabin with two full-fare adults. Individual policy varies, so ask your travel agent for current rates. On some sailings, they might even go free.

Many cruise lines also have their own versions of "frequent passenger" clubs. You can join most without a fee (some, like Celebrity Cruises' Captain's Club, make a charge of $25), and you will be notified first of any special offers that are being made. Discounts can frequently be as high as $1,500 per cabin, so it's worth belonging to a club, especially if you like cruising with a particular line.

Most cruise fares are listed as "per person double occupancy" or "ppd." If you are single and wish to occupy a double cabin on your own, you may have to pay a single supplement (see *Cruising for Romantics*).

However, many lines will let you share a cabin at the standard ppd rate. The line will find you a cabin partner of the same sex, and you can both save money by sharing. The line cannot, however, guarantee that you'll like your partner, but they will invariably specify which cabin categories they have available for sharing.

For those wishing to take their children on a cruise, there are some excellent bargains available for families (see *Cruising for Families*).

CANCELLATIONS AND REFUNDS

It is highly recommended that you take out full cancellation insurance, as cruises (and air transportation to and from them) must be paid in full before your tickets are issued. Without such insurance, if you cancel at the last minute, even for medical reasons, it generally means that you will lose the entire amount. Insurance cover can be obtained from your travel agent for a nominal charge.

Cruise lines usually accept cancellations that are notified more than 30 days before sailing, but all charge full fare if you don't turn up on sailing day, whatever the reason. Other cancellation fees vary from 10 to 100 per cent, depending on the cruise and length of trip. Curiously, many cruise lines do not return port taxes, which are *not* part of the cruise fare.

If you cancel with sufficient notice due to serious medical problems, a doctor's letter should be obtained. This is usually regarded sympathetically by cruise lines.

MEDICAL INSURANCE

Whether you intend to travel overseas or cruise down a local river, and your present medical insurance does not cover you, you should look into extra coverage for your cruise. A "passenger protection program" is a service usually prepackaged by the cruise line, and the charge for same will appear on your final invoice unless you decline. This is worth every penny, and it typically covers such things as evacuation by air ambulance, high-limit baggage, baggage transfers, personal liability, and missed departure.

PORT TAXES/HANDLING CHARGES

These are assessed by individual port authorities and are generally shown with the cruise rates for each itinerary. Port charges will be part of the final payment for your cruise, although they can be changed at any time up to the day of embarkation. The most expensive port charge at the time of press was Bermuda, at $60 per passenger (in 1994, some 589,855 passengers visited this tiny island). The typical handling charges for a cruise ending in America, for example, include a U.S. Customs User/Federal Inspection Fee for each passenger on the cruise.

AIR/SEA PACKAGES

When your cruise fare includes a one-way or round-trip air ticket, the airline arrangements usually can't be changed without having to pay considerably more toward the fare. This is because cruise lines often book space on aircraft on a special group basis in order to obtain the lowest rates. Changing your air ticket or flight within 30 days of your cruise will mean having to pay a surcharge to the cruise line (Regency

Cruises, for example, charges $30 for this "service.")

If you do change, remember that in the event of the airline canceling your flight, the cruise line is under no obligation to help you or return your cruise fare if you don't reach the ship on time. If you are joining a ship in a far-off country, allow some extra days (particularly in winter) just to cover the risk that your domestic airline connections don't work or are canceled.

Because of the group-fare ticket basis by which cruise lines work, be aware that this can also mean that the airline routing to get you to your ship may not always be direct or non-stop. The airlines' use of this hub-and-spoke system can be extremely frustrating for cruise passengers. Because of changes to air schedules, cruise and air tickets are often not sent to passengers until a few days before the cruise. A small number of upscale cruise lines include business-class air tickets.

In Europe, air/sea packages generally start at a major metropolitan airport, while some include first-class rail travel to the airport from outlying districts. In the United States, it is no longer necessary for passengers to depart from a major city, since many cruise lines will include connecting flights from small suburban airports as part of the whole package.

There are many variations on the air/sea theme, but all have the same advantage of offering passengers an all-inclusive price, even down to airport-to-ship transfers and port charges.

Most cruise lines offer the flexibility of jetting out to join a ship in one port and flying home from another. This is especially popular for Mediterranean,

transcanal (Panama Canal) and long cruises. Cunard even has a transatlantic program that lets you cruise one way and then fly back the other. They have taken the idea even further by allowing you to return on specially selected, supersonic Concorde flights for a small additional charge.

Another advantage of almost every air/sea packages is that you only have to check in your baggage once—at the departure airport—for even the baggage transfer from plane to ship is handled for you. This does not, however, include intercontinental fly/cruises, where you must claim your baggage at the airport on arrival in order to clear it through customs.

You may be able to hold an open return air ticket, allowing you to make either a pre- or post-cruise stopover. This depends on the type of contract that exists between a cruise line and its airline partner. Usually, however, you have no stopovers en route, nor can you even change flights.

Whenever the price of an air/sea package is all-inclusive, it is often presented as "free air" in publicity material. Of course, there really is no such thing as a free air ticket—the cost of the air fare is simply hidden in the overall cruise fare.

However, air tickets are not always included. Some of the cruise lines simply don't believe in increasing their rates to cover "free air" or they simply may wish to avoid subsidizing airline tickets. These are, for the most part, upmarket lines that operate long-distance cruises to some of the more exotic destinations. In some countries (such as Germany), the term "free air" cannot be advertised by law.

SAIL 'N' STAY PROGRAMS

A fairly recent concept in the cruise industry is that of going to a specific destination by ship, enjoying the cruise on the way. You then disembark (on an island in the Caribbean or the South Pacific, for example) and stay a week or two, before rejoining the ship when it makes its return weekly or biweekly call. The idea has been adopted by an increasing number of cruise lines in conjunction with some of the hotel and resort properties.

The sail 'n' stay programs are on the increase as cruise lines diversify their offerings. It is also likely that cruise lines currently operating short cruises to the Bahamas will build resorts on Bahamian out-islands, so that their passengers can extend their cruise into a sail 'n' stay vacation.

This concept has yet to take hold in the Mediterranean, although cruise vacation add-ons at resort or city hotels are increasingly popular.

PRE- AND POST-CRUISE PROGRAMS

To extend your cruise, it may be worth looking into the extra stay programs that are offered by many cruise lines. These can be taken either before or after your cruise, and can add another dimension to your cruise vacation.

Hotel add-ons are well noted in most cruise brochures, but you will need to look deeper in order to find some of the more unusual add-ons.

These can include some of the world's most famous and luxurious trains, for example. Such trains as the famed Orient Express (which travels between Venice, London or Paris); the Eastern and Oriental Express (which runs between Bangkok and Singapore); or the Royal Scotsman (which connects London and Edinburgh, with the possibility of additional train cruises around Scotland) all add an extremely scenic land perspective to any luxury cruise.

Accommodations

You've got to feel at home when at sea. And to achieve this, choosing the right accommodations for you is the single most important decision you will have to make. So choose wisely, for if you find your cabin (incorrectly called a "stateroom" by some companies) is too small when you get to the ship, it may be impossible to change it or upgrade it to a higher price category, as the ship could well be completely sold out.

Although you may request a specific cabin when you book, most lines now designate cabins only when deposits have been received and confirmed. They will, however, guarantee the grade and rate requested. If this is not done automatically, or if you come across a disclaimer such as one spotted recently—"All cabin assignments are confirmed upon embarkation of the vessel"—then I would advise that you get a guarantee in writing stating that your cabin will not be changed upon embarkation.

There are really three main types of accommodations to choose from, but there are many variations on each theme: suites (often called penthouse suites, these are the largest of accommodations, with or without private balcony); outside cabins (with large picture window or one or more portholes; they can be either with or without private balcony); and inside cabins (so-called because there is no window or porthole). Here are some tips that you should take into consideration when making your choice.

ABOUT PRIVATE BALCONIES

Cruise lines have devised a new gimmick, and a welcome one—private balconies. A private balcony (also often called a "veranda") is just that: an outside balcony where you can sit, enjoy the view, or even dine. There's something quite wonderful about sitting on one's private veranda eating caviar and sipping champagne, or having breakfast à la deck in some exotic place. It's also pleasant to use to get fresh air, and to escape cold air-conditioned cabins. The value of a private balcony comes into its own in warm weather areas, but choosing a cabin with a balcony for cruises to cold weather areas (such as Alaska) is all but pointless.

Some private balconies are not so private, however. Balconies that are not separated by floor- to-ceiling partitions (as in the case of the *Carnival Destiny*, *Maasdam*, *Norway*, *Oriana*, *Ryndam*, *Statendam*, and *Veendam* for example), don't quite cut it. You get noise from your neighbor. You could also get mountains of smoke from a smoking neighbor in the cabin in front of your own. There is no guarantee. But, when all things are in your favor, a balcony is a wonderful extra. Some ships have balconies that have floor-to-ceiling privacy partitions *and* a light as well (*Century*, *Radisson Diamond*, for example), a real bonus.

If you choose a ship with expensive suites that have forward-facing private

A standard cabin aboard the Holiday *(Carnival Cruise Lines). This shows an "L"-shaped layout of two beds, one of which converts to a sofa for daytime use, plus a "foldaway" third, upper berth.*
Rating ★★★★

balconies at the front of the ship (such as on *Queen Odyssey, Seabourn Pride. Seabourn Spirit, Silver Cloud, Silver Wind,* for example), and notice that although the forward view is excellent when the ship is moving forward, the wind speed can make these balconies all but unusable. In addition, be aware that when the ship drops anchor in ports of call, the noise can be very, very loud (and more disturbing than any early morning alarm!).

Those ships with private balcony cabins (or suites) positioned along the port and starboard sides may be better (such as *Asuka, Century, Crystal Harmony, Crystal Symphony, Royal Princess, Royal Viking Sun, Silver Cloud, Silver Wind, Sun Princess,* for example). If you really want sunshine, however, remember that this will depend on the direction the ship is traveling (and the time of day). The profile section in Part Three of this book gives you the number of cabins with private balconies on each ship. You should look at the ship's deck plan carefully with your travel agent to find where your chosen cabin is located.

HOW MUCH TO PAY

The amount you pay for accommodations on most cruise ships is directly related to the size of the cabin, the location within the ship and the facilities provided. There are various other factors that are also taken into consideration when cruise lines grade their accommodations.

There are no set standards within the cruise industry; each line implements its own system according to ship size, age, construction, and the profit potential. It is unfortunate that cruise lines neglect to give cabin sizes in their brochures, but you'll find the sizes in *The Ratings and Evaluations* section in Part Three of this book.

Before you select your cabin, decide how much you can afford to spend—including airfare (if applicable) and your on-board expenses (don't forget to include the estimated cost of shore excursions, port charges, and tips)—since this will determine the cabin categories available to you. It is advisable to choose the most expensive cabin you can afford, especially if it's your

first cruise, as you will spend some time there. If it is too small (and most cabins are small), you just might suffer from "cabin fever," and so the cruise might fall short of your expectations. Alternatively, it is better to book a low-grade cabin on a good ship than book a high-grade cabin on a poor ship.

If you are in a party of three or more and don't mind sharing a cabin, you'll achieve a substantial saving per person, so you may be able to go to a higher-grade cabin without paying any extra money.

In general, you will get precisely the kind of cabin you pay for.

SIZE OF CABINS

Ships' cabins should be looked upon as hotel rooms in miniature, providing more or less the same facilities. With one difference—that of space. Ships necessarily have space limitations, and therefore tend to utilize every inch efficiently. Viewed by many owners and designers as little more than a convenient place for passengers to sleep, shower and change for dinner, a cabin's space is often compromised in favor of large public rooms and open areas. In some of the smaller inside and outside cabins, changing clothes is a challenge; and to take a shower, you'd need to be an acrobat!

There really is no such thing as an average cabin, as cabin size will depend on the space that is allocated to accommodations within a ship of whatever tonnage measurement and principal dimensions. New ships are fitted with more standardized cabin sizes, because they are made in modular form. They

also have integrated bathrooms, often made from noncombustible phenolic-glass-reinforced plastics, and fitted into the ship during construction.

Generally, the larger the ship, the more generous it will be with regard to cabin space. Cabins can vary from the compact 121 sq. ft. standard cabins on several of the Royal Caribbean Cruises ships to a magnificent 1,515 sq. ft. penthouse suite on Celebrity Cruises' new *Century*.

Remember that cruise ships are operated both for the pleasure of passengers and for the profit of the cruise companies. This is the reason why cabins on many new or modern ships are on the small side. The more cabins that a ship can provide, the more fare-paying passengers can be carried.

Ships of yesteryear were able to offer passengers more spacious cabins simply because there were more days at sea, fewer ports of call, generally less speed, and fewer entertainment rooms. This encouraged many to spend a great deal of time in their cabins, very often entertaining other passengers.

Although most modern ships have smaller cabins, they are certainly adequate for standard-length cruises, and allow maximum space in public rooms for entertainment and social events.

Some of the cruise brochures are more detailed and specific than others when it comes to deck plans and cabin layout diagrams. Deck plans do not normally show the dimensions, but they are drawn to scale, unless otherwise noted.

You can get a good idea of the space in a cabin by examining the cabin plan of the cruise category you are interested in. By looking at the beds (each

83

twin being between 2 feet and 3 feet wide and 6 feet long), you can quite easily figure out how much empty or utilized space (bathroom, closets and so on) there is.

If the cabins appear to be the same size on the deck plan, it's because they *are* the same size, with the exception of suite rooms, which will be substantially larger. This is particularly true on some newer ships, where cabins are standardized.

Ask the cruise line, via your travel agent, for the dimensions of the cabin you have selected, if it is not indicated on the deck plan. This will give you some idea of its size. Pace out a room at home as a means of comparison.

LOCATION OF YOUR CABIN

An "outside" cabin is preferable by far, especially if this is the first time you have been cruising. An "inside" cabin has no portholes or windows, making it more difficult to orient yourself or to gauge the weather or time.

Cabins that are located in the center of a ship are more stable, and they also tend to be noise- and vibration-free. Ships powered by diesel engines (this applies to most new and modern vessels) create and transmit some vibration, especially at the stern. For those who are technically minded, passenger cabins typically result in a noise level of 50-55 dBA (this affects the standard cabins) and 40-50 dBA (this affects the suites and upper-grade cabins).

Take into account your personal habits when choosing the location of your cabin. For example, if you like to go to bed early, don't pick a cabin close to the disco. And if you have trouble walking, select a cabin close to the elevator (and not on a lower deck, where there are none).

Generally, the higher the deck, the higher the cabin price and the better the service—an inheritance from the transoceanic times, when upper deck cabins and suites were sunnier and warmer.

Cabins at the bow (front) of a ship are slightly crescent-shaped, given that the outer wall follows the curvature of the ship's hull. But they are usually roomier and cheaper. However, these forward cabins can be exposed to early morning noises, such as the anchor being dropped at those ports where the ship cannot dock.

Connecting cabins are fine for families or close friends, but remember that the wall between them is usually thin, and each of the neighboring parties can plainly hear anything that's being said next door.

If you book a deluxe upper-deck cabin, check the deck plan carefully; the cabin could have a view of the lifeboats. Many cruise lines now indicate these "obstructed-view" cabins in the brochure. Make sure to read the fine print. Similarly, cabins on promenade decks may have windows which can easily be looked into by passing strollers on deck.

If you select a cabin that is on one of the lower decks, be warned that engine noise and heat become more noticeable, especially at the aft end of the vessel, and around the engine casing. Be aware that on many older ships, elevators will probably not operate to the lowermost decks.

FACILITIES

Cabins will provide some, or all, of the following features:

- Private bathroom (generally small and compact) fitted with shower, wash basin, and toilet. Higher-priced cabins and suites often have full-size bathtubs—and some may even have a whirlpool bath and/or bidet, a hairdryer, and considerably more space.
- Electrical outlets for personal appliances, usually U.S. standard, sometimes both 110 and 220 volts.
- Multichannel radio; on some ships, television (on regular or closed circuit); video equipment.
- Two beds, or a lower and an upper berth (plus, possibly, another one or two upper berths), or a double, queen-or king-size bed (usually in suites or deluxe accommodations). On some ships, twin beds can be pushed together to form a double.
- Telephone, for inter-cabin or ship-to-shore communication.
- Depending on cabin size, a chair, or chair and table, or sofa and table, or even a separate lounge/sitting area (but in higher-priced accommodations only).
- Refrigerator and bar (higher-priced accommodations only).
- Vanity/desk unit with a chair or stool.
- Personal safe.
- Closet space, some drawer space, plus storage room under beds for suitcases.
- Bedside night stand/table unit.
- Towels, soap, shampoo and conditioner. (Many of the ships, and particularly the more "upscale" ones, will provide a much greater selection of items.)

Many first-time cruisers are surprised to find their cabins furnished with twin beds. Double beds in fact were a comparative rarity on the cruise ships except in the higher-priced suite rooms until recently. On some of the ships with small cabins (*Cunard Countess*, *Rhapsody*, *Song of Norway*, *Sun Viking*, for example), the twin beds convert to sofas for daytime use, and at night are converted back by the steward.

The two beds are placed in one of two configurations: parallel (with little space in between) or, preferably, in an "L" shape, giving more floor space and the illusion that the cabin is larger.

On some of the ships (especially the older ones), you will find upper and lower berths. A "berth" is a nautical term for a bed held in a wooden or iron frame. A "pullman berth" tucks away out of sight during the day, usually into the bulkhead or ceiling. You climb up a short ladder at night to get into an upper berth.

THE SUITE LIFE

Suites are the most luxurious and spacious of all the shipboard accommodations. The definition of a suite is that it is a "suite of rooms" and comprises a lounge or sitting room separated from a bedroom by a solid door (not just a curtain), a bedroom with a double, queen- or king-size bed, or large, movable twin beds, and one or more bathrooms. Be warned, however, that many cruise lines inaccurately describe some

accommodations as suites, when in fact they are simply nothing more than larger cabins with a curtain to divide the sitting from the sleeping area.

The bathroom will be quite large (for a ship) and will have a large bath tub (often with a Jacuzzi whirlpool tub) and a shower, hairdryer, plus a toilet, deluxe wash basin and (on some ships) a bidet. Some ships boast gold bathroom fittings in their best suites! Although this is the exception and not the rule, the bathrooms attached to the suites are usually excellent.

Suites should also be equipped with a stereo system, television, VCR video unit, CD player unit, refrigerator and a partially or fully stocked bar, and occupants can command the very best of service round-the-clock (they should have butler service).

On ships such as the *Crown Odyssey* and *QE2*, each suite is decorated in a different style, with authentic or reproduction period furniture, beautiful drapes, and fine furnishings. On the *Century*, *Crystal Harmony*, *Crystal Symphony*, *QE2* and the *Royal Viking Sun*, you'll be attended by a personal butler (on some ships, however, the butler is nothing more than a waiter in a different uniform).

Suite rooms are obviously best for a long voyage, when the ship might cross stretches of ocean for five or more days at a time. They are particularly suitable for impressing a loved one and for entertaining in.

Most of the suites will have their own balcony or veranda, although it's wise to check the deck plan in case the veranda faces the lifeboats or some other obstructive apparatus. Suites are usually sheltered from the noise of the ship and the wind, and should provide considerable privacy. Some of the very best suites are the exclusive and private owner's suites on the *Queen Odyssey*, *Seabourn Pride*, *Seabourn Spirit* and the *Vistafjord*.

This is the Owner's Suite aboard the Queen Odyssey *(Royal Cruise Line). It has a private balcony (not in the photo), and offers some 554 sq. ft. (51.5m²) of private living space.* **Rating ★★★★★**

19TH-CENTURY CRUISING

Cruising today is not the same as it used to be; on the first cruise ships there was little entertainment, and passengers had to clean their own cabins. Orders enforced on all ships sailing from Great Britain in 1849, for example, instructed all passengers to be in their beds by 10 p.m.!

READING A DECK PLAN

Learning to read a deck plan is a relatively easy matter. The plan is always laid out so that the bow (front part of the ship) faces to your right or to the top of a page.

Traditionally, ships have designated the central deck (which is equivalent to the main lobby of a hotel) as the Main Deck. This is where you'll find the purser's office and the other principal business offices. Some of the modern ships, however, do not use the term "Main Deck," preferring a more exclusive- or attractive-sounding name. All ships also have a Boat Deck, so named because this is where the ship's lifeboats are stowed.

In the past, many cruise ships also had a Promenade Deck—an enclosed walkway along the length of the deck on one or both sides of the ship. This was popular with passengers crossing the Atlantic, for when the weather was cold or foggy, they could still take their stroll. It is located between the Main Deck and the Boat Deck, except on some modern ships where the Boat and Promenade decks are interchangeable. When the new generation of specialized cruise ships came into being in

the 1970s, the Promenade Deck disappeared in favor of public entertainment lounges across the full beam of the ship, and the name of the deck was changed. Some of the ships that have been built recently have returned to the idea of a Promenade Deck.

The uppermost decks usually tend to be open and feature sunning space, multisports areas, and running or jogging tracks that may encircle the ship.

The Restaurant Deck has undergone a metamorphosis too. It used to be buried on one of the ship's lower decks so as to avoid the rolling motion of nonstabilized ocean liners. Even on the most luxurious liners, there were often no portholes, because the deck was placed below the waterline. As cruising replaced transportation as the prime source of revenue, newer ships were designed with restaurants set high above the waterline. Big picture windows provide diners with a panoramic view of the port or surrounding sea. The Restaurant Deck can therefore be either above or below Main Deck.

Traditionally, popular-priced cabins have been located below Main Deck, with the high-priced suites occupying space on one or two of the uppermost decks. Suites are always located where the view and privacy are best and the noise is least. In the latest ship designs, however, almost all accommodations areas are located above the Main Deck in order to cut down on the amount of disturbing engine noise and the vibration. The older ships designated their accommodation decks A, B, C, D... and so on, while most of the modern ships have given these decks more appealing names, such as Acapulco, Bimini, Coral, Dolphin, and so on.

The following rates are typical of those you can expect to pay for (a) a 7-day and (b) a 10-day Caribbean cruise on a modern cruise ship. The rates are per person, and include free roundtrip airfare or low-cost air add-ons from principal North American gateways.

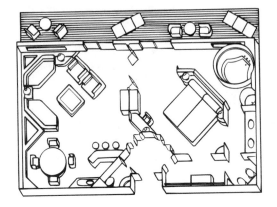

Luxury outside suite with private verandah, separate lounge area, vanity area, extra-large double or queen-sized bed, bathroom with tub, shower, and extensive closet and storage space.
(a)$2,750 (b)$4,000

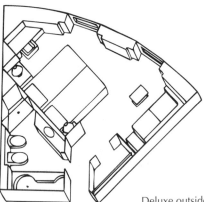

Deluxe outside cabin with lounge area, double or twin beds, bathroom with tub, shower, and ample closet and storage space.
(a)$2,250 (b)$2,850

Note that on some ships, third- and fourth-person berths are available for families or friends wishing to share. These upper pullman berths, not shown on these cabin layouts, are recessed into the wall above the lower beds.

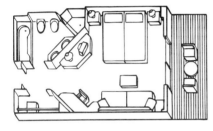

Large outside double with bed and convertible daytime sofabed, bathroom with shower, and good closet space.
(a)$1,750 (b)$2,450

Standard outside double with twin beds (plus a possible upper third/fourth berth), small sitting area, bathroom with shower, and reasonable closet space.
(a)$1,450 (b)$1,975

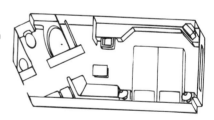

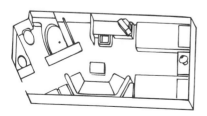

Inside double with two lower beds that may convert into daytime sofabeds (plus a possible upper 3rd/4th berth), bathroom with shower, and fair closet space.
(a)$1,250 (b)$1,750

Cruise Cuisine

The food is still the single most talked and written about aspect of the cruise experience. One of the most sensual pleasures in life is eating; show me the person who is not aroused by the aroma of food being prepared, or who is not charmed by a delicious, satisfying meal in fine surroundings, with a correctly laid table.

There is a special thrill of anticipation that comes with dining out in a fine restaurant. It is the same on board a luxury cruise ship, where gracious dining in elegant, friendly, and comfortable surroundings stimulates an appetite which is already sharpened by the bracing sea air. Some passengers do carry the shipboard dining to the limit, however. Indeed, I've seen plenty of people eat more in one meal than most others do in two or three days!

Attention to presentation, quality, and choice of menu in the honored tradition of the transatlantic luxury liners has made the cruise ships justly famous. Cruise lines know that you'll spend more time eating on board than doing anything else, so their intention is to cater to your palate in every way possible, within the confines of a predetermined budget.

What is spent on food will range from about $7.50 to $30.00 a person a day, depending on the cruise line and standard of cuisine required, although there are exceptions at the higher end, particularly in the Japanese market, where fresh fish and seafood costs are exorbitantly high, and food costs of more than $50 per person per day are normal. Most cruise ships catering to the standard (mass) market spend anything between $7.50 and $15.00 per person per day.

The "intelligent standardization" of the food operation and menus translates to cost-effectiveness in the process of food budgeting for any cruise line. Being able to rationalize expenditure *and* provide maximum passenger satisfaction is today almost a science.

Cruise lines tend to put maximum effort into telling passengers how good their food is, often to the point of being unable to deliver what is shown in their brochures, and thus anticipated by passengers. Generally, however, the level of food provided is good. The best rule of thumb is to ask yourself what you would expect, relative to what you are paying, if you were to eat out in a good restaurant. Does the ship's dining experience meet or exceed your expectations? Would you come back again for the food? If you would, then that particular cruise line has met its promise to feed you with fine food. While gourmet cuisine is enjoyed by a small percentage of people ashore, few ships have the facilities or availability of fresh foods to equal even those of a one-star Michelin-rated restaurant.

The cuisine will, inevitably, vary and this will depend on the nationality and regional influence of the executive chef, his staff and the ship's country of registry or ownership. Thus, choosing a cruise and ship also involves thinking

about the kind of food that will be served on board—and how it is served.

There are perhaps as many different tastes as there are passengers. Some like plain food, some like spicy food. Some like *nouvelle cuisine*, some like meat and potatoes, and lots of it. Some like to try new things, some stick with the same old stuff. It's all a matter of personal taste. So, what the "standard" market cruise lines do is to cater for general tastes. Upscale cruise lines can offer food cooked more or less individually to your liking, but, as in a good restaurant, you get what you pay for. This is why cruise ship standards are so different. Some people are accustomed to drinking coffee out of styrofoam cups and eating food off paper plates at home. Others wouldn't dream of doing that, and expect fine dining, with food correctly served on fine china, just as they do at home.

Some ships have full place settings that include 10 pieces of cutlery, while others provide the correct cutlery just before each course is served (this is more labor-intensive, but the time it takes to lay the cutlery gives the galley more time to get ready for the next course). If you find it bewildering, or don't know which knife and fork to use for which course, the rule is always start at the outermost pair and work towards the innermost pair. The knife and fork closest to where the plate is set will be for the entree (main course). Some ships have special knives for fish courses; others do not, requiring you to use a standard (flat) knife.

While on the subject of place settings, if you are *left-handed*, make sure you tell your waiter at your first meal exactly how you want your cutlery

placed, and to make sure that tea or coffee cup handles are turned in the correct direction. It would be even better if your right- or left-hand preferences were established at the time of booking, and the cruise lines passed on the information to the ship.

Menus for luncheon and dinner are usually displayed outside the dining room each morning so that you can preview the day's meals. On some of the more upmarket ships, menus will be delivered to your suite or cabin each day. When looking at the menu, one thing you'll never have to do is to consider the price—it's all included.

Depending on the ship and cruise, you could sit down to various gourmet specialties, such as duck à l'orange, beef Wellington, lobster thermidor, or prime roast rib of Kansas beef. Or maybe châteaubriand, veal scaloppini, fresh sea bass in dill sauce, or rack of roast English lamb. To top off the meal there could be crème brulée, chocolate mousse, kiwi tart, or that favorite standby, the massed meringue—Baked Alaska—not to mention the tableside flambé choices such as Cherries Jubilee or Crêpes Suzette. And you can always rely on your waiter to bring you a double portion, should you so wish! Of course, these specialties may not be available on all ships. But if you would prefer something that is not on the menu, see the maitre d', give him 24 hours' notice (plus a small tip) and, if the galley can cope, it could well be all your own.

Despite what the glossy brochures say, however, not all meals on all cruise ships are gourmet affairs by any stretch of the imagination. In general, cruise cuisine can be compared favorably to

the kind of "banquet" food served in a good hotel or family restaurant. For a guide to the standard of cruise cuisine, service, and presentation on a particular ship, refer to the ratings in Part Three of this book, but remember that the rating of cruise cuisine is also determined in relation to the per diem cost averages paid by passengers.

Experienced passengers who "collect" cruises have seen it, smelled it, and tasted it all before on cruise ships: real rubber duck—foul (fowl) food, fit only to be stuffed, painted and used as children's toys in their bathtubs! Talk about rock-hard lobster, leather fish, inedible month-old shrimp, third-world, veterinarian-rejected chicken and grenade-quality meats. And not to mention teary-eyed or hammer-proof cheese, soggy, salty crackers, unripe fruits and coffee that looks (and tastes) like army surplus paint! Sadly, it's all there, in the cruise industry's global cafeteria.

One reason that the food on ships cannot always be a "gourmet" experience is that the galley (ship's kitchen) may be striving to turn out hundreds of meals at the same time. What you *will* find is a very fine selection of highly palatable, pleasing, and complete meals served in very comfortable surroundings, in the company of good friends (and *you* don't have to do the cooking!). Add to this the possibility of views out of huge picture windows that overlook a shimmering sea, and perhaps even dining by candlelight. Dining in such a setting is a delightful and relaxed way to spend any evening.

Many cruise lines with large ships now feature buffets for breakfast and luncheon (they don't require as much staff, cutlery, linen or cooked foods), one of the effects of discounted fares. Strangely, passengers don't seem to mind lining up for help-yourself food at the buffets (although it's informal, for the amount of money being paid, sitting down to a meal with service is surely better). Buffets look fine when they are fresh, but after a few minutes of hungry passengers serving themselves, they don't. And, one learns soon enough that the otherwise sweet little old ladies can become ruthlessly competitive when the buffet starting time comes round!

PLATE SERVICE VS SILVER SERVICE

Most fine restaurants ashore now have what is termed "plate service" rather than "silver service." The plate service is when the food is presented as a complete dish, the chef's total concept of how the food should look; its color combinations, the size of the component parts, and its positioning on the plate—all of it together representing the quality of his or her creativity.

In silver service, usually all component parts are brought to the table separately, so that the diner can make the choices regarding the food and what goes on the plate, not the chef. Silver service works best when there is plenty of time to deliver the product. In the setting of most cruise ships, however, silver service is now all but impossible. What some cruise lines class as silver service actually means silver service of vegetables only, with the main item, be it fish, fowl or meat, already positioned on the plate.

On most cruise ships, the "plate service" works well, and means that most people seated at a table will be served at the same time, and can eat together, rather than let their food become cold, as is often the case in silver service, unless several waiters are available to serve one table.

CAVIAR AND CHAMPAGNE

If it's the best caviar you're partial to, you might want to know that Cunard's *QE2* prides itself on being the world's largest single buyer of Beluga caviar (spending about half a million dollars annually), after the Russian and the Ukrainian governments. There are no mother-of-pearl caviar spoons on the *QE2*, however, but you will find them on *Sea Goddess I, Sea Goddess II* and *Song of Flower.*

Although it might seem like it from menu descriptions, most ships do not serve Beluga caviar, but serve the less expensive, and more widely available, Sevruga and Sevruga Malossol (low-salt) caviar. Even more widely served on less exclusive cruise ships, such as those of the Dolphin Cruise Line or Royal Caribbean Cruises, is Norwegian lumpfish caviar—quite different from the highly prized Beluga caviar. The price of caviar is a reflection of the growing rarity of the sturgeon, the fish from which it is derived.

For those who have not tasted good caviar, let me explain that you'll probably find it very salty. That's because the eggs are taken fresh from the female sturgeon, when she is said to be asleep (it takes about 20 years for a female beluga sturgeon to mature).

After the eggs are taken they are passed through a screen to separate them from other fibrous matter. They are then mixed with salt, which acts as a preservative and also promotes the taste. The more salt added, the better the caviar is preserved; the less salt added the finer the taste (Malossol means less salt). The process is done by highly skilled labor, which adds to its cost. The two countries that produce most of the world's caviar are Iran and Russia. In general, Russian caviar is more highly salted than caviar from Iran. And just as each vineyard produces different wines, so each fishery will produce different-tasting caviar.

The Caspian Sea is the spawning ground for 90 per cent of the world's caviar-producing sturgeon. There are three types that are fished for caviar.

1. The giant beluga is hardest to find and therefore the most expensive. It can weigh 1,500lb or more. One fish is capable of yielding as much as 20lb of caviar, whose smoky-grey eggs are the largest (they are also the most delicate).
2. The second most expensive caviar fish is the ossetra. This takes about 13 years to mature, and weighs up to about 40lb. These are the most durable eggs (they are also smaller), and range in color from a darkish brass to olive green.
3. The third caviar fish is the sevruga, which weighs about 6lb. It also has small eggs, ranging in color from soft grey to dark grey.

There is also a fourth type of sturgeon, known as a sterlet, which produces a translucent golden egg, although it is

hard to find today (prior to 1917 all the golden caviar was sent to the Tsar in Russia).

There was a time when sturgeon was found in abundance. So much so that caviar was often placed on the bars of London and New York as a snack to promote the sale of beer and ale.

Caviar is a good natural accompaniment for good champagne, but good champagne (like anything else of high quality) doesn't come cheap. What most ships use as champagne—for the Captain's Welcome Aboard Party for example—just about passes as champagne. Some ships (for example, the newer ships of Princess Cruises) feature a caviar and champagne bar on board, which offers several varieties of caviar, at extra cost of course. Champagne making is a real art (in France itself the production of Champagne is restricted to a very small geographical area). Unlike wine, it is bottled in many sizes, ranging from the minute to the ridiculously huge, and with a variety of names to match:

Quarter bottle:	18.7 centiliters
Half bottle (split):	37.5 centiliters
Bottle:	75 centiliters
Magnum:	2 bottles
Jeroboam:	4 bottles
Rehoboam:	6 bottles
Methuselah:	8 bottles
Salmanazar:	12 bottles
Balthazar:	16 bottles
Nebuchadnezzar:	20 bottles

There are three main grape-growing districts in Champagne: the Montagne de Reims, to the south and east of Reims; the Vallée de la Marne, surrounding the river: and the Côtes des Blancs, south of Epernay. The first two mainly grow the dark pinot-noir and pinot-meunier grapes, while the latter grows the white chardonnay variety. All are used in the making of champagne. Removing the husks before full fermentation prevents the dark grapes coloring the wine red. If a pink champagne is being made, however, the skins are left in the grape mix for a longer time to add color.

Afternoon tea served here in the Queens Room aboard Cunard's 1,740-passenger Queen Elizabeth 2.

Although the Champagne area has been producing wines of renown for a long time, its vintners were unable to keep their bubbles from fizzling out until a monk in the Abbey of Hautvilliers, whose name was Dom Perignon, came up with the solution. The bubbles—escaping carbonic acid gas—had always escaped, until Dom Perignon devised a bottle capable of containing the champagne without it exploding out of the bottle, which was a common occurrence in local cellars. The legacy of this clever monk is that the champagne bottle is the strongest bottle made today. Its thickness is concentrated around the bottle's base and shoulders. Dom Perignon's bottle was aided by the coincidental development of the cork.

Even after his work, champagne was not the perfect elixir we enjoy today. It was quite cloudy due to a residual sediment of dead yeast cells. Its bubbles, therefore, could not be truly relished visually—until la Veuve Cliquot (the Widow Cliquot) devised the system of *remuage* in the last century. Rather than laying the bottles down horizontally for their period of aging, she put them in a special rack, called a *pupitre*, which held them at a 45-degree angle, with the neck of the bottle down. Each day, the bottles are given a short, sharp, quarter turn so as to shake the sediment, which then gradually settles in the neck of the bottle. Once this is complete, a process called *dégorgement* freezes the neck of the bottle. It is then uncorked and internal pressure ejects the ice containing the sediment. Obviously, this means that the bottle is a little less than totally full, so the champagne is topped up with what is called the *dosage*, which is a sweet champagne liqueur. The degree of sweetness of this addition depends on the tastes of the market to which the champagne is ultimately destined. After the *dosage* is added the permanent cork is forced in and wired up. The bottles then remain in the cellar of the winery until they are ordered. Each of the bottles is then washed, labeled and shipped for sale to the consumer.

HEALTHY EATING

Nowadays, with more emphasis being placed on low-cholesterol and low-salt diets, many cruise ships feature "spa" menus—where the heavy, calorie-filled sauces have been replaced by *nouvelle cuisine* and spa cuisine.

Among the best cuisine on a "standard market" cruise is that which is provided on the vessels of Celebrity Cruises—the *Horizon, Meridian,* and *Zenith*—where the three-star Michelin chef Michel Roux is in charge of the menus and overall food product. In the general market, however, you won't get caviar. Going smaller in size but higher in price, the vessels of Renaissance Cruises provide an "800 Club" menu for both lunch and dinner—a complete meal that together adds up to 800 calories. This is an excellent idea for those on a diet.

At the upper (expensive) end of the cruise spectrum, the meals on ships like the *Queen Odyssey, Royal Viking Sun, Sea Goddess I, Sea Goddess II, Seabourn Pride,* and *Seabourn Spirit* can be memorable—they are always cooked to the particular order of the individual passenger.

The difference between the most expensive cruises and the least expensive cruises can frequently be found in details such as the provision of high-quality biscuits made for eating with cheese, or the provision of cappuccino and espresso coffees in the dining room without charge, or the variety of fresh and exotic fruits and the general quality of meats and fish used.

NATIONAL DIFFERENCES

The different nationalities among passengers have their own special needs and requirements that have to be catered for. Here are a few instances of national characteristics which I have noticed and which you may also come across on a cruise:

- British, German and other European passengers like real china egg cups for their boiled eggs for breakfast. When North Americans eat boiled eggs, which is infrequently, they often put the eggs into a bowl and eat them with a fork.
- German passengers tend to prefer breads (especially dark breads) and cheeses for breakfast. And they also have an obvious liking for German draught or bottled beers rather than American canned beers.
- French passengers have a liking for soft, not flaky, croissants, and may request brioche and *confitures*.
- Japanese passengers will be looking for a "bento box" breakfast of fresh steamed Japanese rice, salmon and eel, and vegetable pickles.
- Southern Italians like to have red sauce with just about everything, while northern Italians like less of the red sauces and more flavorings, such as garlic, with their pasta.
- North Americans like coffee with everything—often before, during and after a meal. This is why, even on the most upscale ships, sugar is placed on tables (also for iced tea).
- Most passengers agree that cruise coffee is appalling, but often it is simply the chlorinated water that gives it a different taste. Europeans prefer strong coffee, usually made from the coffee beans of African countries like Kenya. North Americans usually drink the coffee from Colombia or Jamaica.
- European tea drinkers like to drink tea out of tea cups, not coffee mugs (very few cruise ships know how to make a decent cup of tea, so British passengers in particular, should be aware of this).

THE DINING ROOM

On many cruise ships, the running and staffing of dining rooms are contracted out to an outside catering organization specializing in cruise ships. Ships that are continually in waters away from their home country find that professional catering companies do an excellent job, and provide a degree of relief from the operation and staffing of their dining rooms. The quality is generally to a very high standard. However, ships that control their own catering staff and food are often those that go to great lengths to ensure that their passengers are satisfied.

Catering companies tend to change occasionally, so a complete list of them

would probably soon become obsolete. However, here are just a few examples of the principal maritime catering companies:

Apollo Catering	USA
CFCS	Italy/USA
Century Catering	USA
Ligabue Catering	Italy
Stellar Maritime	USA
Trident Catering	USA
World-Wide Catering	USA
Zerbone Catering	Italy

DINING ROOM STAFF

The maître d' is an experienced host, with shrewd perceptions about compatibility; you can trust him when he gives you your table seating. If a table reservation has been arranged prior to boarding, you will find a table seating card in your cabin when you arrive. If this is not the case, you will need to make your reservations with the maître d' or one of his assistants. If you wish to reserve a special table or location in the dining room, do so as soon as possible after boarding .

Unless you are with your own group of friends, you will be seated next to strangers in the dining room. Tables for two are a rarity, except on some small ships and on some of the upmarket liners. Most tables seat six or eight people. It is a good idea to ask to be seated at a larger table, because if you are a couple seated at a table for four and you don't get along with your table partners, there's no one else to talk to. And remember, if the ship is full, it may be difficult to change tables once the cruise has started.

If you are unhappy with any aspect of the dining room operation, the earlier you complain the better. Don't wait until the cruise is over and then send a scathing letter to the cruise line, for then it is too late to do anything positive. See whoever is in charge—they are there to help you to enjoy your meals during the cruise. They want your comments—good or bad.

Each table has at least one waiter and one assistant waiter or busboy. On some ships, up to 30 nationalities may be represented among the dining room staff, who are taught to be courteous, charming, and helpful.

Many ships like to organize special incentive programs, such as a "waiter of the month" competition. This sort of thing helps to keep the staff on their toes, especially if they want to reach the "best" tables. The result is that passengers really do get fine service.

The best waiters are without doubt those who have been trained in the exclusive European hotels or in hotel and catering schools—like the Maritime Catering Institute in Salzburg, Austria. These highly qualified individuals will excel in silver service, and will always be ready with the next course when you want it. They will also know your likes and dislikes by the second night of the cruise. They normally work on the upmarket ships, where dignified professionalism is evident everywhere in the dining room.

SMOKING/NON-SMOKING

Several cruise line companies and their ships have totally non-smoking dining rooms. At the time of this book going

to press they will include all the ships of these shipping cruise lines: CTC Cruise Lines, Carnival Cruise Lines, the Commodore Cruise Line, Curnow Shipping, Epirotiki Cruise Line, Fred Olsen, Hebridean Island Cruises, the Majesty Cruise Line, the Norwegian Cruise Line, the OdessAmerica Cruise Line, Premier Cruise Lines, Princess Cruises, Regency Cruises, the Royal Cruise Line, Transocean Tours, and Windstar Cruises. All other ships feature dining rooms that segregate the smokers from the non-smokers, and most ask that passengers smoke only cigarettes and not cigars or pipes. I expect many more ships will follow this example soon.

Non-smokers who wish to sit in a no-smoking area of the dining room should tell the maître d' or his assistants when reserving a table. Also, you should know that at open seating breakfasts and luncheons in the dining room (or informal buffet dining area), the smokers and non-smokers may be together. If you are bothered by smoke, demand a table in a non-smoking area.

THE CAPTAIN'S TABLE

The captain usually occupies a large table in or near the center of the dining room, the table seating eight or ten people picked from the passenger or "commend" list by the maître d'. Alternatively, the captain may ask personal friends or important company officials to dine with him. If you are invited to the captain's table for dinner, it is gracious to accept, and you'll have the chance to ask all the questions you like about shipboard life.

The captain will not attend meals if he is required on the ship's bridge. When there are two sittings, the captain may have dinner at the first sitting one night, and at the second sitting the next night. On some ships, the captain's guests are changed daily so that more people have a chance to enjoy the experience.

Generally, senior officers also host tables, and being seated with them can be a fascinating experience, especially as they tend to be less formal.

WHICH SITTING?

The best cruise ships feature an open, or single, sitting for meals, where you may dine in unhurried style. "Open sitting" means that you can sit at any table with whom you wish, at whatever time you choose within dining room hours. "Single sitting" means you can choose when you wish to eat, but have regularly assigned tables for the entire cruise. The majority of ships operate a two-sitting arrangement.

The typical first-sitting passengers include: couples (those over 50), families, groups, early-risers, and those passengers who like to dine quickly, and at their normal dining hours at home.

The typical late-sitting passengers include: couples (those under 50), singles, honeymooners, late-risers, and those who like to dine in a leisurely and relaxed style over meals.

Those at the late sitting may not be hungry enough to eat again at the midnight buffet, since it begins about two hours later.

The standard meal times for a two-sitting ship are:

Breakfast:	6:30 a.m./8:30 a.m.
Lunch:	12:00 noon/1:30 p.m.
Dinner:	6:30 p.m./8:30 p.m.

You should note that some ships that operate in Europe (the Mediterranean) may well have even later dinner sittings. Costa Cruises, for example, has its second dinner sitting at 9:00 p.m. instead of the more usual 8:15 p.m. or 8:30 p.m. Dinner hours may vary when the ship is in port to allow for the timing of shore excursions.

You may also find that some of the better seats for the shows and at the movie theater have been taken by those who were on the first sitting. Most ships resolve this problem by scheduling two performances for all the shows at night.

Most ships request that you enter the dining room 15 minutes after the meal has been announced. This is out of consideration for your fellow passengers, your table companions, and the dining room staff. This is especially true for those on the first sitting, but it provides little time to sit and linger over cocktails or after-dinner drinks—one of the drawbacks of the two-sitting arrangement.

SPECIAL REQUIREMENTS

If you are counting calories, are vegetarian or require a salt-free, sugar-restricted, macrobiotic or other diet, let the cruise line know when you first book. The line will then pass the information to the ship, so that your needs can be met. Some of the larger cruise lines, including Carnival Cruise Lines and Royal Caribbean Cruises, now feature a vegetarian entree on all their dinner menus.

Because the food on all the cruises is regarded as "international" or French cuisine, be prepared for dishes that are liberally sprinkled with salt. The vegetables are often cooked with sauces containing dairy products, salt, and sugar. If you want food more to your taste, have a word with the maître d'.

FIRST AND SECOND NIGHTS

For new and experienced cruisers alike, the first evening at sea is exciting—much as the opening night at the theater is. Nowhere is there more a feeling of anticipation than at that first casual dinner when you get a foretaste of the feasting to come.

By contrast, the second night of a cruise tends to be formal, as this is usually the ship captain's welcome-aboard dinner. For this the chef will pull out all the stops to produce a gourmet meal. The dinner follows the captain's cocktail party, which takes place in one of the ship's larger lounges and is an excellent opportunity to meet your fellow passengers and the ship's officers. Toward the end of the party, the captain will give his welcome aboard speech and may also introduce senior members of staff.

THEME NIGHTS

Some of the nights on the cruise will be organized as special theme nights, when waiters dress up fittingly and the menu is planned to suit the occasion.

A TYPICAL DAY

From morning till night, food is on offer to the point of overkill, even on the most modest cruise ship. In fact, on some ships you can eat up to seven meals a day.

Early risers will discover piping hot coffee and tea on deck from about as early as 6 a.m.

A full breakfast, of up to six courses and as many as 60 different items, can be taken in the main dining room. For a more casual meal, you may wish to eat al fresco or buffet style at the outdoor deck café (ideal after an early swim or if you don't wish to dress for the more formal dining room). The choice is obviously more restricted than in the main dining room, but good nonetheless. Times of dining will be set out in your daily program.

A third possibility, especially for romantics, is to have breakfast in your cabin. There's something rather special about waking up and eating breakfast without getting out of bed. Some ships do offer you a full choice of breakfast items, while others opt for the more simple, but usually well-presented, Continental breakfast.

On many ships, the mid-morning bouillon is an established favorite, often served up on one of the open decks—a legacy from the grand days of the transatlantic steamships. Bouillon aboard the *Sagafjord* and *Vistafjord* is served right at your chair-side from trolleys that parade around the promenade deck.

At lunch time, there are at least two choices: a hot lunch with all the trimmings in the dining room, or a buffet-style luncheon in the outdoor café,

featuring light meals, salads, and one or two hot dishes. On some days, this could well turn into a lavish spread, with enough food for a feast (special favorites are the seafood and tropical fruits). And on some ships there will be a separate hot dog and hamburger stand or a pizzeria, where everything is cooked right in front of you, but usually presented with less style than at a McDonald's restaurant.

At around 4 p.m. another throwback to the heyday of the great liners takes place: afternoon tea—of course in the best British tradition—complete with finger sandwiches and cakes. This is often served in one of the main lounges to the accompaniment of live music (it may even be a "tea-dance") or recorded classical music. Afternoon tea usually lasts about an hour (although on some ships it is only half an hour, in which case it is best to be on time so as not to miss out).

Dinner is, of course, the main event of the evening, and apart from the casualness of the first and last nights, it is formal in style.

If you enjoy wine with your dinner, you will find an excellent choice on board. Upmarket ships will carry a selection of wines far more extensive than you will find even in the better restaurants ashore, while other ships will provide some excellent inexpensive wines from the country of the ship's registry or ownership. It is wise to order your wine for the evening meal at lunch time, or at the very latest as soon as you are seated; the wine stewards tend to be extremely busy during the evening meal, and need to draw their stock and possibly have it chilled. Note that if you sail on one of

the smaller ships, the selection of half-bottles of wine will be extremely limited, as most small ships have little space and would rather stock full, rather than half bottles of wine.

A few hours after dinner, there's the midnight buffet—without doubt the most famous of all cruise ship meals. It really is at midnight (until 1 a.m.), and is a spread fit for royalty. Like dinner, it may be based around a different theme each night: a King Neptune seafood buffet one evening, an oriental buffet the next, a tropical fruit fantasy the third, and so on. And the desserts at these buffets are out of this world.

On one night (usually the penultimate evening) there will be a magnificent gala midnight buffet, for which the chefs pull out all the stops. Beautifully sculpted ice-carvings will be on display, each of them fashioned from a 300-lb block of ice. Some of the ships also demonstrate ice-carving.

Even if you are not hungry, stay up to see this display of culinary art—it's something most people never forget.

In addition—or as an alternative—to the midnight buffet, pizza may be served for the late-night disco dancers or the casino crowd.

On a typical day at sea, the ship's bars will be open from about 10 a.m. to late into the night, depending on the bar, its location, and the number of patrons. The details of bar hours are given in the ship's *Daily Program*.

THE EXECUTIVE CHEF

Each ship has its own executive chef who is responsible for planning the menus, ordering enough food (in conjunction with the food manager), organizing his staff and arranging all the meals on the menus.

When a cruise line finds a good executive chef, it is unlikely that they will part company. Many of the best ships employ European chefs who are members of the prestigious Confrérie de la Chaîne des Rôtisseurs, which is the world's oldest gourmet society. The top food and beverage experts work together with their executive chefs, striving for perfection.

One of the principal aims of any good executive chef will be to make sure that menus are never repeated, even on long cruises. He will be inventive enough to offer his passengers dishes that will be new gastronomic experiences for them. On long voyages, the executive chef will work with specially invited guest chefs to offer the passengers a taste of the finest in regional cuisines. Sometimes, he may also purchase fish, seafood, fruit, and various other local produce in "wayside" ports and incorporate them into the menu with a "special of the day" announcement.

THE GALLEY

The galley ("kitchen" for landlubbers) is the very heart of all food preparation on board. At any time of the day or night, there is plenty of activity here—whether baking fresh bread at 2 a.m., making meals and snacks for passengers and crew around the clock, or decorating a special cake for a passenger's birthday celebration.

The staff, from executive chef to pot-washer, must all work together as a

team, each designated a specific role—and there is little room for error.

The galley and preparation areas consist of the following sections:

Fish Preparation Area

This area contains freezers and a fully equipped preparation room, where fish is cleaned and cut to size before it is sent to the galley.

Meat Preparation Area

This area contains separate freezers for meat and poultry. These temperatures are kept at approximately 10ºF. There are also defrosting areas (35ºF to 40ºF). Meat and poultry is sliced and portioned before being sent to the galley.

Soup, Pasta, and Vegetable Preparation Area

Vegetables are cleaned and prepared in this area, pasta is prepared and cooked, and soups are made in huge tureens.

Garde Manger (Cold Kitchen)

This is the area where all cold dishes and salads are prepared, from the simplest sandwich (for room service, for example) to the fine works of art that grace the most wonderful buffets. The area is well equipped with mixing machines, slicing machines and refrigeration cabinets where prepared dishes are stored until required.

Bakery and Pastry Shop

This area provides the raw ingredients for preparing food, and will contain dough mixers, refrigerators, proving ovens, ovens, and containers in all manner of shapes and sizes. Dessert items, pastries, sweets, and other confectionery are prepared and made here.

Dishwashing Area

This area contains huge conveyor-belt dishwashing machines. Wash and rinse temperatures are carefully controlled to comply with the relevant public health regulations. This is where all the special cooking utensils are scrubbed and cleaned, and where the silverware is scrupulously polished.

STANDARDS OF HYGIENE

Galley equipment is in almost constant use. Regular inspections and maintenance help detect potential problems.

Hygiene and correct sanitation are also vital in the galley, and there is continual cleaning of equipment, utensils, bulkheads, floors, and hands. All the staff are required to wear rubber-soled shoes or boots, and the senior officers conduct regular inspections of galleys, equipment and personnel.

Passenger cruise ships sailing from U.S. ports or visiting them are all subject to sanitation inspections by officials from the United States Public Health (USPH) Department of Health and Human Services, under the auspices of the Centers for Disease Control. This is a *voluntary* inspection, not a *mandatory* inspection (it is based on 42 inspection items), and the whole program is paid for by the cruise lines. A similar process takes place in Britain under the Port Health Authority.

On board many ships, a hygiene officer oversees health and sanitation standards. A tour of the galley has proved to be a highlight for passengers on some smaller ships. On larger vessels, passengers are not usually allowed into the galley, due to constant activity

and insurance restrictions. A video of *Behind the Scenes*, for use on in-cabin television, may be provided.

In accordance with internationally accepted standards, the potable water brought on board, or produced by distillation on cruise ships, should contain a free chlorine or bromine residual equal to or greater than 0.2 ppm (parts per million). This is why the drinking water served in the dining room often tastes of chlorine.

ENVIRONMENTAL CONCERNS

The cruise ships refine oil, treat human waste, and incinerate the garbage, but that's not enough today, as pressures continue to mount for clean oceans. Cruise ships and their operating companies have a unique position among all shipping interests. They are not likely to damage the ocean environment as compared with oil tankers, although spillage of any kind is regrettable. Because of ever-increasing regulations and environmental concern, many cruise lines are replacing plastics with more biodegradable and recyclable materials. For example, plastic plates used in certain areas on general market ships should be replaced by china plates, or washable and re-usable hard plastics; the plastic laundry bags should be replaced by paper bags; plastic bottles used for in-cabin amenities should be replaced by containers made of recyclable or re-usable materials. And the cruise lines should make a greater effort to purchase those products that have been produced from recycled paper.

WASTE DISPOSAL

Today's cruise ships need to be capable of efficient handling of garbage and waste materials, as trash generated by passengers and crew must be managed, stored, and disposed of efficiently and economically. The larger the ship, the more waste will obviously be created, and the greater the need for efficient, reliable disposal systems.

Trash includes bottles, cans, corrugated cartons, fabrics, foodstuffs, paper products, plastic containers, as well as medical waste, sludge oil, wet waste, and so on. The sheer magnitude of trash and waste materials can be highly problematic, especially on long cruises that have a large complement of passengers and crew. If solid waste is not burnable, or cannot be disposed of overboard (this type of waste must be bio-degradable), it must be stored aboard ship for later off-loading and disposal on land.

While some of the latest breed of cruise ships are already equipped with "zero-discharge" facilities, other, older, cruise ships still have a way to go when it comes to efficient and economical garbage handling. One method of dealing with food waste is to send it to a waste pulping machine that has been partially filled with water. Cutting mechanisms reduce the waste and allow it to pass through a special sizing ring to be pumped directly overboard or into a holding tank or an incinerator when within three-mile limits. Whichever method of waste disposal is chosen, it, as well as the ship, must meet the extremely stringent demands of Annex V of MARPOL 73/78 international regulations.

103

FOOD & BEVERAGE CONSUMPTION AND STORES

Consumption and stores required for just one transatlantic crossing of *QE2* (five days):

Food Consumption

Beef	9,000 lb
Veal	8,000 lb
Lamb	2,000 lb
Pork	2,500 lb
Chicken	3,500 lb
Duck	1,000 lb
Turkey	1,000 lb
Bacon	2,000 lb
Sausages	2,000 lb
Ham	8,000 lb
Caviar	75 lb
Foie Gras	15 lb
Fish	1,000 lb
Lobsters	1,500 lb
Crabs	800 lb
Tinned fish	1,500 cans
Fresh Vegetables	12,000 lb
Potatoes	3,000 lb
Cereals	800 lb
Rice/Other Grains	3,000 lb
Flour	5,000 lb
Cream	250 gallons
Milk	1,150 gallons
Ice Cream	450 gallons
Butter	2,500 lb
Eggs	43,000
Juices	3,000 gallons
Jam/Marmalade	300 dozen jars
Jam/Marmalade (bulk)	700 lb
Pickles/Condiments	200 bottles
Tea Bags	12,800
Kosher Food	800 lb
Biscuits	2,000 lb
Dog Biscuits	50 lb
Baby Food	600 jars

Bar Consumption

Champagnes	780 bottles
Assorted Wines	1,560 bottles
(the cellar contains 25,000 bottles)	
Whisky	500 bottles
Gin	600 bottles
Rum	240 bottles
Vodka	130 bottles
Brandy	240 bottles
Liqueurs	260 bottles
Port	120 bottles
Sherry	240 bottles
Beer (passengers)	5,230 bottles
Beer (crew)	8,530 cans
Fruit Juice	25,720 pints

The Laundry List

Tablecloths	2,932
Blankets	4,300
Oven Cloths	1,000
Sheets	11,600
Pillow Cases	13,100
Laundry Bags	3,250
Bath Mats	1,650
Hand Towels	15,500
Bath/Other Towels	13,000
Aprons	1,500
Deck Rugs	750

Cruising
for the Physically Challenged

Cruise lines, port authorities, airlines and various allied services are slowly improving their facilities so that those who are wheelchair-bound or otherwise handicapped can enjoy a cruise as fully as possible. At the last count, in the United States alone, some 43 million people—that is one out of every five people over the age of fifteen—were registered as being physically handicapped, while in the U.K. over six million persons were registered as disabled. Not all are in wheelchairs of course, but all of them have needs that the cruise industry is (slowly) working to accommodate.

The main problem areas on cruise ships for the physically challenged are:

a. the cabin itself: the entrance, configuration, the closet hanging rails, and the beds.
b. the cabin bathroom: the grab bars, wheel-in shower stall, toiletries cabinet should all be at an accessible height for the passengers.
c. elevator doorways: the width of the door is important for wheelchair passengers; elevator controls should be at a height suitable for operation from a wheelchair.
d. outside decks: access should be possible through electric-eye doors that open and close automatically rather than through doorways that have to be opened manually; any "lips" at doorways should be ramped.

The very design of ships has traditionally worked against mobility-limited people. To keep out water or to prevent it escaping from a flooded cabin or public area, raised edges (known as "coamings" or "lips") are often placed in doorways and across exit pathways. Also, cabin doorways are so often not wide enough to accommodate even a standard wheelchair. The "standard" cabin door is about 24 inches wide. Cabins designed for disabled people have doors that are about 30 inches wide. "Standard" bathroom doors are normally only about 22 inches wide, whereas those specifically designed for the disabled are about 28-30 inches wide. Do ask your travel agent to confirm the width of these two important access items, and do remember that, while the cabin door may be given as 30 inches, you must allow for the fact that your knuckles on either side of a wheelchair can add three inches to the width of your wheelchair (a "standard" wheelchair is 27 inches wide). The Royal Caribbean Cruises' newest ships, *Legend of the Seas/Splendour of the Seas*, have cabin doorways that are 31 inches wide and elevator doorways that are 43 inches wide. And they also have cabins with verandas for the disabled.

Bathroom doors are a particular problem in this regard, and the door itself, whether it opens outward into the cabin or inward into the bathroom, only compounds the problems

of maneuvering a wheelchair within a cramped space (the four new disabled cabins on *Queen Elizabeth 2,* however, have electrically operated sliding doors into the bathroom, and a completely level entrance into both the cabin and the bathroom). Remember also that bathrooms on most ships are normally small and are full of plumbing fixtures, often at odd angles—extremely awkward when you are trying to move about from the confines of a wheelchair. Bathrooms on newer ships are more accessible, except for the fact that their plumbing is very often located beneath the complete prefabricated module, making the floor higher than that in the cabin, which means a ramp must be fitted in order to "wheel" in.

It was once the policy of almost all cruise lines to discourage the mobility-limited from taking a cruise or traveling anywhere by ship for reasons of safety, insurance and legal liability. But it is now becoming clear that a cruise is the ideal holiday for a physically challenged person as it provides a relaxed environment with plenty of social contact, and organized entertainment and activities. However, despite most cruise brochures declaring that they accept wheelchairs, few ships are well fitted to accommodate them. Some cruise lines, such as Carnival Cruise Lines, openly admit that all public restrooms and cabin bathrooms are inaccessible to wheelchair-bound passengers.

While on the subject of bathrooms, note that many ships have bathroom doors that open inward instead of outward, providing even less space for a wheelchair. An inward opening bathroom door is hard for even ambulatory passengers to cope with, but absolutely useless for anyone in a wheelchair. Many suites have bathroom doors that open inward, while standard-size cabin bathroom doors open outward. Ask your travel agent to check which one applies to your chosen ship and cabin.

The list at the end of this chapter pertains to all the ships presented in Part Three, and provides a guide as to their accessibility (the author personally wheels himself around each ship to check). Once you've decided on your ship and cruise, the next step is to select your accommodations. There are many grades of cabin, depending on size, facilities and location. Select a cruise line that permits you to choose a specific cabin, rather than one which merely allows you to select a price category, then assigns you a cabin immediately prior to your departure date or, worse still, actually at embarkation.

The following tips will help you choose wisely:

• If the ship does not have any specially equipped cabins for the handicapped, then book the best outside cabin in your price range or find a ship that *does* have cabins specially constructed or adapted for the disabled. However, be careful as you may find that even those cruise brochures that state that a ship has "wheelchair accessible" cabins fail to say whether the wheelchair will fit through the *bathroom* door, or whether there is a "lip" at the door. You should also find out whether your wheelchair can fit into the shower area. Get your travel agent to check, and re-check these details. Don't take "I think" as an answer. Get specific measurements.

- Choose a cabin that is close to an elevator. Remember that not all elevators go to all decks, so check the deck plan carefully. For example, the cabins for the physically challenged on the *Radisson Diamond* are located as far away from the elevators as possible. Smaller and older vessels may not even have elevators, making the access to many areas, including the dining room, difficult and sometimes almost impossible.

- Avoid, at all costs, a cabin located down a little alleyway shared by several other cabins, even if the price is attractive. The space along these alleyways is extremely limited and trying to enter one of the cabins in a wheelchair is likely to be a frustrating experience.

- Since cabins that are located amidships are less affected by the motion of the vessel, look for something in the middle of the ship if you're concerned about rough seas, no matter how infrequently they might occur.

- The larger (and therefore the more expensive) the cabin is, the more room you will have to maneuver in. Nowhere does this assume more importance than in the bathroom.

- If your budget allows, pick a cabin that has a bath rather than just a shower, because there will be considerably more room, especially if you are unable to stand comfortably enough.

- Ships that exceed 20,000 grt will have far more spacious alleyways, public areas and (generally) bigger cabins. Ships under 20,000 grt tend to have cabins and passageways that are somewhat confining and therefore difficult to maneuver in.

- Meals on some ships may be served in your cabin, on special request—a decided advantage should you wish to avoid dressing for every meal. There are, however, few ships that have enough actual space in the cabin for real dining tables.

- If you do want to join the other passengers in the dining room and your ship offers two fixed-time sittings for meals, choose the second rather than the first. Then you can linger over your dinner, secure in the knowledge that the waiter won't try to hurry you.

- Space at dining room tables can be somewhat limited on many ships. When making table reservations, therefore, tell the maître d' that you would like a table that leaves plenty of room for your wheelchair, so that it doesn't become an obstacle for the waiters and leaves plenty of room for them—or other passengers—to get past.

- Even if you do find a cruise/travel agent who knows your needs and understands your requirements, try and follow up on all aspects of the booking yourself so that there will be no slip-ups when the day arrives for you to travel.

- Take your own wheelchair with you, as ships carry a very limited number of wheelchairs; in any case these are meant for emergency hospital use only. An alternative is to rent an electric wheelchair, which can be delivered to the ship on your sailing date.

- Hanging rails in the closets on most ships are positioned too high for someone who is wheelchair-bound to reach (even the latest ships seem

to repeat this basic error). There are some cruise ships, however, which do have cabins specially fitted out to suit mobility-limited passengers, in which this and similar problem areas have been dealt with. The cabins on *Queen Elizabeth 2* and *Royal Viking Sun*, for example, are fitted with walk-in closets (the four special cabins on *Queen Elizabeth 2* have a pull-down facility to bring your clothes down to any height you want). In Part Three of this book, the ships which have special cabins are marked either with the number of cabins, or with a "Yes" alongside the entry for Wheelchair Cabins.

- Elevators on many ships are a constant source of difficulty for passengers in wheelchairs. Very often the control buttons are located far too high to reach, especially those buttons for the upper decks.
- Doors on upper decks that open onto a Promenade or Lido Deck are very strong, are difficult to handle, and have high sills. Unless you are ambulatory, or can get out of your wheelchair, these doors can be a source of annoyance, even if there's help around, as they open inward or outward (they should ideally be electrically operated sliding doors).
- Advise any airline you might be traveling with of any special needs well ahead of time so that arrangements can be made to accommodate you without any last-minute problems.
- Advise the cruise line repeatedly of the need for proper transfer facilities, in particular buses or vans with wheelchair ramps.

EMBARKATION

Even if you've alerted the airline and arranged your travel according to your needs, there's still one problem area that can remain when you arrive at your cruise embarkation port to join your ship: the actual boarding. If you embark at ground level, the gangway to the ship may be level or inclined. It will depend on the embarkation deck of the ship and/or the tide in the port.

Alternatively, you may be required to embark from an upper level of the terminal, in which case the gangway could well be of the floating loading-bridge type, such as those used at major airports. Some of these have floors that are totally flat, while others may have raised lips an inch or so in height, spaced every three feet. These are rather awkward to negotiate in a wheelchair, especially if the gangway is made steeper by a rising tide.

I am constantly pressing the cruise lines to provide an anchor emblem in their brochures for those ports of call where ships will be at anchor instead of alongside. If the ship is at anchor, be prepared for an interesting but safe experience. The crew will lower you and your wheelchair into a waiting tender (a ship-to-shore launch) and then, after a short boat-ride, lift you out again onto a rigged gangway. If the sea is calm this maneuver proceeds uneventfully; if the sea is choppy, your embarkation could vary from exciting to harrowing. Fortunately (or not) this type of embarkation is rare unless you are leaving a busy port with several ships all sailing the same day.

The passengers who do not require wheelchairs but are challenged in other

ways, such as those who have impaired sight, hearing or speech, present their own particular requirements. Many of these can be avoided if the person is accompanied by an able-bodied companion, experienced in attending to their special needs. In any event, some cruise lines require physically handicapped passengers to sign a waiver.

The advantages of a cruise for the handicapped are many: ideal place for self-renewal; pure air at sea; no smog; no pollen; no packing and unpacking; spacious public rooms; excellent medical facilities close by; almost any type of dietary requirements can be catered for; a helpful staff; relaxation; good entertainment; gambling (but, as yet, no wheelchair accessible gaming tables, or slot machines); security; no crime on board; many different ports of call and so on.

WHEELCHAIRS

Wheelchair cruise passengers with limited mobility should use a collapsible wheelchair. By limited mobility I mean a person able to get out of the wheelchair and step over a sill or walk with a cane, crutches or other walking device.

The chart on the next two pages indicates the best cruise ships for wheelchair accessibility.

Finally, remember to ask questions before you make a reservation. For example, some of the most important to ask are:

- Does the cruise line's travel insurance (with a cancellation/trip interruption) cover you for any injuries while you are aboard ship?

- Are there any public rooms or public decks on board the ship that are inaccessible to wheelchairs (for instance, it is sometimes difficult to obtain access to the outdoor swimming pool deck)?
- Will you be guaranteed a good viewing place in the main showroom from where you can see the shows, if seated in a wheelchair?
- Will special transportation be provided to transfer you from airport to ship?
- If you need a collapsible wheelchair will one be provided by the cruise line?
- Are passengers required to sign a medical release?
- Do passengers need a doctor's note to qualify for a handicapped cabin?
- Will the crew members be on hand to help, or must the passengers rely on their own traveling companions for help?
- Are the ship's tenders accessible to wheelchairs?
- How do you get from your cabin to the lifeboats (which may be up or down several decks) in an emergency, if the elevators are out of action and cannot be used?

SAILING AS ONE OF THE CREW

For something really different and adventurous, how about sailing yourself? The square-rigged sts *Lord Nelson*, constructed in 1988, is a specially built barque sailing ship with three masts and a total of 18 sails. Designed for the physically challenged and able-bodied to share the challenge of crewing a ship

INDEX TO SHIPS IN THIS BOOK (220 SHIPS)

KEY:

✘ = Not suitable for wheelchair passengers
✓ = Acceptable for wheelchair passengers
✓✓ = Good for wheelchair passengers
✓✓✓ = Highly recommended as most suitable for wheelchair passengers

INDEX TO SHIPS IN THIS BOOK (220 SHIPS)

Princesa Victoria ✘
Queen Elini ✘
Queen Elizabeth 2 ✓✓✓
Queen Odyssey ✘
Radisson Diamond ✓
Regal Empress ✘
Regal Princess ✓✓
Regent Calypso ✘
Regent Isle ✘
Regent Rainbow ✘
Regent Sea ✘
Regent Spirit ✘
Regent Star ✘
Regent Sun ✓
Renaissance One ✘
Renaissance Two ✘
Renaissance Three ✘
Renaissance Four ✘
Renaissance Five ✘
Renaissance Six ✘
Renaissance Seven ✘
Renaissance Eight ✘
Rhapsody ✘
Romantica ✘
Rotterdam ✘
Royal Majesty ✓
Royal Odyssey ✓
Royal Princess ✓
Royal Star ✘
Royal Venture ✘
Royal Viking Sun ✓✓✓
Ryndam ✓
St. Helena ✘
Sagafjord ✓

Sapphire Seas ✘
Sea Goddess I ✘
Sea Goddess II ✘
Sea Prince ✘
Sea Venture ✘
Seabourn Pride ✘
Seabourn Spirit ✘
SeaBreeze I ✘
Seaward ✘
Seawind Crown ✘
Seawing ✘
Sensation ✓
Shota Rustaveli ✘
Silver Cloud ✓
Silver Wind ✓
Sky Princess ✓
Song of America ✘
Song of Flower ✘
Song of Norway ✘
Southern Cross ✘
Sovereign of the Seas ✓
Splendour of the Seas ✓✓
Star Odyssey ✓
Star Pisces ✓
Star Princess ✓
Star/Ship Atlantic ✘
Star/Ship Oceanic ✘
Statendam ✓
Stella Maris ✘
Stella Oceanis ✘
Stella Solaris ✘
Sun Princess ✓✓✓
Sun Viking ✘
SuperStar Gemini ✘

Symphony ✘
Taras Shevchenko ✘
The Azur ✘
Triton ✘
Tropicale ✘
Universe ✘
Veendam ✓
Victoria ✓
Viking Serenade ✓
Vinland Star ✘
Vistafjord ✓
Vistamar ✘
Westerdam ✓
Windward ✓
World Discoverer ✘
World Renaissance ✘
Yamal ✘
Yorktown Clipper ✘
Zenith ✓✓

Sail-Cruise Ships

Club Med I ✘
Club Med II ✘
Le Ponant ✘
Lili Marleen ✘
Sea Cloud ✘
Sir Francis Drake ✘
Star Clipper ✘
Star Flyer ✘
Wind Song ✘
Wind Spirit ✘
Wind Star ✘

1. The following ships of Carnival Cruise Lines have double-width entertainment decks that are good for wheelchair passengers, but the public restrooms are not accessible. In addition, although the cabin bathrooms are equipped with shower stalls and grab bars, the bathrooms have a steep "lip" and are thus not accessible without stepping out of the wheelchair (*Celebration, Ecstasy, Fantasy, Fascination, Holiday, Imagination, Inspiration, Jubilee, Sensation*).

2. The *Crystal Harmony* and *Crystal Symphony* (Crystal Cruises) are the only ships presently in operation that provide special access ramps from an accommodation deck directly to the ship's lifeboats.

3. The *Crown Princess* and *Regal Princess* (Princess Cruises) both have large outside cabins for the disabled, but all have obstructed views.

111

at sea, the 141-foot-long *Lord Nelson* is sailed in both the Mediterranean and Caribbean areas.

Aptly named after arguably Britain's most famous sailor, the ship was built at Wivenhoe, England, at a cost of $5 million for the Jubilee Sailing Trust, headquartered in Southampton, England. All decks are flat, without steps, and there are special lifts for you to get between them, as well as up the ship's side to get aboard. There is even a lift seat to go up the main mast.

Navigation aids do include an audio compass and bright track radar screen for the blind or the partially sighted, and ship-to-shore radio and hydraulic-assist steering.

Down below, all accommodations are accessible to all the physically challenged or able-bodied crew, with specially fitted cabins and bathrooms. In addition, there is a saloon/bar, launderette, library and workshop. Special yachting-type clothing is available on loan. Also the *Lord Nelson's* flat decks, powered lifts, wide companionways and other facilities enable everyone on board to take part on equal terms as part of the ship's crew.

On each voyage, under a professional captain and sailing master, six permanent crew, including a qualified medical purser, guide and instruct the 40-strong crew on each "cruise."

HEARING-IMPAIRED

More than 6 million Americans suffer from hearing loss, and some 1.5 million Americans suffer from a hearing loss of more than 40 per cent. Those affected should be aware of some of the problems on board a ship:

• hearing the announcements on the public address system
• use of telephone
• poor acoustics in the key areas (for example, boarding shore tenders)

Remember to take a spare battery for your hearing aid. More and more new ships have cabins specially fitted with colored signs to help those who are hearing impaired. Norwegian Cruise Line's ships *Dreamward* and *Windward* provide special cabins for the hearing-impaired. Four of the cabins on the *Queen Elizabeth 2* also have illuminated signs to help those who are hearing-impaired. The Crystal Cruises' two ships *Crystal Harmony* and *Crystal Symphony*, as well as Celebrity Cruises' *Century*, are fitted with movie theaters that are equipped with special headsets for use by the hearing-impaired.

When going ashore, particularly on organized excursions, be aware that most destinations are not equipped to handle the hearing-impaired.

Cruising for Romantics

TRAVELING SOLO OR SINGLE

Back in 1932, Warner Bros. released the film *One Way Passage*, a bittersweet story starring Kay Francis and William Powell. Then there was the shipboard affair kindled by Bette Davis and Paul Henried in *Now, Voyager*. Remember Irene Dunne and Charles Boyer in a film called *Love Affair*? Or the same couple in *An Affair to Remember*. All involved ocean-going passenger ships, and romance. Then there was *Gentlemen Prefer Blondes*, in which Marilyn Monroe and Jane Russell starred.

Even in the early 1950s Howard Hughes presented Jane Russell in an RKO movie called *The French Line*, which depicted life on board one of the great ocean liners of the time—the ss *Liberté*—as being exciting, frivolous, promiscuous and romantic! The movie was, in fact, made on board the great ship. Today that same romantic attraction is still very much in vogue.

With more and more singles and solos (those who like to travel alone) in the world today, the possibility of a shipboard romance excites a special attraction. While you may not believe in the notion of mermaids, romance does happen—frequently. Cruise lines, long recognizing this fact, are now trying to help by providing special programs for single passengers. Unfortunately, many solos are turned off cruising because they find it hard to understand why so many lines charge a single occupancy supplement to the fare of someone traveling alone.

By far the most precious commodity aboard any cruise ship is space. Every square foot must be used for essential facilities or revenue-earning areas. Since a single cabin is often as large as a double, and uses the same electrical wiring, plumbing and fixtures—and thus is just as expensive to build—cruise lines naturally feel justified in charging supplements or premiums for those who are occupying single cabins. Singles would probably not object to a smaller cabin, but don't like being charged a supplement or given a poor location.

Where they do exist, single cabins are often among the most expensive, when compared with the per-person rates for the double occupancy cabins. They are also less flexible. From the point of view of the crew, it takes as much time to clean a single cabin as it does a double. And there's only one tip instead of two.

One answer is to construct double cabins only, and then, whenever feasible, sell them as single-occupancy units—this is something that only a handful of cruise lines actually do. Guaranteed singles rates are offered by several lines, but the line and *not* the passenger picks the cabin. If the line doesn't find a roommate, the single passenger may get the cabin to themselves at no extra charge. Ideally, all lines would offer guaranteed singles rates, with no supplement.

> **DID YOU KNOW ...?**
>
> ...that the first passenger ship to exceed 40,000 grt was the White Star Line's *Olympic* of 1911?
>
> ...that the first passenger ship to exceed 80,000 grt was the Compagnie Générale Transatlantique's *Normandie* of 1935 (built at 79,280, and later measured at 82,799 in 1936)?

More than *one million* cruise passengers traveled as singles in 1995! Cruise lines are only now realizing that about a quarter of calls to travel agents are made by singles, single parents, and solos. Singles tend to test the waters by taking short cruises at first. There are lots of singles on the three- and four-day cruises from several U.S. ports (Los Angeles, Miami, Port Canaveral, San Juan) as well as from the port of Piraeus in Greece.

Some cruise lines or tour operators advertise special cruises for singles, but remember that the age range could be anything from 7 to 70. One cruise line in Australia (CTC Cruises) operates 18 to 35 cruises—a nice touch for young people traveling as singles.

While there are some singles who travel with friends or family, many others like to travel alone. For this reason, the cruise lines have now established several programs to accommodate them. One is the "Guaranteed Single" rate, which provides a set price without having to be concerned about which cabin to choose.

A "Guaranteed Share" program is operated by some of the cruise lines.

This allows you to pay the normal double-occupancy rate, but the cruise line will provide another passenger of the same sex to share the double cabin with you.

Some cruise lines do not advertise a guaranteed-share program in their brochures, but will normally try to accommodate such bookings, particularly when demand for space is light. Sometimes, you may end up booking a guaranteed share basis only to find that you end up with a cabin all to yourself. As cruise lines are apt to change such things at short notice, it's best to check with your travel agent for the latest rates, and read the fine print.

For those who want to travel alone and not share a cabin, they can pay either a flat rate for the cabin, or a single "supplement" if they occupy a double cabin. Some lines charge a fixed amount—$250, for instance—as a supplement, no matter what cabin category, ship, itinerary, or length of cruise you require. Single supplements, or solo occupancy rates, vary between lines, and sometimes between ships. The supplement that applies can be found in the ship profile information in Part Three of this book (supplied by

the cruise lines and correct at the time of this book going to press).

CRUISING FOR SINGLE WOMEN

A single woman, a career woman—whether she is single or married—and a widow can take a cruise vacation knowing they are encapsulated in a safe, hassle-free environment. There is perhaps no better way to de-stress, and if you are seeking that special someone, cruising somehow brings people closer together. There's always someone to talk to, whether it be couples or other singles, and cruising is not a "meat market" where you are always under observation. In the dining room, the maître d' will seat you with other singles, or a mix of singles and couples, as you wish.

If you *are* looking for romance, however, beware of the lure of the uniform, of an easy affair or fling with a ship's officer (or member of the crew). They get to see new faces every week, and so the possible risk of sexually transmitted conditions must be borne clearly in mind.

GENTLEMEN CRUISE HOSTS

Because the female to male passenger ratio is high (as much as eight to one on world cruises and other long voyages), especially for cruisers of middle to senior years, some lines employ male social hosts, generally about half a dozen of them, specially recruited to provide dance and bridge partners for passengers. First used to good effect on

Cunard's *Queen Elizabeth 2* in the late 1970s, gentlemen hosts are now employed by a number of cruise lines.

They also host a table in the dining room, appear as dance partners at all cocktail parties and dance classes, and accompany women on shore excursions. These gentlemen, usually over 55 years of age and/or retired, are outgoing, good minglers, well groomed, and enjoy traveling around the world free of charge.

If you are thinking you'd like such a job, do remember that you'll have to dance for several hours most nights, and dance just about every kind of dance well! Crystal Cruises, Cunard Line, Cunard Royal Viking, Ivaran Lines, Regency Cruises, Royal Cruise Line all provide male social hosts, especially on the longer sea voyages or on world cruises.

THE LOVE BOAT CONNECTION

The two famous television shows *The Love Boat* (U.S.) and *Traumschiff* (Germany) have given a tremendous boost to the concept of cruising as the ultimate in romantic vacation, although what is shown on the screen does not quite correspond to reality. Indeed, the captain of one of the ships featured on television, after being asked the difference between his real-life job as captain and that of master of *The Love Boat*, remarked: "On TV they can do a retake if things aren't quite right first time around, whereas I have to get it right first time!"

Ships are indeed romantic places. There is nothing quite like standing on

the aft deck of a cruise ship with the object of your love—with hair blowing in the breeze—as you sail over the moonlit waters to yet another island paradise. Of course, a full moon only occurs once a month, so check the calendar to make sure the timing of *your* moonlit cruise is perfect.

But there is no doubt that cruises are excellent opportunities for meeting people of similar interests. So if you're looking for romance, and if you choose the right ship for your cruise, the odds are in your favor.

GETTING MARRIED ABOARD SHIP

Unlike in all those old black and white movies, a ship's captain can no longer marry you, with one exception—in Japan, where the law still allows couples to marry at sea. If you can't go on a Japanese-registered ship, you should be aware that cruise ship captains are allowed to conduct a marriage vows renewal ceremony.

You *can* get married aboard ship, provided you take along your own registered minister. Some lines, such as American Hawaii Cruises and Carnival Cruise Lines, offer a complete package which includes the services of a minister to marry you, wedding cake, champagne and leis for the bridal party, a band to perform at the ceremony and an album of 24 wedding photos. Carnival Cruise Lines' program includes a marriage ceremony on a beach in St. Thomas. Majesty Cruise Lines offers weddings aboard ship in Miami, and each of five price levels ($375–$825 at time of going to press)

includes notary public services, witnesses and a beautifully designed marriage certificate.

Even if you can't get married aboard ship, you could consider having your wedding reception on one. Many of the cruise lines offer outstanding facilities and provide complete services to help you plan your reception. Contact the director of hotel services at the cruise line of your choice, and you'll be pleased with the way cruise lines go out of their way to help, especially if you follow the reception with a honeymoon cruise.

U.K.-based passengers should know that the P&O Cruises has a series of cruises called the "Red-Letter Anniversary Collection" specially for those celebrating 10, 15, 20, 25, 30, 35, 40, 45, 50, 55 and 60 years of marriage. Gifts you'll receive with the compliments of P&O Cruises include a brass carriage clock by Taylor & Bligh, leather photograph album, or free first-class rail travel from anywhere in the U.K. (check with your travel agent for the latest details).

A cruise also makes not only a fine, no-worry honeymoon vacation, but a delightful belated honeymoon getaway if you had no time to spare when you were married. You'll feel like you're in the middle of a movie set as you sail away to fairytale places, though the ship's a destination in itself.

RENEWAL OF VOWS

There has recently been an upsurge in cruise lines performing the "renewal of vows" ceremonies. A cruise is a wonderful setting for re-affirming to one's

partner the strength of commitment. A handful of ships even have a small chapel where this ceremony can take place, otherwise it can be anywhere aboard ship (a very romantic time is sunrise or sunset on the open deck). The ceremony is conducted, usually by the ship's captain, in a non-denominational text which re-affirms how profound the love and the trust between "partners, lifetime friends and companions," is.

While some companies, such as the Holland America Line, have complete packages that include music, champagne, hors d'oeuvres, certificate, corsages for the women, and so on, other companies do not make a charge (yet). The ship's own photographer usually records the event (it is a revenue-generating photo opportunity) and will have special photo albums embossed with the cruise line's logo.

CRUISING FOR HONEYMOONERS

There is no doubt that cruising is becoming ever more popular as a honeymoon vacation. In fact, U.S.-based Premier Cruise Lines says that more than 5 per cent of its cruise passengers are honeymooners. And there are some real advantages to a honeymoon cruise: you pack and unpack only one time; it's a completely hassle-free and crime-free environment; and you'll get special attention, if you want it. What's more, it's also very easy to budget in advance, as one price often includes the airfare, the cruise, food, entertainment, several ports of call, shore excursions, and pre- and post-cruise hotel stays and other

arrangements. And, once you are married, some cruise lines often offer discounts to entice you to book a future anniversary cruise.

Even nicer is the thought that you won't have to think about cooking meals, as everything will be done for you. You won't have to think about where to eat, or what choice you will have. You can think of the crew as your very own service and kitchen staff.

Although no ship as yet provides bridal suites (hint, hint), many ships do provide cabins with queen-sized or double beds. Some, but by no means all, also provide tables for two in the dining room.

Some cruise ships feature Sunday or Monday departures (from Miami, San Juan, Venice, Singapore, for example), which allow couples to plan a Saturday wedding and reception, and a leisurely travel to the ship of choice. The pre- and post-cruise hotel accommodation can also be arranged by the cruise line.

While most large ships accommodate honeymoon couples really well, if you want to plan a more private, intimate honeymoon, then try one of the smaller, yacht-like cruise vessels, where you'll feel like it's your own private ship on to which you have invited another 50 couples as guests. Highly recommended for a supremely elegant, utterly pampered honeymoon would be the cruises of Renaissance Cruises, the Sea Goddess ships of Cunard Royal Viking, the Seabourn Cruise Line, Radisson Seven Seas Cruises, Showa Line (whose *Oceanic Grace* specializes in weddings, and has huge electric chimes built into the topmost outside deck), Silversea Cruises and the Windstar Cruises. All of them have an open

bridge policy, so you can join the captain on the bridge at almost any time.

While most of the passengers like to socialize in the evenings, it might be more romantic for the honeymooners to take a stroll by themselves on deck, to the forward part of the ship, above the ship's bridge. This will be the quietest (except perhaps for some wind noise), and most dimly lit part of the ship, an ideal spot for star gazing and romancing. Almost all ships are blessed with such places.

Cruise lines offer a variety of honeymoon packages, very much as hotels and resorts on land do. Here's a list of some of the things you can expect from them (note that not all cruise lines provide all services):

- Private captain's cocktail party for honeymooners.
- Tables for two.
- Set of crystal champagne or wine glasses.
- Honeymoon photograph with the captain, and photo album.

- Complimentary champagne (either imported or domestic) or wine.
- Honeymoon cruise certificate.
- Champagne and caviar served up for breakfast.
- Flowers in your suite or cabin.
- Complimentary cake.
- Special T-shirts.

Finally, before you go:
- Remember a copy of your marriage license or certificate, for immigration (or marriage) purposes, as your passports will not yet have been amended.
- Remember to allow extra in your budget for things like shipboard gratuities (tips), shore excursions, and spending money ashore.
- If you need to take your wedding gown aboard for a planned wedding somewhere along the way—perhaps in Hawaii, or Bermuda, for example—there is usually space to hang it in the dressing room next to the stage in the main showroom—especially on larger ships.

Cruising for Families

Yes, you *can* take children on a cruise. In fact, once you get them aboard, you'll hardly see them at all, if you choose the right ship and cruise. On a cruise, families can do different things all at the same time, with parents not having to be concerned about the whereabouts of their children. And where else can you go out for a night on the town without having to drive, and be home in a moment should the babysitter need to contact you?

Dad can sleep in; mom can go for a swim and aerobics classes; the kids can join in the organized activities that go on all day long. Whether you share a cabin with them or whether they have their own separate, though adjoining, cabin, there will be plenty to keep them occupied. On several of the ships which cruise in the Caribbean, you'll even find favorite life-sized cartoon characters on board.

Some cruise lines have token family programs, with limited activities and only a couple of general staff allocated to look after children, even though their brochures might say otherwise. But the cruise lines that are really serious about family cruise programs dedicate complete teams of children's "tweens and teens" counselors, who run special programs that are off-limits to adults. They also have specific facilities such as high chairs in the dining room, cots and real playrooms. Most children's entertainment is designed to run simultaneously with adult programs. For those who cruise with very small children, baby-sitting services may also be available. Cunard's *Queen Elizabeth 2*, for example, has full-time children's nurses and even real English nannies, while P&O Cruises' *Oriana* has a "night nursery" for children of 2 to 5 years of age, so parents can go "out on the town" while being assured their offspring are being well taken care of.

Parents, of course, have long realized that children cost more as they age. For example, children under 2 years old travel free on most cruise lines. But if they are over 2, then they cost money. In case they have to fly, those over 2 also cost more, as they must take up an airline seat.

But there's no doubt that families that cruise together, stay together! There's no better vacation for families than a ship cruise—especially at holiday time—whether it is at Christmas and New Year, Easter or during the long summer school vacation. Active parents can also enjoy the best of all worlds—family togetherness, social contact, and privacy. Cruise ships provide a very safe, crime-free, encapsulated environment, and offer junior cruisers a lot of freedom without parents having to be concerned about where their children are at all times. Cruising has never been more child-friendly or affordable, as the emergence of new lines catering specifically to families has proven. The range of destinations also provides a veritable palette of excursions for both parents and children to enjoy together.

Junior cruisers enjoying one of many planned activities aboard one of the ships of Royal Caribbean Cruises.

A cruise also allows junior cruisers a chance to meet and play with others in their own age group. And because days are quite long on board ship, youngsters will also be able to spend time with their parents or grandparents, as well as with their peers.

A cruise for children is an educational experience. They will tour the ship's bridge, meet senior officers and learn about the navigation, radar and communications equipment, as well as being able to see how the ship operates. They will be exposed to different environments, experience many types of food, travel to and explore new places and participate in any number of exciting activities.

Some cruise ships can be literally crawling with kids, or they can provide quiet moments, shared pleasures, and wonderful memories. On the busiest ships, such as those of Premier Cruise Lines, adults will rarely get to use the swimming pools alone—they will be overwhelmed by so many lively children having a truly good time.

Many cruise lines, recognizing the needs of families, have added a whole variety of children's programs to their roster of daily activities. Some ships have separate swimming pools and play areas for children, as well as playrooms, junior discos, video rooms and teen centers. One cruise company—Carnival Cruise Lines—has created a "Camp Carnival" on its vessels. And Royal Caribbean Cruises has junior counselors on almost all its sailings. Other cruise lines generally have counselors sailing during the summer and other special holiday periods.

Cruise lines that are serious about children split them into five distinct age groups, with various names to match, according to cruise line and program: Toddlers (ages 2-4); Juniors (ages 5-7); Intermediate (ages 8-10): Tweens (ages 11-13); and Teens (ages 14-17). Notably, it often seems to be

children under 12 who get the most from a cruise vacation.

The children and junior cruisers are usually not permitted to participate in adult games, tournaments, quizzes and so on, but have their own versions of them. Also, in compliance with international law, as well as with the policy of most cruise lines, casinos and bars are reserved strictly for passengers aged 18 and over.

One North American cruise company that perhaps best caters to families with children is Premier Cruise Lines, which carries an abundance of children's counselors on every cruise on each of its two red-hulled ships, the *Star/Ship Atlantic* and the *Star/Ship Oceanic*, as well as some famous cartoon characters such as Daffy Duck and Sylvester. Carnival Cruise Lines actually has a 114-foot-long water slide as part of the swimming pool on all its ships (it's even longer on the new *Carnival Destiny*).

Watch out for Disney Cruise lines, which is a new company building two large ships that will cater specifically to families with children. Expected to be the supreme family cruise ships of the future, they will be in the 70,000 grt range and cater to 2,000 passengers, with the whole of the Disney organization to draw from for the shipboard entertainment.

In South-East Asia, the Star Cruise company, based in Singapore, has one ship, the *Langkapuri Star Aquarius,* out of a fleet of five, that has incredible facilities for families with children, including a children's video arcade that is unmatched by anything else at sea. There are also seven restaurants/dining places to choose from.

Parents with babies can rest assured that they will find selected baby foods on board ships that cater to children (along with cribs and high chairs—but do ask your travel agent to check first). If you need something out of the ordinary, or you need that special brand of baby food, do let your travel agent know well in advance. Most cruise lines are very accommodating and will do their best to obtain what is needed, provided enough notice is given, but for parents using organic baby foods, such as those obtained from health food stores, you should be aware that cruise lines buy their supplies from major general food suppliers and not the smaller specialized food houses.

Many ships have really full programs for children during days at sea, although these may be limited when the ship is in port. Ships expect you to take your children with you on organized shore excursions, and sometimes (though not always) there are special prices for children. If the ship has a playroom, it might be wise to find out if it is open and supervised on all days of the cruise. Don't expect your travel agent to know everything. Either ask them to find the answers to your questions, or do some researching yourself.

When going ashore, remember that if you want to take your children swimming or to the beach, it is wise to phone ahead to a local hotel with a beach or pool. Whether it is in the Caribbean, the Mediterranean or the Orient, most hotels will be delighted to show off their property, hoping for future business.

Some cruise ships in the Caribbean area have the use of a "private" island for a day—ideal for children. A life-

guard will be on duty, and there will be watersports and snorkeling equipment you can rent. Note, however, that the beaches on some "private" islands are fine for 200, but with 2,000 on them, they will be crowded, and standing in line for beach barbecues, changing and toilet facilities is a necessary part of the experience.

While the sun and sea might attract the juniors to the warm waters of the Caribbean, those children aged 7 and over will find a Mediterranean or Baltic cruise a delight. They will find it easier to understand, remember and compare the differences between ports of call. They will also have a fine introduction to history, languages and different cultures.

CHILDREN'S RATES

Most cruise lines offer special rates for children sharing their parents' cabin. The cost is often lower than third and fourth person share rates. To get the best possible rates, however, it is wise to book early. And do not overlook booking an inside cabin—you'll rarely be in it anyway.

You should note that while many adult cruise rates include airfare, most children's rates do not! Also, although some lines say children sail "free," they must in fact pay port taxes as well as airfare. The cruise line will get the airfare at the best rate, so there's no need to shop around for the lowest fare.

Unless they have plenty of things to keep them occupied, even the most placid and well-behaved children can become bored and restless. So try to choose a cruise where there are lots of

other children, as they will be best equipped to provide the required entertainment.

SINGLE PARENTS

A single parent traveling with their child(ren) will have their own special needs, and needn't feel left out, either. Female single parents can also feel safe on a cruise, free of the unwanted advances of single men. They will feel more secure than in any hotel. In fact a cruise provides a safe, convenient way for any single parent and child to be together but also have their own space and, in some cases, a guarantee of peer companionship for the child. Only a handful of cruise lines so far have introduced their own version of the "Single Parent Plan." This offers an economical way for single parents to take their child on a cruise, with parent and child sharing a two-berth cabin, or parent and children sharing a three-berth cabin. Single parents will pay approximately one-third the normal single person rate for their children, and there will be plenty of activities for both parent and child to enjoy.

CHILDREN-FRIENDLY CRUISE LINES

The following have been selected by the author for their excellent programs and care: Airtours Cruises, American Hawaii Cruises, Carnival Cruise Lines, Celebrity Cruises, Cunard Line, Norwegian Cruise Line, P&O Cruises, Premier Cruise Lines, Royal Caribbean Cruises, Star Cruise.

Before You Go

BAGGAGE

Cruise lines usually have no limit to the amount of baggage you take on your cruise ship, but as closet space is limited, take only the things you will use. Allow extra space in your luggage for purchases on the trip. Remember that towels, soap, shampoo and shower caps are provided on board.

It is important that you properly tag all your baggage with your name, ship, cabin number, sailing date, and port of embarkation. Tags will be provided by the cruise line along with your ticket. Baggage transfers from airport to ship are generally smooth and problem-free when handled by the cruise line.

Liability for loss or damage to baggage is contained in the passenger contract. If you are not adequately covered for this, you should take out more insurance. The policy should extend from the date of departure until two or three days after your return home. Coverage can be obtained from your cruise/travel agent.

CLOTHING

If you think you might not wear it, don't take it: closet space on most ships is at a premium. Unless you are on an extended cruise, keep your luggage to a minimum. Most of the airlines have a limit of two suitcases at check-in (44lb or 20kg) per person, plus a tote bag or carry-all for small items.

For cruises to tropical areas, where the weather is warm to hot with high humidity, casual wear should include plenty of lightweight cottons and other natural fibers. Synthetic materials do not "breathe" as well and often retain heat. Clothes should, however, be as opaque as possible to counteract the ultraviolet rays of the sun. Also, take a lightweight cotton sweater or two for the evenings, when the ship's air-conditioning will seem even more powerful after a day in the sun.

The same is true for cruises to the Mediterranean, Greek Isles, or North Africa, although there will be little or no humidity most of the year. Certain areas may be dusty as well as dry. In these latitudes, the weather can be changeable and cool in the evenings from October to March, so take extra sweaters.

On cruises to Alaska, the North Cape or to the Norwegian fjords, take some warm comfortable clothing, plus a raincoat or parka for the northernmost port calls. Cruises to Alaska and to the Land of the Midnight Sun only run during the peak summer months, when temperatures are pleasant and when the weather is less likely to be inclement. Unless you are traveling to northern ports such as St. Petersburg during winter, you won't need thermal underwear. However, you will definitely need it—and overcoats, too—if you are taking an adventure cruise to the Antarctic Peninsula or through the Northwest Passage.

In the Far East, what you wear will depend on the time of year. The information package that accompanies your tickets will give recommendations. For a cruise that sets off deep in winter from one of the northern ports (New York or Southampton, for example) and cruises south to find the sun, you should take lightweight cottons plus a few sweaters.

Rainstorms in the tropics are infrequent and don't last long, but they can give you a good soaking, so take inexpensive, but lightweight rain wear for excursions you go on.

In destinations with a strong religious tradition, like Venezuela, Haiti, Dominican Republic, Colombia, and countries in the Far East, do note that shorts or bare shoulders may cause local offense, so cover up.

Aboard ship, dress rules are relaxed during the day, but in the evening what you wear should be tasteful. Men should take a blazer or sports jacket and ties for the dining room and for any "informal" occasions. Transatlantic cruises are normally more elegant.

If you are the athletic type, pack sports clothes for the gymnasium. The ladies should take a leotard and tights for aerobics.

For formal nights (usually two out of every seven), women should wear their best long evening gown, elegant cocktail dress, or a smart pants suit. Gentlemen are expected to wear either a tuxedo or dark business suit. These "rules" are less rigid on short and moderately priced cruises.

There is usually a masquerade night on each cruise, so you may wish to take a costume. Or you can create something on board out of materials that are provided. One of the staff may help, and there may be photographs of past entries to give you ideas. Prizes are awarded for the most creative costume.

No matter where in the world you are traveling, comfortable low- or flat-heeled shoes are a *must* for women, except for formal occasions. Light, airy shoes are best for walking. If you are in the South Pacific or Caribbean and are not used to heat and humidity, your ankles may swell—so, tight shoes are not recommended. Rubber soles are best for walking on the deck of a ship.

FORMAL
Tuxedo (alternatively a dark suit) for men; evening gown or other appropriate formal attire for women.

INFORMAL
Jacket and tie for men; cocktail dress, dressy pants suit, or something similar, for women.

CASUAL
Slacks and jacket on top of sweater or open shirt for men; a blouse with skirt, slacks or similar comfortable attire for women.

On a typical 7-day cruise, the following is what you generally might expect as the dress code for each day:

Sat	Casual
Sun	Formal (Captain's Welcome Aboard Cocktail Party)
Mon	Informal
Tue	Informal
Wed	Informal
Thu	Formal (Captain's Farewell Cocktail Party)
Fri	Casual

DOCUMENTS

A passport is the most practical proof of your citizenship and identification. Although it is not required on all cruises, take it along, if you have one. A voter's registration card and a driver's license are normally acceptable, but are not considered as valid proof of your citizenship.

If you are a non-U.S. citizen taking a cruise from an American port, you must have a valid B-2 multiple-entry visitor's visa stamped in your passport in order to return to the United States at the end of your cruise.

Note: British passport holders do not need a visa to enter the U.S., as the Visa Waiver Program applies.

If you are cruising to areas other than those of the Bahamas, Bermuda, Caribbean, Alaska, Hawaii or Canada, and most of Europe, you may need a tourist visa. Your cruise/travel agent will advise you.

On cruises to the Orient particularly, but also to the Middle East and Africa, you may have to hand in your passport to the purser prior to landing. This helps the customs and immigration officials to "clear" the ship more quickly, and is standard practice. Your passport will be returned when the ship departs, or prior to its arrival in the port of disembarkation.

FLYING

For many people, flying to get to a port of embarkation has become the norm. Most cruise lines now include "free air" as part of the cruise ticket. The effects of rampant discounting, however, have resulted in cruise lines negotiating contracts with airlines that involve passengers sometimes having to travel on flights with absurd connections, even when direct flights are available. In the case of the United States, the introduction of deregulation has resulted in most airlines operating on a "hub and spoke" system, with flights feeding into major centers to connect with other flights. It is now more difficult to find non-stop coast-to-coast flights, as airlines prefer passengers to go through the system to ensure full domestic flights. This is not so prevalent in Europe, but distances are comparatively shorter given the size of each country.

FLYING AND AIR QUALITY

If you are joining a ship in a far-off port and your flight is over six hours duration, you might want to consider paying a little more to move further forward into the Business Class or First Class, rather than go to the Economy Class at the back of the plane. The reason for making this recommendation is simply that the quality of fresh air is better at the front of the plane than it is at the back. There is also a dramatic difference in the quality of air in certain types of aircraft .

It is not easy to change cabin air frequently, because at 40,000 feet the external air can be minus 75°F, and almost completely dry. This air must then be heated to 75°F, and the moisture must be added to the air before it is pumped into the cabin. This all uses fuel. The latest Boeing and Airbus aircraft have tried to cut down on waste

by recycling some of the warm and somewhat moist cabin air. The air is filtered using a mesh to catch bacteria, but this adds to the time taken to change the air completely. What do you do if the air is bad? Tell the senior flight purser, who will ask the engineer to increase the circulation.

Whilst on the subject of air quality, smokers should know that in some countries, smoking is banned on some flights. U.S. carriers forbid smoking on all domestic flights.

FLYING AND JET LAG

If you are flying a long distance to embark on your cruise or to fly home again, you should know that modern air travel is fast, safe, efficient, and comfortable (for the most part). Even experienced travelers, however, may occasionally find that the stresses of international travel persist long after the flight is over. Eastbound flights seem to cause more pronounced jetlag than westbound flights. And while jet aircraft are pressurized, they generally are done so only to some 8,000 feet in altitude, causing discomfort in the ears and the stomach, and swollen feet. The air of the aircraft cabin is also slightly dry. A few precautions should help to reduce the less pleasant effects of flying around the world.

First, you should plan as well in advance of your cruise as you possibly can. It tends to be best to take a daytime flight, so that you can arrive at, or close to, your normal bedtime. Try to remain as quiet as possible for the 24 hours prior to flying, and allow for another five hours of rest after any flight which has crossed more than five time zones.

Enjoy the food and liquor offered during the flight—but in moderation. The best beverages are the nonalcoholic and nonsparkling ones. Smokers may wish to smoke less, as the reduced pressure (and reduced oxygen) means that the effect of carbon monoxide is greater, often resulting in a feeling of depression.

Babies and small children are less affected by changes in time because of their shorter sleeping and waking cycles. But adults generally need more time to adjust. The only way to experience a flight without jet lag is to fly the *Concorde* (London–New York or New York–London). At Mach 2 speed, such a flight does not produce the symptoms of jet lag.

MEDICATIONS

If you are planning a cruise that takes you away from your home country, make sure you take any medicines that you need, plus spare eyeglasses or contact lenses. In many countries it may be difficult to find certain medications. Others may be sold under quite different names. Those traveling on long cruises should ask their doctor for names of alternatives, in case the medicine they are taking is not available.

The ship pharmacy will stock certain standard remedies, but then again, don't expect the ship to have a supply of more unusual or obscure medicines. Remember to take along a doctor's prescription for any medications, especially when you are flying into foreign countries to join a ship, as customs

may be difficult without documentation, particularly those in the Far East.

Also, be advised that if you run out of your medications and you need to get a supply aboard ship, most ships will require that you see the doctor, even if you have a prescription. There is a minimum charge of $15 for the visit, plus the cost of the medication.

Passengers who are diabetic should let spouses/companions carry a supply of insulin and syringes, as well as a quick source of glucose. Make sure you carry a sufficient supply with you, and don't pack it in any luggage that has to be checked in when flying.

MONEY MATTERS

Most of the cruise ships deal primarily in U.S. dollars but some take British pounds, or German marks, or Greek drachmas, or even Australian dollars. Major credit cards and traveler's checks are widely accepted on board. But few lines take personal checks.

Most ships now allow passengers to sign for drinks and assorted other services. On some ships a convenient way to settle expenses is to set up a shipboard credit on embarkation. This is very useful on long voyages. Most lines now have a "cashless" cruising policy, allowing you to pay for all on-board expenses by pre-signed credit card.

PETS

Pets are simply not carried by cruise ships, with two exceptions. One is on the regular scheduled transatlantic services of *Queen Elizabeth 2*, which has

16 air-conditioned kennels (and even a genuine British lamp post), cat containers, plus several special cages for birds. The second is on the regular scheduled South Atlantic service from England to Cape Town and the Ascension Islands on the *St. Helena*. The quarantine and vaccination regulations can be obtained from the consulates of the country of intended entry.

PHOTOGRAPHY

It is hard to find a situation more ideal for photography than a cruise. Your photographs enable you to share your memories with others at home.

Think about where you are going when buying film. It is best to use low-speed film in tropical areas such as the Caribbean or South Pacific, as high-speed film is easily damaged by heat. Take plenty of film with you; standard sizes are available in the ship's shop, but the selection is limited. If you purchase film on a port visit, try to buy it from an air-conditioned store, and check the expiry date.

Keep your film as cool as possible, as the latent image on exposed film is fragile and therefore easily affected by heat. There will be professional photographers on board who may develop film for you—for a fee.

When taking photographs at the various ports of call, respect the wishes of the local inhabitants. Ask permission to photograph someone close-up. Most will smile and tell you to go ahead. But some people are superstitious or truly afraid of having their picture taken and will shy away from you. Don't press the point.

Life Aboard

AIR-CONDITIONING

On all modern cruise ships, cabin temperature is regulated by individually controlled thermostats, so that you can adjust it to suit yourself. The temperature in the public rooms is controlled automatically. On board the ship's air-conditioning is normally kept much cooler than you may be used to, so don't forget to take a sweater or scarf.

BABY-SITTING

On many cruise ships, stewards, stewardesses, and other staff may be available as sitters for an hourly charge. You can make whatever arrangements you need at the purser's office.

BEAUTY SALON/BARBER SHOP

It is advisable to make any appointments for the beauty salon or barber shop as soon after boarding as possible, especially on short cruises. Appointment times fill up rapidly, particularly before social events such as the captain's cocktail party. Charges are comparable to those ashore. The hours of opening will be posted at the salon, and also listed in the *Daily Program*.

BRIDGE VISITS

You should check the *Daily Program* for announcements of visits to the bridge, for which appointment cards can be picked up from the purser's office or cruise staff office. On some ships, bridge visits are not allowed for reasons of insurance and security. On others, although personal visits are forbidden, a *Behind the Scenes* video on how the ship is run may be shown on the in-cabin television system.

CASHLESS CRUISING

It is now quite common to cruise cash-free and settle your account with one easy payment. Often this is arranged by making an imprint of a credit card prior to departure, permitting you to sign for everything. Or you can pay by cash at the end of the cruise.

On many ships, it is no longer possible to pay using cash at the bar, in the beauty salon, or in the shops—a fact bemoaned by older passengers, many of whom often do not use or possess credit cards.

If your cruise ship includes a "private island" on its Bahamas/Caribbean itinerary, you will probably be asked to pay in cash for all beverages, watersports/scuba diving gear and any other items purchased ashore.

Before the end of the cruise, a detailed statement will be delivered to your cabin. Avoid lines by using a credit card for express check out. Some companies that use a "cashless" system may discontinue its use for the last day of the cruise, which can be most irritating for passengers without cash.

CASINO

A large number of cruise ships have a "full" casino, where a range of games are played, such as blackjack, roulette, craps, and baccarat. Playing chips and cash change are available.

Children under 18 are not allowed in the casino. The casino is closed in port due to international customs regulations, and taking photographs in the casino is forbidden. You will find that German and Japanese registered ships are not permitted to operate casinos that give cash prizes.

COMMENT CARDS

On the last day of the cruise you are asked to fill out a company "comment card." Some cruise lines offer "incentives" such as a bottle of champagne and even a free short cruise. Be honest when you fill out this important form, as it can serve as a way of communication between company and passenger. Be warned, however, that on many ships, dining room stewards present "sob" stories of how they will lose their station or section, or even their job, if you don't write "excellent" when you fill out your comment card. Some companies, such as Princess Cruises, provide information on filling out the comment cards, inviting nothing short of an "excellent" rating.

If there *have* been problems with the service, don't write or mark "excellent." Instead, be realistic and mark "good," "fair," or "poor" as the case may be. Otherwise, the cruise line will never know that there are problems and that the service needs improving.

COMMUNICATIONS

Each cruise ship has been designated an internationally recognized call sign, which is made up of a combination of several letters and digits and can be obtained from the cruise line. For each of the ships listed in Part Three of this book, the radio call sign is provided

Fancy a flutter? Many ships operate gambling casinos, with blackjack, roulette and craps among the most popular. There are also slot machines for those who like to do arm exercises. (Fred Olsen Cruise Lines)

(except for those ships which are not yet in service). To receive a call during your cruise, simply give the call sign and name of the ship to those concerned before you leave.

When the ship is at sea, you can call from your cabin (or the ship's radio room) to anywhere in the world:

- by radio-telephone (a slight/moderate background noise might be noticed);
- by satellite (which will be as clear as your own home phone).

The direct dial satellite calls, a service started in 1986, are more expensive, but they are usually completed without delay. Many ships now also have credit card telephones located in public areas aboard ship, which connect instantly at any time of the day or night, via satellite. Satellite calls can still be made when the ship is in port, but radio-telephone calls cannot be made. You could, however, use the local telephones (often at the local post office).

The satellite telephone calls will cost between $5 and $15 per minute, depending on the type of communications equipment the ship carries (the latest system, called Inmarsat-M, is digital and offers lower-priced calls). Cellular telephone calls, such as those operated by the Florida-based Cruise-Phone, typically range from $5.95 to $9.00 per minute. On ships equipped with CruisePhone, payment is made by a major credit card when you make your call. It is more difficult to pay cash for a satellite or cellular telephone call. (The cruise lines should note that many of the older cruisers, especially Europeans, do not own credit cards.)

It is also comforting to know that you can be contacted during your cruise through shore-to-ship calling. Your relatives and friends can reach you by calling the *High Seas Operator* in almost any country (in the United States, dial 1-800-SEA-CALL). Vessels equipped with satellite telephone links can be reached via the *Inmarsat* system, by the caller phoning any local operator and asking for the Inmarsat Operator. When connected, the name of the ship should be given, together with the ocean code (Atlantic is 871; Pacific is 872; Indian Ocean is 873).

Telegrams, telexes, and faxes are all accepted at the purser's office or radio room for transmission when the ship is at sea. Your in-cabin phone can also be used to call any other part of the ship.

CUSTOMS REGULATIONS

All countries vary in the allowances granted by their own customs service, but you will be informed aboard your cruise ship of the allowable amounts for your nationality and residency.

DAILY PROGRAM

The *Daily Program* contains a list of the day's activities, entertainment and social events, and is normally delivered to your cabin the evening before the day which it covers. It is important to read it carefully, so that you know what, when, and where things are happening. If you lose your copy, you can obtain another from the purser's office or your cabin steward.

DECK CHAIRS

Deck chairs and cushions are available from the duty deck steward, and are free of charge on most ships. Specific

locations cannot normally be reserved, except on the few ships where a charge is made, or by arrangement with the deck steward.

DEPARTURE TAX

If you are disembarking in a foreign port, and flying home, be advised that there may well be a departure tax to pay at the airport. Cruise lines often neglect to inform passengers of this, with embarrassing results, especially when you are normally required to pay the departure tax in cash in the local currency of wherever you are.

DISEMBARKATION

During the final part of your cruise, the cruise director will give an informal talk on the customs, immigration, and the disembarkation (sometimes called "debarkation") procedures. At least one member of each family should attend this important talk. This will help simplify and speed up the procedure and avoid confusion at arrival time.

The night before your ship reaches its final destination (in most cases this will be a return to the port you sailed from) you will be given a customs form to fill out. Any duty-free items bought from the ship's shop on board must be included in your allowance, so save the receipts just in case a customs officer wishes to see them.

The night before arrival, your main baggage should be packed and placed outside your cabin door on retiring or before 4 a.m. It will be collected, put in a central baggage area and off-loaded on arrival. Remember to leave out any fragile items and liquor, together with the clothes you intend to wear for disembarkation and onward

travel (it's amazing how many people have packed *everything*, only to find themselves in an embarrassing position on disembarkation day). Anything left in your cabin at this point will be considered hand baggage and has to be hand-carried off when you leave.

On disembarkation day, if you are on a two-sitting ship, be aware that breakfast is usually brought forward by one hour. This means that the first-sitting breakfast could well be as early as 5:30 a.m.! If you are flying home that same day, it's going to turn into a very long day. It might be better to miss breakfast and sleep later, providing announcements on the ship's public address system don't wake you (it's possible on many ships to turn off such announcements).

Even worse than the early breakfast is the fact that you'll be commanded (requested, if you're lucky) to leave your cabin early, only to wait for hours in the crowded public rooms. To add insult to injury, your cabin steward (after he's received his tip, of course) will knock on your door, saying he needs the sheets off the bed so that the cabin can be made up for the incoming passengers. Cruise on a small "upscale" ship and this won't happen.

Before leaving the ship, remember to claim any items you have placed in the ship's safety deposit boxes and leave your cabin key in your cabin. Passengers cannot go ashore until all baggage has been off-loaded, and the customs and/or immigration inspections or pre-inspections have been carried out on board.

In most ports, this takes two to three hours after arrival. Therefore, do not ask people to meet you at arrival

131

time. They will not be allowed to go on board, and you can't get off until all formalities have been completed. Also, leave at least three hours from the time of arrival to catch a connecting flight or other transportation.

Listen for announcements about disembarkation procedures and try not to crowd into the main disembarkation gangway or lobby areas. Once off the ship, you must identify your baggage at the pierside before passing through any further customs (delays are usually minimal). Porters will be there to assist you.

DRUGSTORE

On some ships, there may be a separate drugstore in which a fairly extensive range of standard items will be available, while on others the drugstore will be a small section of the ship's main gift shop. The opening hours will be posted at the store and printed in the *Daily Program*.

ELECTRIC CURRENT

Most cruise ships operating in U.S. waters have standard American 110-volt AC current and sockets. Newer and refurbished ships have 110- and 220-volt AC (alternating current) outlets. A few of the older vessels have 220-volt DC (direct current) outlets; transformers/converters are available.

In general, electrical appliances may only be used on a ship if they operate on AC current. Check with your cabin steward or stewardess before plugging in any electrical appliance more powerful than an electric razor (such as a high-wattage hair dryer), just to make certain that the cabin's circuitry can handle the load.

ENGINE ROOM

On virtually all passenger ships, the engine room is off-limits to passengers, and visits are not allowed, for insurance and security reasons. On some ships, a technical information leaflet may be available from the purser's office. On others, a *Behind the Scenes* video may be shown on the in-cabin television system. For more specific or detailed information, you should contact a member of the ship's engineering staff via the purser's office.

GIFT SHOPS

The gift shop/boutique/drugstore will offer a selection of souvenirs, gifts, toiletries, and duty-free items, as well as a basic stock of essential items. You'll find duty-free goods, such as perfumes, watches, and so on, very competitively priced, and buying on board ship may save you the hassle of shopping ashore. Opening hours will be posted at the store and given in the *Daily Program*.

HEALTH/FITNESS/SPA FACILITIES

Depending on the size of the ship, the health and fitness facilities may include one or more of the following: a gymnasium, weight room, sauna, solarium, exercise classes and jogging track, parcours, massage, swimming pool(s) and whirlpool baths, nutrition lecture and, herbal body wraps, and scuba and snorkel instruction. For information, check with your cruise/travel agent, or, when you are on board, contact the cruise director or the purser's office.

Some ships now have elaborate spas where (for an extra fee) entire days of treatments are on offer. Stress-reducing and relaxation treatments are practiced combined with the use of seawater,

which contains minerals, micro-nutrients and vitamins. Personal massage might include Swedish remedial massage, shiatsu, the Alexander method and aromatherapy treatments.

Few ships today run their own spa facilities, as finding quality personnel to provide consistency of product is time-consuming and difficult. A small number of concession companies now specialize in offering "turn-key" operations. The largest of these is Steiner Transocean, a company that emerged from the 1994 merger between Steiner of London and Coiffeur Transocean, also of London. Steiner Transocean operates the spa and beauty services on more than 100 ships. Good spa operations can be found aboard the *Crystal Harmony*, *Crystal Symphony*, *Europa*, *Norway* and *Queen Elizabeth 2*. All are operated by Steiner Transocean (the exception is *Europa*, which is run like a real German health spa, with medical services and treatments not available on any other cruise ship. This is operated by Polly's Vital Center, Germany). The spa on P&O's new *Oriana* is operated by Champneys, England.

LAUNCH (TENDER) SERVICES

Enclosed motor launches (called "tenders") are employed on those occasions when your cruise ship is unable to berth at a port or island. In these cases, a regular launch service is operated between ship and shore for the duration of the port call. Details of the launch service will be provided in the *Daily Program* and announced over the ship's P.A. system. When stepping on or off a tender, do remember to extend "forearm to forearm" to the person assisting you. Don't grip their hands

because this simply has the effect of immobilizing the helper.

LAUNDERETTE

Some ships are fitted with self-service launderettes, equipped with washers, dryers and ironing facilities, all at no charge. Full-time supervisory staff may be available to assist you, as on the *Queen Elizabeth 2*. (Check the profile information for each individual ship in Part Three of this book).

LAUNDRY AND DRY CLEANING

Most ships offer a full laundry and pressing service. Some ships may also offer dry-cleaning facilities. A detailed list of services (and prices) should be posted in your cabin. Your steward will collect and deliver your laundry or dry cleaning.

LIBRARY

Most cruise ships are equipped with a library offering a large range of books, reference material and periodicals. A small deposit (refundable on return of a book) is sometimes required should you wish to borrow a book from the library. Note that on the small luxury ships, the library is open 24 hours a day, and no deposit is required. On the larger ships, you'll probably find that the library is open only a couple of hours each day, with the exception of those below.

SHIPS WITH THE BEST LIBRARIES

World Explorer	12,000 books
Queen Elizabeth 2	6,000 books
Majesty of the Seas	6,000 books
Monarch of the Seas	6,000 books
Sovereign of the Seas	2,000 books
Crystal Harmony	1,500 books

Cunard's *Queen Elizabeth 2* is, at the present time, the only cruise ship with a full-time, fully qualified librarian—June Applebee—a real treasure.

Sadly, some of the Carnival Cruise Lines ships have superb library rooms and luscious, overstuffed armchairs, but, alas, no books! On many ships, the library is also the place where you can obtain games such as scrabble, backgammon and chess.

LIFEBOAT DRILL

Safety at sea is the number one consideration of all members of the ship's crew. Standards are set by the Safety of Life at Sea (SOLAS) convention of the International Maritime Organization (IMO). For any evacuation procedure to be totally effective and efficient, passengers must know precisely where to go in the unlikely event that an emergency arises. For this reason, and to acquaint passengers with general safety procedures, a lifeboat drill is carried out during the cruise. According to international maritime law, this must take place within 24 hours of embarkation. Some ships sensibly program the passenger lifeboat drill prior to sailing, so as not to take time away from passengers during the cruise.

There have been few recent incidents requiring the evacuation of passengers, although two cruise ships have been totally lost following collisions (*Jupiter* and *Royal Pacific*). Travel by ship, however, still remains one of the safest means of transportation. Even so, it cannot be stressed enough that attendance at lifeboat drill is not only required by the captain, but also makes sense; participation is mandatory. You must, at the very least, know your boat station, and how to get to it, in the event of an emergency requiring evacuation of the ship.

If others are lighthearted about the drill, don't let that affect your seriousness of purpose. Be sure to note your exit and escape pathways and learn how to put on your lifejacket correctly. The drill takes no more than about 15 minutes of your time and is a good investment in playing safe. (The *Royal Pacific* actually sank in a mere 16 minutes in 1992 following a collision.)

Lifejackets are found in your cabin, and instructions as to how to get to your boat station are posted on the back of the cabin door.

LOST PROPERTY

You should contact the purser's office immediately if you lose or find something on the ship. Notices regarding lost and found property may be posted on the bulletin boards.

MAIL

You can buy stamps and post letters on most ships. Some ships use the postal privileges and stamps of their flag of registration, while others buy local stamps at the next port of call. Mail is usually taken ashore by the ship's port agent just before the ship sails for the next port.

If you are sailing on an extended voyage (on a round-the-world cruise, for example), the cruise line will send you a list of all its agents and mailing addresses, together with your tickets and documents, before you leave for the cruise. In this way, you will be able to let your family and friends know where you will be and where you may be contacted at certain times.

MASSAGE

Make any appointments for massage as soon as possible after boarding, in order to get a time and day of your choice. Larger ships have more staff, and offer more flexibility in appointment times. The cost averages $1.00 per minute. On some ships, a massage service is available in your cabin, if it is big enough to accommodate a portable massage table.

MEDICAL SERVICES

All ships carrying over 50 passengers are required, by international maritime convention, to have a fully licensed physician aboard. Usually there is a reasonably equipped hospital in miniature, although the standard of medical practice and of the physicians themselves varies greatly from line to line. Most shipboard doctors are generalists; there are no cardiologists or neurosurgeons. And the doctors are employed as outside contractors and therefore make charges for use of their services. British passengers should note that ships are not covered by the U.K. National Health Service scheme.

For example, Cunard's *Queen Elizabeth 2*, which carries up to 2,825 passengers and crew, has a fully equipped hospital with one surgeon, one doctor, a staff of six nurses and two medical orderlies; contrast this with Carnival's *Sensation*, which carries up to 3,514 passengers and crew, with just one doctor and two nurses.

Regrettably, many cruise lines place a low priority on providing medical services (exceptions: *Europa* and *QE2*, whose medical facilities are truly outstanding, and whose doctors are highly skilled professionals). Most shipboard

physicians are not certified in trauma treatment or medical evacuation procedures, for example. Most ships that cater to North American passengers tend to carry doctors licensed in the United States, Canada, or Britain, but on other ships, doctors come from a variety of countries and disciplines. Some medical organizations, such as the American College of Emergency Physicians, have created a special division for cruise medicine.

Although ships do have some facilities, there is wide variation between standards and equipment. Obviously, any vessel engaged in long-distance cruises, with several days at sea, should have better medical facilities and a better qualified staff than one that is engaged in a standard 7-day Caribbean cruise, with a port of call to make almost every day.

There is, at present, no agreed industry-wide standard relating to the standard of medical certification that is required by cruise ships. Most ship doctors are necessarily of the general practice type, but quite often, short-term contracts can mean poor continuity and differing standards.

Ideally, a ship's medical staff should be certified in Advanced Cardiac Life Support. The minimal standard medical equipment should include:

- Examination room
- Isolation ward/bed
- X-ray machine (to verify the existence of broken or fractured bones)
- ECG (electroencephalogram) cardiac monitor
- Oxygen-saturation monitor (which is used to determine a patient's blood-oxygen level)

- Defibrillator and cardiac monitor
- External pacemaker
- Oxygen, suction and ventilators

Any existing health problems that will require treatment on board must be reported at the time you are booking. Finally, the doctor is the *only* ship's officer who is actually an independent contractor. Aboard ship, that means that standard fees are charged for treatment, including for seasickness shots (except on Russian and Ukrainian registered vessels, where the medical services are free).

MOVIES

On most cruise ships, a movie theater is an essential part of the ship's public-room facilities. The movies are recent, often selected by the cruise director or company entertainment director from a special film- or video-leasing service.

Some of the recently built or modified ships have replaced or supplemented the ship's movie theater with television sets in each cabin. News and events filmed on board are shown as well as video movie features.

NEWS AND SPORTS BULLETINS

The world's news and sports results are reported in the ship's newspaper or placed on the bulletin board—normally located near the purser's office or in the library. For sports results not listed, ask at the purser's office; it may be possible for the office to obtain the results for you.

PASSENGER LISTS

All ships of yesteryear provided passenger lists with each passenger's name and home town. Few companies carry on the tradition (perhaps some passengers are traveling with someone they shouldn't!). Among the companies that still compile a cruise passenger list are: Crystal Cruises, Cunard Line, Cunard Royal Viking, Pearl Cruises (Ocean Cruise Lines), Seabourn Cruise Line, Silversea Cruises, and the Sun Line Cruises.

PHOTOGRAPHS

Professional photographers travel on board to take pictures of passengers throughout the cruise, including their arrival on board. They also cover all main events and social functions, such as the captain's cocktail party.

All the photographs can be viewed without any obligation to purchase (the price is likely to be in excess of $5.00 for a postcard-sized color photograph). They will all be displayed on photo boards either in the main foyer, or in a separate photo gallery. The color and quality of these pictures are usually excellent. Duplicates may be obtained even after your cruise, from the shore-based headquarters of the photographic concessionaire.

POSTCARDS AND WRITING PAPER

These are available from the writing room, library, purser's office, or from your room steward. On many ships, they are available for a modest sum.

PURSER'S OFFICE

This is also known as the reception office, guest relations desk, or information desk. Centrally located, this is the nerve center of the ship for general on-board information and problems. Opening hours are posted outside the office and given in the *Daily Program*.

On some ships, the purser's office is open 24 hours a day.

RELIGIOUS SERVICES

Interdenominational services are conducted on board, usually by the captain or staff captain. A few older ships (and the new ships of Costa Cruises) have a small private chapel. Sometimes denominational services are offered by specially invited or fellow-passenger members of the clergy.

ROOM SERVICE

Beverages and snacks are available at most hours. Liquor is normally limited to the hours when the ship's bars are open. Your room steward will advise you of the services that are offered. There is no charge for this service.

SAFETY ABOARD

Passenger safety is a high priority for all cruise lines. Crew members must attend frequent emergency drills, the lifeboat equipment is regularly tested, and the fire-detecting devices, alarm and fire-fighting systems are checked throughout the ship. If you spot fire or smoke, use the nearest fire alarm box, alert a member of staff, or contact the bridge. Cruise lines should insist on a common language for all crew members, but this is far from the reality.

Be aware that slipping, tripping and falling are the major sources of shipboard injury. This does not mean that ships are unsafe, but there are some things you can do to minimize the chance of injury.

If you *do* suffer from injury aboard a cruise ship, you may think it is the cruise line's fault and you may want to take some kind of legal action against the cruise company concerned; you should be aware of the following:

In the United States, Appendix 46, Section 183(b) of the U.S. Civil Code requires that "the injured passenger notify the cruise line in writing within six months from the date of the injury to file a claim and suit must be filed within one year from the date of injury." Thus, if you file a claim after the one-year period, the cruise line will probably seek a summary judgment for dismissal, which will invariably be granted to it.

It is imperative that you first *read your ticket*. The passenger ticket is a *legal contract* between passenger and cruise line. It will invariably state that you must file suit in the state (or country) designated in the ticket. For example, if a resident of California buys a cruise, and the cruise line is based in Florida, then the suit must be filed in Florida. If you reside in the U.S. and you purchase a cruise in the Mediterranean and the cruise line is based in Italy, for example, then you would have to file suit in Italy. This is known as the Forum Clause.

There is usually a clause in the ticket that will read something like the following:

"The Carrier's legal responsibility for death, injury, illness, damage, delay or other loss or detriment of person or property of whatever kind suffered by the Passenger will, in the first instance, be governed by the Athens Convention relating to the Carriage of Passengers and their Luggage by Sea, 1974, with protocols and amendments, together with the further provisions of the International Convention on Limitation of Liability for Maritime Claims,

1976, with revisions and amendments (hereinafter collectively referred to as the "Convention"). The Carrier shall not be liable for any such death, injury, illness, damage, delay, loss or detriment caused by Act of God, war or warlike operations, civil commotions, labor trouble, interference by Authorities, perils of the sea, or any other cause beyond the control of the Carrier, fire, thefts or any other crime, errors in the navigation or the management of the Vessel, or defect in, or unseaworthiness of hull, machinery, appurtenances, equipment, furnishing or supplies of the Vessel, fault or neglect of pilot, tugs, agents, independent contractors, such as ship's Physician, Passengers or other persons on board not in the Carrier's employ or for any other cause of whatsoever nature except and unless it is proven that such death, injury, illness, damage, delay, loss resulting from Carrier's act or omission was committed with the intent to cause such loss or with knowledge that such loss would probably result therefrom and in that event the Carrier's liability therefore shall not exceed the specified limitations per Passenger in Special Drawing Rights (S.D.R.) as defined in the applicable conventions or in any further revision and/or amendment thereto as shall become applicable."

One area that passengers may not be able to sue the cruise line is in the event of injury or accident when they are on a shore excursion advertised and sold aboard ship. This is because the tour operators of on-shore excursions are usually independently contracted, and do not belong to the cruise line. So, when you buy your shore excursion, ask if the ship's insurance fully covers you under the terms of the passenger ticket contract.

IN YOUR CABIN

- Note that on many ships, particularly older vessels, there are raised lips separating the bathroom from the sleeping area.
- Do not use the fire sprinkler heads that are located on most cabin ceilings as a hanging place for clothes hangers, however light they are.
- On older ships, it is wise to note how the door lock works—some require a key on the inside in order to unlock the door. Leave the key in the lock, so that in the event of a real emergency, you do not have to hunt for the key.

ON DECK

- On older ships, look out for raised lips in doorways leading to open deck areas. Be alert and step, don't trip, over them.
- Wear sensible shoes, with rubber soles (not crepe) when walking on deck or going to pool and lido areas. Do not wear high heels.
- Walk with caution when the outer decks are wet after being washed, or if they are wet after rain—this warning applies especially to metal decks. There's nothing more painful than falling onto a solid steel deck.
- Don't throw a lighted cigarette or cigar end, or knock out your pipe, over the ship's side. The sea might seem like a safe place to throw such items, but the burning ash can easily be sucked into an opening in the ship's side or onto an aft open deck area, only to cause a fire.

HOW TO SURVIVE A SHIPBOARD FIRE
Shipboard fires generate heat, smoke, and often panic. In the unlikely event that you are in one, try to remain calm and think logically and clearly.

When you board the ship and get to your cabin, check the way from there to the nearest emergency exits fore and aft. Count the number of cabin doorways and other distinguishing features to the exits in case you have to escape without the benefit of lighting, or in case a passageway is filled with smoke and you can't see clearly. New ships will more and more make use of the "low location" lighting systems, which are either the electroluminescent or photoluminescent type.

On many new ships, exit signs are located just above floor level, but on older vessels, exit signs may be above your head—virtually useless, as smoke and flames always rise.

You should also note the nearest fire alarm location and know how to use it in the event of dense smoke and/or no lighting. Indeed, all cabins should have pull-out flashlights, but as yet most of them do not.

If you are in your cabin and there is fire in the passageway outside, first put on your lifejacket and feel the cabin door handle. If the door handle is hot, soak a towel in water and use it to turn the handle of the door.

Check the passageway. If everything is clear, walk to the nearest emergency exit or stairway. If there is smoke in the passageway, crawl to the nearest exit. If the exit is blocked, then go to an alternate one.

It may take considerable effort to open a fire door to the exit, as they are very heavy. Never use the elevators, as they may stop at a deck that is on fire or full of smoke, and when the door opens, you may not be able to escape.

In the event of a fire beginning in your cabin, report it immediately by telephone. Then get out of your cabin if you can and close the door behind you to prevent smoke or flames from entering the passageway. Finally, sound the alarm and alert your neighbors.

SAILING TIME

In each port of call, the ship's sailing and all-aboard times will be posted at the gangway where you leave from. The all-aboard time is usually half an hour before sailing time (ships cannot wait for individual passengers who are delayed). On some ships, you will be given an identification card which has to be handed in at the gangway when you return from your visit ashore.

SAUNA

Many ships offer a sauna, which is usually small and compact, and occasionally unisex. In some cases there will be a small charge for its use, especially when it is combined with a massage. Towels are available at the sauna and there is also a small changing area. Opening times will be posted at the sauna and will appear in the information material in your cabin. Reservations are not normally necessary.

SEASICKNESS

Seasickness is rare these days, even in rough weather (less than 3 per cent of all passengers are seasick). Ships have stabilizers—large underwater "fins" on each side of the hull—to counteract any rolling motion. Nevertheless, it is possible to develop some symptoms—

anything from slight nausea to vomiting. What do you do?

Seasickness occurs when the brain receives confusing messages from the body's sensory organs; this causes an imbalance of a mechanism in the inner ear. The mind and brain are accustomed to our walking or riding on a nonmoving surface. If the surface itself moves in another direction, a signal is transmitted to the brain that something's wrong. Continuous mixed signals result in headaches, clammy skin, dizziness, paleness, and yawning, soon followed by bouts of nausea and vomiting. There is still no explanation for the great difference in individual susceptibility to seasickness.

Both old-time sailors and modern physicians have their own remedies, and you can take your choice or try them all:

1. When you notice the first movement of the ship, go out on deck and walk back and forth. You will find that your knees, which are our own form of stabilizer, will start getting their feel of balance and counteraction. This is the sign that you're "getting your sea legs."
2. When you are on deck, focus on a steady point, such as the horizon.
3. Get the breeze into your face, and if nauseous, suck an orange or lemon.
4. Eat lightly. Don't make the mistake of thinking that a heavy meal will keep your stomach well anchored. It won't.
5. A recommended preventive for seasickness is ginger in powder form. (Mix half a teaspoon in a glass of warm water or milk, and drink it before sailing.) This is said to settle

any stomach for a period of up to eight hours.
6. "Sea Bands" (called "Aquastraps" in the U.K.) are a drug-free method of controlling motion sickness. These are slim bands (often in varying colors) that are wrapped around the wrist, with a circular "button" that presses against an acupressure point (*Nei Kuan*) on the lower arm. They should be attached a few minutes before you step aboard and should be worn on both wrists throughout the cruise.
7. Dramamine will be available in tablet form on board the ship.
8. Many now use "the patch." This is called Transderm Scop, or alternatively Transderm V, and is available by prescription. It is like a small sticking plaster, and you position it behind your ear, almost out of sight. For 72 hours it releases into the system a minute quantity of a drug that counteracts seasickness and nausea. Any side-effects are relatively harmless, but check with your physician or ship's doctor. Some of the unpredictable effects that have been observed to occur include acute glaucoma, disorientation, dizziness, intense agitation, and hallucination. After removing the patch, it takes about 12 hours for the reaction to subside.
9. If you are really distressed, the ship's doctor can give you an injection that will cure all discomfort. It may make you drowsy as well, but the last thing on your mind will be staying awake at the movie.

All of this being said, bear in mind that in addition to the stabilizers on the

hull, most cruises are in warm, calm waters and most cruise ships spend much time along the coast or pull into port regularly. The odds are very much against being seasick.

SECURITY

After the tragedy of the *Achille Lauro* hijacking incident in 1985, the United States House of Representatives Committee on the Security of Ports and Vessels, and the United Nations, have suggested ways by which those traveling by cruise ship could expect to receive the same level of protection as those traveling by air. It is satisfying to report that we have seen the progressive formulation of a recognized standard of passenger ship protection. The cruise lines have reached this recognized standard as a result of several factors: a moral obligation which, like safety, is inherent in the industry; the expectation of passengers; and now the firmer and more formal pressures that are being applied across the world by governments and coast guards.

But in spite of these pressures it is still true that the "recognized" standard can be interpreted widely by different companies and ports. The most conscientious cruise lines, ferry operators, and ports follow the standards laid down by International Maritime Security (IMS), a British company that is acknowledged as the world leader in cruise ship, ferry, and port security.

Increasingly, passengers find that at embarkation, as well as at way ports, they are required to go through metal detection devices at the gangway, and baggage will be subject to more stringent inspection procedures. The question of security is now being taken into

account during the final ratings and evaluation of the ships in Part Three.

All cabins are provided with keys, and it is recommended that you keep your cabin door locked at all times when there is no one there. The usual keys are made of metal and operate a mechanical lock, whereas the newer and refurbished ships may have plastic "key cards," which operate electronically coded locks. Cruise lines do not accept responsibility for any money or valuables left in cabins and suggest that you store them in a safety deposit box at the purser's office.

You will be issued with a personal boarding pass when you embark. This serves as a form of identification and must be shown at the gangway each time you board. If you misplace or lose it, let the purser's office know immediately. The system of boarding passes is one of many ways in which cruise lines ensure passenger safety.

SHIPBOARD ETIQUETTE

Cruise lines want you to have a good vacation, but there are some rules that must be observed.

In public rooms, smoking and non-smoking sections are available. In the dining room, however, cigar and pipe smoking are not permitted at all.

If you do have a video camera with you, you must be aware that you will not be allowed to tape any of the professional entertainment shows and cabarets because of the international copyright infringement regulations.

It's all right to be casual when on vacation, but you will not be allowed to enter the ship's dining room in just your bathing suit. Bare feet, likewise, are not permitted.

SPORTS FACILITIES

The variety of sports facilities on board ship will depend on how big the ship is. The facilities will include some of the following: badminton, basketball practice area, golf driving cage, horseshoes, jogging track, miniature putting green, paddle tennis, quoits, ring toss, shuffleboard, skeet shooting, squash (rarely), table tennis, volleyball. Tournaments are arranged by the sports director or the cruise staff. Check the *Daily Program* for times of events.

SUN

If your cruise takes you to the sun, remember that the closer you get to the equator, the more potent and penetrating are the rays. These are most harmful from noon to 2 p.m., when the sun is directly overhead.

If you are taking a short cruise to the Bahamas, Caribbean, or Mexico,

be wary of trying to get the best possible tan in the shortest space of time. Be sure to use a protective sun cream (15–30 factor range), and reapply it every time you go for a swim or soak in the pool or ocean. Start with just 15 minutes' exposure and gradually work your way up to an hour or so. It is better to go home with a suntan than sunburn. If you overdo it, seek immediate help from the ship's doctor.

SWIMMING POOLS

Depending on the ship, it will have indoor or outdoor swimming pools. They may be closed when the ship is in port owing to local health regulations and/or cleaning. Hours of opening will be listed in the *Daily Program*. Diving is not normally allowed, since pools are shallow. Parents should note that pools on most ships are not supervised. Be aware that some ships use excessive

Chess, anyone? This game of giant chess can be found on the open deck of the 11,209-grt, 446-passenger Black Prince *(Fred Olsen Cruise Lines).*

chlorine or bleaching agents for cleanliness, which could cause colors to run on your bathing attire.

TELEVISION

On most new and recently refurbished ships, in-cabin television is standard. Programming may be obtained by a mixture of satellite and video channels. Some ships can "lock-on" to live international news programs (such as those of CNN or BBC World News), or to *text-only* news services (like Oceansat News), for which cruise lines pay a subscription fee per cabin per month. Satellite television reception is often poor, however, because ships at sea are constantly moving out of an extremely narrow beam being downloaded from the satellite and they therefore cannot "track" the signal as accurately as a land-based facility. Some ships sailing in the Caribbean can only pick up the Spanish-language Pan-Am satellite.

TIPPING (GRATUITIES)

Many people find the whole question of tipping awkward and embarrassing. The information given here is meant as a guideline; you should then add your own good judgment.

On some ships, there are subtle suggestions made regarding tips, whereas on others, cruise directors, under the direction of the hotel manager, get carried away and are far too dictatorial as to the practice of tipping. Ships such as those of Princess Cruises offer hints on tipping via the in-cabin video system.

Some of the cruise brochures, like those of Holland America Line, state that "tipping is not required." They may not be required, but they are most definitely expected by the ship's staff.

The industry standard for cruises is roughly as follows:

- Dining room waiter: $3.00-$3.50 per person per day;
- Busboy: $1.50-$1.75 per day;
- Cabin steward/stewardess: $3.00-$3.50 per person per day.

Suite and penthouse passengers should tip $5.00 per person per day to each of the dining room waiters and the suite stewards/stewardesses, as well as to the butler, if there is one (Cunard Line recommends $6 for the butler on *Queen Elizabeth 2*).

Any other gratuities should be given according to services rendered, just as you would tip in any good restaurant or hotel (for example, to the maître d', wine waiter, and barman). On many ships (those that belong to Carnival Cruise Lines, Cunard Line, Norwegian Cruise Line, and Royal Caribbean Cruises, for example), the tip for the barman or bar waiter is automatically added to your bar check, at 15 percent.

Gratuities are usually given on the last evening of a cruise of up to 14 days' duration. For longer cruises, you normally extend half of the tip half way through the cruise and the rest on your last evening.

Note: On some Greek-staffed ships (Epirotiki Cruise Line, Royal Cruise Line, Sun Line Cruises, for example), gratuities are pooled and given to the chief steward, who shares them out at the end of each cruise. A daily amount of $8-$10 per person is the norm.

If you're traveling on a river cruise, you may be asked to tip the cruise director (who is actually more of a cruise manager).

Envelopes for tipping are available from the purser's office, where you can also ask for advice on tipping, or they may be placed in your cabin by your cabin steward/stewardess on the last night of the cruise.

On some of the best-rated ships, such as those listed below, gratuities can be prepaid, so that you do not have to tip at all on board. The ship's staff receive your tips direct from the company. Tipping is all very neat and tidy on: *QE2, Royal Viking Sun, Sagafjord,* and *Vistafjord*.

Gratuities are included in the cruise fare on the following ships, on which no extra tipping is permitted: *Asuka, Club Med I, Club Med II, Oceanic Grace, Radisson Diamond, Royal Viking Sun, Sea Goddess I, Sea Goddess II, Seabourn Pride, Seabourn Spirit, Silver Cloud, Silver Wind, Song of Flower*.

ORIGIN OF THE WORD "TIPS"

Before the introduction of postage stamps, coachmen who carried passengers were often asked to carry a letter or other package. A small recompense was given for this service, called a "tip"—which stands for "to insure personal service." Hence, when in future some special service was provided, particularly in the hospitality industry, tips became an accepted way of saying thank you for services rendered.

TWENTY-FOUR-HOUR CLOCK

On many European-based ships, the 24-hour clock is the standard way of referring to time, in keeping with the practicality of its use in international travel. In spite of the initial strangeness of this system of time-telling, you will soon find it not only simple to use, but far less likely to lead to confusion.

Safe swimming. Passengers enjoying the sun and water at the hydraulically operated, fold-out, floating swimming pool aboard the Black Prince *(Fred Olsen Cruise Lines).*

Up to midday, the hours are shown as 0100 to 1200. Thereafter they proceed from 1300 to 2400. Thus, 1400 is 2 p.m.; 1520 is 3:20 p.m.; and so on.

VALUABLES

A small number of ships have a lock box built into each cabin. However, items of special value should be stored in a safety deposit box in the purser's office. You will then have simple and convenient access to all your valuables during the cruise.

VISITORS

Passes for visitors to see you on board your ship must always be arranged in advance, preferably at the time you make your booking. Announcements will be made when it is time for all visitors to go ashore.

Sadly, Bon Voyage parties, such as those you may have seen in the movies, are virtually a thing of the past. They are no longer possible aboard ship (with the exception of those ships operating around-the-world cruises) owing to greatly increased security concerns and insurance regulations.

WATERSPORTS

Some of the small vessels, such as the *Black Prince*, *Club Med I* and *II*, *Sea Goddess I*, *Sea Goddess II*, *Seabourn Pride*, *Seabourn Spirit*, *Silver Cloud*, *Silver Wind*, *Wind Song*, *Wind Spirit*, and *Wind Star*, have a watersports platform that is lowered from the ship's stern or side. These ships carry with them windsurfers, waterski boats, jet skis, waterskis, and scuba and snorkel equipment, usually at no extra charge. The *Queen Odyssey*, *Seabourn Pride* and *Seabourn Spirit* also feature an enclosed swimming "cage," which is needed for areas of the world where unpleasant fish might be lurking.

Although such facilities look good in the cruise brochures, in many cases ships seem reluctant to make use of them. This is because many itineraries have too few useful anchor ports. Also, the sea must be in an almost flat, calm condition, which is seldom the case. Another more prosaic reason is simply because of strict insurance regulations.

WINE AND LIQUOR

The cost of drinks on board is generally lower than on land, since ships have access to duty-free liquor. Drinks may be ordered in the dining room, at any of the ship's bars or from the room service facility.

In the dining room, you can order wine with your meals from an extensive and reasonably priced wine list. If you want wine with your dinner, try to place your order at lunch time, as waiters are always at their busiest at the evening meal.

On some ships, a duty-free sales point will allow you to purchase wine and liquor for personal consumption in your cabin. Passengers are not normally permitted to bring these purchases into the dining room or into other public rooms, nor indeed any duty-free wine or liquor purchased in port. These regulations are obviously made to protect bar sales, which are a substantial source of on-board revenue for the cruise line.

Indeed, some lines have even introduced a "corkage" fee as part of their policy to deter passengers from bringing their own wines with them into the dining room.

WHAT TO DO IF...

1. Your luggage doesn't arrive at the ship.

If you are traveling as part of the cruise line's air/sea package, the airline is wholly responsible for locating your luggage and delivering it to the next port. If you arranged your own air transportation it is wholly *your* problem. Always have easy-to-read name and address tags both *inside* as well as *outside* your luggage. Keep track of claim documents and give the airline a detailed itinerary and list of port agents (usually included with your documents).

2. *You* miss the ship.

If you miss the ship's departure (due to late or non-performing flight connections, etc.), and you are traveling on an air/sea package, the airline will arrange to get you to the ship. If you are traveling "cruise-only" and have arranged your own air transportation, then *you* are responsible for onward flights, hotel stays and transfers. Many cruise lines now have "deviation" desks, where, for a small fee, you can adjust airline flights and dates to suit personal preferences. If you arrive at the port just as your ship is pulling away, contact the ship's port agent immediately.

3. Your cabin is too small.

Almost all cruise ship cabins are too small! When you book a cruise, you pay for a certain category and type of cabin, but have little or no control over which one you actually get. See the hotel manager/purser as soon as possible, explaining what's wrong with the cabin (noisy, too hot, etc.). If the ship is full (and most are nowadays), it will be difficult to change. However, the hotel manager/purser will probably try to move you from known problem cabins, although they are not required to do so.

4. Your cabin has no air-conditioning, is noisy, or there are other problems.

If there is anything wrong in your cabin, or if there is something wrong with the plumbing in your bathroom, bring it to the attention of the cabin steward immediately. If nothing gets better, complain to the hotel manager/purser. Some cabins, for example, are located above the ship's laundry, generator, or galley (hot); others may be above the disco (noisy). If the ship is full, it may be difficult to change.

5. You have small children and the brochure implied that the ship has special programs for them, but when on board you find out it's not an all-year-round program.

In this instance, either the brochure was misleading, or your travel agent didn't know enough about the ship, or didn't bother to ask the right questions. If you have a genuine cause for complaint, then see your travel agent when you get home. Ships generally try to accommodate your young ones, but may not be covered by their insurance for "looking after" them throughout the day, as the brochure seemed to promise. Again, check thoroughly with your travel agent *before* you book.

6. You don't like your dining room sitting.

Most "standard" market ships operate two sittings for dinner (sometimes for all meals). When you book your cruise, you are asked whether you want first or second sitting. The line will make every attempt to please you.

7. You want a table for two and are put on a table for eight.

Again, see the maître d' and explain why you are not satisfied. A little gratuity may prove helpful.

8. A large group has taken over the ship.
Sometimes, large groups have blocked (pre-booked) several public rooms for meetings (seemingly every hour on the hour in the rooms you want to use). This means the individual passenger (that's you) becomes a second-class citizen. Make your displeasure known to the hotel manager/purser immediately, tell your travel agent and write a follow-up letter to the line when you return home.

9. A port of call is deleted from the itinerary.
If you only took the cruise because the ship goes to the place you've wanted to go for years, then before you go, read the fine print in the brochure. A cruise line is under *no* obligation to perform the stated itinerary. For whatever reason (political unrest, weather, mechanical problems, no berth space, safety, etc.), the ship's captain has the ultimate responsibility.

10. You are unwell aboard ship
Don't worry. All cruise ships carrying more than 50 passengers are required to carry a fully qualified doctor and medical facilities, which will include a small pharmacy. You'll be well taken care of. You should be aware that the ship's medical doctor generally operates as a concession. So, although there are charges for medical services rendered, almost all cruise lines offer insurance packages that include medical coverage for most eventualities. It is wise to take out this insurance when you book.

11. You have a problem with a crew member.
Go immediately to the hotel manager or purser and explain the problem (for single women it could be a persistent cabin steward with a master door key, for example). No one will do anything unless you let them know. Cruise ships try to hire decent staff, but, with 50,000 crew members aboard the world's cruise fleet, there are bound to be a few bad

apples. Insist on a full written report of the incident, which must be entered in the ship's daily log by the staff captain (or deputy captain).

12. You leave some personal belongings on a tour bus.
If you have left something on a tour bus, and you're back on board your ship, first advise the shore excursion manager. If he/she can't be located, advise the purser's office. The shore excursion manager will contact the tour operator ashore and see whether any items have been handed in to their office. In many cases, items are in fact retrieved.

13. You have extra charges on your bill.
Check your itemized bill carefully. Then talk to the purser or reception desk and ask them to show you the charge slips. Make sure you get a copy of your bill, *after* any modifications have been made.

14. The cruise airline's arrangements have you flying from Los Angeles via Timbucktoo to get to your cruise ship.
Well, it's fine if your cruise ship is in Timbucktoo (it shouldn't be, as it's inland). Most cruise lines that have low rates also use the cheapest air routing to get you to your ship. That could mean charter flights from a central hub. It may also mean being dumped off the ship at the end of your cruise very early in the morning. Be warned, you get what you pay for. Ask questions *before* you book.

15. You are unhappy with your cruise experience.
You (or your travel agent) ultimately chose the ship and cruise. But if your ship doesn't meet your specific lifestyle and interests, or the ship performs less well than the brochure promises, then let the cruise line know as soon as possible. If your aggravation is valid, many cruise lines will offer a credit, good towards a future cruise. But do read the fine print on the ticket.

147

Entertainment

THAT'S ENTERTAINMENT!

After food, the most subjective (and talked-about) part of any *mainstream* cruise experience is the entertainment program. Menus always present you with a choice of several foods, whereas the same is not often possible with cruise ship entertainment, which has to be diversified and innovative, but never controversial. Ask 1,000 people what they would like to see as part of any evening's entertainment program, and 1,000 different answers will ensue. It's all a matter of personal taste and choice. Whatever one expects, the days have gone when you would have been entertained by waiters doubling as singers, although a few bar waiters are still known to perform tray-spinning effects to boost their tips!

Many passengers expect to see top notch entertainment, "headline" marquee name cabaret artists, that is, the world's most "popular" singers, and the most dazzling shows with slick special effects, just as one would find in the best venues in Las Vegas, London, or Paris. But there are many reasons why it's not exactly like that. International star acts invariably have an entourage that accompanies them to any venue: their personal manager, their musical director (often a pianist or conductor), a rhythm section (with bass player and drummer), even their hairdresser. On land, one-night shows are possible, but on a ship, an artist cannot always disembark after just one night, especially when it involves moving equipment, costumes, and baggage. They can also lose valuable money-making bookings, and telephone contact. Although they can be contacted at sea, it *is* more difficult, and the telephone number is not their own. This makes the whole business logistically and financially unattractive for all but the very largest ships on fixed itineraries, where a marquee name act might be considered a marketing draw.

When you are at home you can literally bring the world's top talent into your home via television. Cruise ships are a different matter altogether. Most entertainers do not like to be away from their "home base" for longish periods, as they depend so much on the telephone for their work. Most do not like the long contracts that the majority of ships must offer in order to amortize the cost over several weeks.

Entertainers on ships must also *live* with their audiences for several days (sometimes several weeks), something unheard of on land, as well as work on stages that are seldom designed for real live performances.

Many of the older (pre-1970) ships have extremely limited entertainment spaces, and very few ships provide proper dressing rooms and backstage facilities for the storage of costumes, props, or effects, not to mention the extensive sound and lighting equipment most live "name" artists demand or need. Indeed, only the latest ships provide the extensive facilities needed

for presenting the kind of high-tech shows one would find in Las Vegas, London, or New York, for example, with elaborate electronic backdrops, revolving stages, orchestra pits, multi-slide projection, huge stageside video screens, pyrotechnic capabilities, and the latest light-mover and laser technology. Even the latest ships often lack enough dressing room and hanging space for the 150 costumes required in a single typical ship production show.

More emphasis has been placed on entertainment since the mid-1970s. Entertainment on today's large mainstream ships is market-driven. In other words, it is directed toward that segment of the industry that the cruise line's marketing department is specifically targeting (discounting notwithstanding). This is predominantly a family audience, so the entertainment must appeal to as broad an age range as possible—a tall order for any cruise line's director of entertainment.

A cruise line with several ships in its fleet will normally employ an entertainment department that is made up of an entertainment director and several assistants, and most cruise lines have contracts with one or more entertainment agencies that specialize in entertainment for cruise ships.

It is no use, for example, a company booking a juggler who needs a floor-to-ceiling height of 12 feet, but finds that the ship has a show lounge with a height of 7 feet. ("Couldn't he juggle sideways?" I've heard one cruise company executive ask!); or an acrobatic knife-throwing act (and on a moving ship?); or a concert pianist when the ship only has an upright honky-tonk piano; or a singer who sings only in

Production show dancers in costume grace the stage of a Carnival Cruise Lines ship.

English when the passengers are actually German-speaking, and so on.

Indeed, the most difficult audience to cater to is one of mixed nationalities (each of whom will expect entertainers to cater exclusively to their particular linguistic group). Given that cruise lines are now marketing to more international audiences in order to fill ships, the problem of finding the right entertainment is far more acute.

The more upscale cruise lines offer more classical music, even some light opera, and more fine guest lecturers and world-renowned authors than the seven-day package cruises heading for warm-weather destinations.

One area of entertainment that has become part of the experience, and is expected—particularly on the larger, mainstream cruise ships—is that of the glamorous "production show." This is the kind of show one would expect to see in any good Las Vegas show palace, with a team of singers and dancers, a production manager, lavish backdrops, extravagant sets, grand lighting, special effects, and stunning custom-designed costumes. Unfortunately, many cruise line executives, who know nothing about entertainment, regard plumes and huge peacock feathers paraded by showgirls who step, but can't dance, as being desirable. Some cruise ships have "T&A" (tits and ass) shows that are not becoming to either dancer or passenger. Such things went out of vogue about 20 years ago. Shows that offer more creative costuming and real dancing win more votes today.

Those passengers booking the back-to-back seven-day cruises (on alternating eastern and western Caribbean itineraries, for example) should be aware that entertainment is generally geared to seven-day cruises. Thus, you will usually find the same two or three production shows and the same acts on the second week of your cruise. The way to avoid seeing everything twice is to pace yourself by just going to some of the events during the first week and saving the rest for the second week.

Regular cruisegoers will notice that they seem to see the same acts time after time on various ships. For the reasons given above, plus a few more, the criteria narrows the field even though there are many fine land-based acts. In addition, ship entertainers need to love socializing. Successful acts tend to be good mixers, are presentable when in public, don't do drugs or take excess alcohol, are not womanizers (or manizers?), are not late for rehearsals, and must cooperate with the cruise director and his staff, as well as the band. Sadly, with cruise lines forever looking for ways to cut costs, entertainment has of late been a major target for some companies (particularly the smaller ones). Cutting costs translates into bringing on, for example, lower-cost singers (who very often turn out to be non-reading, vocally challenged persons), and bands that can't read charts (musician-speak for musical arrangements) brought on board by cabaret acts.

SHOW BIZ AT SEA

In today's high-tech world, the putting together of a lavish 50–60-minute production show involves the concerted efforts of a range of experienced people from the world of show business, and a cost of $1 million per show is not

unheard of. Weekly running costs (performers' salaries; costume cleaning and repair; royalty payments; replacement audio and video tapes, and so on) all add up to an expensive package for what is often a largely unappreciative and critical audience.

WHO'S WHO

Although production companies differ in their approach, the following list gives some idea of the various people involved behind the scenes.

Executive Producer

His/her task is to transfer the show's concept from design to reality. First, the brief from the cruise line's director of entertainments might be for one new ship production show (the average being two major shows per seven-day cruise). They must first plan the show. After deciding an initial concept, they may then call in the choreographer, vocal coach, and musical arranger for several lengthy meetings, so everyone agrees on the flow of the show.

Choreographer

The choreographer is responsible for auditioning dancers, and for the creation, selection and teaching of all the dance routines. He/she will normally work in conjunction with the executive producer.

Musical Director

His/her job is to coordinate all musical scores and arrangements. He/she may also train the singers in voice and microphone techniques, voice projection, accenting, phrasing, memory and

general presentation, and oversee all session singers and musicians for the recording sessions, click-track tapes, and so on.

Musical Arranger

After the music has been selected, the musical arrangements must be made. For just one song, this can come to a cost of as much as $2,000 for a single arrangement for a 12-piece orchestra.

Costume Designer

He/she must provide creative original designs for a minimum of seven costume changes in one show lasting 45 minutes. Costumes must also be practical, as they will be used repeatedly.

Costume Maker

He/she must purchase all materials, and be able to produce all costumes required by the costume designer, in the time frame allotted.

Graphic Designer

His/her job is to provide all the set designs, whether they are physical one- two- or three-dimensional sets for the stage, or photographic images created on slide film, video, laser disk or other electronic media. The trend is for digital computer technology to play an increasingly important part in creating the images that are to be transferred via an electronic medium.

Lighting Designer

His/her task is to create the lighting patterns and effects for a production show. Sequences and action on stage must be carefully lit to the best advantage. He/she will also present the completed lighting plot to the software

company that will etch the plot into computer-controlled disks to be used every time the show runs.

PRODUCTION SHOW TIMING

A complete, new, large-scale production show, from conception to first performance, will take several months. Here is a breakdown of the time that's needed to put on a hypothetical show.

Month 1
- Production team create show concept.
- Write storybook and submit it to all concerned.
- Second and third meetings of the production team. The set designer provides sketches and graphics.
- Costume designer is contracted to design the costumes for seven scene changes. And you usually need different costumes for each lead singer (one male and one female), and for the dancers.
- Costume maker given order for 70 costumes to be delivered in April.

Month 2
- Advertise for dancers and singers.
- Book a rehearsal theater (with a wooden stage) for dancer auditions.
- Auditions and call-backs for the dancers.
- Book a rehearsal studio (equipped with a piano, microphones and amplifiers) for auditions for singers.
- Auditions and call-backs for the singers.
- Select the suitable talent, issue contracts on behalf of the cruise line

(usually five or six months). Talent will go back to their existing jobs while the new show is put together, making sure that they will be available for rehearsals once they start. Measurements are taken for the costume designer.

Month 3
- Fine-tuning by production team; the timing of scene and costume changes.
- Order sets, backdrops, color slides. Video footage to be made.
- Go into the recording studio.
- Lay down: principal tracks, backing tracks, and click (SMPTE timing) track.
- Mix down and edit tape.
- Produce the "master" and "mother" tapes.
- Produce copies for use aboard ship, as well as backup copies.

Month 4
- Costume fitting; the first dress rehearsal.
- Second costume fitting.

Month 5
- Final rehearsals for intensive two- or three-week period.
- Give details of the ship's mailing address to all cast members, so that they can receive mail while working aboard ship.
- Obtain working visas for all cast.

Month 6
- Crate and freight show costumes, sets, and backdrops.
- Provide the cruise line with details for booking flights and transportation for the performers etc.

- Provide the company's port agents with a name and flight list so they can meet and transfer the cast to the ship.
- Take the show on the high seas.
- After boarding and getting to know the layout of the ship, the entertainers will usually spend a week in intensive rehearsals, often working from midnight to about 5 a.m., while the cast due to come off the ship (for a vacation, or end of contract) is still doing a regular cruise entertainment show.

Month 7

- The opening night for the new show will probably be held on the first formal night of the cruise. No doubt all the ship's senior officers will be in attendance to "judge" the success of the show.

BANDS/MUSICIANS

Before the big production shows and artists can be booked, bands and musicians must be hired, often for long contracts. Polish musicians are favored for a ship's showband, as they are excellent music readers (necessary for all visiting cabaret artists, not to mention the big production shows).

American and British musicians are found on increasingly fewer ships, as cruise lines in the past have experienced too many problems with drugs, drink, and unions. Most musicians work to contracts of about six months. Entertaining lounge duos and solo pianists or singer/pianists are generally hired through an entertainment agency specializing in cruise ships.

Steel bands are recruited from the Caribbean, while other specialist bands (such as popular Country and Western bands) may be invited aboard for special occasions or charters.

OTHER ENTERTAINMENT

Most cruise ships organize acts that, while perhaps not internationally recognized "names," can provide two or three different shows during a seven-day cruise. These will be male/female singers, illusionists, puppeteers, hypnotists, and even circus acts, with wide age-range appeal.

There are comedians, comediennes and comedy duos who perform "clean" material that find employment year-round on what has become known as the "cruise ship circuit." These popular comics enjoy good accommodations, are stars while on board, and often go from ship to ship on a standard rotation every few days. There are raunchy, late-night "adults only" comedy acts on some of the ships with younger, "hip" audiences, but few of them seem to have enough material for two different shows.

The larger a ship, the larger will be the entertainment program. On some ships, the cruise director may "double" as an act, but most companies prefer him/her to be strictly an administrative and social director, allowing more time to be with passengers. Whichever ship and cruise you choose to travel on, you will find that being entertained "live" is an experience far superior to that of sitting at home in front of a television set, watching its clinical presentation. That's show business!

Nautical Notes

The world of ships is a world of its own, and associated with it is a whole language and culture which can sometimes be confusing—but always fascinating—to the newcomer. Here are a few tidbits of nautical information for you, which may contribute to the pleasure of your cruise.

RULES OF THE ROAD

Ships are subject to stringent international regulations. They must keep to the right in shipping lanes, and pass on the right (but there are certain exceptions). When circumstances raise some doubt or shipping lanes are crowded, ships often use their whistles, in the same way an automobile driver uses directional signals to show which way he will turn. When one ship passes another and gives a single blast on its whistle, this means it is turning to starboard (right). Two blasts means a turn to port (left). The other ship acknowledges by repeating the same signal.

Ships switch on their navigational running lights at night—with green for starboard, red for port. Also, they have two white lights on the masts, the forward one lower than the aft one.

Flags and pennants form another part of a ship's communication facilities and are displayed for identification purposes. Each time a country is visited, its national flag is shown. While entering and leaving a port, the ship flies a blue and vertical striped flag to request a pilot, while a half red, half white flag (divided vertically) indicates that a pilot is on board. Cruise lines and other passenger shipping lines also display their own "house" flag, proudly fluttering from the main mast.

A ship's funnel or smokestack is one other means of identification, each line having its own funnel design and color scheme. The size, height, and number of funnels were points worth advertising at the turn of the century. Most ocean liners of the time had four funnels and were called "four-stackers."

Today, perhaps the most distinctive funnel design belongs to those ships of the Royal Caribbean Cruises; some of them actually have a nightclub or lounge perched partway up the stack itself. The view from these is spectacular, although in bad weather it's the room that will move most.

There are numerous customs at sea, many of them older than any maritime law. Superstition has always been an important element, as in the following example quoted in the British Admiralty Manual of Seamanship:

"The custom of breaking a bottle of wine over the stem of a ship when being launched originates from the old practice of toasting prosperity to a ship in a silver goblet of wine, which was then cast into the sea in order to prevent a toast of ill intent being drunk from the same cup. This was a practice that proved too expensive, and it was replaced in 1690 by the breaking of a bottle of wine over the stem."

ON THE WATCH

A ship's working day is made up of six four-hour time periods, known as "watches." In theory, a complement of officers and crew work the same watch round the clock: four hours on followed by eight hours off during any 24-hour period.

To avoid working identical hours day after day, one of the four-hour periods is split further into first and second "dog watches" of two hours each, as follows:

0000-0400 hours	midwatch
0400-0800 hours	morning watch
0800-1200 hours	forenoon watch
1200-1600 hours	afternoon watch
1600-1800 hours	first dog watch
1800-2000 hours	second dog watch
2000-2400 hours	evening watch

On board ship, the tradition is to record time by the striking of bells to indicate the state of the watch. Each bell represents a half hour of time on watch and the duty is ended when eight bells are sounded at midnight, 0400, 0800, 1200, etc.

WIND SPEEDS

A navigational announcement to passengers is normally made once or twice a day, giving the ship's position, temperature and weather information.

Wind velocity is measured on the Beaufort Scale, a method that was first devised in 1805 by Commodore Francis Beaufort, later Admiral and Knight Commander of the Bath, for measuring the force of wind at sea.

Originally, it measured the effect of the wind on a fully rigged man-of-war (which was usually laden with cannon and other heavy ammunition). It became the official way of recording wind velocity in 1874, when it was adopted by the International Meteorological Committee.

You might be confused by the numbering system for wind velocity. There are 12 velocities, known as "force" on the Beaufort Scale. They are as follows:

Force	Speed (mph)	Description/Ocean Surface
0	0-1	Calm; glassy (like a mirror)
1	1-3	Light wind; rippled surface
2	4-7	Light breeze; small wavelets
3	8-12	Gentle breeze; large wavelets, scattered white-caps
4	13-18	Moderate breeze; small waves, frequent white-caps
5	19-24	Fresh breeze; moderate waves, numerous white-caps
6	25-31	Strong breeze; large waves, white foam crests
7	32-38	Moderate gale; streaky white foam
8	39-46	Fresh gale; moderately high waves
9	47-54	Strong gale; high waves
10	55-63	Whole gale, very high waves, curling crests
11	64-73	Storm; extremely high waves, froth and foam, poor visibility
12	73+	Hurricane; huge waves, thundering white spray, nil visibility

KNOTS AND LOGS

A knot is a unit of speed measuring one nautical mile per hour. (A nautical mile is equal to one-sixtieth of a degree of the earth's circumference and measures exactly 6,080.2 feet.) It is about 800 feet—or one-seventh—which is longer than a land mile. Thus, when a ship is traveling at a speed of 20 knots (note: this is never referred to as 20 knots per hour), she is traveling at 20 nautical miles per hour.

This unit of measurement has its origin in the days prior to the advent of modern aids. At that time, sailors used a log and a length of rope in order to measure the distance which their boat had covered, as well as the speed at which it was advancing.

In 1574, a tract by William Bourne, entitled *A Regiment for the Sea*, records the method by which this was done. The log was weighted down at one end while the other end was affixed to a rope. The weighted end, when thrown over the stern into the sea, had the effect of making the log stand upright, thus being visible.

Sailors believed that the log stayed stationary at the spot where it had been cast into the water, while the rope unravelled. By measuring the length of rope used, they could ascertain how far the ship had traveled, and were thus able to calculate its speed.

Sailors first tied knots at regular intervals (eventually fixed at 47 feet 3 inches) along the rope, and counted how many knots had passed through their hands in a specified time (later established as 28 seconds), which was measured by the amount of sand that had run out of an hour glass.

They then used simple multiplication to clearly calculate the number of knots their ship was traveling at over the period of an hour.

The data gathered in this way were put into a special record book—called a logbook. Today, a logbook is used to record the day-to-day details of the life of a ship and its crew, as well as other pertinent information.

LATITUDE AND LONGITUDE

Latitude signifies the distance north or south of the equator, while longitude signifies distance east or west of the 0 degree at Greenwich Observatory in London. Both are recorded in degrees, minutes, and seconds. At the equator, one minute of longitude is equal to one nautical mile, but as the meridians converge after leaving the equator, and meeting at the poles, the size of a degree becomes smaller.

PLIMSOLL MARK

The safety of ships at sea and all those aboard owes much to the 19th-century social reformer, Samuel Plimsoll, a member of the British parliament.

He was specially concerned about the frequent loss of ships due to overloading. In those days there were certain ship owners who would load their vessels down to the gunwales so that they could squeeze every ounce of revenue out of them. They gambled on good weather, good fortune and good seamanship to bring the ships safely into port. Consequently, many ships

went to the bottom of the sea as a result of their buoyancy being seriously impaired by overloading.

Samuel Plimsoll helped to enact the legislation that came to be known as the Merchant Shipping Act of 1875. This required all ship owners to mark all their vessels with a circular disc bisected with a line that would be observed as a measure of their maximum draft, that is, the depth to which a ship's hull could be safely immersed at sea. However, the Merchant Shipping Act of 1890 was even stricter, and required that the Plimsoll mark (or line) had to be positioned on the sides of vessels in accordance with tables that were drawn up by competent authorities. The Plimsoll mark is now found on the ships of every nation.

The Plimsoll mark indicates three different depths: the depth to which a vessel can be loaded in fresh water, which is less buoyant than salt water; the depth in summer, when seas are calmer; and the depth in winter, when the seas are rougher.

THE CHALLENGE OF THE BLUE RIBAND

No award has inspired as much rivalry between shipping lines as the coveted Blue Riband, given to the liner that makes the fastest transatlantic crossing in a particular year. Indeed, possession of the Blue Riband became—and still is—a source of national pride.

By the late 1800s references to the award were already being recorded, but the first real mention of it was made on August 1, 1900, when the *Illustrated London News* reported that the Blue Riband had been won by the *Deutschland*, the Hamburg America Line passenger ship.

Although the great passenger liners of the North Atlantic raced to beat the speed record, there was no actual material award until 1935, when Harold K. Hales (1888-1942), a member of the British parliament, donated a silver challenge trophy to be awarded each year to the steamship line who won the Blue Riband. Speed became so important that newspapers carried daily

PREFIXES

ib – ice-breaker (diesel- or nuclear-powered)

ms – motor ship (diesel power)

mts – motor twin screw (diesel power), or motor turbine ship (steam turbine power)

mv – motor vessel (diesel power)

RMS – Royal Mail Ship

ss – steamship

ssc – semi-submersible craft (swath)

sts – sail training ship

tes – turbo-electric ship (steam turbine power)

ts – turbine steamer (steam turbine power), or twin screw vessel

tsmv – twin screw motor vessel

ys – yacht ship

records of distance steamed by major ships, as well as the duration of each crossing. Average speeds, although not revealed, could be calculated from the figures provided.

Naturally the distance covered can vary with each crossing of the Atlantic. Since 1900 the shortest distance that was recorded for Blue Riband purposes was the 2,807 nautical miles between Sandy Hook, New Jersey, and Queenstown (now Cobh) in Ireland, while the longest distance was 3,199 nautical miles, between Ambrose Light, New Jersey, and Cherbourg, France. Twelve ships have held the record westbound, and ten eastbound.

Some of the world's most illustrious passenger ships are listed among the holders of this prestigious award. For 22 years the Blue Riband was held by the Cunard Line's *Mauretania*, passing briefly, in 1929, to Germany's *Bremen* and in 1930 to that country's *Europa*.

In 1933 the Italian *Rex* took over, only to lose it a mere two years later to France's *Normandie*. Then arrived the *Queen Mary* to vie with the *Normandie* for the award. Both kept the award for a year each, in 1936 and 1937 respectively, until in 1938 Cunard firmly retrieved it with the *Queen Mary*. In 1952, the prize was taken by the new U.S. liner, the *United States*.

The *United States* has the distinction of being the fastest *real* liner ever to win the Blue Riband. Between July 3 and 7, 1952, during an eastbound crossing from Ambrose to Bishop Rock, the ship recorded an average speed of 35.59 knots, although it is claimed that in achieving such a speed, mechanical damage was caused to the extent that any attempt to repeat the

performance was virtually out of the question.

No major passenger ship has been built since the early 1950s to challenge the ss *United States*' record, although with the re-engining of Cunard's *QE2*, it is conceivable that she could attempt to make a Blue Riband crossing, given that she has achieved over 36 knots during her sea trials.

On June 22, 1990, the 243-foot-long, twin-hulled Sea Cat (catamaran-type) passenger ferry (and not a cruise ship) *Hoverspeed Great Britain* made a successful, but somewhat unsporting, bid for the Blue Riband. The vessel, commissioned by Hoverspeed of England to bolster the company's fleet of hovercraft to counter the anticipated competition from the Channel Tunnel, carried only one passenger, and had to refuel three times in mid-ocean, something that no really genuine ocean-going passenger liner has ever had to do. The trophy was awarded despite this, and is now back in England, the country where it first started.

THE BRIDGE

A ship's navigation bridge is manned at all times, both at sea and in port. Besides the captain, who is master of the vessel, other senior officers take "watch" turns for four- or eight-hour periods. In addition, junior officers are continually honing their skills as experienced navigators, awaiting the day when they will be promoted to master of a luxury cruise ship.

Besides the ship's captain, there is a qualified officer on duty at all times— even when the ship is docked in port.

The captain is always in command at times of high risk, such as when the ship is entering or leaving a port, when the density of traffic is particularly high, or when the visibility is severely restricted by poor weather.

Navigation has come a long way since the days of the ancient mariners, who used only the sun and the stars to calculate their course across the oceans. The space-age development of sophisticated navigation devices has enabled us to make giant strides from the less reliable techniques used long ago. Navigation satellites have enabled us to eliminate the guesswork of early navigation (the first global mobile satellite system came into being in 1979).

A ship's navigator today can figure out accurately where the ship is in any weather and at any time. There follows a description of some of the navigation instruments, which will help you to understand the complexities of seamanship today.

System Control

The most sophisticated state of the art machinery and navigation systems are such technical marvels that sailors of yesteryear could not even conceive of their invention. The latest navigation and command system, which is known as the "Electronic Chart Precise Integrated Navigation System" (ECPINS), now combines the electronics of the most up-to-date satellite positioning methods (Global Positioning System) with automatic course plotting, video map displays of the oceans, gyro-compass, echo sounders, sonar doppler log, wind speed, and the various sensors to provide, in a single compact computer unit, a comprehensive at-a-glance display of the ship in relation to the rest of the world, contained in one "real-time" position on a single monitor's electronic chart.

The Compass

A compass is the instrument by which a ship may be steered on a pre-selected course, and by which bearings of *visible* objects can be taken in order to fix a ship's position on a navigation chart. There are two kinds of compass. The magnetic compass uses the inherent magnetic forces within and around the Earth; the gyro-compass, a relatively recent invention, uses the properties of gyroscopic inertia and precession—ideally used to align itself to a true north–south position.

Steering

There are two different methods that can be used to steer a ship:

- Electro-hydraulic steering uses the automatic (telemotor-type) transmission from the wheel itself to the steering gear aft. This is generally used in conditions of heavy traffic, during maneuvers into and out of ports, or on occasions when there is poor visibility.
- Automatic steering (gyro-pilot), a method which is used only in the open sea. This system eliminates the need for having someone at the wheel. However, on every ship, a quartermaster will always be at the wheel, as a backup to the system, for extra safety—and just in case a need should arise to switch from one steering system to another. This changeover from one to the other takes only a few seconds.

Ships and the sea have their own special vocabulary. This list may be of use.

A

Abeam—off the side of the ship, at a right angle to its length

Aft—near, toward or in the rear of the ship

Ahead—something that is ahead of the ship's bow

Alleyway—a passageway or corridor

Alongside—said of a ship when it is beside a pier or another vessel

Amidships—in or toward the middle of the ship; the longitudinal center portion of the ship

Anchor Ball—black ball hoisted above the bow to show that the vessel is anchored

Astern—is the opposite of Ahead (i.e., meaning something behind, or astern, of the ship)

B

Backwash—motion in the water caused by the propeller(s) moving in a reverse (astern) direction

Bar—sandbar, usually caused by tidal or current conditions near the shore

Beam—width of the ship between its two sides at the widest point

Bearing—compass direction, expressed in degrees, from the ship to a particular objective or destination

Below—anything beneath the main deck

Berth—dock, pier, or quay. Also means bed on board ship

Bilge—lowermost spaces of the infra-structure of a ship

Boat Stations—allotted space for each person during lifeboat drill or any other emergency when lifeboats are lowered

Bow—the forwardmost part of the vessel

Bridge—navigational and command control center

Bulkhead—upright partition (wall) dividing the ship into compartments

Bunkers—the space where fuel is stored; "bunkering" means taking on fuel

C

Cable Length—a measured length equaling 100 fathoms or 600 feet

Chart—a nautical map used for navigating

Colors—refers to the national flag or emblem flown by the ship

Companionway—interior stairway

Course—direction in which the ship is headed, in degrees

D

Davit—a device for raising and lowering lifeboats

Deadlight—a ventilated porthole cover to prevent light from entering

Disembark (also Debark)—to leave a ship

Dock—berth, pier or quay

Draft (or Draught)—measurement in feet from the ship's waterline to the lowest point of its keel

E

Embark—to join a ship

F

Fantail—the rear or overhang of the ship

Fathom—distance equal to six feet

Flagstaff—a pole at the stern of a ship where the flag of the ship's country of registry is flown

Free Port—port or place that is free of customs duty and regulations

Funnel—chimney from which the ship's combustion gases are propelled into the atmosphere

G

Galley—the ship's kitchen

Gangway—the stairway or ramp link between ship and shore

Gross Registered Tonnage (grt)—not the weight of the ship but the total of all permanently enclosed spaces above and below decks, with certain exceptions, such as the bridge, radio room, galleys, washing facilities, and other specified areas. It is the basis for harbor dues. New international regulations introduced in 1982 require ship owners to re-measure the grt of their vessels (1 grt = 100 cubic feet of enclosed space/2.83m^3) and not its weight

H

Helm—the apparatus for steering a ship

House Flag—the flag denoting the company to which a ship belongs

Hull—the frame and body of the ship exclusive of masts or superstructure

L

Leeward—the side that is sheltered from the wind

M

Manifest—a list of the ship's passengers, crew, and cargo

N

Nautical Mile—one-sixtieth of a degree of the circumference of the earth, equal to 6,080.2 feet. It is about 800 feet (or one-seventh) longer than a land mile

P

Pilot—a person licensed to navigate ships into or out of a harbor or through difficult waters, and to advise the captain on handling the ship during these procedures

Pitch—the rise and fall of a ship's bow that may occur when the ship is under way

Port—the left side of a ship when facing forward

Q

Quay—berth, dock, or pier

R

Rudder—a finlike device astern and below the waterline, for steering the vessel

S

Screw—a ship's propeller

Stabilizer—a gyroscopically operated retractable "fin" extending from either or both sides of the ship below the waterline to provide a more stable ride

Starboard—the right side of the ship when facing forward

Stern—the aftmost part of the ship which is opposite the bow

T

Tender—a smaller vessel, often a lifeboat, which is used to transport passengers between the ship and shore when the vessel is at anchor

W

Wake—the track of agitated water left behind a ship when in motion

Waterline—the line along the side of a ship's hull which corresponds to the surface of the water

Windward—the side toward which the wind blows

Y

Yaw—the erratic deviation from the ship's set course, usually caused by a heavy sea

Satellite Navigator

Using this latest high-tech piece of equipment, the ship's officers can read, on a small television screen, the ship's position in the open ocean anywhere in the world, at any time, and in any weather, with pinpoint accuracy (that is, within plus or minus 600 feet).

The satellite navigator device uses the information transmitted by a constellation of up to six orbiting satellites. Each of these satellites is in a normal circular polar orbit at an altitude of 450 to 700 nautical miles, and orbits the Earth in about 108 minutes. Data from each gives its current orbital position every two minutes.

Apart from telling the ship where it is, it can continuously provide the distance from any given point, calculate the drift caused by currents and so on, and tell the ship when the next satellite will pass.

The basis of the satellite navigation system is that of the U.S. Navy Satellite System (NNSS). This first became operational in January 1964 as the precision guidance system for the Polaris submarine fleet, and was made available for commercial use in 1967.

The latest system (and more accurate) is the GPS (Global Positioning System), which is now fitted to an increasing number of ships. This uses 24 satellites (18 of which are on-line at any given time) which can provide an accuracy in estimating a ship's position of plus or minus 6 feet. Another variation is the NACOS Navigational Command System. This collects information from a variety of sources: satellites, radar, gyroscopic compass, speed log, surface navigational systems as well as engines, thrusters, rudders, and human input. It then displays relevant computations and information on one screen controlled by a single keyboard.

Radar

Radar is one of the most important discoveries that has ever been made for the development of navigational aids, providing on screen a picture of all solid objects in a range that is selected by the navigator—which is from half a mile to a 72-mile radius. Its greatest asset is possibly as an invaluable aid to collision avoidance with other ships, although it has proven of value in finding a position at a distance when navigational marks or charted coastlines are within its range. Some ships have two or three radar sets with inter-switch units.

Engine Telegraph

These automatic signaling devices are used to communicate orders between the bridge and the engine room. There may be three—one on the bridge and on each bridgewing.

Bow Thruster

This small two-way handle is used to control the bow thrusters—powerful engines in the bow that push the ship away from the dockside without tugs. Some of the new ships may also have thrusters positioned at the stern.

Rudder Angle Indicator

This device is normally positioned in front of, and above, the quartermaster. It provides both the commanding officer and the quartermaster with a constant readout of the degrees of rudder angle, either to port (left) or to starboard (right).

VHF Radio

This is a radio receiver and transmitter, operating on VHF (Very High Frequency) with a "Line-of-Sight" range. It's used for communicating with other ships, pilots, port authorities, etc.

Radio Direction Finder

This operates on radio waves, enabling its operator to take bearings of shore radio stations. By crossing two or more bearings, you find the ship's position.

Depth Indicator

This equipment (which is an echo-sounder) provides a ship with a constant digital monitor readout, together with a printed chart.

Course Recorder

This records and prints all courses followed by the ship at all times.

Clearview Screen

This device makes simple but effective use of centrifugal force, where instead of having an automobile-type windshield wiper, a ship has circular screens that rotate at high speed to clear rain or sea spray away, providing those on the bridge with the best possible view in even the worst weather.

Engine Speed Indicators

These provide a reading of the number of revolutions per minute being generated by the engines. Each engine has a separate indicator, giving the speed in forward or reverse.

Facsimile Recorder

This is a special radio apparatus that is designed to receive meteorological and oceanographic maps, satellite pictures, and other pertinent weather information which is transmitted by maritime broadcast stations that are located all over the world.

Emergency Controls

These include control boards, electric circuits, and other devices to control flooding and fires on board ship.

Fire Control

If anyone sounds the fire alarm, an alarm is automatically set off on the bridge. A red panel light will be illuminated on a large plan of the ship, indicating the section of the ship that has to be checked so that the crew can take immediate action.

In the event of a fire, a ship is sectioned into several distinct zones, each of which can be tightly closed off. In addition, most of the cruise ships have a water-fed sprinkler system that can be activated at the touch of a button, or be automatically activated when sprinkler vials are broken by fire-generated heat.

New electronic fire-detection systems are also installed on ships in order to increase safety further.

Emergency Ventilation Control

This automatic fire damper system also has a manual switch that is activated to stop or control the flow of air (oxygen) to all areas of the ship, in this way reducing the fanning effect on flame and smoke via air-conditioning and fan systems.

Watertight Doors Control

Watertight doors throughout the ship can be closed off, in order to contain the movement of water flooding the

ship. A master switch activates all the doors in a matter of seconds.

All the ships' watertight doors can be operated electrically or manually, which means that nobody can be trapped in a watertight compartment.

Stabilizers Control

The ship's two stabilizing fins can be extended, housed or controlled. They normally operate automatically under the control of a gyroscope located in the engine control room.

THE CRUISER'S PRAYER

"Heavenly Father, look down on us, Your humble, obedient cruise passengers who are doomed to travel the seas and the waterways of this earth, taking photographs, sending postcards, purchasing useless souvenirs and walking around in ill-fitting swimwear.

"We beseech You, oh Lord, to make sure that our plane is not hi-jacked, that our luggage is not lost, and that our over-sized carry-ons go unnoticed.

"Protect all of us from surly and unscrupulous taxi drivers, from avaricious porters and unlicensed, English-speaking guides in foreign places.

"Give us this day Divine guidance in the selection of our cruise ships and our travel agents—so that we may find our bookings and dining room reservations honored, our cabins of generous proportions, that our luggage arrives before the first evening meal.

"We pray that our cabin telephones work, the operator (human or electrical) speaks our tongue and that there are no phone calls from our children forcing us to abandon our cruise early.

"Lead us, dear Lord, to good, inexpensive eating places wherever in the world we go ashore—where the food is superb, the waiters friendly and the wine included in the price of a meal.

"Please grant us a cruise director who doesn't "cream" the spoils of bingo or horse racing, or doesn't stress that we visit only those jewelry stores from which he accepts an offering.

"Grant us the strength to take shore excursions—to visit museums, cathedrals, spice stalls and gift shops listed in the guidebooks.

"Give us the wisdom to tip correctly at the end of our voyage. Forgive us for under-tipping out of ignorance, and over-tipping out of fear. Please make the chief purser and ship's staff love us for what we are and not for what we can contribute to their worldly goods.

"Dear God, restrain our wives from shopping sprees and please protect them from bargains they do not need or cannot afford. Lead them not into temptation in St. Thomas or Hong Kong for they know not what they do.

"Almighty father, restrain our husbands from looking at foreign women and comparing them to us. Save them from making fools of themselves in cafés and nightclubs. Above all, please do not forgive them their trespasses for they know exactly what they do.

"And when our voyage is over and we return home to our loved ones, grant us the favor of finding someone who will look at our home videos and listen to our stories, so our lives as tourists will not have been in vain. This we ask you in the name of our chosen cruise line, and in the name of American Express, Visa, Mastercard, and our banks. Amen."

QUIPS AND QUOTES

Passengers cruising for the first time are the source of all the following questions:

"Do the crew sleep on board?"

"How far above sea level are we?"

"Does this elevator go up as well as down?"

"Will this elevator take me to my cabin?"

"What time's the midnight buffet?"

"Are there two sittings at the midnight buffet?"

"Is dinner in the dining room?"

"How many fjords to the dollar?"

"When the ship's at anchor tomorrow, can we walk ashore?"

"Do we have to stay up until midnight to change our clocks?"

"What time's the 2 o'clock tour?"

"Where's the bus for the walking tour?"

"Are the entertainers paid?"

"Will the ship wait for the tour buses to get back?"

"Will I get wet if I go snorkeling?"

"Do the Chinese do the laundry by hand?"

"Is the mail brought on by plane?"

"Does the ship dock in the middle of town?"

"Who's driving the ship if the captain is at the cocktail party?"

"Is the doctor qualified?"

"Is the island surrounded by water?"

"I'm married, but can I come to the Singles Party?"

"Should I put my luggage outside the cabin before or after I go to sleep?"

Overheard in the dining room:

"Waiter, this vichyssoise is cold."

"Was the fish caught this morning by the crew?"

Overheard on a British islands cruise:

"Windsor Castle is terrific. But why did they build it so close to the airport?"

Overheard on a Greek islands cruise:

"Why did the Greeks build so many ruins?"

Overheard on a round-Japan cruise, in Kagoshima, with Mount Suribaya in the background:

"Can you tell me what time the volcano will erupt—I want to be sure to take a photograph?"

Then there's the cruise line brochure which describes cabin layout: "cabins with double bed can accommodate a third passenger"! (Premier Cruise Lines)

And what about the saying "He let the cat out of the bag?" On board a square-rigger 150 years ago, this would have sent shudders through one's spine—for it meant that a sailor had committed an offense serious enough to have the "cat o' nine tails" extracted from its bag. The "cat" was a whip made of nine lengths of cord, each being about 18 inches long with three knots at the end, all fixed to a rope handle. It could inflict serious injuries, even death upon the victim. It is no longer carried on today's tall ships, having been outlawed by the U.S. Congress in 1850, and then by Britain's Royal Navy in 1879.

Who's Who on Board

Think of a cruise ship as a highly structured floating hotel, in which each of the crew members fills a well-defined role. A look at the chart on pages 150-151 will clarify the hierarchy aboard ship. The highest authority is the captain, and the chain of command works down through the ranks.

All members of the ship's company wear a uniform by which their station and function are instantly identifiable. Rank is also designated by the colors and insignia worn on the sleeves and epaulets of the uniform itself, although the colors in conjunction with the gold braid can vary somewhat. For example, throughout most of the industry, red generally signifies the medical department, but on ships of Italian registry, red signifies the purser's department.

CAPTAIN

The captain is the master of the ship and has absolute dictatorial rights and control over his vessel, officers, crew, and passengers. He is a seaman first, and manager of the ship second. He is also expected to be a generous and worthy host (the social aspect of a captain's job today requires an investment of about a quarter of his time spent with his passengers). When passenger ships are registered for insurance coverage (this is normally with Lloyd's of London), the captain's credentials and past record are reviewed, together with the seaworthiness of the vessel itself.

Although there may be several officers with a master's certificate on the bridge, the captain's authority remains unquestioned. He wears four gold bars on his sleeves and epaulets.

Every ship has a log, a daily record in which notes are recorded of all navigational and pertinent nautical data, details of reports from various department heads and any relevant information on passengers or crew. Maritime law dictates that only the captain is allowed to sign that the daily entries in the log are correct, a necessary part of the job. If a ship was in trouble and had to be abandoned, the log would be the only record of the ship's operation, prevailing conditions, weather information, and the geographical locations that could be reviewed. The captain normally attends various social functions during the course of a cruise, hosts a table in the dining room, and is often seen during the day on walkabout inspection tours of the ship.

STAFF CAPTAIN

The staff captain is second in command and can take over at any time if needed. As the title suggests, the staff captain is concerned not only with what happens on the bridge, but is also involved in the day-to-day running of the ship, its staff and crew, and all the discipline.

In some companies the staff captain takes over when the captain is on leave;

in others there is a "floating" captain who takes all the relief commands. The staff captain also wears four gold bars.

The captain and staff captain work closely together, dividing the duties according to company policy and/or personal interest. At all times, one of these two officers must be on call when the ship is at sea, and most cruise lines insist that one or the other remains on board in any port of call.

The captain earns a top salary, and the staff captain is on almost the same scale. As a matter of interest, despite having as much expertise and responsibility for a passenger load often three times as great as a jumbo jet captain, a ship's captain earns roughly half the salary of that of the pilot.

The airline captain has the added advantage of being able to switch on an automatic pilot to handle almost every navigational task once aloft, and is guided down on to a runway with the assistance of computers and radar. His seagoing counterpart must be able to navigate manually and to negotiate hidden reefs, sandbars, sunken vessels, and marker buoys—including hazards not recorded on any chart.

The seagoing captain also has the very difficult responsibility of docking, maneuvering, and anchoring his ship, often in unfamiliar territory and sometimes in difficult weather conditions.

BRIDGE OFFICERS

Besides the captain and staff captain, other bridge officers include the chief officer, first officer, second officer, and several junior officers. Their job is to ensure the navigation and safe conduct

of the vessel at all times. The bridge is manned 24 hours a day, even in port.

Also on the bridge are the fire-detection systems and controls for the fire and watertight doors, which can be activated by "compartments" if there is a problem on the ship.

CHIEF ENGINEER

A ship's chief engineer (almost always referred to as "Chief") has the ultimate responsibility for the mechanical well-being of a cruise ship. This will include overseeing not only the main and auxiliary engines, but also the air-conditioning, generators, electrical systems, heating, plumbing, ventilation, refrigeration, and the water desalinization systems.

He is trained to handle a multiplicity of on-board systems, and is, in fact, the only person on board who can talk to the captain as an equal. With regard to engineering, he is a mechanical master. He wears four gold bars.

CHIEF RADIO OFFICER

The function of the chief radio officer is to keep the ship in constant touch with the outside world. The radio station is where all the radio, telegraph, telex, and the satellite communication equipment is found. The radio officer is also in charge of the automated telephone exchange.

Today, however, the job has become much simpler with the new automated satellite uplink/downlink systems, and is more concerned with maintenance of this high-tech equipment.

PRINCIPAL MEDICAL OFFICER

On the large cruise ships, the medical department can be very busy, with up to 2,700 passengers and 1,000 crew to attend to. Hopefully, you will meet the doctor socially, not professionally.

On many cruise ships, the hospital is a miniature version of a hospital on land, and may be fitted out with an operating theater, examination rooms, several beds, an X-ray room, and an isolation unit. There is at least one fully qualified doctor on board every cruise ship that is carrying 50 or more passengers, plus a small nursing staff. There may also be a physiotherapist, medical orderlies who may be petty officers, and maybe even a dentist.

HOTEL MANAGER

As head of a "floating hotel" involving almost two-thirds of the entire crew, the hotel manager is responsible for the passenger service, comfort, housekeeping, food, drink, and information services, plus the entertainment—just as in any first-class hotel ashore.

There will also be several junior hotel officers and other staff to whom responsibility for the day-to-day running of the various departments can be delegated.

A hotel manager's two most important associates and aides are the purser and the cruise director. At one time, the purser (called the chief purser on some ships) was responsible for the control of all passenger services. But due to the increasing emphasis that has been placed on food, recreation, com-

fort, and entertainment, the new position of hotel manager has been developed for the cruise ships.

On some ships, hotel managers are simply former chief pursers with a new title and added responsibilities.

If at any time during your cruise you have any unresolved problems or a request that has not been satisfactorily dealt with, contact the hotel manager or deputy hotel manager through the purser's office.

CHIEF PURSER

The chief purser's office is the financial, business, accommodations and information hub of any ship, and will be located in a convenient location in the main lobby area.

The purser's department is responsible for all matters relating to money (including currency exchanges), mail, telexes, telegrams, and telefaxes; it also accepts valuables for safekeeping; and provides a complete information service, sometimes around the clock. The purser is also responsible for all passenger and crew accounts, purchasing and requisitioning of supplies, the shipboard concessions, the on-board printing of items such as the *Daily Program* and menus, and the manning of the telephone switchboard, if the ship does not have an automatic system. The purser's domain also includes relations with customs and immigration officials in all ports of call.

The purser has two main assistants: the hotel purser and the crew purser. The hotel purser is in charge of all passenger business, including accommodations (often under the direction of a

berthing officer), while the crew purser handles all matters relating to the ship's personnel and contracts.

If the cruise ship is based in foreign waters, the crew purser also oversees the crew changeovers and requests, and arranges the flights, baggage, and any other incidental crew matters. Many larger ships have two complete crews, one of which will be on leave while the other works the ship. Often, this works on a continuous rotation basis.

DEPUTY HOTEL MANAGER

The deputy hotel manager can take over from the hotel manager at any time, while his special domain is the food and beverage operation. On some ships, this is run by a concessionaire, who supplies not only the food, but also the dining room and bar staff, in which case the deputy hotel manager's role is that of an aide to both the hotel manager and the chief purser.

CONCIERGE

On some luxury cruise ships, such as those of Crystal Cruises and Cunard Royal Viking, the concierge acts as an invisible liaison officer between the ship and the passenger. The concierge's primary concern is for the well-being and satisfaction of the passengers, and the duties may include setting up private parties, obtaining opera or theater tickets for visits ashore, arranging any special transportation in ports of call, or simply being able to arrange to obtain any items that the passengers cannot find for themselves.

CRUISE DIRECTOR

Without any doubt, the most visible figure on board a ship is the cruise director, who has the ultimate responsibility of planning and operating the passenger entertainment, activities and sports programs, as well as acting as the master of ceremonies for all the shipboard functions and events. The cruise director oversees every area of leisure and recreation on the ship. The position is therefore highly demanding.

Before every ship cruise, the cruise director sketches in all projected activities, entertainment, and movies on a huge chart, showing the program in time slots throughout each day.

He has a number of helpers under his command; these will include the cruise staff and social hosts, the "headliner" and lesser entertainers, the bands and musicians, the lecturers, the recreation, sports and health instructors, and others.

On some larger ships, there may be one or more assistant cruise directors or an entertainment manager, a stage manager, and a social director. Cruise lines label their staff positions in different ways.

A cruise director must plan entertainment, movies and special theme nights with dexterity, taking care not to offend anyone in the process.

On the first day of the cruise, the cruise director will usually invite all the passengers to the main lounge and explain the entertainment program to them, at the same time urging the passengers to take advantage of the many events planned for the cruise. He may also introduce his staff and give a brief ship orientation soon after sailing.

169

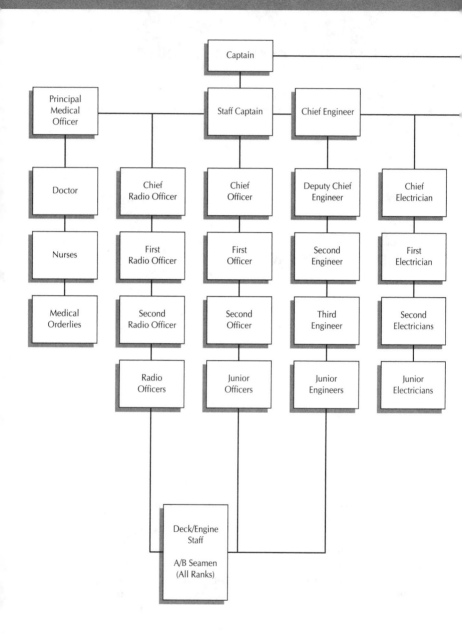

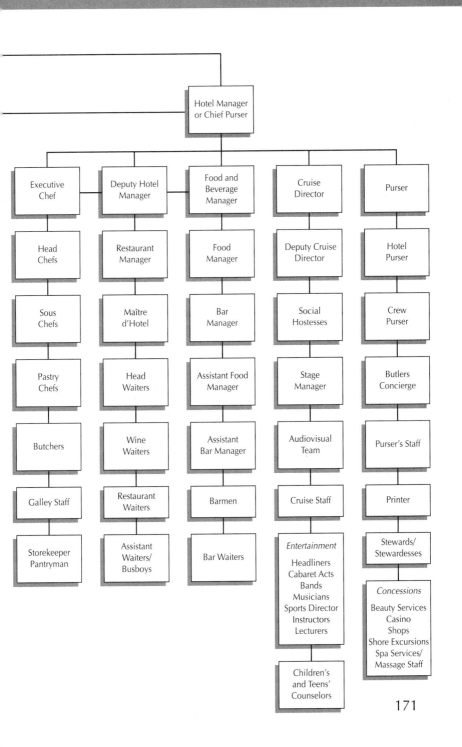

Hotel Manager
or Chief Purser

Executive Chef	Deputy Hotel Manager	Food and Beverage Manager	Cruise Director	Purser
Head Chefs	Restaurant Manager	Food Manager	Deputy Cruise Director	Hotel Purser
Sous Chefs	Maître d'Hotel	Bar Manager	Social Hostesses	Crew Purser
Pastry Chefs	Head Waiters	Assistant Food Manager	Stage Manager	Butlers Concierge
Butchers	Wine Waiters	Assistant Bar Manager	Audiovisual Team	Purser's Staff
Galley Staff	Restaurant Waiters	Barmen	Cruise Staff	Printer
Storekeeper Pantryman	Assistant Waiters/ Busboys	Bar Waiters	*Entertainment* Headliners Cabaret Acts Bands Musicians Sports Director Instructors Lecturers	Stewards/ Stewardesses
			Children's and Teens' Counselors	*Concessions* Beauty Services Casino Shops Shore Excursions Spa Services/ Massage Staff

171

At the start of each cruise, the cruise director usually gives a port lecture, often with audio-visual aids. In this, he will advise the passengers what to do ashore, describe the excursions available, and even offer advice on where to shop. But beware of the cruise director who oversells certain shopping stores, as he could well be on a healthy commission from those stores!

The cruise director may well be an officer, or a "nonsailor" with a showbiz background. A requirement for the job is certainly an ability to deal with difficult entertainers, crew, and passengers!

The cruise director has an office, together with members of his cruise staff, through which he can be reached for anything relating to the entertainment, activities, and sports programs on board. In Part Three of this book, you'll find an evaluation of the cruise director and his staff for each of the ships rated.

Note that on some ships, especially those operated by German companies, the cruise director is more of a cruise manager, and also deals with matters such as immigration, port clearances, and travel arrangements for passengers.

This is how a cruise director also functions on those Russian/Ukrainian-registered ships that are chartered to German tour operators.

SOCIAL HOSTESS

This position was created more for use on the larger cruise ships, where the cruise director needs a female counterpart to act as charming hostess at the various social functions and cocktail parties. The social hostess is not, however, the equivalent of being cruise director, and is not an officer, nor is she required to fulfill lifeboat command roles. She is, however, an important part of the social fabric on larger ships, and, on some, would be required to speak several languages.

She acts as hostess at the Captain's Welcome Aboard party, introducing passengers to the captain; writes invitations to the captain's table and officers' private parties; and would also be required to act as intermediary, in the event of death or serious injury of any passenger, between the ship, passengers and the family members on shore.

Shore Excursions and Shopping

SHORE EXCURSIONS

For some people the idea of a cruise might simply be to get away from it all. Indeed, no matter how many ports the ship visits, some never go ashore, preferring instead to revel in the complete ship-board aspect of cruising. For these people, the ship is the ultimate destination, and they could just as well be on a cruise to nowhere.

For the vast majority, however, the ports offered on a cruise itinerary are important considerations in choosing a cruise, the ship providing the transportation—a means to link the destinations together. The shore excursions, both a challenge and a bane to cruise lines, are proving to be one of the most vital and attractive aspects of the total cruise experience. They are organized so that they are varied enough to suit everyone, from the young and active to the elderly and infirm.

Today you need not feel the least bit uncomfortable or unsure in strange or unusual surroundings, or intimidated by languages other than your own. If you don't want to miss the major sightseeing attractions in each port, you'll find the organized shore excursions the perfect answer. Also, if you do not wish to be on your own, they provide an opportunity to get to know fellow passengers, perhaps with similar interests. Note: when you buy a shore excursion from the cruise line, you are fully covered by insurance; do your own excursion and you will not be covered.

The cruise lines generally plan and oversee shore excursions assuming that you have not seen a place. They aim to show you the most beautiful, striking, and fascinating aspects of a destination in a comfortable manner and at a reasonable price. The shore excursions are operated either by land, sea, or air, or sometimes a combination of all three. They are of varying duration: a half-day of sightseeing; full-day sightseeing, including lunch; evening outings, such as nightclub tours, including admission charges and one or more drinks; and overland excursions, often lasting several days and involving overnight stays in hotels.

On land, buses, rather than taxis or private cars, are so often the principal choice of transportation. This will cut costs and allow the tour operator to narrow the selection of guides to only those most competent, knowledgeable, and fluent in English (or in other languages), while providing some degree of security and control. In the case of air travel (often in small aircraft or by helicopter), the operating companies and all equipment must be thoroughly inspected, as must their safety record.

If shore excursions include travel overland and meals, the quality of any food to be served is taken into account, as are the food preparation areas and hygiene standards of personnel.

Shore excursions are categorized under the heading of "additional on-board expenses" for passengers, and are seen as sources of on-board revenue by

the cruise lines. However, most of the money generated by the sale of shore excursions never reaches the coffers of the cruise lines, but instead goes to third parties—the tour operators in the ports of call. Only a handful of cruise products include shore excursions in the cruise fare, generally those lines that specialize in the "adventure" or "expedition" cruises to unusual and exotic destinations.

Interestingly, passengers often consider shore excursion prices as being high, but they are not aware of the tremendous behind-the-scenes organization required, and the costs involved locally. A considerable amount of time and money is spent by cruise lines setting up suitable shore excursion programs. And the last link in the chain of operation of a successful shore excursion program is the ship's shore excursion office.

SHORE EXCURSION DIRECTOR

In the head office of a cruise line is the shore excursion department, run by the director of shore excursions, who has the responsibility for setting up a successful program, sometimes worldwide. There may also be several staff members involved in the department. Without doubt the best shore excursions are provided by Hapag-Lloyd Cruises, Crystal Cruises, and Cunard.

Directors who work for lines operating worldwide have the greatest challenge, since each cruise undertaken may have a completely different itinerary. Those employed by lines that offer seasonal itineraries, such as those

to Alaska, the Mexican Riviera, the Caribbean, or the Mediterranean, have fewer problems because the itinerary remains unchanged during a complete cruising season.

Perhaps the most challenging of all jobs is that of setting up a comprehensive shore excursion program for a cruise round the world or for a long exotic voyage, where organizing shore excursions so often involves complex overland and flight arrangements and meetings with a number of government tourism officials.

One area that needs attention by the cruise lines is the description of shore excursions. Often, the language used can lead to disappointment and confusion. Ideally, all the cruise lines should adopt the following definitions in their descriptive literature and for their lectures and presentations:

- The term "visit" should be taken to mean actually entering the place or building concerned.
- The term "see" should be taken to mean viewing from the outside (as from a bus, for example).

SHORE EXCURSION OPERATOR

The shore excursion operator is the next link in the chain. Few lines run their own excursions, but instead contract a shore excursion operator for each port of call. They are responsible for providing the best means of transportation, local guides, food, entrance tickets to public buildings, gardens and nightclubs, and other attractions of the excursion.

Cruise lines and ground operators work together in planning or suggesting excursion itineraries, the operator offering the cruise line a "buying price per head" for the excursion or tour package. The margin between the buying price and the selling price to the cruise passenger can be as little as 50 cents or as much as 50 per cent. The average mark-up is about 20-25 per cent, an amount that is far lower than most cruisegoers imagine.

SHORE EXCURSION MANAGER

The cruise ship's representative supervising the entire operation of the shore excursion program is the shore excursion manager. As the eyes and ears of the cruise line, the shore excursion manager is free to recommend to head office that any excursion be suspended if it is not to his satisfaction—which gives him a good deal of authority with the local ground operators. Needless to say, some shore excursion managers can be bribed, to the detriment of passengers, in that some excursions will be downright poor.

The shore excursion manager and staff will be ready on the dockside dispatching the excursions in each port. Any last minute problems or questions you have should be raised then.

SHORE EXCURSION OFFICE

The shore excursion office is normally located in a central position on board, often close to the purser's office, in the main lobby area. This is where you should go for information about the ports of call or to purchase your shore excursion tickets, and where you will find the shore excursion manager and the other members of the department. Please note that the staff cannot normally act as guides or interpreters.

At the shore excursion office you will find details of the excursions and descriptive literature about the ports of call, with information on the history, language, population, currency, main sightseeing attractions, principal shopping areas, beaches and hotels, sports and watersports facilities, transportation, and the principal eating establishments. For more specific information, contact the shore excursion manager or visit the ship's library. On many of the ships, special full-color port booklets or cruise guides may be readily available. Shore excursion office opening times will be listed at the office, and in the *Daily Program*.

BOOKING EXCURSIONS

Early booking of excursions is highly recommended, especially if they are listed as "limited participation." This means that numbers will be restricted, and seats will be sold on a first come, first served basis. On some of the ships, excursions can be booked prior to the sailing date, but sellouts may occur. So, be sure to visit the shore excursion office as soon as you can after boarding and make your reservations early.

Payment for the excursion is normally made via a ship's central billing system, by cash, or traveler's check, or credit card. Note that on most ships, personal checks aren't accepted.

175

The shore excursion office usually attracts long lines shortly after the port lecture is given by the cruise director or the shore excursion manager. You can avoid a wait by reading through the descriptive literature and making your reservations before that talk.

On some cruise ships, prebooking forms for shore excursions will either be forwarded along with your cruise tickets and documents, or you may find them in your cabin on arrival. Prebooking means that you can reserve (and in some cases pay for) excursions before you board or before the shore excursion office is open for business.

As for any cancellations, most ships require a minimum of 24 hours' notice before the advertised shore excursion departure time. Refunds are at the discretion of the cruise line. Should you be unable to go on an excursion or if you change your mind, you will be able, in most cases, to sell your ticket to another passenger. Tickets do not normally have names or cabin numbers on them, except for those which involve air flights or overland arrangements. However, before attempting to resell any tickets, it is wise to check with the shore excursion manager.

CHOOSING THE RIGHT SHORE EXCURSION

As mentioned earlier, at the start of the cruise, the cruise director or the shore excursion manager will give passengers an informal audio-visual lecture on the ports of call on your cruise, together with a brief description of the shore excursions offered. Whether you are a novice or an experienced cruiser, make

an effort to attend this talk. Remember to take a pencil and paper with you to jot down any important points and list the excursions that interest you most.

Look carefully at the shore excursion literature and circle those places that most appeal to you. Then go to the shore excursion office and ask the staff any other questions you may want an answer to before you book.

Here are a few guidelines:

- Shore excursions are put together for general interest. If you want to see something that is not described in the excursion literature, don't take the excursion. Go on your own or with friends.

- In the Caribbean, many of the sightseeing tours cover the same ground. Choose one and then do something different in the next port. (The same is true of the history/archeology excursions operated in the Greek Isles.) It pays to avoid repeating a visit you've made already.

- If you are a history buff, remember that most excursions give very little in-depth history, and the guides are often not acquainted with details beyond a superficial general knowledge. So, pick up a pocket guidebook to the area or check what's on offer in the ship's library.

- City excursions are basically superficial. To get to know a city intimately, it is better to go it alone or with a small group of friends. Travel by taxi or bus directly to the places that are of most interest to you.

- If you enjoy diving or snorkeling, most of the Caribbean cruise ships operate dive-in excursions at a very

reasonable price that includes flippers, mask, and snorkel. Instruction for novices is offered on board, and underwater cameras can often be rented, too.

HELPFUL HINTS

Shore excursions are timed to be most convenient for the greatest number of participants, taking into account the timing of meals on board. Where ships operate two dining room sittings, passengers on the second breakfast sitting may find themselves having to rush their meal in order to participate in a morning excursion. Likewise, those on the afternoon excursions may have to hurry back to get to the first sitting at dinner on time.

Departure times are listed in the descriptive literature and in the *Daily Program*, and will be announced over the ship's public address system. Don't be late, or you may be too late. Note that there are absolutely no refunds if you miss the excursion.

If you are hearing-impaired, make arrangements with the shore excursion manager to assist you in departing for your excursions at the correct times.

Only take along what is necessary; leave any valuables in a safe place on the ship, together with any money and credit cards you do not plan to use. People in sightseeing groups are often targets for pickpockets in major cities such as Barcelona, Caracas, and Rio de Janeiro. Also, beware of the excursion guide who gives you a colored disk to wear for "identification"—he may be marking you as a "rich" tourist for local shopkeepers. You will find it easier—

and also cheaper—to remember your guide's name and the bus number.

Lost or misplaced excursion tickets should be reported immediately to the shore excursion manager. On most of the ships, excursion tickets, once sold, become the sole responsibility of the purchaser, and the cruise line is not generally able to issue replacements. If you place them on the dresser/vanity unit in the cabin, make sure they don't fall down the back, from where there may be no possibility of retrieval. Since tour tickets are not cheap, make sure you place them in a clearly marked envelope right away, and put them in your wallet or purse.

When in foreign ports, convert a little money into the local currency for minor expenses during any tour, or take a supply of U.S. one-dollar bills—useful if you wish to buy a soft drink, for example, or wish to take a taxi to the ship, if you prefer to go shopping rather than go back on the bus.

GOING INDEPENDENTLY

If you do not like to tour with groups of people, you can, of course, go ashore on your own, and in most places this is perfectly safe. In most areas of the world there are no restrictions on independent travel ashore, with the exception of the former countries of the Soviet Union, China, and areas of military importance, together with those countries that stipulate restrictions on individual visas, as in Myanmar (formerly known as Burma). Remember, however, that if you are not on one of the organized excursions, you are *not* covered by the ship's insurance.

Going ashore independently in the major ports of Alaska, the Bahamas, Bermuda, the Caribbean, the Mexican Riviera, the Mediterranean, Canary Islands, the Aegean, and the islands of the South Pacific is ideal for seeing what you want. But in many South American ports, it is wise to go with a friend, especially if you are unfamiliar with the language.

Indeed, in countries where the language is unknown to you, you should always carry some identification (but not your passport), the name of your ship and the area in which it is docked. If the ship is anchored and you take a launch tender ashore, make a note of exactly where the landing place is by observing nearby landmarks, as well as writing down the location. This will be invaluable if you get lost and need to take a taxi back to the launch.

On most ships you'll be given an identification tag or boarding pass at the purser's office or the gangway. This must be handed over every time you return to the ship. Remember that ships have schedules (and sometimes tides) to meet, and that they will not wait for any individual passengers who return late. If the ship is in a launch port in a tropical area and the weather changes for the worse, the ship's captain could well make a decision to depart early to avoid being hemmed in by an approaching storm—it has happened, especially in the Caribbean. If it does, locate the ship's agent in the port, who'll try to get you back on board (and the experience will provide dinner conversation for months).

If you are planning on going to a quiet, secluded beach to swim, first check with the cruise director or shore excursion manager, as certain beaches may be off-limits because of a dangerous undertow, drug pushers, or persistent hawkers. And, if you're thinking of going diving in the sea alone—don't! Not anywhere, not even if you know the area well. Always go diving with at least one companion.

Obviously, going ashore independently does not have to mean going alone. You'll more than likely meet up with others on board ship who prefer to go in their own group rather than with the organized excursion and you can travel with them.

Then again, you don't have to go off the ship in the ports of call at all. You are perfectly free to stay or go from the ship as you please. Sometimes, after several days at sea, you will simply feel like just staying aboard to enjoy the peace and calm while everyone else has left to rush around the port of call.

LOCAL TRANSPORT

In most ports, the same type of transportation is available for sightseeing. You can go by taxi, public bus, rental car, moped, motorcycle, or bicycle.

SIGHTSEEING BY TAXI

If you decide to hire a taxi for sightseeing, be prepared to negotiate the price in advance, and don't pay until you get back to the ship or to your final destination. If you are going with friends, hiring a taxi for a full- or half-day sightseeing trip can often work out far cheaper than renting a car, and you also avoid the hazards of driving. Of

course, prices vary according to where in the world you are, but if you can find a driver who speaks English, or whatever your own national language is, and the taxi is comfortable, even air-conditioned, you're ahead.

Be wary of taxi drivers who wear a badge that claims, "I speak English," for it may be all the English they speak! To be sure, ask the driver a few questions, and make sure that the price you negotiate is clear to both of you. Better still, if your driver speaks only a little English, write down the agreed fare and show it to him. Be sure you know what currency the price represents.

TRAVELING BY BUS

Getting around by public bus can be an inexpensive method of sightseeing and of becoming immersed in the local life. In most countries, public transportation is very safe, but there are, of course, those places where it pays to keep an eye on your wallet or purse.

You will need a small amount of the local currency in order to travel on the bus system. You can usually get what you need on board your ship or from a local bank once at the port.

RENTAL CAR

If you are planning on renting a car for any specific ports of call, try to do so ahead of your cruise; book through your travel agent. This will not only save you much precious time on your arrival in port, but it will go a long way to ensuring that there will be a rental car available when you arrive.

Before departing for your cruise, check to see if your driver's license is valid for the destinations you will visit, as some countries may require you to obtain a local or visitor's license (for a fee) before allowing you to rent a car. Remember also to take along a major credit card, which you will need to make a deposit.

MOPED, MOTORCYCLE, AND BICYCLE

Mopeds and motorcycles are available for hire in many ports. In places such as Bermuda, remember that roadside walls are made of coral and limestone, and can give you nasty abrasions if you scrape them.

Bicycles are a favorite way of getting around in many ports of the world, especially in the Orient. They are inexpensive to rent and you will get some exercise as you pedal. One or two ships (and almost all canal barges) have bicycles on board for passenger use.

THE SHOPPING SCENE

For many cruise ship passengers, "retail therapy," or shopping, is a close second to eating. Indeed, one of the many joys of cruising is going ashore and shopping at leisure. Whether it's for local craftwork, handmade trinkets, articles of clothing, silk and cotton material, jewelry, or liquor, there is something special in store at each destination.

In some places, you will find shopping is a bargain compared with home, depending on the exchange rate, and your local duty and taxation structure.

The best ports for shopping are often those that are "duty free"—meaning that no customs duty is charged on the goods bought.

The best duty-free shopping in the world is in Hong Kong and Singapore, but the Caribbean, situated as it is on the "doorstep" of the United States, is also known for its good-value shopping, with St. Thomas, in the U.S. Virgin Islands, the best known spot. Indeed, there are many people who book a Caribbean cruise only if the itinerary includes St. Thomas.

Cruise lines are happy to go along with this. St. Thomas still offers prices that compare favorably with those on the mainland—particularly the liquor at duty-free prices. But don't forget that you'll have to carry that liquor home (the airlines will not accept it as part of your baggage).

GENERAL HINTS FOR SHOPPING

A good general rule for shopping is: know in advance just what you are looking for, especially if your time is limited. But if time is no problem, browsing can be fun.

When shopping time is included in shore excursions, be careful of those stores repeatedly recommended by the tour guides: the guides are likely to be receiving commissions from the merchants. Do shop around and compare prices before you buy. Excellent shopping hints and recommendations are often given in the cruise director's port lecture at the start of your cruise.

You should know that there are a number of cruise lines operating in the Bahamas, the Caribbean, and the Mexican Riviera who openly engage a company that provides the services of a "shopping lecturer" aboard all or some of their cruise ships. The shopping lecturer does nothing more than promote selected shops, goods, and services heavily, fully authorized by the cruise line (which gets a commission from the establishments they recommend). This relieves the cruise director of any responsibilities, together with any question about his involvement, credibility, and financial remuneration.

You will find in your cabin shopping maps that highlight "selected" stores. Often, they come with a "guarantee" such as that offered by Princess Cruises: "Shop with confidence at each of the recommended stores. Each merchant listed on this map has been carefully selected on the basis of quality, fair dealing and value."

When shopping for local handicrafts, make sure they have definitely been made in the country you are in. It may be that the so-called local product has in fact been made in Taiwan, Hong Kong, or some other country in the Far East. It pays to check.

If you have any specific questions about shopping, put them to the cruise director, shore excursion manager, or one of the cruise staff. Some shopping information may be available in the information literature about the port, and this should be available at the ship's shore excursion office.

Keep in mind that the ship's shops are also duty free, and, in most cases, competitive in price. The shops on board are closed while in port, however, in accordance with international customs regulations.

PART TWO

Coastal Cruises

EUROPE

There is year-round coastal cruising along the shores of Norway to the Land of the Midnight Sun aboard the ships of the Hurtig-Ruten (Norwegian Coastal Express Line). The fleet of 11 ships is comprised of six brand new 450-passenger vessels that are mini-cruise ships, together with a range of older vessels that are small, yet comfortable, working express, real coastal packet steamers. Their principal job is the delivery of mail, small packaged goods and foodstuffs, as well as passengers, to the communities which are spread along the shoreline, between the towns of Bergen and Kirkenes, on the sea route that is frequently called "Highway 1."

This is a 2,500-mile journey (from Bergen in Norway to Kirkenes close to the Russian border), half of which is north of the Arctic Circle, and takes 11 days, but you can join it at any of the 35 ports of call and stay as long as you wish. Most seasoned travelers like to cruise for all of the 11 days. In 1994, the company transported a total of some 286,000 passengers.

The service started over 100 years ago, in 1893, and the three companies that combine to run it have 11 ships. Each ship is of a different size, and, with between 69 and 230 cabins, they can carry a maximum of between 144 and 488 passengers. Three new ships, each designed to carry 488 passengers, as well as 50 cars, were ordered in

1992. The first two, each of which has 230 cabins (with 209 outside and 21 inside) made their debut in 1993, the third in 1994.

Archipelago hopping can be done on Sweden's east coast, too, by sailing in the daytime and staying overnight in one of the many small hotels on the way. One vessel sails from Norrtalje, north of Stockholm, to Oskarshamn, near the Baltic island of Öland, right through the spectacular Swedish archipelago. And you can now cruise from the Finnish city of Lappeenranta to the Estonian city of Viborg without even a visa, thanks to perestroika.

Indeed, the point-to-point coastal transportation between neighboring countries, major cities, and commercial centers is big business in northern Europe. Some of the larger cruise ferries could easily rival major cruise ships in other regions now. They're designed to operate in all weather, their facilities are virtually the same, but with much smaller cabins and with an emphasis on duty-free shopping.

Some would argue that ships such as the huge *Silja Serenade* and *Silja Symphony*, which *are* actually designed for cruising but are used mainly as ferries, are constructed around their duty-free shopping centers. Be that as it may, these super-ferries are nothing short of fantastic as modes of transport and relaxation. And it would take a separate book to list them all, along with their owning companies, as they tend to change hands rather often.

SCOTLAND

The fishing town of Oban, some two hours west of Glasgow by road, perhaps seems an unlikely point to start a cruise, but it is the base to one of the world's very finest vacation ships. The former MacBrayne ferry the *Hebridean Princess* is an absolute gem, with Laura Ashley-style interiors; it carries passengers around some of Scotland's most magnificent coastline and islands. Do remember to take plenty of warm clothing, however, as the weather can be somewhat unkind.

UNITED STATES

In the United States, coastal vessels, flying the red, white, and blue flag, offer a change of style and pace from the big oceangoing liners. On these cruises, informality is the order of the day. Accommodating up to 160 passengers, the ships tend to be more like a private party or club—there's no pretentiousness. And unlike major cruise ships, these small vessels are rarely out of sight of land. The owners seek out lesser-known cruise areas, offering in-depth visits to destinations inaccessible to larger ships, both along the east coast, and in Alaska.

During the last few years, there has been little growth in this segment of the cruise market. If you are the sort of person who prefers a small country inn to a larger resort, this type of cruise just might appeal to you. The ships, each of which measures under 100 grt and each of which is classed as a "D"-class vessel, are not subject to the bureaucratic regulations nor the union rules that sounded the death knell for large U.S.-registered ships, and which are restricted to cruising to no more than 20 miles off shore.

The 138-passenger Yorktown Clipper *(Clipper Cruise Lines) sails the inland waterways in North and Central America.* **Rating ★★★**

You cruise in comfort at up to 12 knots. All the public room facilities are limited, and because the vessels are of American registry, there's no casino on board. As far as entertainment goes, passengers are usually left to their own devices, although there may sometimes be a piano. Most of these vessels are in port during the evening, so you can go ashore for the local nightlife. Getting ashore is extremely easy; the passengers can be off in a matter of minutes, with no waiting at the gangway.

Accommodations, though they are not elaborate, have all-outside cabins, each with its own large picture window and private bathroom. The cabins are small but quite cozy. Closet space is very limited, so take only what you absolutely need. The only drawback to all-outside cabins is that some do open directly on to the deck—not convenient when it rains. And the fact that cabins are closer to the engines means that noise is considerable throughout these vessels. The quietest cabins are at the bow, and most cruising is done during the day so that passengers will be able to sleep better at night. Tall passengers should note that the overall length of beds on most of these vessels does not exceed 6 feet maximum.

The principal evening event on these cruises is dinner in the dining room, which accommodates all passengers at once. This can be a family-style affair, with passengers at long tables, and the food passed around. The cuisine is decidedly American, with fresh local specialties.

These vessels usually have three or four decks, and no elevators. Stairs can be on the steep side, and are not recommended for people with walking difficulties. This kind of cruise is good for those who do enjoy a family-type cruise experience in pleasant surroundings. The maxim "You just relax, we'll move the scenery" is very appropriate in this case.

Only three of the coastal and inland cruise vessels are featured in Part Three of this book, since they are small and specialized and have limited facilities. You should be aware that on these cruises you may have a linen change only once or twice a week, and you may not get a "turn-down" service. The typical cabin sizes range from 73 sq. ft. (6.7m²) to 232 sq. ft. (21.5m²).

River and Barge Cruises

Whether you want to cruise down the River Nile, along the mighty Amazon or along the lesser Orinoco, the stately Volga, the primal Sepik, the magnificent Rhine, the "blue" Danube, the mystical Irrawaddy (which has been renamed the Ayeyarwady) or along the "yellow" Yangtze—to say nothing of the Don and the Dnieper, the Elbe, or Australia's Murray—there's a cruise and vessel ready for you.

What sort of person enjoys cruising on river vessels? Well, cruise ship passengers who survive very well without dressing up, bingo, casinos, discos, and entertainment, and those who like a totally unstructured lifestyle.

RIVER CRUISING: EUROPE

Cruising down one of Europe's great waterways is an experience in itself—quite different from sailing on an open sea, where motion has to be taken into consideration (rivers are always calm). These cruises provide you with a constant change of scenery, often passing through several countries, each with their own history and architecture, in a week-long journey. The river vessels are always close to land and offer you the chance to visit cities and areas that are inaccessible to large ships. Indeed, watching stunning scenery slip past your floating hotel is one of the most relaxing and refreshing ways to absorb the beauty that has inspired poets and artists through the centuries. A cruise on the Danube, for example, will take you through four countries, and from the Black Forest to the Black Sea.

In 1840-41, the Marquess of Londonderry, a member of the British aristocracy, traveled across Europe along the Rhine and Danube rivers. He then wrote about these experiences, which were published in 1842 in a charming book entitled *A Steam Voyage to Constantinople*. And who could forget the romance implied in Johann Strauss's famous waltz "The Blue Danube." The new Rhine-Main-Danube waterway is now open, and at 2,175 miles it is the longest waterway in Europe. It connects 14 countries from Rotterdam on the North Sea to Sulina and Izmail on the Black Sea, and offers river travelers some of the most fascinating sights anywhere in the world.

River vessels are long and low in the water, and their masts must fold down in order to negotiate the low bridges found along most of Europe's rivers. Although they are small when compared to oceangoing cruise ships, these vessels do have a unique and friendly international atmosphere. The most modern of them do offer the discreet luxury of a small floating hotel, and some of them actually have several public rooms, including a large dining room. They typically have three or four decks. Most are air-conditioned, and the newest will also feature an observation lounge, bar, heated swimming pool (some of them may even have a heated indoor pool), a sauna,

185

solarium, whirlpool, gymnasium, massage, hairdresser, and shop kiosk.

Although the cabins may be small, with limited closet space, they will be mostly outside (facing the river), have a private bathroom, and will be very comfortable for a one-week journey. Cabins are largest on the *Mozart*, at 205 sq. ft., while most other river vessel cabins will be smaller. All of the cabins are generally clean and tidy, as well as functional. Many of the cabins on the most modern vessels feature a personal safe, a mini-bar, a television, and an alarm clock/radio. You will find that the ceilings are quite low, and that the beds are quite short, too. In general, shore excursions must be booked at the same time as you book your cabin, as only unsold space will be available on board the ship.

In Europe, river cruising has now reached a very sophisticated level, and you can be assured of good service and meals of a consistently high European standard. The dining is quite pleasant, although not quite a gourmet experience (excepting those vessels that are catered by Austrian and Swiss companies). Lunch is normally a buffet affair. For dinner, a set menu, consisting of three or four courses, is the norm, except for the most upscale vessels. Without doubt the best cuisine can be found aboard the *Danube Princess*, *Mozart* and *Prussian Princess*, although reasonably decent cuisine is served on many other river vessels.

Typical rates for river cruises are from $800 to more than $3,000 per person for a one-week cruise (prices increase for the most popular periods), including meals, cabin with private facilities, side trips and airport/railway transfers. If you are already in Europe, many cruises can be purchased "cruise-only" for greater flexibility.

TIP: It's best to go for an outside cabin on a deck that doesn't have a promenade deck walkway outside it. Normally, cabins on the lowest deck have a four-berth configuration. It doesn't matter which side of the vessel you're on, as you'll see a river bank and scenery on both sides.

DID YOU KNOW ...?

...that the last four-funnel passenger ship was Cunard's *Aquitania* (1914-1949)?

...that Alaska has two time zones? Most of Alaska is one hour behind Pacific Standard Time, while the Aleutian Islands are two hours behind Pacific Standard Time.

...that the Pacific Ocean has a tide of 22 feet, while the Atlantic Ocean has a tide of only 8 inches?

Informality is the order of the day, and, because rivers are calm by nature, you can't get seasick (you can also see land on both sides almost all the time).

RIVER CRUISING: RUSSIA

Perhaps the best way to get to know Russia is on a river/inland waterways cruise. Often referred to as the "Waterways of the Tsars," the country benefits as a cruise destination from the well-developed network of rivers, lakes and canals. Geographically, the river routes for tourists are divided into these three main areas:

- Those in Central European Russia.
- Those in Northwestern European Russia.
- Those in Asian Russia.

Rechtflot is the Russian government's management overlord. It consists of some 21 shipping companies, with the combined fleet made up of more than 5,000 vessels. The largest is the United Volga River Shipping Company, which alone has more than 2,000 river vessels. It carries more than 50 million passengers and about 100 million tons of cargo each year. The Moscow River Shipping Company is the next largest, operates more than 1,000 vessels and transports as many as 11 million passengers and more than 60 million tons of cargo each year.

In the Central Basin, Moscow is the hub of river tourism, and the newly opened waterways between Moscow and St. Petersburg allow a seven-day cruise link between the present and former capitals.

Best known Russian rivers are the Don, Moskva, Neva and Volga, but the lesser known Belaja, Dvina (and North Dvina) Irtysh, Kama, Ob (longest river in Siberia), Oka, Svir, Tura and Vyatka connect the great system of rivers and lakes in the vast Russian hinterland.

Many Russian vessels are chartered to foreign (non-Russian) cruise wholesalers and tour packagers. The vessels are well equipped, air-conditioned and almost always clean and tidy. I would advise you to choose one that has its food (especially the food) and hotel services catered by the Swiss company Flotel. Try the *Kirov*.

One unusual Russian river vessel worth mentioning, the *Rossiya*, is used for state visits and is extremely elegant and fitted throughout with exceptionally fine materials. Cruises include the services of a cruise manager and specialist lecturers, and some companies also specialize in "home stays" before or after the cruise as part of an attractive cultural package. A Russian entry visa is required for non-Russian visitors, and this can be obtained for you by the cruise/tour company.

RIVER CRUISING: THE NILE

A journey along the Nile—the world's longest (and historically the greatest) river—is a journey that takes you back in time, to over 4,000 years before the birth of Christ—when the Pharaohs believed they were immortal. Even though time has proved them mistaken, the people that lived along the river banks formed one of the greatest civilizations the world has known. And the scenery has changed little in over

2,000 years; the best way to see it is of course by river boat.

There are approximately 140 vessels cruising the Nile, many offering excellent standards of comfort, food and service. Most have a swimming pool, lounge, piano bar and a disco. A specialist lecturer in Ancient Egyptian history accompanies almost all sailings, which cruise the 140 miles between Aswan and Luxor in four or five days. Extended cruises, typically of seven or eight days, cover about 295 miles, and visit Dendera and Abydos. The longest cruises, which take 10-12 days, cover 590 miles, and include visits to Sohag, El Amarna, Tuna El Gabal and Ashmuneim, ending in Cairo. In all, there are over 7,000 departures every year! If you're worried about the recent spate of terrorist attacks on passengers, note that these have only occurred on the Cairo to Aswan cruise section. But the best and most fascinating Nile cruising is between Aswan and Luxor, and this is normally not touched by the terrorist groups.

Most Nile cruises include all sightseeing excursions, which are accompanied by experienced, trained guides who may be resident on board, or who may meet the boat at each place of call. Multi-lingual guides also accompany each cruise.

RIVER CRUISING: CHINA

There are now several new river vessels featuring cruises along the Yangtze, the world's third longest river, particularly through the area known as the Three Yangtze River Gorges, which is a 100-mile stretch between Nanjin Pass in the east and White King City in the west. The Three Gorges are Xiling, Wu and Qutang. Also, the Lesser Three Gorges (or Three Small Gorges) are, for many, a more impressive sight, sometimes as part of the main cruise, but also reached by small river vessels from Wushan. Take a cabin with a balcony—it's worth the extra money, and the view is better. Note that in China, rats and rivers often go together, so be aware that rat poison may well be found under your bed.

Arguably, the best river vessels in China are the new *Elaine*, *Jeannie* and *Sheena* (Regal China Cruises), a trio that cater superbly well to 258 passengers. The vessels have both Chinese- and Western-style restaurants, beauty salon, health club with sauna, and eight private mah-jong and karaoke rooms. Fine Asian hospitality and service prevail, and cabins are always supplied with fresh towels and hot tea. There are several other operators, but do check on the facilities, meet-and-greet service and the newness of the vessels before booking. The best time of the year to go is May–June, and late August–October (July and early August are extremely hot and humid).

If you do want to cruise this area sometime in the future you should be aware that a $20 billion-plus hydroelectric Sanxia (three gorges) dam, the world's largest (first envisioned by Sun Yat-Sen in 1919), is going to be constructed, essentially blocking off this major tourism attraction by creating a 370-mile-long reservoir. Construction is scheduled to start after the winter of 1997/1998, which means that there will be no more river cruises after then if work goes ahead as scheduled.

IRAWADDY RIVER (MYANMAR)

How about the Road to Mandalay? For those visiting the eastern countries, the Eastern and Oriental Express company in November 1995 launched a new luxury river cruise vessel in Myanmar (formerly known as Burma).

The vessel, which has been christened the *Road to Mandalay*, operates between Bangkok and Yangon (Rangoon), on the Ayeyarwady (Irrawaddy) River. The vessel departs weekly to cruise between Mandalay and Pagan. Included is a visit to the Shwedagon Pagoda (this is at its best at night) and a tour of the city of Yangon.

RIVER MURRAY (AUSTRALIA)

The fifth largest river in the world, the Murray was the lifeblood of the pioneers who lived in the driest continent on earth. Today the river flows for more than 1,250 miles across a third of Australia. Paddlewheel boats such as the *Murray Princess* offer all the amenities you will find on America's *Mississippi Queen*. There are even six cabins for the physically disabled.

BARGE CRUISING: EUROPE

Smaller than river vessels, and more accurately called boats, "hotel barges" ply the inland waterways and canals of Europe from April to November, when the weather is generally good. Barge cruises are usually of three, six, or 13 days' duration, and they offer a completely informal atmosphere, for up to a dozen passengers. These barges cruise along slowly in the daytime, and moor early each evening, to give you time to pay a visit to the local village, and to get a restful night's sleep.

Hotel barges are even more intimate than river vessels, and offer a different experience. You go ashore on your own during the day and at night. Shopping opportunities are limited, and evening entertainment is always impromptu. Most of the barges carry between eight and 24 passengers.

Hotel barges tend to be beautifully fitted out with rich wood paneling, full carpeting, custom-built furniture and tastefully chosen fabrics. Each barge has a dining room/lounge-bar and is equipped with the passenger's comfort in mind. Each barge captain takes special pride in his vessel, often acquiring some rare memorabilia to be incorporated into the decor.

Locally grown fresh foods are usually purchased and prepared each day by a caring crew, allowing you to live well and feel like a house guest. Most of the barges can also be chartered for exclusive use—so you can just take your family and friends, for example.

The waterways of France, especially, offer beauty, tranquility and a diversity of interests, and barge cruising is an excellent way of exploring an area not previously visited. Most cruises include a visit to a famous vineyard and wine cellar, as well as side-trips to places of historic, architectural or scenic interests. You will be accompanied by a crew member familiar with the surrounding countryside. You can even go hot-air ballooning over the local countryside, and land to a welcome glass of

189

champagne and your flight certificate. Although ballooning is an expensive extra, the experience of floating within earshot of châteaux, villages and over pastoral landscapes is something you can always treasure.

How you dine on board a barge will depend on which barge and area you choose; dining will range from home-style cooking to outstanding *nouvelle cuisine*, with all the trimmings. And the hotel barges will have English or English-speaking French crews.

Barging on the canals often means going through a constant succession of locks. Nowhere is this more enjoyable and entertaining than in the Burgundy region of France where, between Dijon and Macon, for example, a barge can negotiate as many as 54 locks during a six-day cruise. Interestingly, all lock-keepers in France are women!

Typical rates range from $600 to more than $3,000 per person for a six-day cruise. I don't recommend taking children. Rates include cabin with private facilities, all meals, excellent wine with lunch and dinner, other beverages, use of bicycles, side trips and air-port/railway transfers. Some operators also provide a hotel the night before or after the cruise. Clothing, by the way, is totally casual at all times, but at the beginning and end of the season, the weather can be unreliable, so make sure you take sweaters and rain gear.

STEAMBOATING: U.S.A.

The most famous of all river cruises in the United States are those aboard the steamboats of the mighty Mississippi River. Mark Twain, an outspoken fan of Mississippi cruising, at one time said: "When man can go 700 miles an hour, he'll want to go seven again."

The grand traditions of the steamboat era are maintained by the brand new *American Queen*, and by the older, smaller *Delta Queen* and *Mississippi Queen* (Delta Queen Steamboat Company), all of which are powered by steam engines that drive huge wooden paddlewheels at the stern.

The smaller and older of the three boats, the 180-passenger *Delta Queen*, was built on Scotland's Clydeside in

This is the Mississippi Queen (Delta Queen Steamboat Company), seen steamboating down the Mississippi River in the U.S.A.

1926 and is on the U.S. National Register of Historic Places. She came to the nation's attention when President Carter spent a week aboard in 1979.

Half a century younger, the 400-passenger *Mississippi Queen* was built at a cost of some $27 million in Jefferson, Indiana, the place where nearly 5,000 steamboats were built during the 19th century. (And the *Mississippi Queen* itself was designed by the creator of Cunard's *Queen Elizabeth 2*, James Gardner of London.) Each of the steamboats feature one of the rarest of musical instruments—a real "steam piano," driven by the boat's engine.

A spanking new, 222-cabin, 436-passenger American-built steamboat, which was christened *American Queen* (Delta Queen Steamboat Company, who now also owns American Hawaii Cruises), debuted in June 1995. Built at a cost of $60 million by McDermott Shipyard, Morgan City, Louisiana, the riverboat is fitted out with vintage tandem compound horizontal reciprocating steam engines (circa 1930) that originally drove a steam dredge called the *Kennedy*. The engines are used to drive the 60-ton stern paddle wheel, made up of individual bucket boards (the paddles) that are 30 feet long and

2 feet wide. The *American Queen* is the 30th steamboat built for the Delta Queen Steamboat Company.

Traveling on one of these steamboats makes you feel like you're stepping back into the past and into the world of American folklore. You will be surrounded by a certain charm and old-world graciousness, as well as by delightful woods, brass and flowing staircases. And once every year, the two boats battle each other in the Great Steamboat Race—a 10-day extravaganza in which the *Delta Queen* battles her larger sister, the *Mississippi Queen*.

Steamboat cruises last from two to 12 days, and during the year there are several theme cruises, with big bands and lively entertainment. These boats cruise up and down the Mississippi and Ohio rivers.

As for food on the steamboats, it is generally very much "American" fare. That means you will be eating steak, shrimp, Creole sauces, fried foods, and few fresh vegetables.

Traveling on the river is a great way of taking a vacation and avoiding the crush of congested roads and airports. And of course there are no immigration or customs officials and procedures in the heartland of America.

Expedition Cruises

"The risk one runs in exploring a coast in these unknown and icy seas is so very great that I can be so bold to say no man will ever venture farther than I have done and that the lands to the south will never be explored."

So wrote Captain James Cook in 1774. His voyage was a feat of great courage, for not only did he take the risk of entering an unknown sea, but his ship, the *Resolution*, was far too fragile a vessel (462 tons) to undertake such a trip. Yet there is no landscape quite so breathtaking and compelling as the polar regions of the south, and there is no experience so unforgettable as a visit there. Today's would-be Captain Cooks have the curiosity and drive to move into adventure cruising.

Given that we have so many opportunities to cruise in places such as Alaska and the Baltic, the Caribbean, the Mediterranean, and the Mexican Riviera areas, you may be surprised to discover a small but growing group of enthusiasts heading out for strange and remote waters. But there are countless virtually untouched areas to be visited by the more adventurous. Passengers tend to be more self-reliant and more interested in doing or learning than in being entertained.

On an expedition cruise, passengers play an active part in every aspect of the voyage, which tends to be intensively oriented toward visiting interesting destinations, exploring areas and studying nature. You will find naturalists, historians, and specialist lecturers, rather than entertainers, on board each ship to provide background information and observations about wildlife. Each participant receives his or her personal *log book*—which is illustrated and written by the renowned wildlife artists and writers who accompany each cruise. This log book documents the entire expedition and serves as a great source of information, as well as a complete *mémoire* of the voyage. All the companies that offer these adventure cruises provide expedition parka and waterproof boots.

Imagine walking on pack ice in the Arctic Circle, exploring a teeming penguin rookery on Antarctica or the Falkland Islands, searching for the "lost" peoples in Melanesia, cruising close to the source of the Amazon, gazing at species of flora and fauna in the Galapagos Islands (Darwin's laboratory), or watching an authentic dragon (from a comfortable distance, of course). This is what expedition cruising is all about, and it is not really recommended for the novice cruisegoer.

Because of the briefings, the lectures, and the laboratory at sea, there is a strong cultural and intellectual aspect to these expedition cruises. There is no formal entertainment as such; passengers enjoy this type of cruise more for the camaraderie and educational experience than anything else. The vessels themselves are designed and equipped to sail through ice-laden waters, and yet have a shallow enough draft to glide over coral reefs.

Expedition cruise vessels can, nevertheless, provide comfortable and even elegant surroundings for as many as 200 passengers; they have a highly trained and knowledgeable staff, and they offer first-class food and service. Without traditional cruise ports to stop at, the ship must be self-sufficient, capable of long-range cruising, as well as being environmentally friendly.

Expedition cruising was inspired by people's desire to find out more about this remarkable planet we live on—its incredible animal, bird, and marine life. This type of cruise was pioneered in the late 1960s by Lars-Eric Lindblad, a Swedish-American who was determined to turn the experience of travel into adventure by opening up parts of the world that tourists had never visited.

After chartering several vessels for adventure cruises to Antarctica, Lindblad then organized the design and construction of a ship capable of going almost anywhere in comfort and safety. In 1969, this ship, *Lindblad Explorer*, was launched.

In the years that followed, the ship earned an enviable reputation in the adventure travel area. Lindblad's company sold the ship to Salen-Lindblad Cruising in 1982. They subsequently resold her to Society Expeditions, who renamed her the *Society Explorer*. She is now operated by another adventure travel company, Abercrombie & Kent, as the *Explorer*. See Part Three, where details and ratings are provided.

Today there is only a handful of adventure/expedition cruise companies that are in operation. They provide in-depth expertise and specially constructed vessels, usually with ice-hardened hulls that are capable of venturing into the vast reaches of the Arctic regions and Antarctica.

ADVENTURE CRUISE AREAS

Buddha was once asked to express verbally what life meant to him. For a moment he was still—then, without speaking, he held up a single rose. This is what several "destinations" on this planet are like, in that there are no words that can adequately describe them—they have instead to be experienced, just as a single rose.

The principal adventure cruise areas of the world at the moment are: Alaska and the Aleutians, Amazonia and the Orinoco, Antarctica, Australasia and the Great Barrier Reef, Chilean fjords, the Galapagos Archipelago, Indonesia, Melanesia, the Northwest Passage, and Polynesia and the South Pacific. Other adventure cruise destinations growing in popularity are Baha California and the Sea of Cortez, Greenland, the Red Sea, East Africa, the Réunion Islands and the Seychelles, West Africa and the Ivory Coast, and the South China Seas and China Coast.

In order to put together their special cruise expeditions, the staff at the various companies turn to knowledgeable sources and advisers. Scientific institutions are consulted, experienced world explorers are questioned, and naturalists provide up-to-date reports on wildlife sightings, migrations and other natural phenomena. Although some days are scheduled for relaxation or preparing for the days ahead, participants are kept active both physically and mentally. And speaking of physical

activity, it is unwise to consider such an adventure cruise if you are not completely ambulatory.

ANTARCTICA

Perhaps the most intriguing "destination" on earth is Antarctica, which was first sighted only in 1820 by the American sealer Nathaniel Palmer, a British naval officer Edward Bransfield and a Russian ship's captain Fabian Bellingshausen. For most, it's nothing but a wind-swept frozen wasteland (it has been calculated that the ice mass contains almost 90 per cent of the snow and ice in the world). For others, however, it represents the last pristine place on earth, empty of people, commerce and pollution, yet offering awesome scenery and a truly wonderful abundance of marine and bird life. There are no germs, and not a single tree. Over 6,000 people visited the continent during 1992—the first and only

smoke-free continent on earth—and yet the first human to arrive did so within a generation of man landing on the moon. There is not a single permanent human inhabitant of the continent, whose ice is as much as two miles thick. Its total land mass equals more than all the rivers and lakes on earth and exceeds that of China and India combined. The continent has a raw beauty and ever-changing landscape. Once part of the ancient land mass known as Gondwanaland (which also included Africa, South America, India, Australasia and Madagascar), it is, perhaps, the closest we have to another planet, and has so fragile an ecosystem that it needs international protection.

Although visited by "soft" expedition cruise ships and even "normal"-sized cruise ships with ice-hardened hulls (capable of carrying as many as 800 passengers), you should know that the more remote "far side"—the Oates and Scott Coasts, McMurdo Sound and the famous Ross Ice Shelf—can

The 138-passenger World Discoverer *(Clipper Adventure Cruises) has over 50 Antarctic voyages to her credit.*
Rating ★★★★+

only be visited by "real" ice-breaker expedition ships such as the *Kapitan Dranitsyn*, *Khlebnikov*, and *World Discoverer*, as the winds can easily get up to 100 m.p.h. or more in this part of the continent.

GALAPAGOS

A word of advice about the Galapagos Islands: don't even think about taking a cruise with a "foreign-flag" expedition ship. The Ecuadoreans jealously guard their island, and prohibit the movement of virtually all the non-Ecuadorean-registered cruise vessels within its boundaries. Thus, the best way to get to see this place that Charles Darwin loved is to fly to Quito and then cruise on an Ecuadorean-registered vessel such as the *Isabella II* (no doctor on board) or *Santa Cruz* (it does have a doctor on board).

GREENLAND

The world's largest island, Greenland, in the Arctic Circle, is technically a desert that is 82 per cent covered with ice (actually it is compressed snow), which can be as thick as 11,000 feet. This country's rocks are among the world's oldest (the 3.8 billion-year-old Isukasia formations) and its ecosystem is one of the newest. Forget Alaska, the glacier at Jacobshavn (also known as Ilulissat) is the fastest moving in the world, and creates a new iceberg every five minutes. Greenland is said to have more dogs than people, and these provide the principal means of transport for the Greenlanders.

THE ENVIRONMENT

Since the increase in peoples' environmental awareness, cruise adventurers have banded together to protect the environment from further damage. In future, only the ships that are capable of meeting new "zero discharge" standards, like those introduced in the Arctic by the Canadian Coast Guard, will be allowed to proceed through environmentally sensitive areas.

The expedition companies themselves are deeply concerned about the environment, and they spend a good deal of time and money in educating both crews and passengers about safe environmental procedures.

In the course of the past two years an "Antarctic traveler code" has been created, the rules of which are enforced by all the expedition cruise companies, based on the Antarctic Conservation Act of 1978, and adopted by the U.S. Congress to protect and preserve the ecosystem, the flora, and the fauna of the Antarctic continent. By law, every U.S. citizen who travels to Antarctica must adhere to the Act.

Briefly, the Act makes it unlawful to take native animals or birds, to collect any special native plant or to introduce species, to enter certain special areas (SPAs), or to discharge or dispose of any pollutants, unless authorized by regulation or permit issued under the Act. To "take" a native mammal or a bird means to remove, harass, molest, harm, pursue, hunt, shoot, kill, trap, capture, restrain, or to tag any such wildlife, or to attempt to do as such.

Under the Act, violations are subject to civil penalties, including a fine of up to $10,000 and a term of one

The Explorer *(Society Expeditions) anchors off South Georgia Island, close to a nearby rookery of 75,000 King penguins.* **Rating ★★★**

year's imprisonment for each violation. A copy of the Act is found in the library of each adventure/expedition ship which visits the continent.

Will there ever be large cruise ships cruising to Antarctica? Not in the foreseeable future, as ships are limited to a maximum 400 passengers, so the likelihood of a *Legend of the Seas* or *Sensation* zooming in on the penguins with 2,000-plus passengers is hardly likely.

THE COMPANIES

Abercrombie & Kent
This is a well-known company that operates the older, but still highly suitable *Explorer* (ex-*Society Explorer*).

Hanseatic Tours
This is the company that operates the *Bremen* (ex-*Frontier Spirit*) as well as *Hanseatic*, which are the latest in high-tech luxury expedition cruise vessels. Both vessels are engaged in offering destination-intensive itineraries. The ships have truly luxurious appointments, and are targeted to appeal to both English-speaking and German-speaking passengers.

Quark Expeditions
This company, which was formed by the former president of Salen Lindblad Cruising (which was purchased by NYK of Japan in 1991), called Quark Expeditions, is the U.S. general sales agent for one or more of the Russian-owned nuclear- or diesel-powered icebreakers, which are fitted out with a range of outstanding amenities and decent creature comforts for up to 100 passengers. Among the vessels available for charter are the *Kapitan Dranitsyn* and the *Yamal*. In the U.K. the company is represented by Noble Caledonia Limited of London.

Society Expeditions

This company operates the more luxurious *World Discoverer*—a fine expedition cruise vessel, which features full creature comforts and a range of fascinating itineraries. In addition, the ship is often available for charter.

Special Expeditions

This company operates the *Polaris*, a small expedition vessel, featuring fine appointments and full creature comforts (see profile section for details). In addition, it has two small vessels, the *Sea Bird* and *Sea Lion* (ex-Exploration Cruise Lines vessels), which operate "soft" expedition cruises along some of the specially protected coastal areas in the United States, including Alaska.

THE NORTHWEST PASSAGE

In 1984, the Salen Lindblad Cruising company made maritime history by successfully negotiating a westbound voyage through the Northwest Passage, a 41-day epic which started from St. John's, Newfoundland, in Canada and ended at Yokohama in Japan. The expedition cruise had taken two years of planning, and was sold out just days after it was announced.

The search for a Northwest Passage to the Orient attracted brave explorers for more than four centuries. Despite

numerous attempts and some loss of life, including Henry Hudson in 1610, a "white passage" to the East remained an elusive dream. Amundsen's 47-ton ship the *Gjoa* eventually navigated the route in 1906, taking three years to do so. It was not until 1943 that a Canadian ship, the *St. Roch*, became the first vessel in history to make the passage in a single season. The *Lindblad Explorer* became the 34th vessel, and the first cruise vessel, to complete the journey through the Northwest Passage.

THE NORTHEAST PASSAGE

Quark Expeditions had the good fortune of making maritime history in July/August 1991 when a Russian icebreaker, *Sovetskiy Soyuz*, made a spectacular 21-day voyage to negotiate a passage from Murmansk, Russia, to Nome, Alaska, across the North Pole. The ship followed the trail which had been set in 1909 by Admiral Peary, who crossed the North Pole accompanied by 56 Eskimos, setting out on his journey by sled from Ellesmere Island. Although the polar ice cap had been navigated before by U.S. nuclear submarines *Skate* and *Nautilus*—as well as by dirigible and airplane—this was the first passenger ship to make the hazardous crossing. The planning for this expedition took over two years.

Sail-Cruise Ships

Thinking of a cruise but really want to sail? Been cruising on a conventional Caribbean cruise ship that is more like an endurance test? Whatever happened to the *romance* of sailing? Think no more, for the answer, to quote a movie title, is "back to the future."

If you're active, think about cruising under sail, with towering masts and washing-powder-white sails to power you along. There's simply nothing that beats the thrill of being aboard a multi-masted tall ship, sailing under thousands of square feet of canvas through waters that mariners have sailed across for centuries.

This is what cruising in the old traditional manner is all about, on board authentic sailing ships, on contemporary copies of clipper ships, or on the very latest high-tech cruise-sail ships. Even the most jaded of cruise passengers will love the exhilaration of being under sail.

Tall ships provide either a genuine sail-powered experience like those of the past (*Lili Marleen, Sea Cloud, Sir Francis Drake, Star Clipper, Star Flyer*), or they are contemporary vessels built to emulate sail-powered vessels, but which are actually *sail-assisted* vessels in an ultra-chic form (*Club Med I, Club Med II, Le Ponant, Wind Song, Wind Spirit, Wind Star*).

Whichever you choose, there are no rigid schedules, and life aboard equates to a totally unstructured lifestyle, apart from meal times. Weather conditions may often dictate whether a scheduled port visit will be made or not, but passengers sailing on these vessels are usually unconcerned with being ashore anywhere. They would rather savor the thrill of being one with nature, albeit in a comfortable, civilized setting, but without having to do the hard work themselves.

REAL TALL SHIPS

While we have all been dreaming of adventure, a pocketful of designers and yachtsmen have committed their pen to paper, hand in pocket and rigging to mast, and come up with a pot-pourri of stunning vessels to delight the eye and refresh the spirit.

Ships of the Star Clippers company, *Star Clipper* and *Star Flyer*, are *working* four-masted barentine clipper ships that rely on the wind about 80 per cent of the time. Their diesel engines are used only as a backup in emergencies, for generating electrical power and for desalinating approximately 40 tons of seawater each day for shipboard needs. The crew perform almost every task on these ships, including hoisting, trimming, winching, and repairing the sails. The whole sail-cruise experience evokes the feeling of sailing on some famous private yacht at the turn of the century. Star Clippers' two modern clipper ships were born in the mind of a ship-loving owner, Mikaël Krafft.

When growing up, Krafft, himself a yachtsman (he actually sails a 128-foot

schooner) in his native Sweden, was told tales of the four-masted barkentine-rigged clipper ships of yesteryear—the last one had been built 140 years ago. Krafft turned his boyhood dreams into reality in 1991, with the introduction of the tallest of the tall ships in the world, the Belgian-built *Star Flyer*. It has sails hoisted aloft on four masts, the tallest being 226 feet high. One year later, the almost identical *Star Clipper* emerged from the same shipyard as *Star Flyer*.

These are no ordinary clipper ships; they are built for passengers, who share in the experience of the trade winds of the Caribbean. With accommodations for as many as 180 passengers, the new breed of clipper ships are the only ones that are fully certified under the U.S. Coast Guard regulations. In addition to this, they also carry Lloyd's Register of Shipping's highest rating—a rating which has not been bestowed on any other sailing vessel since 1911.

Star Flyer, the first clipper sailing ship to be built for 140 years, became the first commercial sailing vessel to cross the North Atlantic in 90 years, and one of only a handful of sailing ships ever to be allowed into the Port of Miami under full sail. It is no exaggeration to say that to be aboard the Star Clippers is to seem to have died and gone to the yachtsman's heaven.

While the rigging and sails above decks are totally traditional, accommodations below decks are extremely well equipped, though not as lavish as those on the Club Meds and Windstars. Spacious cabins are each equipped with twin beds that convert into a double bed, individually controlled air-conditioning, two-channel audio, color television (they didn't have those in 1840), personal safe, and private bathroom

This is 170-passenger Star Flyer *(Star Clipper) under full sail. She is a true clipper ship, but with all modern amenities.* **Rating ★★★★**

with shower, toilet, sink, and even a hairdryer (the deluxe cabins also go to the extent of having a bathtub and a refrigerator).

Take minimal clothing, for these ships are the ultimate in casual dress. No jacket and tie are needed in the dining room, which can accommodate all the passengers at once in an open seating. Short-sleeved shirts and short trousers for the men, very casual shorts and tops for the ladies, are the order of the day (and night). The deck crew are real sailors, brought up with yachts and tall ships—and most wouldn't set foot on a cruise ship.

Passengers gather each morning for "captain's story-time." The captain also explains the sailing maneuvers when changing the rigging or directing the ship as it sails into port. Passengers are encouraged to lend a hand, pulling on thick ropes to haul up the main sail. And they love it. At the end of the cruise, tipping (at a suggested $8 per passenger per day) is pooled and is distributed to all members of the crew.

Passengers are provided with many of the amenities of large modern cruise vessels, such as air-conditioning, cashless cruising, occasional live music, a small shop, and a pool to swim in. There is no dress code, so you can be as relaxed as you wish. At 9 a.m. each day the captain, sometimes in two or three languages, gives a daily briefing of the important events of the day, such as what time he expects to enter port, the wind and the sea conditions, and when passengers can help furl or unfurl the sails if they so wish.

The Star Clippers also carry a fine range of watersports craft for the use of passengers—at no extra charge (except scuba diving). The equipment includes a water-ski boat, sailfish, scuba diving, and snorkeling gear.

While cuisine aboard the Star Clippers is perhaps less than the advertised excellence (as far as presentation and choice are concerned), one has to take into account the tiny galley and preparation space provided. Seating in the dining room is awkward for "correct"

A typical cabin aboard the 148-passenger three Windstar Cruises ships. Each has a twin or queen-size bed; stocked mini-bar; multi-channel television and videocassette player; CD-player; direct-dial telephone; private bath with shower.
Rating ★★★★+

service, and consists of six-seat tables set along the sides of the room. However, this *is* supposed to be a casual experience.

The above comments also apply in general to the beautiful, elegant *Sea Cloud*, which is an authentic 1930s three-masted barkentine whose masts are as high as a 20-story building. She was the largest private yacht ever built, when she was constructed in 1931 by E. F. Hutton for his wife, Marjorie Merriweather Post. Built for $1 million in the Krupp shipyard in Kiel, Germany, this steel-hulled yacht is immensely impressive. The cuisine is quite superb, although the choices are limited. This ship has some beautiful cabins, including two lavish owner's suites (both of them with fireplaces and a French canopy bed) left over from her private yacht days, and gorgeous hand-crafted interiors.

In addition to retained and refurbished original suites and cabins, with their paneling, antiques and dressers, some newer, smaller cabins were also added when a consortium of German yachtsmen purchased the ship. Recent owners spent $7.5 million refurbishing her. Many original oil paintings adorn her inner walls. Now owned and operated under charter, *Sea Cloud* sails in both the Caribbean and the Mediterranean waters and is a tribute to elegant times past. The wood-paneled dining room is splendid.

Another brand new three-masted barkentine, owned and operated by German entrepreneur Peter Deilmann, the *Lili Marleen* is the culmination of a lifelong dream. Built in 1994, this vessel cruises the Caribbean during the winter and the Mediterranean during the summer, and caters specifically to the German-speaking market.

Another vintage vessel, called the *Sir Francis Drake*, also offers you a real working tall ship experience, albeit in a much more casual setting than the Star Clippers or *Sea Cloud*. With carpeted cabins that each have a private bathroom, the ship caters to a more casual clientele than the Star Clippers or *Sea Cloud*. You will find that the cuisine is very basic, though not as basic as that which you will find on the ships of Windjammer Barefoot Cruises or the Maine Windjammer Association.

CONTEMPORARY SAIL-CRUISE SHIPS

At the other extreme, if you like sailing but want all your needs taken care of automatically (no energy needed), look no further than the *Club Med I* and *Club Med II* (Club Mediterranée)— with five masts the world's largest sail-cruise ships—and *Wind Song*, *Wind Spirit*, and the *Wind Star* (Windstar Cruises), each with four masts. How so? Nary a hand touches the sails. It's all controlled by computer from an ultra-high-tech bridge. These ships are the contemporary ocean-going robots.

Club Med ships are first and foremost cruise vessels with very impressive sails and tall aluminum masts, while Windstar Cruises' ships carry less than half the number of passengers of the Club Med ships (and fewer than the Star Clippers). From a yachtsman's point of view, the sail-to-power ratio is laughable. And that's why these cruise ships with sails have engine power to get them into and out of port. (The

Star Clippers, by contrast, do it by sail alone, except when there isn't any wind—which isn't often.) The Windstar ships were built first. You should be aware that on some itineraries, when there's little wind, you could well be under motor power for most of the cruise, with only a few hours spent under sail. Windstar and Club Med ships would probably be under sail for no more than 40 per cent of the time they were at sea.

It was a Norwegian living in New York, Karl Andren, who first turned the concept of a cruise vessel with sails into reality. "Boyhood dream stuff," he said. The shipyard he chose to build his ships, the Société Nouvelle des Ateliers et Chantiers du Havre (ACH, as it is known in Le Havre), enjoyed the challenge of building the most unusual vessels. The shipyard had great expertise in the design and construction of cable-laying ships using the hydraulic power of servomechanisms—a concept that was adopted for the Windstar computer-controlled sail rig. Gilbert Fournier, the president of the shipyard, and an expert computer programmer, was fascinated with this ship project. Three Windstar ships were delivered (a fourth was planned but never built). These ships carry mainly North American passengers, whereas the Club Med ships are geared to cater principally to French-speaking passengers.

The Windstar and Club Med ships offer luxurious accommodations, outstanding full-service meals, and a fine-tuned service. These vessels also have entertainment (however the GOs—Gentils Organisateurs—on Club Med ships can only provide amateurish holiday-camp-style entertainment), and several public rooms, all of which have contemporary sophisticated decor.

Another, slightly smaller but very chic, new entrant is the ultra-sleek *Le Ponant*. This three-masted ship caters to just 64 French-speaking passengers in elegant, yet casual, real high-tech surroundings, developing the original Windstar concept to a very advanced state of 1990s technology.

Aboard the Club Meds, Star Clippers, Windstars and *Le Ponant*, watersports take over in the Caribbean when you're not ashore sampling the delights of smaller islands like St. Barthelemy, St. Eustatius, or Les Isles du Saintes, where the huge "white-whale" cruise ships can't go. The Club Meds, Windstars and *Le Ponant* feature an aft, fold-down watersports platform. On-board equipment includes scuba diving gear (you can undertake a full certification course), snorkeling equipment, water-ski boat, windsail boats and rubber Zodiacs to whisk you off to private, unspoiled beaches.

A separate section in Part Three compares these beautiful ships.

World Cruises and Classic Voyages

THE WORLD CRUISE

The ultimate classic voyage for any experienced traveler is a world cruise. This is usually defined as the complete circumnavigation of the earth in a continuous one-way voyage that extends for about three months or longer. The ports of call are carefully planned for their interest and their diversity, and the entire trip can go on for as long as four months.

Voyages that go from cold to warm climates—almost always during January, February and March, when the weather in the Orient is at its best—give you the experience of crisp, clear days, sparkling nights, delicious food, tasteful entertainment, superb accommodations, delightful company, and unforgettable memories. It is for some the cultural, social, and travel experience of a lifetime, and for the few who can afford it, an annual event!

The concept of the world sea cruise first became popular in the 1920s, although it has existed since the 1880s. The first round-the-world voyage was made by the Portuguese navigator Ferdinand Magellan in 1539.

A world cruise on a modern ship means experiencing stabilized, air-conditioned comfort in luxury cabins, and extraordinary sightseeing and excursions on shore and overland. And on some ships, such as the Cunard Royal

The superb 600-passenger Europa *(Hapag-Lloyd Cruises) operates one world cruise and several long cruises each year.* **Rating ★★★★★+**

Viking's venerable *Sagafjord*, every passenger will get to dine with the captain at least once.

A world cruise, which lasts between 80 and 110 days, gives you the opportunity to indulge yourself. Although at first the idea may sound totally extravagant, it need not be, and fares can be as low as $100 per day—to more than $3,000 per day. Alternatively, you can book just a segment of the cruise if that fits your pocket and interest.

How much a world cruise costs will depend on your choice of ship and accommodations. For 1996, a double occupancy cruise fare will vary from about $8,000 to more than $100,000 per person. *QE2*'s split-level penthouse suites, for example, can cost more than $360,000 each (based on two persons occupying a suite)! Gratuities alone would be more than $2,000 for the full voyage! At the other end of the scale, a Russian/Ukrainian-registered vessel is the least expensive way of going round the word by ship. It almost pays not to stay home; the trip will cost less than $100 per person per day—and that includes gratuities!

PLANNING AND PREPARATION

Few enterprises can match the complexity of planning and preparing for a world cruise. More than 675,000 main meals will be prepared in the ship's galleys during a *QE2* world cruise, for example. Several hundred professional entertainers, specialist lecturers, bands, and musicians must all be booked up about a year in advance of the trip. Crew changeovers during the cruise must be organized. A ship the size of Cunard's *QE2* requires two major crew changes during the three-month-long voyage. This normally involves chartering a jumbo jet to and from the relevant port of call. Airline tickets must be arranged for personnel flying in to join the ship—in the right port, and at the right time.

Because a modern world cruise ship has to be totally self-contained, a warehouse-full of spare parts (electrical, plumbing and engineering supplies, for example) must be planned for, ordered,

DID YOU KNOW ...?

... that the first floating eclipse expedition was led by U.S. astronomer Ted Pedas in 1972, when 800 passengers sailed to a spectacular rendezvous with totality in the North Atlantic?

...that a whole county in Iowa raises all its beef cattle for Carnival Cruise Lines?

...that one current cruise ship has two names: *Seawind Crown*, which is also called *Vasco da Gama*?

P&O Cruises' 1,399-passenger Canberra *is one example of a low-budget ship that operates a world cruise each year. It's better, and probably cheaper, than staying home!*
Rating ★★★

loaded, and stored somewhere aboard ship prior to sailing. For just about every shipboard department, the same basic consideration will apply: once at sea, it will be impossible to pick up a replacement projector bulb, air-conditioning belt, table tennis ball, saxophone reed, or anything else that the ship might run out of.

The cruise director will have his/her hands full planning entertainment and social events for a long voyage—not like the "old days" when an occasional game of bingo, or the horse racing, or the daily tote would satisfy passengers.

Another preparation will include reserving fuel at various ports on the itinerary. How much fuel does a cruise ship use? Well, that depends on the size of the ship. On the *Canberra's* 90-day world cruise, the 44,807-grt liner would steam 53 feet per gallon of fuel, at a cruising speed of 20 knots.

A cruise line must give advance notice of the date and time that pilots will be needed, together with requirements for tugs, docking services, customs and immigration authorities, or meetings with local dignitaries and the press. Then there's the organization of dockside labor and stevedoring services at each port of call, plus planning and contracting of bus or transportation services for shore excursions.

The complexity of the preparations requires the concerted efforts of many departments and people on every continent to bring about, with precise timing, this ultimate cruising experience for travelers.

OTHER CLASSIC VOYAGES

Cruises to exotic destinations—China, the Orient, the South Pacific, around Africa and in the Indian Ocean, and around South America—offer all the delights that are associated with a world cruise. The cruise can be shorter and hence less expensive, yet offer the same elegance and comfort, splendid food, delightful ambiance and interesting, well-traveled fellow passengers.

An exotic voyage can be a totally self-contained cruise to a specific destination, lasting anywhere from 30 days to more than 100. Or you can book a segment of a world cruise to begin at one of its ports of call, getting off at another port. "Segmenting" is ideal for those who wish to be a part of a world cruise but have neither the time nor the money for the prolonged extravagance of a three- to four-month cruise vacation.

The segment cruising idea necessarily involves flying either to or from your cruise, or both. You can travel to join your exotic cruise at principal ports such as Genoa, Rio de Janeiro, Acapulco, Honolulu, Sydney, Hong Kong, Singapore, Bangkok, Colombo, Bombay, Mombasa, and at Athens, depending on the ship and cruise.

Ships that already cruise worldwide during the year offer the most experienced world cruises or segments. Even though most of these accommodate a maximum number of 750 passengers, they often operate at about 75 per cent capacity round the world, thus providing their passengers with considerably more space to move around in than they would normally have.

WORLD CRUISE FLEET

The following list includes ships which are at the moment scheduled for world cruises in 1996.

Albatros (Phoenix Seereisen)
Asuka (NYK Cruises)
Azerbaydzhan (CTC Cruise Lines)
Canberra (P&O Cruises)
Crystal Symphony (Crystal Cruises)

Oriana (P&O Cruises)
Europa (Hapag Lloyd Cruises)
Kazakhstan II (Delphin Seereisen)
Maxim Gorki (Phoenix Seereisen)
Odessa (Transocean Tours)
Queen Elizabeth 2 (Cunard Line)
Regent Sea (Regency Cruises)
Rotterdam (Holland America Line)
Royal Odyssey (Royal Cruise Line)
Royal Viking Sun
   (Cunard Royal Viking)
Sagafjord (Cunard Royal Viking)
Victoria (P&O Cruises)

GOING P.O.S.H.

This colloquialism for "grand" or "first rate" has its origin in the days of ocean steamship travel between England and India. The wealthy passengers would, at some considerable extra cost, book their round trip passage as "Port Outward, Starboard Home." In this way they would secure cabins on what was thought to be the cooler side of the ship while crossing the unbearably hot Indian Ocean in the sun. Abbreviated as P.O.S.H., the expression soon came to be applied to first-class passengers who could afford that luxury (*Brewers Dictionary of Phrase & Fable*, Cassell).

However, the reality is that the monsoon winds that blow in and out of the Asian area shift between winter and summer, so that the sheltered side of a ship would change according to the season. Further, in looking at deck plans of ships of the period, it appears that most cabins were located *centrally*, with indoor promenades or corridors along each side, so the actual definition of the origin of P.O.S.H. could be said to be taken as artistic license.

Crossings

By "crossings," I mean crossings of the North Atlantic, that is, 3,000 miles or so of it, from the Old World to the New World—or vice versa, although crossings might also include any other major ocean, such as the Pacific or the Indian Ocean.

Crossing the North Atlantic by ship is an adventure, when time seems to be suspended—the most delicious way of enjoying life aboard ship. It actually takes little more than a long weekend. After the embarkation procedures have been completed, you will be shown to the gangway. Cross the gangway from pier to ship and you are in another world—a world that provides a complete antidote to the pressures of contemporary life ashore, and allows you to engage in the fine art of doing nothing, if you so wish. After the exhilaration of a North Atlantic crossing, the anticipation of landfall among passengers throughout any ship is nothing short of electric.

ATLANTIC OCEAN

Hemmed in by the polar ice caps, the Atlantic Ocean divides Europe and Africa from the Americas. It is three times the size of North America, and contains the world's longest mountain range, which extends (undersea) over 7,000 miles and rises to more than 6,000 feet above the ocean floor. The only points of this ridge that rise to the surface are at St. Helena (Ascension),

St. Paul's Rocks (in the Azores,) and Tristan da Cunha. The ocean's average width is 2,500 miles.

Although half the size of the Pacific Ocean, the Atlantic receives more than half of the water drainage of the world (four times that of the Pacific Ocean). Its average depth is 18,900 feet and its greatest depth, which is known as the Milwaukee Depth, goes down beyond 30,240 feet deep.

Crossing the North Atlantic by passenger vessel should really be considered an art form. I have done it myself more than 130 times, and always enjoy it immensely. As a former professional musician, I often consider crossings as rests, in musical parlance, for both are described as "passages." Indeed, musicians do often "hear" rests in between notes. So if ports of call are the musical notes of a voyage, then the rests are the days at sea—a temporary interlude, when the indulgence of the person and psyche are of paramount importance.

Experienced mariners will tell you that a ship only behaves like a ship when it is on a crossing, as that's what a real ship is built for. Yet the days when ships were built specifically for crossings are almost gone. The only ship left offering a regularly scheduled transatlantic service (a "crossing") is Cunard's *QE2*, the 70,267-grt ship which was superbly designed to hold well against the very worst weather the Atlantic has to offer. Indeed, captains work harder on an Atlantic crossing than on regular cruising schedules.

The most unpredictable weather in the world, together with fog off the Grand Banks of Newfoundland, can mean that the ship's captain will spend tortuous hours on the bridge, with little time for socializing. And when it's foggy, the crew of the *QE2* is often pestered by passengers eager to know if the ship has yet approached latitude 41°46' north, longitude 50°14' west— which is where the *Titanic* struck an Arctic iceberg on that fateful April night in 1912.

There is something that is magical in "doing a crossing." It takes you back to the days when hordes of passengers turned up at the piers of the ports of New York, Southampton, Cherbourg, or Hamburg, accompanied by chauffeurs and steamer trunks, jewels and finery ablaze in a show of what they thought was the finest in life. Movie stars of the 1920s, 1930s and 1940s often traveled abroad on the largest liners of the day, to arrive refreshed, ready to dazzle their European public.

There is also the excitement and anticipation that precedes a crossing— the hubbub and bustle of check-in, of crossing the threshold of the gangway before being welcomed into the calmness aboard and then escorted to one's accommodations for the next several days. Once the umbilical cord of the gangway is severed, bow and stern mooring lines are cast off, and with three long blasts on its deep whistle the *QE2* is pried gently from her berth. She sails silently down the waterway, away from the world, as pretty as a picture, as serene as a Rolls-Royce, and as sure as the Bank of England. The passengers on deck observe the foolhardy yachtsmen dangerously cutting under the raked bows of the *QE2*, while numerous motorboats try to keep up with the giant liner as she edges down the Hudson River, past Battery Park

The one and only Queen Elizabeth 2 *(or* QE2 *as she is affectionately known), with her greyhound-like, sleek profile, long foredeck and massive funnel. She is the last of the great transatlantic superliners. (Cunard).* **Rating ★★★★★ to ★★★★**

City, the Statue of Liberty, the restored Ellis Island, and then out toward the Verrazano-Narrows Bridge and out to the open sea. Coming the other way, arriving in New York by ship is one of the world's most thrilling travel experiences. Following a five-day westbound crossing on the *QE2*, where days are 25 hours long (they are 23 hours long on an eastbound crossing), everything else is an anticlimax.

The *QE2* can accommodate up to 40 cars per crossing—just in case you really don't want to be separated from your wheels. It also provides kennels, so that you can even take your pet, although when crossing eastbound to Southampton, do remember that they will have to be quarantined for up to six months. The *QE2* is a distillation of over 150 years of transatlantic traditions, an oasis of creature comforts offered by no other ship.

Apart from the *QE2*'s regular crossings, there are a number of cruise lines today who feature transatlantic crossings. Although little more than repositioning of cruises—a way of moving ships which cruise the Mediterranean in summer to the Caribbean in winter, and vice versa—they do offer more chances to experience the romance and adventure of a crossing, usually in the spring and in the fall. Perhaps the most unusual transatlantic crossings—made twice a year—are aboard the sail-cruise vessel *Star Flyer*—a four-masted barkentine vessel that can carry 180 passengers, totally under sail.

Most cruise ships performing repositioning crossings actually cross the Atlantic by using the "sunny southern route"—that is, they set sail from southern ports such as Ft. Lauderdale,

San Juan, or Barbados, and end the journey in Lisbon, Genoa, or Copenhagen via the Azores or the Canary Islands off the coast of northern Africa. In this way they avoid the more difficult weather that is often encountered in the North Atlantic. The crossings take longer, however, and last between eight and 12 days.

QUEEN ELIZABETH 2: MILESTONES OVER THE YEARS

The *Queen Elizabeth 2* is a very special ship—part liner, part cruise ship—a real legend in her own lifetime, and the only ship offering regularly scheduled crossings all year. I worked aboard her in two roles: from December 1968 to October 1969 as leader of a jazz group; and then from 1977 to 1980 as the shore excursion manager/deputy cruise director.

Instead of allowing the ship to deteriorate, Cunard has spent a vast sum of money on refurbishments over time, the most recent being a $60 million refit in November/December 1994 that greatly improved the flow of passenger on and off the ship, and further enhanced and increased her already considerable facilities and amenities.

During the ship's initial planning stages, the naval architect Dan Wallace and the director of engineering Tom Kameen were responsible for the ship's design, which was to be for a high-speed, twin-screw ship capable of carrying out safely a five-day transatlantic crossing. Cunard's chairman, Sir Basil Smallpiece, invited James Gardner and Dennis Lennon, well known industrial

designers, to be general design co-ordinators. Gardner concentrated on the exterior aesthetics, while Lennon, in addition to designing the restaurant interiors—the basic shape of which had already been determined by constructional and operational requirements—was also involved with the introduction of a design signature that would be immediately apparent anywhere on the ship; for example, in staircases and corridors. The aim was that the interior design of QE2 would emphasize the "classless" ship concept.

1955

Preparation work for a large liner such as QE2 had already been underway for some time by 1955. It had involved introducing an intensive weight-saving exercise in the design of Cunard's Sylvania, which was then under construction at Glasgow's famous Clydebank shipyards. By agreement with the ship builder, John Brown's, various experimental features were built into this ship. Most of these were successful and provided many weight-saving devices which were to be adopted some 10 years later for the QE2. These included lightweight furniture, fiberglass shower units, new types of deck coverings, as well as new construction and joinery methods.

In conjunction with British Steel's research section, a new type of girder was developed and tested. This girder had large holes for the various services (piping, wiring, etc.) cut in during fabrication, with the depth of the girder being slightly increased in order to compensate for the reduced tension. The result was a girder that was much lighter than the standard ones of the

time, and which was used experimentally in the Sylvania—a ship which was pioneering the way ships were built in terms of advanced construction techniques and materials usage.

October 1963

Construction plans and financing were announced by the Cunard Line company in England.

December 30, 1964

The contract to build was signed by Sir John Brocklebank, then chairman of Cunard, and Lord Aberconway, then chairman of Upper Clyde Shipbuilders (formerly John Brown's), a consortium of five major shipyards on the upper reaches of the River Clyde in Scotland. Some 300 British workers contributed to the building and furnishing of the ship. The contract price was £25.5 million, but this inevitably escalated as a result of increases in wage rates and costs of material during the building period. On completion, the total cost was approximately £30 million.

Coincidental with the building of QE2 was the financial improvement of the Cunard Group, which meant that in 1968 the company was able to forgo part of a loan negotiated with the Board of Trade. This was in addition to the loan of £17.6 million obtained in 1964 under the British government's shipbuilding credit scheme. There was never any question of a direct construction subsidy from the government; Cunard was entirely responsible for meeting the full cost of QE2. A condition of the loan was that the proceeds of the sale of the Queen Elizabeth would be paid to the finance company who provided the loan.

July 4, 1965

America's Independence Day—which also happened to be the 125th anniversary of the maiden voyage of Cunard's first ship, *Britannia*, in 1840—was the day the first prefabricated section of the keel for hull number 736 of *QE2* was laid in the shipyard on Clydebank.

September 20, 1967

"I name this ship *Queen Elizabeth the Second*. May God bless her and all who sail in her." With these historic words, Queen Elizabeth II named the new liner—not after herself, as some had claimed, but simply because this was the second ship to bear that name (the first *Queen Elizabeth* was still in operation at that time). Apparently it was an impulse on the part of the queen to add "second" to the name, which no one, not even at Cunard headquarters, had expected, as it had been secretly agreed to name the ship simply *Queen Elizabeth*. Ahead of her lay a year of fitting out; the new ship was to fill two roles—those of transatlantic express liner and leisure cruise ship.

On the transatlantic run, she was to be a two-class ship. It was decided that class distinction would be completely absent in the naming of public spaces, rooms and decks. The passengers occupying the best accommodations would simply have certain spaces and rooms reserved expressly for their use.

In addition, there was to be single-sitting dining in the Grill Room and Columbia Restaurants, but two sittings would be held in the Britannia Restaurant. However, the greater part of the accommodations would be open to all on board without restrictions. The passengers would then be allotted a restaurant according to the accommodations that had been chosen.

December 1968

Queen Elizabeth 2 (or just *QE2* as she became affectionately known) sailed gracefully out of Gourock, Scotland, with 600 John Brown men aboard, still doing the final fitting-out work. A brochure had advertised a Christmas Cruise, but those who had booked were informed it had been canceled when Cunard Line refused to take delivery of the ship because she was not completed. Instead, the workmen had a good Christmas (the beer flowed freely). The *QE2*'s captain was Commodore William ("Bill") Warwick and its cruise director was Bryan Vickers. I was aboard.

April 18, 1969

The *QE2* was commissioned.

April 22, 1969

In a demonstration of local support, coat hangers for the crew were donated by the District Spastics Association of Southampton, England—*QE2*'s home port. The Cunard Line finally accepted delivery of the new ship from the builders and embarked on a "Preview Cruise" to the ports of Las Palmas, Tenerife and Lisbon. I was aboard with my own jazz trio, which performed each night in what was then the ship's most elegant nightclub (for first-class passengers only)—the Q4 Room (no longer in existence, although it was the "in" place to be in those days).

I remember well that the featured film was *2001: A Space Odyssey*, and that an English rock band called The Applejacks was playing. The ship actu-

ally had four "go-go" dancers, and they worked in the 736 Room (the discotheque of the day, but which is now the exclusive Queens Grill—according to many, the finest restaurant afloat). Twice each day, passengers gathered for a classical concert staged in the Upper Deck Library.

May 2, 1969, Maiden Voyage

The *QE2* set sail from the port of Southampton on her maiden voyage. Her Majesty Queen Elizabeth II and her husband, the Duke of Edinburgh, paid an official visit to the ship prior to sailing. Five days later the ship arrived in New York harbor to a tumultuous welcome. She was greeted to the city by Mayor John Lindsay. I was aboard.

June 1970

The *QE2* crosses from Southampton to New York in 3 days, 20 hours and 42 minutes, at an average speed of 30.36 knots. A casino is also added as U.S. gaming laws are relaxed.

October 1970

The *QE2*'s inaugural long cruise gets underway—a 37-day voyage around North America, South America and Africa.

January 9, 1971

In a dramatic rescue in the Grenadines, *QE2* takes on board 501 passengers and crew from the burning wreck of the 19,828-grt French Line cruise ship *Antilles*, and lands them at Barbados.

January 1975, World Cruise

QE2's first world cruise sets off. It is to be a successful voyage, and the ship is welcomed enthusiastically with celebrations and parties in all her ports of call. She proves herself newsworthy.

May 1975

QE2 meets "Operation Tall Ships" in Tenerife, Canary Islands.

1977, Refit

The Britannia Restaurant is converted into Tables of the World (later nicknamed "Stables of the World")—the largest of the ship's four restaurants. America also made a contribution to the changing face of the *QE2*, and in Bethlehem Steel Shipyard in Bayonne, New Jersey, two ultra-deluxe suites, appropriately called *Queen Mary* and *Queen Elizabeth*, were added.

The Grill Room was renamed the Princess Grill and the 736 Club (formerly a discotheque) was transformed into the Queens Grill. At the same time, the under-used 24-hour Coffee Shop was divided up and reworked into the galley (kitchen) space and the Queens Grill Lounge/Bar, one of the most elegant and prestigious spaces afloat anywhere

The forward Lookout Bar on the Upper Deck was, sadly, changed into an enlarged galley for the Tables of the World. The London Gallery, an experimental art gallery with paintings for sale, was converted into the Reading Room—a restful space for the first-class passengers.

On the Upper Deck amidships, the Portside Promenade and Library were transformed into a full casino and re-christened The Players Club. Meanwhile, the Theatre Bar was converted into a discotheque for the younger passengers, although this change never really became a success

As the brochures often state (and this picture shows) you can do all, or almost nothing, aboard a cruise ship.

1978
The National Geographic organization made a feature film about the great liners, featuring *QE2*.

January 1979
QE2 operated her tenth world cruise. Included in the itinerary was a maiden transit of the Suez Canal, which was experienced by the greatest number of passengers ever.

May 1982, the Falklands
QE2 was requisitioned by the British government for service as a troop ship in the Falkland Islands. The requisition came just as she was crossing from New York to Southampton after her inaugural visit to Philadelphia.

When she arrived in Southampton, it took only seven days to convert her into a troop ship, complete with helicopter landing pads. All the furniture, artworks, slot machines, pianos and plants were off-loaded and placed into storage at the Pickford's warehouse in Southampton.

August 1982
QE2 sets sail for engine trials following a nine-week-long refit to reconvert her to passenger service. The Golden Door Spa at Sea was added. The Q4 Room (the nightclub where I entertained passengers with a small jazz combo when the ship made its debut in 1969) was converted into the Club Lido.

The ship's hull was painted pebble grey—not a pretty sight! *QE2* sailed on a transatlantic crossing for the first time since her Falklands service.

April 1983
For the first time, *QE2* was paired for holiday packages with British Airways' supersonic aircraft, Concorde.

213

May 1983

QE2 honors New York's leading ladies with an afternoon tea and a British fashion show as part of the "Britain Salutes New York" festivities. Guests of honor included city council woman Carol Bellamy.

October 1983, Marathon

QE2 enters a five-man team in the New York City Marathon. A collection is made by the ship for the National Lifeboat Association and Guide Dogs for the Blind charities. As a result, a guide dog, whose picture is hung on a wall aboard the ship, was subsequently christened "Marathon."

January 1984

A "magrodome" sliding glass roof was fitted on to the Club Lido indoor/outdoor leisure center (this later proved to be only moderately successful). As a sign of the times, the Reading Room was changed into a Computer Center, which fast became an extremely popular facility. Later in the year, Cunard signed a $40 million contract with British Airways. Nowadays more than 10,000 passengers take a round-trip in completely unique style—one leisurely crossing on QE2, the other at supersonic speed on the Concorde, between London and New York.

June 1984

The first seagoing branch of Harrods was opened on board QE2 by the film and stage actress Hermione Gingold.

December 1984

The refurbishment of the Columbia Restaurant, with its decor being transformed by softer colors and lighting.

January 1985

American Express opened the first seagoing finance center aboard ship. It was located in the 2-Deck lobby.

July 1985

Captain Robert ("Bob") Arnott, QE2's longest serving captain, retires.

January 1986

The first regular television programming at sea began operating, courtesy of NBC-TV. Passengers watched the Superbowl live in Lima, Peru, while on the ship's annual world cruise.

March 1986

The prestigious International Herald Tribune became the first newspaper to be printed on board ship, by means of its transmission to QE2 via satellite.

May 1986

A royal touch is provided by Queen Elizabeth, the Queen Mother, who visits QE2 in Southampton for the Cunarder Queen Mary's 50th anniversary celebrations.

October 1986, Refit

QE2 makes her last voyage as a steam ship, prior to entering the Lloyd Werft shipyard in Bremerhaven in Germany for a six-month-long, huge $160 million refit. Her steam engines and three boilers were exchanged for a nine-unit, diesel-electric propulsion system, and her two fixed-pitch six-bladed propellers were replaced by two skewbacked, controllable-pitch, five-bladed propellers weighing 42 tons each. A new and fatter funnel was constructed, designed to prevent any soot from falling on to her expansive open decks.

The refit took 179 days and a workforce of men from 34 different countries was involved.

April 29, 1987

QE2 undertakes her inaugural crossing from Southampton to New York under diesel-electric power. A flotilla of small craft led by millionaire publisher Malcolm Forbes' famed yacht, the *Highlander*, escort the "new" QE2 past the Statue of Liberty.

May 8, 1994

QE2 slides gracefully as a Rolls Royce away from her berth at Southampton Docks. There were no outward celebrations on the deck: no champagne, no streamers, no cruise staff—in fact nothing to show that this was the silver anniversary of her maiden voyage from Southampton to New York some 25 years earlier. On the bridge for the historic moment were the ship's first captain, Commodore William Warwick (now retired, but then commodore of the Cunard fleet and captain of QE2 on her maiden crossing in May 1969), his son, Ron Warwick, a Cunard captain, and the ship's present master, Captain John Burton-Hall. There were five passengers aboard who had been on the original crossing, of whom I was one.

The only sign of this special occasion was a large banner draped over a section of the Ocean Terminal, which conveyed the simple message, "Congratulations from ABP" (Associated British Ports). It was a celebration of another kind, however, with jazz music giants George Shearing, Gerry Mulligan, Ronnie Scott and others playing their way across the North Atlantic.

November 1994, Refit

QE2 was placed into drydock at the Blohm & Voss shipyard in Hamburg, Germany, for one month for an extensive refit. She underwent a dramatic $45 million interior refurbishment, including numerous structural changes designed to facilitate better passenger flow and even more dining (and other facility) choices. All cabin bathrooms were replaced (a mammoth task), and several new suites were added, as well as an enlarged library, a new shop with books and memorabilia, a multimedia center, and a florist shop. The Club Lido magrodome-covered pool was replaced with a new, informal al fresco buffet dining area, called The Lido, complete with its own separate preparation galley and bar. The Mauretania Restaurant was re-named the Caronia Restaurant, together with a superb new Crystal Bar (which includes a long model of the *Caronia*, the former Cunard world cruise ship). In addition, the Columbia Restaurant became the Mauretania Restaurant (a magnificent 16-foot-long model of the *Mauretania* of 1907 is displayed proudly at the head of the "D" stairway outside the restaurant, and a new Captain's Dining Area was added. The three Grill Rooms remain (but Queens Grill was completely refurbished, and banquette seating was replaced by individual seating). The original Princess Grill has survived, while the second Princess Grill had its name changed to Britannia Grill. A new private "key club" was established in the former Boardroom.

The shops are still located on the upper level of the showlounge, but the horseshoe-shaped stairway behind the

stage has been blocked off, thus creating a dedicated showlounge. A new Golden Lion Pub is now occupies the former Theatre Bar location.

The Midships Bar was totally refurbished, expanded, and rechristened the Chart Room, with charts of many ports of call in three stages (current chart, chart from the turn of the century, and one from over a hundred years ago). The Yacht Club is greatly enlarged into a new nightclub created from the space that was gained from an extension of the aft deck.

Unfortunately, the German shipyard where she underwent the refit didn't deliver the ship to Cunard in a completed state and, as a result, the company received bad press for having an unfinished ship and a great many unhappy passengers. All was resolved in the weeks following the refit, however, and she is now the stunning, majestic ship that one would expect.

THE FUTURE

During the past 25 years, QE2 has become one of the most popular and successful liners ever built. She has sailed more than three-and-a-half million nautical miles, catering to more than 1.5 million passengers on over 1,000 voyages. Her interiors have been changed into those reminiscent of the ocean liners of yesteryear, which is what passengers have always expected of this ship. Until now, however, the interiors have been disappointing, built as she was in the late 1960s, when contemporary design favored the extensive use of plastic laminates (some 2 million square feet of Formica laminates were used in her original interiors). Now completed, the new enhancements provide deserved space, grace, and pace.

Perhaps in her next refit the Midships Lobby could be made into a two-deck-high affair, with all ship's passenger services—such as the purser's office, bank, and housekeeping office—located on the upper level of the expanded lobby, with passengers embarking into the lower level.

Will the QE2 survive into the 21st century? All the signs point to the fact that she will, if only to provide a regularly scheduled transatlantic service (many of her regular passengers do not fly). In the face of stiff competition from all the new ships with their high-tech toys and playgrounds, this super-liner simply cannot compete for cruise business. The exception, however, is when she operates her annual round-the-world cruise, when her speed helps her cross the world's vast oceans faster than any other cruise ship afloat, and provides passengers with more time in ports of call.

PART THREE

How a Ship is Evaluated

I have been evaluating and rating cruise ships and the cruise product professionally since 1980, and have continually refined the rating and evaluation system. In 1995, the system was altered dramatically in order to take into account the many changes in cruise product, the delivery of the cruise product, service standards, and the new features that have been built into the latest ships, providing passengers with more choices. I have thus further refined the system to take into account more of the passenger "software" and actual cruise product that is experienced.

This section includes 220 ocean-going cruise ships, expedition ships and tall ships that were in service when this book was completed in July 1995. All except 12 new ships have been carefully evaluated, taking into account more than 300 separate inspection points based on personal sailings and visits to ships. For the sake of clarity, the inspections are channeled into 15 sections. With a possible 10 points per section, the maximum possible score for any ship is thus 150 points.

Expedition cruise vessels and tall sail-cruise ships cannot be judged according to the same criteria as "normal" cruise ships because they are purpose-built and many have unique features that reflect the type of expeditions or sailing experiences they offer. I have thus adopted a weighting system for any exceptional cases.

I have also taken into consideration the fact that passengers of different nationalities expect different things from their cruise experiences. The passenger expectations on ships that operate in the Mediterranean with European passengers (particularly older vessels), for example, vary considerably from those of North American passengers, who often want the latest in high-tech interiors, facilities, and features, while their European counterparts enjoy older ships with more traditional fittings and fixtures, and less razzle-dazzle entertainment.

The stars beside the name of the ship at the top of each page relate directly to the Overall Rating. The highest number of stars awarded is five (★★★★★), the lowest is one (★). A plus (+) indicates that a ship deserves just that little bit more than the number of stars given.

Overall Rating	Number of Stars
135.1-150.0	★★★★★+
125.1-135.0	★★★★★
115.1-125.0	★★★★+
105.1-115.0	★★★★
100.1-105.0	★★★+
90.1-100.0	★★★
85.1-90.0	★★+
80.1-85.0	★★
80.1 or less	★

Cruise lines are in the business of creating and selling cruise products and

vacation packages of (marketed and perceived) excellence. Thus the common factor of all cruise ships is quality. Therefore, in appraising the cruise industry, it is inevitable that scores will be on the high side, and the difference in score from one ship to another may be very slight. This explains why of the 220 cruise vessels evaluated, some 178 have achieved three stars or more.

COMMENTS

The smaller details and my personal comments on each ship may help you determine what is best for you. These have been separated into four parts:

+ (positive comments)
- (negative comments)
Dining (comments on cuisine, service, and the dining room experience), and
General Comments (comments about the ship or product).

Needless to say, there is no such thing as a "standard" cruise ship. They come in all sizes and shapes, and a wide variety of internal layouts, facilities, appointments, and levels of service—as do hotels and resorts on land. The one thing all ships do have in common is gross registered tonnage, often abbreviated to grt. This is an international measurement that is used for ship classification purposes.

Since size is often the key to the kind of facilities, level of comfort, and, of course, number of passengers on board, I have found it prudent to adopt a weighting system. It is not possible to evaluate a small ship such as

the *Renaissance III* or *Sea Goddess I* fairly against a large ships such as *Crystal Symphony* or *Sun Princess* using precisely the same criteria. The weighting system takes into account prices, food quality, and, in particular, the level of service from and the attitude of the crew (hospitality). The rating of expedition cruise vessels also includes garbage compacting and incineration, waste disposal, as well as compliance with the most recent environmental and safety regulations (MARPOL V).

The results, comments, and ratings are strictly personal, and are intended to guide you in formulating your own opinions and cruise plans. They are also intended to help travel agents to differentiate between the many cruise ships and cruise products in today's expanding market.

CHANGES IN THE RATINGS

Cruise lines, ship owners, and operators should note that ratings, like stocks and shares, *can go down as well as up*, even when things have supposedly been improved aboard their ships. This is explained by increased competition, the introduction of newer ships with better custom-designed facilities, and other market- or passenger-driven factors. With an increasing number of ships in the marketplace, and the building of ships for niche operations, tougher evaluations have become increasingly important.

When discounting was introduced in order to stimulate the demand for cruises in certain markets, so too were more cost-cutting measures. As a

result, cruise cuisine and service standards have suffered cut-backs in the past few years. The ratings now reflect this trend more accurately. It is encouraging that cruise lines are now playing "catch up" to those considered the best in their respective (unwritten) class.

Ratings and evaluations cover four principal areas:

1) The Ship
2) Accommodations
3) Cuisine/Service
4) Cruise Product

1) THE SHIP

Ship: Condition/Cleanliness

Cleanliness and hygiene standards have become and increasingly important in all aspects of everyday life, and even more so aboard cruise ships, which really are a microcosm of modern society.

This score reflects the general condition of the ship, both internally and externally. It takes into account: the ship's age and maintenance requirements; the condition of the hull, exterior paint, decking materials, caulking, swimming pool surrounds, deck furniture, lifeboats, life rafts, and life-preserving equipment; interior cleanliness with regard to the public restrooms, elevators, floor coverings, carpeting, wall coverings, stairways, passageways, doorways, other access points, crew stairways, alleyways, accommodations and galleys; food preparation, food storage rooms, and refrigeration units; and garbage handling, compacting, incineration, and waste disposal facilities.

Ship: Space/Flow/Comfort

This score reflects the use of common passenger spaces including: outside deck areas; sunbathing and sheltered deck space; swimming pools; outdoor and indoor promenades; interior spaces—density and passenger flow, and ceiling height; lobby areas, stairways and passageways, and public restrooms and facilities; lighting, direction signs, air-conditioning, smoke extraction and ventilation flow; the degree of comfort or crowding (passenger space ratio), density, and crew to passenger ratio.

Ship: Decor/Furnishings

This score reflects: the overall interior design and decor, including appearance and condition; color combinations and visual appeal; hard and soft furnishings (including suitability and practicality); wood (and imitation wood) paneling, veneers, and use of glass and plastics; carpet material, tuft density, color and pattern practicality, and fit and finish (including seams and edging); chair design and comfort; ceiling treatments, bulkheads and treatments; reflective surfaces; artwork quality, suitability and aesthetic appeal; and color definition and lighting.

Ship: Fitness Facilities

This score reflects: the health spa, its location and its accessibility; the gymnasium, exercise room, and fitness, sports and games facilities; spa treatments and rejuvenation programs; swimming pools, whirlpools, grand baths, saunas, steam rooms, and massage rooms (size and cleanliness); and running, jogging and walking tracks.

2) ACCOMMODATIONS

Cabins: Comfort/Facilities

This score reflects the design and layout of cabins, balconies, beds and berths, furniture (its placement and practicality), and other fittings; closets and other hanging space, drawer space, and bedside tables; vanity unit, bathroom facilities, washbasin, cabinets, and toiletries storage; lighting, air-conditioning and ventilation; audio-visual facilities; quality and degree of luxuriousness; and bulkhead insulation, noise, and vibration levels.

Cabins: Software

This score reflects the soft furnishings and details in cabins such as: the information manual (list of services), paper and postcards (including personalized stationery); telephone directory; laundry lists; tea- and coffee-making equipment; fresh flowers (if any), fruit (if any); and bathroom amenities kits, bathrobes, slippers, and the size, thickness, quality and material content of towels.

3) CUISINE

This section is perhaps the most important, as food is often the main feature of today's cruise package. Cruise lines put maximum emphasis on telling passengers how good their food is, often to the point of being unable to deliver what is promised. Generally, however, the standard of food is good.

The rule of thumb is: if you were to eat out in a good restaurant, what would you expect? Does the ship meet your expectations? Would you come back again for the food?

There are perhaps as many different tastes as there are passengers. The "standard" market cruise lines cater for a wide range of tastes. Upscale cruise lines can offer food cooked individually to your taste. Generally, as in any good restaurant, you get what you pay for. Over the past two years, many cruise lines have been cutting back on their food (and service), and this has had more effect on the ratings for 1996.

Food: Dining Room/Cuisine

This score reflects: the main dining room's physical structure, window treatments, seating (alcoves and individual chairs, with or without armrests), lighting and ambiance, table set-ups, the quality and condition of linen, china, and cutlery, and table centerpieces (flowers); menus, food quality, presentation, food combinations, culinary creativity, variety, appeal, taste, palatability, freshness, color, balance, garnishes, and decorations; appetizers, soups, pastas, flambeaus, and so on; fresh fruit and cakes; the wine list; and the price range.

Food: Buffets/Informal Dining

This score reflects: the hardware (including the provision of sneeze guards, tongs, ice containers and ladles, and serving utensils); buffet displays, appeal and presentation, trays and set-ups, correct food temperatures; breakfast, luncheon, deck buffets, midnight buffets, and late-night snacks; decorative elements such as ice carvings; and staff attitude, service, and communication skills.

Food: Quality of Ingredients

This score reflects the overall quality of ingredients used, including: consistency and portion size; grades of meat, fish and fowl; and the price paid by the cruise company for its food product per passenger per day. It is the quality of ingredients that most dictates the eventual presentation, aesthetic appeal and quality of the finished product—as well as its taste.

SERVICE

Service: Dining Room

This score reflects the professionalism of all restaurant staff: Maitre d' Hotel, dining room managers, head section waiters, and waiters and assistant waiters (busboys). It includes correct place settings and service, communication skills, attitude, flair, and finesse.

Service: Bars/Lounges

This score reflects: lighting and ambiance; service in bars and lounges; noise levels; communication skills (between bartenders and bar staff and passengers in particular); staff attitude, personality, flair and finesse; and the correct use of glasses,

Service: Cabins

This score reflects: the cleaning and housekeeping staff, butlers, cabin stewards and stewardesses, and supervisory staff; efficiency and professionalism; visibility and availability; attention to cleanliness and extra attention to detail; in-cabin food service; promptness, speed and accuracy; linen provision and changes; and language and communication skills.

4) CRUISE PRODUCT

Cruise: Entertainment

This score reflects the overall entertainment program and content as designed and targeted to specific passenger demographics. Cruise ship entertainment has to appeal to passengers who are of widely varying ages and types.

The rating includes: the physical plant (stage/bandstand); proficiency of technical support, lighting, follow spotlight operation, and set and backdrop design; sound and light systems, recorded click-tracks and cues, and special effects; the variety, quality and timing of large-scale production shows, including content, story and plot, cohesion, set design, creativeness of costumes, relevancy, quality, choreography, and vocal content; cabaret; variety shows; singers; visual acts; bands and solo musicians.

Cruise: Activities Program

This score reflects the variety, quality and quantity of daytime activities and events. The rating includes: the cruise director and cruise staff (including their visibility, availability, ability and professionalism); sports and exercise programs; participation games; special-interest programs; mind-enrichment lectures and demonstrations; variety, content and timing of activities; and staff attitude and competence in running activities.

Cruise: Overall Hospitality

This score reflects the level of hospitality of the crew and their attention to detail and personal satisfaction. It includes: the professionalism of senior

officers, middle management, supervisors, cruise staff, and general crew; social contact, appearance and dress codes; atmosphere and ambiance; motivation; communication skills (of crucial importance); and the general ambiance and impression created.

Watersports Facilities

This score reflects: the watersports equipment that is carried (including banana boat, jet skis, scuba tanks and snorkeling equipment); the waterski boat; windsurfers; watersports instruction programs, overall staff supervision; the marina (usually located aft) or side-retractable watersports platforms; and the enclosed swimming area (if applicable).

NOTES

Expedition Cruise Ships/Tall Ships/Wind-Sail Ships

These are highly specialized vessels that offer a particular kind of cruise experience. Consequently, they do not feature the same facilities as the majority of "standard" cruise ships, and their ratings are calculated in a different manner. The total score awarded is based on the cruise experience offered, the range and quality of on-board facilities, the product itself, and the extent to which the company is concerned for the environment.

Expedition Ships

These vessels are constructed for in-depth expedition cruising, with special ice-hardened hulls and the classification to operate legally in ecologically and environmentally sensitive areas.

They are given a rating and a total score based on a number of relevant extra criteria. These include: classification of service; suitability for expeditions; cleanliness, hygiene, and sanitation; wet and dry garbage treatment and handling; concern for the environment; itineraries; shore expeditions; lecture facilities and lecturers; expedition leaders; medical facilities; evacuation provisions; operation of the inflatable Zodiac landing craft; helicopter; air and ground transportation; ticketing and documentation; and the experience and reputation of the expedition company concerned.

Tall Ships/Sail-Cruise Experience

These ships are either specially constructed so as to provide a genuine sail-powered experience (*Lili Marleen*, *Sea Cloud*, *Sir Francis Drake*, *Star Clipper*, *Star Flyer*), or they are contemporary vessels that have been built to emulate sail-powered vessels but are really sail-assisted (*Club Med I*, *Club Med II*, *Le Ponant*, *Wind Song*, *Wind Spirit*, *Wind Star*).

They provide another dimension to the cruise experience, and, as with true expedition ships, cannot be evaluated in precisely the same way as other oceangoing cruise ships.

Their rating also includes a number of extra, relevant criteria. These include the following: on-board sail-cruise experience; relaxation facilities; provision of in-cabin entertainment facilities; existence or otherwise of open bridge policy; watersports facilities; expert lecturers and instructors; privacy and quiet spaces; destinations; and environmental policy.

223

WHAT MAKES A FIVE-STARS-PLUS (★★★★★+) CRUISE SHIP

Ship owners and cruise marketing directors often proudly describe their products as "luxury" and of a "five-star-plus" or "five-star" standard. However, in reality, very few ships deserve this designation. To merit it requires a combination of discreet sophistication and impeccable service; almost every individual need must be anticipated, and every amenity within the structural provisions of today's passenger ships must be provided. The cruise product should allow for a completely relaxed and hassle-free vacation.

The items listed are just some of the things required of any ship that is aiming for the highest rating of Five-Stars-Plus. Ships that do not meet any of the following criteria will have points deducted accordingly. This is the reason that cruise ship and cruise product ratings vary so enormously (from five-stars-plus down to one star), and hence the value of this book.

The training of crew to the highest levels of service is the responsibility of any ship owner who is competing for passengers willing to pay between $500 and $3,000 per person per day. Passengers want and demand what they perceive as "value for money"—no matter what amount is paid. Crew members that cannot communicate with passengers well, in their own language, will inevitably fail to provide the same level of contact or service to them.

While the introduction of rampant discounting has lowered the expectation level of many passengers, the level and quality of service demanded by those paying the topmost rates is quite justified.

Hardware (The Ship Itself)

- The Passenger Space Ratio must be 35.0 or better (based on two per suite/cabin and obtained by dividing the gross register tonnage (grt) by the number of passenger beds).
- The ship must be kept in pristine condition, with no visible signs of rusting steel work.
- Safety must be of the utmost importance, with thoroughly trained fire crews, constant drills, and single-language communications for all emergency procedures.
- All lifeboat davits and safety equipment must be fully functional, and inspected by senior shipboard management once each week.
- Paintwork must be immaculate at all times (ships must be constantly painted, and a five-stars-plus rating will not be considered for any ship that defers painting and minor maintenance items to drydock time only).
- All exterior fittings, gangway mechanisms, lighting, to be in pristine condition. Any faulty equipment must be replaced, and no wear and tear will be tolerated.
- All gangways are to be in immaculate condition, with non-slip stair treads and wood or rubber-grip or similar handrails.
- No light bulbs to be missing (not working) from the "string of lights" between the bow, mast, funnel and stern.
- Shuttle buses to be provided in ports of call where a city or town center is

more than a few minutes away from the ship.

SOFTWARE (DECOR, HOSPITALITY AND SERVICE STANDARDS)

Accommodations

• Accommodations designated as "suites" *must* have a day (lounge) area and a completely separate bedroom with a closing (and lockable) door. Cabins should certainly not be described as "suites" if there is simply a curtain separating the sleeping area from the lounge area.

• The minimum cabin size must be 200 sq.ft. (18.5 sq.m.).

• Cabin placement and insulation to be of such thickness that a telephone ringing in an adjacent cabin cannot be heard.

• Privacy curtains to be installed between cabin entrance and sleeping or lounge area.

• Fresh flowers are to be placed in all cabins.

• Personalized stationery in all suites (and in all cabins on any ship with fewer than 300 passengers).

• Leather-bound stationery/cabin service folder should be provided.

• 100% cotton (or 100% cotton loop) towels (to include hand towel, face towel, shower towel, large bath towel). Bath towels should be a minimum size of 48 inches by 30 inches.

• 100% cotton bed linen, including pillowcases, should be provided (points deducted for cotton/polyester mix). Bed linen should ideally feature the cruise line's logo.

• Thick 100% cotton ankle-length bathrobe, which must be changed daily, should be provided.

• Special pillows for those passengers who are "allergy-sensitive" are to be available.

• Minimum of six storage drawers per passenger.

• Walk-in closets for all top-grade accommodations, and for "suites."

• Illuminated closets for all other cabins, with wooden (not plastic) hangers, tie rail, and shoe horn.

• Full or half-tiled bathroom with bathtub and shower (bidet in all suites).

• Refrigerator or mini-bar (fully stocked), with appropriate glassware, paper napkins, coasters, and cocktail stirrers.

• Separate make-up desk with mirror (could serve as a writing desk).

• Hairdryer (built-in or free standing).

• Enclosed toiletries cabinet and storage space.

• Audio-visual entertainment center to include color television and VCR player (preferably also a CD player), and enclosed cabinet where possible. One remote control for all units.

• Three channels of audio including one classical channel.

• Lunch and dinner menus delivered daily to all suites and upper-grade cabins.

• Direct-dial satellite-linked telephone.

• Lockable personal safe (must be easy to operate, either with a key, or digitally, but not with a credit card).

• No sharp edges on furniture (rounded edges and corners only).

• Electrical sockets must be labeled with the correct voltage.

- Course-by-course in-suite or in-cabin meal service, with individual chairs and adjustable-height dining table.
- Amenities kits to contain (minimum): shampoo, conditioner, body lotion, quality soap, sewing kit and emery board.
- Wood (fire-retardant treated) rather than metal cabinetry and drawers.
- World news to be delivered to all cabins each day.
- In each port of call, newspapers should be made available (where possible).
- "Butler Service" should include pressing of clothes on embarkation, if needed, and canapés at 6:00 p.m. daily, correctly presented on a silver or other display tray.
- Balcony furniture to have cushions or pads for seating areas, wiped down daily.
- Canvas (not plastic) laundry bags for personal self-service launderette use.
- Bottled water is to be provided without charge and replaced daily.
- Umbrellas for all passengers (ships of up to 300 passengers), and for all passengers in "suites" on ships of over 300 passengers.
- Service pantries located opposite passenger cabins to have "silent closing" device fitted.

Dining/Cuisine

- Waiters should be able to recognize whether a passenger is right- or left-handed and set or change tableware accordingly.
- Place settings must include proper fish knives and forks.
- There must be no "spotting" on cutlery.

- The finest quality plateware, with different patterns for dining room, informal dining and cabin service items, should be used.
- Finger bowls must be provided for courses that include the use of fingers (mussels in shells, for example).
- Dining room meals to be placed on linen tablecloth with linen napkins, and changed for each meal.
- Finest quality glassware, and correct wine glasses, must be used.
- Special (off-menu) orders must be possible at any time in the dining room (by giving reasonable notice).
- Tableside cooking and presentation of whole fish, carved meats, poultry, pasta and flambeau dessert items.
- Dessert trolley and cheese trolley (both with cover) should be used when possible. A minimum four types of biscuits/crackers should be offered.
- Beluga or Sevruga caviar in unlimited quantities, and at any time, served with the correct style of mother-of-pearl or bone (not metal) caviar spoons.
- Meals individually cooked to order on ships of under 300 passengers.
- All sauces must be presented in the correct sauce boats, and never in bottles.
- Bottled water must be provided, without charge, in all dining areas. Silver pitchers should be towel-wrapped to prevent condensation from dripping.
- Afternoon tea to have a minimum of six different types of teas available, plus herbal teas. No "supermarket" blended varieties.
- Paper doilies should be placed under all teacups for afternoon tea service.

- Cappuccino/espresso coffees should be available without charge in the dining room and at least two bars/lounges. A crystallized sugar stick should be provided.
- No packeted sugar to be used in the dining room. All sugars should be presented in porcelain or stainless steel bowls (with attached lid, and spoon). No sugar should be on the table during meals; only when tea/coffee is served.
- Course-by-course in-cabin dining at any time (in all cabins for ships of under 300 passengers; in "penthouse" or "suite" categories for ships of over 300 passengers).
- The wine list and stock should equal that of a one-star Michelin restaurant ashore, with a minimum of: three types of champagne; 30 white wines; 30 red wines; and 5 rosé or "blush" wines. Non- and low-alcoholic and organic wines should also be offered.
- Wine sommelier service with appropriate decanters, correct-sized glassware, and leather-bound wine list.
- Bartenders that know your correct name and remember your favorite drinks.
- Dress codes must be enforced at all times in the dining room.
- Senior officers and social staff to host passenger tables each evening (preferably on a rotation basis).
- Nutritional information (to include approximate calorie, fat, protein content) should be available to passengers requesting same, perhaps in an alternative menu.
- Waiters are to wear name badges (on the same side) at all times, and should provide efficient service

without touching passengers at any time. In a fixed (not open) seating arrangement, they should ideally learn and use passengers' surnames when addressing them. The language of a formal dining room should be used whenever possible ("would you like coffee, sir/madam?" and not "coffee sir?"). Hands should be properly manicured and nails should not be overly long nor in poor trim.

- Waiters should not offer "recommended" dishes, except when asked to do so by the executive chef/maître d'. Instead, they should merely describe accurately how each dish is prepared and presented.
- Waiters must always serve to the correct side of the passenger. Likewise, they (or their assistants/busboys) must always take finished plates away from the correct side of the passenger. There should be no leaning over tables except when absolutely necessary (large alcove tables, for example).
- Waiters (or assistant waiters/busboys) should not, at any time, take away a finished plate from any table while other passengers at the same table are still eating the same course.

General
- Meet and greet staff should be at the airport to offer "refreshment packs" for passengers arriving on long-haul flights.
- All luggage must be transported as "seamlessly" as possible without being handled by the passenger.
- White-gloved staff members must escort passengers to their suites or cabins upon embarkation.

- "No" should not be heard as an answer to any reasonable request.
- Ticket documentation box must include leather ticket/document wallet, and leather key card or boarding pass holder.
- Camera to be positioned on the bridge, facing forward, for in-cabin television system.
- Newspapers to be provided in ports of call whenever possible.
- Room service for simple items such as coffee, tea, croissants, etc., must take no more than five minutes.
- Room service for complete meals and complex orders must take no longer than 15 minutes.
- Full book and video library access 24 hours per day without charges of any kind (except on unreturned items).
- Complimentary self-service launderette.
- Concierge or similar to attend to personal comfort details, arrangement of private cocktail parties, etc.
- Tender service that is continuous when in port, and not at designated times. Tenders must have clean cushioned seating areas, and tender stations ashore must have first-aid kits.
- Tour operators ashore must be told that each unit of transportation must have a practical first-aid kit suitable for most emergencies.
- Fresh flowers or pot pourri should be provided in all cabin bathrooms.
- Fresh flowers (not plastic) should be provided in shore tenders.
- Oriental rugs in lobby areas and public restrooms.
- Pot pourri baskets or flower baskets should be provided in all public restrooms.

- Separate gangway for crew members (tidal conditions permitting).
- Cushions placed on seats and backs of all outdoor chairs (at the poolside, indoor/outdoor cafés, for example).
- The highest level of security, which should include combination passenger ID/charge cards.
- Baggage to be placed outside cabins upon retiring on the last night of the cruise (and not at any time specified before 3 a.m. on the morning of arrival).
- All port taxes and gratuities must be included.
- The crew must communicate in a single language (maritime tradition states "English") for all safety procedures.
- Crew alleyways to have individual steel garbage cans (not plastic) with separation of paper and plastic.

Outdoor Decks/Leisure Areas
- Deck chaise longue chairs must be wood, aluminum or stainless steel (not plastic).
- Thick cushioned pads must be provided on all outdoor deck lounge chairs. Towels must be rolled up and placed on them each morning (weather permitting).
- A fresh supply of 100% cotton towels must be available at all times.
- Swimming pools and whirlpools available 24 hours, except in the event of cleaning, refilling, or other maintenance.
- Shower stalls must have wall-mounted dispensers for soap, shampoo, etc.
- Deck beverage service available on all open decks with seating areas, not just the principal deck.

The Ratings and Evaluations

Ship Profiles
Technical and specific information on each ship is given, followed by a point by point evaluation and a summary including positive and negative points.

Prefixes
The prefixes on the name of a ship are used to denote the type of propulsion system that is being used:

ib = ice-breaker (diesel or nuclear)
ms = motor ship (diesel)
mts = motor twin screw (diesel) or motor turbine ship (steam)
mv = motor vessel (diesel)
msy = motor sailing yacht
RMS = Royal Mail Ship
ss = steam ship
ssc = semi-submersible craft (swath)
sts = sail training ship
tes = turbo-electric ship (steam)
ts = turbine steamer (steam) or twin screw vessel
tsmv = twin screw motor vessel
ys = yacht ship

Cruise Areas
Main cruising areas (e.g. Caribbean).

Length
Cruise length is given only for ships featuring year-round cruises to destinations such as the Bahamas.

Cruise Line
The cruise line and operator will be different if the company that owns the vessel does not market and operate it.

First Entered Service
Where two dates are given, the first is the ship's maiden passenger voyage when new, the second the date it began service for the present operator.

Christened By
Where two names are given, the first is the person who christened the ship when first built, the second the person who christened the ship for its present owner/operator.

Interior Design
The name of the principal coordinating architect is given, but it should be noted that most new ships are often the result of a complex partnership of several designers. Older ships (which were smaller) often had a single interior designer.

Propulsion
The number of main engines is given, together with the output (at 100%), expressed either as:
bhp = brake horsepower
kW = kilowatts generated
shp = shaft horsepower

Propellers
Included is the type of propeller, where known.
CP = controllable (variable) pitch
FP = fixed (direct) pitch

Passenger Capacity
The number of passengers is based on:
a) Two beds/berths per cabin, plus all

single cabins; b) All available beds/berths filled.

Passenger Space Ratio
Achieved by dividing the gross registered tonnage (grt) by the number of passengers.

Cabin Size Range
From the smallest cabin to the largest suite, in square feet and square meters, rounded up to the nearest number.

Wheelchair Cabins
Cabins designed to accommodate passengers with mobility problems.

NOTE
In the **Other Comments** section at the bottom of each page, all gratuities are usually at extra cost unless included in the price, and extra gratuities are strictly prohibited. Likewise, insurance and port taxes are also at extra cost unless specifically stated as included.

The Ratings

SHIP	CRUISE LINE	RATING	STARS
Royal Viking Sun	Cunard Royal Viking	136.8	★★★★★+
Europa	Hapag-Lloyd Cruises	136.5	★★★★★+
Sea Goddess I	Cunard Royal Viking	136.5	★★★★★+
Sea Goddess II	Cunard Royal Viking	136.5	★★★★★+
Seabourn Pride	Seabourn Cruise Line	136.2	★★★★★+
Seabourn Spirit	Seabourn Cruise Line	136.2	★★★★★+
Crystal Symphony	Crystal Cruises	135.3	★★★★★+
Crystal Harmony	Crystal Cruises	135.1	★★★★★+
Vistafjord	Cunard Royal Viking	135.1	★★★★★+
Queen Elizabeth 2	Cunard (Grill Class)	134.4	★★★★★
Queen Odyssey	Royal Cruise Line	134.3	★★★★★
Song of Flower	Radisson Seven Seas Cruises	133.8	★★★★★
Silver Wind	Silversea Cruises	133.6	★★★★★
Hanseatic	Hanseatic Tours	133.5	★★★★★
Silver Cloud	Silversea Cruises	133.5	★★★★★
Sagafjord	Cunard Royal Viking	132.6	★★★★★
Asuka	NYK Cruises	128.7	★★★★★
Hebridean Princess	Hebridean Island Cruises	126.2	★★★★★
Radisson Diamond	Radisson Seven Seas Cruises	126.1	★★★★★
Zenith	Celebrity Cruises	126.0	★★★★★
Horizon	Celebrity Cruises	125.1	★★★★★
Sea Cloud	Sea Cloud Cruises	125.1	★★★★★
Queen Elizabeth 2	Cunard (Deluxe Class)	124.8	★★★★+
Oriana	P&O Cruises	124.4	★★★★+
Legend of the Seas	Royal Caribbean Cruises	124.4	★★★★+
Oceanic Grace	Oceanic Cruises	124.3	★★★★+
Bremen	Hanseatic Tours	123.1	★★★★+
Le Ponant	Compagnie des Isles du Ponant	122.4	★★★★+
Megastar Aries	Star Cruise	121.6	★★★★+
Megastar Taurus	Star Cruise	121.6	★★★★+

Cruise Ship Directory and Ratings

SHIP	CRUISE LINE	RATING	STARS
Astor	AquaMarin Cruises	117.9	★★★★+
Royal Princess	Princess Cruises	120.3	★★★★+
Club Med II	Club Mediterranée	117.9	★★★★+
Club Med I	Club Mediterranée	117.8	★★★★+
Berlin	Deilmann Reederei	117.6	★★★★+
Star Princess	Princess Cruises	117.4	★★★★+
Wind Song	Windstar Cruises	117.1	★★★★+
Wind Spirit	Windstar Cruises	117.1	★★★★+
Wind Star	Windstar Cruises	117.1	★★★★+
Sky Princess	Princess Cruises	116.9	★★★★+
Monarch of the Seas	Royal Caribbean Cruises	116.6	★★★★+
Majesty of the Seas	Royal Caribbean Cruises	116.4	★★★★+
Regal Princess	Princess Cruises	116.4	★★★★+
Sovereign of the Seas	Royal Caribbean Cruises	116.4	★★★★+
CostaRomantica	Costa Cruises	116.1	★★★★+
Langkapuri Star Aquarius	Star Cruise	116.1	★★★★+
Crown Princess	Princess Cruises	115.9	★★★★+
World Discoverer	Society Expeditions	115.7	★★★★+
Star Pisces	Star Cruise	115.5	★★★★+
Meridian	Celebrity Cruises	115.4	★★★★+
Crown Odyssey	Royal Cruise Line	114.8	★★★★
Queen Elizabeth 2	Cunard (Premium Class)	114.8	★★★★
Nordic Empress	Royal Caribbean Cruises	114.7	★★★★
Windward	Norwegian Cruise Line	114.7	★★★★
Dreamward	Norwegian Cruise Line	114.6	★★★★
Royal Odyssey	Royal Cruise Line	114.3	★★★★
Marco Polo	Orient Lines	114.1	★★★★
Renaissance Five	Renaissance Cruises	114.1	★★★★
Renaissance Six	Renaissance Cruises	114.1	★★★★
Renaissance Seven	Renaissance Cruises	114.1	★★★★
Renaissance Eight	Renaissance Cruises	114.1	★★★★
Orient Venus	Japan Cruise Line	114.0	★★★★
Star Odyssey	Royal Cruise Line	114.0	★★★★
Royal Majesty	Majesty Cruise Line	113.8	★★★★
Ryndam	Holland America Line	114.2	★★★★

SHIP	CRUISE LINE	RATING	STARS
Maasdam	Holland America Line	114.0	★★★★
Statendam	Holland America Line	113.9	★★★★
Columbus Caravelle	Odessa Cruise Company	113.3	★★★★
Island Princess	Princess Cruises	113.2	★★★★
Pacific Princess	Princess Cruises	113.2	★★★★
Americana	Ivaran Lines	112.9	★★★★
Golden Princess	Princess Cruises	112.8	★★★★
Italia Prima	Nina Cruise Line	112.8	★★★★
CostaClassica	Costa Cruises	112.5	★★★★
Renaissance One	Renaissance Cruises	112.0	★★★★
Renaissance Two	Renaissance Cruises	112.0	★★★★
Renaissance Three	Renaissance Cruises	112.0	★★★★
Renaissance Four	Renaissance Cruises	112.0	★★★★
Imagination	Carnival Cruise Lines	111.2	★★★★
Cunard Crown Dynasty	Cunard Crown Cruises	111.1	★★★★
Norway	Norwegian Cruise Line	111.0	★★★★
Star/Ship Atlantic	Premier Cruise Lines	111.0	★★★★
Seaward	Norwegian Cruise Line	110.9	★★★★
Superstar Gemini	Star Cruise	110.2	★★★★
Nippon Maru	Mitsui OSK Passenger Line	110.1	★★★★
Arkona	Deutsche Seetouristik	110.0	★★★★
Nautican	Cruise Lines International	110.0	★★★★
Fascination	Carnival Cruise Lines	109.5	★★★★
Sensation	Carnival Cruise Lines	109.4	★★★★
Westerdam	Holland America Line	109.4	★★★★
CostaRiviera	Costa Cruises	108.7	★★★★
Polaris	Special Expeditions	108.5	★★★★
Maxim Gorki	Phoenix Seereisen	108.4	★★★★
Star Clipper	Star Clippers	108.4	★★★★
Star Flyer	Star Clippers	108.4	★★★★
Nieuw Amsterdam	Holland America Line	108.2	★★★★
Noordam	Holland America Line	108.2	★★★★
Song of America	Royal Caribbean Cruises	108.2	★★★★
Star/Ship Oceanic	Premier Cruise Lines	107.5	★★★★
Victoria	P&O Cruises	107.4	★★★★
Fuji Maru	Mitsui OSK Passenger Line	107.3	★★★★

Cruise Ship Directory and Ratings

SHIP	CRUISE LINE	RATING	STARS
Ecstasy	Carnival Cruise Lines	106.5	★★★★
Fantasy	Carnival Cruise Lines	106.5	★★★★
Stella Solaris	Sun Line Cruises	106.3	★★★★
Celebration	Carnival Cruise Lines	105.7	★★★★
Viking Serenade	Royal Caribbean Cruises	105.6	★★★★
Holiday	Carnival Cruise Lines	105.5	★★★★
Jubilee	Carnival Cruise Lines	105.2	★★★★
CostaAllegra	Costa Cruises	105.1	★★★★
Caledonian Star	Noble Caledonian	104.9	★★★+
CostaMarina	Costa Cruises	104.5	★★★+
EugenioCosta	Costa Cruises	104.5	★★★+
Tropicale	Carnival Cruise Lines	104.3	★★★+
Seawind Crown	Seawind Cruise Line	104.2	★★★+
Song of Norway	Royal Caribbean Cruises	103.8	★★★+
The Azur	Festival Cruises	103.8	★★★+
World Renaissance	Epirotiki Cruise Line	103.8	★★★+
Southern Cross	CTC Cruise Lines	103.3	★★★+
Yamal	Murmansk Shipping	103.2	★★★+
Black Prince	Fred Olsen Cruise Line	103.0	★★★+
Carousel	Airtours Cruises	102.9	★★★+
Vistamar	Mar Line Shipping	102.7	★★★+
Odessa	Black Sea Shipping	101.9	★★★+
Rhapsody	StarLauro Cruises	101.8	★★★+
Rotterdam	Holland America Line	101.8	★★★+
CostaPlaya	Costa Cruises	101.7	★★★+
Daphne	Costa Cruises	101.7	★★★+
Kazakhstan II	Delphin Seereisen	101.7	★★★+
Triton	Epirotiki Cruise Line	101.6	★★★+
Olympic	Epirotiki Cruise Line	101.3	★★★+
Cunard Countess	Cunard Crown Cruises	101.1	★★★+
Festivale	Carnival Cruise Lines	101.1	★★★+
Regent Sun	Regency Cruises	100.3	★★★+
Sun Viking	Royal Caribbean Cruises	100.8	★★★+
Ocean Majesty	Majestic International Cruises	99.9	★★★

SHIP	CRUISE LINE	RATING	STARS
Kapitan Dranitsyn	Murmansk Shipping	99.8	★★★
Kapitan Khlebnikov	Far East Shipping	99.8	★★★
Monterey	Starlauro Cruises	99.6	★★★
Baltica	Sunshine Cruise Line	99.5	★★★
Canberra	P&O Cruises	99.4	★★★
Orpheus	Epirotiki Cruise Line	99.4	★★★
Regent Isle	Regency Cruises	99.4	★★★
Bali Sea Dancer	P&O Spice Island Cruises	99.2	★★★
Albatros	Phoenix Seereisen	99.1	★★★
Stella Maris	Sun Line Cruises	98.9	★★★
Seawing	Airtours	98.9	★★★
Symphony	StarLauro Cruises	98.8	★★★
Bolero	Festival Cruise Line	98.2	★★★
Regent Calypso	Regency Cruises	98.0	★★★
Stella Oceanis	Sun Line Cruises	97.7	★★★
OceanBreeze	Dolphin Cruise Line	97.6	★★★
Explorer	Abercrombie & Kent	97.5	★★★
Don Juan	Royal Hispania Cruises	97.0	★★★
Royal Star	Star Line	97.0	★★★
Regent Sea	Regency Cruises	96.7	★★★
Sea Prince	Sunshine Cruise Line	96.6	★★★
Odysseus	Epirotiki Cruise Line	96.2	★★★
SeaBreeze I	Dolphin Cruise Line	95.9	★★★
Regent Rainbow	Regency Cruises	95.3	★★★
Constitution	American Hawaii Cruises	95.2	★★★
Independence	American Hawaii Cruises	95.2	★★★
Mermoz	Paquet Cruises	95.0	★★★
Regent Star	Regency Cruises	95.0	★★★
Dolphin IV	Dolphin Cruise Line	94.7	★★★
Regent Spirit	Regency Cruises	94.7	★★★
Amerikanis	Fantasy Cruises	94.5	★★★
Aegean Dolphin	Dolphin Hellas Shipping	94.1	★★★
Funchal	Arcalia Shipping	92.6	★★★
Yorktown Clipper	Clipper Cruise Line	92.8	★★★
Ausonia	Ausonia Cruises	92.5	★★★
Princesa Victoria	Louis Cruise Lines	92.5	★★★

SHIP	CRUISE LINE	RATING	STARS
Astra II	Neckermann Seereisen	91.7	★★★
Fairstar	P&O Holidays	91.5	★★★
Sea Venture	Royal Venture Cruise Line	91.5	★★★
Nantucket Clipper	Clipper Cruise Line	91.4	★★★
Princesa Marissa	Louis Cruise Lines	91.4	★★★
Taras Shevchenko	Primexpress Cruises	91.4	★★★
Enchanted Isle	New Commodore Cruise Line	91.0	★★★
Enchanted Seas	New Commodore Cruise Line	91.0	★★★
Leisure World	New Century Tours	90.3	★★★
Universe	World Explorer Cruises	90.3	★★★
Azerbaydzhan	CTC Cruise Lines	90.2	★★★
Royal Venture	Royal Venture Cruise Line	90.2	★★★
Kareliya	CTC Cruise Lines	90.1	★★★
La Palma	Intercruise	89.8	★★+
Shota Rustaveli	Black Sea Shipping	89.7	★★+
Regal Empress	Regal Cruises	89.5	★★+
Alla Tarasova	Murmansk Shipping	89.1	★★+
Ilich	Baltic Line	88.6	★★+
Andaman Princess	Cruise Lines International	88.2	★★+
Atalante	Paradise Cruises	87.6	★★+
Ivan Franko	Black Sea Shipping	87.0	★★+
Princesa Amorosa	Louis Cruise Lines	86.3	★★+
Dimitri Shostakovich	Black Sea Shipping	84.8	★★
Konstantin Simonov	Baltic Line	84.8	★★
Lev Tolstoi	Transocean Cruise Lines	84.8	★★
Mikhail Sholokhov	Far Eastern Shipping	84.8	★★
Astra	Caravella Shipping	84.7	★★
Princesa Cypria	Louis Cruise Lines	84.7	★★
Sir Francis Drake	Tall Ship Adventures	83.4	★★
Antonina Nezhdanova	Far East Shipping	83.0	★★
Fedor Shalyapin	Black Sea Shipping	82.8	★★
Orient Star	Pacific Cruise Company	82.3	★★
Vinland Star	Vinland Cruises	82.1	★★
Sapphire Seas	Discovery Cruises	81.9	★★

SHIP	CRUISE LINE	RATING	STARS
Leonid Sobinov	Black Sea Shipping	81.7	★★
Klaudia Yelanskaya	Murmansk shipping	79.2	★
Ayvasovskiy	Soviet Danube Shipping	78.1	★
Romantica	Ambassador Cruises	77.7	★
Queen Elini	Vergina Cruises	76.5	★

mv Aegean Dolphin ★★★

OPERATES

3- AND 4-DAY MEDITERRANEAN CRUISES

Cruise Line	Dolphin Hellas Shipping	Elevators	2
Former Names	Narcis/Alkyon	Casino Yes Slot Machines	Yes
Gross Tonnage	11,563	Swimming Pools (outside) 1 (inside)	0
Builder	Santierul N. Galatz (Romania)	Whirlpools 0 Gymnasium	Yes
Reconstruction:	Perama Shipyards (Greece)	Sauna/Steam Room Yes/No Massage	Yes
Original Cost	n/a	Self-Service Launderette	Yes
Christened By	Captain A. Angelopoulos	Movie Theater/Seats	Yes/176
Entered Service	1974/May 1988	Library Yes Children's Facilities	No
Interior Design	A&M Katzourakis	Watersports Facilities	None
Country of Registry	Greece (SWEO)	Classification Society	Lloyd's Register
Tel No 113-0627 Fax No	113-0627		
Length (ft/m)	460.9/140.50	**RATINGS**	**SCORE**
Beam (ft/m) 67.2/20.50 Draft (ft/m)	20.3/6.20	Ship: Condition/Cleanliness	6.6
Propulsion	diesel-mech (10,296kW)	Ship: Space/Flow/Comfort	6.7
Propellers	2 (CP)	Ship: Decor/Furnishings	6.9
Decks 8 Crew	190	Ship: Fitness Facilities	6.1
Pass. Capacity (basis 2) 576 (all berths)	670	Cabins: Comfort/Facilities	6.7
Pass. Space Ratio (basis 2) 20.0 (all berths)	17.2	Cabins: Software	7.0
Officers Greek Dining Staff	International	Food: Dining Room/Cuisine	6.1
Total Cabins	288	Food: Buffets/Informal Dining	5.8
Size Range (sq ft/m)	135-290/12.5-27.0	Food: Quality of Ingredients	5.6
Outside Cabins 202 Inside Cabins	86	Service: Dining Room	6.4
Single Cabins 0 Supplement	50%	Service: Bars	6.3
Balcony Cabins 0 Wheelchair Cabins	Yes	Service: Cabins	6.6
Cabin Current	220 AC	Cruise: Entertainment	5.6
Refrigerator	Yes	Cruise: Activities Program	5.7
Cabin TV Yes VCR	No	Cruise: Hospitality Standard	6.0
Dining Rooms 1 Sittings	2	OVERALL RATING	94.1

+ The public rooms are tastefully decorated in contemporary colors, but with much use of mirrored surfaces. There's a good showroom, laid out amphitheater-style. The Belvedere Lounge, set high atop ship and forward, features a smart piano bar and good views. The mostly outside cabins are reasonably spacious for ship size and have picture windows. Bathrobes provided. Dialysis station is a bonus. Service quite attentive.

— This ship always appears to be listing. Crowded open decks and limited sunning space when the ship is full. There's no library. Cabins do not have enough drawer or closet space for two. The cabin bathrooms themselves are small. Too many loud announcements, in several languages, are irritating.

Dining The dining room, set low down, is bright and cheerful, but rather cramped, and has mostly large tables (no tables for two). Features a mixed Continental cuisine, with limited choice, particularly of breads, cheeses and fruits.

Other Comments This ship's profile looks quite smart, following an extensive $26 million conversion/stretch in 1988, but is somewhat angular. This ship is for Europeans, and will cruise you in comfortable but densely populated surroundings, and at a fairly decent price, but don't expect much finesse.

ms Aida

OPERATES

VARIOUS CRUISES WORLDWIDE

Cruise Line	Deutsche Seetouristik		
Former Names	-		
Gross Tonnage	36,800		
Builder	Kvaerner Masa-Yards		
Original Cost	DM300 million		
Christened By	n/a		
Entered Service	July 7, 1996		
Interior Design	Partner Ship Design		
Country of Registry	Germany		
Tel No	n/a	Fax No	n/a
Length (ft/m)		633.2/193.0	
Beam (ft/m) 90.5/27.6	Draft (ft/m)	20.3/6.2	
Propulsion	diesel (21,720kw)		
Propellers		2 (CP)	
Decks	7	Crew	370
Pass. Capacity (basis 2) 1,186	(all berths) 1,230		
Pass. Space Ratio (basis 2) 32.5	(all berths) 29.9		
Officers German	Dining Staff	German	
Total Cabins	593		
Size Range (sq ft/m)	136.7-387.5/12.7-36.0		
Outside Cabins 391	Inside Cabins	202	
Single Cabins 0	Supplement	75%	
Balcony Cabins 4	Wheelchair Cabins	3	
Cabin Current	220 AC		
Refrigerator	No		
Cabin TV Yes	VCR	No	
Dining Rooms 1	Sittings	2	
Elevators	5		

Casino	No	Slot Machines	0
Swimming Pools (outside) 1		(inside)	0
Whirlpools	3	Gymnasium	Yes
Sauna/Steam Room Yes/Yes		Massage	Yes
Self-Service Launderette			Yes
Movie Theater/Seats			No
Library			Yes
Children's Facilities			Yes
Watersports Facilities			No
Classification Society		Germanischer Lloyd	

RATINGS	SCORE
Ship: Condition/Cleanliness	NYR
Ship: Space/Flow/Comfort	NYR
Ship: Decor/Furnishings	NYR
Ship: Fitness Facilities	NYR
Cabins: Comfort/Facilities	NYR
Cabins: Software	NYR
Food: Dining Room/Cuisine	NYR
Food: Buffets/Informal Dining	NYR
Food: Quality of Ingredients	NYR
Service: Dining Room	NYR
Service: Bars	NYR
Service: Cabins	NYR
Cruise: Entertainment	NYR
Cruise: Activities Program	NYR
Cruise: Hospitality Standard	NYR
OVERALL RATING	

+ She has a sleek, contemporary profile, and is well proportioned, with a swept-back funnel. There is an outdoor teakwood wrap-around promenade deck, good for strolling. Has an observation lounge set high atop the ship overlooking the bow, and a wide array of intimate public rooms and spaces. The accommodations consist of outside de luxe cabins, and "club class" cabins (mix of outside and inside standards, many with one bed and convertible daytime sofa bed). Four suites also have forward-facing private balconies and more luxurious furnishings and fittings.

— Cabins have somewhat limited drawer space, so you won't need many clothes.

Dining The dining room is very attractive, and has tables for four, six or eight. As on other Deutsche Seetouristik ships, the standard of food is quite good, with adequate presentation and decent service.

Other Comments This brand new ship, which looks externally very similar to the *Royal Majesty*, has diesel-mechanical propulsion and provides a replacement for the company's beloved *Arkona*, which has been on long-term charter to the company. Caters almost exclusively to German-speaking passengers. I expect this ship to operate a round-the-world cruise in 1997. A sister ship has is also on order, due for delivery in 1997.

ts Albatros ★★★

Cruise Line	Phoenix Seereisen	Casino Yes	Slot Machines Yes
Former Names Dawn Princess/FairWind/Sylvania		Swimming Pools (outside) 3	(inside) 0
Gross Tonnage	24,803	Whirlpools 0	Gymnasium Yes
Builder	John Brown & Co. (UK)	Sauna/Steam Room Yes/No	Massage Yes
Original Cost	n/a	Self-Service Launderette	No
Christened By	n/a	Movie Theater/Seats	No
Entered Service	Jun 5, 1957/Aug 18, 1993	Library	No
Interior Design	Barbara Dorn	Children's Facilities	No
Country of Registry	Bahamas (C6LV3)	Watersports Facilities	None
Tel No 130-6132 Fax No 130-6133		Classification Society	Lloyd's Register
Length (ft/m)	608.2/185.40		

RATINGS	SCORE
Ship: Condition/Cleanliness	6.3
Ship: Space/Flow/Comfort	6.1
Ship: Decor/Furnishings	6.6
Ship: Fitness Facilities	5.0
Cabins: Comfort/Facilities	6.4
Cabins: Software	6.7
Food: Dining Room/Cuisine	6.8
Food: Buffets/Informal Dining	6.6
Food: Quality of Ingredients	6.7
Service: Dining Room	6.8
Service: Bars	7.0
Service: Cabins	7.2
Cruise: Entertainment	7.3
Cruise: Activities Program	6.6
Cruise: Hospitality Standard	7.0
OVERALL RATING	99.1

Beam (ft/m) 80.3/24.49 Draft (ft/m) 29.3/8.94	
Propulsion	steam turbine (18,300kW)
Propellers	2 (FP)
Decks 11 Crew	330
Pass. Capacity (basis 2) 940 (all berths) 1,100	
Pass. Space Ratio (basis 2) 26.3 (all berths) 22.5	
Officers Italian Dining Staff International	
Total Cabins	470
Size Range (sq ft/m)	90-241/8.3-22.3
Outside Cabins 239 Inside Cabins	231
Single Cabins 0 Supplement	Set rates
Balcony Cabins 0 Wheelchair Cabins 0	
Cabin Current	110 AC
Refrigerator	Category A only
Cabin TV No VCR	No
Dining Rooms 2 Sittings	1
Elevators	3

+ This is a sturdily constructed ship, stable at sea, and is quite well maintained. A second swimming pool, fitted into a former cargo hold, is for children. There is plenty of dark wood paneling and trim, with solid brass accents used throughout. Has a good-sized library. Wide range of cabin sizes and configurations, all with heavy-duty furniture. Features excellent and extensive itineraries that provide much of interest to those seeking to cruise in an older style of ship in very casual surroundings. Young, willing Phoenix Seereisen staff.

— There's not much open deck and sunning space, especially when full. Public rooms are few, always crowded, and full of cigarette smoke.

Dining The two dining rooms are really quite charming, but the tables are close together. The menu is not very creative, and there is limited choice. Service is friendly and attentive, in true European style.

Other Comments This all-white ship was built in true vintage ocean liner style, and has a large centrally placed funnel. Furnishings consist of heavy, patterned fabrics that are very comfortable. This unpretentious ship does have an interesting old-world ambiance and charm that somehow help to make up for the lack of finesse associated with more upscale and expensive products. Principally for German-speaking passengers.

ms Alla Tarasova ★★+

OPERATES

ARCTIC AND ANTARCTIC CRUISES

Cruise Line	Murmansk Shipping Company		
Former Names			-
Gross Tonnage			3,941
Builder	Brodgradiliste Uljanik (Yugoslavia)		
Original Cost	n/a	Christened By	n/a
Entered Service			1976
Interior Design			n/a
Country of Registry			Russia (UHJG)
Tel No	n/a	Fax No	n/a
Length (ft/m)			328.1/100.01
Beam (ft/m) 53.2/16.24		Draft (ft/m)	15.2/4.65
Propulsion			diesel (3,884kW)
Propellers			1 (FP)
Decks	3	Crew	80
Pass. Capacity (basis 2) 100		(all berths) 100	
Pass. Space Ratio (basis 2) 39.4		(all berths) 39.4	
Officers	Russian	Dining Staff	East European
Total Cabins			50
Size Range (sq ft/m)			n/a
Outside Cabins	50	Inside Cabins	0
Single Cabins	0	Supplement	Set rates
Balcony Cabins	0	Wheelchair Cabins	0
Cabin Current			220 AC
Refrigerator			No
Cabin TV	No	VCR	No
Dining Rooms	1	Sittings	1
Elevators			0
Casino	No	Slot Machines	No

Swimming Pools (outside)			No
(inside)			No
Whirlpools	No	Gymnasium	No
Sauna/Steam Room No/No		Massage	No
Self-Service Launderette			No
Movie Theater/Seats			No
Library			Yes
Children's Facilities			No
Watersports Facilities			No
Classification Society			RS

RATINGS	SCORE
Ship: Condition/Cleanliness	7.9
Ship: Space/Flow/Comfort	5.5
Ship: Decor/Furnishings	6.8
Ship: Fitness Facilities	3.0
Cabins: Comfort/Facilities	5.8
Cabins: Software	6.2
Food: Dining Room/Cuisine	6.5
Food: Buffets/Informal Dining	5.9
Food: Quality of Ingredients	6.0
Service: Dining Room	6.4
Service: Bars	6.5
Service: Cabins	6.8
Cruise: Entertainment	4.2
Cruise: Activities Program	4.7
Cruise: Hospitality Standard	6.9
OVERALL RATING	89.1

+ This ship has an ice-strengthened hull. Nicely refurbished in 1992, this little ship now specializes in close-in destination cruising. Tidy, neat and clean throughout, with fairly attractive, though rather plain, decor that is comfortable. All cabins are outside and have lower beds, with private bathroom, shower and toilet. Many cabins can be used by single cruisegoers. Two larger cabins (called suites, which they are not) are quite well equipped. The dress code is very informal. Has a small number of Zodiac rubber landing craft for shore exploring and tendering.

— Has very limited public spaces. Cabins have tiny bathrooms (of the "me first, you next" variety). Poor library needs better selection of books. There's no forward observation lounge.

Dining Pleasant, though somewhat dark dining room seats everyone at one sitting. Catering is often done by a European company. There are limited menu choices, but the food is quite wholesome, although fresh produce is rarely used. Limited selection of breads, cheeses and fruits.

Other Comments Named after a famous Russian actress, this ship is not as glamorous as the new ships, but she is very cozy and caters to travelers rather than cruisegoers.

mv Americana ★★★★

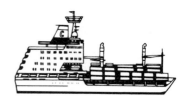

OPERATES

51-52-DAY SOUTH AMERICA CRUISES

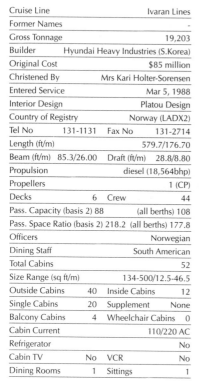

Cruise Line	Ivaran Lines	Elevators	2
Former Names	-	Casino Yes	Slot Machines Yes
Gross Tonnage	19,203	Swimming Pools (outside) 1	(inside) 0
Builder	Hyundai Heavy Industries (S.Korea)	Whirlpools 1	Gymnasium Yes
Original Cost	$85 million	Sauna/Steam Room Yes/No	Massage Yes
Christened By	Mrs Kari Holter-Sorensen	Self-Service Launderette	Yes
Entered Service	Mar 5, 1988	Movie Theater/Seats	No
Interior Design	Platou Design	Library Yes	Children's Facilities No
Country of Registry	Norway (LADX2)	Watersports Facilities	None
Tel No 131-1131 Fax No 131-2714		Classification Society	Det Norske Veritas

Length (ft/m)	579.7/176.70
Beam (ft/m) 85.3/26.00 Draft (ft/m) 28.8/8.80	
Propulsion	diesel (18,564bhp)
Propellers	1 (CP)
Decks 6 Crew	44
Pass. Capacity (basis 2) 88	(all berths) 108
Pass. Space Ratio (basis 2) 218.2 (all berths) 177.8	
Officers	Norwegian
Dining Staff	South American
Total Cabins	52
Size Range (sq ft/m)	134-500/12.5-46.5
Outside Cabins 40 Inside Cabins	12
Single Cabins 20 Supplement	None
Balcony Cabins 4 Wheelchair Cabins	0
Cabin Current	110/220 AC
Refrigerator	No
Cabin TV No VCR	No
Dining Rooms 1 Sittings	1

RATINGS	SCORE
Ship: Condition/Cleanliness	8.6
Ship: Space/Flow/Comfort	7.4
Ship: Decor/Furnishings	8.1
Ship: Fitness Facilities	7.3
Cabins: Comfort/Facilities	8.0
Cabins: Software	8.1
Food: Dining Room/Cuisine	7.8
Food: Buffets/Informal Dining	7.2
Food: Quality of Ingredients	7.7
Service: Dining Room	7.8
Service: Bars	7.6
Service: Cabins	7.4
Cruise: Entertainment	6.0
Cruise: Activities Program	6.2
Cruise: Hospitality Standard	7.7
OVERALL RATING	112.9

+ The incredible space ratio is because this is a well-designed freighter-cruise ship with excellent passenger facilities placed astern of a 1,120-capacity container section. Elegant and beautifully finished interior. Plenty of live tropical plants, soft leather chairs and space are appreciated. Has a neat double-spiral staircase. Two owners' suites are lavish, with separate bedroom and living room, and big picture windows. Other cabins are lovely, well equipped, with restful decor and excellent soft furnishings. Several single cabins. Generous sheltered and open sunning space. Well-stocked library. Gentlemen "hosts" carried on all voyages.

— No wrap-around promenade deck, no room service (except on doctor's orders), and no cushioned pads for outdoor deck lounge chairs. Has a steep gangway in ports of call.

Dining Elegant dining room has beautiful table settings and china, and overlooks the sea. Cuisine, while not elaborate, is appealing, well prepared, and features Norwegian and Continental fare. Breakfast and lunch are buffet-style.

Other Comments A minimum of 50 passengers assures priority berths in ports. For the older passenger with time to spare, who enjoys privacy and quiet, as well as the chance to explore places alone. This is the ultimate in contemporary freighter-cruise travel, with a fine itinerary. Passengers are mostly experienced cruisegoers of age 60 and up. Port taxes are included.

ss Amerikanis ★★★

OPERATES
7-DAY EUROPE CRUISES

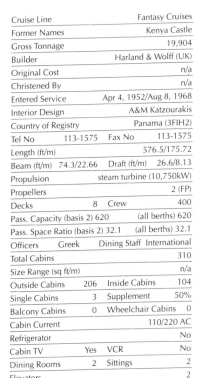

Cruise Line	Fantasy Cruises		
Former Names	Kenya Castle		
Gross Tonnage	19,904		
Builder	Harland & Wolff (UK)		
Original Cost	n/a		
Christened By	n/a		
Entered Service	Apr 4, 1952/Aug 8, 1968		
Interior Design	A&M Katzourakis		
Country of Registry	Panama (3FIH2)		
Tel No	113-1575	Fax No	113-1575
Length (ft/m)			576.5/175.72
Beam (ft/m) 74.3/22.66		Draft (ft/m)	26.6/8.13
Propulsion		steam turbine (10,750kW)	
Propellers			2 (FP)
Decks	8	Crew	400
Pass. Capacity (basis 2) 620		(all berths) 620	
Pass. Space Ratio (basis 2) 32.1		(all berths) 32.1	
Officers Greek		Dining Staff International	
Total Cabins			310
Size Range (sq ft/m)			n/a
Outside Cabins	206	Inside Cabins	104
Single Cabins	3	Supplement	50%
Balcony Cabins	0	Wheelchair Cabins	0
Cabin Current			110/220 AC
Refrigerator			No
Cabin TV	Yes	VCR	No
Dining Rooms	2	Sittings	2
Elevators			2

Casino	Yes	Slot Machines	Yes
Swimming Pools (outside) 2		(inside)	0
Whirlpools	0	Gymnasium	Yes
Sauna/Steam Room Yes/No		Massage	Yes
Self-Service Launderette			No
Movie Theater/Seats			Yes/115
Library			Yes
Children's Facilities			Yes
Watersports Facilities			None
Classification Society			Lloyd's Register

RATINGS	SCORE
Ship: Condition/Cleanliness	6.1
Ship: Space/Flow/Comfort	6.0
Ship: Decor/Furnishings	6.7
Ship: Fitness Facilities	4.7
Cabins: Comfort/Facilities	6.8
Cabins: Software	7.6
Food: Dining Room/Cuisine	6.5
Food: Buffets/Informal Dining	5.8
Food: Quality of Ingredients	5.5
Service: Dining Room	6.6
Service: Bars	6.2
Service: Cabins	6.7
Cruise: Entertainment	6.6
Cruise: Activities Program	6.3
Cruise: Hospitality Standard	6.4
OVERALL RATING	94.5

+ Provides inexpensive, good value-for-money cruises at a very realistic price. Has a wide range of cabin sizes and styles. Some cabins have excellent closet and drawer space, heavy-duty fittings and good soundproofing. Interesting artwork throughout. Well-planned destination-intensive itineraries. Good if you like older ships, with their wood and brass interiors and basic features.

— Often there are long embarkation and disembarkation lines, as well as for buffets. Dated fixtures, and slow, tired elevators. The service is almost friendly, quite basic and lacks finesse.

Dining A cramped dining room, with tables very close together (although there are tables for two) means it is difficult for waiters to provide decent service, but most passengers seem quite satisfied. The food is of a reasonable quality and presentation, but better quality ingredients would improve the dining experience. Poor selection of breads and fruits.

Other Comments This older ship with classic fifties liner styling and a long history of service to several passenger lines has been extremely well maintained. Her interior decor is now much lighter after a recent make-over, although the ship is, remember, over 40 years old, and it's time she was retired.

mv Andaman Princess ★★+

OPERATES

7-DAY ANDAMAN SEA/GULF OF THAILAND CRUISES

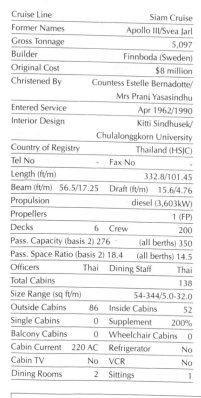

Cruise Line	Siam Cruise
Former Names	Apollo III/Svea Jarl
Gross Tonnage	5,097
Builder	Finnboda (Sweden)
Original Cost	$8 million
Christened By	Countess Estelle Bernadotte/ Mrs Prani Yasasindhu
Entered Service	Apr 1962/1990
Interior Design	Kitti Sindhusek/ Chulalonggkorn University
Country of Registry	Thailand (HSJC)
Tel No	- Fax No -
Length (ft/m)	332.8/101.45
Beam (ft/m) 56.5/17.25	Draft (ft/m) 15.6/4.76
Propulsion	diesel (3,603kW)
Propellers	1 (FP)
Decks 6	Crew 200
Pass. Capacity (basis 2) 276	(all berths) 350
Pass. Space Ratio (basis 2) 18.4	(all berths) 14.5
Officers Thai	Dining Staff Thai
Total Cabins	138
Size Range (sq ft/m)	54-344/5.0-32.0
Outside Cabins 86	Inside Cabins 52
Single Cabins 0	Supplement 200%
Balcony Cabins 0	Wheelchair Cabins 0
Cabin Current 220 AC	Refrigerator No
Cabin TV No	VCR No
Dining Rooms 2	Sittings 1

Elevators			2
Casino	Yes	Slot Machines	Yes
Swimming Pools (outside) 0		(inside)	0
Whirlpools 1 (large, indoor)		Gymnasium	Yes
Sauna/Steam Room Yes/No		Massage	Yes
Self-Service Launderette			No
Movie Theater/Seats			No
Library	No	Children's Facilities	Yes
Watersports Facilities			None
Classification Society			Lloyd's Register

RATINGS	SCORE
Ship: Condition/Cleanliness	5.6
Ship: Space/Flow/Comfort	5.8
Ship: Decor/Furnishings	6.0
Ship: Fitness Facilities	3.7
Cabins: Comfort/Facilities	6.0
Cabins: Software	6.1
Food: Dining Room/Cuisine	6.1
Food: Buffets/Informal Dining	5.8
Food: Quality of Ingredients	6.0
Service: Dining Room	6.6
Service: Bars	6.3
Service: Cabins	6.4
Cruise: Entertainment	5.4
Cruise: Activities Program	5.6
Cruise: Hospitality Standard	6.8
OVERALL RATING	88.2

+ Her original steam engines were exchanged for diesel propulsion in 1981. Lovely brass staircase. Lots of original wood paneling throughout. Snorkels and masks provided free, while underwater cameras can be rented. Has a Fuji express photo lab for instant service. Good children's learning center teaches three alphabets. Except for 12 suites, most of which have lifeboat views, most cabins are small, cleanly appointed, and quite comfortable. All have been refurbished. Closet and storage space is limited.

— There's no outdoor deck space at all, but then Asian passengers seldom like sunbathing. Passageways are narrow and cramped.

Dining The two dining rooms are quite charming and have acres of lovely original wood paneling. The food is typically good quality Thai and Chinese, with attentive service from a very willing staff. There is also a 24-hour coffee shop for casual snacks.

Other Comments Charming ex-Swedish night ferry with aft-placed funnel has seen many internal changes. An extensive refurbishment has equipped the ship for specialized cruising. This is the first attempt at operating a full-service cruise ship by Thai owners for Asian passengers, but it is not the luxury experience it claims to be yet. It is, however, an excellent way to experience cruising in Thai waters at modest rates.

ms Antonina Nezhdanova ★★

OPERATES
VARIOUS CRUISES

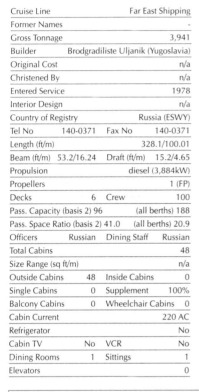

Cruise Line	Far East Shipping	Casino	No	Slot Machines	No
Former Names	-	Swimming Pools (outside)	1	(inside)	No
Gross Tonnage	3,941	Whirlpools	No	Gymnasium	No
Builder	Brodgradiliste Uljanik (Yugoslavia)	Sauna/Steam Room	Yes/No	Massage	No
Original Cost	n/a	Self-Service Launderette			No
Christened By	n/a	Movie Theater/Seats			Yes/75
Entered Service	1978	Library			Yes
Interior Design	n/a	Children's Facilities			No
Country of Registry	Russia (ESWY)	Watersports Facilities			None
Tel No 140-0371 Fax No 140-0371		Classification Society			RS
Length (ft/m)	328.1/100.01				
Beam (ft/m) 53.2/16.24 Draft (ft/m) 15.2/4.65		**RATINGS**			**SCORE**
Propulsion	diesel (3,884kW)	Ship: Condition/Cleanliness			5.3
Propellers	1 (FP)	Ship: Space/Flow/Comfort			5.5
Decks 6 Crew 100		Ship: Decor/Furnishings			6.1
Pass. Capacity (basis 2) 96 (all berths) 188		Ship: Fitness Facilities			3.0
Pass. Space Ratio (basis 2) 41.0 (all berths) 20.9		Cabins: Comfort/Facilities			5.7
Officers Russian Dining Staff Russian		Cabins: Software			6.0
Total Cabins 48		Food: Dining Room/Cuisine			6.0
Size Range (sq ft/m) n/a		Food: Buffets/Informal Dining			5.4
Outside Cabins 48 Inside Cabins 0		Food: Quality of Ingredients			6.0
Single Cabins 0 Supplement 100%		Service: Dining Room			6.2
Balcony Cabins 0 Wheelchair Cabins 0		Service: Bars			6.4
Cabin Current 220 AC		Service: Cabins			6.5
Refrigerator No		Cruise: Entertainment			4.2
Cabin TV No VCR No		Cruise: Activities Program			4.6
Dining Rooms 1 Sittings 1		Cruise: Hospitality Standard			6.1
Elevators 0		OVERALL RATING			83.0

+ Intimate, small ship with well-balanced profile is one of a series of eight identical sisters. Some have now been sold while others are sometimes chartered to European operators. Has an ice-hardened hull suitable for some "soft" expedition cruising. Good open deck space for the size of the vessel. Has an outdoor observation deck plus an enclosed promenade deck for inclement weather. Charming forward music lounge has wooden dance floor. Rich, highly polished wood paneling throughout. Lovely winding brass-railed main staircase. Cabins are compact and spartan, but most can accommodate four persons, and stewardess service is basically sound.

— There's no indoor observation lounge. Poor lecture room with non-existent ventilation. Poor accounting system (no cashless cruising). Announcements are too loud and rather military in style. This is simply too small a ship for much open water cruising.

Dining The dining room is dark and unappealing, even though it has portholes. The food is an eclectic mixture, and certainly not memorable, with its heavy sauces and salt in everything. Very limited menu choice. Poor selection of cheeses and fruits. Willing waitress service.

Other Comments This ship is small, yet comfortable, and has plenty of character. Often chartered to Western operators for "soft" expedition-style cruises.

ms Arkona ★★★★

OPERATES
EUROPE CRUISES

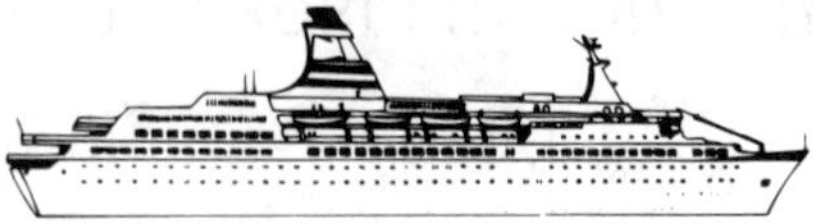

Cruise Line	Deutsche Seetouristik		
Former Names	Astor (I)		
Gross Tonnage	18,591		
Builder	Howaldtswerke Deutsche Werft (Germany)		
Original Cost	$55 million		
Christened By	Ms Lisa Weithuchter		
Entered Service	Dec 23, 1981/Oct 15, 1985		
Interior Design	Hans Sabert		
Country of Registry	Germany (Y5CC)		
Tel No	112-1511	Fax No	112-1512
Length (ft/m)	539.2/164.35		
Beam (ft/m)	74.1/22.60	Draft (ft/m)	20.0/6.11
Propulsion/Propellers	diesel (9,700kW)/2 (CP)		
Decks	8	Crew	243
Pass. Capacity (basis 2)	516	(all berths)	618
Pass. Space Ratio (basis 2)	36.0	(all berths)	30.1
Officers	German	Dining Staff	East European
Total Cabins	258		
Size Range (sq ft/m)	n/a		
Outside Cabins	176	Inside Cabins	82
Single Cabins	0	Supplement	40-75%
Balcony Cabins	0	Wheelchair Cabins	0
Cabin Current	220 AC		
Refrigerator	No (suites have minibar)		
Cabin TV	Yes	VCR	No
Dining Rooms	1	Sittings	2
Elevators	3		

Casino	No	Slot Machines	No
Swimming Pools (outside)	1	(inside)	1
Whirlpools	0	Gymnasium	Yes
Sauna/Steam Room	Yes/No	Massage	Yes
Self-Service Launderette	No		
Movie Theater/Seats	Yes/80		
Library	Yes		
Children's Facilities	No		
Watersports Facilities	None		
Classification Society	Germanischer Lloyd		

RATINGS	**SCORE**
Ship: Condition/Cleanliness	8.1
Ship: Space/Flow/Comfort	8.0
Ship: Decor/Furnishings	7.9
Ship: Fitness Facilities	6.7
Cabins: Comfort/Facilities	7.8
Cabins: Software	7.8
Food: Dining Room/Cuisine	7.7
Food: Buffets/Informal Dining	7.6
Food: Quality of Ingredients	7.7
Service: Dining Room	6.8
Service: Bars	6.7
Service: Cabins	6.8
Cruise: Entertainment	6.6
Cruise: Activities Program	6.5
Cruise: Hospitality Standard	7.3
OVERALL RATING	110.0

+ Well-constructed ship has a handsome profile. Good open deck and sunning space, with gorgeous teakwood decking and rails. Beautifully appointed interior fittings and decor, with much rosewood paneling and trim. Subdued lighting and soothing ambiance, highlighted by fine artwork throughout. Has good meetings facilities, a fine library, and, more important, an excellent pub with draught German beer. Excellent indoor spa and fitness center. Boat Deck suite rooms are simply lovely. Other cabins are well equipped and decorated. Bathrooms are compact but fully tiled, with good toiletry cabinet. Good traditional European hotel service.

– No wrap-around promenade deck. Atmosphere a little starchy. Many smokers.

Dining The Arkona Restaurant, located high in the ship, has big picture windows and is quite elegant, with dark wood paneling and restful decor. The food is adequate to very good, though choice is somewhat limited. The occasional formal candlelight dinners are romantic. Limited cabin service menu.

Other Comments This ship cruises under long-term charter to German operators, and features good value-for-money cruising in contemporary comfort with German-speaking passengers who appreciate quality, fine surroundings, good food, and excellent destination-intensive itineraries. Port taxes are included.

ms Astra ★★

OPERATES

VARIOUS MEDITERRANEAN CRUISES

Cruise Line	Caravella Shipping		
Former Names	Istra		
Gross Tonnage	5,635		
Builder	Brodgradiliste (Yugoslavia)		
Original Cost	n/a		
Christened By	n/a		
Entered Service	1965/May 22, 1993		
Interior Design	n/a		
Country of Registry	Russia (UIZK)		
Tel No	140-3475	Fax No	140-3475
Length (ft/m)	383.8/116.8m		
Beam (ft/m) 54.1/16.5m	Draft (ft/m)	18.3/5.6m	
Propulsion	diesel (11,030kW)		
Propellers	2 (FP)		
Decks	5	Crew	120
Pass. Capacity (basis 2) 282	(all berths) 282		
Pass. Space Ratio (basis 2) 19.9	(all berths) 19.9		
Officers Russian	Dining Staff Russian/German		
Total Cabins	141		
Size Range (sq ft/m)	n/a		
Outside Cabins	83	Inside Cabins	58
Single Cabins	0	Supplement	Set rates
Balcony Cabins	0	Wheelchair Cabins	0
Cabin Current	220 AC		
Refrigerator	No		
Cabin TV	No	VCR	No
Dining Rooms	1	Sittings	1
Elevators	0		

Casino	No	Slot Machines	No
Swimming Pools (outside) 1	(inside)		0
Whirlpools	0	Gymnasium	No
Sauna/Steam Room No/No	Massage		No
Self-Service Launderette			No
Movie Theater/Seats			No
Library			Yes
Children's Facilities			No
Watersports Facilities			None
Classification Society		Russian Survey	

RATINGS	SCORE
Ship: Condition/Cleanliness	5.6
Ship: Space/Flow/Comfort	5.0
Ship: Decor/Furnishings	6.0
Ship: Fitness Facilities	4.0
Cabins: Comfort/Facilities	5.1
Cabins: Software	5.4
Food: Dining Room/Cuisine	6.2
Food: Buffets/Informal Dining	5.7
Food: Quality of Ingredients	5.7
Service: Dining Room	6.3
Service: Bars	6.4
Service: Cabins	6.5
Cruise: Entertainment	5.0
Cruise: Activities Program	5.8
Cruise: Hospitality Standard	6.0
OVERALL RATING	84.7

+ This small ship is quite attractive, and is particularly good for "nooks and crannies" ports of call. Has an enclosed teak promenade deck. Interior decor is attractive in general. Features interesting itineraries. A two-deck-high Lido Bar is attractive. Very casual dress code and unpretentious relaxed ambiance. The service staff are very friendly and most attentive.

— Few public rooms, and little open deck space. Maintenance and cleanliness need a lot more attention. Teakwood decking is in poor condition. Upper berths in cabins do not have sufficient grab ("anti-fall-out") protection. Public rooms are always busy and it's hard to get away from the cigarette smokers. The crew tend to put themselves first, passengers second.

Dining Although the dining room is quite warm and attractive, and features decent place settings, there are no tables for two, and tables are close together. The food itself is limited in choice and variety. The selection of vegetables, fresh fruits and breads could be better. Ukrainian waitresses are quite charming, but, although friendly and attentive, there's no finesse.

Other Comments This small ship has a typical low-built early sixties profile. At present the ship is cruising for the German and Russian markets, with passengers cruising on a price-sensitive budget.

ms Astra II ★★★

OPERATES

BALTIC AND
MEDITERRANEAN CRUISES

Cruise Line		Caravella Shipping/
		Neckermann Seerederei
Former Names		Golden Odyssey
Gross Tonnage		10,563
Builder		Helsingor Skibsvog (Denmark)
Original Cost		$22 million
Christened By		-
Entered Service		Sept 5, 1974/Oct 1995
Interior Design		John Terzoglou
Country of Registry		Bahamas (SXTD)
Tel No	110-4672	Fax No 110-3461
Length (ft/m)		426.8/130.10
Beam (ft/m)	62.9/19.20	Draft (ft/m) 17.0/5.20
Propulsion		diesel (11,033kW)
Propellers		2 (CP)
Decks	7	Crew 215
Pass. Capacity (basis 2) 460		(all berths) 489
Pass. Space Ratio (basis 2) 22.9		(all berths) 21.6
Officers	East European	Dining Staff Ukrainian
Total Cabins		227
Size (sq ft./m.):		121-262 sq ft.
Outside Cabins	181	Inside Cabins 46
Single Cabins		0
Single Supplement		100%
Balcony Cabins	0	Wheelchair Cabins 0
Cabin Current	110 AC	Refrigerator No
Cabin TV	No	VCR No
Dining Rooms	1	Sittings 1

Elevators			2
Casino	No	Slot Machines	No
Swimming Pools (outside) 1		(inside)	0
Whirlpools	0	Gymnasium	Yes
Sauna/Steam Room	Yes/No	Massage	Yes
Self-Service Launderette			No
Movie Theater/Seats			Yes/154
Library			Yes
Children's Facilities/Playroom:			No
Classification Society			Lloyd's Register

RATINGS	SCORE
Ship: Condition/Cleanliness	6.3
Ship: Space/Flow/Comfort	6.1
Ship: Decor/Furnishings	6.0
Ship: Fitness Facilities	4.0
Cabins: Comfort/Facilities	6.1
Cabins: Software	6.5
Food: Dining Room/Cuisine	6.2
Food: Buffets/Informal Dining	5.8
Food: Quality of Ingredients	5.6
Service: Dining Room	6.7
Service: Bars	6.8
Service: Cabins	7.1
Cruise: Entertainment	6.2
Cruise: Activities Program	5.7
Cruise: Hospitality Standard	6.6
OVERALL RATING	91.7

+ Sleek-looking small ship has a well-balanced, compact, almost contemporary profile. Well maintained, although now 20 years old. Elegant, intimate ship with a loyal following, for good reason. The ship is very clean and tidy throughout. Outdoor promenade deck. Good selection of public rooms for ship size. Cabins, although not large, are tastefully furnished and decorated, with a fair amount of closet and drawer space, and pleasant artwork. Attentive staff offer fine-tuned personal service that is personable without being condescending.

— The cabins are small, as are the bathrooms, and towels also are small. Has a steep, narrow gangway in many ports. The plumbing is tired and troublesome at times.

Dining Very comfortable dining room, with good quality Continental food that is well presented. The menu choice is good, and the food is geared specifically to German tastes.

Other Comments This ship, now owned by Caravella Shipping, offers comfortable surroundings, at a moderate price, to a well-chosen palette of destinations. Ideally suited to passengers who want a small ship atmosphere and who don't like big ships. Under charter to Neckermann Seereisen for 225 days each year until the year 2002.

ms Astor ★★★★+

OPERATES

VARIOUS CRUISES WORLDWIDE

Cruise Line	AquaMarin Cruises	Casino	No	Slot Machines	No
Former Names	Fedor Dostoyevsky/Astor (II)	Swimming Pools (outside)	1	(inside)	1
Gross Tonnage	20,158	Whirlpools	0	Gymnasium	Yes
Builder Howaldtswerke Deutsche Werft (Germany)		Sauna/Steam Room	Yes/No	Massage	Yes
Original Cost	$65 million	Self-Service Launderette			Yes
Christened By	Frau Inta Gleich	Movie Theater/Seats			No
Entered Service	Feb 2, 1987/Nov 1995	Library			Yes
Interior Design	Hans Sabert	Children's Facilities			Yes
Country of Registry	Bahamas (C6JR3)	Watersports Facilities			None
Tel No 140-2771/140-2772 Fax No 140-0125		Classification Society			RS

Length (ft/m)	579.0/176.50
Beam (ft/m) 74.1/22.61 Draft (ft/m) 20.0/6.10	

RATINGS	SCORE
Propulsion diesel (15,400kW)	Ship: Condition/Cleanliness	8.0
Propellers 2 (CP)	Ship: Space/Flow/Comfort	8.2
Decks 7 Crew 295	Ship: Decor/Furnishings	8.2
Pass. Capacity (basis 2) 590 (all berths) 650	Ship: Fitness Facilities	7.5
Pass. Space Ratio (basis 2) 34.1 (all berths) 31.0	Cabins: Comfort/Facilities	8.0
Officers Russian	Cabins: Software	8.1
Dining Staff European	Food: Dining Room/Cuisine	7.7
Total Cabins 295	Food: Buffets/Informal Dining	7.5
Size Range (sq ft/m) n/a	Food: Quality of Ingredients	7.4
Outside Cabins 199 Inside Cabins 96	Service: Dining Room	7.7
Single Cabins 0 Supplement Set rates	Service: Bars	7.7
Balcony Cabins 0 Wheelchair Cabins 0	Service: Cabins	7.9
Cabin Current 220 AC Refrigerator Yes	Cruise: Entertainment	7.7
Cabin TV Yes VCR No	Cruise: Activities Program	7.6
Dining Rooms 1 Sittings 2	Cruise: Hospitality Standard	8.7
Elevators 3	OVERALL RATING	117.9

+ Very attractive ship with raked, squarish funnel. Finest ship in the Russian/Ukrainian-owned fleet. Built in the best German tradition. Almost everything is absolutely top quality. Fine teakwood decking and rails and polished wood everywhere. Excellent worldwide itineraries. Basketball court. Supremely comfortable and varied public rooms and conference facilities. Wood-paneled tavern with German beer on draught is a fine retreat. Fine mix of traditional and contemporary styling. Well-designed interior fitness center and pool. Dark-wood-accented cabins are superbly equipped and tastefully decorated in fresh pastel colors. There is plenty of closet and drawer space. Good bathrooms, with toiletries cabinet.

— Deck service could be better. Poor cabin service menu.

Dining Exquisite dining room is one of the nicest afloat. Service is friendly, although food quality needs more attention, with presentation and choice below the standard of the rest of the product. Buffets are limited.

Other Comments Nice continental atmosphere. Has mostly German-speaking passengers. This ship provides style, comfort, and elegance, and a fine leisurely cruise experience. Port taxes, insurance, and gratuities are included.

ms Asuka ★★★★★

OPERATES

ASIA/CIRCLE JAPAN/
SOUTH PACIFIC CRUISES

Cruise Line	NYK Cruises	Elevators		5
Former Names	-	Casino	Yes	Slot Machines Yes
Gross Tonnage	28,717	Swimming Pools (outside) 1	(inside)	0
Builder	Mitsubishi Heavy Industries (Japan)	Whirlpools	3	Gymnasium Yes
Original Cost	$86 million	Sauna/Steam Room Yes/Yes	Massage	Yes
Christened By	Mr Jiro Nemoto	Self-Service Launderette		Yes
Entered Service	Dec 1991	Movie Theater/Seats		Yes/97
Interior Design	Kenmochi Design/Robert Tillberg	Library	Yes	Children's Facilities No
Country of Registry	Japan (JPBG)	Watersports Facilities		None
Tel No 120-4654/-4660 Fax No 120-4662		Classification Society	Nippon Kaiji Kyokai	
Length (ft/m)	632.5/192.81			

Beam (ft/m) 81.0/24.70 Draft (ft/m) 20.3/6.20	
Propulsion/Propellers diesel (17,300kW)/2 (CP)	
Decks 8 Crew 243	
Pass. Capacity (basis 2) 584 (all berths) 604	
Pass. Space Ratio (basis 2) 49.1 (all berths) 47.5	
Officers Japanese	
Dining Staff Japanese/Filipino	
Total Cabins 292	
Size Range (sq ft/m) 182-650/17.0-60.3	
Outside Cabins 292 Inside Cabins 0	
Single Cabins 0 Supplement 100%	
Balcony Cabins 100 (all have binoculars)	
Wheelchair Cabins 2	
Cabin Current 110 AC Refrigerator All cabins	
Cabin TV Yes VCR No	
Dining Rooms 1 (+ sushi restaurant)	
Sittings 2	

RATINGS	SCORE
Ship: Condition/Cleanliness	9.1
Ship: Space/Flow/Comfort	8.3
Ship: Decor/Furnishings	8.8
Ship: Fitness Facilities	8.6
Cabins: Comfort/Facilities	8.7
Cabins: Software	8.6
Food: Dining Room/Cuisine	8.8
Food: Buffets/Informal Dining	8.1
Food: Quality of Ingredients	8.7
Service: Dining Room	8.7
Service: Bars	8.6
Service: Cabins	8.4
Cruise: Entertainment	8.6
Cruise: Activities Program	7.4
Cruise: Hospitality Standard	9.3
OVERALL RATING	128.7

+ Handsome exterior styling, with good open deck space. Good meetings facilities with high-tech equipment. Wrap-around outdoor promenade deck. Excellent and spacious true Japanese grand bath. Many intimate public rooms. Elegant interior decor and pleasing colors. Superb "club" suites. Excellent insulation between cabins. Good closet and drawer space. Tea-making units and bathtubs in all cabins. Traditional "Watushi" tatami room. Features sushi-making classes. Cellular pay telephones. Good entertainment.

— "Cake-layer" stacking of public rooms hampers passenger flow. Standard cabin bathrooms are rather small. No butler service in the "club" suites. Balcony door handles are awkward in the suites. Massage room is located away from the grand bath area and should be integrated.

Dining The dining room has good space around tables, but there are not enough tables for two. Japanese and Western food. Features traditional Japanese breakfast and luncheon, and Western-style dinners. Excellent Hotel Okura chain menus and food. Chinaware is Wedgwood. The sushi bar features fresh seafood, beautifully presented. Traditional Washitsu tatami room for tea ceremonies.

Other Comments This is the first all-new large ship specially designed for the Japanese cruise market. Children under 10 not allowed. Gratuities are neither expected, nor permitted.

ms Atalante ★★+

OPERATES

*3- AND 4-DAY EGYPT/
ISRAEL CRUISES*

Cruise Line	Paradise Cruises
Former Names	Tahitien
Gross Tonnage	13,113
Builder	Arsenal de la Marine Nationale
	Française (France)
Original Cost	n/a
Christened By	n/a
Entered Service	May 4, 1953/Dec 18, 1992
Interior Design	n/a
Country of Registry	Cyprus (P3XW4)
Tel No 357-9-545600	Fax No 357-9-370298
Length (ft/m)	548.5/167.20
Beam (ft/m) 67.9/20.70	Draft (ft/m) 25.5/7.80
Propulsion	diesel (7,700kW)
Propellers	2 (FP)
Decks 5	Crew 160
Pass. Capacity (basis 2) 484	(all berths) 635
Pass. Space Ratio (basis 2) 27.0	(all berths) 20.6
Officers Greek	Dining Staff International
Total Cabins	242
Size Range (sq ft/m)	n/a
Outside Cabins 188	Inside Cabins 54
Single Cabins 2	Supplement 50%
Balcony Cabins 0	Wheelchair Cabins 18
Cabin Current	220 AC/200 DC
Refrigerator	Top grade cabins only
Cabin TV Yes	VCR No
Dining Rooms 1	Sittings 2

Elevators			0
Casino	Yes	Slot Machines	Yes
Swimming Pools (outside) 2		(inside)	0
Whirlpools	0	Gymnasium	No
Sauna/Steam Room No/No		Massage	No
Self-Service Launderette			No
Movie Theater/Seats	No	Library	No
Children's Facilities			No
Watersports Facilities			None
Classification Society			Bureau Veritas

RATINGS	SCORE
Ship: Condition/Cleanliness	6.2
Ship: Space/Flow/Comfort	6.3
Ship: Decor/Furnishings	6.3
Ship: Fitness Facilities	4.4
Cabins: Comfort/Facilities	6.4
Cabins: Software	6.5
Food: Dining Room/Cuisine	5.8
Food: Buffets/Informal Dining	5.6
Food: Quality of Ingredients	5.4
Service: Dining Room	6.1
Service: Bars	6.1
Service: Cabins	6.3
Cruise: Entertainment	5.0
Cruise: Activities Program	5.2
Cruise: Hospitality Standard	6.0
OVERALL RATING	87.6

+ This former passenger-car liner has a small, squat funnel amidships and a long foredeck. She is a very stable ship at sea, with a deep draft, and rides well. There is a generous amount of open deck and sunning space, but the outdoor decking is worn in several places. The interior decor is also dated and worn, yet adequate and comfortable for those who do not want the glitz of newer ships. Cabins are small and rather spartan, although most have been recently redecorated in pastel shades. There is limited closet space, but you don't need much clothing for this casual cruise environment.

— The vessel has a very awkward layout. The nightlife is disco-loud. There's no finesse anywhere, although the staff are reasonably enthusiastic. New cabins installed in 1993 are subject to extreme squeaks and are noisy (difficult to sleep in).

Dining The dining room is low down in the ship and musty. The food is quite basic, that's all—with little choice. Poor selection of breads, fruits and cheeses. Buffets are minimal and could be more attractive.

Other Comments The number of public rooms is very limited, but recent decor changes are for the better. This ship is for the young, budget-minded cruiser wanting to party and travel without much service.

ts Ausonia ★★★

6-11 DAY EUROPE CRUISES

Cruise Line	Grimaldi Cruises	Casino	No	Slot Machines	No
Former Names	-	Swimming Pools (outside) 1	(inside)	0
Gross Tonnage	12,609	Whirlpools	1	Gymnasium	No
Builder	Cantieri Riuniti dell' Adriatico (Italy)	Sauna/Steam Room Yes/No	Massage	Yes
Original Cost	n/a	Self-Service Launderette	No
Christened By	n/a	Movie Theater/Seats	Yes/125
Entered Service	Sep 23, 1957	Library	No
Interior Design	n/a	Children's Facilities	No
Country of Registry	Italy (IBAX)	Watersports Facilities	None
Tel No 115-0673 Fax No 115-0673	Classification Society	Lloyd's Register
Length (ft/m)	522.5/159.26		

Beam (ft/m) 69.8/21.29 Draft (ft/m) 21.4/6.54	**RATINGS**
Propulsion steam turbine (12,799kW)	

RATINGS	SCORE
Ship: Condition/Cleanliness	7.5
Ship: Space/Flow/Comfort	7.2
Ship: Decor/Furnishings	7.0
Ship: Fitness Facilities	4.7
Cabins: Comfort/Facilities	6.1
Cabins: Software	6.2
Food: Dining Room/Cuisine	6.4
Food: Buffets/Informal Dining	5.7
Food: Quality of Ingredients	6.0
Service: Dining Room	6.1
Service: Bars	6.1
Service: Cabins	6.3
Cruise: Entertainment	5.5
Cruise: Activities Program	5.7
Cruise: Hospitality Standard	6.0
OVERALL RATING	92.5

Propellers	2 (FP)
Decks 8 Crew	210
Pass. Capacity (basis 2) 506 (all berths) 808
Pass. Space Ratio (basis 2) 24.9 (all berths) 15.6
Officers Italian Dining Staff Italian
Total Cabins	253
Size Range (sq ft/m)	n/a
Outside Cabins 154 Inside Cabins 99
Single Cabins 8 Supplement 100%
Balcony Cabins 0 Wheelchair Cabins 0
Cabin Current 220 AC Refrigerator No
Cabin TV Yes (upper grade cabins only)
VCR	No
Dining Rooms 2 Sittings 2
Elevators	1

+ Well-maintained ship with classic, swept-back lines and profile. Quite clean and tidy. Good open deck and sunning space. Ship underwent much mechanical and galley upgrading in late 1990. Also, the upgraded public areas are light and spacious. Ballroom is pleasantly decorated in blues and creams. Small, compact, yet reasonably comfortable cabins were refurbished in 1989–90. All have private facilities; uppermost cabin grades have full bathtub, others have showers, while two new suites feature whirlpool baths. There are several family cabins.

— Passengers are very heavy smokers and it's almost impossible to get away from it. Has a steep gangway in most ports.

Dining The dining rooms are set high up, and have good ocean views, but are extremely noisy. Friendly, efficient and bubbly Italian service throughout. Good Continental food, with some excellent pasta, although sauces are very heavy. Midnight pizza parties very popular. Poor selection of fruits and cheeses.

Other Comments This ship operates in four languages (announcements are long, loud and constant) and offers regular Mediterranean cruise service in very comfortable surroundings, with Italian flair, but no finesse in either food or service.

ms Ayvasovskiy ★

OPERATES

7 DAY BLACK SEA/
MEDITERRANEAN CRUISES

Cruise Line		Eurocruises
Former Names		-
Gross Tonnage		7,127
Builder		Alsthom Atlantique
Original Cost		n/a
Christened By		n/a
Entered Service		1976
Interior Design		n/a
Country of Registry		Russia (UHVL)
Tel No 140-1204	Fax No	140-1204
Length (ft/m)		398.6/121.50
Beam (ft/m) 57.4/17.50	Draft (ft/m)	14.4/4.40
Propulsion		diesel (7,650kW)
Propellers		2 (CP)
Decks 4	Crew	130
Pass. Capacity (basis 2) 248	(all berths)	664
Pass. Space Ratio (basis 2) 28.7	(all berths)	10.7
Officers Ukrainian	Dining Staff	Ukrainian
Total Cabins		84
Size Range (sq ft/m)		n/a
Outside Cabins 84	Inside Cabins	0
Single Cabins 0	Supplement	60%
Balcony Cabins 0	Wheelchair Cabins	0
Cabin Current		220 AC
Refrigerator		No
Cabin TV No	VCR	No
Dining Rooms 1	Sittings	2
Elevators		0

Casino	No	Slot Machines	Yes
Swimming Pools (outside) 1		(inside)	0
Whirlpools	0	Gymnasium	No
Sauna/Steam Room Yes/No		Massage	No
Self-Service Launderette			No
Movie Theater/Seats			No
Library			No
Children's Facilities			No
Watersports Facilities			None
Classification Society			CIS

RATINGS	SCORE
Ship: Condition/Cleanliness	5.2
Ship: Space/Flow/Comfort	4.9
Ship: Decor/Furnishings	5.7
Ship: Fitness Facilities	4.0
Cabins: Comfort/Facilities	5.4
Cabins: Software	5.2
Food: Dining Room/Cuisine	5.2
Food: Buffets/Informal Dining	5.1
Food: Quality of Ingredients	5.3
Service: Dining Room	6.0
Service: Bars	6.0
Service: Cabins	6.1
Cruise: Entertainment	4.2
Cruise: Activities Program	4.2
Cruise: Hospitality Standard	5.6
OVERALL RATING	78.1

+ This attractive and well-proportioned small ship now sails on a seven-day itinerary during the summer months, to Greece, Italy, and Turkey. Has forward outdoor observation area. The ship does have small indoor pool, which is unusual for a ship of this small size. Cabins are all outside.

— Has a very small amount of open deck space, and no wrap-around outdoor promenade deck. Has only a limited amount of public room space. There's a steep gangway in most ports. Cabins (except for four "suites") are small and spartan, with little closet and drawer space for a seven-day cruise, and tiny bathrooms.

Dining Comfortable, almost attractive dining room has large picture windows. Table set-ups are minimal. The food is barely adequate, with little choice. Poor bread, rolls, cheeses, and fruit selection. The service, however, is pleasant, from the Ukrainian waitresses, but it is completely without finesse.

Other Comments Although the number of public rooms is limited, this ship provides a somewhat international ambiance with passengers from a mix of Western and Eastern European countries. If you don't expect any elegance and finesse from this cruise product, you might actually enjoy it.

ms Azerbaydzhan ★★★

OPERATES
VARIOUS CRUISES

Cruise Line	CTC Cruise Lines	Elevators		1
Former Names	-	Casino	Yes	Slot Machines	Yes
Gross Tonnage	15,065	Swimming Pools (outside) 1	(inside)	0
Builder	Wartsila (Finland)	Whirlpools	0	Gymnasium	Yes
Original Cost	$25 million	Sauna/Steam Room Yes/No	Massage	Yes
Christened By	n/a	Self-Service Launderette		Yes
Entered Service	Jan 1976	Movie Theater/Seats		Yes/145
Interior Design	Lloyd Werft	Library	Yes Children's Facilities Yes
Country of Registry	Ukraine (UFZX)	Watersports Facilities		None
Tel No 140-0740 Fax No 140-0740		Classification Society Ukraine Register of Shipping
Length (ft/m)	512.5/156.24			

Beam (ft/m) 72.3/22.05	Draft (ft/m) 19.4/5.92	**RATINGS**	**SCORE**
Propulsion	diesel (13,430kW)	Ship: Condition/Cleanliness	6.2
Propellers	2 (CP)	Ship: Space/Flow/Comfort	6.1
Decks 8	Crew 240	Ship: Decor/Furnishings	6.0
Pass. Capacity (basis 2) 460	(all berths) 635	Ship: Fitness Facilities	4.7
Pass. Space Ratio (basis 2) 32.7	(all berths) 23.7	Cabins: Comfort/Facilities	6.1
Officers	Ukrainian	Cabins: Software	6.3
Dining Staff	European/Ukrainian	Food: Dining Room/Cuisine	5.8
Total Cabins	230	Food: Buffets/Informal Dining	5.2
Size Range (sq ft/m)	150-428/14.0-39.7	Food: Quality of Ingredients	5.4
Outside Cabins 112	Inside Cabins 118	Service: Dining Room	6.5
Single Cabins 0	Supplement 50%	Service: Bars	7.1
Balcony Cabins 0	Wheelchair Cabins 0	Service: Cabins	7.2
Cabin Current	220 AC	Cruise: Entertainment	5.2
Refrigerator	Boat deck cabins only	Cruise: Activities Program	5.7
Cabin TV Boat Deck cabins only	VCR No	Cruise: Hospitality Standard	6.7
Dining Rooms 2	Sittings 1	OVERALL RATING	90.2

+ This smart-looking ship has a squared funnel housing. Suites and deluxe cabins are large and very nicely furnished, and have wood-paneled walls and cabinetry. Other cabins are small, have clean lines and are simply furnished, without much closet and drawer space, but they are quite adequate and comfortable. Smart, but quite basic, the ship provides a civilized way to get to and from Australia (once each way each year). Good for price-sensitive travelers. Good European itineraries.

— There are really too many inside cabins. The cabin insulation in general is poor. Has a steep, narrow gangway in most ports. Inflexible staff need more hospitality training.

Dining Has two rather plain, but cozy dining rooms; one is for smokers, the other for non-smokers. Attentive and friendly waitress service, but there's no real finesse. The cuisine is so-so, with limited choice, yet is presented nicely, and service comes with a smile.

Other Comments This ship has an informal, unpretentious ambiance. This ship, and CTC Cruises, will provide a good cruise experience for a modest price, principally for British and other European passengers. Has British (low-budget) entertainment, and Ukrainian crew show. Port taxes are included.

mv Bali Sea Dancer ★★★

OPERATES

3- AND 4-DAY INDONESIA CRUISES

Cruise Line	P&O Spice Island Cruises	Casino	No	Slot Machines	No
Former Names	Illiria	Swimming Pools (outside) 1	(inside)	0
Gross Tonnage	3,852	Whirlpools	0	Gymnasium	No
Builder	Cantieri Navale Pellegrino (Italy)	Sauna/Steam Room No/No	Massage	No
Original Cost	n/a	Self-Service Launderette	No
Christened By	n/a	Movie Theater/Seats:	No
Entered Service	1962	Library	Yes	Children's Facilities No
Interior Design	n/a	Watersports Facilities	None
Country of Registry	Liberia (ELIP6)	Classification Society	American Bureau
Tel No	124-1440 Fax No	124-1441		of Shipping
Length (ft/m)	332.6/101.40		

Beam (ft/m) 48.0/14.66	Draft (ft/m)	16.4/5.02	
Propulsion		diesel (4,281kW)	
Propellers		2 (FP)	
Decks	4	Crew	90
Pass. Capacity (basis 2) 143		(all berths) 148	
Pass. Space Ratio (basis 2) 26.9		(all berths) 26.0	
Officers	Greek	Dining Staff	Greek
Total Cabins			74
Size Range (sq ft/m)			n/a
Outside Cabins	64	Inside Cabins	10
Single Cabins	9	Supplement	Set rates
Balcony Cabins	0	Wheelchair Cabins	0
Cabin Current			220 AC
Refrigerator			No
Cabin TV	No	VCR	No
Dining Rooms	1	Sittings	Open
Elevators			0

RATINGS	SCORE
Ship: Condition/Cleanliness	7.0
Ship: Space/Flow/Comfort	7.0
Ship: Decor/Furnishings	7.4
Ship: Fitness Facilities	3.6
Cabins: Comfort/Facilities	7.0
Cabins: Software	7.1
Food: Dining Room/Cuisine	7.0
Food: Buffets/Informal Dining	6.7
Food: Quality of Ingredients	7.0
Service: Dining Room	7.1
Service: Bars	7.0
Service: Cabins	7.3
Cruise: Lecturers	6.3
Cruise: Activities Program	4.6
Cruise: Hospitality Standard	7.1
OVERALL RATING	99.2

+ A real gem of a ship, formerly used for worldwide cruises for nature-lovers. Quite small and compact, and ideal for her present operating area. The ship is very clean throughout and quite well maintained despite her age. Well equipped, and the limited number of public rooms have pleasing decor and fabrics, all recently refurbished. The main lounge has fluted columns, and there is a well-stocked reference library. There are some interesting works of art throughout. Good lecture program. The cabins are reasonably spacious for the size of the ship, and have wood trim. All have private bathroom with shower, except two deluxe cabins, which have full bathtub. Fine, attentive, yet unobtrusive service from the all-Greek crew.

— The cabins have little closet and drawer space, and bathrooms are small.

Dining Charming dining room is reminiscent of classical Greece. The cuisine is Continental. Open seating dining (sit where and with whom you like). Menu choice (American and Continental cuisine) is generally sound, but the selection of breads, cheeses and fruits is limited.

Other Comments This small ship will provide a very comfortable destination-oriented expedition cruise experience for those seeking to get close to the natural, ecologically interesting world.

mts Baltica ★★★

Cruise Line/Operator	Sunshine Cruise Line		
Former Names	Danae/Therisos Express/		
	Port Melbourne		
Gross Tonnage	17,074		
Builder	Swan, Hunter (UK)		
Original Cost	n/a		
Christened By	n/a		
Entered Service	Jul 1955/1994		
Interior Design	n/a		
Country of Registry	Panama (3FEX4)		
Tel No 134-6425	Fax No 134-6425		
Length (ft/m)	532.7/162.39		
Beam (ft/m) 70.0/21.34	Draft (ft/m) 41.9/12.8		
Propulsion	diesel (9,850kW)		
Propellers	2 (FP)		
Decks 7	Crew 240		
Pass. Capacity (basis 2) 544	(all berths) 657		
Pass. Space Ratio (basis 2) 31.3	(all berths) 25.9		
Officers	Scandinavian		
Dining Staff	International		
Total Cabins	272		
Size (sq ft/m):	200.0-270.0/18.5-25.0		
Outside Cabins 226	Inside Cabins 46		
Single Cabins 0	Supplement 50%		
Balcony Cabins 6	Wheelchair Cabins 0		
Cabin Current	220 AC		
Refrigerator	No		
Dining Rooms 1	Sittings 2		

Elevators			2
Casino	Yes	Slot Machines	Yes
Swimming Pools (outside) 1		(inside)	0
Whirlpools	2	Gymnasium	Yes
Sauna:	Yes	Massage	Yes
Movie Theater/Seats:			Yes/275
Cabin TV	No	Library	Yes
Children's Facilities/Playroom:			No
Classification Society		American Bureau	
		of Shipping	

RATINGS	SCORE
Ship: Condition/Cleanliness	6.5
Ship: Space/Flow/Comfort	7.1
Ship: Decor/Furnishings	7.0
Ship: Fitness Facilities	5.5
Cabins: Comfort/Facilities	6.8
Cabins: Software	7.0
Food: Dining Room/Cuisine	7.1
Food: Buffets/Informal Dining	6.2
Food: Quality of Ingredients	6.5
Service: Dining Room	7.1
Service: Bars	7.0
Service: Cabins	7.1
Cruise: Entertainment	5.6
Cruise: Activities Program	6.0
Cruise: Hospitality Standard	7.0
OVERALL RATING	99.5

+ Solidly built ship with good lines. Has a good amount of open deck space for sunning. Pleasant old-world ambiance. Features high-quality interior appointments that are solidly made. Spacious public rooms, although the decor is somewhat conservative. Roomy, traditional theater with three audio channels for simultaneous translation for international conventions. Good-sized cabins have heavy-duty furniture and fittings and lots of closet and drawer space.

— There is no forward observation lounge. Cabins located under the disco can suffer from thumping noise late at night. The lower-grade cabins are very spartan.

Dining The dining room is decorated quite nicely. Features Continental/European cuisine and service that is quite attentive as there is only one sitting.

Other Comments This ship will provide a comfortable, though by no means glamorous, short cruise for its mainly European/Scandinavian clientele looking for a no-frills experience.

mv Berlin ★★★★+

OPERATES

VARIOUS CRUISES WORLDWIDE

Cruise Line	Deilmann Reederei		
Former Names	Princess Mahsuri		
Gross Tonnage	9,570		
Builder	Hawaldtswerke Deutsche		
	Werft (Germany)		
Original Cost	n/a	Christened By	n/a
Entered Service	Jun 9, 1980		
Interior Design	HDW/Nobiskrug shipyard		
Country of Registry	Germany (DLRC)		
Tel No	112-0251	Fax No	112-0251
Length (ft/m)	457.0/139.30		
Beam (ft/m) 57.5/17.52	Draft (ft/m)	15.7/4.80	
Propulsion	diesel (7,060kW)		
Propellers	2 (CP)		
Decks	8	Crew	210
Pass. Capacity (basis 2) 422	(all berths) 448		
Pass. Space Ratio (basis 2) 22.6	(all berths) 21.3		
Officers	German	Dining Staff	German
Total Cabins	211		
Size Range (sq ft/m)	93-192/8.6-17.8		
Outside Cabins	158	Inside Cabins	53
Single Cabins 0	Supplement Rates on request		
Balcony Cabins	0	Wheelchair Cabins	0
Cabin Current	220 AC		
Refrigerator	Promenade/Main Deck cabins only		
Cabin TV	Yes	VCR	No
Dining Rooms	2	Sittings	2
Elevators	2		

Casino	No	Slot Machines	No
Swimming Pools (outside) 1	(inside)		1
Whirlpools	0	Gymnasium	Yes
Sauna/Steam Room Yes/No	Massage		Yes
Self-Service Launderette			No
Movie Theater/Seats			Yes/330
Library			Yes
Children's Facilities			On request
Watersports Facilities			None
Classification Society		Germanischer Lloyd	

RATINGS	SCORE
Ship: Condition/Cleanliness	8.2
Ship: Space/Flow/Comfort	7.9
Ship: Decor/Furnishings	8.0
Ship: Fitness Facilities	6.8
Cabins: Comfort/Facilities	7.8
Cabins: Software	7.8
Food: Dining Room/Cuisine	8.0
Food: Buffets/Informal Dining	8.1
Food: Quality of Ingredients	7.8
Service: Dining Room	7.9
Service: Bars	7.8
Service: Cabins	7.7
Cruise: Entertainment	7.9
Cruise: Activities Program	7.8
Cruise: Hospitality Standard	8.1
OVERALL RATING	117.6

+ Handsome contemporary ship, with crisp, clean all-white lines and well-balanced profile. Has an ice-strengthened hull. Star of the long-running German television show *Traumschiff* (Dream Ship). Very tidy throughout, this is a well-appointed ship with elegant, tasteful, though somewhat dark European decor. Beautiful collection of original oil paintings from the owner's personal collection. Cabins are small, but very comfortable and well equipped. Bathrooms have shower units, no bathtubs. Intimate, highly personable atmosphere.

— No forward observation lounge. Has a small swimming pool. Interior passageways are quite narrow.

Dining Lovely dining room has big picture windows, and several tables for two. Attentive, professional and correct European service with a smile. The food caters strictly to German tastes, with cream sauces accompanying entrees. Good selection of breads and cheeses.

Other Comments Stretched in 1986. Continental passenger mix. Outstanding health spa treatments. This charming ship will provide a rather exclusive destination-intensive cruise experience in elegant, intimate, and contemporary surroundings for the discerning German-speaking passenger who doesn't need constant entertainment. Insurance and gratuities are included.

ms Black Prince ★★★+

Cruise Line	Fred Olsen Cruise Lines
Former Names	-
Gross Tonnage	11,209
Builder	Fender Werft (Germany)
Original Cost	$20 million
Christened By	Lady Doris Denny
Entered Service	1966
Interior Design	Platou Design
Country of Registry	Norway (LATE2)
Tel No 131-3217 Fax No 131-3217	
Length (ft/m)	470.4/143.40
Beam (ft/m) 66.6/20.30 Draft (ft/m)	20.0/6.10
Propulsion	diesel (12,310kW)
Propellers	2 (CP)
Decks 7 Crew	200
Pass. Capacity (basis 2) 446 (all berths) 517	
Pass. Space Ratio (basis 2) 25.1 (all berths) 21.6	
Officers European Dining Staff Filipino/Thai	
Total Cabins	238
Size Range (sq ft/m)	80-226/7.5-21.0
Outside Cabins 168 Inside Cabins 70	
Single Cabins 30 Supplement Set rates	
Balcony Cabins 0 Wheelchair Cabins 2	
Cabin Current	230 AC
Refrigerator	Upper grade cabins only
Cabin TV Yes VCR	No
Dining Rooms 2 Sittings	1
Elevators	2

Casino	Yes	Slot Machines	No
Swimming Pools (outside) 2		(inside)	0
Whirlpools	2	Gymnasium	Yes
Sauna/Steam Room Yes/No		Massage	Yes
Self-Service Launderette			No
Movie Theater/Seats	No	Library	Yes
Children's Facilities			Yes
Watersports Facilities	Aft marina pool, Zodiacs, windsurfers, waterski		
Classification Society		Det Norske Veritas	

RATINGS	SCORE
Ship: Condition/Cleanliness	7.1
Ship: Space/Flow/Comfort	7.0
Ship: Decor/Furnishings	7.1
Ship: Fitness Facilities	5.8
Cabins: Comfort/Facilities	6.6
Cabins: Software	6.8
Food: Dining Room/Cuisine	7.0
Food: Buffets/Informal Dining	6.6
Food: Quality of Ingredients	6.8
Service: Dining Room	7.0
Service: Bars	6.7
Service: Cabins	7.1
Cruise: Entertainment	7.3
Cruise: Activities Program	6.4
Cruise: Hospitality Standard	7.7
OVERALL RATING	103.0

+ Well-maintained ship, and run with family pride. Good indoor fitness center. Life-size chess game is fun. Features a popular 60 ft hydraulic "marina park" and free-float swimming pool surround that extends aft of the mother ship (only used in very calm waters). Restrained decor and ambiance, with much of the soft furnishings hand tailored on board. Outside suites are good. Other cabins are small, but well equipped and tastefully decorated. An ironing room is provided. Large number of single cabins. The two-level showlounge is quite pleasant.

— Often difficult to get away from smokers. Sadly, there is a charge for room service. Many cabins have poor air-conditioning. Entertainment is a low-cost, tightly budgeted affair.

Dining The two main dining rooms (both non-smoking) have big picture windows. First- and second-sitting diners sometimes exchange sittings, a good arrangement. Food is generally of high quality, but there should be more menu choice, particularly at buffet lunches. Communication with the Filipino waiters can prove frustrating.

Other Comments Solidly built white ship, converted to a full cruise ship in 1986, has a somewhat ungainly profile. Lots of repeat passengers who wouldn't dream of trying another vessel. Well suited to the informal British market, particularly for passengers of senior years. Currency aboard: UK Sterling (£). Recommended gratuities: UK£4.00 per passenger per day.

ms Bolero ★★★

OPERATES

7-DAY MEDITERRANEAN CRUISES

Cruise Line	Festival Cruises
Former Names	Starward
Gross Tonnage	16,107
Builder	A.G. Weser (Germany)
Original Cost	n/a
Christened By	Ms Olga Mowinckel
Entered Service	Dec 1, 1968/October 1995
Interior Design	Tage Wandborg
Country of Registry	Bahamas (C6CM4)
Tel No	110-4163	Fax No	110-4163
Length (ft/m)	525.3/160.13
Beam (ft/m) 74.9/22.84	Draft (ft/m)	20.4/6.22
Propulsion	diesel (12,950kW)
Propellers	2 (CP)
Decks	7	Crew	315
Pass. Capacity (basis 2) 758	(all berths) 1,022
Pass. Space Ratio (basis 2) 21.2	(all berths) 15.7
Officers Norwegian	Dining Staff International
Total Cabins	379
Size Range (sq ft/m)	90-225/8.3-21.0
Outside Cabins	229	Inside Cabins	150
Single Cabins	0	Supplement 50-100%
Balcony Cabins	0	Wheelchair Cabins	0
Cabin Current	110 AC
Refrigerator	Category 1 only
Cabin TV	No	VCR	No
Dining Rooms	1	Sittings	2
Elevators	4

Casino	Yes	Slot Machines	Yes
Swimming Pools (outside) 2	(inside)	0
Whirlpools	0	Gymnasium	Yes
Sauna/Steam Room Yes/No	Massage	Yes
Self-Service Launderette	No
Movie Theater/Seats	Yes/204
Library	Yes
Children's Facilities	No
Watersports Facilities	None
Classification Society	Det Norske Veritas

RATINGS	SCORE
Ship: Condition/Cleanliness	6.9
Ship: Space/Flow/Comfort	6.4
Ship: Decor/Furnishings	6.9
Ship: Fitness Facilities	4.9
Cabins: Comfort/Facilities	6.1
Cabins: Software	6.4
Food: Dining Room/Cuisine	7.1
Food: Buffets/Informal Dining	6.4
Food: Quality of Ingredients	6.4
Service: Dining Room	7.1
Service: Bars	7.0
Service: Cabins	7.2
Cruise: Entertainment	6.4
Cruise: Activities Program	6.2
Cruise: Hospitality Standard	6.9
OVERALL RATING	98.2

+ This ship has a fairly smart-looking upper profile with dual swept-back funnels. Reasonable choice of public rooms feature clean, modern furnishings and upbeat, cheerful decor throughout. Good balconied theater. Except for five good-sized suites, the cabins are quite compact units that are moderately comfortable, with bright, contemporary colors, and quite adequate for a one-week cruise.

— Has a less than handsome duck-tailed sponson stern. Reasonable open deck and sunning space, but this high-density vessel really feels crowded when full. Noisy diesels throb in many parts of the vessel. Cabin closet and drawer space are poor, and metal drawers are tinny.

Dining Has a charming dining room, with some tables overlooking the stern. Reasonably good cruise food and menu choice, as on the sister ship *The Azur*. Service comes with a smile. Has a limited selection of breads, fruits and cheeses.

Other Comments Formerly owned by Norwegian Cruise Line and acquired in 1995 by Festival Cruises, the ship has a warm, friendly ambiance. Although it's hard for this ship to compete with larger ships, this is a comfortably sized vessel for Mediterranean cruises, and is operated specifically for European passengers. The ship will provide a well-tuned cruise experience in comfortable, though not elegant, surroundings, at a decent price.

ms Bremen ★★★★+

OPERATES

WORLDWIDE EXPEDITION CRUISES
(INCLUDING ANTARCTICA)

Cruise Line	Hapag-Lloyd Tours/Hanseatic Tours		Casino	No	Slot Machines No
Former Names		Frontier Spirit	Swimming Pools (outside) 1		(inside) 0
Gross Tonnage		6,752	Whirlpools	0	Gymnasium Yes
Builder	Mitsubishi Heavy Industries (Japan)		Sauna/Steam Room Yes/No		Massage No
Original Cost		$42 million	Self-Service Launderette		Yes
Christened By		Mrs Kaoru Kanetaka/	Lecture/Film Room:		Yes (seats 164)
		Mrs Wedemeier	Library	Yes Zodiacs	12
Entered Service	Nov 6, 1990/Nov 20, 1993		Helicopter Pad		Yes
Interior Design		Wilfried Kohnemann	Watersports Facilities		None
Country of Registry		Bahamas (C6JC3)	Classification Society		Lloyd's Register
Tel No 110-3404	Fax No	110-3405			
Length (ft/m)		365.8/111.51	**RATINGS**		**SCORE**
Beam (ft/m) 55.7/17.00	Draft (ft/m)	15.7/4.80	Ship: Condition/Cleanliness		8.6
Propulsion		diesel (4,855kW)	Ship: Space/Flow/Comfort		8.2
Propellers		2 (CP)	Ship: Expedition Equipment		8.5
Decks 6	Crew	94	Ship: Decor/Furnishings		8.3
Pass. Capacity (basis 2) 164		(all berths) 184	Cabins: Comfort/Facilities		8.2
Pass. Space Ratio (basis 2) 41.1		(all berths) 36.6	Cabins: Software		8.1
Officers European	Dining Staff	Filipino	Food: Dining Room/Cuisine		8.1
Total Cabins		82	Food: Buffets/Informal Dining		7.8
Size Range (sq ft/m)	175-322/16.2-30.0		Food: Quality of Ingredients		8.0
Outside Cabins 82	Inside Cabins	0	Service: Dining Room		8.0
Single Cabins 0	Supplement On request		Service: Bars		8.2
Balcony Cabins 18	Wheelchair Cabins	2	Service: Cabins		8.0
Cabin Current 110 AC	Refrigerator	No	Cruise: Itineraries/Operations		8.5
Cabin TV Yes	VCR	Yes	Cruise: Lecture Program		8.4
Dining Rooms		1 (open seating)	Cruise: Hospitality Standard		8.2
Elevators		2	OVERALL RATING		123.1

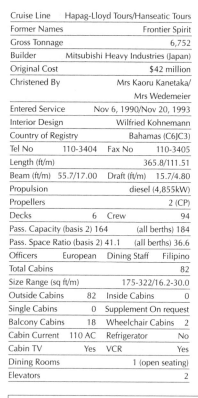

+ This purpose-built expedition cruise vessel (ex-*Frontier Spirit*) has a handsome contemporary profile and the latest equipment. Its wide beam provides great stability, and long cruising range and ice-hardened hull give access to the most remote destinations. Zero-discharge waste handling and the highest ice classification make her usable anywhere. All equipment for in-depth marine and shore excursions provided. The all-outside cabins are spacious and well equipped. Some cabins also have a small balcony, a first on an expedition cruise vessel. Fine, well-planned destination-intensive itineraries, good documentation and port information. Soft drinks in refrigerators are replenished daily, at no charge.

— Has a steep gangway. The sauna is tiny. Cabins don't have much drawer space.

Dining Dining room is quite charming. Food is excellent, with high-quality ingredients, although it is highly salted. Good breads, pastries, cheeses and fruits. Service is very good, with bilingual (German- and English-speaking) waiters and waitresses immaculately dressed.

Other Comments This ship will provide you with an outstanding learning and expedition experience. Well-chosen itineraries and thoughtful passenger care are combined with a high degree of comfort. The ship's interiors were upgraded in late 1993. Caters principally to German-speaking passengers. Insurance, port taxes and gratuities are included.

mv Caledonian Star ★★★+

OPERATES
WORLDWIDE EXPEDITION CRUISES

Cruise Line	Noble Caledonia/Special Expeditions		
Former Names	North Star/Marburg/Lindmar		
Gross Tonnage			3,095
Builder	A.G. Weser Seebeckwerft (Germany)		
Original Cost			n/a
Christened By		Ms Barbro Svensson	
Entered Service			1966/1984
Interior Design			Robert Tillberg
Country of Registry			Bahamas (C6BE4)
Tel No	110-4706	Fax No	110-4766
Length (ft/m)			292.6/89.20
Beam (ft/m)	45.9/14.00	Draft (ft/m)	20.3/6.20
Propulsion			diesel (3,236kW)
Propellers			1 (FP)
Decks	6	Crew	60
Pass. Capacity (basis 2) 120		(all berths) 150	
Pass. Space Ratio (basis 2) 25.7		(all berths) 20.6	
Officers	Scandinavian	Dining Staff	Filipino
Total Cabins			61
Size Range (sq ft/m)		192-269/17.8-25.0	
Outside Cabins	68	Inside Cabins	0
Single Cabins			2
Supplement			On request
Balcony Cabins	0	Wheelchair Cabins	0
Cabin Current			110/220 AC
Refrigerator			All cabins
Cabin TV	Yes	VCR	Yes
Dining Rooms			1 (open sitting)

Elevators			0
Casino	Yes	Slot Machines	Yes
Swimming Pools (outside)			1
Whirlpools	0	Gymnasium	No
Sauna/Steam Room	No/No	Massage	No
Self-Service Launderette			No
Lecture/Film Room	No	Library	Yes
Zodiacs	4	Helicopter Pad	No
Watersports Facilities			None
Classification Society		Det Norske Veritas	

RATINGS	SCORE
Ship: Condition/Cleanliness	7.2
Ship: Space/Flow/Comfort	5.6
Ship: Expedition Equipment	7.1
Ship: Decor/Furnishings	7.0
Cabins: Comfort/Facilities	5.8
Cabins: Software	6.0
Food: Dining Room/Cuisine	7.4
Food: Buffets/Informal Dining	6.7
Food: Quality of Ingredients	7.0
Service: Dining Room	7.4
Service: Bars	7.5
Service: Cabins	7.6
Cruise: Itineraries/Operations	7.5
Cruise: Lecture Program	7.6
Cruise: Hospitality Standard	7.5
OVERALL RATING	104.9

+ Reasonably handsome ship is extremely well maintained. Has an open-bridge policy. Warm, intimate ambiance. Good range of public rooms. The all-outside cabins are compact but comfortable, and decorated in warm, muted tones. All have minibar-refrigerator, VCR, and good closet and drawer space. Comfortable and unpretentious, with a casual dress code. Carries Zodiac landing craft for in-depth excursions, and an enclosed, contemporary shore tender. Fine lecture room/library also has videos for in-cabin use. Excellent lecturers on every cruise make this a real life-enrichment and learning experience for an intellectual clientele.

— Interior stairways are a little steep. Exterior stairway to Zodiac embarkation point is steep. Ceilings are plain. Noise from the diesel engines (generators) is irksome. Communication can sometimes prove frustrating.

Dining The dining room is small but charming, and chairs are quite small. European cuisine is slanted toward British tastes, with high-quality, very fresh ingredients, but not a lot of menu choice. Attentive and friendly service.

Other Comments This comfortable ship provides a well-tuned destination-intensive, soft expedition cruise experience, at a very reasonable price, and attracts many loyal repeat passengers, most of whom are British.

tes Canberra ★★★

OPERATES

14-DAY EUROPE CRUISES

Cruise Line	P&O Cruises
Former Names	-
Gross Tonnage	44,807
Builder	Harland & Wolff (UK)
Original Cost	UK£17,021,000
Christened By	Dame Pattie Menzies, GBE
Entered Service	Jun 2, 1961
Interior Design	Sir High Casson/
	John Wright/Barbara Oakley
Country of Registry	Great Britain (GBVC)
Tel No 144-0205 Fax No 144-0205	
Length (ft/m)	818.5/249.49
Beam (ft/m) 102.5/31.25 Draft (ft/m) 32.2/9.84	
Propulsion	turbo-electric (64,876kW)
Propellers	2 (FP)
Decks 10 Crew	860
Pass. Capacity (basis 2) 1,399 (all berths) 1,641	
Pass. Space Ratio (basis 2) 32.0 (all berths) 27.3	
Officers British Dining Staff British/Goan	
Total Cabins	780 (236 without facilities)
Size Range (sq ft/m)	63-525/5.8-48.7
Outside Cabins 462 Inside Cabins	318
Single Cabins 161 Supplement	Set rates
Balcony Cabins 0 Wheelchair Cabins	0
Cabin Current	230 AC
Refrigerator	Categories AA/AB/AC/AD only
Cabin TV Yes (upper grade cabins only) VCR No	
Dining Rooms 2 Sittings	2

Elevators			6
Casino	Yes	Slot Machines	Yes
Swimming Pools (outside) 3		(inside)	0
Whirlpools	0	Gymnasium	Yes
Sauna/Steam Room No/No		Massage	Yes
Self-Service Launderette			Yes
Movie Theater/Seats			Yes/460
Library	Yes	Children's Facilities	Yes
Watersports Facilities			None
Classification Society			Lloyd's Register

RATINGS	SCORE
Ship: Condition/Cleanliness	6.6
Ship: Space/Flow/Comfort	7.0
Ship: Decor/Furnishings	6.7
Ship: Fitness Facilities	6.1
Cabins: Comfort/Facilities	6.3
Cabins: Software	6.4
Food: Dining Room/Cuisine	6.1
Food: Buffets/Informal Dining	5.6
Food: Quality of Ingredients	6.0
Service: Dining Room	7.1
Service: Bars	7.2
Service: Cabins	7.3
Cruise: Entertainment	7.3
Cruise: Activities Program	6.6
Cruise: Hospitality Standard	7.1
OVERALL RATING	99.4

+ White ship has good open deck and sunning space, and British-style canvas deck chairs. Constant upgrading has changed some public rooms, added new features and decor. Popular favorites are the Crow's Nest Bar and Cricketer's Club. Lots of good wood paneling. Luxury suites are good, with heavy-duty wood furniture. Wide range and variety of other cabins to choose from. This is an excellent ship for families with children, who will discover all the nooks and crannies. Efficient, courteous service from Goanese stewards.

— Expect long lines for shore tenders, buffets and disembarkation. Some cabins share nearby bathroom facilities. Cabins on "B" Deck have obstructed views. There are simply too many repetitive announcements. Smokers seem to be everywhere.

Dining Atlantic (large) and Pacific (smaller) restaurants feature British and "colonial" cuisine. Good curries, plentiful meat, fish and desserts, but lacks lobster, shrimp and pasta dishes. Poor bread selection. Senior officers host tables nightly.

Other Comments Often dubbed the "great white whale," this ship is probably due for retirement soon. She will provide you with a cruise vacation package in very comfortable, though not elegant, surroundings at an affordable price. All port taxes and insurance are included for British passengers. Allow about UK£3.00 per person, per day for gratuities.

ms Carnival Destiny

OPERATES

7-DAY CARIBBEAN CRUISES

Cruise Line	Carnival Cruise Lines	Swimming Pools (outside)	3 (1 with magrodome)	
Former Names	-	(inside)		1
Gross Tonnage	100,000	Whirlpools	n/a	Gymnasium	Yes
Builder	Fincantieri (Italy)	Sauna/Steam Room	Yes/Yes	Massage	Yes
Original Cost	$400 million	Self-service Launderette		No
Christened By	n/a	Movie Theater/Seats	1/1,040 (showlounge)	
Entered Service	Fall 1996	Library		Yes
Interior Design	Joe Farcus	Children's Facilities/Playroom:		Yes
Country of Registry	Panama	Watersports Facilities		None
Tel No	n/a	Fax No	n/a	Classification Society	Lloyd's Register
Length (ft/m)	892.3/272.0			
Beam (ft/m) 116.0/35.3 Draft (ft/m) 27.0/8.2		**RATINGS**		**SCORE**
Propulsion	diesel-electric (63,400kW)	Ship: Condition/Cleanliness		NYR
Propellers	2 (CP)	Ship: Space/Flow/Comfort		NYR
Decks	12 Crew 1,000	Ship: Decor/Furnishings		NYR
Pass. Capacity (basis 2) 2,642 (all berths) 3,350		Ship: Fitness Facilities		NYR
Pass. Space Ratio (basis 2) 37.8 (all berths) 29.8		Cabins: Comfort/Facilities		NYR
Officers Italian Dining Staff International		Cabins: Software		NYR
Total Cabins	1,321	Food: Dining Room/Cuisine		NYR
Size Range (sq ft/m)	180-483/16.7-44.8	Food: Buffets/Informal Dining		NYR
Outside Cabins 740 Inside Cabins 519		Food: Quality of Ingredients		NYR
Single Cabins 0 Supplement 50-100%		Service: Dining Room		NYR
Balcony Cabins 418 Wheelchair Cabins 0		Service: Bars		NYR
Cabin Current 110 AC Refrigerator Suites only		Service: Cabins		NYR
Cabin TV Yes VCR No		Cruise: Entertainment		NYR
Dining Rooms 2 Sittings 2		Cruise: Activities Program		NYR
Elevators	13	Cruise: Hospitality Standard		NYR
Casino Yes Slot Machines Yes		OVERALL RATING		NYR

+ Although the bow is extremely short, this ship has the most balanced profile of all the ships in the Carnival fleet. A retractable glass dome in three sections (magrodome) over the aft swimming pool provides shelter in inclement weather conditions. Amidships is the longest water slide afloat (at over 100ft in length), and tiered sunbathing decks between two pools and several hot tubs.

Inside the ship, Joe Farcus, the interior designer, has outdone himself. It is grand, quite superb, and a fantasy land for the senses. Like its predecessors, this ship will feature a double-wide indoor promenade, glass-domed atrium and Nautica Spa. The three-level showlounge is simply stunning, and features a revolving stage, hydraulic orchestra pit, and seating on two levels, with the upper level tiered through two decks, as well as a proscenium over the stage that acts as a scenery loft. Over half of all outside cabins have private balconies (with glass rather than steel balustrades, for better ocean views), with the balconies extending from the ship's side. The balconies also feature bright fluorescent lighting. The standard cabins are a good size, and come equipped with all the basics, although the furniture is square and angular, with no rounded edges. Three decks of cabins (eight on each deck, each with private balcony) overlook the stern.

From the viewpoint of safety, passengers will be able to embark directly into the lifeboats from their secured position without having to wait for them to be lowered, thus saving time in the event of a real emergency. Well done.

— This is a big ship, with lots of people, and that will mean lines, particularly for shore excursions, buffets, embarkation and disembarkation (even though the Port of Miami has greatly improved terminal facilities specifically for this ship, with some 90 check-in desks). In cabins with balconies, the partition between each balcony is open at top and bottom, so you will be able to hear noise from neighbors, or smell their smoke.

Dining The ship's two dining rooms (forward: 706 seats; aft: 1,090 seats) each span two decks, and incorporate a dozen pyramid-shaped domes and chandeliers. The aft dining room features a two-deck-high wall of glass overlooking the stern. There are tables for four, six and eight (and a few tables for two). Dining room entrances have comfortable drinking areas for pre-dinner cocktails. The menus, which have been upgraded during the past year, feature a better selection than before, with more choices, and better quality entree items. Also two decks high is the Lido Bar and Grill, the ship's informal eatery, which is adjacent to the aft pool and can be covered by the magrodome in inclement weather.

Other Comments Besides the shipyard, some 700 sub-contractors were involved in building this, presently the world's largest cruise ship, and Carnival's 11th new ship in the past 15 years. This ship is destined to become the floating playground of the young-in-mind set that likes constant stimulation and lots of noise in order to play while on a vacation at sea. It promises to be the ultimate adult playground at sea, a live board game with every move executed in typically grand, colorful Carnival style.

ms Carousel ★★★+

OPERATES

7-DAY MEDITERRANEAN CRUISES

Cruise Line	Airtours Cruises		
Former Names	Nordic Prince		
Gross Tonnage	23,200		
Builder	Wartsila (Finland)		
Original Cost	$13.5 million		
Christened By	Ms Ingrid Bergman		
Entered Service	Jul 31, 1971/May 6, 1995		
Interior Design	Njal Eide		
Country of Registry	Norway (LAPJ3)		
Tel No 131-0547	Fax No 131-0547		
Length (ft/m)	637.5/194.32		
Beam (ft/m) 78.8/24.03	Draft (ft/m) 21.9/6.70		
Propulsion	diesel (13,400kW)		
Propellers	2 (CP)		
Decks 7	Crew 434		
Pass. Capacity (basis 2) 1,062	(all berths) 1,200		
Pass. Space Ratio (basis 2) 21.8	(all berths) 19.3		
Officers European	Dining Staff International		
Total Cabins	531		
Size Range (sq ft/m)	120-483/11.1-44.8		
Outside Cabins 345	Inside Cabins 186		
Single Cabins 0	Supplement 50-100%		
Balcony Cabins 0	Wheelchair Cabins 0		
Cabin Current	110 AC		
Refrigerator	Owner's suite only		
Cabin TV No	VCR No		
Dining Rooms 1	Sittings 2		
Elevators	4		

Casino Yes	Slot Machines	Yes
Swimming Pools (outside) 1	(inside)	0
Whirlpools 0	Gymnasium	Yes
Sauna/Steam Room Yes/No	Massage	Yes
Self-Service Launderette		No
Movie Theater/Seats		No
Library		No
Children's Facilities		No
Watersports Facilities		None
Classification Society	Det Norske Veritas	

RATINGS	SCORE
Ship: Condition/Cleanliness	7.5
Ship: Space/Flow/Comfort	6.6
Ship: Decor/Furnishings	7.0
Ship: Fitness Facilities	6.6
Cabins: Comfort/Facilities	5.8
Cabins: Software	7.7
Food: Dining Room/Cuisine	6.6
Food: Buffets/Informal Dining	6.3
Food: Quality of Ingredients	6.8
Service: Dining Room	6.6
Service: Bars	6.5
Service: Cabins	6.1
Cruise: Entertainment	7.6
Cruise: Activities Program	7.6
Cruise: Hospitality Standard	7.6
OVERALL RATING	102.9

+ Fairly smart, modish look with nicely raked bow. Polished outdoor wrap-around promenade deck and wooden railings. Good interior layout and passenger flow, with clean, bright decor. Good wooden paneling and trim. Casual dress code for unstuffy cruising. Very affordable for families with children. Good pre- and post-cruise hotel programs.

— Cabins are not assigned until you arrive at the ship. Expect lines for embarkation, disembarkation, buffets, and shore tenders. Open deck space for sunning is crowded and noisy. Passageways are narrow. Cabins are very small, with mediocre closets, and almost no storage space. Too many announcements. "Blue coat" social staff provide the entertainment.

Dining Good general dining room operation, although food all seems to taste the same. No tables for two. Limited selection of breads and fruits. Attentive, friendly but rather hurried dining room service that means you eat rather than dine.

Other Comments The ship, acquired by Airtours Cruises in 1995, will provide you with an activity-filled cruise product in comfortable, but noisy, surroundings. Airtours packages things well, and this ship is ideal for families on a limited budget. Currency is UK£ Sterling. Note that cabin voltage is 110 volts, so bring adapters. Tipping is recommended at UK£5.00 per day. Insurance is included (but you are charged for it unless you decline coverage).

ms Celebration ★★★★

OPERATES

7-DAY CARIBBEAN CRUISES
(YEAR-ROUND)

Cruise Line	Carnival Cruise Lines
Former Names	-
Gross Tonnage	47,262
Builder	Kockums (Sweden)
Original Cost	$135 million
Christened By	Ms Kathie Lee Gifford
Entered Service	Mar 14, 1987
Interior Design	Joe Farcus
Country of Registry	Liberia (ELFT8)
Tel No 124-0526 Fax No	124-0526
Length (ft/m)	732.6/223.30
Beam (ft/m) 92.5/28.20 Draft (ft/m)	25.5/7.80
Propulsion	diesel (23,520kW)
Propellers	2 (CP)
Decks 10 Crew	670
Pass. Capacity (basis 2) 1,486 (all berths)	1,896
Pass. Space Ratio (basis 2) 31.8 (all berths)	24.9
Officers Italian Dining Staff	International
Total Cabins	743
Size Range (sq ft/m)	185/17.1
Outside Cabins 453 Inside Cabins	290
Single Cabins	0
Supplement	50% (cat.1-3)/100% (cat.4-12)
Balcony Cabins 10 Wheelchair Cabins	14
Cabin Current	110 AC
Refrigerator	Category 12 only
Cabin TV Yes VCR	No
Dining Rooms 2 Sittings	2

Elevators			8
Casino	Yes	Slot Machines	Yes
Swimming Pools (outside) 3		(inside)	0
Whirlpools	2	Gymnasium	Yes
Sauna/Steam Room Yes/No		Massage	Yes
Self-Service Launderette			Yes
Movie Theater/Seats	No	Library	Yes
Children's Facilities			Yes
Watersports Facilities			None
Classification Society		Lloyd's Register	

RATINGS	SCORE
Ship: Condition/Cleanliness	7.8
Ship: Space/Flow/Comfort	7.6
Ship: Decor/Furnishings	6.4
Ship: Fitness Facilities	7.8
Cabins: Comfort/Facilities	7.6
Cabins: Software	7.4
Food: Dining Room/Cuisine	6.7
Food: Buffets/Informal Dining	6.4
Food: Quality of Ingredients	5.3
Service: Dining Room	7.0
Service: Bars	7.2
Service: Cabins	6.4
Cruise: Entertainment	8.0
Cruise: Activities Program	7.8
Cruise: Hospitality Standard	6.3
OVERALL RATING	105.7

+ Double-width indoor promenades and good selection of public rooms. Colorful artwork. Nautically themed decor in Wheelhouse Bar-Grill. Features New Orleans-themed decor throughout the public rooms. Cabins, most of which are identical, are generously sized, very comfortable and well equipped. Especially good are ten suites with private balconies. Huge, very active, noisy casino. Party atmosphere good for anyone wanting a stimulating cruise experience. Wide range of entertainment and activities. Excellent for families with children.

— Swimming pools are small, but open deck space is quite good. Expect long lines for embarkation, disembarkation, buffets and shore tenders. Dining rooms cramped and noisy. Disappointing buffets. Nowhere to go for privacy and quiet. Too many announcements.

Dining The two dining rooms are cramped when full, and extremely noisy (both, however, are non-smoking). Quantity, not quality, prevails, and not much is spent on the food product.

Other Comments Flamboyant interior decor in public rooms is stimulating, not restful, except for the beautiful, and unused, Admiral's Library, the only quiet room aboard. This ship offers dazzle and sizzle for the whole family and provides a good choice for a first cruise, if you like lots of people, lots of noise, and lively action around you.

ms Century

Cruise Line	Celebrity Cruises
Former Names	-
Gross Tonnage	70,000
Builder	Meyer Werft (Germany)
Original Cost	$320 million
Christened By	Mrs Christina Chandris
Entered Service	Dec 20, 1995
Interior Design	Katzourakis/McNeece
Country of Registry	Liberia
Tel No	n/a	Fax No	n/a
Length (ft/m)	807.1/246.00
Beam (ft/m) 105.6/32.20	Draft (ft/m)	24.6/7.50
Propulsion	diesel (29,250kW)
Propellers	2 (CP)
Decks	10	Crew	843
Pass. Capacity (basis 2) 1,750	(all berths) 2,150
Pass. Space Ratio (basis 2) 40.0	(all berths) 40.0
Officers	Greek	Dining Staff	International
Total Cabins	875
Size Range (sq ft/m)	172-1,173/15.7-108.9
Outside Cabins	571	Inside Cabins	304
Single Cabins	0	Supplement	Set rates
Balcony Cabins	61	Wheelchair Cabins	8
Cabin TV	Yes	VCR Upper grades only
Dining Rooms	2	Sittings	2
Elevators	9
Cabin Current	110/220 AC
Casino	Yes	Slot Machines	Yes

Swimming Pools (outside)			2
Swimming Pools (inside)		1 hydropool
Whirlpools	4	Gymnasium	Yes
Sauna/Steam Room	Yes	Massage	Yes
Self-service Launderette			No
Movie Theater/Seats			Yes/190
Library			Yes
Children's Facilities/Playroom:			Yes
Watersports Facilities			None
Classification Society		Lloyd's Register

RATINGS	SCORE
Ship: Condition/Cleanliness	NYR
Ship: Space/Flow/Comfort	NYR
Ship: Decor/Furnishings	NYR
Ship: Fitness Facilities	NYR
Cabins: Comfort/Facilities	NYR
Cabins: Software	NYR
Food: Dining Room/Cuisine	NYR
Food: Buffets/Informal Dining	NYR
Food: Quality of Ingredients	NYR
Service: Dining Room	NYR
Service: Bars	NYR
Service: Cabins	NYR
Cruise: Entertainment	NYR
Cruise: Activities Program	NYR
Cruise: Hospitality Standard	NYR
OVERALL RATING	

+ This ship, which looks, externally, like a larger version of the popular *Horizon/Zenith*, is well balanced despite its squarish stern and has the distinctive Celebrity Cruises "X" funnel ("X" being the Greek letter "C," which stands for Chandris, the owning company). With a very high passenger space ratio for such a large ship, there should not be any sense of crowding, and passenger flow is very well thought out. This is a contemporary ship full of superlatives. Features a stunning two-level, 1,000 seat showlounge/theater, three-deck-high main foyer, and 4.5 acres of open deck space, together with a stunning array of other public rooms and enhanced passenger facilities. An outstanding AquaSpa (9,340 sq ft/867.6m^2), set forward and high, has huge panoramic windows and the latest high-tech equipment, all set in a Japanese environment, complete with shoji screens and Japanese rock garden.

The wide passageways provide plenty of indoor space for strolling, so there's no feeling of being crowded, and passenger flow is excellent. Also has a dedicated movie theater, which doubles as a conference and meeting center with all the latest audio-visual technology, as well as three-language simultaneous translation, and headsets for the hearing-impaired. Michael's Club is destined to become the favorite watering place for those who smoke, with decor reminiscent of a real English gentlemen's club.

A wide variety of cabin types includes 18 family cabins, each with two lower beds, two fold-away beds and one upper berth. All cabins throughout the ship have interactive television and entertainment systems (you can even go shopping interactively), as well as hairdryers in the bathrooms, and 100% cotton towels. All cabins also have a personal safe, mini-bar refrigerator and hairdryer and are very nicely equipped and decorated, with warm wood-finish furniture and none of the "boxy" feel of cabins on many ships as a result of the placement of vanity and audio-video consoles at an angle. In addition, all suites will feature butler service and in-cabin dining facilities.

The ultimate in accommodations aboard this ship are two beautifully decorated Presidential Suites of 1,173 sq ft (109m^2), each, located mid-ships in the most desirable position (can be combined with the adjacent mini-suite via an inter-connecting door, to provide a total of 1,515 sq ft (140.7m^2) of living space, the largest at sea today). Each has a marble-floored foyer, living room with mahogany wood floor and hand-woven rug; separate dining area with six-seat dining table; butler's pantry with wet bar, wine bar with private label stock, refrigerator and microwave; huge private balcony with dining table for two, chaise lounge chairs with cushioned pads, hot tub and dimmer-controlled lighting; master bedroom dressed with fine fabrics and draperies, Egyptian cotton bed linens, king-sized bed; all-marble bathroom with jet-spray shower and whirlpool bath; walk-in closet with abundant storage space. Interactive Sony audio and video facilities for booking shore excursions, ordering room service and purchasing goods from the ship's boutiques, so you don't have to leave your quarters if you don't wish to, especially if you don't like the ports of call! Naturally, electrically operated blinds and other goodies are standard, with everything controlled from a special unit.

— Because this is a large ship, you should expect some lines to form for embarkation, disembarkation, shore excursions, and informal buffet meals, although Celebrity Cruises staff will do their best to minimize any discomfort, and embarkation will be staggered. Disembarkation is the one weak link in the Celebrity operation. The dining room chairs should, but do not, have armrests. There are no cabins for singles.

Dining Features a really grand staircase that connects the upper and lower levels of the two-level dining room, each level with its own finishing galley. The design of the two galleys is excellent, and is such that food that should be hot *will* arrive hot at the table. There is also a huge indoor/outdoor lido café, called Islands, with four well-designed serving stations, as well as special grill serving stations located adjacent to the swimming pools, and a Sky Bar located on a second level.

An in-suite dining alternative (for all meals, including full dinners) will be featured for the two Presidential and 48 Century suites. Celebrity Cruises has established an enviable reputation for fine dining aboard its ships, and this tradition will be continued. Michel Roux, whose design of Celebrity Cruises' menus and tight control over their correct cooking and delivery, will assure consistency of product.

Other Comments This latest, and largest ship for Celebrity Cruises (almost 50% larger than *Horizon/Zenith*) is expected to provide the best of contemporary features for its passengers, and has taken over the itineraries of the *Zenith*. The ship, though large, is quite stunning, not only from a passenger facilities point of view, but also from the standpoint of technical and engineering excellence, and the over-indulgence of fire and safety equipment. The ship also provides an extremely high crew/passenger ratio of 1.9, the highest of any new large cruise ship, and is thus expected to provide a high level of service for its passengers. This ship looks set to become a most sought-after ship on which to take a seven-day Caribbean cruise.

ms Columbus Caravelle ★★★★

OPERATES

BALTIC AND SOUTHEAST
ASIA CRUISES

Cruise Line	Odessa Cruise Company
Former Names	Sally Caravelle/Delfin Caravelle
Gross Tonnage	7,560
Builder	Rauma Yards (Finland)
Original Cost	$60 million
Christened By	Mrs Leena Matomaki
Entered Service	Jul 1990/Jan 10, 1995
Interior Design	Arto Kukkasiemi
Country of Registry	Bahamas (C6KP5)
Tel No 130-5133	Fax No 130-5133
Length (ft/m)	381.8/116.40
Beam (ft/m) 55.7/17.00	Draft (ft/m) 14.4/4.40
Propulsion/Propellers	diesel (6,000kW)/2 (CP)
Decks 5	Crew 120
Pass. Capacity (basis 2) 250	(all berths) 303
Pass. Space Ratio (basis 2) 29.0	(all berths) 25.0
Officers	Ukrainian
Dining Staff	East/West European
Total Cabins	178
Size Range (sq ft/m)	78-243/7.2-22.5
Outside Cabins 98	Inside Cabins 80
Single Cabins 78	Supplement None
Balcony Cabins 8	Wheelchair Cabins 2
Cabin Current 220 AC	Refrigerator All cabins
Cabin TV Yes	VCR Yes
Dining Rooms 1	Sittings 1
Elevators	2
Casino No	Slot Machines No

Swimming Pools (outside) 1		(inside)	0
Whirlpools	1	Gymnasium	No
Sauna/Steam Room			Yes (2)/No
Massage			Yes
Self-Service Launderette			No
Lecture Room/Theater/Seats			Yes/156
Library	Yes	Children's Facilities	No
Watersports Facilities			None
Classification Society			American Bureau of Shipping

RATINGS	SCORE
Ship: Condition/Cleanliness	7.9
Ship: Space/Flow/Comfort	7.7
Ship: Decor/Furnishings	8.8
Ship: Fitness Facilities	6.2
Cabins: Comfort/Facilities	7.9
Cabins: Software	7.9
Food: Dining Room/Cuisine	7.7
Food: Buffets/Informal Dining	7.1
Food: Quality of Ingredients	7.3
Service: Dining Room	7.6
Service: Bars	7.7
Service: Cabins	8.8
Cruise: Entertainment	7.0
Cruise: Activities Program	6.0
Cruise: Hospitality Standard	7.7
OVERALL RATING	113.3

+ Twin swept-back outboard funnels highlight the smart exterior design of this small cruise ship, with its ice-hardened hull and shallow draft. Carries rubber landing craft for flexible, in-depth destination-oriented soft expedition cruise itineraries. All cabins are quiet, as they are located forward, with public rooms aft. Has an attractive wintergarden area and forward observation bar. Good outdoor observation decks. Well-designed lecture facilities. Contemporary interior design uses pleasing colors and complementary fabrics. Cabins are furnished to a high standard. Eight suites feature private balcony and whirlpool bathtub. Bathrobes for all. Large number of single cabins makes this a good vessel for solo cruising.

— Soundproofing between cabins is poor. Cabin bathrooms have small towels.

Dining Spacious dining room has light decor and good ambiance, and accommodates all passengers at one sitting. Service is by Russian and Ukrainian waitresses. The food quality is good, but menu choice is rather limited.

Other Comments This ship, under charter for part of the year to Transocean Cruise Lines, presently cruises from Singapore during the winter season as the *Lido Star*. Her slightly smaller sister ship, which cruises from Kota Kinabalu, is called *Delfin Star* (not listed in this edition due to lack of space).

ss Constitution ★★★

OPERATES

*7-DAY HAWAII CRUISES
(YEAR-ROUND)*

Cruise Line	American Hawaii Cruises
Former Names	Oceanic Constitution
Gross Tonnage	30,090
Builder	Bethlehem Shipbuilders (USA)
Original Cost	$20 million
Christened By	Mrs Charles Bey
Entered Service	Jun 6, 1951/Jun 5, 1982
Interior Design	Henry Dreyfuss
Country of Registry	USA (KAEG)
Tel No - Fax No	-
Length (ft/m)	681.7/207.80
Beam (ft/m) 88.9/27.10 Draft (ft/m)	30.1/9.20
Propulsion	steam turbine (40,456kW)
Propellers	2 (FP)
Decks 9 Crew	315
Pass. Capacity (basis 2) 796 (all berths)	1,004
Pass. Space Ratio (basis 2) 37.8 (all berths)	29.9
Officers American Dining Staff	American
Total Cabins	398
Size Range (sq ft/m)	75-410/7.0-38.0
Outside Cabins 179 Inside Cabins	219
Single Cabins 9 Supplement	60-100%
Balcony Cabins 0 Wheelchair Cabins	0
Cabin Current	110 AC
Refrigerator	Category 0/AA/A only
Cabin TV No VCR	No
Dining Rooms 2 Sittings	2
Elevators	4

Casino	No	Slot Machines	No
Swimming Pools (outside) 2		(inside)	0
Whirlpools	0	Gymnasium	Yes
Sauna/Steam Room Yes/No		Massage	Yes
Self-Service Launderette			Yes
Movie Theater/Seats			Yes/144
Library	Yes	Children's Facilities	Yes
Watersports Facilities			None
Classification Society		American Bureau of Shipping	

RATINGS	SCORE
Ship: Condition/Cleanliness	6.2
Ship: Space/Flow/Comfort	6.8
Ship: Decor/Furnishings	6.1
Ship: Fitness Facilities	5.8
Cabins: Comfort/Facilities	6.2
Cabins: Software	7.0
Food: Dining Room/Cuisine	6.3
Food: Buffets/Informal Dining	6.1
Food: Quality of Ingredients	6.4
Service: Dining Room	6.6
Service: Bars	6.7
Service: Cabins	6.4
Cruise: Entertainment	6.0
Cruise: Activities Program	6.2
Cruise: Hospitality Standard	6.4
OVERALL RATING	95.2

+ American-built, registered and crewed, this ship has expansive open deck space and two freshwater swimming pools. Wrap-around outdoor promenade deck. Public areas are spacious, with high ceilings. Varied range of cabin types and configurations, most of which offer ample room, decent closet and drawer space, and bright decor. Heavy-duty furniture and fittings are designed for unkind oceans. Some outside cabins have windows that open.

— Solidly constructed vessel is now over 40 years old and needs more than a facelift. Poor air-conditioning in several places. Awkward interior layout, with numerous dead-end passageways. Room service is slow. Showlounge is too small and always crowded. Drinks prices excessive. No stabilizers, so the ship rolls...and rolls. Public bathrooms are old.

Dining Two dining rooms are quite spacious, with well-spaced tables. Typically American-Polynesian food, but presentation and menu choice could be better. Poor bread selection. Good self-service buffet. Very expensive wine list (most are Californian). Service comes with a smile, but is slow and lacks finesse. First evening's dinner is buffet-style.

Other Comments Families with children cruise during the summer and other school holidays, otherwise passengers are 50+. Returns to service in June 1996 following a one-year refit. Note that the rating and evaluation above was done prior to this extensive refit.

mv CostaAllegra ★★★★

OPERATES

7-13 DAY CARIBBEAN AND MEDITERRANEAN CRUISES

Cruise Line	Costa Cruises
Former Names	Annie Johnson
Gross Tonnage	28,430
Builder	Mariotti Shipyards (Italy)
Original Cost	$175 million
Christened By	Adrienne Greene, Cheryl Myerson,
Dorothy Maitland, Bernice Rosmarin, Nancy Lian
Entered Service	Dec 19, 1992
Interior Design	Guido Canali
Country of Registry	Italy (ICRA)
Tel No 115-1562 Fax No	115-1557
Length (ft/m)	616.7/187.94
Beam (ft/m) 84.6/25.75 Draft (ft/m)	27.1/8.22
Propulsion/Propellers	diesel (19,200kW)/2 (CP)
Decks 8 Crew	405
Pass. Capacity (basis 2) 810 (all berths)	1,066
Pass. Space Ratio (basis 2) 35.1 (all berths)	26.6
Officers Italian Dining Staff	Italian/International
Total Cabins	405
Size Range (sq ft/m)	105-266/9.8-24.7
Outside Cabins 218 Inside Cabins	187
Single Cabins 0 Supplement	50%
Balcony Cabins	10
Wheelchair Cabins	8 (inside)
Cabin Current	110 AC
Refrigerator	Grand suites only
Cabin TV Yes VCR	No
Dining Rooms 1 Sittings	2

Elevators			4
Casino	Yes	Slot Machines	Yes
Swimming Pools (outside) 1		(inside)	0
Whirlpools	3	Gymnasium	Yes
Sauna/Steam Room Yes/Yes		Massage	No
Self-Service Launderette			No
Movie Theater/Seats			Yes/370
Library	Yes	Children's Facilities	Yes
Watersports Facilities			None
Classification Society			RINA

RATINGS	SCORE
Ship: Condition/Cleanliness	7.8
Ship: Space/Flow/Comfort	7.6
Ship: Decor/Furnishings	7.7
Ship: Fitness Facilities	6.6
Cabins: Comfort/Facilities	6.7
Cabins: Software	7.3
Food: Dining Room/Cuisine	7.0
Food: Buffets/Informal Dining	6.7
Food: Quality of Ingredients	6.6
Service: Dining Room	7.3
Service: Bars	7.2
Service: Cabins	6.8
Cruise: Entertainment	6.6
Cruise: Activities Program	6.7
Cruise: Hospitality Standard	6.5
OVERALL RATING	105.1

+ Slightly longer and larger than her sister ship *CostaMarina*, this ship enjoys better quality interior fit and finish. Has a high glass-to-steel ratio, with numerous glass domes and walls admitting light. Good outdoor deck and sunning space. Cushioned pads provided for outdoor lounge chairs. Interesting glass-enclosed stern. Surprisingly fine interior decor with restful colors and soft furnishings. Decks are named after famous Italian painters.

— Angular-looking ship. Upright funnel takes getting used to. No forward observation lounge. Nice domed decorative ceilings. There are many small inside cabins, and all cabins suffer from poor soundproofing. Expect long lines at buffets. Many pillars obstruct sightlines in showroom. Pompous attitude of officers should be addressed.

Dining The dining room is quite spacious and has window views on three sides, but there are no tables for two. Dinner is later when the ship operates in Europe. The cuisine is mostly Continental with many Italian dishes featured, and generally excellent service from a bubbly staff. Good fresh pasta dishes served daily. Fruit and cheese selection is poor.

Other Comments This ship will provide a good first cruise experience for young adults who enjoy European service and a real upbeat, elegant atmosphere with an Italian accent.

mv CostaClassica ★★★★

OPERATES

*7-DAY CARIBBEAN AND
EUROPE CRUISES*

Cruise Line	Costa Cruises		
Former Names	-		
Gross Tonnage	53,700		
Builder	Fincantieri (Italy)		
Original Cost	$325 million		
Christened By	Emilia Costa Viganego/		
	Angie Dickenson		
Entered Service	Jan 25, 1992		
Interior Design	Gregotti Associates		
Country of Registry	Italy (ICIC)		
Tel No	115-1312	Fax No	115-1313
Length (ft/m)			718.5/220.61
Beam (ft/m) 98.4/30.8	Draft (ft/m)		25.0/7.60
Propulsion	diesel (22,800kW)		
Propellers			2 (CP)
Decks	10	Crew	590
Pass. Capacity (basis 2) 1,308	(all berths) 1,766		
Pass. Space Ratio (basis 2) 41.0	(all berths) 30.4		
Officers Italian	Dining Staff Italian/International		
Total Cabins			654
Size Range (sq ft/m)			185-430/17.2-40.0
Outside Cabins	438	Inside Cabins	216
Single Cabins	0	Supplement	50%
Balcony Cabins			10
Wheelchair Cabins			6 (inside)
Cabin Current	110 AC	Refrigerator Suites only	
Cabin TV	Yes	VCR	No
Dining Rooms	1	Sittings	2

Elevators			8
Casino	Yes	Slot Machines	Yes
Swimming Pools (outside) 2	(inside)		0
Whirlpools	4	Gymnasium	Yes
Sauna/Steam Room Yes/Yes	Massage		Yes
Self-Service Launderette			No
Movie Theater/Seats			Yes/577
Library	Yes	Children's Facilities	Yes
Watersports Facilities			None
Classification Society			RINA

RATINGS	SCORE
Ship: Condition/Cleanliness	8.0
Ship: Space/Flow/Comfort	8.0
Ship: Decor/Furnishings	8.1
Ship: Fitness Facilities	8.2
Cabins: Comfort/Facilities	8.0
Cabins: Software	8.0
Food: Dining Room/Cuisine	7.2
Food: Buffets/Informal Dining	6.4
Food: Quality of Ingredients	6.5
Service: Dining Room	7.7
Service: Bars	7.6
Service: Cabins	7.8
Cruise: Entertainment	6.7
Cruise: Activities Program	7.1
Cruise: Hospitality Standard	7.2
OVERALL RATING	112.5

+ Contemporary, innovative Italian design. Good business and conference facilities. Has fascinating artwork, including six hermaphrodite statues in one lounge. Fine multi-tiered amphitheater-style showroom. Cabins are generously sized and have cherrywood veneered cabinetry, useful sliding doors to bathroom and closets, and good cabin soundproofing.

— The interior is best described as an innovative design project that almost works. Forward observation lounge/nightclub sits atop ship like a lump of cheese, and fails as a nightclub. Multi-level atrium is stark, angular and cold. Poor informal buffet area. Indifferent service. Uncarpeted, marble-covered staircases are institutional. Long lines for embarkation, disembarkation shore tenders, and buffets.

Dining Dining room has a lovely, indented white ceiling, but is noisy. Good number of tables for two. Changeable wall panels create a European Renaissance atmosphere, albeit at the expense of blocking windows. Dinner on European cruises is late. Reasonable Continental cuisine, with many Italian (salty) dishes, but presentation, quality, and service are poor. Alfresco Café (outdoors) is good. Steep charge for lounge afternoon tea should stop. Breakfast and luncheon buffets are poor, and long lines mean crowding. Poor bread rolls and fruit.

Other Comments This ship has brought Costa into the mainstream—Italian-style.

mv CostaMarina ★★★+

CRUISE AREA

MEDITERRANEAN AND
SOUTH AMERICA CRUISES

Cruise Line	Costa Cruises	Casino	Yes	Slot Machines Yes
Former Names	Axel Johnson	Swimming Pools (outside) 1		(inside) 0
Gross Tonnage	25,441	Whirlpools	3	Gymnasium Yes
Builder	Marriotti Shipyards (Italy)	Sauna/Steam Room Yes/Yes		Massage Yes
Original Cost	$130 million	Self-Service Launderette		No
Christened By	Ersiliaa Bracaloni Pitorri/	Movie Theater/Seats		Yes/442
	Annette Funicello	Library		Yes
Entered Service	Jul 22, 1990	Children's Facilities		Yes
Interior Design	Guido Canali	Watersports Facilities		None
Country of Registry	Italy (IBNC)	Classification Society		RINA

Tel No 115-0610 Fax No 115-0611	
Length (ft/m) 571.8/174.25	
Beam (ft/m) 84.6/25.75 Draft (ft/m) 26.1/8.20	
Propulsion diesel (19,152kW)	
Propellers 2 (CP)	
Decks 8 Crew 390	
Pass. Capacity (basis 2) 772 (all berths) 1,025	
Pass. Space Ratio (basis 2) 31.8 (all berths) 24.0	
Officers Italian Dining Staff Italian/International	
Total Cabins 386	
Size Range (sq ft/m) 104-258/9.7-24.6	
Outside Cabins 183 Inside Cabins 203	
Single Cabins 14 Supplement 50%	
Balcony Cabins 0 Wheelchair Cabins 8 (inside)	
Cabin Current 110 AC Refrigerator No	
Cabin TV Yes VCR No	
Dining Rooms 1 Sittings 2	
Elevators 4	

RATINGS	SCORE
Ship: Condition/Cleanliness	7.8
Ship: Space/Flow/Comfort	7.6
Ship: Decor/Furnishings	7.7
Ship: Fitness Facilities	6.6
Cabins: Comfort/Facilities	6.7
Cabins: Software	7.2
Food: Dining Room/Cuisine	6.8
Food: Buffets/Informal Dining	6.6
Food: Quality of Ingredients	6.6
Service: Dining Room	7.3
Service: Bars	7.2
Service: Cabins	6.8
Cruise: Entertainment	6.6
Cruise: Activities Program	6.5
Cruise: Hospitality Standard	6.5
OVERALL RATING	104.5

+ High glass-to-steel ratio, with numerous glass domes and walls. Good passenger flow throughout her public room spaces. There are some well-stocked boutiques for shopping. The outside cabins are quite comfortable, yet plain. The illuminated cabin numbers are novel.

— Fit and finish is below the standard of competing ships in same price category. Very limited open deck and sunning space. There's no forward observation lounge. Has tiny swimming pool. Simply too many inside cabins. Poor sightlines in showroom with too many (14) pillars. Poor library.

Dining The dining room, located aft, has ocean views on three sides, is reasonably spacious, and reached by escalator. Awful lime green (institutional) color. There are only two tables for two. Table candle lights are poor quality. Good pasta, Continental cuisine, and bubbly service.

Other Comments Interesting, angular looking mid-sized ship. Has a cutaway stern replaced virtually by glass wall, and stark upright funnel cluster. Most public rooms located above accommodation decks. This very Italian ship will provide a good first cruise experience for young adults, but is much better suited to European passengers.

ms CostaPlaya ★★★+

OPERATES

7-DAY CARIBBEAN
(INCLUDING CUBA) CRUISES

Cruise Line		Costa Cruises	
Former Names		Pearl/Ocean Pearl/	
		Pearl of Scandinavia/Finnstar	
Gross Tonnage		12,475	
Builder		Wartsila (Finland)	
Original Cost		n/a	
Christened By	HRH Princess Galyani Vadhana	
Entered Service		May 25, 1967/Nov 1995	
Interior Design		A&M Katzourakis	
Country of Registry		Bahamas (C6DC)	
Tel No	110-4105	Fax No	130-5352
Length (ft/m)		517.4/157.7	
Beam (ft/m)	65.9/20.10	Draft (ft/m)	19.0/5.80
Propulsion		diesel (12,060kW)	
Propellers		2 (CP)	
Decks	9	Crew	232
Pass. Capacity (basis 2) 489		(all berths) 739	
Pass. Space Ratio (basis 2) 25.5		(all berths) 16.8	
Officers British	Dining Staff	European/Filipino
Total Cabins		250	
Size Range (sq ft/m)		n/a	
Outside Cabins	188	Inside Cabins	62
Single Cabins	11	Supplement	75-100%
Balcony Cabins	0	Wheelchair Cabins	6
Cabin Current		110/220 AC	
Refrigerator		No	
Cabin TV	No	VCR	No
Dining Rooms	1	Sittings	2

Elevators			2
Casino	Yes	Slot Machines	Yes
Swimming Pools (outside) 1		(inside)	1
Whirlpools	0	Gymnasium	Yes
Sauna/Steam Room Yes/No		Massage	Yes
Self-Service Launderette			No
Movie Theater/Seats			Yes/62
Library	Yes	Children's Facilities No	
Watersports Facilities			None
Classification Society			Bureau Veritas

RATINGS	SCORE
Ship: Condition/Cleanliness	6.7
Ship: Space/Flow/Comfort	5.9
Ship: Decor/Furnishings	7.1
Ship: Fitness Facilities	5.7
Cabins: Comfort/Facilities	7.0
Cabins: Software	7.2
Food: Dining Room/Cuisine	7.0
Food: Buffets/Informal Dining	6.6
Food: Quality of Ingredients	6.6
Service: Dining Room	7.4
Service: Bars	7.1
Service: Cabins	7.1
Cruise: Entertainment	6.6
Cruise: Activities Program	6.4
Cruise: Hospitality Standard	7.3
OVERALL RATING	101.7

+ Mildly attractive profile. Tasteful decor includes many earth tones, and some interesting artwork. Lovely refinished woods give much warmth. Indonesian and Filipino hotel staff provide personal service with a smile, although standards have declined. Explorer Deck cabins (called "suites" by the line) are quite spacious, with lots of wood paneling and portholes that open. Other cabins are quite roomy and well equipped, with lots of closet, drawer and storage space. Top-price accommodations have bathtubs, others have showers.

— Awkward layout with some dead-end passageways. Too many announcements. Ship could be cleaner. Cabin soft furnishings worn, and air-conditioning controls not clearly calibrated.

Dining The dining room is very attractive, set high in the ship and located forward, with excellent ocean views. The food is quite creative, but presentation is uninspiring. Breads and pastry items are poor, and there's a limited selection of cheeses and fruits.

Other Comments Originally built as a ferry, this ship was reconstructed in 1988 as a cruise vessel. After sailing for 12 years in the Far East, the ship was repositioned to the Caribbean area in September 1995, operating seven-day cruises. This ship provides a low-cost way for European passengers (mainly German and Italian) to experience the Caribbean and Cuba in comfort and style, and at a realistic price.

ss CostaRiviera ★★★★

OPERATES

7-DAY CARIBBEAN AND
MEDITERRANEAN CRUISES

Cruise Line	Costa Cruises	Elevators	7
Former Names	American Adventure/	Casino Yes	Slot Machines Yes
	CostaRiviera/Guglielmo Marconi	Swimming Pools (outside) 3	(inside) 0
Gross Tonnage	31,500	Whirlpools 3	Gymnasium Yes
Builder	Cantieri Riuniti dell' Adriatico (Italy)	Sauna/Steam Room Yes/No	Massage Yes
Original Cost	$33.7 million (reconstruction)	Self-Service Launderette	Yes
Christened By	Ms Connie Stevens/4 children	Movie Theater/Seats	Yes/186
Entered Service	Nov 18, 1963/Dec 18, 1993	Library Yes	Children's Facilities No
Interior Design	Jeffrey Howard	Watersports Facilities	None
Country of Registry	Italy (IBBG)	Classification Society	RINA
Tel No 115-0146 Fax No 115-0146			
Length (ft/m)	700.9/213.65	**RATINGS**	**SCORE**
Beam (ft/m) 94.1/28.71 Draft (ft/m) 28.3/8.65		Ship: Condition/Cleanliness	8.0
Propulsion	steam turbine (32,800kW)	Ship: Space/Flow/Comfort	7.4
Propellers	2 (FP)	Ship: Decor/Furnishings	7.6
Decks 8 Crew	654	Ship: Fitness Facilities	6.2
Pass. Capacity (basis 2) 924 (all berths) 1,500		Cabins: Comfort/Facilities	7.2
Pass. Space Ratio (basis 2) 34.0 (all berths) 21.0		Cabins: Software	7.3
Officers Italian Dining Staff International		Food: Dining Room/Cuisine	7.2
Total Cabins	462	Food: Buffets/Informal Dining	6.6
Size Range (sq ft/m)	150-210/14.0-19.5	Food: Quality of Ingredients	6.7
Outside Cabins 286 Inside Cabins 176		Service: Dining Room	7.4
Single Cabins 0 Supplement 100%		Service: Bars	7.5
Balcony Cabins 0 Wheelchair Cabins 0		Service: Cabins	7.4
Cabin Current	110/220 AC	Cruise: Entertainment	7.4
Refrigerator	No	Cruise: Activities Program	7.3
Cabin TV No VCR No		Cruise: Hospitality Standard	7.5
Dining Rooms 1 Sittings 2		OVERALL RATING	108.7

+ Solidly built ship is stable at sea and rides well, owing to her deep draft. Built-up fore and aft decks provide a good amount of open deck and sunning space. The interior styling, colors, appointments, and everything else is geared to families. Good array of public rooms. The cabins are for cozy families. Many cabins are for families of five or six, and many others will accommodate four. Has a very casual, bubbly ambiance and relaxed dress code.

— The ship lacks a forward observation lounge. Cabin insulation is not good, and bathrooms are very small. Expect lines for embarkation, disembarkation, buffets, and shore excursions. Too many announcements.

Dining Dining room is large and bubbly, but quite plain and unattractive, especially the ceiling. Good Continental food, with plentiful pasta, pizza, buffets. Good service from an international staff comes with a smile, but this is not for those who like quiet dining.

Other Comments Reconstructed former three-class ocean liner completely refurbished in 1993 in theme-park style for families, then refurbished again for Italian family cruising in 1994. This ship will cruise you in comfortable family-filled surroundings for a modest price, and is lots of fun. Think of this as a colorful, activity-filled ship, particularly catering to an Italian family clientele.

275

mv CostaRomantica ★★★★+

OPERATES

7-DAY CARIBBEAN AND
EUROPE CRUISES

Cruise Line	Costa Cruises	Elevators		8
Former Names	-	Casino Yes	Slot Machines	Yes
Gross Tonnage	56,800	Swimming Pools (outside) 2	(inside)	0
Builder	Fincantieri (Italy)	Whirlpools 4	Gymnasium	Yes
Original Cost	$325 million	Sauna/Steam Room Yes/No	Massage	Yes
Christened By	Maria Alessandra Fantoni Costa	Self-Service Launderette		No
Entered Service	Nov 21, 1993	Movie Theater/Seats		Yes/626
Interior Design	Gregotti Associates	Library Yes	Children's Facilities	Yes
Country of Registry	Italy (IBCR)	Watersports Facilities		None
Tel No 115-1757 Fax No	115-1760	Classification Society		RINA
Length (ft/m)	718.5/220.61			

RATINGS	SCORE
Ship: Condition/Cleanliness	8.4
Ship: Space/Flow/Comfort	8.4
Ship: Decor/Furnishings	8.6
Ship: Fitness Facilities	8.2
Cabins: Comfort/Facilities	8.2
Cabins: Software	8.0
Food: Dining Room/Cuisine	7.5
Food: Buffets/Informal Dining	6.6
Food: Quality of Ingredients	6.6
Service: Dining Room	7.6
Service: Bars	7.3
Service: Cabins	7.6
Cruise: Entertainment	7.9
Cruise: Activities Program	7.6
Cruise: Hospitality Standard	7.6
OVERALL RATING	116.1

Beam (ft/m) 98.4/30.89	Draft (ft/m)	25.0/7.60
Propulsion	diesel (22,800kW)
Propellers	2 (CP)
Decks 10	Crew	600
Pass. Capacity (basis 2) 1,356	(all berths) 1,782
Pass. Space Ratio (basis 2) 41.8	(all berths) 31.8
Officers Italian Dining Staff Italian/International
Total Cabins	678
Size Range (sq ft/m)	185-430/17.2-40.0
Outside Cabins 462	Inside Cabins	216
Single Cabins 0	Supplement	50%
Balcony Cabins	10
Wheelchair Cabins	6 (inside)
Cabin Current	110 AC
Refrigerator	Suites/Mini-suites only
Cabin TV Yes	VCR	No
Dining Rooms 1	Sittings	2

+ Sister ship to *CostaClassica*, but with better interior design. Excellent business and conference facilities. Decor is tasteful, and will appeal to both Europeans and sophisticated North Americans. Multi-level atrium is open and spacious, with a revolving mobile sculpture. Good amphitheater-style two-deck-high, multi-tiered showroom, and has interesting artwork. Also has a small chapel (in a different location to that on her sister ship). Apart from 16 suites and 18 mini-suites, which are superb, almost all cabins are of a generous size, with nicely finished cherrywood cabinetry. Good number of triple and quad cabins, ideal for families.

— Layout and flow somewhat disjointed. Showroom has stark upright seating, and sightlines are interrupted by 10 large pillars. Cabin bathrooms and showers are small. Expect long lines for embarkation, disembarkation, shore tenders, and buffets.

Dining Dining room is better designed and a little less noisy than on *CostaClassica*, with many tables for two. Reasonable Continental cuisine, but presentation, quality, and service need more attention. Poor selection of bread rolls and fruits. However, pastas are fine. Much improved and more practical buffet layout than on her sister ship.

Other Comments Bold, contemporary ship has upright funnel cluster typical of Italian styling today. Well established in Europe, Costa goes cruising Italian-style, something it does well.

ms CostaVictoria

Cruise Line	Costa Cruises	Casino	Yes	Slot Machines	Yes
Former Names	-	Swimming Pools (outside) 2	(inside)	1
Gross Tonnage	74,000	Whirlpools	8	Gymnasium	Yes
Builder	Bremer Vulkan (Germany)	Sauna/Steam Room Yes/No	Massage	Yes
Original Cost	$350 million	Self-Service Launderette		Yes
Christened By	n/a	Movie Theater/Seats		Yes/950
Entered Service	June 1996	Library		Yes
Interior Design Gregotti Associates/Robert Tillberg	Children's Facilities/Playroom:		Yes
Country of Registry	Liberia	Watersports Facilities		none
Tel No n/a Fax No	n/a	Classification Society		RINA
Length (ft/m)	823.0/251.0			
Beam (ft/m) 105.5/32.25 Draft (ft/m)	25.6/7.80	**RATINGS**		**SCORE**
Propulsion	diesel (30,000kW)	Ship: Condition/Cleanliness		NYR
Propellers	2 (CP)	Ship: Space/Flow/Comfort		NYR
Decks 14 Crew	780	Ship: Decor/Furnishings		NYR
Pass. Capacity (basis 2) 1,950 (all berths) 2,250	Ship: Fitness Facilities		NYR
Pass. Space Ratio (basis 2) 37.9 (all berths) 32.8	Cabins: Comfort/Facilities		NYR
Officers Italian Dining Staff European	Cabins: Software		NYR
Total Cabins	965	Food: Dining Room/Cuisine		NYR
Size Range (sq ft/m)	150-721/15.0-67.0	Food: Buffets/Informal Dining		NYR
Outside Cabins 625 Inside Cabins	340	Food: Quality of Ingredients		NYR
Single Cabins 0 Supplement	50%	Service: Dining Room		NYR
Balcony Cabins 6 Wheelchair Cabins 6	Service: Bars		NYR
Cabin Current	110/220 AC	Service: Cabins		NYR
Refrigerator	Yes	Cruise: Entertainment		NYR
Cabin TV Yes VCR	No	Cruise: Activities Program		NYR
Dining Rooms 2 Sittings	2	Cruise: Hospitality Standard		NYR
Elevators	12	OVERALL RATING		

+ Has an outdoor wrap-around promenade deck, large jogging track, and a four-deck-high observation lounge; on one side of it is a waterfall, while balconies open forward of the lounge: a stunning room. Seven-deck-high atrium has four glass elevators that go right up to the crystal dome. Features a large forward shopping gallery with ocean-view walls. Unusual for a new ship, there is an indoor swimming pool, and an indoor jogging track. Also has a tennis court. There are six suites and 14 mini-suites; some 65% of all cabins are outside. Good, bubbly staff will help passengers enjoy life Italian-style.

— None known at press time, although as with any large ship, there will be lines for embarkation, disembarkation, and shore excursions.

Dining The main dining room is expansive. The ship also features a two-deck-high al fresco-style café with indoor/outdoor seating (under sail-cloth canvas for the outdoor section).

Other Comments The ship's profile is similar to that of an enlarged version of the successful and popular *CostaClassica* and *CostaRomantica*. Costa Cruises now has a very contemporary fleet, operating in the Caribbean and Mediterranean, having replaced all its older tonnage in the past five years. A sister ship, slightly longer and with 1,050 cabins (but unnamed at press time) is due in June 1997.

ms Crown Dynasty ★★★★

OPERATES

7-DAY ALASKA AND CARIBBEAN CRUISES

Cruise Line	Cunard Crown Cruises	Elevators		4
Former Names	-	Casino	Yes	Slot Machines Yes
Gross Tonnage	19,089	Swimming Pools (outside) 1	(inside)	0
Builder	Union Navale de Levante (Spain)	Whirlpools	3	Gymnasium Yes
Original Cost	$100 million	Sauna/Steam Room Yes/No	Massage	Yes
Christened By	Mrs Betty Ford	Self-Service Launderette		No
Entered Service	Jul 17, 1993	Movie Theater/Seats	No	Library No
Interior Design	Yran & Storbraaten	Children's Facilities		No
Country of Registry	Panama (3FJX3)	Watersports Facilities		None
Tel No 133-7757 Fax No 133-7761		Classification Society		Det Norske Veritas
Length (ft/m)	537.4/163.81			
Beam (ft/m) 73.8/22.5 Draft (ft/m) 17.7/5.40		**RATINGS**		**SCORE**
Propulsion diesel (13,200kW) Propellers 2 (CP)		Ship: Condition/Cleanliness		8.3
Decks	7 Crew 330	Ship: Space/Flow/Comfort		7.8
Pass. Capacity (basis 2) 800	(all berths) 916	Ship: Decor/Furnishings		8.1
Pass. Space Ratio (basis 2) 23.8	(all berths) 20.8	Ship: Fitness Facilities		8.0
Officers	European/Scandinavian	Cabins: Comfort/Facilities		7.8
Dining Staff	Filipino	Cabins: Software		8.0
Total Cabins	401	Food: Dining Room/Cuisine		7.6
Size Range (sq ft/m)	140-350/13.0-32.5	Food: Buffets/Informal Dining		6.8
Outside Cabins 277 Inside Cabins 124		Food: Quality of Ingredients		6.5
Single Cabins 0 Supplement 50-100%		Service: Dining Room		7.8
Balcony Cabins 10 Wheelchair Cabins 4		Service: Bars		7.5
Cabin Current	110/220 AC	Service: Cabins		7.1
Refrigerator	Category 1 only	Cruise: Entertainment		7.8
Cabin TV Yes VCR No		Cruise: Activities Program		4.8
Dining Rooms	1	Cruise: Hospitality Standard		7.2
Sittings	2 (open seating breakfast/lunch)	OVERALL RATING		111.1

+ Handsome exterior styling. Good open deck and sunning space. Well-designed five-deck-high glass-walled atrium and off-center stairways add a sense of spaciousness. Clever interior design connects passengers with sea and light. Pleasant artwork. Interior decor in public spaces is warm and inviting, with contemporary, but not brash, art deco color combinations. Nicely furnished, wood-trimmed cabins feature large picture windows and come well equipped, complete with vanity desk unit, a good amount of drawer space, curtained windows, and personal safe. Bathrooms are somewhat compact, but are nicely fitted out and have an excellent shower stall.

— Cabins have poor soundproofing. Tiny health spa. Poorly designed showlounge is liable to congestion. Long lines for buffets and tenders. Passengers in cabins on Deck 4 are disturbed by anyone running or jogging on the open deck above, as insulation is poor.

Dining Attractive dining room is cramped, and there are no tables for two, but ambiance is warm. Cuisine is disappointing, and lacks presentation. A varied menu is provided but food arrives invariably overcooked (a problem of distance from the galley).

Other Comments This sleek mid-sized ship is handsome, and is a refreshing change for those that don't want to cruise on larger ships. Gratuities are included for UK passengers.

ms Crown Odyssey ★★★★

OPERATES

VARIOUS CRUISES WORLDWIDE

Cruise Line	Royal Cruise Line	Casino Yes	Slot Machines Yes
Former Names	-	Swimming Pools (outside) 1	(inside) 1
Gross Tonnage	34,242	Whirlpools 4	Gymnasium Yes
Builder	Meyer Werft (Germany)	Sauna/Steam Room Yes/No	Massage Yes
Original Cost	$178 million	Self-Service Launderette	Yes
Christened By	Ms Irene Panagopoulos	Movie Theater/Seats	Yes/215
Entered Service	Jun 7, 1988	Library	Yes
Interior Design	Katzourakis/Terzoglou	Children's Facilities	No
Country of Registry	Bahamas (C6II4)	Watersports Facilities	None
Tel No 110-4673 Fax No	110-4674	Classification Society	Lloyd's Register
Length (ft/m)	615.9/187.75		
Beam (ft/m) 92.5/28.20 Draft (ft/m)	23.8/7.26	**RATINGS**	**SCORE**
Propulsion	diesel (21,330kW)	Ship: Condition/Cleanliness	8.4
Propellers	2 (CP)	Ship: Space/Flow/Comfort	8.2
Decks 10 Crew	470	Ship: Decor/Furnishings	8.2
Pass. Capacity (basis 2) 1,052 (all berths) 1,221		Ship: Fitness Facilities	7.8
Pass. Space Ratio (basis 2) 32.5 (all berths) 28.0		Cabins: Comfort/Facilities	8.3
Officers Greek Dining Staff	Greek	Cabins: Software	8.2
Total Cabins	526	Food: Dining Room/Cuisine	7.5
Size Range (sq ft/m)	154-615/14.3-57.0	Food: Buffets/Informal Dining	6.8
Outside Cabins 412 Inside Cabins	114	Food: Quality of Ingredients	6.7
Single Cabins 0 Supplement	100%	Service: Dining Room	7.5
Balcony Cabins 16 Wheelchair Cabins	4	Service: Bars	7.6
Cabin Current	110 AC	Service: Cabins	7.4
Refrigerator	Categories AA/AB only	Cruise: Entertainment	7.4
Cabin TV No VCR	No	Cruise: Activities Program	7.1
Dining Rooms 1 Sittings	2	Cruise: Hospitality Standard	7.7
Elevators	4	OVERALL RATING	114.8

+ This well-designed and built ship has a handsome profile with generally good passenger flow, ample space, and fine quality interiors. Well-planned and interesting itineraries. Spacious layout and many public rooms. Generous warm woods and marble used. Has a wrap-around outdoor promenade deck. Excellent Roman-style indoor spa, pool and facilities. Good theater-style showroom, but sightlines could be better. Suites are spacious; each is decorated in a different style. Most cabins have good closet and drawer space, and come well equipped. Cabin soundproofing is good. Non-smoking cabins are available. Friendly staff.

— Expect long lines for tenders, embarkation, disembarkation (especially), elevators, and buffets. Cruise cuisine is moderately good, but needs upgrading. There are no padded mattresses for the deck lounge chairs.

Dining Large, noisy, dining room features a stained-glass ceiling and comfortable seating. The Continental cuisine is not gourmet either in quality or presentation, but is adequate. The waiters are excellent, and very attentive, though sometimes too friendly.

Other Comments Excellent for the older passenger, this ship exudes style and charm, for a moderately decent price. The gentlemen "host" program is excellent. You'll be pampered with refined living at sea aboard this ship, although discounting has led to some decline in quality.

mv Crown Princess ★★★★+

OPERATES

*7-DAY ALASKA AND CARIBBEAN
CRUISES*

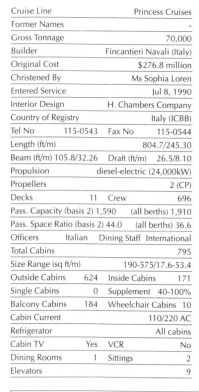

Cruise Line	Princess Cruises		
Former Names	-		
Gross Tonnage	70,000		
Builder	Fincantieri Navali (Italy)		
Original Cost	$276.8 million		
Christened By	Ms Sophia Loren		
Entered Service	Jul 8, 1990		
Interior Design	H. Chambers Company		
Country of Registry	Italy (ICBB)		
Tel No 115-0543	Fax No 115-0544		
Length (ft/m)	804.7/245.30		
Beam (ft/m) 105.8/32.26	Draft (ft/m) 26.5/8.10		
Propulsion	diesel-electric (24,000kW)		
Propellers	2 (CP)		
Decks 11	Crew 696		
Pass. Capacity (basis 2) 1,590	(all berths) 1,910		
Pass. Space Ratio (basis 2) 44.0	(all berths) 36.6		
Officers Italian	Dining Staff International		
Total Cabins	795		
Size Range (sq ft/m)	190-575/17.6-53.4		
Outside Cabins 624	Inside Cabins 171		
Single Cabins 0	Supplement 40-100%		
Balcony Cabins 184	Wheelchair Cabins 10		
Cabin Current	110/220 AC		
Refrigerator	All cabins		
Cabin TV Yes	VCR No		
Dining Rooms 1	Sittings 2		
Elevators	9		

Casino	Yes	Slot Machines	Yes
Swimming Pools (outside) 2		(inside)	0
Whirlpools	4	Gymnasium	Yes
Sauna/Steam Room Yes/No		Massage	Yes
Self-Service Launderette			Yes
Movie Theater/Seats			Yes/169
Library			Yes
Children's Facilities			No
Watersports Facilities			None
Classification Society		Lloyd's Register	

RATINGS	SCORE
Ship: Condition/Cleanliness	8.0
Ship: Space/Flow/Comfort	7.8
Ship: Decor/Furnishings	7.9
Ship: Fitness Facilities	8.0
Cabins: Comfort/Facilities	8.1
Cabins: Software	8.2
Food: Dining Room/Cuisine	7.2
Food: Buffets/Informal Dining	7.0
Food: Quality of Ingredients	7.3
Service: Dining Room	7.4
Service: Bars	7.7
Service: Cabins	7.8
Cruise: Entertainment	8.1
Cruise: Activities Program	7.8
Cruise: Hospitality Standard	7.6
OVERALL RATING	115.9

+ Innovative styling mixed with traditional features, and spacious interior layout. Good swimming pool deck. An observation dome features large casino, dance floor and live music. Good health spa facilities. Strikingly elegant three-deck-high atrium features grand staircase with fountain sculpture (real, stand-up cocktail parties are held here). Understated pastel decor is highlighted by colorful artwork. Well-designed cabins have large bathrooms, good soundproofing, walk-in closets, refrigerator, safe, and interactive video system.

— No wrap-around outdoor promenade deck (the only walking space is along the sides of the ship). When full, there is not enough outdoor space, and little connection with outside. No non-enclosed forward viewing space. Too many pillars in public rooms obstruct sightlines. Internal layout somewhat disjointed. Cabins for the physically challenged have obstructed views. Expect lines for embarkation, disembarkation, buffets, shore excursions, and tenders.

Dining Large dining room lacks tables for two. Some interesting tables overlook the stern. Disappointing, stodgy cuisine, with poor creativity and presentation. Pasta dishes are good. Service is reasonable, but perfunctory. There is an excellent, but small, pizzeria.

Other Comments This ship provides a decent cruise environment in elegant and comfortable surroundings, with service by a lukewarm staff.

mv Crystal Harmony ★★★★★+

OPERATES
VARIOUS CRUISES WORLDWIDE

Cruise Line			Crystal Cruises
Former Names		- Gross Tonnage	48,621
Builder		Mitsubishi Heavy Industries (Japan)	
Original Cost			$240 million
Christened By			Ms Mary Tyler Moore
Entered Service			Jul 24, 1990
Interior Design			Robert Tillberg
Country of Registry			Bahamas (C6IP2)
Tel No	110-3237	Fax No	110-3242
Length (ft/m)			790.5/240.96
Beam (ft/m) 97.1/29.60		Draft (ft/m)	24.6/7.50
Propulsion		diesel-electric (32,800kW)	
Propellers			2 (CP)
Decks 8	Crew 545	Total Cabins	480
Pass. Capacity (basis 2) 960		(all berths) 1,010	
Pass. Space Ratio (basis 2) 50.6		(all berths) 48.9	
Officers			Scandinavian/Japanese
Dining Staff			European/Filipino
Size Range (sq ft/m)			183-948/17.0-88.0
Outside Cabins	461	Inside Cabins	19
Single Cabins	0	Supplement	20-100%
Balcony Cabins	260	Wheelchair Cabins	4
Cabin Current			115/220 AC
Refrigerator			All cabins
Cabin TV	Yes	VCR	Yes
Dining Rooms		3 (2 alternative restaurants)	
Sittings		2 (dinner only, main restaurant)	
Elevators			8

Casino	Yes	Slot Machines	Yes
Swimming Pools (outside)		2 (1 with magrodome)	
(inside)			0
Whirlpools	2	Gymnasium	Yes
Sauna/Steam Room Yes/Yes		Massage	Yes
Self-Service Launderette			Yes
Movie Theater/Seats			Yes/270
Library	Yes	Children's Facilities	Yes
Classification Society			Lloyd's Register/
			Nippon Kaiji Kyokai

RATINGS	SCORE
Ship: Condition/Cleanliness	9.1
Ship: Space/Flow/Comfort	9.5
Ship: Decor/Furnishings	9.2
Ship: Fitness Facilities	9.0
Cabins: Comfort/Facilities	8.7
Cabins: Software	9.0
Food: Dining Room/Cuisine	8.8
Food: Buffets/Informal Dining	8.8
Food: Quality of Ingredients	8.6
Service: Dining Room	9.1
Service: Bars	9.0
Service: Cabins	9.0
Cruise: Entertainment	9.1
Cruise: Activities Program	8.7
Cruise: Hospitality Standard	9.5
OVERALL RATING	135.1

+ Handsome contemporary ship with raked clipper bow and well-balanced, sleek flowing lines. Excellent open deck, sunning space, and sports facilities. One of two outdoor swimming pools has a swim-up bar and can be covered by a magrodome. There's almost no sense of crowding anywhere, a superb example of comfort by design, quality construction and engineering. Has wrap-around teakwood deck for walking. Fine assortment of public entertainment lounges and small intimate rooms. Outstanding are the Vista (observation) Lounge and the supremely tranquil, elegant Palm Court, one of the nicest rooms afloat. A Business Center features laptop computer, printer, satellite fax, phone.

Has an excellent book and video library. Theater features high-definition video projection, and special headsets for the hearing-impaired. Useful self-service launderette on each deck. Fine quality fabrics and soft furnishings, china, flatware and silver are used. Fine in-cabin television programming, and close-captioned videos for the hearing-impaired.
Spacious, well-designed accommodations, including four spectacular Crystal penthouses that feature a huge private balcony and lounge, bedroom with queen-sized bed and electric curtains, and stunning ocean-view bathroom. Five butlers feature the best in personal service in the top category suites (Penthouse Deck 10 with a total of 132 beds), where all room service food arrives on sterling silver trays. More than 50% of all cabins have private

balconies, and are supremely comfortable. Even in standard cabins, there's plenty of drawer space, some recently added to lower-grade cabins, although closet hanging space is somewhat limited for long voyages. Excellent cabin soundproofing. Generously sized Caswell-Massey personal bathroom amenities. Very friendly, well-trained, highly professional staff and excellent teamwork, under the direction of an all-European middle management. It is the extra attention to detail that makes a cruise on this ship so special, such as few announcements, and no background music anywhere.

— The main dining room features two sittings for dinner (the earlier sitting is too rushed). There should be separate entrances for the two alternative restaurants (at present one entrance serves both). Except for the penthouse suites, cabin bathrooms are somewhat compact, and closet space is quite limited, particularly on longer voyages. Some cabins (grades G and I), but no public rooms, have obstructed views.

Dining The dining room is elegant, with plenty of space around each table, well-placed waiter service stations, and a good number of tables for two. Food is attractively presented and well served (silver service). It is of a very high standard, with fine quality ingredients used throughout. Features a mixture of European specialties and North American favorites. The menus are extremely varied, and special orders are available, as is caviar and many other niceties. All in all, the food is most acceptable and, with the choice of the two alternative dining spots, provides consistently high ratings from passengers.

Dinner in the main dining room is in two sittings, but with two alternative restaurants, off-menu choices and a fine hand-picked European staff and impeccable service, dining is memorable.

Pasta specialties are made each day on request to the head waiters. For those who enjoy caviar, it is available, but is Sevruga (Malossol) and not Beluga. The wine list is superb. Afternoon Tea (and coffee) in the Palm Court is delightful, and refreshed constantly. Superlative choice of sandwiches, cakes and pastries. Needless to say, service is generally excellent.

Two alternative restaurants—Prego (superb pasta dishes), and Kyoto, with pseudo-Japanese specialties (there's no extra charge, other than a recommended $5 waiter gratuity per meal that should be included in the cruise fare)—are intimate, have great views and feature fine food.

Other Comments This ship has just about everything for the discerning, seasoned traveler that wants and is prepared to pay for good style, space, and the comfort and the facilities of a large vessel capable of longer voyages. This ship is without doubt an outstanding example of the latest style in contemporary grand hotels afloat and provides abundant choices and flexibility. Following a refit in 1995, some of the public rooms have been expanded. You'll be surrounded by a cocoon of creative comfort and pampering to the highest degree. Insurance and gratuities are extra, but should be included.

ms Crystal Symphony ★★★★★+

OPERATES

ALASKA/AUSTRALASIA/SOUTHEAST ASIA CRUISES

Cruise Line	Crystal Cruises	Elevators		8
Gross Tonnage	50,202	Casino	Yes Slot Machines	Yes
Builder	Masa-Yards (Finland)	Swimming Pools (outside)	2 (1 with magrodome)
Original Cost	$300 million	(inside)		0
Christened By	Ms Angela Lansbury	Whirlpools	2 Gymnasium	Yes
Entered Service	May 4, 1995	Sauna/Steam Room Yes/Yes	Massage	Yes
Interior Design	Robert Tillberg	Self-Service Launderette		Yes
Country of Registry	Bahamas (C6MY5)	Movie Theater/Seats		Yes/143
Tel No	630-916820/30/40/50/60	Library	Yes Children's Facilities	Yes
Fax No	130-6716	Classification Society	Lloyd's Register
Length (ft/m)	777.8/237.10			
Beam (ft/m) 98.0/30.20	Draft (ft/m) 24.9/7.60	**RATINGS**		**SCORE**
Propulsion	diesel-electric (33,880kW)	Ship: Condition/Cleanliness		9.3
Propellers	2 (CP)	Ship: Space/Flow/Comfort		9.5
Decks 8	Crew 530	Ship: Decor/Furnishings		9.3
Pass. Capacity (basis 2) 960	(all berths) 1,010	Ship: Fitness Facilities		9.1
Pass. Space Ratio (basis 2) 52.2	(all berths) 49.7	Cabins: Comfort/Facilities		8.7
Officers Scandinavian	Dining Staff European	Cabins: Software		9.0
Total Cabins	480	Food: Dining Room/Cuisine		8.8
Size Range (sq ft/m)	202-982/18.7-91.2	Food: Buffets/Informal Dining		8.6
Outside Cabins 480	Inside Cabins 0	Food: Quality of Ingredients		8.6
Single Cabins 0	Supplement 20-100%	Service: Dining Room		9.1
Balcony Cabins 276	Wheelchair Cabins 7	Service: Bars		9.0
Cabin Current	110/220 AC	Service: Cabins		9.0
Refrigerator	All cabins	Cruise: Entertainment		9.1
Cabin TV Yes	VCR Yes	Cruise: Activities Program		8.7
Dining Rooms	3	Cruise: Hospitality Standard		9.5
Sittings	2 (dinner only, main dining room)	OVERALL RATING		135.3

+ This is a contemporary ship that has nicely raked clipper bow and well-balanced lines. Has excellent open deck, sunning space, and sports facilities. The aft of two outdoor swimming pools can be covered by a magrodome in inclement weather. No sense of crowding anywhere, a superb example of comfort by design, high-quality construction and engineering. Has a wide wrap-around teakwood deck, uncluttered by lounge chairs.
Interior decor is restful, with color combinations that don't jar the senses. Has a good mixture of public entertainment lounges and small intimate rooms. Outstanding is the Palm Court, a forward observation lounge that is tranquil, and one of the nicest rooms afloat (it is larger than on the sister ship). There's an excellent book, video and CD-ROM library (combined with a Business Center). The theater (smaller than on the sister ship) features high-definition video projection, and headsets for the hearing-impaired. Useful self-service launderette on each deck. Fine quality fabrics and soft furnishings, china, flatware and silver are used. Excellent in-cabin television programming (including CNN and ESPN), and close-captioned videos for the hearing-impaired.
Spacious, well-designed accommodations include two spectacular 982 sq ft (91.2m²) Crystal penthouses with a huge balcony and lounge, bedroom with queen-sized bed, and stunning ocean-view bathroom with large whirlpool bath. Butlers feature the best in personal service in the top category suites on Penthouse Deck 10, where all room service food arrives on sterling

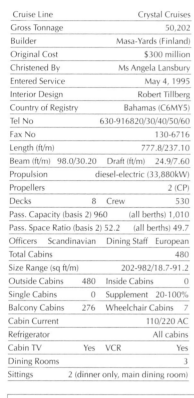

silver trays, and lots of extra goodies are provided for occupants. All other cabins (called "penthouses" by Crystal Cruises) on Deck 10 are worth the asking price, being extremely spacious, supremely comfortable and quiet units equipped with everything necessary for refined, private living at sea.

More than 50% of all cabins have private balconies, are very well equipped and extremely comfortable, with excellent sound insulation. Even in the lowest category of standard cabins, there's plenty of drawer space, but the 7.25 ft (2.2m) of closet hanging space may prove somewhat limited for long voyages. Has generously sized personal bathroom amenities, duvets and down pillows. European stewardesses provide excellent service and attention. Highly professional and attentive staff. It is the extra attention to detail that make a cruise on this ship so special, such as very few announcements.

— Some might not like the "apartment block" look of the ship's exterior, it's the look of the future, as balconies become the norm. Balcony partitions are not floor to ceiling (so you can hear your neighbors). The main dining room features two sittings for dinner (the earlier sitting is too rushed). Some cabins (grades G and I), but no public rooms, have obstructed views. Except for the penthouse suites, cabin bathrooms are somewhat compact. There's no wrap-around passageway on Deck 6 as there is on the sister ship (dead-ends lead to the two alternative restaurants). A privacy curtain should be placed between entrance and sleeping area in all non-Penthouse Deck cabins.

Dining The main dining room is quite elegant, with crisp design and plenty of space around each table, well-placed waiter service stations, and ample tables for two. The main dining room is somewhat noisy at times, and not conducive to a fine dining experience. It is well laid out, and features a raised, circular central section. There are tables for two (many of them positioned adjacent to large windows), four, six or eight.

Food is attractively presented and well served (mix of plate and silver service). It is of a high standard, with fine quality ingredients used. Features mainly European dishes. Menus are extremely varied, and feature a good selection of meat, fish and vegetarian dishes. Special (off-menu) orders are available, as is caviar and other culinary niceties.

Overall, the food is most acceptable for a large ship and, with the choice of the two alternative dining spots, receives high passenger praise. Dinner in the main dining room is in two sittings, but with two alternative restaurants, off-menu choices, a fine European staff and excellent service, dining can be quite memorable.

Fresh pasta and dessert flambeau specialties are made each day by the head waiters at tableside. The wine list is excellent.

Afternoon Tea in the Palm Court is a delightful daily event.

The Lido provides breakfast and luncheon buffets that are fairly standard fare.

Two alternative dining rooms, the 75-seat "Prego" (serving Italian cuisine), and the 84-seat "Jade Garden" (serving contemporary Chinese dishes), are appreciably larger and set on a lower deck (Deck 6) than on the sister ship, and each restaurant has a separate entrance and themed decor. They both provide an excellent standard of culinary fare, with food individually cooked to order, at no extra charge (but the recommended $5 waiter gratuity per meal should be included in the cruise fare).

In addition, The Bistro provides a fine array of snacks, cakes, coffees, and teas throughout the day, with unusual, Crystal-logo china.

Other Comments Besides abundant space, it's the staff that makes this cruise experience really special. They are a fine-tuned, well-trained group whose middle name is hospitality. With few design defects, *Crystal Symphony* is a refined ship in today's contemporary cruise industry, and a fine sea-going resort for those that want the newest in furnishings and surroundings. There are subtle differences between this and sister ship *Crystal Harmony*, notably in the repositioning of the two alternative restaurants, to a lower deck; the doubling in size of the popular Crystal Cove and the Lido Cafe.

Gratuities should be included on a ship so highly rated (they can be pre-paid, however). Port taxes and insurance are extra.

mv Cunard Countess ★★★+

OPERATES

7- AND 14-DAY CARIBBEAN CRUISES (YEAR-ROUND)

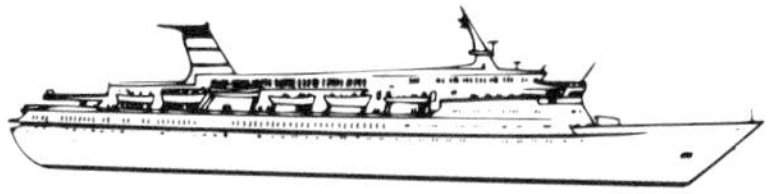

Cruise Line			Cunard Crown Cruises
Former Names			-
Gross Tonnage			17,593
Builder			Burmeister & Wein (Denmark)
Original Cost			UK£12 million
Christened By			Mrs Janet Armstrong
Entered Service			Aug 7, 1976
Interior Design			McNeece Design
Country of Registry			Bahamas (CBCF)
Tel No	110-4676	Fax No	110-4676
Length (ft/m)			536.6/163.56
Beam (ft/m)	74.9/22.84	Draft (ft/m)	19.0/5.82
Propulsion			diesel (15,670kW)
Propellers			2 (CP)
Decks	8	Crew	360
Pass. Capacity (basis 2)	812	(all berths)	959
Pass. Space Ratio (basis 2)	21.6	(all berths)	18.3
Officers	British	Dining Staff	International
Total Cabins			406
Size Range (sq ft/m)			88-265/8.1-24.6
Outside Cabins	249	Inside Cabins	149
Single Cabins	0	Supplement	50%
Balcony Cabins	0	Wheelchair Cabins	0
Cabin Current			110/220 AC
Refrigerator			Grades 1, 2 only
Cabin TV	No	VCR	No
Dining Rooms	1	Sittings	2
Elevators			2

Casino	Yes	Slot Machines	Yes
Swimming Pools (outside)	1	(inside)	0
Whirlpools	2	Gymnasium	Yes
Sauna/Steam Room	Yes/No	Massage	No
Self-Service Launderette			No
Movie Theater/Seats			Yes/126
Library			Yes
Children's Facilities			No
Watersports Facilities			None
Classification Society			Lloyd's Register

RATINGS	SCORE
Ship: Condition/Cleanliness	6.1
Ship: Space/Flow/Comfort	6.3
Ship: Decor/Furnishings	6.6
Ship: Fitness Facilities	6.7
Cabins: Comfort/Facilities	5.8
Cabins: Software	7.7
Food: Dining Room/Cuisine	6.6
Food: Buffets/Informal Dining	6.1
Food: Quality of Ingredients	6.2
Service: Dining Room	7.0
Service: Bars	6.8
Service: Cabins	7.2
Cruise: Entertainment	7.3
Cruise: Activities Program	7.1
Cruise: Hospitality Standard	7.6
OVERALL RATING	101.1

+ Has a modern profile, with clean lines and a distinctive swept-back red funnel. Good selection of public rooms have attractive, light colors and decor. Good indoor-outdoor entertainment nightclub incorporates an aft open deck area. The cabins, mostly of a standard (small) size, are furnished with much lighter colors and better combinations, are small, space-efficient units with metal fixtures and thin walls.

– High-density vessel. Poor cabin insulation, which means you hear your neighbors brushing their hair. Cabins on the lowest deck (2 Deck) suffer from vibration and the odor of fuel. Outside decks need attention. The cabin service snack menu should be upgraded. Cramped charter flights are a turn-off, but then, the price is right.

Dining Pleasant dining room has large picture windows. Reasonable banquet food standard, tailored for UK passengers. Out of the ordinary requests difficult. Poor fruit and cheese selection. Good, cheerful service from an attentive staff, but it lacks the finesse that made Cunard famous.

Other Comments Passengers seeking a casual, destination-intensive cruise will probably like this, and come back for more. Good mainly for a destination-oriented and informal first Caribbean cruise experience. Gratuities included for UK passengers only.

mts Daphne ★★★+

OPERATES

12-DAY EUROPE/
MEDITERRANEAN CRUISES

Cruise Line	Costa Cruise Lines/Prestige Cruises	Casino	Yes
Former Names	Therisos Express/Port Sydney	
Gross Tonnage	9,436	
Builder	Swan, Hunter (UK)	
Original Cost	n/a	
Christened By	n/a	
Entered Service	Mar 1955/Jul 26, 1975	
Interior Design	A&M Katzourakis	
Country of Registry	Liberia (ELLU8)	
Tel No 124-6505 Fax No 124-3127		
Length (ft/m)	532.7/162.39	

Casino	Yes	Slot Machines	Yes
Swimming Pools (outside) 1		(inside)	0
Whirlpools	2	Gymnasium	Yes
Sauna/Steam Room Yes/No		Massage	Yes
Self-Service Launderette			Yes
Movie Theater/Seats			Yes/200
Library			Yes
Children's Facilities			No
Watersports Facilities			None
Classification Society			RINA

Beam (ft/m) 70.2/21.42	Draft (ft/m)	28.4/8.66
Propulsion		diesel (9,850kW)
Propellers		2 (FP)
Decks	7	Crew	260
Pass. Capacity (basis 2) 412		(all berths) 508
Pass. Space Ratio (basis 2) 22.9		(all berths) 18.5
Officers		Italian
Dining Staff		Italian/International
Total Cabins		206
Size Range (sq ft/m)		150-349/14.0-32.5
Outside Cabins	189	Inside Cabins	17
Single Cabins	0	Supplement	50%
Balcony Cabins	6	Wheelchair Cabins	0
Cabin Current 220 DC		Refrigerator Suites only
Cabin TV Suites only	VCR		No
Dining Rooms	1	Sittings	1
Elevators		2

RATINGS	SCORE
Ship: Condition/Cleanliness	7.1
Ship: Space/Flow/Comfort	7.2
Ship: Decor/Furnishings	7.1
Ship: Fitness Facilities	5.7
Cabins: Comfort/Facilities	7.0
Cabins: Software	7.2
Food: Dining Room/Cuisine	7.2
Food: Buffets/Informal Dining	6.6
Food: Quality of Ingredients	6.7
Service: Dining Room	7.1
Service: Bars	7.0
Service: Cabins	7.1
Cruise: Entertainment	5.7
Cruise: Activities Program	6.0
Cruise: Hospitality Standard	7.0
OVERALL RATING	101.7

+ This ship has an expansive outdoor deck and plenty of sunning space. Well-maintained vessel. Features bright, contemporary decor in the public rooms. Has a large, fine theater, which is especially good for meetings and groups. Other public rooms have fairly high ceilings. Has very spacious cabins with good, solid fittings and heavy-duty doors. There's plenty of closet and drawer space, and very good insulation between each cabin. The cabin bathrooms are of a generous size.

— There's no forward-looking observation lounge, and no wrap-around promenade deck.

Dining The dining room is quite charming, and has uncluttered seating. Has friendly, attentive and quite bubbly European service with many Italian waiters, but there's little finesse. The food is generally good, especially the pasta, of which there is plenty.

Other Comments Identical in outward appearance to sister *Danae* (presently operating as *Baltica*). Originally constructed as a general cargo vessel, she was well reconstructed as a cruise ship. This is a very comfortable ship, built to a high standard. This ship maintains an air of intimacy, has a fine range of public rooms, and represents good value when cruising on itineraries longer than a week.

mv Dimitriy Shostakovich ★★

OPERATES
14-DAY EUROPE CRUISES

Cruise Line	Black Sea Shipping		
Former Names	-		
Gross Tonnage	10,303		
Builder	A. Warski (Poland)		
Original Cost	n/a	Christened By	n/a
Entered Service	1980		
Interior Design	n/a		
Country of Registry	Ukraine (UMYN)		
Tel No	140-1336	Fax No	140-1336
Length (ft/m)	450.0/137.15		
Beam (ft/m) 68.8/21.00	Draft (ft/m)	17.3/5.28	
Propulsion	diesel (12,800kW)		
Propellers	2 (CP)		
Decks	7	Crew	150
Pass. Capacity (basis 2) 278	(all berths) 494		
Pass. Space Ratio (basis 2) 37.0	(all berths) 20.8		
Officers	Russian/Ukrainian		
Dining Staff	East European		
Total Cabins	139		
Size Range (sq ft/m)	100-320/9.3-29.7		
Outside Cabins	66	Inside Cabins	73
Single Cabins	0	Supplement	100%
Balcony Cabins	0	Wheelchair Cabins	0
Cabin Current	220 AC		
Refrigerator	No		
Cabin TV	No	VCR	No
Dining Rooms	1	Sittings	1
Elevators	1		

Casino	No	Slot Machines	No
Swimming Pools (outside) 1	(inside)		0
Whirlpools	0	Gymnasium	Yes
Sauna/Steam Room Yes/No	Massage		Yes
Self-Service Launderette			No
Movie Theater/Seats			No
Library			Yes
Children's Facilities			No
Watersports Facilities			None
Classification Society			RS

RATINGS	SCORE
Ship: Condition/Cleanliness	6.6
Ship: Space/Flow/Comfort	6.2
Ship: Decor/Furnishings	6.0
Ship: Fitness Facilities	5.6
Cabins: Comfort/Facilities	5.5
Cabins: Software	6.1
Food: Dining Room/Cuisine	5.3
Food: Buffets/Informal Dining	5.1
Food: Quality of Ingredients	5.1
Service: Dining Room	6.1
Service: Bars	6.2
Service: Cabins	6.2
Cruise: Entertainment	4.3
Cruise: Activities Program	4.7
Cruise: Hospitality Standard	5.8
OVERALL RATING	84.8

+ Has a fully enclosed bridge, as well as an ice-hardened hull, good for cold-weather cruise areas. One of a series of five Polish-built vessels intended for all-weather line voyages.

— Lacks a forward observation lounge. Limited open deck and sunning space and tiny swimming pool. Limited choice of public rooms.

Dining The dining room is reasonably comfortable, and everyone dines in one sitting, with food served family style. The food is pretty basic, no more, and menu choice is very limited, as is the selection of breads, cheeses, and fruits.

Other Comments This ship has a square, angular profile with upright stern, stubby bow and fat funnel. Interior decor is rather spartan, yet the ambiance is comfortable, made better by tropical plants. Cabins, some with upper pullman berths, are small and utilitarian in fittings and furnishings, but adequate. Bathrooms are small, however. This ship features a regular 14-day itinerary that provides a destination-oriented, basic cruise experience for an international clientele, at modest rates, nothing more.

ss Dolphin IV ★★★

OPERATES

*2- DAY BAHAMAS CRUISES
(YEAR-ROUND)*

Cruise Line	Dolphin Cruise Line	Elevators		1
Former Names	Ithaca/Amelia De Melo/Zion	Casino	Yes	Slot Machines Yes
Gross Tonnage	13,000	Swimming Pools (outside) 1	(inside)	0
Builder	Howaldtswerke Deutsche	Whirlpools	1	Gymnasium Yes
	Werft (Germany)	Sauna/Steam Room No/No	Massage	No
Original Cost	n/a	Self-Service Launderette		No
Christened By	n/a	Movie Theater/Seats No	Library	No
Entered Service	Mar 9, 1956/Jan 17, 1979	Children's Facilities		Yes
Interior Design	n/a	Watersports Facilities		None
Country of Registry	Bahamas (HOOG)	Classification Society		Lloyd's Register
Tel No	- Fax No -			
Length (ft/m)	501.2/152.77	**RATINGS**		**SCORE**
Beam (ft/m) 65.1/19.87	Draft (ft/m) 27.5/8.40	Ship: Condition/Cleanliness		6.3
Propulsion	steam turbine (7,723kW)	Ship: Space/Flow/Comfort		5.7
Propellers	1 (FP)	Ship: Decor/Furnishings		6.3
Decks 7	Crew 290	Ship: Fitness Facilities		4.5
Pass. Capacity (basis 2) 588	(all berths) 684	Cabins: Comfort/Facilities		6.4
Pass. Space Ratio (basis 2) 22.1	(all berths) 19.0	Cabins: Software		6.5
Officers Greek	Dining Staff International	Food: Dining Room/Cuisine		7.0
Total Cabins	281	Food: Buffets/Informal Dining		6.3
Size Range (sq ft/m)	73-258/6.7-24.0	Food: Quality of Ingredients		6.6
Outside Cabins 206	Inside Cabins 75	Service: Dining Room		6.6
Single Cabins 0	Supplement 50%	Service: Bars		6.6
Balcony Cabins 0	Wheelchair Cabins 0	Service: Cabins		7.0
Cabin Current	110/220 AC	Cruise: Entertainment		6.4
Refrigerator	No	Cruise: Activities Program		6.0
Cabin TV No	VCR No	Cruise: Hospitality Standard		6.5
Dining Rooms 1	Sittings 2	OVERALL RATING		94.7

+ Attractive-looking older ship with pleasing lines, even with its now very noticeable center-sag. The ship's public rooms are well decorated in clean, crisp, contemporary colors, with much use of reflective surfaces. There is a good shopping area. The showroom is reasonable, but the stage would be better at the opposite end, and seating is uncomfortable for long periods. The cabins are small, yet comfortable and quite adequate for short cruises. Friendly staff and ambiance.

— The open deck and sunning area are cramped owing to the ship's high passenger density. Has a very claustrophobic discotheque. The cabins on lower decks suffer from noise (and the smell of diesel) from the engine-room. Entertainment is rather weak and low budget.

Dining Charming dining room has warm ambiance, but is narrow and has a low ceiling. The food is reasonably good, even creative, but ingredients aren't the best. Service is moderately good, but is hurried and lacking in finesse, although the staff are friendly and try to please. Good buffet displays.

Other Comments This ship has a good, friendly, and lively ambiance and is recommended for short, fun cruises for the young, active set, but I wonder how much longer this ship can compete with the bright new ships that offer more facilities, and indeed more of everything.

mv Don Juan ★★★

OPERATES

7-DAY MEDITERRANEAN CRUISES

Cruise Line	Royal Hispania Cruises
Former Names	Crown del Mar/
	Las Palmas de Gran Canarias
Gross Tonnage	10,000
Builder	Union Navale de Levante (Spain)
Original Cost	n/a
Christened By	n/a
Entered Service	1967/Jul 1, 1994
Interior Design	G.M.O. Design
Country of Registry	Panama (3EYM6)
Tel No 135-1264	Fax No 135-1264
Length (ft/m)	428.8/130.70
Beam (ft/m) 62.9/19.20	Draft (ft/m) 18.0/5.50
Propulsion	diesel-electric (11,769kW)
Propellers	2 (CP)
Decks 5	Crew 195
Pass. Capacity (basis 2) 448	(all berths) 469
Pass. Space Ratio (basis 2) 22.3	(all berths) 21.3
Officers Norwegian	Dining Staff Filipino
Total Cabins 209	Size Range (sq ft/m) n/a
Outside Cabins 130	Inside Cabins 79
Single Cabins 0	Supplement 100%
Balcony Cabins 0	Wheelchair Cabins 1
Cabin Current	110/220 AC
Refrigerator	No
Cabin TV	Yes
Dining Rooms 1	Sittings 2
Elevators	1

Casino	Yes	Slot Machines	Yes
Swimming Pools (outside)	1	(inside)	0
Whirlpools	2	Gymnasium	No
Sauna/Steam Room	Yes/No	Massage	Yes
Self-Service Launderette			No
Movie Theater/Seats			No
Library			No
Children's Facilities/Playroom			Yes
Watersports Facilities			None
Classification Society		Lloyd's Register	

RATINGS	SCORE
Ship: Condition/Cleanliness	7.0
Ship: Space/Flow/Comfort	6.6
Ship: Decor/Furnishings	7.6
Ship: Fitness Facilities	4.3
Cabins: Comfort/Facilities	6.9
Cabins: Software	7.1
Food: Dining Room/Cuisine	6.0
Food: Buffets/Informal Dining	5.8
Food: Quality of Ingredients	6.0
Service: Dining Room	7.0
Service: Bars	7.1
Service: Cabins	7.2
Cruise: Entertainment	5.7
Cruise: Activities Program	6.0
Cruise: Hospitality Standard	6.7
OVERALL RATING	97.0

+ Has a good amount of open deck space. Inside, soft earth tones are used. Has a three-deck high atrium. Five suites, located just below the navigation bridge, command forward views, are well furnished, and have full bathtubs (most other cabins have showers), but no balconies. Standard cabins are adequate at best.

— Most public rooms are set below accommodation decks, except for one forward observation lounge. The showroom is set between accommodation decks, which makes it noisy at night for some passengers. Standard cabins have almost no drawer space, little closet space, and small bathrooms. There are no cushioned pads for deck lounge chairs. The ship seems to have a permanent list.

Dining The dining room is set low down, and has ocean views, but it's a little dark and somber. There are no tables for two. Cuisine is barely adequate, and menu choice is very limited. Reasonably attentive service staff throughout, but there's no finesse, and it's hard to communicate.

Other Comments Refurbished in 1994, this former Spanish ferry sports a new, though somewhat angular look. This ship will provide a comfortable cruise experience, but forget the word "luxury," for this is quite basic.

ms Dreamward ★★★★

Cruise Line	Norwegian Cruise Line
Former Names	-
Gross Tonnage	39,217
Builder	Chantiers de l'Atlantique (France)
Original Cost	$240 million
Christened By	Ms Diana Ross
Entered Service	Dec 6, 1992
Interior Design	Yran & Storbraaten
Country of Registry	Bahamas (C6LG5)
Tel No	130-5510	Fax No	130-5507
Length (ft/m)	623.3/190.00
Beam (ft/m) 93.5/28.50	Draft (ft/m)	22.3/6.80
Propulsion	diesel (18,480kW)
Propellers	2 (CP)
Decks	11	Crew	483
Pass. Capacity (basis 2) 1,246	(all berths) 1,450
Pass. Space Ratio (basis 2) 32.9	(all berths) 28.2
Officers Norwegian	Dining Staff International
Total Cabins	623
Size Range (sq ft/m)	140-350/13.0-32.5
Outside Cabins 530	Inside Cabins	93
Single Cabins 0	Supplement 50-100%
Balcony Cabins	48
Wheelchair Cabins 6 (+ 30 for hearing-impaired)
Cabin Current	110 AC
Refrigerator	Category 1/2/3 only
Cabin TV Yes	VCR	No
Dining Rooms 4	Sittings	2

Elevators			7
Casino	Yes	Slot Machines	Yes
Swimming Pools (outside) 2		(inside)	0
Whirlpools	2	Gymnasium	Yes
Sauna/Steam Room Yes/No		Massage	Yes
Self-Service Launderette			No
Movie Theater/Seats	No	Library	Yes
Children's Facilities			Yes
Watersports Facilities			None
Classification Society		Det Norske Veritas

RATINGS	SCORE
Ship: Condition/Cleanliness	8.6
Ship: Space/Flow/Comfort	7.9
Ship: Decor/Furnishings	8.1
Ship: Fitness Facilities	8.0
Cabins: Comfort/Facilities	7.8
Cabins: Software	8.0
Food: Dining Room/Cuisine	7.2
Food: Buffets/Informal Dining	6.3
Food: Quality of Ingredients	6.4
Service: Dining Room	7.6
Service: Bars	7.5
Service: Cabins	7.5
Cruise: Entertainment	8.2
Cruise: Activities Program	7.8
Cruise: Hospitality Standard	7.7
OVERALL RATING	114.6

+ Built first, this sister to *Windward* has a handsome, well-balanced profile, despite its large, square funnel. Has inboard lifeboats and red rubber-covered promenade deck. Much innovative design incorporated, with good passenger flow. Inside, the ship absorbs passengers well even when full. The tiered pool deck is innovative, and the aft sun terraces are a plus. Pastel interior color scheme is soothing. Cabins feature wood-trimmed cabinetry, and warm decor, but there's almost no drawer space (closets have shelves), so take minimal clothing. All cabins have a sitting area, but this takes away free space, making movement tight. Bathrooms are small. Special cabins for hearing impaired are innovative.

— Entrance lobby is uninviting. Carpeted stairwell steps are tinny. Room service menu poor. The casino is intimate, but cramped.

Dining There are three main Dining Rooms: The Sun Terrace, The Terraces, The Four Seasons (all have the same menu and food), plus The Bistro (for casual dining) and Sports Bar for breakfast, luncheon and teatime buffets (poor). The food is adequate, but not memorable. Service is perfunctory, at best. The wine list is good, with very moderate prices.

Other Comments This ship is proving to be highly successful for NCL's sports-minded passengers. Provides a good alternative to the mega-ships and mega-crowds.

ms Ecstasy ★★★★

OPERATES

*3- AND 4-DAY CARIBBEAN
CRUISES (YEAR-ROUND)*

Cruise Line	Carnival Cruise Lines
Former Names	-
Gross Tonnage	70,367
Builder	Kvaerner Masa-Yards (Finland)
Original Cost	$275 million
Christened By	Ms Kathie Lee Gifford
Entered Service	Jun 2, 1991
Interior Design	Joe Farcus
Country of Registry	Liberia (ELNC5)
Tel No 124-4233 Fax No	124-4234
Length (ft/m)	855.8/260.60
Beam (ft/m) 104.0/31.40 Draft (ft/m)	25.9/7.89
Propulsion	diesel-electric (42,240kW)
Propellers	2 (CP)
Decks 10 Crew	920
Pass. Capacity (basis 2) 2,040 (all berths)	2,594
Pass. Space Ratio (basis 2) 34.4 (all berths)	27.1
Officers Italian Dining Staff	International
Total Cabins	1,020
Size Range (sq ft/m)	185-421/17.0-39.0
Outside Cabins 618 Inside Cabins	402
Single Cabins	0
Supplement	50% (cat.1-3)/100% (cat.4-12)
Balcony Cabins 54 Wheelchair Cabins	20
Cabin Current	110 AC
Refrigerator	Category 11/12 only
Cabin TV Yes VCR	No
Dining Rooms 2 Sittings	2

Elevators			14
Casino	Yes	Slot Machines	Yes
Swimming Pools (outside) 3		(inside)	0
Whirlpools	6	Gymnasium	Yes
Sauna/Steam Room Yes/Yes		Massage	Yes
Self-Service Launderette			Yes
Movie Theater/Seats	No	Library	Yes
Children's Facilities			Yes
Watersports Facilities			None
Classification Society			Lloyd's Register

RATINGS	SCORE
Ship: Condition/Cleanliness	8.0
Ship: Space/Flow/Comfort	7.8
Ship: Decor/Furnishings	6.8
Ship: Fitness Facilities	7.8
Cabins: Comfort/Facilities	7.6
Cabins: Software	7.4
Food: Dining Room/Cuisine	6.7
Food: Buffets/Informal Dining	6.5
Food: Quality of Ingredients	5.3
Service: Dining Room	7.0
Service: Bars	7.2
Service: Cabins	6.4
Cruise: Entertainment	7.9
Cruise: Activities Program	7.8
Cruise: Hospitality Standard	6.3
OVERALL RATING	106.5

+ This big ship has good passenger flow, and clever interior design. Vintage Rolls Royce on indoor promenade. Fine health spa. Stunning 10-ton sculpture graces marble and glass atrium that spans seven decks. Lovely library, but few books. Plain, but comfortable cabins are quite roomy and practical, with good storage space and practical bathrooms. Suites are attractive. Chinatown Lounge has hanging lanterns and smoking dragon. This ship will provide a great introduction to cruising for the novice passenger seeking an action-packed, dare I say, orgasmic, short cruise experience in contemporary surroundings, with the minimum of fuss and finesse, lots of enthusiasm and a real swinging party atmosphere. You'll have a fine time if you like nightlife and silly games, even if the line does emphasize the "fun" theme constantly.

— Neon lighting in the interior decor. Color combinations are too vivid. Too many people, too many annoying announcements, and too much hustling for drinks. Long lines for embarkation, disembarkation, and buffets.

Dining The two dining rooms have attractive decor and colors, but are large, crowded, and very noisy. The food is adequate, no more (despite being upgraded). Service is robotic.

Other Comments Life in the fast lane, this is cruising in theme-park fantasy land. An enthusiastic staff will make sure you have fun, and that's what Carnival does best.

ss Enchanted Isle ★★★

OPERATES

*7-DAY MEXICO CRUISES
(YEAR-ROUND)*

Cruise Line	New Commodore Cruise Line	Casino	Yes	Slot Machines	Yes
Former Names	Commodore Hotel/Enchanted Isle/	Swimming Pools (outside) 1		(inside)	0
Bermuda Star/Veendam/Monarch Star/Argentina		Whirlpools	0	Gymnasium	Yes
Gross Tonnage	23,395	Sauna/Steam Room Yes/No		Massage	Yes
Builder	Ingalls Shipbuilding (USA)	Self-Service Launderette			No
Original Cost	$26 million	Movie Theater/Seats			Yes/200
Christened By	n/a	Library			No
Entered Service	Dec 12, 1958/Feb 4, 1995	Children's Facilities			Yes
Interior Design	VFD Interiors	Watersports Facilities			None
Country of Registry	Panama (3FMG2)	Classification Society		Lloyd's Register

Tel No	133-3171 Fax No	133-3201
Length (ft/m)		617.5/188.22
Beam (ft/m) 88.1/26.88	Draft (ft/m)	27.2/8.30
Propulsion	steam turbine (19,000kW)	
Propellers		2 (FP)
Decks	9 Crew	350
Pass. Capacity (basis 2) 729	(all berths) 729	
Pass. Space Ratio (basis 2) 32.0	(all berths) 32.0	
Officers European	Dining Staff	International
Total Cabins		366
Size Range (sq ft/m)		104-293/9.6-27.2
Outside Cabins	290 Inside Cabins	76
Single Cabins	3 Supplement	50-100%
Balcony Cabins	0 Wheelchair Cabins	0
Cabin Current		110 AC
Refrigerator	No Cabin TV	No
Dining Rooms	1 Sittings	2
Elevators		3

RATINGS	SCORE
Ship: Condition/Cleanliness	6.4
Ship: Space/Flow/Comfort	6.2
Ship: Decor/Furnishings	6.6
Ship: Fitness Facilities	4.5
Cabins: Comfort/Facilities	6.3
Cabins: Software	6.6
Food: Dining Room/Cuisine	6.3
Food: Buffets/Informal Dining	5.8
Food: Quality of Ingredients	6.0
Service: Dining Room	6.0
Service: Bars	6.2
Service: Cabins	6.4
Cruise: Entertainment	6.0
Cruise: Activities Program	5.6
Cruise: Hospitality Standard	6.1
OVERALL RATING	91.0

+ Nice ocean liner profile with big, but false, funnel. Stable sea ship that has been quite well maintained. The ship has a rather homely, matronly look and ambiance. Good exterior teakwood decking. Good choice of public rooms and open deck areas. The cabins are quite spacious, with solid, heavy-duty furniture and fittings.

— The interior is by no means glamorous, though it is quite pleasant, but becoming rather dated and worn. Poor sightlines in showlounge.

Dining The dining room is located on a lower deck and needs more light. Buffets are really limited. The dining room food is decent, but menu choice is limited. Service is attentive and friendly, but there's no finesse.

Other Comments Large casino is not at all inviting. This ship will provide a decent first-time cruise experience, in a fun atmosphere, at a down to earth price, providing you don't expect too much.

ss Enchanted Seas ★★★

OPERATES

7-DAY CARIBBEAN CRUISES
(YEAR-ROUND)

Cruise Line	New Commodore Cruise Line
Former Names	Queen of Bermuda, Canada Star,
Liberte, Island Sun, Volendam, Monarch Sun, Brazil
Gross Tonnage			23,879
Builder	Ingalls Shipbuilding (USA)
Original Cost			$26 million
Christened By	Mrs Emmett J. McCormack
Entered Service	Sep 12, 1958/Nov 3, 1990
Interior Design			n/a
Country of Registry	Bahamas (3FMF2)
Tel No	113-1605	Fax No	133-1605
Length (ft/m)			617.4/188.20
Beam (ft/m)	84.3/25.70	Draft (ft/m)	27.2/8.30
Propulsion	steam turbine (19,000kW)
Propellers			2 (FP)
Decks	8	Crew	365
Pass. Capacity (basis 2) 740		(all berths) 846
Pass. Space Ratio (basis 2) 32.2		(all berths) 28.2
Officers	European	Dining Staff	International
Total Cabins			371
Size Range (sq ft/m)			104-293/9.6-27.2
Outside Cabins	290	Inside Cabins	79
Single Cabins	2	Supplement	50-100%
Balcony Cabins	0	Wheelchair Cabins	0
Cabin Current	110 AC	Refrigerator	No
Cabin TV	Yes	VCR	No
Dining Rooms	1	Sittings	2
Elevators			3

Casino	Yes	Slot Machines	Yes
Swimming Pools (outside) 2		(inside)	0
Whirlpools	0	Gymnasium	Yes
Sauna/Steam Room	No/No	Massage	Yes
Self-Service Launderette			No
Movie Theater/Seats			Yes/200
Library	Yes	Children's Facilities	Yes
Watersports Facilities			None
Classification Society			American Bureau
			of Shipping

RATINGS	SCORE
Ship: Condition/Cleanliness	6.4
Ship: Space/Flow/Comfort	6.2
Ship: Decor/Furnishings	6.6
Ship: Fitness Facilities	4.5
Cabins: Comfort/Facilities	6.3
Cabins: Software	6.6
Food: Dining Room/Cuisine	6.3
Food: Buffets/Informal Dining	5.8
Food: Quality of Ingredients	6.0
Service: Dining Room	6.0
Service: Bars	6.2
Service: Cabins	6.4
Cruise: Entertainment	6.0
Cruise: Activities Program	5.6
Cruise: Hospitality Standard	6.1
OVERALL RATING	91.0

+ Somewhat traditional ocean liner profile. Extensively refurbished. Beautifully finished outdoor teakwood decks. Being an older ship, there are spacious outdoor promenade areas for walking. The public rooms are quite spacious and well equipped, with high ceilings, and pleasing decor and colors that don't jar the senses. The showroom is quite good, but cannot compare with those on larger, more modern, ships. Has a large casino. There's plenty of sheltered and open sunning space. Two outdoor pools are well used. Cabins are of a generous size, with nice, heavy-duty furniture and fittings.

— Expect long lines for casual buffet meals. Poor sightlines in showlounge.

Dining Charming dining room has large windows which provide more light and a better ambiance. The menu choice is somewhat limited, but service is attentive and comes with a smile, even if it's without finesse. Poor selection of bread rolls, cheeses, and fruits.

Other Comments This ship will provide you with an enjoyable first cruise experience in comfort surroundings reminiscent of old world style, at a very reasonable price. However, with all the discounting, service and product delivery standards have been lowered.

ts EugenioCosta ★★★+

Cruise Line	Costa Crociere	Casino	Yes	Slot Machines	Yes
Former Names	Eugenio C	Swimming Pools (outside) 2	(inside)	0
Gross Tonnage	32,753	Whirlpools	1	Gymnasium	Yes
Builder	Cantieri Riuniti dell' Adriatico (Italy)	Sauna/Steam Room Yes/No	Massage	Yes
Original Cost	$24.5 million	Self-Service Launderette		Yes
Christened By	Pinuccia Costa Musso	Movie Theater/Seats		Yes/230
Entered Service	Aug 31, 1966/Dec 18, 1994	Library		Yes
Interior Design	Architects Zoncada/De Jorio	Children's Facilities		Yes
Country of Registry	Italy (ICVV)	Watersports Facilities		None
Tel No 115-0116 Fax No 115-0116		Classification Society		RINA
Length (ft/m)	713.2/217.39			
Beam (ft/m) 96.1/29.39 Draft (ft/m) 28.3/8.63		**RATINGS**		**SCORE**
Propulsion	steam turbine (40,456kW)	Ship: Condition/Cleanliness		7.1
Propellers	2 (FP)	Ship: Space/Flow/Comfort		7.3
Decks 10 Crew 480		Ship: Decor/Furnishings		7.6
Pass. Capacity (basis 2) 1,012 (all berths) 1,418		Ship: Fitness Facilities		6.3
Pass. Space Ratio (basis 2) 32.3 (all berths) 23.0		Cabins: Comfort/Facilities		7.3
Officers	Italian	Cabins: Software		7.4
Dining Staff	Italian/International	Food: Dining Room/Cuisine		6.7
Total Cabins	506 (8 without facilities)	Food: Buffets/Informal Dining		6.3
Size Range (sq ft/m)	93-236/8.7-22.0	Food: Quality of Ingredients		6.7
Outside Cabins 271 Inside Cabins 235		Service: Dining Room		7.3
Single Cabins 0 Supplement 50%		Service: Bars		7.3
Balcony Cabins 0 Wheelchair Cabins 0		Service: Cabins		7.6
Cabin Current 127 AC Refrigerator No		Cruise: Entertainment		6.1
Cabin TV No VCR No		Cruise: Activities Program		6.4
Dining Rooms 1 Sittings 2		Cruise: Hospitality Standard		7.1
Elevators	5	OVERALL RATING		104.5

+ She has good teakwood decking outdoors and good open deck and sunning space. Spacious array of public rooms feature new, theme-park decor and colors. There's a good range of accommodations, with many different styles, sizes, and configurations of cabins. This ship is comfortable throughout, and provides good value cruising for families in a no-ties required setting that is unashamedly an ultra-casual, high-density, floating all-year-round summer camp.

— Long lines for embarkation, disembarkation, buffets, and shore tenders. Many passengers smoke heavily, and it's almost impossible to get away from them. Non-smokers should choose another ship.

Dining Pasta dishes are excellent, but other dishes can only be described as adequate, and certainly not memorable. Poor selection of breads, cheeses, and fruits.

Other Comments This well-proportioned ex-ocean liner has the graceful flowing lines of a sixties ocean liner and twin slender funnels aft. Provides good value cruises for its mainly Italian-speaking clientele.

ms Europa ★★★★★+

OPERATES

VARIOUS CRUISES WORLDWIDE

Cruise Line	Hapag-Lloyd Cruises		
Former Names	- Gross Tonnage 37,012		
Builder	Bremer Vulkan (Germany)		
Original Cost	$120 million		
Christened By	Mrs Simone Veil		
Entered Service	Jan 8, 1982		
Interior Design	Wilfried Kohnemann		
Country of Registry	Germany (DLAL)		
Tel No 112-0756	Fax No 112-0756		
Length (ft/m)	654.9/199.63		
Beam (ft/m) 93.8/28.60	Draft (ft/m) 27.6/8.42		
Propulsion	diesel (21,270kW)		
Propellers	2 (CP)		
Decks 10	Crew 300		
Pass. Capacity (basis 2) 600	(all berths) 600		
Pass. Space Ratio (basis 2) 61.6	(all berths) 61.6		
Officers German	Dining Staff European		
Total Cabins	316		
Size Range (sq ft/m)	150-420/14.0-39.0		
Outside Cabins 260	Inside Cabins 56		
Single Cabins	32		
Supplement	On request		
Balcony Cabins 0	Wheelchair Cabins 1		
Cabin Current	110/220 AC		
Refrigerator	All cabins		
Cabin TV Yes	VCR Yes		
Dining Rooms 1	Sittings 1		
Elevators	4		

Casino	No	Slot Machines	No
Swimming Pools (outside)		2 (1 magdrodome)	
Swimming Pools (inside)		1 (fresh water)	
Whirlpools	0	Gymnasium	Yes
Sauna/Steam Room Yes/Yes		Massage	Yes
Self-Service Launderette			Yes
Movie Theater/Seats			Yes/238
Library	Yes	Children's Facilities	No
Watersports Facilities			None
Classification Society		Germanischer Lloyd	

RATINGS	SCORE
Ship: Condition/Cleanliness	9.5
Ship: Space/Flow/Comfort	9.5
Ship: Decor/Furnishings	9.4
Ship: Fitness Facilities	9.6
Cabins: Comfort/Facilities	9.3
Cabins: Software	9.2
Food: Dining Room/Cuisine	9.1
Food: Buffets/Informal Dining	9.0
Food: Quality of Ingredients	8.8
Service: Dining Room	8.8
Service: Bars	8.8
Service: Cabins	9.0
Cruise: Entertainment	8.7
Cruise: Activities Program	8.6
Cruise: Hospitality Standard	9.2
OVERALL RATING	136.5

+ Beautifully designed, handsome contemporary ship presents a well-balanced, almost sleek profile. Superb, stable, and well-behaved ship at sea. Immaculate maintenance and care. Outstanding outdoor deck and sunning space, including a private nudist deck. The all-white Belvedere Lounge, the ship's forward observation lounge, is one of the most elegant rooms afloat. Every cabin on this ship is superb, and all were completely refurbished in 1995. All feature lighted closets, dark wood cabinetry with rounded edges, several full-length mirrors, television and VCR, mini-bar refrigerator, personal safe, hairdryer and excellent cabin insulation. Refreshingly, not a trace of horse racing, gambling tables or slot machines. There is an incredible amount of space per passenger, even when the ship is full. Dark, restful colors in public rooms and cabins, and subtly hidden lighting throughout. There is some fine artwork featured throughout. Outstanding health spa and rejuvenation facilities, with many treatments not available on any other ship, and the most professional spa staff to be found anywhere. It is run by Polly's Vital Center (Polly Hillbrunner) from Kitzbühel, Austria, one of the world's most famous personal and bodycare clinics. All cabins feature mini-bar refrigerator with complimentary soft drinks, beer, and personal safe. Excellent cabin insulation. Impeccable European staff and service that is very formal and proper. This is a ship of the very highest quality and spaciousness. There are no announcements. This ship deserves praise for

providing a most elegant cruise experience in supremely luxurious and quiet, spacious surroundings. The qualities of elegance, space, and grace abound everywhere.

— There is no wrap-around outdoor promenade deck (only a half-length promenade). There are no cabins with private balconies.

Dining The dining room is extremely spacious, and with a single sitting for all meals is quite unhurried. Fine, traditional silver service and plenty of space between tables provide an elegant dining experience. Menus are not repeated, even on long cruises. Excellent quality food ingredients and presentation. Caviar (both Russian and Iranian) is always available, as are special orders and tableside flambeau items. The food and cuisine are of course geared to German (including Austrian and Swiss) tastes, which means a wide variety of fish and meat dishes, as well as many breads and cheeses.

Other Comments Although now fourteen years old, the ship looks like a three-year-old vessel, and is aging gracefully. Although there are no balcony cabins or wrap-around promenade deck, it's the food and service that are really outstanding.

If you are looking for a restful, restorative cruise, with fine quality European entertainment, outstanding, seldom repeated worldwide itineraries, superb food and service, then this German-language ship is probably unbeatable. The passengers are almost entirely German-speaking, so don't book unless you understand this (some staff do speak English). It's just about the ultimate totally relaxing cruise experience, to be enjoyed particularly on long cruises with plenty of days at sea. Port taxes and insurance are included.

In 1997, the company will celebrate its 150th anniversary; perhaps there will soon be a new ship on the horizon.

mv Explorer ★★★

OPERATES

WORLDWIDE EXPEDITION CRUISES
(INCLUDING ANTARCTICA)

Cruise Line	Abercrombie & Kent
Former Names	Society Explorer/
	Lindblad Explorer/World Explorer
Gross Tonnage	2,398
Builder	Nystad Varv Shipyard (Finland)
Original Cost	$2.5 million
Christened By	Mrs Sonja Lindblad
Entered Service	1969/Mar 14, 1993
Interior Design	n/a
Country of Registry	Liberia (ELJD8)
Tel No 124-1223 Fax No	124-1223
Length (ft/m)	239.1/72.88
Beam (ft/m) 46.0/14.03 Draft (ft/m)	13.7/4.20
Propulsion	diesel (2,795kW)
Propellers	1 (FP)
Decks 6 Crew	71
Pass. Capacity (basis 2) 100 (all berths)	114
Pass. Space Ratio (basis 2) 23.9 (all berths)	21.0
Officers	European
Dining Staff	European/Filipino
Total Cabins 50 Size Range (sq ft/m)	n/a
Outside Cabins 50 Inside Cabins	0
Single Cabins	8
Supplement	40-70% (all others)
Balcony Cabins 0 Wheelchair Cabins	0
Cabin Current 220 AC Refrigerator	No
Cabin TV No VCR	No
Dining Rooms	1 (open seating)

Elevators			0
Casino No Slot Machines			No
Swimming Pools (outside)			1
Whirlpools 0 Exercise Room			Yes
Sauna/Steam Room Yes/No Massage			Yes
Self-Service Launderette			No
Lecture/Film Room Yes Library			Yes
Zodiacs Yes Helicopter Pad			No
Watersports Facilities			None
Classification Society		Det Norske Veritas	

RATINGS	SCORE
Ship: Condition/Cleanliness	6.0
Ship: Space/Flow/Comfort	5.6
Ship: Expedition Equipment	6.7
Ship: Decor/Furnishings	6.2
Cabins: Comfort/Facilities	5.5
Cabins: Software	5.4
Food: Dining Room/Cuisine	6.4
Food: Buffets/Informal Dining	6.1
Food: Quality of Ingredients	6.0
Service: Dining Room	7.0
Service: Bars	6.6
Service: Cabins	7.0
Cruise: Itineraries/Operations	7.8
Cruise: Lecture Program	7.6
Cruise: Hospitality Standard	7.6
OVERALL RATING	97.5

+ Well fitted out with all necessary equipment, including Zodiac rubber landing craft. Now ageing and showing signs of wear and tear. National Geographic maps presented in all cabins. Tasteful interior decor in public rooms. Large reference library. Outstanding lecturers and nature specialists placed on board by Abercrombie & Kent.

— The cabins are extremely small and utilitarian, with little closet, drawer, and storage space. Even so, they are just about adequate for an expedition; bathrooms are really tiny, however, and don't have much room even for toiletries.

Dining Intimate dining room is cheerful, though noisy, but seats all passengers at one sitting. Good, creatively presented food (but there's little choice) and wine list. Smiling, attentive, and genuinely friendly service, but it's quite casual.

Other Comments This specialist, unpretentious expedition cruise vessel with ice-hardened hull has a well-balanced profile and is extremely maneuverable, although she is now looking tired, and maintenance could be improved. This is cruising for the serious adventurer who wants to explore the world, yet have some of the basic creature comforts of home within reach. All shore excursions, and gratuities, are included.

tss Fairstar ★★★

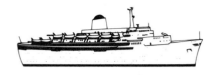

Cruise Line	P&O Holidays		
Former Names	Oxfordshire		
Gross Tonnage	23,764		
Builder	Fairfield Shipbuilding (UK)		
Original Cost	n/a		
Christened By	Lady Dorothea Head		
Entered Service	Feb 1957/Aug 20, 1973		
Interior Design	n/a		
Country of Registry	Liberia (5MXH)		
Tel No 124-0245	Fax No	124-0245	
Length (ft/m)	609.4/185.76		
Beam (ft/m) 78.2/23.86	Draft (ft/m)	27.5/8.41	
Propulsion	steam turbine (13,400kW)		
Propellers	2 (FP)		
Decks 10	Crew	460	
Pass. Capacity (basis 2) 976	(all berths) 1,598		
Pass. Space Ratio (basis 2) 24.3	(all berths) 14.8		
Officers Italian	Dining Staff	Italian/Indonesian	
Total Cabins	488 (68 without facilities)		
Size Range (sq ft/m)	86-301/8.0-28.0		
Outside Cabins 169	Inside Cabins	319	
Single Cabins	0		
Supplement	On request		
Balcony Cabins 0	Wheelchair Cabins	0	
Cabin Current 115 AC	Refrigerator	No	
Cabin TV No	VCR	No	
Dining Rooms 2	Sittings	2	
Elevators	4		

Casino	Yes	Slot Machines	Yes
Swimming Pools (outside) 1		(inside)	0
Whirlpools	0	Gymnasium	Yes
Sauna/Steam Room No/No		Massage	No
Self-Service Launderette			No
Movie Theater/Seats			Yes/360
Library			No
Children's Facilities			Yes
Watersports Facilities			None
Classification Society			Lloyd's Register

RATINGS	SCORE
Ship: Condition/Cleanliness	6.0
Ship: Space/Flow/Comfort	5.1
Ship: Decor/Furnishings	6.6
Ship: Fitness Facilities	4.7
Cabins: Comfort/Facilities	5.3
Cabins: Software	6.2
Food: Dining Room/Cuisine	6.5
Food: Buffets/Informal Dining	6.2
Food: Quality of Ingredients	5.7
Service: Dining Room	7.7
Service: Bars	6.7
Service: Cabins	6.6
Cruise: Entertainment	6.1
Cruise: Activities Program	6.1
Cruise: Hospitality Standard	6.0
OVERALL RATING	91.5

+ Well-constructed older ship has classic lines and profile has new dolphin logo on her funnel. Well maintained. New late-night Brasserie Delfino is popular. Sail-cloth awning around swimming pool provides shade. Has a recently added arcade shopping area. Good for families with children, with plenty of noisy activities. Other cabins fine for two, crowded with more. There is a curfew for children at night.

— Limited open deck and sunning space. Long lines for embarkation, disembarkation, shore tenders, and buffets. No sophistication anywhere. Public rooms are barely adequate for the number of passengers, and it's difficult to get away from smokers. Too many duty-free shops, and lines. Take books to read (there's no library). Has really small cabin bathrooms, most with exposed plumbing. There are too many irritating announcements, like at summer camp.

Dining The dining rooms, although crowded and noisy, have plenty of tables for two. The cuisine is low-budget banquet food, and is strictly quantity, not quality, although it's adequate, and there's always plenty of good pasta. There is an excellent pizzeria.

Other Comments Lacks any sort of glamor, but makes up for it in spirit and boisterous cruise atmosphere. Excellent value for money cruise product for younger "down-under" passengers who want a lively, active, noisy, fun-filled cruise.

ms Fantasy ★★★★

Cruise Line	Carnival Cruise Lines	Elevators	14
Former Names	-	Casino Yes	Slot Machines Yes
Gross Tonnage	70,367	Swimming Pools (outside) 3	(inside) 0
Builder	Kvaerner Masa-Yards (Finland)	Whirlpools 6	Gymnasium Yes
Original Cost	$225 million	Sauna/Steam Room Yes/Yes	Massage Yes
Christened By	Mrs Tellervo Koivisto	Self-Service Launderette	Yes
Entered Service	Mar 2, 1990	Movie Theater/Seats No	Library Yes
Interior Design	Joe Farcus	Children's Facilities	Yes
Country of Registry	Liberia (ELKI6)	Watersports Facilities	None
Tel No 124-2660 Fax No 124-2661		Classification Society	Lloyd's Register
Length (ft/m)	855.8/263.60		
Beam (ft/m) 104.0/31.40 Draft (ft/m) 25.9/7.90		**RATINGS**	**SCORE**
Propulsion	diesel-electric (42,240kW)	Ship: Condition/Cleanliness	8.0
Propellers	2 (CP)	Ship: Space/Flow/Comfort	7.8
Decks 10 Crew	920	Ship: Decor/Furnishings	6.8
Pass. Capacity (basis 2) 2,044 (all berths) 2,634		Ship: Fitness Facilities	7.8
Pass. Space Ratio (basis 2) 34.4 (all berths) 26.7		Cabins: Comfort/Facilities	7.6
Officers Italian Dining Staff International		Cabins: Software	7.4
Total Cabins	1,022	Food: Dining Room/Cuisine	6.7
Size Range (sq ft/m)	185-421/17.0-39.0	Food: Buffets/Informal Dining	6.5
Outside Cabins 620 Inside Cabins 402		Food: Quality of Ingredients	5.3
Single Cabins	0	Service: Dining Room	7.0
Supplement	50% (cat.1-3)/100% (cat.4-12)	Service: Bars	7.2
Balcony Cabins 54 Wheelchair Cabins 20		Service: Cabins	6.4
Cabin Current	110 AC	Cruise: Entertainment	7.9
Refrigerator	Category 11/12 only	Cruise: Activities Program	7.8
Cabin TV Yes VCR No		Cruise: Hospitality Standard	6.3
Dining Rooms 2 Sittings 2		OVERALL RATING	106.5

+ Although externally angular and not handsome, this is one of eight identical megaships for Carnival. Features vibrant colors and extensive use of neon lighting for sensory stimulation. Six-deck-high atrium features spectacular artistic centerpiece. Expansive open deck areas. Public entertainment lounges, bars, and clubs galore, with something for everyone. Delightful library and quiet reading room, but few books. Dazzling colors and 21st-century-themed designs in handsome public rooms connected by wide indoor boulevards. Lavish multi-tiered showroom. Three-deck-high glass enclosed health spa. Banked jogging track. Gigantic casino has non-stop action.

— Expect long lines for embarkation, disembarkation, shore excursions, and buffets. Too many annoying announcements and hustling for drinks. Large shop, poor merchandise.

Dining The two large dining rooms are noisy, but the decor is attractive. The food is very disappointing (despite being upgraded). The service is basic, and pushy, with no finesse.

Other Comments First of a series of eight sister ships. Although the cuisine is so-so, the real fun begins at sundown, when Carnival excels in sound, lights, and razzle-dazzle shows. From the futuristic Electricity Disco to the ancient Cleopatra's Bar, this ship will entertain you well.

ms Fascination ★★★★

OPERATES

*7-DAY CARIBBEAN CRUISES
(YEAR-ROUND)*

Cruise Line	Carnival Cruise Lines
Former Names	-
Gross Tonnage	70,367
Builder	Kvaerner Masa-Yards (Finland)
Original Cost	$315 million
Christened By	Mrs Jean Farcus
Entered Service	Jul 29, 1994
Interior Design	Joe Farcus
Country of Registry	Liberia (3EWK9)
Tel No 134-6374 Fax No 134-6375	
Length (ft/m)	855.0/260.60
Beam (ft/m) 104.9/31.69 Draft (ft/m) 25.7/7.86	
Propulsion	diesel-electric (42,240kW)
Propellers	2 (CP)
Decks	10 Crew 920
Pass. Capacity (basis 2) 2,040 (all berths) 2,594	
Pass. Space Ratio (basis 2) 34.4 (all berths) 26.7	
Officers Italian Dining Staff International	
Total Cabins	1,020
Size Range (sq ft/m)	185-421/17.0-39.0
Outside Cabins 618 Inside Cabins 402	
Single Cabins	20
Supplement 50% (cat. 1-3)/100% (cat. 4-12)	
Balcony Cabins 26 Wheelchair Cabins 0	
Cabin Current	110 AC
Refrigerator	Category 11/12 only
Cabin TV Yes VCR No	
Dining Rooms 2 Sittings 2	

Elevators			14
Casino	Yes	Slot Machines	Yes
Swimming Pools (outside) 3		(inside)	0
Whirlpools	6	Gymnasium	Yes
Sauna/Steam Room Yes/Yes		Massage	Yes
Self-Service Launderette			Yes
Movie Theater/Seats	No	Library	Yes
Children's Facilities			Yes
Watersports Facilities			None
Classification Society			Lloyd's Register

RATINGS	SCORE
Ship: Condition/Cleanliness	8.5
Ship: Space/Flow/Comfort	7.8
Ship: Decor/Furnishings	8.7
Ship: Fitness Facilities	7.8
Cabins: Comfort/Facilities	7.6
Cabins: Software	7.4
Food: Dining Room/Cuisine	6.7
Food: Buffets/Informal Dining	6.5
Food: Quality of Ingredients	5.3
Service: Dining Room	7.1
Service: Bars	7.2
Service: Cabins	6.5
Cruise: Entertainment	8.2
Cruise: Activities Program	7.8
Cruise: Hospitality Standard	6.4
OVERALL RATING	109.5

+ One of a series of eight identical megaships for Carnival reflects the fine creative interior design work of Joe Farcus. Almost vibration-free service from diesel electric propulsion system. The atrium lobby is six decks high, with cool marble and hot neon, topped by large glass dome, and a spectacular artistic centerpiece. Expansive open deck areas, but never enough when the ship is full. 28 outside suites have whirlpool tubs and elegant decor. Public entertainment lounges, bars, and clubs galore, with something for everyone. Sophisticated Hollywood design theme in handsome public rooms connected by wide indoor boulevards crave your indulgence, as will the photo opportunities with life-like figures from the movies. Lavish multi-tiered showroom and fine razzle-dazzle shows. Has a three-deck-high glass-enclosed health spa and gymnasium. Gigantic casino has non-stop action.

— As with all large ships, expect long lines for embarkation, disembarkation, shore excursions, and buffets.

Dining Two huge, noisy dining rooms (both are non-smoking) with the usual efficient, assertive service. Improved cuisine so-so, but first-time passengers seem to accept it.

Other Comments The real fun begins at sundown, when Carnival excels in decibels. This ship will entertain you in timely fashion.

ts Fedor Shalyapin ★★+

OPERATES
EUROPE CRUISES

Cruise Line	Black Sea Shipping	Casino	No	Slot Machines	No
Former Names	Franconia/Ivernia	Swimming Pools (outside) 1	(inside)	0
Gross Tonnage	21,406	Whirlpools	0	Gymnasium	Yes
Builder	John Brown & Co. (UK)	Sauna/Steam Room Yes/No	Massage	No
Original Cost	n/a	Self-Service Launderette	No
Christened By	Mrs C.D. Howe	Movie Theater/Seats	Yes/260
Entered Service	Jul 1, 1955/Nov 20, 1973	Library	Yes
Interior Design	n/a	Children's Facilities	Yes
Country of Registry	Ukraine (UZLA)	Watersports Facilities	None
Tel No - Fax No -		Classification Society	Bureau Veritas/RS
Length (ft/m)	607.9/185.30		
Beam (ft/m) 79.7/24.30 Draft (ft/m) 28.8/8.80		**RATINGS**	**SCORE**
Propulsion	steam turbine (18,300kW)	Ship: Condition/Cleanliness	5.6
Propellers	2 (FP)	Ship: Space/Flow/Comfort	6.4
Decks 7 Crew 380		Ship: Decor/Furnishings	6.1
Pass. Capacity (basis 2) 576 (all berths) 800		Ship: Fitness Facilities	4.2
Pass. Space Ratio (basis 2) 37.1 (all berths) 26.7		Cabins: Comfort/Facilities	5.8
Officers Russian Dining Staff East European		Cabins: Software	6.0
Total Cabins	292	Food: Dining Room/Cuisine	5.1
Size Range (sq ft/m)	90-241/8.3-22.3	Food: Buffets/Informal Dining	5.0
Outside Cabins 159 Inside Cabins 133		Food: Quality of Ingredients	5.0
Single Cabins 0 Supplement 100%		Service: Dining Room	5.9
Balcony Cabins 0 Wheelchair Cabins 0		Service: Bars	6.1
Cabin Current	110/220 AC	Service: Cabins	6.2
Refrigerator	No	Cruise: Entertainment	5.0
Cabin TV No VCR No		Cruise: Activities Program	4.8
Dining Rooms 2 Sittings 2		Cruise: Hospitality Standard	5.6
Elevators	3	OVERALL RATING	82.8

+ Well-built older former transatlantic ship with classic steamship profile and single, large funnel looks good on the outside. Features two good indoor promenades. There are many different cabin configurations to choose from. Some (former first-class) cabins are quite large and have solid, heavy-duty fittings and furniture, mostly original, from her former transatlantic service days.

— Public rooms rather poor, with the exception of the Music Salon and Theater, and her interiors are now looking quite tired. They could also be cleaner. The furniture and fittings are quite worn and in need of extensive refurbishing. There are too many announcements.

Dining The unappetizing, somber dining room is located on a lower deck. The food, which is limited in choice, needs better presentation. The staff are quite friendly and attentive, but need better direction and supervision.

Other Comments An ex-Cunard transatlantic liner, well preserved from the fifties. This ship will appeal mainly to low-budget continental European passengers. Although the price may be right, this ship is not really up to Western standards, and provides no more than a mediocre cruise experience; it would be better retired or used as a floating hotel. Gratuities are not included.

tss Festivale ★★★+

OPERATES

7-DAY CARIBBEAN CRUISES
(YEAR-ROUND)

Cruise Line	Carnival Cruise Lines	Casino	Yes Slot Machines	Yes
Former Names	TransVaal Castle/S.A. Vaal	Swimming Pools (outside) 3	(inside)	0
Gross Tonnage	38,175	Whirlpools	0 Gymnasium	Yes
Builder	John Brown & Co. (UK)	Sauna/Steam Room Yes/No	Massage	Yes
Original Cost	n/a	Self-Service Launderette	No (has ironing room)	
Christened By	Mrs Clara Zonis	Movie Theater/Seats		Yes/202
Entered Service	Jan 18, 1962/Oct 28, 1978	Library		Yes
Interior Design	Joe Farcus	Children's Facilities		Yes
Country of Registry	Bahamas (C6KP)	Watersports Facilities		None
Tel No 110-3150 Fax No	110-3150	Classification Society	Lloyd's Register	
Length (ft/m)	760.1/231.70			

RATINGS	SCORE
Ship: Condition/Cleanliness	7.3
Ship: Space/Flow/Comfort	7.5
Ship: Decor/Furnishings	6.2
Ship: Fitness Facilities	6.9
Cabins: Comfort/Facilities	7.5
Cabins: Software	7.2
Food: Dining Room/Cuisine	6.2
Food: Buffets/Informal Dining	6.2
Food: Quality of Ingredients	5.3
Service: Dining Room	6.7
Service: Bars	6.5
Service: Cabins	6.4
Cruise: Entertainment	8.0
Cruise: Activities Program	7.1
Cruise: Hospitality Standard	6.1
OVERALL RATING	101.1

Beam (ft/m) 90.1/27.49	Draft (ft/m)	31.9/9.75
Propulsion	steam turbine (32,800kW)	
Propellers		2 (FP)
Decks 9	Crew	580
Pass. Capacity (basis 2) 1,146	(all berths) 1,400	
Pass. Space Ratio (basis 2) 33.3	(all berths) 27.2	
Officers Italian	Dining Staff	International
Total Cabins		580
Size Range (sq ft/m)	50-167/4.6-15.5	
Outside Cabins 272	Inside Cabins	308
Single Cabins		14
Supplement 50% (cat. 1-3/100% (cat.4-12)		
Balcony Cabins 10	Wheelchair Cabins	0
Cabin Current 110 AC	Refrigerator	No
Cabin TV No	VCR	No
Dining Rooms 1	Sittings	2
Elevators		4

+ Classic former ocean liner styling with superb, well-balanced profile and long, tiered foredeck. She looks like a real ship, and has a good amount of open deck space. Carnival have maintained the ship incredibly well. The interiors retain much of the original wood and brass fittings intact from her former days as a Union Castle liner. Has a good array of public rooms. Fascinating steel art deco staircase. Cabins are spacious, with plenty of closet and drawer space, and heavy-duty fittings. Some large cabins are especially good for families.

— Contemporary colors blend well, but are perhaps too bold. Outside cabins on Veranda deck have obstructed views. The staff are not overly friendly, hustle for drinks, and English is a problem for some. Expect long lines for embarkation, disembarkation, shore tenders, and buffets. There are too many repetitive announcements.

Dining Dining room, located low down, is bright, cheerful, and noisy. There are no tables for two. The food, and its quality, are a letdown. Service is fair, but is hurried and lacks polish.

Other Comments This is a real fun ship experience, with lively casino action, for singles and the young at heart who want a stimulating, not relaxing, vacation. Moderate rates and good value for money for party-goers. I expect this ship will be moved to European waters before long.

mv Fuji Maru ★★★★

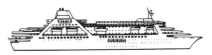

OPERATES

JAPAN/SOUTH EAST ASIA CRUISES

Cruise Line		Mitsui OSK Passenger Line
Former Names	-	Gross Tonnage 23,340
Builder		Mitsubishi (Japan)
Original Cost		$55 million
Christened By		Mr Shintaro Ishiwara
Entered Service		Apr 29, 1989
Interior Design	Osamu Higuchi/Mikiya Murakami	
Country of Registry		Japan (JBTQ)
Tel No 120-0467	Fax No	120-0470
Length (ft/m)		547.9/167.00
Beam (ft/m) 78.7/24.00	Draft (ft/m)	21.4/6.55
Propulsion		diesel (15,740kW)
Propellers		2 (CP)
Decks 8	Crew	190
Pass. Capacity (basis 2) 328	(all berths) 603	
Pass. Space Ratio (basis 2) 71.1	(all berths) 38.7	
Officers Japanese	Dining Staff Japanese/Filipino	
Total Cabins		164
Size Range (sq ft/m)	182-376/17.0-35.0	
Outside Cabins 164	Inside Cabins	0
Single Cabins 0	Supplement	25-60%
Balcony Cabins 0	Wheelchair Cabins	2
Cabin Current		100 AC
Refrigerator	Suites, Deluxe cabins only	
Cabin TV Yes	VCR	No
Dining Rooms 1	Sittings	1
Elevators		5
Casino Yes*	Slot Machines	No

Swimming Pools (outside) 1	(inside)	0
Whirlpools	0 (4 Japanese Baths)	
Gymnasium		Yes
Sauna/Steam Room Yes/No	Massage	Yes*
Self-Service Launderette		Yes
Movie Theater/Seats Yes/142	Library	Yes
Children's Facilities		Yes*
Watersports Facilities		None
Classification Society	Nippon Kaiji Kyokai	

* = on leisure cruises only

RATINGS	SCORE
Ship: Condition/Cleanliness	7.5
Ship: Space/Flow/Comfort	7.8
Ship: Decor/Furnishings	7.6
Ship: Fitness Facilities	6.4
Cabins: Comfort/Facilities	6.7
Cabins: Software	7.1
Food: Dining Room/Cuisine	7.3
Food: Buffets/Informal Dining	6.6
Food: Quality of Ingredients	7.0
Service: Dining Room	7.3
Service: Bars	7.4
Service: Cabins	6.9
Cruise: Entertainment	6.7
Cruise: Activities Program	6.7
Cruise: Hospitality Standard	8.3
OVERALL RATING	107.3

+ Well thought out and flexible multi-functional design, principally for incentives, conventions, as a seminar and training ship and individual passengers. Extensive lecture and conference rooms, the largest of which is two decks high, seats 600, and converts into a sports stadium or hall for industrial product introductions. Elegant lobby and two-level atrium. Classic wood-paneled library. Has two Japanese-style grand baths, and traditional "Washitsu" tatami mat room. "Hanaguruma" owner's room is elegant for small formal functions. Sakura Salon is soothing, with Western and traditional Japanese design. High-tech media and television system throughout (bilingual multiplex televisions in crew cabins). Two suites are lovely, and deluxe cabins are of a high standard, with full bathtubs. Other simply furnished cabins are ideal for seminar and school usage. Folded blankets are lovely.

— Indoor areas clean and tidy, but some outdoor upper decks need attention.

Dining The dining room is attractive, has a high ceiling, but bright lighting. Japanese or Western cuisine for all meals. The food is of a good standard, with simple, but colorful, presentation. There are several beverage machines.

Other Comments Good exhibition, training, and educational charter cruise ship with up to date facilities, although not ideally designed for individual passengers. No tipping is allowed.

ms Funchal ★★★

OPERATES

EUROPE CRUISES

Cruise Line	Arcalia Shipping
Former Names	-
Gross Tonnage	9,846
Builder	Helsingor Skibsvog (Denmark)
Original Cost	n/a
Christened By	n/a
Entered Service	Oct 31, 1961/May 1976
Interior Design	George Potamianos
Country of Registry	Panama (3EHK4)
Tel No 133-0320 Fax No	133-6716
Length (ft/m)	518.3/158.00
Beam (ft/m) 62.5/19.08 Draft (ft/m)	21.4/6.53
Propulsion	diesel (7,356kW)
Propellers	2 (FP)
Decks 6 Crew	155
Pass. Capacity (basis 2) 406 (all berths)	460
Pass. Space Ratio (basis 2) 24.2 (all berths)	21.4
Officers European Dining Staff	European
Total Cabins	222
Size Range (sq ft/m)	n/a
Outside Cabins 134 Inside Cabins	88
Single Cabins 38 Supplement	Set rates
Balcony Cabins 0 Wheelchair Cabins	0
Cabin Current	220 AC
Refrigerator	No
Cabin TV No VCR	No
Dining Rooms 1 Sittings	1
Elevators	2

Casino	Yes	Slot Machines	Yes
Swimming Pools (outside) 1		(inside)	0
Whirlpools	0	Gymnasium	Yes
Sauna/Steam Room Yes/No		Massage	No
Self-Service Launderette			No
Movie Theater/Seats			No
Library			Yes
Children's Facilities			No
Watersports Facilities			None
Classification Society		Lloyd's Register	

RATINGS	SCORE
Ship: Condition/Cleanliness	6.3
Ship: Space/Flow/Comfort	6.3
Ship: Decor/Furnishings	6.7
Ship: Fitness Facilities	4.0
Cabins: Comfort/Facilities	6.1
Cabins: Software	6.2
Food: Dining Room/Cuisine	6.1
Food: Buffets/Informal Dining	6.0
Food: Quality of Ingredients	6.0
Service: Dining Room	6.6
Service: Bars	6.7
Service: Cabins	6.8
Cruise: Entertainment	6.0
Cruise: Activities Program	5.8
Cruise: Hospitality Standard	7.0
OVERALL RATING	92.6

+ This tidy-looking small ship has a classic, well-balanced, but now dated profile. She has been quite well maintained. Has a very warm, charming, and attentive staff, and a loyal passenger following. Although showing her age, she has twin sheltered promenade decks for those who enjoy strolling. The refurbished public rooms are well laid out, with plenty of wood paneling and wood trim. The cabins are very compact, yet quite well equipped, with just enough closet and drawer space. They are decorated in pleasing colors.

— Cabin bathrooms are very small and utilitarian. Some back-to-back cabins share bathrooms (a red light goes on in the opposing cabin when the bathroom is in use).

Dining The dining room is quite tastefully decorated, and has a real cozy, old-world atmosphere. The food, which is Scandinavian in style (that means plenty of fish and seafood), is surprisingly good, as is the service. There is a limited selection of cheeses and fruits.

Other Comments Very popular with northern Europeans, this ship offers a destination-oriented cruise experience in comfortable surroundings, ideally suited to singles and couples seeking good value for money, but North Americans may find the ship to be too eclectic. Good if you like small, older ships with their accompanying eccentricities. Often marketed by Fritiskryys, a Swedish tour operator.

ms Golden Princess ★★★★

Cruise Line	Princess Cruises	Elevators	5
Former Names	Sunward/Birka Queen/	Casino Yes	Slot Machines Yes
	Royal Viking Sky	Swimming Pools (outside) 2	(inside) 0
Gross Tonnage	28,078	Whirlpools 0	Gymnasium Yes
Builder	Wartsila (Finland)	Sauna/Steam Room Yes/Yes	Massage Yes
Original Cost	$22.5 million	Self-Service Launderette	Yes
Christened By	Mrs Vesla Darre Hirsch	Movie Theater/Seats	Yes/156
Entered Service	Jun 13, 1973/Jun 13, 1993	Library Yes	Children's Facilities Yes
Interior Design	Njal Eide	Watersports Facilities	None
Country of Registry	Bahamas (C6CN3)	Classification Society	Det Norske Veritas

Tel No 110-4505	Fax No 110-4506	
Length (ft/m)		674.1/205.47
Beam (ft/m) 82.6/25.20	Draft (ft/m) 24.7/7.55	
Propulsion		diesel (13,400kW)
Propellers		2 (CP)
Decks 8	Crew	435
Pass. Capacity (basis 2) 804	(all berths) 867	
Pass. Space Ratio (basis 2) 34.9	(all berths) 32.3	
Officers Scandinavian	Dining Staff International	
Total Cabins		402
Size Range (sq ft/m)		136-580/12.6-53.8
Outside Cabins 351	Inside Cabins	51
Single Cabins 38	Supplement	25-100%
Balcony Cabins 9	Wheelchair Cabins	0
Cabin Current		110/220 AC
Refrigerator	Category 1/2/3/4/5/6 only	
Cabin TV Yes	VCR	No
Dining Rooms 1	Sittings	2

RATINGS	SCORE
Ship: Condition/Cleanliness	7.0
Ship: Space/Flow/Comfort	8.0
Ship: Decor/Furnishings	7.4
Ship: Fitness Facilities	7.7
Cabins: Comfort/Facilities	7.6
Cabins: Software	7.5
Food: Dining Room/Cuisine	7.6
Food: Buffets/Informal Dining	7.2
Food: Quality of Ingredients	7.0
Service: Dining Room	7.6
Service: Bars	7.6
Service: Cabins	7.7
Cruise: Entertainment	7.6
Cruise: Activities Program	7.5
Cruise: Hospitality Standard	7.8
OVERALL RATING	112.8

+ Handsome outer styling. Beautifully balanced, and with sharply raked bow. Plenty of open deck and sunning space. Fine outdoor wrap-around promenade deck. Lively casino. Excellent fitness and sports facilities. Tasteful decor following extensive refurbishment. Suites are spacious and nicely equipped. All cabins are well appointed, and have good closet, drawer, and storage space. Most bathrooms are good, although some have awkward access.

— The ship is now looking very tired, and maintenance is inconsistent. Cabins have tinny metal drawers. Plumbing is getting to be unreliable.

Dining The spacious dining room has a high ceiling, low noise level, and provides an elegant setting for cuisine that is now improving, but presentation could be better. Overall food quality is in line with that of other similarly priced ships, and the company is introducing upgraded menus. Pasta dishes prepared nightly by the head waiters are always a highlight. Poor bread rolls, pastry items, and fruits. The wine list contains nearly 80 selections.

Other Comments This ship was stretched in 1982, and will provide a good cruise experience in spacious, nicely furnished surroundings. The ship charter ends in July 1996, when it is expected that she will be returned to her owners, who need to spend a considerable sum of money to bring her up to standard again.

ms Grandeur of the Seas

OPERATES

CARIBBEAN CRUISES

Cruise Line	Royal Caribbean Cruises
Former Names	-
Gross Tonnage	73,600
Builder	Kvaerner-Masa Yards (Finland)
Original Cost	$300 million
Christened By	n/a
Entered Service	November 1996
Interior Design	Njal Eide
Country of Registry	n/a
Tel No	n/a	Fax No	n/a
Length (ft/m)	915.6/279.1
Beam (ft/m) 105.6/32.2	Draft (ft/m)	25.0/7.62
Propulsion	diesel-electric (50,400kW)
Propellers	2 (FP)
Decks	11	Crew	768
Pass. Capacity (basis 2) 1,954	(all berths) 2,432
Pass. Space Ratio (basis 2) 37.6	(all berths) 30.2
Officers Norwegian	Dining Staff International
Total Cabins	977
Size Range (sq ft/m)	137-1,147/12.8-106.6
Outside Cabins	578	Inside Cabins	399
Single Cabins	0	Supplement	50%
Balcony Cabins	212	Wheelchair Cabins	14
Cabin Current	110/220 AC
Refrigerator	Some cabins
Cabin TV	Yes	VCR	Some cabins
Dining Rooms	1	Sittings	2
Elevators	9

Casino	Yes	Slot Machines	Yes
Swimming Pools (outside)			1
(inside)	1 (indoor/outdoor w/glass roof)
Whirlpools	6	Gymnasium	Yes
Sauna/Steam Room Yes/Yes	Massage	Yes
Self-Service Launderette			No
Movie Theater/Seats	No	Library	Yes
Children's Facilities/Playroom			Yes
Watersports Facilities			None
Classification Society	Det Norske Veritas

RATINGS	SCORE
Ship: Condition/Cleanliness	NYR
Ship: Space/Flow/Comfort	NYR
Ship: Decor/Furnishings	NYR
Ship: Fitness Facilities	NYR
Cabins: Comfort/Facilities	NYR
Cabins: Software	NYR
Food: Dining Room/Cuisine	NYR
Food: Buffets/Informal Dining	NYR
Food: Quality of Ingredients	NYR
Service: Dining Room	NYR
Service: Bars	NYR
Service: Cabins	NYR
Cruise: Entertainment	NYR
Cruise: Activities Program	NYR
Cruise: Hospitality Standard	NYR
OVERALL RATING	

+ This ship has a lengthy design profile, with a funnel placed well aft and a well-rounded stern (as on the Sovereign of the Seas-class ships). There will be a fine nightclub located high atop the ship, forward of the funnel and overlooking the swimming pool deck, as on the *Legend of the Seas/Splendour of the Seas*, with access provided by a multi-deck-high atrium.

— None known at press time.

Dining General comments regarding the food operation of Legend of the S*eas/Splendour of the Seas* will apply, but you can also expect some innovative options to be included.

Other Comments This is another new ship design for Royal Caribbean Cruises, with what should prove to be an excellent passenger flow. Ideal for first-time cruisegoers who want fine, comfortable new surroundings, and all the very latest in facilities, entertainment lounges and high-tech sophistication in one neat, well-packaged, and, rather predictably, a fine-tuned cruise vacation.

ms Hanseatic ★★★★★

OPERATES

*WORLDWIDE EXPEDITION CRUISES
(INCLUDING ANTARCTICA)*

Cruise Line	Hanseatic Tours	Swimming Pools (outside)	1
Former Names	-	Whirlpools 1	Exercise Room Yes
Gross Tonnage	8,378	Sauna/Steam Room Yes/No	Massage Yes
Builder	Rauma Yards (Finland)	Self-Service Launderette	No
Original Cost	$68 million	Lecture/Film Room	Yes (seats 160)
Christened By	Ms Dagmar Berghoff	Library Yes	Zodiacs 14
Entered Service	Mar 27, 1993	Helicopter Pad	Yes
Interior Design	Wilfried Koehnemann	Watersports Facilities	banana boat,
Country of Registry	Bahamas (C6KA9)		glass-bottom boat
Tel No 110-3726 Fax No	110-3727	Classification Society	Det Norske Veritas
Length (ft/m)	402.6/122.74		
Beam (ft/m) 59.0/18.00 Draft (ft/m)	15.4/4.70	**RATINGS**	**SCORE**
Propulsion	diesel (5,880kW)	Ship: Condition/Cleanliness	9.2
Propellers	2 (CP)	Ship: Space/Flow/Comfort	9.0
Decks 6 Crew	125	Ship: Expedition Equipment	9.2
Pass. Capacity (basis 2) 160 (all berths) 200		Ship: Decor/Furnishings	9.1
Pass. Space Ratio (basis 2) 52.3 (all berths) 41.8		Cabins: Comfort/Facilities	9.1
Officers German Dining Staff European/Filipino		Cabins: Software	9.0
Total Cabins	94	Food: Dining Room/Cuisine	8.7
Size Range (sq ft/m)	232-471/21.5-43.7	Food: Buffets/Informal Dining	8.6
Outside Cabins 94 Inside Cabins	0	Food: Quality of Ingredients	8.6
Single Cabins	0	Service: Dining Room	8.7
Supplement	On Request	Service: Bars	8.7
Balcony Cabins 0 Wheelchair Cabins	2	Service: Cabins	8.7
Cabin Current 220 AC Refrigerator	Yes	Cruise: Itineraries/Operations	9.1
Cabin TV Yes VCR	No	Cruise: Lecture Program	8.8
Dining Rooms 1 Sittings	open seating	Cruise: Hospitality Standard	9.0
Elevators	2	OVERALL RATING	133.5

+ Fine luxury ship, fittings and furnishings, under long-term charter to Hanseatic Tours. Has fully enclosed bridge, ice-hardened hull with highest classification, the latest high-tech navigation equipment, and an open bridge policy. Staff are very helpful. Special shoe-washing room provided. The all-outside cabins, located forward, are large and well appointed, and include separate lounge area, mini-bar, television. Bathrooms have bathtub and bathrobe. There are only two types of cabins; 34 have double beds, others have twin beds. Bridge Deck suites and cabins have butler service and full in-cabin dining privileges. Outstanding, well-planned itineraries. Informal ambiance. Has outstanding lecturers and naturalists.

— This ship is principally for German-speaking and English-speaking passengers, so other nationalities may find it hard to integrate.

Dining The dining room is elegant, warm, and welcoming, and features fine Rosenthal china and silverware. The cuisine and service are first rate, with high-quality ingredients used. Very creative and nicely presented. Excellent selection of breads, cheeses, and fruits.

Other Comments This ship provides destination-intensive, nature and life-enrichment expedition cruises in elegant surroundings to some fascinating places. Port taxes, insurance, gratuities and most shore excursions are included (except for those in Europe).

mv Hebridean Princess ★★★★★

OPERATES

7-DAY SCOTTISH COAST CRUISES

Cruise Line	Hebridean Islands Cruises	Casino	No	Slot Machines	No
Former Names	Columba	Swimming Pools (outside)	0	(inside)	0
Gross Tonnage	2,112	Whirlpools	0	Gymnasium	Yes
Builder	Hall Russell (Scotland)	Sauna/Steam Room No/No	Massage	No
Original Cost	n/a	Self-Service Launderette	No
Christened By	HRH the Duchess of York	Movie Theater/Seats	No
Entered Service	1964/Apr 26, 1989	Library	Yes
Interior Design	Susan Binns	Children's Facilities	No
Country of Registry	Scotland (GNHV)	Watersports Facilities	None
Tel No 144-0772 Fax No 144-0772	Classification Society	Lloyd's Register

Length (ft/m)	235.0/71.6
Beam (ft/m) 46.0/14.0 Draft (ft/m)	10.0/3.0
Propulsion	diesel (1,790kW)
Propellers	2 (FP)
Decks 5 Crew	35
Pass. Capacity (basis 2) 48	(all berths) 55
Pass. Space Ratio (basis 2) 44.0	(all berths) 38.4
Officers British Dining Staff	British
Total Cabins	29
Size Range (sq ft/m)	112-367/10.4-34.0
Outside Cabins 4 Inside Cabins	0
Single Cabins 10 Supplement	None
Balcony Cabins 4 Wheelchair Cabins	0
Cabin Current	240 AC
Refrigerator	Yes
Cabin TV Yes VCR Yes (some cabins)
Dining Rooms 1 Sittings	1
Elevators	0

RATINGS	SCORE
Ship: Condition/Cleanliness	8.6
Ship: Space/Flow/Comfort	8.4
Ship: Facilities	9.0
Ship: Expedition Equipment	8.0
Ship: Fitness/Watersports Facilities	6.0
Cabins: Comfort/Facilities	8.3
Cabins: Software	9.0
Food: Dining Room/Cuisine	9.1
Food: Buffets/Informal Dining	8.8
Food: Quality of Ingredients	8.5
Service: Dining Room	8.6
Service: Bars	8.5
Service: Cabins	8.4
Cruise: Entertainment/Lecture Program	7.7
Cruise: Hospitality Standard	9.3
OVERALL RATING	126.2

+ This is a charming little ship that combines stately home service with a warm country cottage ambiance. Features a real brick-walled fireplace in the Tiree Lounge. Cabins all have different color schemes and names (there are no numbers, and, refreshingly, no door locks). All are individually designed and created (with sweeping Laura Ashley-style drapes), and come in a range of configurations: double-bed, twin-bed, or single-bed. All except three have private bathroom with bath or shower; some have gold-plated bathroom fittings. Brass cabin portholes actually open. Three recently added cabins are outfitted in Scottish Baronial style, and all have real Victorian bathroom fittings. Use of the ship's small boats, speedboat, bicycles, and fishing gear is included in the price, as are entrance fees to gardens, castles, and other attractions. Specialist guides accompany all cruises.

— This 30-year-old ship is strong, but does have structural limitations and noisy diesel engines that cause some vibration (however, the engines don't run at night, and the ship anchors well before bedtime). It's always cold (and often very wet) in the Scottish islands, so take plenty of warm clothing that can be layered.

Dining The dining room is totally no-smoking. Outstanding cuisine is about the same quality and presentation as the Sea Goddess ships. Fresh produce is purchased locally—a welcome change from the mass catering of most cruise ships. Although there are no flambé items (the

galley has electric, not gas, cookers), what is created is beautifully presented and of the very highest standard.

Breakfast menus alternate every two nights and feature special dishes in addition to the traditional Scottish fare. Although there's waiter service for most things, there's also a delightful buffet table display for breakfast and luncheon. Freshly squeezed orange juice (difficult to obtain on most cruise ships) is always available.

The ship carries an extensive wine list, with prices that are quite moderate. There are also 18 types of whisky available (including some fine single malts) at the bars, along with some fine premium and vintage cognacs (most expensive being a 50-year-old Remy Martin Louis XIII). Very personal and attentive service throughout.

Other Comments Small is beautiful. Inspector Hercules Poirot would be right at home here. With no lines and no noise, it is a pleasure to cruise on this ship, and a fine way to see some of the most beautiful scenery in the world—the Scottish Highlands and islands. This cruise is a superb Scottish Island Fling. You are met at the rail station or airport in Glasgow and taken to Oban to join the ship. Direct bookings accepted. She is the only cruise vessel in the world with an all-British crew, and, although expensive, is one of the world's best kept travel secrets.

ms Holiday ★★★★

Cruise Line		Carnival Cruise Lines
Former Names		-
Gross Tonnage		46,052
Builder		Aalborg Vaerft (Denmark)
Original Cost		$170 million
Christened By		Mrs Lin Arison
Entered Service		Jul 13, 1985
Interior Design		Joe Farcus
Country of Registry		Bahamas (C6KM)
Tel No 110-3216	Fax No	110-3216
Length (ft/m)		726.9/221.57
Beam (ft/m) 92.4/28.17	Draft (ft/m)	25.5/7.77
Propulsion		diesel (22,360kW)
Propellers		2 (CP)
Decks 9	Crew	660
Pass. Capacity (basis 2) 1,452	(all berths)	1,800
Pass. Space Ratio (basis 2) 31.7	(all berths)	25.5
Officers Italian	Dining Staff	International
Total Cabins		726
Size Range (sq ft/m)		185-190/17.0-17.6
Outside Cabins 447	Inside Cabins	279
Single Cabins		0
Supplement	50% (cat. 1-3)/100% (cat. 4-12)	
Balcony Cabins 10	Wheelchair Cabins	15
Cabin Current		110 AC
Refrigerator		Category 12 only
Cabin TV Yes	VCR	No
Dining Rooms 2	Sittings	2

Elevators			8
Casino	Yes	Slot Machines	Yes
Swimming Pools (outside) 3		(inside)	0
Whirlpools	2	Gymnasium	Yes
Sauna/Steam Room Yes/No		Massage	Yes
Self-Service Launderette			Yes
Movie Theater/Seats	No	Library	Yes
Children's Facilities			Yes
Watersports Facilities			None
Classification Society			Lloyd's Register

RATINGS	SCORE
Ship: Condition/Cleanliness	7.8
Ship: Space/Flow/Comfort	7.6
Ship: Decor/Furnishings	6.4
Ship: Fitness Facilities	7.8
Cabins: Comfort/Facilities	7.6
Cabins: Software	7.4
Food: Dining Room/Cuisine	6.7
Food: Buffets/Informal Dining	6.4
Food: Quality of Ingredients	5.3
Service: Dining Room	7.0
Service: Bars	7.2
Service: Cabins	6.4
Cruise: Entertainment	8.0
Cruise: Activities Program	7.6
Cruise: Hospitality Standard	6.3
OVERALL RATING	105.5

+ Distinctive swept-back wing-tipped funnel. Numerous public rooms on two entertainment decks, with Broadway-themed interior decor. Has bright decor in all public rooms except for the elegant Carnegie Library. Double-wide indoor promenade, with real red and cream bus (used as a snack cafe). Stunning multi-tiered showroom. Excellent casino with round-the-clock action. Plenty of dazzle and sizzle entertainment. Children's facilities include virtual reality machines. Cabins are quite spacious, and attractively decorated.

— Bold, slab-sided contemporary ship with short, rakish bow and stubby stern—typical of new buildings today. Expect long lines for embarkation, disembarkation, shore tenders, and buffets. Constant hustling for drinks, but at least it's done with a knowing smile. Noisy.

Dining The two dining rooms (both are non-smoking) have low ceilings, making the raised center sections seem rather crowded, and very noisy. Food is quantity, not quality. Service is average, and hurried. Buffets are very basic, as is the selection of breads, rolls, and fruit.

Other Comments This ship, now over 10 years old, is ideal for a first cruise experience in very comfortable, lively surroundings, and for the active set who enjoy constant stimulation and a fun-filled atmosphere, at an attractive price. There's no doubt that Carnival does it well, but once is enough, then you'll want to move to a more upscale ship.

mv Horizon ★★★★★

OPERATES

7-DAY ALASKA AND CARIBBEAN CRUISES

Cruise Line	Celebrity Cruises	Casino	Yes	Slot Machines Yes
Former Names	-	Swimming Pools (outside) 2	(inside)	0
Gross Tonnage	46,811	Whirlpools	3	Gymnasium Yes
Builder	Meyer Werft (Germany)	Sauna/Steam Room Yes/No	Massage	Yes
Original Cost	$185 million	Self-Service Launderette		No
Christened By	Mrs D. J. Chandris	Movie Theater/Seats		Yes/850
Entered Service	May 26, 1990	Library		Yes
Interior Design	Katzourakis/McNeece	Children's Facilities		Yes
Country of Registry	Liberia (ELNG6)	Watersports Facilities		None
Tel No 124-3527 Fax No 124-3532		Classification Society		Lloyd's Register
Length (ft/m)	680.7/207.49			
Beam (ft/m) 95.1/29.00 Draft (ft/m) 23.6/7.20		**RATINGS**		**SCORE**
Propulsion	diesel (19,960kW)	Ship: Condition/Cleanliness		9.0
Propellers	2 (CP)	Ship: Space/Flow/Comfort		8.7
Decks 9 Crew	645	Ship: Decor/Furnishings		8.6
Pass. Capacity (basis 2) 1,354 (all berths) 1,660		Ship: Fitness Facilities		8.1
Pass. Space Ratio (basis 2) 34.5 (all berths) 28.1		Cabins: Comfort/Facilities		8.2
Officers Greek Dining Staff International		Cabins: Software		8.1
Total Cabins	677	Food: Dining Room/Cuisine		8.4
Size Range (sq ft/m)	185-334/17.0-31.0	Food: Buffets/Informal Dining		8.0
Outside Cabins 529 Inside Cabins	148	Food: Quality of Ingredients		8.0
Single Cabins 0 Supplement Set rates		Service: Dining Room		8.2
Balcony Cabins 0 Wheelchair Cabins 4		Service: Bars		8.1
Cabin Current	110 AC	Service: Cabins		8.2
Refrigerator	No	Cruise: Entertainment		8.6
Cabin TV Yes VCR	No	Cruise: Activities Program		8.3
Dining Rooms 1 Sittings	2	Cruise: Hospitality Standard		8.6
Elevators	7	OVERALL RATING		125.1

+ Handsome contemporary ship. Spacious public rooms, with good passenger flow. Elegant furnishings and appointments. Soothing pastel colors. Wood-paneled casino has a stately home feel. Two-level showroom has excellent sightlines. The lobby is unusual, with its peachy Miami Beach Art Deco look. Cabins have fine quality fittings, tastefully decorated and above average size, with excellent closet and drawer space and good insulation. Suites have butler service. Elegant entertainment, with some of the best production shows afloat, and a good cruise staff.

— No self-service launderette, nor cabins with balconies. Too many announcements at times. No cushioned pads for the deck lounge chairs. Bathroom towels are small and too skimpy.

Dining Celebrity Cruises has achieved an enviable reputation for providing fine quality food, presentation, and service. The menu is excellent, with a wide variety of dishes. The dining room is large, yet feels small and elegant, with several tables for two. Informal cafe features good breakfast and lunch buffets, and an outdoor grill serves fast food items. Separate menu for vegetarians and children. Caviar (at extra charge) is available in the America's Cup Club.

Other Comments This ship delivers a well-defined North American cruise experience at a most modest price. It represents outstanding value for money, hence its very high rating.

ms Ilich ★★+

OPERATES

*2/5-DAY BALTIC CRUISES
(YEAR-ROUND)*

Cruise Line			Baltic Line
Former Names			Skandia/Bore I
Gross Tonnage			8,528
Builder			Wartsila (Finland)
Original Cost	n/a	Christened By	n/a
Entered Service			1973
Interior Design			n/a
Country of Registry			Russia (UPWX)
Tel No	140-0777	Fax No	140-0777
Length (ft/m)			419.9/128.00
Beam (ft/m)	72.1/22.00	Draft (ft/m)	19.3/5.90
Propulsion			diesel (2,460kW)
Propellers			2 (CP)
Decks	5	Crew	160
Pass. Capacity (basis 2) 350		(all berths) 380	
Pass. Space Ratio (basis 2) 24.3		(all berths) 22.4	
Officers			Russian
Dining Staff			Ukrainian/Scandinavian
Total Cabins			175
Size Range (sq ft/m)			86-130/8.0-12.0
Outside Cabins	92	Inside Cabins	83
Single Cabins	0	Supplement	100%
Balcony Cabins	0	Wheelchair Cabins	0
Cabin Current			220 AC
Refrigerator			No
Cabin TV	No	VCR	No
Dining Rooms	2	Sittings	2
Elevators			0

Casino	Yes	Slot Machines	Yes
Swimming Pools (outside) 0		(inside)	1
Whirlpools	0	Gymnasium	No
Sauna/Steam Room Yes/No		Massage	No
Self-Service Launderette			No
Movie Theater/Seats			No
Library			No
Children's Facilities			Yes
Watersports Facilities			None
Classification Society			Lloyd's Register

RATINGS	SCORE
Ship: Condition/Cleanliness	6.2
Ship: Space/Flow/Comfort	6.1
Ship: Decor/Furnishings	6.2
Ship: Fitness Facilities	3.8
Cabins: Comfort/Facilities	5.1
Cabins: Software	5.6
Food: Dining Room/Cuisine	6.4
Food: Buffets/Informal Dining	6.1
Food: Quality of Ingredients	6.2
Service: Dining Room	6.4
Service: Bars	6.6
Service: Cabins	6.6
Cruise: Entertainment	5.8
Cruise: Activities Program	5.4
Cruise: Hospitality Standard	6.1
OVERALL RATING	88.6

+ This conventional-looking small former ferry is an ideal size for Baltic cruising. Features short cruises between Stockholm, St. Petersburg and Riga (two full nights in St. Petersburg). Has six small, but well utilized conference rooms. Entertainment is limited, but the crew show is good. Good facilities for families with children. Has a small indoor pool and numerous saunas.

— Very limited outdoor deck and sunning space, but it's not really needed as the weather is often on the chilly side. Cabins are very small, with spartan furnishings, and closet and drawer space is extremely limited. Cabin bathrooms are really tiny. A small number of cabins do not have private facilities, so check carefully before booking.

Dining There are two restaurants (one à la carte) that are quite comfortable, plus several lounges. The food is quite adequate, though don't expect gourmet presentation or selection. Good service from a friendly, multilingual staff.

Other Comments This tidy little ship provides a comfortable cruise experience, but in a densely populated environment. However, for short cruises, the ship will provide a reasonable cruise experience for those on a limited budget, nothing more.

ms Imagination ★★★★

OPERATES

7-DAY WESTERN CARIBBEAN CRUISES (YEAR-ROUND)

Cruise Line	Carnival Cruise Lines	Elevators		14
Former Names	-	Casino	Yes	Slot Machines Yes
Gross Tonnage	70,367	Swimming Pools (outside) 3	(inside)	0
Builder	Kvaerner Masa-Yards (Finland)	Whirlpools	6	Gymnasium Yes
Original Cost	$330 million	Sauna/Steam Room Yes/Yes	Massage	Yes
Christened By	Jodi Dickinson	Self-Service Launderette		Yes
Entered Service	July 1, 1995	Movie Theater/Seats No	Library	Yes
Interior Design	Joe Farcus	Children's Facilities		Yes
Country of Registry	Panama (3EWJ9)	Watersports Facilities		None
Tel No 134-7673 Fax No	134-7674	Classification Society		Lloyd's Register
Length (ft/m)	855.0/260.60			
Beam (ft/m) 104.0/31.40 Draft (ft/m)	25.9/7.90	**RATINGS**		**SCORE**
Propulsion	diesel-electric (42,240kW)	Ship: Condition/Cleanliness		9.2
Propellers	2 (CP)	Ship: Space/Flow/Comfort		8.1
Decks 10 Crew	920	Ship: Decor/Furnishings		8.4
Pass. Capacity (basis 2) 2,040 (all berths) 2,594		Ship: Fitness Facilities		8.0
Pass. Space Ratio (basis 2) 34.4 (all berths) 26.7		Cabins: Comfort/Facilities		7.6
Officers Italian Dining Staff International		Cabins: Software		7.4
Total Cabins	1,020	Food: Dining Room/Cuisine		6.7
Size Range (sq ft/m)	185-421/17.0-39.0	Food: Buffets/Informal Dining		7.0
Outside Cabins 620 Inside Cabins	402	Food: Quality of Ingredients		5.3
Single Cabins	0	Service: Dining Room		7.0
Supplement 50% (cat. 1-3)/100% (cat. 4-12)		Service: Bars		7.2
Balcony Cabins 54 Wheelchair Cabins 20		Service: Cabins		6.4
Cabin Current	110 AC	Cruise: Entertainment		8.6
Refrigerator	Category 11/12 only	Cruise: Activities Program		7.8
Cabin TV Yes VCR	No	Cruise: Hospitality Standard		6.5
Dining Rooms 2 Sittings	2	OVERALL RATING		111.2

+ Fifth in a series of eight Carnival megaships that reflects the creative talents of interior designer Joe Farcus, whose philosophy is that the cruise ship environment provides an escape from routine. Ethereal decor in public rooms connected by wide indoor boulevards. Fine artistic centerpiece in the atrium. Expansive open deck areas and an excellent health spa. There's also a $1 million living art collection. Ship buffs will like the six Stephen Card paintings of clipper ships in the Grand Bar. The Victorian-era-style library is a curious room, with intentionally mismatched furnishings, fine oriental rugs, and even some books. Lavish yet elegant multi-tiered showroom and fine, frenetic razzle-dazzle shows.

— Some would say that the sensory and auditory indulgence is a little over the top. There are too many announcements. Expect lines for embarkation, disembarkation, buffets, shore tenders, and excursions, and no quiet spaces aboard to get away from crowds. Aggressive hustling for drinks. Cabin bathroom amenities are minimal.

Dining Two large, noisy dining rooms have the usual efficient, programmed, assertive service. The improved cuisine is fair. One plus is a 24-hour pizzeria.

Other Comments Has a forthright, angular appearance typical of today's space-creative designs. This ship will entertain those who are young at heart in fine fashion.

ss Independence ★★★

OPERATES

7-DAY HAWAII CRUISES (YEAR-ROUND)

Cruise Line	American Hawaii Cruises	Elevators	4
Former Names	Oceanic Independence/Sea Luck I	Casino	No	Slot Machines	No
Gross Tonnage	30,090	Swimming Pools (outside) 2	(inside)	0
Builder	Bethlehem Shipbuilders (USA)	Whirlpools	0	Gymnasium	Yes
Original Cost	$25 million	Sauna/Steam Room	Yes/No	Massage	Yes
Christened By	Mrs John Slater	Self-Service Launderette		Yes
Entered Service	Feb 10, 1951/Jun 15, 1980	Movie Theater/Seats		Yes/144
Interior Design	Henry Dreyfuss/	Library	Yes	Children's Facilities Yes
	Dian Cleve/Henry Beer	Classification Society		American Bureau
Country of Registry	USA (KPHI)			of Shipping

Tel No 808-847-3172 Fax No 808-848-0406	
Length (ft/m)	682.4/208.01

RATINGS	**SCORE**
Ship: Condition/Cleanliness	6.2
Ship: Space/Flow/Comfort	6.8
Ship: Decor/Furnishings	6.1
Ship: Fitness Facilities	5.8
Cabins: Comfort/Facilities	6.2
Cabins: Software	7.0
Food: Dining Room/Cuisine	6.3
Food: Buffets/Informal Dining	6.1
Food: Quality of Ingredients	6.4
Service: Dining Room	6.6
Service: Bars	6.7
Service: Cabins	6.4
Cruise: Entertainment	6.0
Cruise: Activities Program	6.2
Cruise: Hospitality Standard	6.4
OVERALL RATING	95.2

Beam (ft/m) 89.1/27.18	Draft (ft/m) 30.1/9.19		
Propulsion	steam turbine (40,456kW)		
Propellers	2 (FP)		
Decks	9	Crew	315
Pass. Capacity (basis 2) 809	(all berths) 1,025		
Pass. Space Ratio (basis 2) 37.1	(all berths) 29.3		
Officers	American	Dining Staff	American
Total Cabins			414
Size Range (sq ft/m)		70-375/6.5-34.8	
Outside Cabins	203	Inside Cabins	211
Single Cabins	19	Supplement	60-100%
Balcony Cabins	0	Wheelchair Cabins	0
Cabin Current			110 AC
Refrigerator		Category O/AA/A only	
Cabin TV	No	VCR	No
Dining Rooms	1	Sittings	2

+ American-built, crewed, and registered, this ship has spacious public rooms with high ceilings (not as attractive as on sister ship *Constitution*). Has good facilities for meetings. Expansive open deck space for sun-worshippers. Wrap-around outdoor promenade deck. New Hawaii-themed decor is an improvement. Wide range of cabin types and configurations, all of which offer ample room to move in, plus decent closet and drawer space and fairly bright decor. Has heavy-duty furniture and fittings, designed for unkind oceans. Local Hawaiian artists have their artwork featured on board. Dress is very casual.

— Now over 40 years old. Slow room service. Showlounge is not large enough and is always crowded. Cabin bathrooms are small. Drinks prices are high. There are no stabilizers, so the ship rolls in any inclement weather, which is often.

Dining Dining room is set low down, and without an ocean view (bi-level forward section is more elegant), but it's fairly cheerful, and has tables for two, four, and six. The cuisine is American, with quantity, not quality. Good self-service buffet area.

Other Comments Laid-back atmosphere prevails, with Aloha smiles. This is a destination-intensive cruise on a ship that is still tired, despite a $30 million refurbishment in 1994.

ms Inspiration

OPERATES

*7-DAY CARIBBEAN CRUISES
(YEAR-ROUND)*

Cruise Line	Carnival Cruise Lines	Elevators	14
Former Names	-	Casino	Yes
Gross Tonnage	70,367	Swimming Pools (outside) 3	(inside)
Builder	Kvaerner Masa-Yards (Finland)	Whirlpools	6
Original Cost	$270 million	Sauna/Steam Room Yes/Yes	Massage
Christened By	n/a	Self-Service Launderette	
Entered Service	Mar 1996	Movie Theater/Seats No	Library
Interior Design	Joe Farcus	Children's Facilities	
Country of Registry	Panama	Watersports Facilities	None
Tel No	n/a Fax No n/a	Classification Society	Lloyd's Register
Length (ft/m)	855.0/260.60		

Elevators	14
Casino Yes	Slot Machines Yes
Swimming Pools (outside) 3	(inside) 0
Whirlpools 6	Gymnasium Yes
Sauna/Steam Room Yes/Yes	Massage Yes
Self-Service Launderette	Yes
Movie Theater/Seats No	Library Yes
Children's Facilities	Yes
Watersports Facilities	None
Classification Society	Lloyd's Register

Beam (ft/m) 104.0/31.40 Draft (ft/m)	25.9/7.90
Propulsion	diesel-electric (42,240kW)
Propellers	2 (CP)
Decks 10 Crew	920
Pass. Capacity (basis 2) 2,040 (all berths)	2,594
Pass. Space Ratio (basis 2) 34.4 (all berths)	26.7
Officers Italian Dining Staff	International
Total Cabins	1,020
Size Range (sq ft/m)	185-421/17.0-39.0
Outside Cabins 620 Inside Cabins	402
Single Cabins	0
Supplement 50% (cat. 1-3)/100% (cat. 4-12)	
Balcony Cabins 54 Wheelchair Cabins	20
Cabin Current	110 AC
Refrigerator	Category 11/12 only
Cabin TV Yes VCR	No
Dining Rooms 2 Sittings	2

RATINGS	SCORE
Ship: Condition/Cleanliness	NYR
Ship: Space/Flow/Comfort	NYR
Ship: Decor/Furnishings	NYR
Ship: Fitness Facilities	NYR
Cabins: Comfort/Facilities	NYR
Cabins: Software	NYR
Food: Dining Room/Cuisine	NYR
Food: Buffets/Informal Dining	NYR
Food: Quality of Ingredients	NYR
Service: Dining Room	NYR
Service: Bars	NYR
Service: Cabins	NYR
Cruise: Entertainment	NYR
Cruise: Activities Program	NYR
Cruise: Hospitality Standard	NYR
OVERALL RATING	

+ Like her sister ships, has a dramatic six-deck-high atrium, with cool marble and hot neon, topped by a glass dome, and features a spectacular artistic centerpiece. Expansive open deck areas and excellent health spa. Outside suites have whirlpool tubs. Public entertainment lounges, bars, and clubs galore, with something for everyone. Dazzling colors and design themes in handsome public rooms connected by wide indoor boulevards beg your attention. $1 million art collection, much of it bright and vocal. The library is a lovely room, but there are almost no books. Lavish, but elegant multi-tiered showroom and high-energy razzle-dazzle shows. Three-deck-high glass-enclosed health spa. Huge casino has non-stop action.

— Would be sensory overkill for some. Too many announcements. Expect long lines for embarkation, disembarkation, shore tenders, and buffets. Aggressive hustling for drinks.

Dining Has two huge, noisy dining rooms with usual efficient, assertive service. Improved cuisine so-so, but it's not Carnival's strong point. Service is attentive, but programmed.

Other Comments Has a bold, angular appearance that is typical of today's space-creative designs. Poor food, but forget it, the real fun begins at sundown, when Carnival excels. This ship will entertain you well, with sensory indulgence. It's a ship to play on, and probably you'll never get bored!

ms Island Princess ★★★★

Cruise Line	Princess Cruises	Casino	Yes
Former Names	Island Venture		
Gross Tonnage	19,907		
Builder	Rheinstahl Nordseewerke (Germany)		

Cruise Line	Princess Cruises
Former Names	Island Venture
Gross Tonnage	19,907
Builder	Rheinstahl Nordseewerke (Germany)
Original Cost	$25 million
Christened By	n/a
Entered Service	Feb 5, 1972/1974
Interior Design	Robert Tillberg
Country of Registry	Great Britain (GBBM)
Tel No 144-0214	Fax No 144-0214
Length (ft/m)	553.6/168.74
Beam (ft/m) 80.8/24.64	Draft (ft/m) 24.5/7.49
Propulsion	diesel (13,400kW)
Propellers	2 (CP)
Decks 7	Crew 350
Pass. Capacity (basis 2) 610	(all berths) 717
Pass. Space Ratio (basis 2) 32.6	(all berths) 27.7
Officers British	Dining Staff International
Total Cabins	305
Size Range (sq ft/m)	126-443/11.7-41.0
Outside Cabins 238	Inside Cabins 67
Single Cabins 2	Supplement 40-100%
Balcony Cabins 0	Wheelchair Cabins 4
Cabin Current	110/220 AC
Refrigerator	Category A/B/C/D/DD only
Cabin TV Yes	VCR No
Dining Rooms 1	Sittings 2
Elevators	4

Casino	Yes	Slot Machines	Yes
Swimming Pools (outside) 2		(inside)	0
Whirlpools	0	Gymnasium	Yes
Sauna/Steam Room Yes/No		Massage	Yes
Self-Service Launderette			No
Movie Theater/Seats			Yes/250
Library			Yes
Children's Facilities			No
Watersports Facilities			None
Classification Society			Lloyd's Register

RATINGS	SCORE
Ship: Condition/Cleanliness	7.7
Ship: Space/Flow/Comfort	7.6
Ship: Decor/Furnishings	8.0
Ship: Fitness Facilities	6.2
Cabins: Comfort/Facilities	7.5
Cabins: Software	7.6
Food: Dining Room/Cuisine	7.3
Food: Buffets/Informal Dining	7.0
Food: Quality of Ingredients	6.7
Service: Dining Room	7.9
Service: Bars	8.0
Service: Cabins	7.8
Cruise: Entertainment	8.1
Cruise: Activities Program	7.8
Cruise: Hospitality Standard	8.0
OVERALL RATING	113.2

+ Very attractive profile and exterior styling for this 24-year-old ship. Has very pleasing lines, and recently underwent a dramatic facelift and refurbishment program. Sharply dressed officers and crew. Extremely spacious public areas, with wide passageways and high ceilings in public rooms. Pleasant two-deck-high lobby. Tasteful decor, with pastel colors and pleasing artwork. Forward observation lounge also acts as an indoor buffet dining area. The suites are quite large and well designed. Other cabins have ample room, are well equipped, with plenty of closet and drawer space. Bathrobes and upgraded amenities provided in all cabins.

— There is no wrap-around outdoor promenade deck.

Dining Features a lovely dining room (non-smoking), with decent service from an attentive staff. Food quality is basically good, if uncreative, and standards that had slipped for a couple of years are now improving again. Good pasta dishes. Poor bread rolls, pastry items, and fruits.

Other Comments Quality prevails aboard. This mid-sized ship is ageing well, is quite elegant, and will provide a good cruise experience from start to finish, in very comfortable surroundings, for the older passenger that wants plenty of space and doesn't want to be part of the larger, more impersonal ships.

mv Italia Prima ★★★★

OPERATES

VARIOUS CRUISES WORLDWIDE

Cruise Line	Nina Cruise Line		
Former Names	Volkerfreundschaft/		
	Stockholm/Fridtjof Nansen		
Gross Tonnage	15,000		
Builder	Varco Chiapella (Italy)		
Original Cost	$150 million (reconstruction)		
Christened By	Dr. Margarita Tasi		
Entered Service	Feb 21, 1948/May 27, 1994		
Interior Design	Giuseppe De Jorio		
Country of Registry	Italy (ICZU)		
Tel No 115-2210/-2214	Fax No115-2211/-2215		
Length (ft/m)	525.2/160.10		
Beam (ft/m) 68.8/21.04	Draft (ft/m)	24.6/7.5	
Propulsion	diesel (11,200kW)		
Propellers	2 (CP)		
Decks	7	Crew	260
Pass. Capacity (basis 2) 540		(all berths) 600	
Pass. Space Ratio (basis 2) 27.7		(all berths) 25.0	
Officers	Italian		
Dining Staff	Croatian/Italian/Ukrainian		
Total Cabins	260		
Size Range (sq ft/m)	129-376/12.0-35.0		
Outside Cabins	221	Inside Cabins	39
Single Cabins	0	Supplement	35%
Balcony Cabins	0	Wheelchair Cabins	0
Cabin Current110/220 AC	Refrigerator		Yes
Cabin TV	Yes	VCR	No
Dining Rooms	1	Sittings	1

Elevators			2
Casino	Yes	Slot Machines	Yes
Swimming Pools (outside) 1		(inside)	0
Whirlpools	1	Gymnasium	Yes
Sauna/Steam Room		Yes/Yes (Turkish Bath)	
Massage			Yes
Self-Service Launderette			No
Movie Theater/Seats			Yes/400
Library	Yes	Children's Facilities	No
Classification Society			RINA

RATINGS	SCORE
Ship: Condition/Cleanliness	8.4
Ship: Space/Flow/Comfort	8.3
Ship: Decor/Furnishings	8.8
Ship: Fitness Facilities	6.7
Cabins: Comfort/Facilities	8.3
Cabins: Software	8.6
Food: Dining Room/Cuisine	7.7
Food: Buffets/Informal Dining	6.3
Food: Quality of Ingredients	6.4
Service: Dining Room	7.3
Service: Bars	7.0
Service: Cabins	7.6
Cruise: Entertainment	7.2
Cruise: Activities Program	6.3
Cruise: Hospitality Standard	7.9
OVERALL RATING	112.8

+ Has a wrap-around outdoor promenade deck and wooden "steamer" chairs. Fine selection of public rooms to choose from, including a good 400-seat auditorium for meetings. Lovely interiors with excellent fit and finish, and fine quality materials. Contemporary decor, with good selection of artwork. All cabins have bathtubs and mini-bars. 38 suites feature Jacuzzi bathtubs. Also has a Turkish bath, which is quite unusual on today's ships.

— No forward observation lounge. Small swimming pool is really a "dip" pool. Movie theater seats are not staggered. The cabins on Sole Deck forward have lifeboat-obstructed views. No cushioned pads for deck chairs. Steep gangway designed for European, not Caribbean, ports.

Dining The large dining room, set low down, is attractive and has tables for two, four, six, and eight. Features distinctive Italian cuisine, with excellent pasta. There is a good selection of Italian wines (house wines are included for lunch and dinner). Also has a pizzeria. There is a limited selection of breads, fruits, and cheeses, and the cabin service menu is poor.

Other Comments This ex-ocean liner made history when she rammed and sank the *Andrea Doria* in 1956. Reconstructed as a cruise ship in 1994. She is under charter for most of each year to Neckermann Seereisen, and thus caters mainly to a German-speaking clientele (for the rest of the year she caters to other Europeans).

ms Ivan Franko ★★+

OPERATES
EUROPE CRUISES

Cruise Line	Black Sea Shipping	Casino	No	Slot Machines	No
Former Names	-	Swimming Pools (outside) 1	(inside)	1
Gross Tonnage	20,064	Whirlpools	0	Gymnasium	Yes
Builder	VEB Mathias Thesen (Germany)	Sauna/Steam Room Yes/No	Massage	Yes
Original Cost	n/a Christened By n/a	Self-Service Launderette		No
Entered Service	Nov 14, 1964	Movie Theater/Seats		Yes/130
Interior Design	Shipyard	Library		Yes
Country of Registry	Ukraine (USLI)	Children's Facilities		No
Tel No 140-0233 Fax No 140-0233		Watersports Facilities		None
Length (ft/m)	577.4/176.00	Classification Society		RS
Beam (ft/m) 77.4/23.60 Draft (ft/m) 26.8/8.17				
Propulsion	diesel (15,700kW)			
Propellers	2 (CP)	**RATINGS**		**SCORE**
Decks 8 Crew 340		Ship: Condition/Cleanliness		6.0
Pass. Capacity (basis 2) 580 (all berths) 714		Ship: Space/Flow/Comfort		6.2
Pass. Space Ratio (basis 2) 34.5 (all berths) 28.1		Ship: Decor/Furnishings		6.0
Officers	Russian	Ship: Fitness Facilities		5.0
Dining Staff	Ukrainian	Cabins: Comfort/Facilities		5.9
Total Cabins	290	Cabins: Software		6.1
Size Range (sq ft/m)	n/a	Food: Dining Room/Cuisine		5.3
Outside Cabins 287 Inside Cabins 3		Food: Buffets/Informal Dining		5.1
Single Cabins 0 Supplement 100%		Food: Quality of Ingredients		5.2
Balcony Cabins 3 Wheelchair Cabins 0		Service: Dining Room		6.2
Cabin Current	220 AC	Service: Bars		6.7
Refrigerator	No	Service: Cabins		7.1
Cabin TV No VCR No		Cruise: Entertainment		5.1
Dining Rooms 2 Sittings 2		Cruise: Activities Program		5.4
Elevators	3	Cruise: Hospitality Standard		5.7
		OVERALL RATING		87.0

✛ Classic lines and traditional profile with strong ice-hardened hull, which means that this ship is very stable at sea, even in unkind weather conditions. There is a good selection of public rooms to choose from, and most have fairly high ceilings. The interior decor also looks tired and worn, but the wood paneling does add a degree of warmth and coziness.

— Black hull with white superstructure now looks tired and worn. The ship needs better maintenance and cleaning. The stairwells are uncarpeted and quite institutional. The cabins are almost all outside, but are simply and skimpily furnished, and some have no private facilities. There is little closet and drawer space, and bathrooms are small.

Dining The dining room is operated more like a cafeteria than a restaurant. Food is heavy, salty, poorly presented and choice is limited. Poor selection of breads, cheeses, and fruits. The service is unrefined, and there is much room for improvement. The staff are willing, however, but need more direction from management.

Other Comments This ship is in need of a major refurbishment and upgrading. Good for families on a low budget, but there's no finesse anywhere, and the operation is not up to international standards.

ms Jubilee ★★★★

OPERATES

7-DAY MEXICAN RIVIERA CRUISES
(YEAR-ROUND)

Cruise Line	Carnival Cruise Lines	Elevators	8
Former Names	-	Casino Yes Slot Machines	Yes
Gross Tonnage	47,262	Swimming Pools (outside) 3 (inside)	0
Builder	Kockums (Sweden)	Whirlpools 2 Gymnasium	Yes
Original Cost	$135 million	Sauna/Steam Room Yes/No Massage	Yes
Christened By	Mrs Yvonne Ryding	Self-Service Launderette	Yes
Entered Service	Jul 6, 1986	Movie Theater/Seats No Library	Yes
Interior Design	Joe Farcus	Children's Facilities	Yes
Country of Registry	Liberia (ELFK6)	Watersports Facilities	None
Tel No 124-0503 Fax No	124-0503	Classification Society	Lloyd's Register
Length (ft/m)	733.0/223.40		

Beam (ft/m) 92.5/28.20 Draft (ft/m) 24.9/7.60	**RATINGS**	**SCORE**
Propulsion diesel (23,520kW)	Ship: Condition/Cleanliness	7.6
Propellers 2 (CP)	Ship: Space/Flow/Comfort	7.6
Decks 10 Crew 670	Ship: Decor/Furnishings	6.4
Pass. Capacity (basis 2) 1,486 (all berths) 1,896	Ship: Fitness Facilities	7.8
Pass. Space Ratio (basis 2) 31.8 (all berths) 24.9	Cabins: Comfort/Facilities	7.6
Officers Italian Dining Staff International	Cabins: Software	7.4
Total Cabins 743	Food: Dining Room/Cuisine	6.7
Size Range (sq ft/m) 185-420/17.0-39.0	Food: Buffets/Informal Dining	6.4
Outside Cabins 453 Inside Cabins 290	Food: Quality of Ingredients	5.3
Single Cabins 0	Service: Dining Room	7.0
Supplement 50% (cat.1-3)/100% (cat.4-12)	Service: Bars	7.1
Balcony Cabins 10 Wheelchair Cabins 14	Service: Cabins	6.4
Cabin Current 110 AC	Cruise: Entertainment	8.0
Refrigerator Category 12 only	Cruise: Activities Program	7.6
Cabin TV Yes VCR No	Cruise: Hospitality Standard	6.3
Dining Rooms 2 Sittings 2	OVERALL RATING	105.2

+ This large ship has a short, rakish bow. Distinctive swept-back funnel. Flamboyant, vivid colors in all public rooms except for the elegant Churchill's Library, which has few books. Huge casino has round-the-clock action. Cabins are quite spacious, neatly equipped, and have attractive decor. Especially nice are ten large suites. Outside cabins feature large picture windows. Numerous public rooms spread throughout two entertainment decks. Excellent double-wide promenade deck features a white gazebo. Stimulating multi-tiered Atlantis Lounge showroom has huge theater stage. Constant entertainment and activities.

— Has rather glitzy decor that is designed to stimulate, not relax you. Expect long lines for embarkation, disembarkation, shore tenders, and buffets. There are simply too many annoying and unnecessary announcements. Constant hustling for drinks.

Dining The two dining rooms (both non-smoking) are attractive, but have low ceilings, and a raised center section is cramped. The food, though upgraded, is still very much a low-budget Americana affair. Poor selection of breads, rolls, and fruit. Service is hurried and lacks finesse.

Other Comments This ship provides novice cruisers with an excellent, action-filled and noisy first cruise experience in crowded surroundings. Fun-filled and stimulating for party-goers. Good for singles who want lots of life and constant action. Provides very good value.

mv Kapitan Dranitsyn ★★★

OPERATES

*ARCTIC/ANTARCTICA EXPEDITION
CRUISES*

Cruise Line	Murmansk Shipping/ Quark Expeditions		
Former Names	-		
Gross Tonnage	12,288		
Builder	Wartsila (Finland)		
Original Cost	n/a		
Christened By	L.I. Soboleb		
Entered Service	Dec 7, 1980		
Interior Design	n/a		
Country of Registry	Russia (URNN)		
Tel No 140-5675	Fax No 140-5660		
Length (ft/m)	434.6/132.49		
Beam (ft/m) 86.9/26.50	Draft (ft/m) 27.8/8.50		
Propulsion	diesel-electric (22,000hp)		
Propellers	3 (CP)		
Decks 4	Crew 90		
Pass. Capacity (basis 2) 112	(all berths) 112		
Pass. Space Ratio (basis 2) 109.7	(all berths) 109.7		
Officers	Russian		
Dining Staff	Russian/Ukrainian		
Total Cabins	50		
Size Range (sq ft/m)	129-269/12.0-25.0		
Outside Cabins 50	Inside Cabins 0		
Single Cabins 0	Supplement 80%		
Balcony Cabins 0	Wheelchair Cabins 0		
Cabin Current 220 AC	Refrigerator No		
Cabin TV No	VCR No		
Dining Rooms 1	Sittings 1		

Elevators			0
Casino No	Slot Machines		No
Swimming Pools (outside) 0	(inside)		1
Whirlpools 0	Gymnasium		Yes
Sauna/Steam Room Yes/No	Massage		No
Lecture/Film Room No	Library		Yes
Zodiacs			4
Helicopter Pad	Yes (1 helicopter)		
Watersports Facilities	None		
Classification Society	RS		

RATINGS	SCORE
Ship: Condition/Cleanliness	7.0
Ship: Space/Flow/Comfort	6.0
Ship: Expedition Equipment	8.7
Ship: Decor/Furnishings	5.4
Cabins: Comfort/Facilities	5.6
Cabins: Software	5.8
Food: Dining Room/Cuisine	6.7
Food: Buffets/Informal Dining	6.1
Food: Quality of Ingredients	6.5
Service: Dining Room	6.4
Service: Bars	6.3
Service: Cabins	6.6
Cruise: Itineraries/Operations	7.7
Cruise: Lecture Program	7.6
Cruise: Hospitality Standard	7.4
OVERALL RATING	99.8

+ This real, working icebreaker, one of a fleet of 10, has an incredibly thick hull, forthright profile and a bow like an inverted whale head. Diesel-electric engines allow her to plough through ice several feet thick. Plenty of open deck and observation space. The cabins are spread over four decks and all have private facilities, and plenty of storage space. There is always a team of excellent naturalists and lecturers aboard. Heavy parka and boots are provided for passengers, who really become participants in this kind of hands-on expedition cruising.

— Basic cruise amenities and spartan decor.

Dining Hearty food, and generous portions, with an emphasis on fish, is served by hearty waitresses in a dining room that is comfortable and practical without being the slightest bit pretentious. The food production and presentation is supervised by Scandinavian advisors, who import Western foods specifically for these chartered voyages.

Other Comments The funnel is placed amidships and the accommodation block is placed forwards. This vessel is particularly good for tough expedition cruising, and will provide practical surroundings, a friendly, very experienced, and dedicated crew, and excellent value for money in true expeditionary style.

mv Kapitan Khlebnikov ★★★

OPERATES

ARCTIC/ANTARCTICA EXPEDITION CRUISES

Cruise Line		Far East Shipping/Quark Expeditions	
Former Names			-
Gross Tonnage			12,288
Builder			Wartsila (Finland)
Original Cost	n/a	Christened By	n/a
Entered Service			1981
Interior Design			n/a
Country of Registry			Russia (UTSU)
Tel No	140-0676	Fax No	140-0676
Length (ft/m)			434.6/132.49
Beam (ft/m)	86.9/26.50	Draft (ft/m)	27.8/8.50
Propulsion			diesel-electric (22,000hp)
Propellers			3 (CP)
Decks	4	Crew	90
Pass. Capacity (basis 2)	112	(all berths)	112
Pass. Space Ratio (basis 2)	109.7	(all berths)	109.7
Officers			Russian
Dining Staff			Russian/Ukrainian
Total Cabins			50
Size Range (sq ft/m)			n/a
Outside Cabins	50	Inside Cabins	0
Single Cabins	0	Supplement	80%
Balcony Cabins	0	Wheelchair Cabins	0
Cabin Current	220 AC	Refrigerator	No
Cabin TV	No	VCR	No
Dining Rooms	1	Sittings	1
Elevators			0
Casino	No	Slot Machines	No

Swimming Pools (outside)	0	(inside)	1
Whirlpools	0	Gymnasium	Yes
Sauna/Steam Room			Yes (2)/No
Massage			No
Lecture/Film Room			No
Library			Yes
Zodiacs			4
Helicopter Pad			Yes (1 helicopter)
Watersports Facilities			None
Classification Society			RS

RATINGS	SCORE
Ship: Condition/Cleanliness	7.0
Ship: Space/Flow/Comfort	6.0
Ship: Expedition Equipment	8.7
Ship: Decor/Furnishings	5.4
Cabins: Comfort/Facilities	5.6
Cabins: Software	5.8
Food: Dining Room/Cuisine	6.7
Food: Buffets/Informal Dining	6.1
Food: Quality of Ingredients	6.5
Service: Dining Room	6.4
Service: Bars	6.3
Service: Cabins	6.6
Cruise: Itineraries/Operations	7.7
Cruise: Lecture Program	7.6
Cruise: Hospitality Standard	7.4
OVERALL RATING	99.8

+ This real, working icebreaker, one of a large fleet, has an incredibly thick hull and forthright profile. Funnel is placed amidships and the accommodations forwards. Open-bridge policy. Ample open deck and observation space. Cabins are spread over four decks and all have private facilities, and plenty of storage space. This vessel is particularly good for expedition cruises to Antarctica and the Arctic, and will provide comfortable surroundings, a friendly, very experienced, and dedicated crew, and excellent value for money in true expeditionary style. Interesting naturalists and lecturers aboard. Heavy parka and boots are provided for passengers, who become participants in this hands-on-style expedition cruising.

— Has basic amenities and rather spartan, but practical decor.

Dining Hearty food, and generous portions, with an emphasis on fish, is served by hearty waitresses in a dining room that is comfortable and practical without being the slightest bit pretentious. The food production and presentation is supervised by Scandinavian advisors, who import Western foods specifically for these chartered voyages.

Other Comments Her tough diesel-electric engines allow her to plough through ice several meters thick. Another vessel in the same configuration and series is *Kapitan Dranitsyn*.

ms Kareliya ★★★

OPERATES

7-DAY EUROPE CRUISES

Cruise Line	CTC Cruise Lines
Former Names	Leonid Brezhnev
Gross Tonnage	15,065
Builder	Wartsila (Finland)
Original Cost	$25 million
Christened By	Mrs Landeman
Entered Service	Dec 19, 1976/Mar 13, 1981
Interior Design	Wartsila/Lloyd Werft
Country of Registry	Ukraine (URRN)
Tel No 140-0261 Fax No	140-0261
Length (ft/m)	512.6/156.27
Beam (ft/m) 71.8/21.90 Draft (ft/m)	19.4/5.92
Propulsion	diesel (13,430kW)
Propellers	2 (CP)
Decks 8 Crew	250
Pass. Capacity (basis 2) 472	(all berths) 644
Pass. Space Ratio (basis 2) 31.1	(all berths) 23.3
Officers	Ukrainian
Dining Staff	British/Ukrainian
Total Cabins	236
Size Range (sq ft/m)	90-428/8.4-38.0
Outside Cabins 110 Inside Cabins	126
Single Cabins 0 Supplement	50%
Balcony Cabins 0 Wheelchair Cabins	0
Cabin Current	220 AC
Refrigerator	Boat Deck cabins only
Cabin TV Boat Deck cabins only VCR	No
Dining Rooms 2 Sittings	1

Elevators			2
Casino	Yes	Slot Machines	Yes
Swimming Pools (outside) 1		(inside)	0
Whirlpools	0	Gymnasium	Yes
Sauna/Steam Room Yes/No		Massage	Yes
Self-Service Launderette			Yes
Movie Theater/Seats			Yes/140
Library	Yes	Children's Facilities	Yes
Watersports Facilities			None
Classification Society Ukraine Register of Shipping			

RATINGS	SCORE
Ship: Condition/Cleanliness	6.3
Ship: Space/Flow/Comfort	6.2
Ship: Decor/Furnishings	6.1
Ship: Fitness Facilities	4.7
Cabins: Comfort/Facilities	6.1
Cabins: Software	6.3
Food: Dining Room/Cuisine	5.9
Food: Buffets/Informal Dining	5.2
Food: Quality of Ingredients	5.4
Service: Dining Room	6.5
Service: Bars	7.0
Service: Cabins	7.3
Cruise: Entertainment	4.7
Cruise: Activities Program	5.6
Cruise: Hospitality Standard	6.8
OVERALL RATING	90.1

+ Smart-looking vessel sports a large square funnel. Has pleasing interior, but the decor is uncoordinated. Her newer facilities provide more public rooms. The library and book selection have improved. Boat Deck suites are large and well equipped. Other cabins are on the small side, but adequate, with reasonable closet space. Features a wide range of interesting and popular itineraries.

— Some inner cabins share bathrooms. There's little drawer space in most cabins – hard for long voyages. Cabin bathrooms are small and utilitarian, with little space for toiletries. Has a steep gangway in many ports. No cabin service menu. Sadly, no fresh flowers anywhere.

Dining The two dining rooms (one for smokers, one for non-smokers) are quite attractive, but noisy, with service by Ukrainian waitresses who try hard, although there's no finesse, and more direction is needed. The menu choice is very limited, and quality needs improving. Poor selection of breads, fruits, and cheeses.

Other Comments This ship provides comfortable, reasonably warm and friendly surroundings. Caters primarily to British passengers seeking a destination-intensive cruise in comfortable surroundings, at a modest price. Port taxes are included. Gratuities are not compulsory, but expected.

ms Kazakhstan II ★★★+

OPERATES

VARIOUS CRUISES WORLDWIDE

Cruise Line	Delphin Seereisen	Casino	Yes	Slot Machines Yes
Former Names	Belorussiya	Swimming Pools (outside) 1	(inside)	0
Gross Tonnage	16,600	Whirlpools	0 Gymnasium	Yes
Builder	Wartsila (Finland)	Sauna/Steam Room Yes/No	Massage	Yes
Original Cost	$25 million	Self-Service Launderette		Yes
Christened By	Mrs Stepanova	Movie Theater/Seats		Yes/143
Entered Service	Jan 15, 1975/Dec 22, 1993	Library		Yes
Interior Design	Lloyd Werft	Children's Facilities		No
Country of Registry	Ukraine (UUDP)	Watersports Facilities		None
Tel No 140-0204 Fax No	140-0204	Classification Society Ukraine Register of Shipping		
Length (ft/m)	512.5/156.24			

| Beam (ft/m) 71.8/21.90 Draft (ft/m): 19.4/5.92 |
| Propulsion | diesel (13,430kW) |
| Propellers | 2 (CP) |

RATINGS	SCORE
Ship: Condition/Cleanliness	7.7
Ship: Space/Flow/Comfort	6.6
Ship: Decor/Furnishings	7.4
Ship: Fitness Facilities	6.5
Cabins: Comfort/Facilities	6.7
Cabins: Software	7.2
Food: Dining Room/Cuisine	6.2
Food: Buffets/Informal Dining	6.1
Food: Quality of Ingredients	6.0
Service: Dining Room	7.3
Service: Bars	7.4
Service: Cabins	7.3
Cruise: Entertainment	6.4
Cruise: Activities Program	6.2
Cruise: Hospitality Standard	6.7
OVERALL RATING	101.7

Decks	8	Crew	250
Pass. Capacity (basis 2) 474		(all berths) 640	
Pass. Space Ratio (basis 2) 35.02		(all berths) 25.9	
Officers Ukrainian		Dining Staff Ukrainian	
Total Cabins			237
Size Range (sq ft/m)		150-492/14.0-45.7	
Outside Cabins 129	Inside Cabins		108
Single Cabins 0	Supplement		50%
Balcony Cabins 0	Wheelchair Cabins		0
Cabin Current			220 AC
Refrigerator		Boat deck cabins only	
Cabin TV Boat deck cabins only		VCR	No
Dining Rooms 2	Sittings		1
Elevators			1

+ Has good outdoor promenade decks. New facilities added following an extensive refit and refurbishment program that improved almost all public areas and added new fitness facilities and much better outdoor pool/lido deck. The suites on Boat Deck are extremely large and well equipped. Other cabins are compact, and adequate, although bathrooms are small. The ship has smart interior decor and furnishings.

— Has poor cabin insulation and little drawer space. Service, while quite friendly, shows little finesse, and communication is sometimes frustrating.

Dining Has two dining rooms, one each for smokers and non-smokers. The food, while attractively presented, and quite reasonable, is of a limited choice and quality, although the catering is improving slowly. Limited selection of breads, cheeses, and fruits, and buffets are very simple.

Other Comments This smart-looking modern ship has a square, contemporary funnel, and has been smartly refurbished throughout following a shipyard roll-over incident. This ship will provide a comfortable cruise experience for an international, but mostly German-speaking, clientele at an extremely attractive price, but there's little finesse, and it's not a luxury product, nor does it pretend to be. Port taxes, insurance, and gratuities are included.

ms Klaudia Yelanskaya ★

OPERATES

ARCTIC CRUISES

Cruise Line	Murmansk Shipping
Former Names	-
Gross Tonnage	3,941
Builder	Brodgradiliste Uljanik (Yugoslavia)
Original Cost	n/a
Christened By	n/a
Entered Service	1976
Interior Design	n/a
Country of Registry	Russia (UMZQ)
Tel No 140-1764 Fax No	140-1764
Length (ft/m)	328.1/100.01
Beam (ft/m) 53.2/16.24 Draft (ft/m)	15.2/4.65
Propulsion	diesel (3,884kW)
Propellers	1 (FP)
Decks 6 Crew	80
Pass. Capacity (basis 2) 104 (all berths)	186
Pass. Space Ratio (basis 2) 37.8 (all berths)	21.1
Officers	Russian
Dining Staff	Russian/Ukrainian
Total Cabins	52
Size Range (sq ft/m)	n/a
Outside Cabins 52 Inside Cabins	0
Single Cabins 0 Supplement	100%
Balcony Cabins 0 Wheelchair Cabins	0
Cabin Current 220 AC Refrigerator	No
Cabin TV No VCR	No
Dining Rooms 1 Sittings	1
Elevators	0

Casino	No	Slot Machines	No
Swimming Pools (outside) 1		(inside)	No
Whirlpools	No	Gymnasium	No
Sauna/Steam Room Yes/No		Massage	No
Self-Service Launderette			No
Movie Theater/Seats			Yes/75
Library			Yes
Children's Facilities			No
Watersports Facilities			None
Classification Society			RS

RATINGS	SCORE
Ship: Condition/Cleanliness	5.6
Ship: Space/Flow/Comfort	4.8
Ship: Decor/Furnishings	6.0
Ship: Fitness Facilities	3.0
Cabins: Comfort/Facilities	5.5
Cabins: Software	5.7
Food: Dining Room/Cuisine	5.3
Food: Buffets/Informal Dining	5.0
Food: Quality of Ingredients	4.6
Service: Dining Room	6.0
Service: Bars	6.2
Service: Cabins	6.4
Cruise: Entertainment	5.0
Cruise: Activities Program	4.4
Cruise: Hospitality Standard	5.7
OVERALL RATING	79.2

+ Intimate, small ship with well-balanced profile is one of a series of eight identical sisters often chartered to European operators. Has an ice-hardened hull suitable for "soft" expedition cruising. Good open deck spaces for ship size. Recently underwent extensive refurbishment. Outdoor observation deck and enclosed promenade deck for inclement weather. Charming forward music lounge has wooden dance floor. Rich, highly polished wood paneling throughout and winding brass-railed main staircase. Good movie theater-lecture room.

− Cabins are compact and spartan, and most can accommodate four persons, but space really is tight, and there's little closet and drawer space.

Dining Comfortable dining room has ocean views, but no tables for two. Limited choice of food, which is hearty, but service is friendly and quite attentive. Poor selection of breads, fruits, and cheeses.

Other Comments Although small, and not glamorous at all, this is a comfortable ship that has plenty of character. The ship is often chartered to Western tour operators for part of a year for soft expedition-style cruises, where all shore excursions, and visas, are normally included, and rated accordingly.

mv Konstantin Simonov ★★

OPERATES

3-DAY BALTIC CRUISES

Cruise Line	Baltic Line	Casino	No	Slot Machines Yes
Former Names	-	Swimming Pools (outside) 1		(inside) 0
Gross Tonnage	9,885	Whirlpools	0	Gymnasium No
Builder	Szszecin (Poland)	Sauna/Steam Room Yes/No		Massage Yes
Original Cost	n/a	Self-Service Launderette		No
Christened By	n/a	Movie Theater/Seats		No
Entered Service	1982	Library		Yes
Interior Design	n/a	Children's Facilities		No
Country of Registry	Russia	Watersports Facilities		None
Tel No - Fax No	-	Classification Society		RS
Length (ft/m)	441.2/134.50			

Beam (ft/m) 68.8/21.00	Draft (ft/m)	17.3/5.28	
Propulsion		diesel (12,800kW)	
Propellers			2 (CP)
Decks 6	Crew		160
Pass. Capacity (basis 2) 278		(all berths) 492	
Pass. Space Ratio (basis 2) 35.5		(all berths) 20.0	
Officers Russian	Dining Staff	Russian	
Total Cabins			139
Size Range (sq ft/m)		100-320/9.2-29.7	
Outside Cabins 50	Inside Cabins		89
Single Cabins 0	Supplement		100%
Balcony Cabins 0	Wheelchair Cabins		0
Cabin Current			220 AC
Refrigerator	Suites and deluxe cabins only		
Cabin TV Suites only	VCR		No
Dining Rooms 2	Sittings		1
Elevators			1

RATINGS	SCORE
Ship: Condition/Cleanliness	6.6
Ship: Space/Flow/Comfort	6.2
Ship: Decor/Furnishings	6.0
Ship: Fitness Facilities	5.6
Cabins: Comfort/Facilities	5.5
Cabins: Software	6.1
Food: Dining Room/Cuisine	5.3
Food: Buffets/Informal Dining	5.1
Food: Quality of Ingredients	5.1
Service: Dining Room	6.1
Service: Bars	6.2
Service: Cabins	6.2
Cruise: Entertainment	4.3
Cruise: Activities Program	4.7
Cruise: Hospitality Standard	5.8
OVERALL RATING	84.8

+ Has a fully enclosed bridge for all-weather operation. One of a series of five vessels intended for line voyages and short cruises. The interior decor is rather spartan and totally void of glitz. The ambiance is reasonably friendly. The suites are large and well equipped. Standard cabins are small and some are fitted with upper pullman berths. Most are utilitarian in fittings and furnishings, but quite adequate.

— Lacks a forward observation lounge. Has very limited open deck and sunning space and tiny swimming pool. Both public room and cabin soft furnishings could be better.

Dining There are several dining rooms and cafeterias to choose from. The food quality varies depending on dining area chosen, but is quite adequate, no more, and menu choice is very limited.

Other Comments This ship has a square, angular profile with square stern, stubby bow and a fat, squat funnel. Wide choice of cabins. Choice of several bars. Service lacks training and finesse. Has Finnish cruise staff. Provides a basic low-cost cruise experience for an international clientele wanting to visit St. Petersburg, at modest rates, nothing more.

ms La Palma ★★+

Cruise Line	Intercruise	Elevators	0
Former Names	Delphi/La Perla/	Casino Yes	Slot Machines Yes
	Ferdinand De Lesseps	Swimming Pools (outside) 1	(inside) 0
Gross Tonnage	11,608	Whirlpools 0	Gymnasium No
Builder Forges et Chantiers de la Gironde (France)		Sauna/Steam Room No/No	Massage No
Original Cost	n/a	Self-Service Launderette	No
Christened By	George D. Louris	Movie Theater/Seats No	Library Yes
Entered Service	Oct 3, 1952/Apr 1978	Children's Facilities	No
Interior Design	George D. Louris	Watersports Facilities	None
Country of Registry	Greece (SXBS)	Classification Society	Grecian Lloyd
Tel No 113-0506 Fax No 113-0506			
Length (ft/m)	492.4/150.09	**RATINGS**	**SCORE**
Beam (ft/m) 62.6/19.10 Draft (ft/m) 22.0/6.72		Ship: Condition/Cleanliness	6.1
Propulsion	diesel (9,100kW)	Ship: Space/Flow/Comfort	6.3
Propellers	2 (FP)	Ship: Decor/Furnishings	6.5
Decks 7 Crew	230	Ship: Fitness Facilities	4.0
Pass. Capacity (basis 2) 648 (all berths) 832		Cabins: Comfort/Facilities	6.2
Pass. Space Ratio (basis 2) 17.9 (all berths) 13.9		Cabins: Software	6.3
Officers Greek Dining Staff Greek		Food: Dining Room/Cuisine	6.2
Total Cabins	324	Food: Buffets/Informal Dining	5.8
Size Range (sq ft/m)	105-215/9.7-20.0	Food: Quality of Ingredients	6.0
Outside Cabins 176 Inside Cabins	148	Service: Dining Room	6.4
Single Cabins 5 Supplement Set rates		Service: Bars	6.2
Balcony Cabins 0 Wheelchair Cabins 0		Service: Cabins	6.5
Cabin Current	110/220 AC	Cruise: Entertainment	5.4
Refrigerator	Category AS/A only	Cruise: Activities Program	5.6
Cabin TV Yes (DeLuxe cabins only) VCR No		Cruise: Hospitality Standard	6.3
Dining Rooms 1 Sittings	2	OVERALL RATING	89.8

+ Basically a well-maintained vessel. Plenty of open deck and sunning space except when ship is full. Water slide into swimming pool for children. This is one of only two ships to feature an isolated nudist sunbathing deck (the other being Hapag-Lloyd's *Europa*). Has a popular Bavarian beer garden on deck. Cheerful interior decor, with plenty of wood and wood trim throughout. Ten suites are very spacious and nicely furnished, while other cabins are moderately so. All have private facilities and all have been refurbished.

— Has steep gangway in most ports of call. Beverages are extremely expensive.

Dining Dining room is set low down, but is quite cozy. The continental cuisine is adequate, but there is little choice, especially for non-meat eaters. Poor selection of breads, cheeses, and fruits. Service comes with a smile, but without any finesse.

Other Comments Traditional older styling, with low funnel profile. Passageways have floor-to-ceiling carpeting which is difficult to keep clean, but provides good insulation. This is a high-density ship that caters best to young couples, families, and active singles on a very modest budget. Flexible scheduling means passengers can embark and disembark at almost every port and take a full cruise, or segment. Mostly multinational European passengers, and multilingual staff. Cruise rate is moderate.

mv Langkapuri Star Aquarius ★★★★+

OPERATES

*2/3-DAY SOUTH-EAST ASIA CRUISES
(YEAR-ROUND)*

Cruise Line			Star Cruise
Former Names	Athena	Gross Tonnage	40,022
Builder			Wartsila (Finland)
Original Cost			SEK650 million
Christened By			Ms Marianne Myrsten
Entered Service			Apr 1989/Dec 23, 1993
Interior Design			Robert Tillberg/PM design
Country of Registry			Panama (3FRG)
Tel No			02-011-719543
Fax No			02-011-719514
Length (ft/m)			579.3/176.6
Beam (ft/m)	97.1/29.6	Draft (ft/m)	20.3/6.2
Propulsion			diesel (23,760kW)
Propellers			2 (CP)
Decks	12	Crew	750
Pass. Capacity (basis 2) 1,530		(all berths) 1,900	
Pass. Space Ratio (basis 2) 26.1		(all berths) 21.0	
Officers	Scandinavian	Dining Staff	Filipino
Total Cabins			718
Size Range (sq ft/m)			67-145/6.3-13.5
Outside Cabins	303	Inside Cabins	415
Single Cabins	42	Supplement	Set rates
Balcony Cabins	0	Wheelchair Cabins	6
Cabin Current	220 AC	Refrigerator	No
Cabin TV	Yes	VCR	No
Dining Rooms			4 (+3 cafes)
Sittings			1
Elevators			5

Casino	Yes	Slot Machines	Yes
Swimming Pools (outside) 1		(inside)	1
Whirlpools	6	Gymnasium	Yes
Sauna/Steam Room Yes/Yes		Massage	Yes
Self-Service Launderette			No
Movie Theater/Seats			Yes (2)/210 each
Library			Yes
Children's Facilities			Yes
Watersports Facilities			None
Classification Society			Det Norske Veritas

RATINGS	SCORE
Ship: Condition/Cleanliness	8.4
Ship: Space/Flow/Comfort	7.7
Ship: Decor/Furnishings	8.4
Ship: Fitness Facilities	8.3
Cabins: Comfort/Facilities	6.0
Cabins: Software	7.6
Food: Dining Room/Cuisine	8.3
Food: Buffets/Informal Dining	7.8
Food: Quality of Ingredients	8.1
Service: Dining Room	7.8
Service: Bars	7.3
Service: Cabins	7.2
Cruise: Entertainment	7.5
Cruise: Activities Program	7.0
Cruise: Hospitality Standard	8.7
OVERALL RATING	116.1

+ This ex-Viking Line ferry has been skillfully converted into a cruise vessel specifically for the Asian family market, with a reduction in berths to 1,900 (from 2,200). The ship sports a deep blue hull, and a blue band around the funnel base. Scandinavian design combined with a touch of the Orient, this ship even has a helipad. Features a large duty-free shopping center and supermarket. There is very imperial casino for VIPs, which is large and has a 13-feet-high, finely detailed ceiling and regal decor (there's also a second casino for general passenger use). Has a karaoke lounge and eight private karaoke rooms.

Except for some very large suites for top-paying passengers, the cabins are very small, and come with just basic facilities (some are for families, with quad occupancy). The top suites, each of which is decorated in luxurious materials, feature two bathrooms, butler service, and a private club meeting room, private sundeck, and spa.

Besides a general Universe Fitness and Health Bar (with juice bar and low-calorie items), there is also a superb health club for men (King Neptune), offering an extensive range of features and facilities, including a gymnasium, indoor pool, and two whirlpools, plus all massage, steam, and sauna facilities.

There are 11 meeting rooms (all have audio-visual facilities), two conference auditoriums and a business center, with full secretarial support, computers, fax, telex, and copy machines. Has outstanding family facilities for children and teens, with a wide assortment of computers and

video game machines in the huge children's entertainment and play center. There's also free ice cream for kids.

— Such a high-density ship means crowded public rooms, and long lines for shore visits, buffets, embarkation, and disembarkation. The standard cabin bathrooms really are very small indeed. The amount of open deck space is quite limited, but is possibly sufficient for the Asian market.

Dining With seven restaurants to choose from, there's a wide choice of cuisine and dining styles. This ship has a real Chinese Restaurant called Ocean Palace (Cantonese and Sichuan cuisine) with a Hong Kong chef, and live fish tanks from which to select your seafood, as well as private dining rooms; Kamogawa Japanese restaurant, including sushi bar and waitresses in kimonos, as well as private tatami rooms; Marco Polo Italian restaurant (featuring candlelight dining); Spice Island buffet restaurant for laksa, satay, and hawker delights; Mariner buffet, with food to choose from large open-concept kitchen stalls, and children's buffet; Castaway Cafe, which features afternoon teas and coffees; Blue Lagoon, for fast food snacks (open 24 hours a day).

Other Comments With a low, very attractive ticket price, everything on board (including food, except for the buffet restaurant) costs extra, so a cruise for the family can end up being quite expensive. The ship does, however, offer a tremendous number of choices for the whole family, and the service and hospitality is superb (better than any ship out of Miami, for example), and really fine-tuned. Gratuities are strictly forbidden.

ms Leeward

OPERATES

*3- AND 4-DAY BAHAMAS/MEXICO
CRUISES (YEAR-ROUND)*

Cruise Line	Norwegian Cruise Line	Casino	Yes	Slot Machines	Yes
Former Names	Sally Albatros/Viking Saga	Swimming Pools (outside) 1	(inside)		0
Gross Tonnage	25,000	Whirlpools	1	Gymnasium	Yes
Builder	Wartsila (Finland)	Sauna/Steam Room Yes/No	Massage		Yes
Original Cost	n/a Christened By n/a	Self-Service Launderette			No
Entered Service	1980/Oct 20, 1995	Movie Theater/Seats			No
Interior Design	L. Heikkinen/Yran & Storbraaten	Library			No
Country of Registry	Bahamas	Children's Facilities/Playroom			Yes
Tel No	n/a Fax No n/a	Watersports Facilities			None
Length (ft/m)	492.1/150.0	Classification Society		Bureau Veritas	
Beam (ft/m) 82.6/25.2	Draft (ft/m) 18.0/5.5				
Propulsion	diesel (19,120kW)	**RATINGS**			**SCORE**
Propellers	2 (CP)	Ship: Condition/Cleanliness			NYR
Decks 7	Crew 400	Ship: Space/Flow/Comfort			NYR
Pass. Capacity (basis 2) 950	(all berths) 1,150	Ship: Decor/Furnishings			NYR
Pass. Space Ratio (basis 2) 26.3	(all berths) 21.7	Ship: Fitness Facilities			NYR
Officers	Norwegian	Cabins: Comfort/Facilities			NYR
Dining Staff	International	Cabins: Software			NYR
Total Cabins	475 (548)	Food: Dining Room/Cuisine			NYR
Size Range (sq ft/m)	53-387/5.0-36.0	Food: Buffets/Informal Dining			NYR
Outside Cabins 219	Inside Cabins 256	Food: Quality of Ingredients			NYR
Single Cabins 0	Supplement 50-100%	Service: Dining Room			NYR
Balcony Cabins 10	Wheelchair Cabins 2	Service: Bars			NYR
Cabin Current	110/220 AC	Service: Cabins			NYR
Refrigerator	No	Cruise: Entertainment			NYR
Cabin TV Yes	VCR No	Cruise: Activities Program			NYR
Dining Rooms 2	Sittings 2	Cruise: Hospitality Standard			NYR
Elevators	4	OVERALL RATING			

+ Sleek, swept-back wedge-shaped design with steeply tiered aft decks. Has a teakwood wrap-around outdoor promenade deck for joggers and strollers, large spa and recreation center. Glitzy but pleasant lobby. Features contemporary, bright decor, with modern artworks. Good showlounge, with tiered seating. Pleasing ambiance. Some top-grade cabins have angled private balconies. Six cabins specially designed for allergy sufferers. Sports fans will like the Sports Bar and Grill, an informal television-filled long bar and adjacent fast food joint.

— There's hardly any bow to this ship. No forward observation lounge. This is a high-density ship with ceilings that are a little low in some areas. Cabins are very small and bathrooms are *tiny*. Many outside cabins on Deck 6 have obstructed views.

Dining Besides the two principal dining rooms, located aft, there's also Le Bistro, an 80-seat informal and alternative dining area for pasta and other lighter fare. Service is generally good, but hurried. Menu choice is good, and presentation is reasonable, but no finesse. Limited selection of breads, cheeses, and fruits.

Other Comments A 1995 refit cost $60 million. Has a flat, squared-off stern, with car deck ramps (ideal for the Miami–Cuba run). Also has a fully unclosed bridge. Presently under a four-year charter to Norwegian Cruise Line for short cruises, for which the ship is well suited.

ms Legend of the Seas ★★★★+

OPERATES

7-10 DAY ALASKA, HAWAII AND
PANAMA CANAL CRUISES

Cruise Line	Royal Caribbean Cruises	Casino	Yes Slot Machines	Yes
Former Names	-	Swimming Pools (outside)	2 (1 with sliding roof)	
Gross Tonnage	70,950	Swimming Pools (inside)		0
Builder	Chantiers de l'Atlantique (France)	Whirlpools	4 Gymnasium	Yes
Original Cost	$325 million	Sauna/Steam Room Yes/Yes	Massage	Yes
Christened By	Mrs Cindy Pritzker	Self-Service Launderette		No
Entered Service	May 16, 1995	Movie Theater/Seats	No Library	Yes
Interior Design	Njal Eide	Children's Facilities		Yes
Country of Registry	Panama (ELRR5)	Watersports Facilities		None
Tel No 363-600710 Fax No	363-600712	Classification Society	Det Norske Veritas	
Length (ft/m)	867.0/264.20			
Beam (ft/m) 105.0/32.00 Draft (ft/m)	24.5/7.46	**RATINGS**		**SCORE**
Propulsion	diesel (40,200kW)	Ship: Condition/Cleanliness		9.3
Propellers	2 (CP)	Ship: Space/Flow/Comfort		9.1
Decks 11 Crew	732	Ship: Decor/Furnishings		9.1
Pass. Capacity (basis 2) 1,804 (all berths) 2,064		Ship: Fitness Facilities		9.0
Pass. Space Ratio (basis 2) 39.3 (all berths) 34.3		Cabins: Comfort/Facilities		8.6
Officers Norwegian Dining Staff International		Cabins: Software		8.7
Total Cabins	902	Food: Dining Room/Cuisine		8.1
Size Range (sq ft/m)	138-1,148/12.8-106.6	Food: Buffets/Informal Dining		7.7
Outside Cabins 575 Inside Cabins	327	Food: Quality of Ingredients		7.1
Single Cabins 0 Supplement	Set rates	Service: Dining Room		7.9
Balcony Cabins 231 Wheelchair Cabins	17	Service: Bars		7.6
Cabin Current	110/220 AC	Service: Cabins		7.6
Refrigerator	Upper grades only	Cruise: Entertainment		8.5
Cabin TV Yes VCR	Suites only	Cruise: Activities Program		7.9
Dining Rooms 1 Sittings	2	Cruise: Hospitality Standard		8.2
Elevators	11	**OVERALL RATING**		**124.4**

+ This ship's contemporary profile looks somewhat unbalanced (though it soon grows on you), but she does have a nicely tiered stern. The pool deck amidships overhangs the hull to provide an extremely wide deck, while still allowing the ship to navigate the Panama Canal. With engines placed midships, there is little noise and no noticeable vibration, and the ship has an operating speed capability of 24 knots. Inside the ship, the interior decor is quite stunning and colorful (it's too glitzy for European tastes). The outside light is brought inside in many places, with an extensive amount of glass area that provides extensive contact with sea and air (there is, in fact, over two acres of glass). Features an innovative single-level sliding glass roof (not a magrodome) over the more formal setting of one of two swimming pools, thus providing a multi-activity, all-weather indoor-outdoor area, called The Solarium. The glass roof provides shelter for the Roman-style pool and adjacent health and fitness facilities (which are superb) and slides aft to cover the miniature golf course when required (both can't be covered at the same time, however).

There are two full entertainment decks to play on, sandwiched between five decks full of cabins. The tiered and balconied showlounge, which covers two decks, is expansive and has excellent sightlines, very comfortable seats; several large-scale production shows are provided here, and there's an orchestra "pit" that can be raised or lowered as required. A multi-tiered seven-deck-high atrium lobby, complete with a huge stainless steel sculpture, connects with

the impressive Viking Crown Lounge via glass-walled elevators. The casino is really expansive, overly glitzy and packed absolutely full to the gills. The Library, which has a bust of Shakespeare outside, is a fine facility, with over 2,000 books.

Golfers will (hopefully) enjoy the 18-hole, 6,000 sq ft (557.5m²) miniature golf course, aptly named "Legend of the Links" (it's the first of its kind on any cruise ship). It has the topography of a real championship course, complete with trees, foliage, grass, bridges, water hazards, and lighting for play at night. The holes themselves are 155-230 sq ft.

Royal Caribbean Cruises has thankfully realized that small cabins do not happy passengers make. The company has therefore set about designing a ship with much larger standard cabins than any of its previous vessels. Some cabins on Deck 8 also have a larger door for wheelchair access in addition to the 17 cabins for the physically handicapped, and the ship is very accessible, with lots of ramped areas and sloping decks. All cabins have sitting area, and beds that convert to double configuration, and there's ample closet and drawer space, although there's not much space around the bed, and the showers could have been better. Cabins with balconies have glass railings rather than steel/wood to provide less intrusive sightlines. The largest accommodations, named The Royal Suite, is beautifully designed; there's even a baby grand piano, whirlpool, and all the comfort toys; it is finely decorated, and is a superb living space for those that can afford the best. Adjacent to the best cabins are several quiet sitting areas amidships.

— There is, sadly, no separate movie theater on this large ship. The casino could be somewhat disorienting, with its mirrored walls and lights flashing everywhere, although it's no different to those found in Las Vegas fantasy gaming halls. As with any large ship, you can expect to find yourself standing in lines for embarkation, disembarkation, buffets, and shore excursions, although the company does its best to minimize such lines. Seventeen cabin categories is really too many. Sadly, there are no cabins for singles.

Dining The two-deck-high dining room has dramatic two-deck-high glass side walls, so many passengers both upstairs and downstairs can see both the ocean and each other in reflection (it would, perhaps, have been even better located at the stern), but it is quite noisy when full (call it atmosphere). There is also a cavernous indoor-outdoor cafe, located towards the bow and above the bridge, as well as a good-sized snack area, which provide more informal dining choices. Menus and food choices were much improved in 1995, and presentation has also been improved. In addition, full vegetarian menus were also introduced. Royal Caribbean Cruises delivers consistently good, programmed food and service, with waiters that are smartly dressed and very attentive. Special orders are seldom possible, however, there's no decent caviar, and tableside carving and flambeau items are not possible.

Overall Comments A natural evolution, this ship is an outstanding new cruise vessel for the many repeat passengers who appreciate Royal Caribbean's consistent delivery of a well-integrated, fine-tuned, very comfortable and well-liked product. With larger cabins, and a ship of excellent decor and contemporary style, *Legend of the Seas* is poised to take Royal Caribbean passengers, most of whom are typically from middle-America, into a much upgraded cruise experience from that of the company's other ships. The ship provides an excellent value for money cruise experience for all ages.

ms Leisure World ★★★

CRUISE AREA

*1-4 DAY SOUTH-EAST ASIA CRUISES
(YEAR-ROUND)*

Cruise Line	New Century Tours	Elevators	4
Former Names	Fantasy World/Asean World/	Casino	Yes Slot Machines Yes
	Shangri-La World/Skyward	Swimming Pools (outside) 1	(inside) 0
Gross Tonnage	16,254	Whirlpools 0	Gymnasium Yes
Builder	Seebeckwerft (Germany)	Sauna/Steam Room Yes/No	Massage Yes
Original Cost	n/a	Self-Service Launderette	No
Christened By	Lin Arison	Movie Theater/Seats	Yes/180
Entered Service	Dec 21, 1969/1990	Library Yes	Children's Facilities Yes
Interior Design	Tage Wandborg	Watersports Facilities	None
Country of Registry	BVI (C6CM5)	Classification Society	Det Norske Veritas

Tel No 110-4164 Fax No 110-4164	
Length (ft/m) 525.3/160.13	
Beam (ft/m) 74.9/22.84 Draft (ft/m) 20.6/6.29	
Propulsion diesel (12,950kW)	
Propellers 2 (CP)	
Decks 8 Crew 250	
Pass. Capacity (basis 2) 730 (all berths) 1,071	
Pass. Space Ratio (basis 2) 22.2 (all berths) 15.1	
Officers International Dining Staff International	
Total Cabins 365	
Size Range (sq ft/m) 90-330/8.3-30.5	
Outside Cabins 219 Inside Cabins 145	
Single Cabins 0 Supplement 100%	
Balcony Cabins 0 Wheelchair Cabins 0	
Cabin Current 110/220 AC	
Refrigerator No	
Cabin TV No VCR No	
Dining Rooms 1 Sittings 2	

RATINGS	SCORE
Ship: Condition/Cleanliness	6.1
Ship: Space/Flow/Comfort	6.2
Ship: Decor/Furnishings	6.3
Ship: Fitness Facilities	5.7
Cabins: Comfort/Facilities	6.0
Cabins: Software	6.5
Food: Dining Room/Cuisine	6.2
Food: Buffets/Informal Dining	5.7
Food: Quality of Ingredients	5.6
Service: Dining Room	6.1
Service: Bars	6.0
Service: Cabins	6.2
Cruise: Entertainment	5.7
Cruise: Activities Program	5.9
Cruise: Hospitality Standard	6.1
OVERALL RATING	90.3

+ Attractive but somewhat dated, seventies-looking ship has a distinctive daytime sun lounge set high and forward against the ship's mast. Refurbished interior features light, airy decor in clean, crisp colors. Lounge and bar atop ship has plenty of light. Pleasant balconied theater. Good karaoke lounge for sing-alongs, and the casino action is constant and noisy.

— Very high-density ship means crowded public areas and long lines for buffets and elevators. Except for 10 suites, the cabins are small and have very limited closet and drawer space and tinny metal furniture, as well as poor cabin soundproofing. The staff lack finesse. Despite what the brochures proclaim, this is not a luxury ship. Attracts many gamblers.

Dining The dining room, although attractive, is cramped and extremely noisy, and food service is fast and without finesse. Choice of à la carte menu or Asian/Western buffet. There's a mixture of Asian and Western dishes. The food quality is so-so, but then the price is reasonably low. Cheerful, but rather hurried service from a staff that lacks finesse, and wine service that is quite poor.

Other Comments Adequate for short cruises. This ship is fine for active passengers wanting an upbeat cruise experience at a fair price, in comfortable, friendly, but not elegant, surroundings.

ss Leonid Sobinov ★★

OPERATES

14-DAY EUROPE CRUISES

Cruise Line	Baltic Shipping	Elevators		3
Former Names	Carmania/Saxonia	Casino	No	Slot Machines	No
Gross Tonnage	21,846	Swimming Pools (outside) 1	(inside)	0
Builder	John Brown Shipyard (Scotland)	Whirlpools	0	Gymnasium	No
Original Cost	n/a	Sauna/Steam Room No/No	Massage	No
Christened By	Lady Winston Churchill	Self-Service Launderette		No
Entered Service	Sep 2, 1954/Feb 25, 1974	Movie Theater/Seats	Yes	Library	Yes
Interior Design	n/a	Children's Facilities		Yes
Country of Registry	Malta	Watersports Facilities		None
Tel No 125-6223 Fax No	125-6223	Classification Society		RS
Length (ft/m)	604/184.00			

Beam (ft/m) 80.0/24.40 Draft (ft/m)	26.2/8.00
Propulsion	steam turbine (18,300kW)

RATINGS	SCORE
Ship: Condition/Cleanliness	4.1
Ship: Space/Flow/Comfort	5.3
Ship: Decor/Furnishings	5.3
Ship: Fitness Facilities	4.1
Cabins: Comfort/Facilities	5.3
Cabins: Software	5.6
Food: Dining Room/Cuisine	5.4
Food: Buffets/Informal Dining	5.1
Food: Quality of Ingredients	5.2
Service: Dining Room	6.5
Service: Bars	6.4
Service: Cabins	6.6
Cruise: Entertainment	5.3
Cruise: Activities Program	5.4
Cruise: Hospitality Standard	6.1
OVERALL RATING	81.7

Propellers		2 (FP)
Decks	7	Crew	400
Pass. Capacity (basis 2) 700	(all berths) 925
Pass. Space Ratio (basis 2) 31.2	(all berths) 23.6
Officers		Russian/Ukrainian
Dining Staff		Russian/Ukrainian
Total Cabins		288
Size Range (sq ft/m)	90-241/8.3-22.3
Outside Cabins	158	Inside Cabins	130
Single Cabins	0	Supplement	100%
Balcony Cabins	0	Wheelchair Cabins	0
Cabin Current		110/220 AC
Refrigerator		No
Cabin TV	No	VCR	No
Dining Rooms	1	Sittings	2

+ This former Cunard ocean liner has classic lines and a deep-draft, go-anywhere hull shape. Renamed after a famous operatic singer. Solidly built – they don't build ships like this any more. Has a good wrap-around outdoor promenade deck, as one would expect from a former transatlantic ship, and a kidney-shaped swimming pool. There's a good array of public rooms, bars, and lounges. Features acres of good wood paneling, and much brass-trimmed furniture throughout. The cabins are reasonably spacious and have heavy-duty fittings and furnishings, but they are well worn, and a major refurbishment now would prove expensive.

— In her heyday, this ship had a pleasant, welcoming interior decor, but she is now becoming a little neglected. Outside, there are areas of major rust showing, and the wood decking could be better.

Dining The dining room is reasonably practical, but the decor and lighting are now very dated. The cuisine is very basic, with very poor selection of breads, fruits, and cheeses. Outside, on the port side, is an interesting and popular Steak Bar.

Other Comments The ship is still much in its original condition as it was in the fifties, when she operated for Cunard. This is cheap and cheerful cruising for a European-based passenger mix, but it's time the old girl was retired.

mv Lev Tolstoi ★★

OPERATES
EUROPE CRUISES

Cruise Line	Transocean Tours		
Former Names	-		
Gross Tonnage	12,600		
Builder	Szszecin (Poland)		
Original Cost	n/a	Christened By	-
Entered Service	1982		
Interior Design	-		
Country of Registry	Ukraine (UWSU)		
Tel No	140-1354	Fax No	140-1354
Length (ft/m)	441.2/134.50		
Beam (ft/m) 68.8/21.00	Draft (ft/m)	17.3/5.28	
Propulsion	diesel (12,800kW)		
Propellers	2 (CP)		
Decks	6	Crew	150
Pass. Capacity (basis 2) 264	(all berths) 290		
Pass. Space Ratio (basis 2) 47.7	(all berths) 43.4		
Officers	Ukrainian		
Dining Staff	Russian/Ukrainian		
Total Cabins	132		
Size Range (sq ft/m)	100-320/9.2-29.7		
Outside Cabins	58	Inside Cabins	74
Single Cabins	0	Supplement	100%
Balcony Cabins	0	Wheelchair Cabins	0
Cabin Current 220 AC	Refrigerator	No	
Cabin TV	Only in two deluxe cabins		
VCR	No		
Dining Rooms	1	Sittings	1
Elevators	1		

Casino	Yes	Slot Machines	Yes
Swimming Pools (outside) 1	(inside)	0	
Whirlpools	0	Gymnasium	Yes
Sauna/Steam Room Yes/No	Massage	Yes	
Self-Service Launderette			No
Movie Theater/Seats			No
Library			Yes
Children's Facilities			No
Watersports Facilities			None
Classification Society			RS

RATINGS	SCORE
Ship: Condition/Cleanliness	6.6
Ship: Space/Flow/Comfort	6.2
Ship: Decor/Furnishings	6.0
Ship: Fitness Facilities	5.6
Cabins: Comfort/Facilities	5.5
Cabins: Software	6.1
Food: Dining Room/Cuisine	5.3
Food: Buffets/Informal Dining	5.1
Food: Quality of Ingredients	5.1
Service: Dining Room	6.1
Service: Bars	6.2
Service: Cabins	6.2
Cruise: Entertainment	4.3
Cruise: Activities Program	4.7
Cruise: Hospitality Standard	5.8
OVERALL RATING	84.8

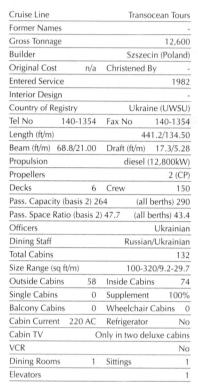

+ This ship has a square, angular profile with boxy stern, stubby bow and a fat funnel – otherwise she's handsome! Has a fully enclosed bridge for all-weather operation. One of a series of five Polish-built vessels intended for line voyages but now used as a cruise ship. Attractive itineraries. The interior decor is quite smart, with soft pastel colors, and the ambiance is friendly and comfortable, and there is no glitz. Some cabins are fitted with upper pullman berths. Apart from seven large cabins, all are small and somewhat spartan in fittings and furnishings, and there's little drawer space.

– There is no forward observation lounge. Has a limited amount of open deck and sunning space and a tiny swimming pool that is really a "dip" pool.

Dining The dining room is plain, yet attractive, and has large picture windows with white chiffon curtains. The cuisine is meat and potatoes basic and adequate, but the food is highly salted. Service is provided by charming and attractive Ukrainian waitresses.

Other Comments Service is somewhat perfunctory, but getting better. Now under charter to Transocean Tours, whose staff are excellent. Passengers can also drive to the port and take their cars with them on the cruise. This ship provides a basic, inexpensive cruise experience for a mostly German-speaking clientele, at modest rates, but don't expect too much.

ms Maasdam ★★★★

OPERATES

7-DAY ALASKA AND
CARIBBEAN CRUISES

Cruise Line	Holland America Line
Former Names	-
Gross Tonnage	55,451
Builder	Fincantieri (Italy)
Original Cost	$215 million
Christened By	Ms June Allyson
Entered Service	Dec 3, 1993
Interior Design	VFD Interiors/Joe Farcus
Country of Registry	Bahamas (C6VF)
Tel No 130-6156 Fax No 130-6157	
Length (ft/m)	719.3/219.30
Beam (ft/m) 101.0/30.80 Draft (ft/m) 24.6/7.50	
Propulsion	diesel-electric (34,560kW)
Propellers	2 (CP)
Decks 10 Crew	588
Pass. Capacity (basis 2) 1,264 (all berths) 1,627	
Pass. Space Ratio (basis 2) 43.8 (all berths) 34.0	
Officers	Dutch
Dining Staff	Filipino/Indonesian
Total Cabins	632
Size Range (sq ft/m)	187-1,126/17.3-104.5
Outside Cabins 501 Inside Cabins 131	
Single Cabins 0 Supplement 50-100%	
Balcony Cabins 150 Wheelchair Cabins 6	
Cabin Current	110/220 AC
Refrigerator	Category PS/S/A/B only
Cabin TV Yes VCR No	
Dining Rooms 1 Sittings 2	

Elevators			12
Casino	Yes	Slot Machines	Yes
Swimming Pools (outside)			1
Swimming Pools (inside)		1 (magrodome)	
Whirlpools	2	Gymnasium	Yes
Sauna/Steam Room Yes/No		Massage	Yes
Self-Service Launderette			Yes
Movie Theater/Seats			Yes/249
Library	Yes	Children's Facilities	No
Classification Society		Lloyd's Register	

RATINGS	SCORE
Ship: Condition/Cleanliness	8.7
Ship: Space/Flow/Comfort	8.4
Ship: Decor/Furnishings	8.5
Ship: Fitness Facilities	7.7
Cabins: Comfort/Facilities	8.1
Cabins: Software	8.1
Food: Dining Room/Cuisine	6.8
Food: Buffets/Informal Dining	6.7
Food: Quality of Ingredients	6.7
Service: Dining Room	6.1
Service: Bars	7.2
Service: Cabins	8.0
Cruise: Entertainment	7.0
Cruise: Activities Program	7.7
Cruise: Hospitality Standard	8.3
OVERALL RATING	114.0

+ The decor is softer, more sophisticated, and far less eclectic than on sister ship *Statendam*. Antiques and artwork are stunning, and beautifully displayed. Fine flower arrangements in public areas. Has good passenger flow. Three-deck-high atrium foyer. A "magrodome" roof covers the large indoor-outdoor swimming pool/whirlpools and central lido area. Two-deck-high showroom is well thought out, but the ceiling is low and balcony sightlines are not good. Relaxing reference (no fiction) library. 28 suites, each able to accommodate four, feature an in-suite dining alternative. Other cabins are spacious, tastefully decorated and well laid out.

— Expect lines for embarkation, disembarkation, buffets, shore tenders, and shore excursions. Cabin closet space is tight. Communication with staff is often frustrating. No division of smoking and no-smoking areas at the outdoor Lido Cafe. No bell-push outside suites. Extra charge for self-service launderette machines.

Dining The two-level dining room, located at the stern (upper level for smokers, lower level for non-smokers) is dramatic, with panoramic views on three sides. Open seating breakfast and lunch, two sittings for dinner. Food and service standards are going down.

Other Comments This is a well-built, quality ship, but the cruise product itself needs some fine-tuning in the food, service, and communication departments.

ms Majesty of the Seas ★★★★+

Cruise Line	Royal Caribbean Cruises		
Former Names	-		
Gross Tonnage	73,941		
Builder	Chantiers de l'Atlantique		
Original Cost	$300 million		
Christened By	H.M. Queen Sonja of Norway		
Entered Service	Apr 26, 1992		
Interior Design	Njal Eide		
Country of Registry	Norway (LAOI4)		
Tel No 131-3370	Fax No 131-3370		
Length (ft/m)	873.6/266.30		
Beam (ft/m) 105.9/32.30	Draft (ft/m) 24.9/7.60		
Propulsion	diesel (21,844kW)		
Propellers	2 (CP)		
Decks 12	Crew 822		
Pass. Capacity (basis 2) 2,354	(all berths) 2,744		
Pass. Space Ratio (basis 2) 31.4	(all berths) 26.9		
Officers Norwegian	Dining Staff International		
Total Cabins	1,177		
Size Range (sq ft/m)	120-446/11.0-41.5		
Outside Cabins 732	Inside Cabins 445		
Single Cabins 0	Supplement 50%		
Balcony Cabins 62	Wheelchair Cabins 4		
Cabin Current	110 AC		
Refrigerator	Category R/A only		
Cabin TV Yes	VCR No		
Dining Rooms 2	Sittings 2		
Elevators	18		

Casino	Yes	Slot Machines	Yes
Swimming Pools (outside)	2	(inside)	0
Whirlpools	2	Gymnasium	Yes
Sauna/Steam Room	Yes/No	Massage	Yes
Self-Service Launderette			No
Movie Theater/Seats			Yes/200
Library			Yes
Children's Facilities			Yes
Watersports Facilities			None
Classification Society		Det Norske Veritas	

RATINGS	SCORE
Ship: Condition/Cleanliness	8.0
Ship: Space/Flow/Comfort	8.0
Ship: Decor/Furnishings	7.9
Ship: Fitness Facilities	7.6
Cabins: Comfort/Facilities	7.6
Cabins: Software	7.7
Food: Dining Room/Cuisine	7.9
Food: Buffets/Informal Dining	7.6
Food: Quality of Ingredients	7.1
Service: Dining Room	7.7
Service: Bars	7.6
Service: Cabins	7.6
Cruise: Entertainment	8.2
Cruise: Activities Program	7.9
Cruise: Hospitality Standard	8.0
OVERALL RATING	116.4

+ Spacious, well-designed interior, with excellent signage. RCCL's trademark Viking Crown lounge and bar surrounds funnel and provides stunning view. Beautiful, well-stocked library adds class. Five-deck-high Centrum is a focal point. While suites are more spacious, most cabins are small, but attractively decorated. Special "family suites," located amidships, sleep four. Excellent headline name cabaret and extensive general entertainment program.

— Deck space cramped when full. Cabins are small. Too many announcements. Expect long lines for embarkation, disembarkation, buffets, and shore tenders.

Dining Two musical-themed dining rooms are large, attractive, and colorful. Dining operation is well orchestrated, with emphasis on highly programmed service that is hurried.
Food is consistently good, but not memorable. Features French, Oriental, Italian, Caribbean, and American theme nights, with waiters/busboys in appropriate costumes. Extensive wine list. Staff are overly friendly, even intrusive.

Other Comments You'll be overwhelmed by the public spaces, and underwhelmed by the size of the cabins. Well-run, fine-tuned, highly programmed cruise product geared particularly to those passengers seeking an action-packed cruise vacation in seven days, at a moderately good price, with around 2,500 fellow passengers.

mv Marco Polo ★★★★

OPERATES
EAST EUROPEAN, ORIENT, PACIFIC AND INDIAN OCEAN CRUISES

Cruise Line		Orient Lines	Elevators		4
Former Names		Aleksandr Pushkin	Casino	Yes	Slot Machines Yes
Gross Tonnage		20,502	Swimming Pools (outside) 1		(inside) 0
Builder	VEB Mathias Thesen (Germany)		Whirlpools	3	Gymnasium Yes
Original Cost		n/a	Sauna/Steam Room Yes/No		Massage Yes
Christened By		Patricia Herrod	Self-Service Launderette		No
Entered Service	Apr 13, 1966/Oct 30, 1993		Movie Theater/Seats	No	Library Yes
Interior Design		A&M Katzourakis	Children's Facilities	No	Zodiacs 10
Country of Registry		Bahamas (C6JZ7)	Helipad:		Yes
Tel No 630-869310 Fax No		130-6216	Classification Society		Bureau Veritas
Length (ft/m)		578.4/176.28			

Beam (ft/m) 77.4/23.60	Draft (ft/m)	26.8/8.17
Propulsion		diesel (14,444kW)
Propellers		2 (CP)
Decks 8	Crew	356
Pass. Capacity (basis 2) 848		(all berths) 915
Pass. Space Ratio (basis 2) 24.1		(all berths) 22.4
Officers European	Dining Staff	Filipino
Total Cabins		425
Size Range (sq ft/m)		120-480/11.0-44.5
Outside Cabins 294	Inside Cabins	131
Single Cabins (doubles sold for single occupancy)		
Supplement		25%
Balcony Cabins 0	Wheelchair Cabins	2
Cabin Current		110/220 AC
Refrigerator		Suites/Jr. suites only
Cabin TV Yes	VCR	No
Dining Rooms 2	Sittings	2

RATINGS	SCORE
Ship: Condition/Cleanliness	8.0
Ship: Space/Flow/Comfort	7.7
Ship: Decor/Furnishings	8.0
Ship: Fitness Facilities	7.6
Cabins: Comfort/Facilities	7.7
Cabins: Software	7.7
Food: Dining Room/Cuisine	8.3
Food: Buffets/Informal Dining	8.1
Food: Quality of Ingredients	7.8
Service: Dining Room	7.7
Service: Bars	7.5
Service: Cabins	7.7
Cruise: Entertainment	5.8
Cruise: Activities Program	6.8
Cruise: Hospitality Standard	7.7
OVERALL RATING	114.1

+ Has a good profile, a strong ice-strengthened hull, and huge storage spaces for long voyages. Completely refitted and refurbished, she now features destination-intensive cruises at very realistic prices. Fitted with the latest navigational aids and biological waste treatment center. There's even a helicopter landing pad. Tasteful interior decor, with careful use of mirrored surfaces, and colors that do not clash. She is a comfortable vessel throughout and rides well. Cabins are adequate, no more.

— Some Upper Deck and Sky Deck cabins have lifeboat-obstructed views. Cabin software and detail is not the high point of this ship. There are not enough elevators. Expect long lines for Zodiac shore tenders.

Dining The main dining room is nicely decorated, practical in design, and functions well, but it's noisy and tables are very close together. There are tables for two to ten. Fine place settings and china. The food itself is of a very high standard, with good presentation. The wine list is limited, but reasonably priced.

Other Comments Specialist expedition lecturers lead some cruises, while others will have a program of fine lecturers and specialists. Excellent and well-planned destination-intensive itineraries. Gratuities are not included. Port taxes are included for E.U. passengers only.

ts Maxim Gorki ★★★★

OPERATES
EUROPE CRUISES

Cruise Line	Phoenix Seereisen/Sovcomflot		
Former Names	Hanseatic/Hamburg		
Gross Tonnage	24,981		
Builder	Howaldtswerke Deutsche		
	Werft (Germany)		
Original Cost	UK£5.6 million		
Christened By	n/a		
Entered Service	Mar 28, 1969/Jan 1974		
Interior Design	n/a		
Country of Registry	Bahamas (C6IQ5)		
Tel No	130-5670/140-2204		
Fax No	130-5671/140-2205		
Length (ft/m)	638.8/194.72		
Beam (ft/m) 87.3/26.62	Draft (ft/m)	27.0/8.25	
Propulsion	steam turbine (16,900kW)		
Propellers		2 (FP)	
Decks	10	Crew	340
Pass. Capacity (basis 2) 650		(all berths) 788	
Pass. Space Ratio (basis 2) 38.4		(all berths) 31.7	
Officers	Russian/Ukrainian		
Dining Staff	Russian/Ukrainian		
Total Cabins	326	Size Range (sq ft/m) n/a	
Outside Cabins	210	Inside Cabins	116
Single Cabins	2	Supplement	20-50%
Balcony Cabins	0	Wheelchair Cabins	0
Cabin Current	220 AC	Refrigerator Suites only	
Cabin TV	Yes	VCR	No
Dining Rooms	3	Sittings	1

Elevators			4
Casino	No	Slot Machines	No
Swimming Pools (outside) 1		(inside)	1
Whirlpools	0	Gymnasium	Yes
Sauna/Steam Room Yes/No		Massage	Yes
Self-Service Launderette			Yes
Movie Theater/Seats			Yes/290
Library			Yes
Children's Facilities			No
Classification Society		Det Norske Veritas	

RATINGS	SCORE
Ship: Condition/Cleanliness	7.8
Ship: Space/Flow/Comfort	8.0
Ship: Decor/Furnishings	7.9
Ship: Fitness Facilities	6.8
Cabins: Comfort/Facilities	6.5
Cabins: Software	6.9
Food: Dining Room/Cuisine	7.1
Food: Buffets/Informal Dining	6.7
Food: Quality of Ingredients	6.8
Service: Dining Room	7.4
Service: Bars	7.5
Service: Cabins	7.6
Cruise: Entertainment	7.4
Cruise: Activities Program	6.8
Cruise: Hospitality Standard	7.2
OVERALL RATING	108.4

+ This all-white ship has long, pleasing lines and outer styling, easily identified by its odd-looking, platform-topped funnel. Generally well maintained, with more facilities added during her last refurbishment. Has good open deck and sunning space. Well-designed public rooms. Good wood paneling throughout. Fine Russian crew show. The cabins are spacious, and many have wood paneling and trim; large bathrooms feature a full bathtub in all except 20 cabins. Superb deluxe cabins are fully equipped, and have huge picture windows, while others have portholes. In-cabin Russian and German satellite TV programs.

— Now 25 years old, the ship needs refurbishing extensively, particularly the wood paneling. Old-fashioned entertainment facilities. The decor, while restful, is dark and dull.

Dining The three nicely decorated restaurants are set low down, but are cheerfully decorated. Excellent lager on draught, and water fountains on all accommodation decks. Moderately good food, and wine at lunch and dinner is included, but more choice, and better presentation, would be welcome. Attentive, courteous service from a well-meaning staff.

Other Comments This ship provides an excellent cruise experience in very comfortable, almost elegant, surroundings, at a modest price. Particularly targeted to German-speaking passengers who appreciate good value. Port taxes, insurance and gratuities are included.

ms Megastar Aries ★★★★+

OPERATES

*7-DAY SOUTH-EAST ASIA CRUISES
(YEAR-ROUND)*

Cruise Line		Star Cruise
Former Names		Aurora I/Lady Diana
Gross Tonnage		3,300
Builder		Flender Werft (Germany)
Original Cost		$35 million
Christened By		Ms Carol Theodore
Entered Service		Jan 5, 1992/Nov 1994
Interior Design		Giorgio Vafiadis
Country of Registry		Bahamas (C6KP6)
Tel No	130-5141	Fax No 130-5144
Length (ft/m)		269.6/82.2
Beam (ft/m) 45.9/14.0	Draft (ft/m)	10.9/3.3
Propulsion		diesel (3,356kW)
Propellers		2 (CP)
Decks	4	Crew 59
Pass. Capacity (basis 2) 80		(all berths) 80
Pass. Space Ratio (basis 2) 41.2		(all berths) 41.2
Officers Scandinavian	Dining Staff	Asian
Total Cabins		44
Size Range (sq ft/m)		250-430/23.0-40.0
Outside Cabins	44	Inside Cabins 0
Single Cabins	6	Supplement Set rates
Balcony Cabins	0	Wheelchair Cabins 0
Cabin Current		110/220 AC
Refrigerator		All cabins
Cabin TV Yes	VCR	Yes
Dining Rooms	1	Sittings Open
Elevators		0

Casino	No	Slot Machines	No
Swimming Pools (outside) 1		(inside)	0
Whirlpools	0	Gymnasium	No
Sauna/Steam Room No/No		Massage	No
Self-Service Launderette			No
Movie Theater/Seats			No
Library			Yes
Children's Facilities			No
Watersports Facilities			None
Classification Society		Germanischer Lloyd	

RATINGS	SCORE
Ship: Condition/Cleanliness	8.8
Ship: Space/Flow/Comfort	7.7
Ship: Facilities	8.4
Ship: Decor/Furnishings	8.8
Ship: Fitness/Watersports Facilities	7.2
Cabins: Comfort/Facilities	8.1
Cabins: Software	8.4
Food: Dining Room/Cuisine	8.2
Food: Buffets/Informal Dining	7.7
Food: Quality of Ingredients	8.2
Service: Dining Room	7.7
Service: Bars	7.7
Service: Cabins	7.9
Cruise: Entertainment/Lecture Program	8.1
Cruise: Hospitality Standard	8.7
OVERALL RATING	121.6

+ Features teakwood decks for strolling, and real wooden "steamer" deck chairs. Warm friendly ambiance. Features wood-accented trim and fine soft furnishings, plush chairs and couches, and always fresh flowers. Has a good library. Personal fax machine in each cabin. Has large cabins for ship size, and most are very comfortable, with big picture windows. The bathrooms, which are enormous for the size of the ship, have clean, crisp colors. All cabins have unobstructed views. This is strictly a private club at sea, for VIPs.

− No wrap-around outdoor promenade deck. The swimming pool is tiny – it's really a "dip" pool. Public room space is limited. The ship, being small, rolls in heavy seas.

Dining The dining room is charming, intimate and very comfortable, with smart contemporary decor. The cuisine is Asian and International in style, and food is well prepared and nicely presented, although there is not a great deal of menu choice. Fine china and flatware.

Other Comments Rather like having the privileges of a private yacht, without the burden of ownership, this ship travels off the beaten path to take you in style and comfort. Port taxes are included.

ms Megastar Taurus ★★★★+

OPERATES
7-DAY SOUTH-EAST ASIA CRUISES
(YEAR-ROUND)

Cruise Line	Star Cruise		
Former Names	Aurora II/Lady Sarah		
Gross Tonnage	3,300		
Builder	Flender Werft (Germany)		
Original Cost	$35 million		
Christened By	Ms Jeanne Buiter		
Entered Service	Feb 27, 1992/Jan 1995		
Interior Design	Giorgio Vafiadis		
Country of Registry	Bahamas (C6KP7)		
Tel No 130-5151	Fax No 130-5154		
Length (ft/m)	269.6/82.2		
Beam (ft/m) 45.9/14.0	Draft (ft/m) 10.9/3.3		
Propulsion	diesel (3,356kW)		
Propellers	2 (CP)		
Decks 4	Crew 59		
Pass. Capacity (basis 2) 80	(all berths) 80		
Pass. Space Ratio (basis 2) 41.2	(all berths) 41.2		
Officers Scandinavian	Dining Staff Asian		
Total Cabins	44		
Size Range (sq ft/m)	250-430/23.0-40.0		
Outside Cabins 44	Inside Cabins 0		
Single Cabins 6	Supplement Set rates		
Balcony Cabins 0	Wheelchair Cabins 0		
Cabin Current	110/220 AC		
Refrigerator	All cabins		
Cabin TV Yes	VCR Yes		
Dining Rooms 1	Sittings Open		
Elevators	0		

Casino No	Slot Machines	No
Swimming Pools (outside) 1	(inside)	0
Whirlpools 0	Gymnasium	No
Sauna/Steam Room No/No	Massage	No
Self-Service Launderette		No
Movie Theater/Seats		No
Library		Yes
Children's Facilities		No
Watersports Facilities		None
Classification Society	Germanischer Lloyd	

RATINGS	SCORE
Ship: Condition/Cleanliness	8.8
Ship: Space/Flow/Comfort	7.7
Ship: Facilities	8.4
Ship: Decor/Furnishings	8.8
Ship: Fitness/Watersports Facilities	7.2
Cabins: Comfort/Facilities	8.1
Cabins: Software	8.4
Food: Dining Room/Cuisine	8.2
Food: Buffets/Informal Dining	7.7
Food: Quality of Ingredients	8.2
Service: Dining Room	7.7
Service: Bars	7.7
Service: Cabins	7.9
Cruise: Entertainment/Lecture Program	8.1
Cruise: Hospitality Standard	8.7
OVERALL RATING	121.6

+ Smart-looking ship has a low, sleek profile and royal blue hull. Designed for highly personal cruising. Features teakwood outdoor decks and real wooden "steamer" chairs. Cabins are large, have big picture windows, and are superbly equipped with fine woods, writing desk, and fax machine. All cabins have unobstructed views, and bathrooms are large. Limited public spaces, yet these are good for those VIPs seeking a private club ambiance in new and highly sophisticated surroundings, with a small number of fellow travelers.

— There is no wrap-around outdoor promenade deck. The swimming pool is tiny—it's really a "dip" pool. Public room space is limited. The ship, being small, rolls in heavy seas.

Dining The dining room is charming, intimate and very comfortable, with smart contemporary decor. The cuisine is Asian and International in style, and food is well prepared and nicely presented, although there is not a great deal of menu choice. Features fine china and flatware.

Other Comments One of a pair of identical ships originally created for the defunct Windsor Line, but sold before delivery. Great style and fine personal service. Rather like having the privileges of a private yacht, without the burden of ownership. Port taxes are included.

ss Meridian ★★★★+

OPERATES

7-DAY BERMUDA AND 10/11-DAY CARIBBEAN CRUISES

Cruise Line	Celebrity Cruises	Casino	Yes	Slot Machines	Yes
Former Names	Galileo/Galileo Galilei	Swimming Pools (outside) 1	(inside)	0
Gross Tonnage	30,440	Whirlpools	3	Gymnasium	Yes
Builder	Cantieri Riuniti dell' Adriatico (Italy)	Sauna/Steam Room Yes/No	Massage	Yes
Original Cost	n/a	Self-Service Launderette		No
Christened By	Mrs Jeanne Chandris	Movie Theater/Seats		Yes/218
Entered Service	Apr 22, 1963/Feb 1990	Library		Yes
Interior Design	A&M Katzourakis	Children's Facilities		Yes
Country of Registry	Panama (3FIP2)	Watersports Facilities		None
Tel No 110-3143 Fax No 110-3145		Classification Society		Lloyd's Register
Length (ft/m)	700.9/213.65			

Beam (ft/m) 94.1/28.71 Draft (ft/m) 28.3/8.64			
Propulsion	steam turbine (32,800kW)	**RATINGS**	**SCORE**
Propellers	2 (FP)	Ship: Condition/Cleanliness	7.6
Decks	8 Crew	580	Ship: Space/Flow/Comfort	7.3
Pass. Capacity (basis 2) 1,106 (all berths) 1,398		Ship: Decor/Furnishings	7.6
Pass. Space Ratio (basis 2) 27.5 (all berths 21.7		Ship: Fitness Facilities	7.0
Officers Greek Dining Staff International		Cabins: Comfort/Facilities	7.4
Total Cabins	553	Cabins: Software	8.2
Size Range (sq ft/m)	n/a	Food: Dining Room/Cuisine	8.3
Outside Cabins 295 Inside Cabins 258		Food: Buffets/Informal Dining	7.9
Single Cabins 0 Supplement Set rates		Food: Quality of Ingredients	8.0
Balcony Cabins 0 Wheelchair Cabins 2		Service: Dining Room	8.0
Cabin Current	110/220 AC	Service: Bars	7.5
Refrigerator	Suites only	Service: Cabins	7.8
Cabin TV No VCR No		Cruise: Entertainment	7.6
		Cruise: Activities Program	7.5
Dining Rooms 1 Sittings 2		Cruise: Hospitality Standard	7.7
Elevators	3	OVERALL RATING	115.4

+ Well-balanced classic ship profile, with rakish bow, rounded stern and new funnel. Expansive sheltered deck areas and open deck sunning space. Wide selection of cabin sizes and configurations, and all are well equipped. Captain's Deck suites have skylights, are large, comfortable, and well equipped. Public rooms have high ceilings and soft, very elegant pastel decor and color tones throughout, with good use of mirrored surfaces. Large casino. Charming twin garden lounges for quiet reading.

— No forward observation lounge. Expect lines for embarkation, disembarkation, shore tenders, and buffets, especially during the summer Bermuda season when the ship is often under charter. Cabin bathrooms are small. No cushioned pads for deck lounge chairs.

Dining The dining room is warm and inviting. Fine, French-influenced cuisine with varied menus created by three-star Michelin master chef Michel Roux. Good selection of pastries and dessert items. The service, by a mainly European staff, is friendly, attentive, and polished. Very attractive and well-presented buffets.

Other Comments This ship delivers an excellent, friendly cruise experience, with fine service and outstanding value for money at very realistic rates. Very highly recommended and especially suited to the longer 10- and 11-day cruise itineraries, which are outstanding.

ms Mermoz ★★★

OPERATES

*14-DAY CARIBBEANAND
EUROPE CRUISES*

Cruise Line			Paquet Cruises
Former Names			Jean Mermoz
Gross Tonnage			13,691
Builder		Chantiers de l'Atlantique (France)	
Original Cost	n/a	Christened By	n/a
Entered Service			May 1957/Sep 1970
Interior Design			Marc Held
Country of Registry			Bahamas (C6BB3)
Tel No	110-4216	Fax No	110-4216
Length (ft/m)			531.5/162.01
Beam (ft/m)	65.0/19.82	Draft (ft/m)	20.9/6.40
Propulsion			diesel (8,000kW)
Propellers			2 (FP)
Decks	9	Crew	320
Pass. Capacity (basis 2) 533		(all berths) 662	
Pass. Space Ratio (basis 2) 25.6		(all berths) 20.6	
Officers			French
Dining Staff			French/Indonesian
Total Cabins			275
Size Range (sq ft/m)			n/a
Outside Cabins	217	Inside Cabins	58
Single Cabins	17	Supplement	75-100%
Balcony Cabins	0	Wheelchair Cabins	0
Cabin Current			110/220 AC
Refrigerator			No
Cabin TV	No	VCR	No
Dining Rooms	2	Sittings	1
Elevators			2

Casino	Yes	Slot Machines	Yes
Swimming Pools (outside) 2		(inside)	0
Whirlpools	Yes	Gymnasium	No
Sauna/Steam Room Yes/No		Massage	Yes
Self-Service Launderette			No
Movie Theater/Seats			Yes/240
Library			Yes
Children's Facilities			No
Watersports Facilities			None
Classification Society			Bureau Veritas

RATINGS	SCORE
Ship: Condition/Cleanliness	5.5
Ship: Space/Flow/Comfort	5.7
Ship: Decor/Furnishings	6.0
Ship: Fitness Facilities	4.7
Cabins: Comfort/Facilities	4.8
Cabins: Software	5.8
Food: Dining Room/Cuisine	7.6
Food: Buffets/Informal Dining	6.9
Food: Quality of Ingredients	7.5
Service: Dining Room	7.3
Service: Bars	7.3
Service: Cabins	7.4
Cruise: Entertainment	6.3
Cruise: Activities Program	5.6
Cruise: Hospitality Standard	6.6
OVERALL RATING	95.0

+ Delightful chic art deco interior decor, with earth tone color scheme throughout and a real "colonial" ambiance feel. Quaint and typically French in ambiance and service. Spa and solarium are good, with emphasis on hydrotherapy. The annual Classical Music Festival cruise is a real cultural delight. Much artwork and models are of interest to ship lovers. Cabins are not large, and only basically equipped, but they are tastefully furnished, cozy, and comfortable, with solid fixtures and lots of wood everywhere. Good closet and drawer space. Bathrobes provided for everyone.

— There is no forward observation lounge. The cabin bathrooms are very small. There is a steep, narrow gangway in some ports.

Dining Outstanding cuisine that is extremely creative, especially during special theme cruises. Fine grill room and food. There is also a 65,000-bottle wine cellar, and wine is complementary with dinner.

Other Comments Traditional older ship with good lines and a rather dated profile. Eclectic interiors. This ship has a wonderful, idiosyncratic French character, flair, ambiance, and is for those who enjoy being with French-speaking passengers wishing to cruise at a moderate price.

ms Mikhail Sholokhov ★★

OPERATES

INDONESIA/SOUTH PACIFIC CRUISES

Cruise Line	Far Eastern Shipping
Former Names	-
Gross Tonnage	9,878
Builder	Adolf Warski Werft (Poland)
Original Cost	n/a
Christened By	n/a
Entered Service	1986
Interior Design	n/a
Country of Registry	Russia (UKSK)
Tel No 140-0360 Fax No	140-0360
Length (ft/m)	441.0/134.40
Beam (ft/m) 68.8/21.00 Draft (ft/m)	18.3/5.60
Propulsion	diesel (12,800kW)
Propellers	2 (CP)
Decks 7 Crew	168
Pass. Capacity (basis 2) 234 (all berths)	412
Pass. Space Ratio (basis 2) 42.2 (all berths)	23.9
Officers	Russian/Ukrainian
Dining Staff	East European
Total Cabins	117
Size Range (sq ft/m)	100-320/9.2-29.7
Outside Cabins 71 Inside Cabins	46
Single Cabins 0 Supplement	100%
Balcony Cabins 0 Wheelchair Cabins	0
Cabin Current	220 AC
Refrigerator	No
Cabin TV No VCR	No
Dining Rooms 1 Sittings	1

Elevators			1
Casino	No	Slot Machines	No
Swimming Pools (outside) 1		(inside)	0
Whirlpools	0	Gymnasium	Yes
Sauna/Steam Room Yes/No		Massage	Yes
Self-Service Launderette			No
Movie Theater/Seats	No	Library	Yes
Children's Facilities			No
Watersports Facilities			None
Classification Society			RS

RATINGS	SCORE
Ship: Condition/Cleanliness	6.6
Ship: Space/Flow/Comfort	6.2
Ship: Decor/Furnishings	6.0
Ship: Fitness Facilities	5.6
Cabins: Comfort/Facilities	5.5
Cabins: Software	6.1
Food: Dining Room/Cuisine	5.3
Food: Buffets/Informal Dining	5.1
Food: Quality of Ingredients	5.1
Service: Dining Room	6.1
Service: Bars	6.2
Service: Cabins	6.2
Cruise: Entertainment	4.3
Cruise: Activities Program	4.7
Cruise: Hospitality Standard	5.8
OVERALL RATING	84.8

+ This ship has an ice-hardened hull and fully enclosed bridge for all-weather operations. One of a series of five built in Poland. Attractive, though dated decor in the limited number of public rooms.

— This is a somewhat boxy looking vessel with a stubby bow and huge square funnel. Has reasonably good open deck and sunning space, but the swimming pool is very small. Limited number of public rooms. There's no cashless cruising here.

Dining The dining room is cheerful, and dining is family style. Food and menu choice are reasonable, no more. Service is perfunctory, but the female waitress staff do try.

Other Comments Interior decor is reasonably pleasant, but somewhat spartan. Cabins are small, space-efficient units that have little warmth. Operates mainly in the Indonesian islands and the South Pacific. This ship provides a reasonable cruise experience that is definitely for the budget-conscious. Don't expect any finesse.

ms Monarch of the Seas ★★★★+

OPERATES

7-DAY CARIBBEAN CRUISES
(YEAR-ROUND)

Cruise Line	Royal Caribbean Cruises	Casino Yes	Slot Machines Yes
Former Names	-	Swimming Pools (outside) 2	(inside) 0
Gross Tonnage	73,941	Whirlpools 2	Gymnasium Yes
Builder	Chantiers de l'Atlantique	Sauna/Steam Room Yes/No	Massage Yes
Original Cost	$300 million	Self-Service Launderette	No
Christened By	Ms Lauren Bacall	Movie Theater/Seats	Yes (2)/146 each
Entered Service	Nov 17, 1991	Library	Yes
Interior Design	Njal Eide	Children's Facilities	Yes
Country of Registry	Norway (LAMU4)	Watersports Facilities	None
Tel No 131-2764 Fax No	131-2764	Classification Society	Det Norske Veritas
Length (ft/m)	873.6/266.30		

Beam (ft/m) 105.9/32.30 Draft (ft/m) 24.9/7.60	
Propulsion diesel (21,844kW)	
Propellers 2 (CP)	
Decks 12 Crew 822	
Pass. Capacity (basis 2) 2,354 (all berths) 2,744	
Pass. Space Ratio (basis 2) 31.0 (all berths) 26.9	
Officers Norwegian Dining Staff International	
Total Cabins 1,177	
Size Range (sq ft/m) 120-441/11.1-41.5	
Outside Cabins 732 Inside Cabins 445	
Single Cabins 0 Supplement 50-100%	
Balcony Cabins 62 Wheelchair Cabins 4	
Cabin Current 110 AC	
Refrigerator Category R/A only	
Cabin TV Yes VCR No	
Dining Rooms 2 Sittings 2	
Elevators 18	

RATINGS	SCORE
Ship: Condition/Cleanliness	8.0
Ship: Space/Flow/Comfort	8.0
Ship: Decor/Furnishings	7.9
Ship: Fitness Facilities	7.6
Cabins: Comfort/Facilities	7.6
Cabins: Software	7.7
Food: Dining Room/Cuisine	7.9
Food: Buffets/Informal Dining	7.6
Food: Quality of Ingredients	7.1
Service: Dining Room	7.7
Service: Bars	7.6
Service: Cabins	7.8
Cruise: Entertainment	8.2
Cruise: Activities Program	7.9
Cruise: Hospitality Standard	8.0
OVERALL RATING	116.6

+ Almost identical in size and appearance to sister *Sovereign of the Seas,* but with improved internal layout, public room features, passenger flow and signage. Surprisingly stable and smooth sailing. Many public rooms, from large to small. RCCL's trademark Viking Crown lounge and bar surrounds funnel and provides a stunning view. Five-deck-high atrium is the interior focal point, and glass-walled elevators. Exceptionally fine library. While suites are more spacious, most cabins are small, but comfortable, and attractively decorated. Special "family suites," located amidships, sleep four. Has good childrens' and teens' programs.

— This ship has small cabins, but the line's philosophy is that you won't spend much time in your cabin. Poor room service menu. Too many announcements. Expect long lines for disembarkation, buffets, and shore tenders.

Dining The two musical-themed dining rooms are large (no tables for two), but have good service and food. Most nights are themed (French, Oriental, Italian, Caribbean, American), with waiters and busboys in appropriate costumes. Good wine list.

Other Comments Provides excellent facilities, with consistently good, well-operated but highly programmed service from an attentive, though robotic, staff. This translates to a rather impersonal but activity-filled cruise experience as one of over 2,000 passengers each week.

ss Monterey ★★★

OPERATES
4 TO 11-DAY EUROPE CRUISES

Cruise Line	Starlauro Cruises	Casino	Yes	Slot Machines	Yes
Former Names	Free State Mariner	Swimming Pools (outside) 1	(inside)	0
Gross Tonnage	21,051	Whirlpools	2	Gymnasium	Yes
Builder	Bethlehem Steel Corp. (USA)	Sauna/Steam Room	Yes/No	Massage	Yes
Original Cost	n/a	Christened By	n/a	Self-Service Launderette	No
Entered Service	Dec 18, 1952/Aug 27, 1988	Movie Theater/Seats	Yes/107
Interior Design	Platou Design	Library	Yes	Children's Facilities	No
Country of Registry	Liberia (3EAH8)	Watersports Facilities	None
Tel No 133-3517 Fax No 133-3517	Classification Society	American Bureau
Length (ft/m)	563.6/171.81		of Shipping

Beam (ft/m) 76.3/23.27 Draft (ft/m) 29.3/8.95	
Propulsion	steam turbine (14,400kW)
Propellers	1 (FP)
Decks 4 Crew 280	
Pass. Capacity (basis 2) 600 (all berths) 638	
Pass. Space Ratio (basis 2) 35.0 (all berths) 32.9	
Officers	Italian
Dining Staff	International
Total Cabins 300 Size Range (sq ft/m) n/a	
Outside Cabins 171 Inside Cabins 129	
Single Cabins 0 Supplement Set rates	
Balcony Cabins 0 Wheelchair Cabins 0	
Cabin Current	110 AC
Refrigerator	Category 13, 14 only
Cabin TV	Category 13, 14 only
VCR	No
Dining Rooms 1 Sittings 2	
Elevators	2

RATINGS	SCORE
Ship: Condition/Cleanliness	6.3
Ship: Space/Flow/Comfort	6.4
Ship: Decor/Furnishings	6.4
Ship: Fitness Facilities	5.3
Cabins: Comfort/Facilities	6.8
Cabins: Software	7.1
Food: Dining Room/Cuisine	6.7
Food: Buffets/Informal Dining	6.2
Food: Quality of Ingredients	6.6
Service: Dining Room	7.7
Service: Bars	7.0
Service: Cabins	7.4
Cruise: Entertainment	6.4
Cruise: Activities Program	6.0
Cruise: Hospitality Standard	7.3
OVERALL RATING	99.6

+ This ship has a traditional fifties liner profile. This is a very stable sea ship with an almost vertical bow and an overhanging aircraft-carrier-like stern that is not at all handsome. She was refurbished in moderate art deco style, when a new sports deck was added. Good sheltered and open deck space. Very friendly, bubbly Italian crew and atmosphere. There is a wide choice of cabin sizes and configurations – but only the top three categories have full bathtubs. Has extremely spacious suites; other cabins are very roomy, well-equipped units. Bathrobes are provided.

— Lacks a forward observation lounge. There is too much cold steel, and not enough warmth in the interior decoration. Cabins forward on Boat Deck have lifeboat-obstructed views.

Dining The charming two-tier dining room is set low down, and decorated in soft pink tones, so the ambiance is quite charming, but it is noisy when full. Features Continental cuisine, with some excellent pasta dishes. Poor selection of breads, cheeses, and fruits. Service is friendly and attentive, in typical Italian style, but somewhat hurried.

Other Comments This ship will cruise you in reasonably elegant style and surroundings, with mainly European, and particularly Italian-speaking passengers. Currency aboard: Lire. Port taxes are included.

mv Nantucket Clipper ★★★

OPERATES

*7 TO 14-DAY US/CANADA COAST
AND VIRGIN ISLANDS CRUISES*

Cruise Line	Clipper Cruise Line
Former Names	-
Gross Tonnage	1,471
Builder	Jeffboat (USA)
Original Cost	$9 million
Christened By	Ms Christiane Ebsworth
Entered Service	Dec 23, 1984
Interior Design	n/a
Country of Registry	USA (WSQ8373)
Tel No none	Fax No none
Length (ft/m)	207.0/63.00
Beam (ft/m) 37.0/11.20	Draft (ft/m) 8.0/2.40
Propulsion	diesel (700kW)
Propellers	2 (FP)
Decks 4	Crew 37
Pass. Capacity (basis 2) 102	(all berths) 102
Pass. Space Ratio (basis 2) 14.4	(all berths) 14.4
Officers	American
Dining Staff	American
Total Cabins	51
Size Range (sq ft/m)	121-138/11.2-12.8
Outside Cabins 51	Inside Cabins 0
Single Cabins 0	Supplement Set rates
Balcony Cabins 0	Wheelchair Cabins 0
Cabin Current 110 AC	Refrigerator No
Cabin TV No	VCR No
Dining Rooms 1	Sittings 1
Elevators 0	

Casino	No	Slot Machines	No
Swimming Pools (outside) 0		(inside)	0
Whirlpools	0	Gymnasium	No
Sauna/Steam Room No/No		Massage	No
Self-Service Launderette			No
Movie Theater/Seats			No
Library	Yes	Children's Facilities No
Watersports Facilities			None
Classification Society		American Bureau
			of Shipping

RATINGS	SCORE
Ship: Condition/Cleanliness	6.4
Ship: Space/Flow/Comfort	4.0
Ship: Decor/Furnishings	6.8
Ship: Fitness Facilities	3.0
Cabins: Comfort/Facilities	6.1
Cabins: Software	6.5
Food: Dining Room/Cuisine	7.1
Food: Buffets/Informal Dining	6.2
Food: Quality of Ingredients	7.0
Service: Dining Room	7.1
Service: Bars	7.0
Service: Cabins	7.3
Cruise: Entertainment	4.0
Cruise: Activities Program	5.6
Cruise: Hospitality Standard	7.3
OVERALL RATING	91.4

+ This small, shallow draft vessel is specially built for coastal and inland cruises and is very maneuverable. Well maintained. Extremely high-density ship has only two public rooms – the dining room and an observation lounge. Wrap-around open teakwood walking deck. Passengers can visit the bridge at any time. The all-outside cabins (in four categories) are very small, but somehow comfortable and tastefully furnished, with wood-accented trim, and good sound insulation.

— Has very small cabins. High engine noise level when under way. The per diem price is high for what you get, and air fare is extra.

Dining The dining room is warm and inviting, and has large picture windows. There are table assignments only for dinner, which is at a single sitting. There are no tables for two. Features simple and plain cuisine, with limited menu choice and small portions.

Other Comments Service is by young, friendly all-American college-age types. This is most definitely an "Americana" experience for those seeking particularly to learn more about the coastal ports around the USA. Casual and unstructured lifestyle, rather like a small, but not luxurious, country club afloat, with much attention to detail. Not to be compared with big ship ocean cruising. No mindless activities or corny games.

ms Nautican ★★★★

OPERATES

3, 5 AND 7-DAY SOUTH EAST ASIA CRUISES (YEAR-ROUND)

Cruise Line	Cruise Lines International
Former Names	Crown Monarch
Gross Tonnage	15,271
Builder	Union Navale de Levante (Spain)
Original Cost	$95 million
Christened By	Mrs Gunvar "Gigi" Grundstad
Entered Service	Dec 1, 1990/Oct 30, 1994
Interior Design	Oliver Design
Country of Registry	Panama (3EGA8)
Tel No 133-3627 Fax No	133-3630
Length (ft/m)	494.4/150.72
Beam (ft/m) 67.6/20.62 Draft (ft/m)	17.7/5.40
Propulsion	diesel (13,680kW)
Propellers	2 (CP)
Decks 7 Crew	215
Pass. Capacity (basis 2) 510 (all berths)	556
Pass. Space Ratio (basis 2) 29.9 (all berths)	27.4
Officers	International
Dining Staff	Filipino/Burmese
Total Cabins	255
Size Range (sq ft/m)	145-398/13.5-37.0
Outside Cabins 225 Inside Cabins	30
Single Cabins 0 Supplement	50-100%
Balcony Cabins 10 Wheelchair Cabins	5
Cabin Current	110 AC
Refrigerator	Category 1 only
Cabin TV Yes VCR	No
Dining Rooms 1 Sittings	2

Elevators			4
Casino	Yes	Slot Machines	Yes
Swimming Pools (outside) 1		(inside)	0
Whirlpools	2	Gymnasium	Yes
Sauna/Steam Room Yes/No		Massage	Yes
Self-Service Launderette			No
Movie Theater/Seats	No	Library	Yes
Children's Facilities			No
Watersports Facilities			None
Classification Society		Det Norske Veritas	

RATINGS	SCORE
Ship: Condition/Cleanliness	7.4
Ship: Space/Flow/Comfort	7.7
Ship: Decor/Furnishings	8.6
Ship: Fitness Facilities	7.1
Cabins: Comfort/Facilities	7.7
Cabins: Software	7.9
Food: Dining Room/Cuisine	7.5
Food: Buffets/Informal Dining	6.8
Food: Quality of Ingredients	6.6
Service: Dining Room	7.4
Service: Bars	7.2
Service: Cabins	7.5
Cruise: Entertainment	7.1
Cruise: Activities Program	6.0
Cruise: Hospitality Standard	7.5
OVERALL RATING	110.0

+ This is a handsome, highly maneuverable small ship with swept-back funnel and fine, well-balanced profile. Has reasonably good open deck and sunning space. Lifeboats are well located to avoid obstructed views. Numerous public rooms to choose from, all tastefully decorated and very comfortable. Well-designed interior has an excellent layout and good passenger flow. Suites with private balconies are excellent. All other cabins are nicely appointed and have elegant, pleasing decor and wood accents, and double-to-twin convertible beds, with floral-patterned bedspreads. Most cabins are large for the ship size.

— The indoor/outdoor cafe is poorly designed and has very limited seating and traffic flow. Poor cabin soundproofing. Disappointing cuisine needs attention and some upgrading, as does the service.

Dining The dining room is quite charming, elegantly appointed, and has real wood chairs with arm rests, warm decor, and an informal atmosphere. The food is generally good, with generous portions, but choice is limited. Service is good to excellent, from a friendly and attentive staff.

Other Comments This ship, under charter from Effjohn, will provide Asian passengers with a pleasant cruise experience in comfortable, contemporary surroundings, at a modest price.

ms Nieuw Amsterdam ★★★★

OPERATES

*7-DAY ALASKA AND
CARIBBEAN CRUISES*

Cruise Line	Holland America Line
Former Names	-
Gross Tonnage	33,930
Builder	Chantiers de l'Atlantique (France)
Original Cost	$150 million
Christened By	HRH Princess Margriet
Entered Service	Jul 9, 1983
Interior Design	VFD Interiors
Country of Registry	Netherlands Antilles (PJCH)
Tel No 115-0123 Fax No 114-0123	
Length (ft/m)	704.2/214.66
Beam (ft/m) 89.4/27.26 Draft (ft/m) 24.6/7.52	
Propulsion	diesel (21,600kW)
Propellers	2 (CP)
Decks 10 Crew	542
Pass. Capacity (basis 2) 1,210 (all berths) 1,350	
Pass. Space Ratio (basis 2) 28.0 (all berths) 25.1	
Officers	Dutch
Dining Staff	Filipino/Indonesian
Total Cabins	605
Size Range (sq ft/m)	152-295/14.0-27.5
Outside Cabins 411 Inside Cabins 194	
Single Cabins 0 Supplement 50-100%	
Balcony Cabins 0 Wheelchair Cabins 4	
Cabin Current	110/220 AC
Refrigerator	Category A only
Cabin TV Yes VCR	No
Dining Rooms 1 Sittings	2

Elevators			7
Casino	Yes	Slot Machines	Yes
Swimming Pools (outside) 2		(inside)	0
Whirlpools	1	Gymnasium	Yes
Sauna/Steam Room Yes/No		Massage	Yes
Self-Service Launderette			Yes
Movie Theater/Seats			Yes/230
Library	Yes	Children's Facilities	No
Watersports Facilities			None
Classification Society			Lloyd's Register

RATINGS	SCORE
Ship: Condition/Cleanliness	8.0
Ship: Space/Flow/Comfort	8.2
Ship: Decor/Furnishings	8.0
Ship: Fitness Facilities	6.7
Cabins: Comfort/Facilities	8.0
Cabins: Software	7.6
Food: Dining Room/Cuisine	6.1
Food: Buffets/Informal Dining	6.0
Food: Quality of Ingredients	6.0
Service: Dining Room	6.6
Service: Bars	7.3
Service: Cabins	8.1
Cruise: Entertainment	6.7
Cruise: Activities Program	7.1
Cruise: Hospitality Standard	7.8
OVERALL RATING	108.2

+ Has nicely raked bow. Plenty of open deck space. Traditional teakwood outdoor decks, including wrap-around promenade deck. Spacious interior design and layout, with soothing color combinations. Much polished teak and rosewood paneling. Stunning antiques and artwork. Explorers' Lounge is relaxing for after-meal coffee and live chamber music. Balconied main lounge reminiscent of former ocean liner era. Spacious and well-equipped cabins have quality furniture and fittings, wood paneling, good counter and storage space, and good-sized bathrooms. Top three categories have full bathtubs. Several cabins have king- or queen-sized beds, and cabin insulation is good.

— Suffers from vibration at stern. Indonesian waiters try hard, but communication is at times frustrating. Some cabins on Boat and Navigation Decks have obstructed views. Expect long lines for buffets and shore tenders. Has poor entertainment.

Dining The dining room is large and attractive, with ample space. Open seating for breakfast and lunch, two sittings for dinner. Food is attractively presented, but not adventurous, and the quality has deteriorated lately. Poor choice of breads, bread rolls, and fruits.

Other Comments Recommended for seasoned, senior-age travelers wanting a quality, traditional cruise experience, in elegant surroundings, at a realistic and moderate price level.

ms Nippon Maru ★★★★

OPERATES
JAPAN/SOUTH EAST ASIA CRUISES

Cruise Line		Mitsui OSK Passenger Line	
Former Names			-
Gross Tonnage			21,903
Builder	Mitsubishi Heavy Industries (Japan)		
Original Cost			$59.4 million
Christened By		Mr Susumi Temporin	
Entered Service			Sep 27, 1990
Interior Design	Osamu Higuchi/Mikiya Murakami		
Country of Registry			Japan (JNNU)
Tel No	120-0462	Fax No	120-0462
Length (ft/m)			546.7/166.65
Beam (ft/m)	78.7/24.00	Draft (ft/m)	21.4/6.55
Propulsion			diesel (15,740kW)
Propellers			2 (CP)
Decks	7	Crew	160
Pass. Capacity (basis 2)	408	(all berths)	607
Pass. Space Ratio (basis 2)	53.6	(all berths)	36.0
Officers	Japanese	Dining Staff	Japanese
Total Cabins			204
Size Range (sq ft/m)			150-430/14.0-40.0
Outside Cabins	189	Inside Cabins	15
Single Cabins	0	Supplement	25-60%
Balcony Cabins	0	Wheelchair Cabins	2
Cabin Current	100 AC	Refrigerator	Yes
Cabin TV	Yes	VCR	No
Dining Rooms	1	Sittings	1
Elevators			5
Casino	Yes*	Slot Machines	No

Swimming Pools (outside) 1	(inside)		0
Whirlpools			4 (Japanese baths)
Gymnasium			Yes
Sauna/Steam Room Yes/No	Massage		Yes*
Self-Service Launderette			Yes
Movie Theater/Seats			Yes/135
Library			Yes
Children's Facilities			Yes*
Classification Society		Nippon Kaiji Kyokai	

* = On leisure cruises only

RATINGS	SCORE
Ship: Condition/Cleanliness	8.0
Ship: Space/Flow/Comfort	7.7
Ship: Decor/Furnishings	8.2
Ship: Fitness Facilities	6.6
Cabins: Comfort/Facilities	7.3
Cabins: Software	7.2
Food: Dining Room/Cuisine	7.5
Food: Buffets/Informal Dining	6.7
Food: Quality of Ingredients	7.1
Service: Dining Room	7.5
Service: Bars	7.4
Service: Cabins	7.0
Cruise: Entertainment	6.8
Cruise: Activities Program	6.8
Cruise: Hospitality Standard	8.3
OVERALL RATING	110.1

+ Traditional profile and single funnel aft of midships. Public rooms have high ceilings. The ship has an elegant, dramatic six-deck-high atrium. Specifically built and outfitted for the domestic Japanese seminar/lecture marketplace and individual passengers. Excellent teakwood decking. Well-designed public rooms have high-quality furnishings and soothing color combinations. Features true Japanese baths, as well as a "Washitsu" tatami room. Most cabins located forward, public rooms aft. Nicely decorated suites and deluxe cabins.

— Interior decor is plain and unexciting. The showlounge could be improved somewhat.

Dining The dining room is quite basic, and features both traditional Japanese cuisine and some Western dishes. One sitting for leisure cruises and two sittings for ship charter cruises. The food presentation standard is good but simplistic, and menu choice is limited.

Other Comments Has a small outdoor swimming pool with magrodome sliding glass roof. Balconied main lounge. Tastefully decorated suites and deluxe cabins with good storage space. While suites and deluxe cabins are quite elegant and well equipped, the standard cabins, which form the majority, are quite small and spartan, though adequate. This ship is principally for Japanese individual passengers who want to cruise at moderate rates without the extra luxury touches one might expect in a top hotel. No tipping is allowed.

ms Noordam ★★★★

Cruise Line	Holland America Line	Elevators	7
Former Names	-	Casino	Yes	Slot Machines	Yes
Gross Tonnage	33,930	Swimming Pools (outside) 2	(inside)	0
Builder	Chantiers de l'Atlantique (France)	Whirlpools	1	Gymnasium	Yes
Original Cost	$160 million	Sauna/Steam Room Yes/No	Massage	Yes
Christened By	Mrs Beatrijs van De Wallbake	Self-Service Launderette	Yes
Entered Service	Apr 8, 1984	Movie Theater/Seats	Yes/230
Interior Design	VFD Interiors	Library Yes	Children's Facilities	No
Country of Registry	Netherlands Antilles (PJCO)	Watersports Facilities	None
Tel No 175-0105 Fax No	175-0110	Classification Society	Lloyd's Register
Length (ft/m)	704.2/214.66		
Beam (ft/m) 89.4/27.26 Draft (ft/m)	24.2/7.40	**RATINGS**	**SCORE**
Propulsion	diesel (21,600kW)	Ship: Condition/Cleanliness	8.0
Propellers	2 (CP)	Ship: Space/Flow/Comfort	8.2
Decks 10 Crew	530	Ship: Decor/Furnishings	8.0
Pass. Capacity (basis 2) 1,210 (all berths) 1,350		Ship: Fitness Facilities	6.7
Pass. Space Ratio (basis 2) 28.0 (all berths) 25.1		Cabins: Comfort/Facilities	8.0
Officers	Dutch	Cabins: Software	7.6
Dining Staff	Filipino/Indonesian	Food: Dining Room/Cuisine	6.1
Total Cabins	605	Food: Buffets/Informal Dining	6.0
Size Range (sq ft/m)	152-295/14..0-27.5	Food: Quality of Ingredients	6.0
Outside Cabins 411 Inside Cabins	194	Service: Dining Room	6.6
Single Cabins 0 Supplement	50-100%	Service: Bars	7.3
Balcony Cabins 0 Wheelchair Cabins	4	Service: Cabins	8.1
Cabin Current	110/220 AC	Cruise: Entertainment	6.7
Refrigerator	Category A only	Cruise: Activities Program	7.1
Cabin TV Yes VCR	No	Cruise: Hospitality Standard	7.8
Dining Rooms 1 Sittings	2	OVERALL RATING	108.2

+ Traditional teakwood outdoor decks, including wrap-around promenade. Outstanding 17th- and 18th-century artwork and Dutch artifacts, well displayed. Flower bouquets are lovely. Crow's Nest observation lounge is a good retreat. Explorers' Lounge is fine for after-dinner coffees with live chamber music. Good indoor/outdoor dining area. Spacious and practical cabins have plenty of storage space, good closets and decent bathrooms (top three categories have full bathtubs). All cabins are well equipped, and have good insulation.

— Some cabins on Boat and Navigation Decks have obstructed views. Expect lines for buffets. Has poor entertainment. Frustrating trying to communicate with newer staff.

Dining Charming and spacious dining room. Open seating for breakfast and lunch, two sittings for dinner. Generally good service from Indonesian staff—always with a smile. Features international cuisine with an American flavor, but ingredients are not the best in quality, and entrees are tasteless. Poor choice of breads, rolls, and fruits.

Other Comments Identical squarish exterior to *Nieuw Amsterdam* with same squat, angular design, but different interior colors and decor. This ship will cruise you (leave the children at home, please, for they'll be out of place here) for a week in an elegant style, but at an affordable, realistic price.

ms Nordic Empress ★★★★

OPERATES

*3- AND 4-DAY BAHAMAS CRUISES
(YEAR-ROUND)*

Cruise Line	Royal Caribbean Cruises	Casino	Yes
Former Names	-	Slot Machines	Yes-220
Gross Tonnage	48,563	Swimming Pools (outside) 2	(inside) 0
Builder	Chantiers de l'Atlantique (France)	Whirlpools 4	Gymnasium Yes
Original Cost	$170 million	Sauna/Steam Room Yes/No	Massage Yes
Christened By	Ms Gloria Estefan	Self-Service Launderette	No
Entered Service	Jun 25, 1990	Movie Theater/Seats No	Library No
Interior Design	Njal Eide	Children's Facilities	Yes
Country of Registry	Liberia (ELJV7)	Watersports Facilities	None
Tel No 124-3540 Fax No	124-3547	Classification Society	Det Norske Veritas
Length (ft/m)	692.2/211.00		
Beam (ft/m) 100.7/30.70 Draft (ft/m)	23.2/7.10	**RATINGS**	**SCORE**
Propulsion	diesel (16,200kW)	Ship: Condition/Cleanliness	8.0
Propellers	2 (CP)	Ship: Space/Flow/Comfort	7.6
Decks 12 Crew	671	Ship: Decor/Furnishings	7.6
Pass. Capacity (basis 2) 1,600 (all berths)	2,020	Ship: Fitness Facilities	7.3
Pass. Space Ratio (basis 2) 30.2 (all berths)	24.0	Cabins: Comfort/Facilities	7.2
Officers Scandinavian Dining Staff	International	Cabins: Software	7.7
Total Cabins	800	Food: Dining Room/Cuisine	7.8
Size Range (sq ft/m)	117-269/10.8-25.0	Food: Buffets/Informal Dining	7.6
Outside Cabins 471 Inside Cabins	329	Food: Quality of Ingredients	7.1
Single Cabins 0 Supplement	50-100%	Service: Dining Room	7.7
Balcony Cabins 69 Wheelchair Cabins	4	Service: Bars	7.6
Cabin Current	110 AC	Service: Cabins	7.6
Refrigerator	Category R/A only	Cruise: Entertainment	8.2
Cabin TV Yes VCR	No	Cruise: Activities Program	7.9
Dining Rooms 1 Sittings	2	Cruise: Hospitality Standard	7.8
Elevators	7	OVERALL RATING	114.7

+ Contemporary ship with short bow and squared stern looks quite stunning. Designed specifically for the short cruise market, for which the ship is well suited. Has outdoor polished wood wrap-around promenade deck. Dramatic use of glass-enclosed viewing spaces. Stunning nine-deck-high atrium is focal point. Lots of crystal and brass to reflect light. Ingenious use of lighting effects in interiors. Tri-level casino has sailcloth ceiling. Superb outdoor pool deck designed for evenings under the stars. Viking Crown Lounge, aft of the funnel, is a bi-level nightclub-disco. Nine cabins have private balconies overlooking the stern. All cabins convert to double bed configuration and are very small, though comfortable.

— Expect lines for embarkation, disembarkation, and buffets. Two-level showroom has poor sightlines in balcony. Constant repetitive announcements are irritating.

Dining Two-level musical-themed dining room is delightful, though noisy, and has huge windows overlooking the stern. The dining room operation is well orchestrated, with emphasis on highly programmed service with some finesse. The food is consistently good, but not memorable. Menu choices are varied. Wine list is quite extensive.

Other Comments This is a glamorous, well-designed ship for short party atmosphere cruises, with high passenger density, and lots of activities designed for the whole family.

ss Norway ★★★★

Cruise Line	Norwegian Cruise Line
Former Names	France
Gross Tonnage	76,049
Builder	Chantiers de l'Atlantique (France)
Original Cost	$80 million
Christened By	Madame Charles de Gaulle
Entered Service	Feb 3, 1962/Jun 1, 1980
Interior Design	Tage Wandborg/Angelo Donghia
Country of Registry	Bahamas (C6CM7)
Tel No 110-4603 Fax No 110-4604	
Length (ft/m)	1035.1/315.50
Beam (ft/m) 109.9/33.50 Draft (ft/m) 35.4/10.80	
Propulsion	steam turbine (29,850kW)
Propellers	4 (FP)
Decks 12 Crew	875
Pass. Capacity (basis 2) 2,044 (all berths) 2,370	
Pass. Space Ratio (basis 2) 37.2 (all berths) 32.8	
Officers Norwegian Dining Staff International	
Total Cabins	1,013
Size Range (sq ft/m)	100-957/9.2-89.0
Outside Cabins 647 Inside Cabins 366	
Single Cabins 20 Supplement 50-100%	
Balcony Cabins 56 Wheelchair Cabins 10	
Cabin Current	110 AC
Refrigerator Category 1/2/3/4/5/owner's suite only	
Cabin TV Yes VCR	No
Dining Rooms 2 Sittings	2
Elevators	13

Casino Yes Slot Machines Yes	
Swimming Pools (outside)	2
Swimming Pools (inside) 1 (plus Aquacize Pool)	
Whirlpools 2 Gymnasium Yes	
Sauna/Steam Room Yes/No Massage Yes	
Self-Service Launderette	Yes
Movie Theater/Seats	Yes/840
Library Yes Children's Facilities Yes	
Watersports Facilities	None
Classification Society	Bureau Veritas

RATINGS	SCORE
Ship: Condition/Cleanliness	7.7
Ship: Space/Flow/Comfort	7.5
Ship: Decor/Furnishings	7.3
Ship: Fitness Facilities	8.0
Cabins: Comfort/Facilities	7.8
Cabins: Software	6.7
Food: Dining Room/Cuisine	7.5
Food: Buffets/Informal Dining	7.2
Food: Quality of Ingredients	6.4
Service: Dining Room	7.2
Service: Bars	7.1
Service: Cabins	7.5
Cruise: Entertainment	8.2
Cruise: Activities Program	7.6
Cruise: Hospitality Standard	7.3
OVERALL RATING	111.0

✚ Legendary grand former classic ocean liner *France* was for many years the world's largest cruise ship. The 1993 refurbishment refreshed her interiors, and some rooms now feature art deco touches reminiscent of the former ocean liner she once was. Has two different color schemes in the forward and aft sections, which help first-time passengers to find their way around. Has two glass-enclosed decks atop the ship that house 135 outside suites and junior suites, and lower the profile of the two wing-tip funnels considerably, but the balconies are not very private. The public rooms are, for the most part, quite pleasing. Soft furnishings and much marble freshened the ship's interior recently. Two large landing craft provide fast, efficient transportation ashore. Has well-varnished outdoor decks. Good Roman Spa and spa programs. Extensive jogging track (but it can't be used before 8:00 a.m. as it's located above some of the most expensive cabins). Club Internationale is an elegant carryover from her former days, and still the perfect meeting place for cocktails and sophisticated evenings. Excellent proscenium theater for dazzle and sizzle production shows. Large active casino. Very wide range of suites and cabins—from really luxurious and spacious outside suites to tiny inside cabins. All have high ceilings, long beds, good closet and drawer space and full amenities. Outstanding owner's suites are extremely lavish. Take the family, as children and teens will have a fine time aboard this ship. She's so large, there are plenty of places to play.

— Expect long lines everywhere: for embarkation, disembarkation, shore excursions, shore tenders, breakfast, and lunch buffets. Poor deck and sunning space when the ship is full. Doesn't dock anywhere because of its size and deep draft (a problem for the non-ambulatory). Roman Spa fitness facilities incur hefty extra charge, plus a 12% tip added. There are too many announcements, making for too much of a holiday camp atmosphere.

Dining There are two large dining rooms – nicest is the Windward, with its fine domed ceiling, while the Leeward has a fine balcony. There are few tables for two, however, and tables are close together. The food is not memorable, and, for most, the menus are uninspiring and quite disappointing. Poor bread rolls and fruit. Service ranges from poor to very good. Le Bistro offers a taste of Italy in "South Miami Beach" style, at no extra charge. The cuisine is reasonable American hotel banquet food, no more, although it has become better in the past year or so. Good, moderately priced wine list.

Other Comments Like Cunard's *QE2*, the *Norway* is a floating city herself. All suite occupants should have a private dining room. Recommended for active passengers and families with children of all ages. This ship will provide an action-packed, sun-filled cruise in comfortable, but rather overpopulated surroundings, at a decent price.

ss OceanBreeze ★★★

OPERATES

3- AND 4-DAY BAHAMAS CRUISES (YEAR-ROUND)

Cruise Line		Dolphin Cruise Line
Former Names		Azure Seas/Calypso/
		Monarch Star/Southern Cross
Gross Tonnage		21,486
Builder		Harland & Wolff (UK)
Original Cost		n/a
Christened By		HRH Queen Elizabeth II
Entered Service		Mar 29, 1955/May 31, 1992
Interior Design		A&M Katzourakis
Country of Registry		Panama (ELLY4)
Tel No 124-6254	Fax No	124-6254
Length (ft/m)		603.8/184.06
Beam (ft/m) 80.0/24.41	Draft (ft/m)	26.1/7.97
Propulsion	steam turbine (14,900kW)	
Propellers		2 (FP)
Decks 9	Crew	380
Pass. Capacity (basis 2) 782	(all berths) 946	
Pass. Space Ratio (basis 2) 27.4	(all berths) 22.7	
Officers International	Dining Staff International	
Total Cabins		391
Size Range (sq ft/m)		99-400/90.0-37.0
Outside Cabins 241	Inside Cabins	150
Single Cabins 0	Supplement	50%
Balcony Cabins 0	Wheelchair Cabins	0
Cabin Current		110/220 AC
Refrigerator		No
Cabin TV No	VCR	No
Dining Rooms 1	Sittings	2

Elevators			2
Casino	Yes	Slot Machines	Yes
Swimming Pools (outside) 1		(inside)	0
Whirlpools	1	Gymnasium	Yes
Sauna/Steam Room Yes/No		Massage	No
Self-Service Launderette			No
Movie Theater/Seats			Yes/55
Library	Yes	Children's Facilities	No
Watersports Facilities			None
Classification Society			Bureau Veritas

RATINGS	SCORE
Ship: Condition/Cleanliness	6.5
Ship: Space/Flow/Comfort	5.9
Ship: Decor/Furnishings	6.5
Ship: Fitness Facilities	4.5
Cabins: Comfort/Facilities	6.3
Cabins: Software	6.5
Food: Dining Room/Cuisine	7.0
Food: Buffets/Informal Dining	6.8
Food: Quality of Ingredients	6.6
Service: Dining Room	6.8
Service: Bars	6.9
Service: Cabins	7.1
Cruise: Entertainment	6.8
Cruise: Activities Program	6.6
Cruise: Hospitality Standard	6.8
OVERALL RATING	97.6

+ Older ship has long, low profile and single funnel astern. Well maintained, although showing her age in places. Good open deck and sunning space. Two-level casino is beautifully decorated, in art deco style, and action-packed, in what used to be the movie theater. Cabins are reasonably comfortable and nicely decorated in earth tones, and, though not large, they are well equipped, and have heavy-duty fittings. Has a good children's program for families.

— Expect lines for embarkation, disembarkation, shore excursions, and buffets. There are lots of smokers among passenger carry. Many crew members do not speak English well.

Dining The dining room is located low down in the ship, but has a warm and very cheerful ambiance, though the chairs do not have armrests. The food is generally quite good, and there's plenty of it, but it isn't gourmet food at all, despite what the brochure claims. Service is quite reasonable and attentive, but there's no finesse. Limited choice of cheeses and fruits.

Other Comments This is a good ship for those wanting a decent cruise experience for a modest price, in casual surroundings, to the southern Caribbean and Panama Canal (on alternating itineraries). At the start and end of the cruise you have to deal with the awful, crowded Aruba airport, so be prepared.

ms Ocean Majesty ★★★

OPERATES

7-DAY AEGEAN/
MEDITERRANEAN CRUISES

Cruise Line	Majestic International Cruises		
Former Names	Homeric/Olympic/Ocean Majesty/		
	Kypros Star/Juan March		
Gross Tonnage	10,417		
Builder	Union de Levante (Spain)		
Original Cost	$65 million		
Christened By	Chios Breeze Marine		
Entered Service	1966/Apr 15, 1994		
Interior Design	D. Androutsopoulos & Assoc.		
Country of Registry	Greece (SZWX)		
Tel No 113-2141	Fax No 113-2142		
Length (ft/m)	443.8/135.30		
Beam (ft/m) 62.9/19.20	Draft (ft/m) 19.5/5.95		
Propulsion/Propellers	diesel (12,200kW)/2 (CP)		
Decks 8	Crew 235		
Pass. Capacity (basis 2) 535	(all berths) 621		
Pass. Space Ratio (basis 2) 19.4	(all berths) 16.7		
Officers Greek	Dining Staff Greek		
Total Cabins	273		
Size Range (sq ft/m)	96-182/9.0-17.0		
Outside Cabins 186	Inside Cabins 87		
Single Cabins 11	Supplement 50%		
Balcony Cabins 8	Wheelchair Cabins 2		
Cabin Current	110/220 AC		
Refrigerator	Suites only		
Cabin TV Suites only	VCR No		
Dining Rooms 1	Sittings 2		
Elevators	3		

Casino	Yes	Slot Machines	Yes
Swimming Pools (outside) 1		(inside)	0
Whirlpools		1 Gymnasium	Yes
Sauna/Steam Room Yes/No		Massage	Yes
Self-Service Launderette			No
Movie Theater/Seats	No	Library	Yes
Children's Facilities			Yes
Watersports Facilities			None
Classification Society		American Bureau	
		of Shipping	

RATINGS	SCORE
Ship: Condition/Cleanliness	7.3
Ship: Space/Flow/Comfort	6.6
Ship: Decor/Furnishings	7.7
Ship: Fitness Facilities	4.4
Cabins: Comfort/Facilities	6.9
Cabins: Software	7.1
Food: Dining Room/Cuisine	6.6
Food: Buffets/Informal Dining	6.4
Food: Quality of Ingredients	6.0
Service: Dining Room	7.3
Service: Bars	7.2
Service: Cabins	7.3
Cruise: Entertainment	5.9
Cruise: Activities Program	6.1
Cruise: Hospitality Standard	7.1
OVERALL RATING	99.9

+ This ship has a pleasing, balanced, almost handsome profile with an aft funnel. Has several good, practical public rooms, bars and lounges, furnished with fine quality materials and fabrics. The decor includes an abundance of highly polished mirrored surfaces. Cabins are small and functional, but with little closet and drawer space.

— This is a high-density vessel, so expect lines for embarkation, disembarkation, shore excursions, and buffets. Open deck and sunning space is limited. Cabin bathrooms are extremely small. Rather awkward interior layout and steep interior stairways with short steps.

Dining The dining room is set low down, and, although quite attractive, it is also extremely noisy (particularly at the tables adjacent to the waiter stations). No tables for two. The cuisine is Continental, with the emphasis on Greek preparation and presentation. Limited selection of breads, fruits, and cheeses, and buffets are generally simple and unimaginative affairs.

Other Comments A former Spanish ro-ro vessel (sister vessel to the present *Don Juan*), this ship has undergone an extensive transformation into a cruise vessel, with the exception of hull, shaft, and propellers, all completed in 1994. The conversion was good, but her built-up stern is not really handsome. Cruising on this ship will provide a busy, destination-oriented experience in surroundings that are quite comfortable, but nothing special.

ms Oceanic Grace ★★★★+

OPERATES

JAPAN/SOUTH EAST ASIA CRUISES

Cruise Line	Oceanic Cruises/Showa Line		
Former Names	-		
Gross Tonnage	5,218		
Builder	NKK Tsu Shipyard (Japan)		
Original Cost	$40 million		
Christened By	Ms Mineko Takamine		
Entered Service	Apr 22, 1989		
Interior Design	Studio Acht		
Country of Registry	Japan (JMIA)		
Tel No 120-1634	Fax No	120-6134	
Length (ft/m)	337.5/102.90		
Beam (ft/m) 50.5/15.40	Draft (ft/m)	14.1/4.30	
Propulsion	diesel (5,192kW)		
Propellers	2 (CP)		
Decks 4	Crew	70	
Pass. Capacity (basis 2) 120	(all berths) 120		
Pass. Space Ratio (basis 2) 43.4	(all berths) 43.4		
Officers Japanese	Dining Staff International		
Total Cabins	60		
Size Range (sq ft/m)	196-260/18.2-24.0		
Outside Cabins 60	Inside Cabins	0	
Single Cabins	0		
Supplement	$355 per day (any cabin)		
Balcony Cabins 8	Wheelchair Cabins	1	
Cabin Current 115 AC	Refrigerator All cabins		
Cabin TV Yes	VCR	Yes	
Dining Rooms 1	Sittings	1	
Elevators	1		

Casino	No	Slot Machines	No
Swimming Pools (outside) 1		(inside)	0
Whirlpools	1	Gymnasium	Yes
Sauna/Steam Room Yes/Yes		Massage	Yes
Self-Service Launderette			No
Movie Theater/Seats No		Library	Yes
Children's Facilities			No
Watersports Facilities		Aft platform, scuba,	
	snorkel, water-ski, Zodiacs		
Classification Society		Nippon Kaiji Kyokai	

RATINGS	SCORE
Ship: Condition/Cleanliness	8.7
Ship: Space/Flow/Comfort	8.2
Ship: Decor/Furnishings	8.4
Ship: Fitness/Watersports	8.6
Cabins: Comfort/Facilities	8.4
Cabins: Software	8.2
Food: Dining Room/Cuisine	8.7
Food: Buffets/Informal Dining	8.5
Food: Quality of Ingredients	8.7
Service: Dining Room	8.2
Service: Bars	8.3
Service: Cabins	8.1
Cruise: Entertainment	7.3
Cruise: Activities Program	7.3
Cruise: Hospitality Standard	8.7
OVERALL RATING	124.3

+ Has impressive contemporary looks and twin outboard funnels. Has a decompression chamber for scuba divers. Plenty of open deck and sunning space. Teakwood jogging track. Integrated, balanced East-West interior design concept, decor and color combinations. Clean, sophisticated decor throughout. Can be used as a two-class ship for "membership club" cruising. Tastefully furnished all-outside cabins feature blond wood cabinetry, three-sided mirrors, personal safe, mini-bar/refrigerator, safe, tea-making unit, cotton bathrobes, slippers, shoe horn, clothes brush and deep, full-sized bathtub.

— The small swimming pool is really a "dip" pool. Cabins with balconies have awkward balcony door handles. Bathroom toilet seats are too high, particularly for Japanese passengers. Watersports equipment is not used on the short cruises around the Japan coast. Room service items are at extra charge.

Dining Warm and inviting dining room features the freshest of foods from local ports of call. Features Japanese cuisine. Chefs and hotel staff are provided by the superb Palace Hotel in Tokyo.

Other Comments This is an excellent ship for watersports aficionados. Scuba equipment rental is extra. Port taxes are included. Gratuities are neither expected nor allowed.

mv Odessa ★★★+

OPERATES

VARIOUS CRUISES WORLDWIDE

Cruise Line	Black Sea Shipping	Casino	No
Former Names	Copenhagen	Swimming Pools (outside)	1
Gross Tonnage	13,252	Whirlpools	0
Builder	Vickers Ltd (UK)	Sauna/Steam Room	Yes/No
Original Cost	n/a	Self-Service Launderette	
Christened By	n/a	Movie Theater/Seats	
Entered Service	Jul 18, 1975/	Library	
Interior Design	n/a	Children's Facilities	
Country of Registry	Ukraine (ENTC)	Watersports Facilities	
Tel No 140-2777 Fax No	140-0223	Classification Society	

Casino	No
Slot Machines	Yes
Swimming Pools (outside) 1	(inside) 0
Whirlpools 0	Gymnasium Yes
Sauna/Steam Room Yes/No	Massage Yes
Self-Service Launderette	No
Movie Theater/Seats	Yes/152
Library	Yes
Children's Facilities	No
Watersports Facilities	None
Classification Society	Lloyd's Register

Length (ft/m)	447.1/136.30
Beam (ft/m) 70.6/21.52 Draft (ft/m)	19.0/5.81
Propulsion	diesel (11,950kW)
Propellers	2 (CP)
Decks 5 Crew	250
Pass. Capacity (basis 2) 482	(all berths) 570
Pass. Space Ratio (basis 2) 27.4	(all berths) 23.2
Officers	Russian/Ukrainian
Dining Staff	Russian/Ukrainian
Total Cabins	241
Size Range (sq ft/m)	109-375/10.0-34.8
Outside Cabins 241 Inside Cabins	0
Single Cabins 0 Supplement	50-100%
Balcony Cabins 0 Wheelchair Cabins	0
Cabin Current 220 AC Refrigerator	Suites only
Cabin TV Yes VCR	No
Dining Rooms 1 Sittings	2
Elevators	4

RATINGS	SCORE
Ship: Condition/Cleanliness	7.1
Ship: Space/Flow/Comfort	7.0
Ship: Decor/Furnishings	7.7
Ship: Fitness Facilities	5.5
Cabins: Comfort/Facilities	7.0
Cabins: Software	7.4
Food: Dining Room/Cuisine	6.8
Food: Buffets/Informal Dining	6.5
Food: Quality of Ingredients	6.6
Service: Dining Room	6.7
Service: Bars	6.5
Service: Cabins	7.0
Cruise: Entertainment	6.6
Cruise: Activities Program	6.3
Cruise: Hospitality Standard	7.2
OVERALL RATING	101.9

+ Handsome smaller ship has well-balanced traditional lines and profile. Maintenance and cleanliness are good. There is a good selection of public rooms, lounges and bars, most with very tasteful decor. Has a neat three-deck-high spiral staircase topped with glass skylight. Attractive balconied theater. All cabins are outside, completely new, somewhat small, but very tastefully furnished, with good closet and drawer space, and pastel colors. Artwork has been upgraded. Bathrobes provided in all cabins.

— Has a steep, narrow gangway in many ports.

Dining The charming Odessa restaurant is set high up in the ship and has intricate artwork on integral columns. Service is quite attentive from very attractive Ukrainian waitresses. The food product has been upgraded recently, but it's still quite basic, and there's a limited selection of breads, cheeses, and fruits.

Other Comments Neat, tidy ship that often operates worldwide under charter to various operators.

mts Odysseus ★★★

OPERATES

*3, 4 AND 7-DAY SOUTHERN
EUROPE CRUISES*

Cruise Line	Epirotiki Cruise Line	Casino	Yes	Slot Machines Yes
Former Names	Aquamarine/Marco Polo/	Swimming Pools (outside) 1		(inside) 0
	Princesa Isabel	Whirlpools	4	Gymnasium Yes
Gross Tonnage	12,000	Sauna/Steam Room Yes/No		Massage Yes
Builder	Society Espanola Shipyard (Spain)	Self-Service Launderette		No
Original Cost	n/a	Movie Theater/Seats		Yes/145
Christened By	n/a	Library		Yes
Entered Service	1962/Spring 1987	Children's Facilities		No
Interior Design	Arminio Lozzi	Watersports Facilities		None
Country of Registry	Greece (J4GU)	Classification Society		Lloyd's Register

Tel No	113-0652	Fax No	113-0252

RATINGS	SCORE
Length (ft/m)	483.1/147.30		

Beam (ft/m)	61.2/18.67	Draft (ft/m)	24.1/7.35
Propulsion		diesel (6,766kW)	
Propellers			2 (CP)
Decks	7	Crew	194
Pass. Capacity (basis 2) 454		(all berths) 484	
Pass. Space Ratio (basis 2) 26.4		(all berths) 24.7	
Officers	Greek	Dining Staff	Greek
Total Cabins			226
Size Range (sq ft/m)		102-280/9.5-26.0	
Outside Cabins	183	Inside Cabins	43
Single Cabins	0	Supplement	50%
Balcony Cabins	0	Wheelchair Cabins	0
Cabin Current	110 AC	Refrigerator	No
Cabin TV	No	VCR	No
Dining Rooms	2	Sittings	2
Elevators			1

RATINGS	SCORE
Ship: Condition/Cleanliness	6.9
Ship: Space/Flow/Comfort	6.5
Ship: Decor/Furnishings	6.8
Ship: Fitness Facilities	3.7
Cabins: Comfort/Facilities	6.4
Cabins: Software	6.9
Food: Dining Room/Cuisine	6.6
Food: Buffets/Informal Dining	6.3
Food: Quality of Ingredients	6.0
Service: Dining Room	7.3
Service: Bars	7.2
Service: Cabins	7.3
Cruise: Entertainment	5.4
Cruise: Activities Program	5.7
Cruise: Hospitality Standard	7.2
OVERALL RATING	96.2

+ This attractive-looking vessel has a balanced profile, and was acquired and completely reconstructed by Epirotiki in 1987. There is ample open deck and sunning space. Has twin teak-decked sheltered promenades. There is a good range of public rooms featuring pleasing Mediterranean decor, and some decent artwork throughout. The Taverna is especially popular with the younger set. Attractive, quite roomy, mostly outside cabins have convertible sofa-bed (a few have double beds), good closet and drawer space, and tasteful wood trim.

– Has steep gangway in most ports. The cabin bathrooms are small, particularly the shower stalls.

Dining The dining room is quite charming, though it tends to be noisy. Food is typically continental, and features several Greek dishes. Warm, attentive service in true Epirotiki style, but the menu choice is rather limited. The quality and selection of breads, cheeses, and fruits could be better.

Other Comments This ship is for those who want to cruise at modest cost, in warm surroundings, on a very comfortable vessel, in the Aegean and Mediterranean areas. Often chartered by learning enrichment tour operators.

tts Olympic ★★★+

OPERATES

*7-DAY AEGEAN/
MEDITERRANEAN CRUISES*

Cruise Line	Epirotiki Cruise Line
Former Names	FiestaMarina/Carnivale/
	Empress of Britain/Queen Anna Maria
Gross Tonnage	31,500
Builder	Fairfield Shipbuilding (UK)
Original Cost	UK£7,500,000
Christened By	H.M. Queen Elizabeth II/
	Ms Dayanara Torres
Entered Service	Apr 20, 1956/1994
Interior Design	Joe Farcus
Country of Registry	Greece

Tel No	n/a	Fax No	n/a
Length (ft/m)			640.0/195.08
Beam (ft/m) 87.0/26.51	Draft (ft/m)		29.0/8.84
Propulsion	steam turbine (22,400kW)		
Propellers			2 (FP)
Decks	9	Crew	550
Pass. Capacity (basis 2) 976	(all berths) 1,386		
Pass. Space Ratio (basis 2) 32.2	(all berths) 22.7		
Officers	Greek	Dining Staff	Greek
Total Cabins	488	Size Range (sq ft/m) n/a	
Outside Cabins	221	Inside Cabins	267
Single Cabins			0
Supplement	50% (cat.1-3)/100% (cat.4-12)		
Balcony Cabins	0	Wheelchair Cabins	0
Cabin Current	110 AC	Refrigerator	No
Cabin TV	No	VCR	No
Dining Rooms	1	Sittings	2

Elevators			4
Casino	Yes	Slot Machines	Yes
Swimming Pools (outside) 2		(inside)	1
Whirlpools	1	Gymnasium	Yes
Sauna/Steam Room Yes/No		Massage	Yes
Self-Service Launderette		No (has ironing room)	
Movie Theater/Seats			Yes/180
Library	No	Children's Facilities Yes	
Watersports Facilities			None
Classification Society		Lloyd's Register	

RATINGS	SCORE
Ship: Condition/Cleanliness	6.7
Ship: Space/Flow/Comfort	6.3
Ship: Decor/Furnishings	7.3
Ship: Fitness Facilities	5.3
Cabins: Comfort/Facilities	6.2
Cabins: Software	6.5
Food: Dining Room/Cuisine	7.1
Food: Buffets/Informal Dining	6.6
Food: Quality of Ingredients	6.2
Service: Dining Room	7.1
Service: Bars	7.2
Service: Cabins	7.3
Cruise: Entertainment	7.5
Cruise: Activities Program	6.5
Cruise: Hospitality Standard	7.5
OVERALL RATING	101.3

+ This solidly built former ocean liner has a midships funnel, while teak outdoor and glass-enclosed indoor promenade decks encircle the ship. Has had an extensive recent refurbishment. The interior colors are quite stimulating, and the public rooms have rather jazzy decor. The casino is large for a Europe-based ship. Has some delightful original woods and polished brass throughout her public spaces. Large whirlpool added, and new colorful tiled outdoor deck. There is a wide range of cabins, most of them large, some with rich wood furniture, all of them redecorated recently. Many cabins have third and fourth berths.

— She's an old ship, and the cabin bathrooms are small. Constant multilingual announcements are irritating. Expect long lines for embarkation, disembarkation, buffets, and shore excursions.

Dining The dining room is crowded, and noisy, but nicely redecorated. The food, be aware, is not for gourmets.

Other Comments Epirotiki Cruise Line provide good family cruising in an unsophisticated and very casual setting, for a first cruise at a decent price, to some fascinating destinations.

ms Oriana ★★★★+

OPERATES

12 TO 90-DAY VARIOUS CRUISES
WORLDWIDE

Cruise Line/Operator:	P&O Cruises	Casino Yes	Slot Machines Yes
Former Names	-	Swimming Pools (outside) 3	(inside) 0
Gross Tonnage	69,153	Whirlpools 5	Gymnasium Yes
Builder	Meyer Werft (Germany)	Sauna/Steam Room Yes/Yes	Massage Yes
Original Cost	UK£200 million	Self-Service Launderette	Yes
Christened By	H.R.H. Queen Elizabeth II	Movie Theater/Seats	Yes/189
Entered Service	Apr 9, 1995	Library	Yes
Interior Design	Tillberg/McNeece/Yran	Children's Facilities	Yes
Country of Registry	Great Britain (GVSN)	Watersports Facilities	None
Tel No 145-3403 Fax No	145-3404	Classification Society	Lloyd's Register
Length (ft/m)	853.0/260.0		
Beam (ft/m) 105.6/32.2 Draft (ft/m)	25.9/7.9	**RATINGS**	**SCORE**
Propulsion	diesel (47,750kW)	Ship: Condition/Cleanliness	9.2
Propellers	2 (CP)	Ship: Space/Flow/Comfort	9.0
Decks 10 Crew	760	Ship: Decor/Furnishings	9.2
Pass. Capacity (basis 2) 1,828 (all berths)	1,975	Ship: Fitness Facilities	8.7
Pass. Space Ratio (basis 2) 37.8 (all berths)	35.0	Cabins: Comfort/Facilities	8.7
Officers British Dining Staff	International	Cabins: Software	9.0
Total Cabins	914	Food: Dining Room/Cuisine	7.7
Size Range (sq ft/m)	151-501/14.0-46.5	Food: Buffets/Informal Dining	7.1
Outside Cabins 594 Inside Cabins	320	Food: Quality of Ingredients	7.5
Single Cabins 112 Supplement	Set rates	Service: Dining Room	8.2
Balcony Cabins 118 Wheelchair Cabins	8	Service: Bars	8.1
Cabin Current	110/220 AC	Service: Cabins	8.2
Refrigerator	Yes	Cruise: Entertainment	8.7
Cabin TV Yes VCR	Suites only	Cruise: Activities Program	7.0
Dining Rooms 2 Sittings	2	Cruise: Hospitality Standard	8.1
Elevators	10	OVERALL RATING	124.4

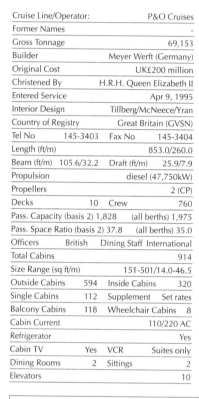

+ The ship is, thankfully, quite conventional, and is evolutionary rather than revolutionary. Capable of speedy long distance cruising. Has the largest stabilizers of any ship, covering an area of 231 sq ft (21.5m^2). She is a ship that takes Canberra's traditional appointments and public rooms and adds more up-to-date touches, together with better facilities and passenger flow, and a feeling of timeless elegance.

Her interiors are gentle and unabrasive, mild and assuring; warm, welcoming, relaxing, and restrained. Splendid amount of open deck and sunning space, important for her outdoors-loving British passengers. Has an extra-wide wrap-around outdoor promenade deck. Features inboard lifeboats as do so many ships today. The stern superstructure is nicely rounded and has several tiers that overlook an aft deck, pool and children's outdoor facilities. Inside, the well laid-out design provides good horizontal passenger flow and wide passageways. Noticeable are the fine detailed ceiling treatments. Being a ship for all types of people, specific areas have been designed to attract different age groups and lifestyles.

There is a four-deck-high atrium and waterfall; it is elegant but not glitzy, topped by a dome of Tiffany glass. The large number of public entertainment rooms provides plenty of choice. The Theatre Royal, designed by John Wyckham, is decorated in rich reds and created specifically for drama and light theatrical presentations. It has individually air-conditioned seats, an orchestra pit, revolving stage and excellent acoustics. Anderson's Lounge (named after the

founder members of the Peninsular Steam Navigation Company in the 1830s) features a series of 19th century marine paintings, and is decorated in the manner of a British gentleman's club. Although there's no fireplace, it's the most popular lounge.

The fine, restful library has a well-chosen selection of hardback books (a librarian would be a useful addition), skillfully crafted tables and some extremely comfortable chairs. Lord's Tavern is, without doubt, the most sporting place to pitch a beverage or two, decorated as it is in cricket memorabilia (indeed the ship's interior designer, John McNeece's own house stands on the site of the original Lord's cricket ground in London). Thackeray's (writing room) is named after William Makepeace Thackeray, a former P&O passenger. Carpeting throughout the ship is of excellent quality, much of it custom designed and made (100% wool). There are some outstanding pieces of sculpture that provide a living museum afloat, and original artwork by all-British artists that include tapestries and sculptures.

The health spa, run by Champney's, is located forward and atop ship, is quite large, and provides all the latest alternative therapy treatments. The co-ed sauna is a large facility (most ships have separate saunas for men and women).

Wide range of well-equipped cabin configurations and categories, including family cabins with extra beds (110 cabins can accommodate four persons). Some suites and cabins with balconies have an inter-connecting door, and include a trouser press, ironing board and iron, neatly tucked into a cupboard, binoculars, umbrella, a large atlas, and a second television. Bathrooms, however, are disappointing, with an ordinary sink; I expected a marble unit. The whirlpool bathtubs are good, however, although they have high sides to step over.

There is much use of rich, warm limed oak or cherrywood in the cabins, which makes even the least expensive four-berth cabin seem inviting. There's also a good number of cabins for single passengers. Bathrooms are compact, and feature art deco-style cabinets and lighting. Children and teens have their own "Club Oriana" programs with their own rooms ("Peter Pan" and "Decibels"), and outdoor pool for the children. There's also a special "night nursery" for small children (ages 2 to 5). The cabins also have a baby listening facility.

The most expensive suites are pleasant, but not at all impressive when compared to suites on other contemporary ships, although they do have a trouser press, ironing board and iron as part of their furnishings, as well as sliding glazed panels between bedroom and sitting room, and private balcony.

— Suite bathrooms are inferior to those on other like-sized ships. The theater seats would provide better stage sightlines if they had been staggered. The Pacific Lounge has too many pillars that obstruct sightlines. The aerobic exercise room and health spa are not connected (you first must go out of the spa, into a foyer, and then into the exercise room). Expect lines for embarkation, disembarkation, buffets, the Reception Desk, and shore tenders.

Dining The two restaurants, Peninsular, and Oriental, allocated according to the cabin grade and cabin chosen, are midships and aft. Both are quite handsome (each has tables for two, four, six, or eight). Both have interesting ceilings, chandeliers and decor. Oriental Restaurant has windows on three sides, including the stern. Has Anton Mosimann-designed signature dishes. The time allotted for meals, however, is quite short; thus, "eat and run" instead of "dining" tends to be the norm. Meals are fairly non-memorable, standard fare, and presentation is rather lacking, although I expect this to improve.

The light and airy indoor/outdoor Conservatory buffet café offers alternative light breakfast and luncheon buffets, and 24-hour self-service beverage stands. For the British market, an alternative restaurant featuring Indian food would have been a useful addition.

Other Comments Oriana is the first cruise ship specifically designed for the growing British market. This is a ship and not a hotel, however, something that will please the P&O traditionalists, and provide a fine cruise experience principally for British passengers who don't want to fly to get to their cruise ship.

Finally, port taxes and insurance are included for British passengers. For gratuities, allow about UK£3.00 per person, per day.

ms Orient Star ★★

OPERATES

VARIOUS SOUTHEAST ASIA CRUISES

Cruise Line	Pacific Cruise Company		
Former Names	Olga Sadovskaya		
Gross Tonnage	3,941		
Builder	Brodgradiliste Uljanik (Yugoslavia)		
Original Cost	n/a		
Christened By	n/a		
Entered Service	1977/1994		
Interior Design	n/a		
Country of Registry	Russia (ESWY)		
Tel No	140-0371	Fax No	140-0371
Length (ft/m)	328.1/100.01		
Beam (ft/m) 53.2/16.24	Draft (ft/m)	15.2/4.65	
Propulsion	diesel (3,884kW)		
Propellers	1 (FP)		
Decks	6	Crew	100
Pass. Capacity (basis 2) 96	(all berths) 188		
Pass. Space Ratio (basis 2) 41.0	(all berths) 20.9		
Officers	Russian		
Dining Staff	Russian/Ukrainian		
Total Cabins	48		
Size Range (sq ft/m)	n/a		
Outside Cabins	48	Inside Cabins	0
Single Cabins	0	Supplement	100%
Balcony Cabins	0	Wheelchair Cabins	0
Cabin Current	220 AC	Refrigerator	No
Cabin TV	No	VCR	No
Dining Rooms	1	Sittings	1
Elevators	0		

Casino	No	Slot Machines	No
Swimming Pools (outside) 1	(inside)	No	
Whirlpools	No	Gymnasium	No
Sauna/Steam Room Yes/No	Massage	No	
Self-Service Launderette	No		
Movie Theater/Seats	Yes/75		
Library	Yes		
Children's Facilities	No		
Watersports Facilities	None		
Classification Society	RS		

RATINGS	SCORE
Ship: Condition/Cleanliness	5.3
Ship: Space/Flow/Comfort	5.5
Ship: Decor/Furnishings	6.1
Ship: Fitness Facilities	3.0
Cabins: Comfort/Facilities	5.7
Cabins: Software	6.0
Food: Dining Room/Cuisine	5.8
Food: Buffets/Informal Dining	5.3
Food: Quality of Ingredients	5.6
Service: Dining Room	6.2
Service: Bars	6.4
Service: Cabins	6.5
Cruise: Entertainment	4.2
Cruise: Activities Program	4.6
Cruise: Hospitality Standard	6.1
OVERALL RATING	82.3

+ Intimate small ship has a well-balanced profile. Has an ice-hardened hull suitable for soft expedition cruising. Reasonable open deck space for ship size. Recently underwent extensive refurbishment. Outdoor observation deck and enclosed promenade deck for inclement weather. Charming forward music lounge has wooden dance floor. Rich, highly polished wood paneling throughout. Lovely winding brass-railed main staircase. Good cinema/lecture room.

— The cabins are very compact and spartan, but most can accommodate four persons. Has a steep, narrow gangway in ports of call. The cabin insulation is rather poor.

Dining Comfortable dining room has ocean views. Limited choice of food, but service is friendly and quite attentive. Poor selection of breads, fruits, and cheeses.

Other Comments This ship is very small, yet reasonably comfortable, and has plenty of character, but don't expect much finesse from the service aspects of the cruise.

mv Orient Venus ★★★★

OPERATES

VARIOUS JAPAN/SOUTH EAST ASIA CRUISES

Cruise Line	Japan Cruise Line		
	(Nippon Cruise Kyakusen)		
Former Names	-		
Gross Tonnage	21,884		
Builder	Ishikawajima Heavy Industries (Japan)		
Original Cost	$150 million		
Christened By	Mr Yasuo Iritani		
Entered Service	Jul 1990		
Interior Design	Daimaru Design & Engineering		
Country of Registry	Japan (JFYU)		
Tel No	120-1731	Fax No	120-1731
Length (ft/m)	570.8/174.00		
Beam (ft/m) 78.7/24.00	Draft (ft/m)	21.3/6.52	
Propulsion	diesel (18,540bhp)		
Propellers	2 (CP)		
Decks	8	Crew	120
Pass. Capacity (basis 2) 390	(all berths) 606		
Pass. Space Ratio (basis 2) 56.1	(all berths) 36.1		
Officers	Japanese		
Dining Staff	Japanese/Asian		
Total Cabins	195		
Size Range (sq ft/m)	183-592/17.0-55.0		
Outside Cabins	195	Inside Cabins	0
Single Cabins	0	Supplement	100%
Balcony Cabins	2	Wheelchair Cabins	0
Cabin Current	110 AC	Refrigerator	All cabins
Cabin TV	Yes	VCR	No
Dining Rooms	2	Sittings	1

Elevators			3
Casino	No	Slot Machines	No
Swimming Pools (outside) 1		(inside)	0
Whirlpools	0	Gymnasium	Yes
Sauna/Steam Room	No/No	Massage	No
Self-Service Launderette			Yes
Movie Theater/Seats			Yes/606
Library	Yes	Children's Facilities	No
Watersports Facilities			None
Classification Society		Nippon Kaiji Kyokai	

RATINGS	SCORE
Ship: Condition/Cleanliness	8.1
Ship: Space/Flow/Comfort	8.0
Ship: Decor/Furnishings	8.0
Ship: Fitness Facilities	7.8
Cabins: Comfort/Facilities	7.8
Cabins: Software	7.5
Food: Dining Room/Cuisine	7.4
Food: Buffets/Informal Dining	7.2
Food: Quality of Ingredients	7.0
Service: Dining Room	7.7
Service: Bars	7.8
Service: Cabins	7.6
Cruise: Entertainment	7.0
Cruise: Activities Program	7.2
Cruise: Hospitality Standard	7.9
OVERALL RATING	114.0

+ New conventional-shaped ship has a graceful profile. Night and Day lounge set at funnel base looking forward over swimming pool. Expansive open deck and sunning space. Windows of the Orient is a small attractive, peaceful forward observation lounge. Superb conference facilities with small conference room and main lecture room with 620 moveable seats. Fine array of public rooms with tasteful and very inviting decor throughout. Horseshoe-shaped main lounge has fine sightlines to platform stage. Expansive open sunning deck aft of funnel. Four cabin grades provide variety of well-equipped, all-outside, Western-style cabins. Two suites are huge and have private balconies.

— Does not really cater to individual passengers well. The decor is rather plain in many public rooms.

Dining Very attractive main dining room. Romanesque Grill is unusual, with classic period decor and high, elegant ceiling. Features reasonably good, but rather commercial Japanese cuisine exclusively.

Other Comments This Western-style ship will provide its mostly Japanese corporate passengers with extremely comfortable surroundings, and a superb cruise and seminar/learning environment and experience.

mts Orpheus ★★★

OPERATES
14-DAY SOUTHERN EUROPE CRUISES

Cruise Line	Epirotiki Cruise Line/Swan Hellenic		Casino	No	Slot Machines	No
Former Names	Thesus/Munster I/Munster		Swimming Pools (outside) 1	(inside)	0
Gross Tonnage	5,092		Whirlpools	0	Gymnasium	No
Builder	Harland & Wolff (UK)		Sauna/Steam Room No/No	Massage	No
Original Cost	n/a		Self-Service Launderette	No
Christened By	n/a		Movie Theater/Seats	No
Entered Service	1952/1969		Library	Yes
Interior Design	Arminio Lozzi		Children's Facilities	No
Country of Registry	Greece (SXUI)		Watersports Facilities	None
Tel No 113-3165 Fax No 113-3165			Classification Society	Lloyd's Register

Length (ft/m)	374.8/114.26
Beam (ft/m) 50.1/15.30 Draft (ft/m) 16.0/4.88	

RATINGS	SCORE
Propulsion	diesel (4,119kW)		Ship: Condition/Cleanliness	6.6
Propellers	2 (FP)		Ship: Space/Flow/Comfort	6.4
Decks 6 Crew 140		Ship: Decor/Furnishings	6.7
Pass. Capacity (basis 2) 304 (all berths) 310		Ship: Fitness Facilities	3.9
Pass. Space Ratio (basis 2) 16.7 (all berths) 16.4		Cabins: Comfort/Facilities	6.0
Officers Greek Dining Staff Greek		Cabins: Software	6.7
Total Cabins 152		Food: Dining Room/Cuisine	6.7
Size Range (sq ft/m) n/a		Food: Buffets/Informal Dining	6.2
Outside Cabins 117 Inside Cabins 35		Food: Quality of Ingredients	6.0
Single Cabins 7 Supplement 50-90%		Service: Dining Room	7.5
Balcony Cabins 0 Wheelchair Cabins 0		Service: Bars	7.2
Cabin Current 220 AC		Service: Cabins	7.4
Refrigerator No		Cruise: Entertainment	7.2
Cabin TV No VCR No		Cruise: Activities Program	7.0
Dining Rooms 1 Sittings Open		Cruise: Hospitality Standard	7.9
Elevators 0		OVERALL RATING	99.4

+ Traditional ship profile, with small, squat funnel. Charming and very well maintained. Ample open deck and sunning space for a ship of this size, including a wrap-around outdoor promenade deck. Comfortable public rooms with Mediterranean decor, good fabrics, and fine artwork. Cabins are compact but nicely appointed and quite adequate. Informality is the order of the day. The ship itself is secondary (there is speculation she will be replaced in 1996 by another ship), but has a very homely ambiance, and operates on a long-term charter to Swan Hellenic for a program of outstanding, in-depth life-enrichment cruises. Repeat passengers are known, rather proudly, as "Swans."

— High density means that public rooms are always crowded when the ship is full. There is a limited amount of closet, drawer, and storage space.

Dining The dining room is quite attractive and features an open seating policy. Attentive, friendly service from single-nationality crew. The food itself is quite reasonable, but certainly not memorable, and the selection of breads, cheeses, and fruits is limited.

Other Comments The company features a cast of excellent guest lecturers who provide informed, yet informal presentations aboard all cruises. Insurance, gratuities and all shore excursions are included for the ship's mainly British passengers.

mv Pacific Princess ★★★★

Cruise Line	Princess Cruises
Former Names	Sea Venture
Gross Tonnage	20,636
Builder	Rheinstahl Nordseewerke (Germany)
Original Cost	$25 million
Christened By	n/a
Entered Service	May 14, 1971/Apr 1975
Interior Design	Robert Tillberg
Country of Registry	Great Britain (GBCF)
Tel No 144-0212 Fax No	144-0212
Length (ft/m)	553.6/168.74
Beam (ft/m) 80.8/24.64 Draft (ft/m)	25.2/7.70
Propulsion	diesel (13,240kW)
Propellers	2 (CP)
Decks 7 Crew	350
Pass. Capacity (basis 2) 610 (all berths)	717
Pass. Space Ratio (basis 2) 33.8 (all berths)	28.7
Officers British Dining Staff	International
Total Cabins	305
Size Range (sq ft/m)	126-443/11.7-41.0
Outside Cabins 238 Inside Cabins	67
Single Cabins 2 Supplement	25-100%
Balcony Cabins 0 Wheelchair Cabins	4
Cabin Current	110/220 AC
Refrigerator	Category A/B/C/D/DD only
Cabin TV Yes VCR	No
Dining Rooms 1 Sittings	2
Elevators	4

Casino	Yes	Slot Machines	Yes
Swimming Pools (outside) 2		(inside)	0
Whirlpools	0	Gymnasium	Yes
Sauna/Steam Room Yes/No		Massage	Yes
Self-Service Launderette			No
Movie Theater/Seats			Yes/250
Library			Yes
Children's Facilities			No
Watersports Facilities			None
Classification Society			Lloyd's Register

RATINGS	SCORE
Ship: Condition/Cleanliness	7.7
Ship: Space/Flow/Comfort	7.6
Ship: Decor/Furnishings	8.0
Ship: Fitness Facilities	6.2
Cabins: Comfort/Facilities	7.5
Cabins: Software	7.6
Food: Dining Room/Cuisine	7.3
Food: Buffets/Informal Dining	7.0
Food: Quality of Ingredients	6.7
Service: Dining Room	7.9
Service: Bars	8.0
Service: Cabins	7.8
Cruise: Entertainment	8.1
Cruise: Activities Program	7.8
Cruise: Hospitality Standard	8.0
OVERALL RATING	113.2

+ This is a well-proportioned, handsome ship with high superstructure and quite graceful lines. Has been recently upgraded and is well maintained. Has plenty of good open deck space and decent sunning areas. Spacious public areas have wide passageways. One swimming pool has magrodome roof for use in inclement weather. Tasteful earth-toned decor throughout, with complementary artwork. Good movie theater. Suites and all other cabins are quite roomy and well appointed. Excellent production shows and general entertainment. Very smartly dressed officers and crew. Bathrobes for all passengers

— No wrap-around outdoor promenade deck, and the present teak decking is badly worn in many places. The outdoor lido deck's buffet area is untidy.

Dining The dining room (non-smoking) is located on a lower deck, but has nice, light decor and feels comfortable and spacious. Good service and fairly good food, although standards have been slipping, as a result of discounted fares.

Other Comments This ship is definitely for the older passenger, is quite elegant and moderately expensive, but will cruise you in very comfortable, elegant surroundings, in style. However, it is small compared to Princess Cruises' newer ships and cannot offer the same range of facilities and services.

ms Polaris ★★★★

OPERATES

WORLDWIDE EXPEDITION CRUISES

Cruise Line	Special Expeditions	Swimming Pools (outside)	0
Former Names	Lindblad Polaris/Oresund	Whirlpools 0 Exercise Room	No
Gross Tonnage	2,214	Sauna/Steam Room Yes/No Massage	No
Builder	Aalborg Vaerft (Denmark)	Self-Service Launderette	No
Original Cost	n/a	Lecture/Film Room	No
Christened By	n/a	Library	Yes
Entered Service	1960/May 6, 1987	Zodiacs	8
Interior Design	G. Unnar Svensson	Helicopter Pad	No
Country of Registry	Bahamas (C6CB8)	Watersports Facilities	None
Tel No 110-4424 Fax No	110-3276	Classification Society	Bureau Veritas
Length (ft/m)	236.6/72.12		
Beam (ft/m) 42.7/13.03 Draft (ft/m)	13.7/4.30	**RATINGS**	**SCORE**
Propulsion	diesel (2,354kW)	Ship: Condition/Cleanliness	7.3
Propellers	2 (CP)	Ship: Space/Flow/Comfort	5.7
Decks 4 Crew	43	Ship: Expedition Equipment	7.6
Pass. Capacity (basis 2) 82	(all berths) 84	Ship: Decor/Furnishings	7.4
Pass. Space Ratio (basis 2) 27.0	(all berths) 26.3	Cabins: Comfort/Facilities	5.6
Officers Swedish Dining Staff	Filipino	Cabins: Software	6.4
Total Cabins	41	Food: Dining Room/Cuisine	7.6
Size Range (sq ft/m)	100-230/9.2-21.3	Food: Buffets/Informal Dining	7.3
Outside Cabins 41 Inside Cabins	0	Food: Quality of Ingredients	6.9
Single Cabins 0 Supplement	50%	Service: Dining Room	7.7
Balcony Cabins 0 Wheelchair Cabins	0	Service: Bars	7.5
Cabin Current 220 AC Refrigerator	No	Service: Cabins	7.6
Cabin TV No VCR	No	Cruise: Itineraries/Operations	8.0
Dining Rooms	1 (open seating)	Cruise: Lecture Program	7.8
Elevators	0	Cruise: Hospitality Standard	8.1
Casino No Slot Machines	No	OVERALL RATING	108.5

+ This "soft" expedition cruise vessel, of modest proportions, sports a dark blue hull and white superstructure. Well maintained. Sports a fantail and improved aft outdoor lounge area. Carries Zodiacs and a glass-bottom boat. Tidy Scandinavian interior furnishings and decor, with lots of wood trim. The cabins are quite roomy and nicely appointed, but there's little drawer space. Some have been refurbished, and feature large (lower) beds with wooden headboards. Each has a hairdryer. Cabin keys are not used. Friendly, very intimate atmosphere on board. Excellent lecturers and nature observers, and a restful, well-stocked library.

— There are few public rooms. There is no cabin service menu. Cabin bathrooms are really tiny.

Dining Dining room has big picture windows. Seating is now at individual tables for improved access. Has very good food, with major emphasis on fish and seafood dishes. There is also a fine wine list. Breakfast and lunch are buffet-style. Friendly service from a caring, attentive staff.

Other Comments There is no formal entertainment, and no one needs it, but there are always specialist lecturers accompanying all cruises. This is a delightful vessel to choose for your next destination- and learning-intensive "soft" expedition cruise experience.

mts Princesa Amorosa ★★+

OPERATES
7-DAY MEDITERRANEAN CRUISES

Cruise Line	Louis Cruise Lines	Casino	Yes	Slot Machines	Yes

Cruise Line	Louis Cruise Lines
Former Names	Galaxias/Galaxy/Scottish Coast
Gross Tonnage	5,026
Builder	Harland & Wolff (UK)
Original Cost	n/a
Christened By	Mr Costakis Loizou
Entered Service	1957/July 2, 1990
Interior Design	P. Yapanis
Country of Registry	Cyprus (P3NE3)
Tel No none Fax No	none
Length (ft/m)	342.2/104.32
Beam (ft/m) 52.6/16.06 Draft (ft/m)	15.7/4.81
Propulsion	diesel 4,781kW)
Propellers	2 (FP)
Decks 6 Crew	130
Pass. Capacity (basis 2) 284 (all berths)	327
Pass. Space Ratio (basis 2) 17.6 (all berths)	15.3
Officers	Cypriot/Greek
Dining Staff	International
Total Cabins	142
Size Range (sq ft/m)	107.6-172.2/10.0-16.0
Outside Cabins 115 Inside Cabins	27
Single Cabins 0 Supplement	50%
Balcony Cabins 0 Wheelchair Cabins	0
Cabin Current 220 AC Refrigerator	No
Cabin TV No VCR	No
Dining Rooms 1 Sittings	2
Elevators	0

Casino	Yes	Slot Machines	Yes
Swimming Pools (outside) 1		(inside)	0
Whirlpools	0	Gymnasium	No
Sauna/Steam Room No/No		Massage	No
Self-Service Launderette			No
Movie Theater/Seats			No
Library			Yes
Children's Facilities			No
Watersports Facilities			None
Classification Society			Lloyd's Register

RATINGS	SCORE
Ship: Condition/Cleanliness	5.6
Ship: Space/Flow/Comfort	5.2
Ship: Decor/Furnishings	6.0
Ship: Fitness Facilities	4.0
Cabins: Comfort/Facilities	5.8
Cabins: Software	6.1
Food: Dining Room/Cuisine	6.1
Food: Buffets/Informal Dining	5.9
Food: Quality of Ingredients	5.8
Service: Dining Room	6.6
Service: Bars	6.2
Service: Cabins	6.3
Cruise: Entertainment	5.0
Cruise: Activities Program	5.1
Cruise: Hospitality Standard	6.6
OVERALL RATING	86.3

+ This older vessel has fairly spacious open decks for her size. Interesting maroon wrought iron staircase balustrades show her former British heritage. Public rooms have been refurbished. Earth-tone colors used to good effect, creating a mild sense of spaciousness. Most cabins are outside and are quite comfortable, with crisp Mediterranean colors and some wood trim, but they are small, and bathrooms do show their age. Pleasant lounge and bar for socializing, with comfortable seating and warm decor. The ambiance aboard is delightfully warm and friendly.

— Limited number of public rooms and facilities. Has a steep, narrow gangway in some ports. The swimming pool is really only a "dip" pool. Cabins above the disco are noisy.

Dining The dining room has portholes and is quite cheery. Food is decidedly Mediterranean, with reasonable choice, and excellent presentation. Full vegetarian menu available. Service is quite cheerful, and the staff try hard. Both à la carte and buffet meals are featured.

Other Comments This small white ship is quite old, but still in good shape (seeing the bridge is like stepping back in time), and she is a hardy, stable ship at sea. She was purchased by her present owners in 1989. This ship is crowded when full, but offers a reasonably pleasant cruise experience if your expectations are not too high.

mv Princesa Cypria ★★

Cruise Line	Louis Cruise Lines	Elevators	2
Former Names	Asia Angel/Lu Jiang/	Casino	Yes Slot Machines Yes
	Princesse Margrethe	Swimming Pools (outside) 0	(inside) 0
Gross Tonnage	9,984	Whirlpools 0	Gymnasium No
Builder	Cantieri del Terreno (Italy)	Sauna/Steam Room No/No	Massage No
Original Cost	n/a	Self-Service Launderette	No
Christened By	Mr Costakis Loizou	Movie Theater/Seats No	Library No
Entered Service	1968/July 1, 1989	Children's Facilities	No
Interior Design	A. Lozzi/P. Yapanis	Watersports Facilities	None
Country of Registry	Cyprus (P3CQ3)	Classification Society	Det Norske Veritas
Tel No none Fax No	none		
Length (ft/m)	409.9/124.95	**RATINGS**	**SCORE**
Beam (ft/m) 63.1/19.25 Draft (ft/m)	20.9/5.40	Ship: Condition/Cleanliness	5.4
Propulsion	diesel (12,000bhp)	Ship: Space/Flow/Comfort	5.3
Propellers	2 (FP)	Ship: Decor/Furnishings	6.1
Decks 6 Crew	180	Ship: Fitness Facilities	4.1
Pass. Capacity (basis 2) 548	(all berths) 633	Cabins: Comfort/Facilities	6.0
Pass. Space Ratio (basis 2) 18.2	(all berths) 15.7	Cabins: Software	6.2
Officers	Greek/Cypriot	Food: Dining Room/Cuisine	5.9
Dining Staff	International	Food: Buffets/Informal Dining	5.7
Total Cabins	274	Food: Quality of Ingredients	5.6
Size Range (sq ft/m)	n/a	Service: Dining Room	6.0
Outside Cabins 144 Inside Cabins	129	Service: Bars	6.2
Single Cabins 0 Supplement	50%	Service: Cabins	6.3
Balcony Cabins 0 Wheelchair Cabins	0	Cruise: Entertainment	5.2
Cabin Current 220 AC Refrigerator	No	Cruise: Activities Program	5.0
Cabin TV No VCR	No	Cruise: Hospitality Standard	5.7
Dining Rooms 2 Sittings Open (Buffets)		OVERALL RATING	84.7

+ Offers a low-cost way to visit several ports. The public rooms are basically attractive. She has a very warm atmosphere, and lovers of old ships will find the ship very pleasant.

— Low foredeck is typical of this former ferry, whose profile is stubby and poorly balanced, particularly at the stern, where some new cabins have been added. Open deck and sunning space is very limited. Exterior maintenance needs more work. She is an extremely high density ship, which means public rooms are always crowded. Low ceilings and too many support pillars create a rather confined feeling. Has very small and spartan cabins with virtually no closet and drawer space, and some 103 are without private facilities. Bathrooms are tiny. Expect lines for buffets and shore excursions when the ship is full.

Dining One dining room is located high up and forward and has large picture windows, while a second is set amidships. The food is adequate, and basic, but no more, and service comes without finesse. In a word—it is disappointing.

Other Comments Carries both cars and passengers on short voyages. This vessel is for cruisegoers looking for really low fares, and completely unpretentious surroundings, in a cruise that goes to the Holy Land.

mv Princesa Marissa ★★★

OPERATES

2 AND 3-DAY EGYPT/ISRAEL CRUISES (YEAR-ROUND)

Cruise Line	Louis Cruise Lines		
Former Names	Finnhansa/Princessan		
Gross Tonnage	10,487		
Builder	Wartsila (Finland)		
Original Cost	n/a		
Christened By	Mr Costakis Loizou		
Entered Service	1966/1 June, 1987		
Interior Design	G. Petrides/P. Yapanis		
Country of Registry	Cyprus (P3HO2)		
Tel No	none	Fax No	none
Length (ft/m)		440.6/134.30	
Beam (ft/m) 65.2/19.90	Draft (ft/m)	18.7/5.70	
Propulsion		diesel (10,300kW)	
Propellers		2 (CP)	
Decks	9	Crew	185
Pass. Capacity (basis 2) 628		(all berths) 839	
Pass. Space Ratio (basis 2) 16.6		(all berths) 12.4	
Officers		Cypriot/Greek	
Dining Staff		International	
Total Cabins		314	
Size Range (sq ft/m)		75.3-226.0/7.0-21.0	
Outside Cabins	148	Inside Cabins	166
Single Cabins	0	Supplement	50%
Balcony Cabins	0	Wheelchair Cabins	0
Cabin Current		220 AC	
Refrigerator		No	
Cabin TV	No	VCR	No
Dining Rooms	2	Sittings	2

Elevators			1
Casino	Yes	Slot Machines	Yes
Swimming Pools (outside) 0		(inside)	0
Whirlpools	0	Gymnasium	No
Sauna/Steam Room Yes/No		Massage	No
Self-Service Launderette			No
Movie Theater/Seats	No	Library	No
Children's Facilities			Yes
Watersports Facilities			None
Classification Society		Det Norske Veritas	

RATINGS	SCORE
Ship: Condition/Cleanliness	6.1
Ship: Space/Flow/Comfort	6.0
Ship: Decor/Furnishings	5.8
Ship: Fitness Facilities	5.6
Cabins: Comfort/Facilities	6.7
Cabins: Software	7.0
Food: Dining Room/Cuisine	5.8
Food: Buffets/Informal Dining	5.8
Food: Quality of Ingredients	5.3
Service: Dining Room	6.0
Service: Bars	5.8
Service: Cabins	6.1
Cruise: Entertainment	5.1
Cruise: Activities Program	5.3
Cruise: Hospitality Standard	6.0
OVERALL RATING	91.4

+ Her interiors are very smart and tidy, and the ship is quite well maintained. The public room decor is very attractive, with warm colors and with well-designed fabrics and soft furnishings. Has small conference facilities. Standard cabins are quite smart and functional. A whole section of new cabins, added in 1995, are of a good size, have picture windows, and decor is bright and cheerful. They also have excellent bathrooms.

— High passenger density. Also has low ceilings, typical of ferry construction. Limited open deck and sunning space. Few crew for so many passengers. Passengers must board through the aft car deck, but it all works and is no real hardship.

Dining The two dining rooms are quite attractive (the forward one is more intimate). Both à la carte and buffet-style meals are featured, and the menu includes three entrees. There is also a full vegetarian menu. Comfortable dining chairs. Good breads and ice cream sundaes.

Other Comments This former passenger-car ferry has a square stern, twin funnels and a short, somewhat stubby bow. This high-density vessel offers transportation, low fares, and food that is attractively presented. She is quite popular with Swedish passengers, who simply want an unsophisticated cruise in unstuffy surroundings. This ship provides year-round short cruises that represent very good value for money, and include all shore excursions in Egypt and Israel.

mv Princesa Victoria ★★★

OPERATES

2 AND 3-DAY EGYPT/ISRAEL CRUISES

Cruise Line	Louis Cruise Lines	Casino	Yes	Slot Machines	Yes
Former Names	The Victoria/Victoria/	Swimming Pools (outside) 2	(inside)	0
	Dunottar Castle	Whirlpools	0	Gymnasium	Yes
Gross Tonnage	14,583	Sauna/Steam Room Yes/No	Massage	No
Builder	Harland & Wolff (UK)	Self-Service Launderette	No
Original Cost	n/a	Movie Theater/Seats	Yes/250
Christened By	Mr Costakis Loizou	Library	Yes
Entered Service	Jul 3, 1936/Jan 15, 1993	Children's Facilities	Yes
Interior Design	A&M Katzourakis	Watersports Facilities	None
Country of Registry	Cyprus (P3YG4)	Classification Society	Lloyd's Register

Tel No 110-1627 Fax No 110-1630	
Length (ft/m) 572.8/174.60	
Beam (ft/m) 71.9/21.92 Draft (ft/m) 27.8/8.50	
Propulsion diesel (10,450kW)	
Propellers 2 (FP)	
Decks 7 Crew 230	
Pass. Capacity (basis 2) 566 (all berths) 750	
Pass. Space Ratio (basis 2) 25.7 (all berths) 19.4	
Officers Cypriot/Greek Dining Staff International	
Total Cabins 287	
Size Range (sq ft/m) 156.0-258.3/14.5-24.0	
Outside Cabins 216 Inside Cabins 71	
Single Cabins 8 Supplement 50%	
Balcony Cabins 0 Wheelchair Cabins 0	
Cabin Current 115 AC Refrigerator Suites only	
Cabin TV Yes VCR No	
Dining Rooms 1 Sittings 2	
Elevators 3	

RATINGS	SCORE
Ship: Condition/Cleanliness	6.5
Ship: Space/Flow/Comfort	6.0
Ship: Decor/Furnishings	6.1
Ship: Fitness Facilities	5.3
Cabins: Comfort/Facilities	6.8
Cabins: Software	7.0
Food: Dining Room/Cuisine	6.6
Food: Buffets/Informal Dining	6.1
Food: Quality of Ingredients	5.7
Service: Dining Room	6.3
Service: Bars	6.0
Service: Cabins	6.3
Cruise: Entertainment	5.6
Cruise: Activities Program	5.5
Cruise: Hospitality Standard	6.7
OVERALL RATING	92.5

+ This ship has been well maintained, despite her age. The center stairway is real art deco-style. Good amount of open deck space. Friendly ambiance aboard. Cabins are quite spacious, with heavy-duty furniture and fittings. Suite rooms are cavernous, and large bathrooms come with deep, full bathtubs.

— The Riviera Club is a contemporary room that's totally out of keeping with the rest of ship. Repetitive announcements are irritating. Poor separation of smokers and non-smokers. You'll find lines for buffets. There are no showers at the twin swimming pools.

Dining The dining room is set low down, but is comfortable, and has a fine two-deck-high center section with barrel-shaped ceiling, and with music balcony and lots of wood paneling. The standard of cuisine is good, particularly for the price you pay. There are three entrees, as well as a complete vegetarian menu. Salads, bakery items, and fruits are reasonable.

Other Comments This is a solidly constructed ship of vintage years that has a classic liner profile. Provides a good cruise experience for first-time cruisers, in pleasant surroundings, and at a most realistic price. Represents outstanding value for money, particularly for those seeking an add-on to their hotel vacation in Cyprus.

mts Queen Elini ★

Cruise Line	Vergina Cruises	Casino No	Slot Machines No
Former Names	City of Rhodos/33 Orientales	Swimming Pools (outside) 1	(inside) 0
Gross Tonnage	6,497	Whirlpools 0	Gymnasium No
Builder	Society Espanola de	Sauna/Steam Room No/No	Massage No
	Construciones Navale (Spain)	Self-Service Launderette	No
Original Cost	n/a	Movie Theater/Seats	No
Christened By	n/a	Library No	Children's Facilities No
Entered Service	1966/1995	Watersports Facilities	None
Interior Design	n/a	Classification Society	American Bureau
Country of Registry	Greece (SYXO)		of Shipping
Tel No 113-3131 Fax No 113-3131			
Length (ft/m)	427.5/130.31	**RATINGS**	**SCORE**
Beam (ft/m) 56.7/17.30 Draft (ft/m) 13.8/4.21		Ship: Condition/Cleanliness	5.4
Propulsion	diesel (5,737kW)	Ship: Space/Flow/Comfort	4.4
Propellers	2 (FP)	Ship: Decor/Furnishings	5.6
Decks 5 Crew 160		Ship: Fitness Facilities	3.0
Pass. Capacity (basis 2) 416 (all berths) 503		Cabins: Comfort/Facilities	5.3
Pass. Space Ratio (basis 2) 15.6 (all berths) 12.9		Cabins: Software	5.5
Officers Greek Dining Staff Greek		Food: Dining Room/Cuisine	5.2
Total Cabins	208	Food: Buffets/Informal Dining	5.0
Size Range (sq ft/m)	n/a	Food: Quality of Ingredients	4.9
Outside Cabins 144 Inside Cabins 64		Service: Dining Room	6.0
Single Cabins 0 Supplement 100%		Service: Bars	5.8
Balcony Cabins 0 Wheelchair Cabins 0		Service: Cabins	6.0
Cabin Current 220 AC Refrigerator No		Cruise: Entertainment	4.6
Cabin TV No VCR No		Cruise: Activities Program	4.8
Dining Rooms 1 Sittings 2		Cruise: Hospitality Standard	5.0
Elevators 0		OVERALL RATING	76.5

+ The public rooms are aft, away from cabins, so noise in them is minimized. Has a long, unattractive profile (this ship was rebuilt from a former Argentinean coastal ferry), but it's alright for the passenger who wants a low-grade cruise experience. Except for some "suites," the cabins are small and barely adequate.

— This very high-density vessel is cramped even when not full. Has only two main public rooms plus a dining room. Has a small swimming pool, and not much open deck space for sunning. Cabin bathrooms are *tiny*, and spartan. The ship's decor is well worn, unclean, and needs some refurbishment. There are too many announcements. Steep gangway in most ports.

Dining The dining room is mildly attractive, but has a low ceiling and is very noisy. The cuisine, in a word, is basic, low-budget food that is unattractively presented and quite mediocre. Limited selection of breads, cheeses and fruits. The service is adequate, but there's not even a flicker of finesse.

Other Comments This ship, now getting a little long in the tooth, caters to those who need to cruise on a very limited budget, don't mind noise, or crowded places. Recently acquired by Vergina Cruises, a division of Vergina Lines, the Piraeus-based ferry company. Operates seasonally to Egypt and Israel.

tsmv Queen Elizabeth 2 ★★★★★ *to* ★★★★

OPERATES

5-DAY SCHEDULED TRANSATLANTIC SERVICE AND CARIBBEAN/ EUROPE/WORLD CRUISES

Cruise Line	Cunard	Casino	Yes	Slot Machines Yes
Former Names	-	Swimming Pools (outside) 1	(inside)	2
Gross Tonnage	70,327	Whirlpools	4	Gymnasium Yes
Builder	Upper Clyde Shipbuilders (UK)	Sauna/Steam Room Yes/Yes	Massage	Yes
Original Cost	UK£29,091,000	Self-Service Launderette		Yes (12 machines)
Christened By	H.M. Queen Elizabeth II	Movie Theater/Seats		Yes/531
Entered Service	May 2, 1969	Library Yes	Children's Facilities Yes	
Interior Design	Dennis Lennon & Partners	Watersports Facilities		None
Country of Registry	Great Britain (GBTT)	Classification Society		Lloyd's Register

Tel No 144-0412 Fax No 144-1331		Ratings:			
Length (ft/m)	963.0/293.50	(a) Grill Class; (b) Deluxe Class; (c) Premium Class			
Beam (ft/m) 105.1/32.03 Draft (ft/m) 32.4/9.87		**RATINGS SCORE**	**(a)**	**(b)**	**(c)**
Propulsion	diesel-electric (99,900kW)	Ship: Condition/Cleanliness	9.1	8.6	7.7
Propellers	2 (CP)	Ship: Space/Flow/Comfort	9.1	8.4	7.6
Decks 13 Crew	1,015	Ship: Decor/Furnishings	9.1	8.5	7.8
Pass. Capacity (basis 2) 1,756 (all berths) 1,892		Ship: Fitness Facilities	9.0	9.0	9.0
Pass. Space Ratio (basis 2) 40.0 (all berths) 37.1		Cabins: Comfort/Facilities	9.2	8.5	7.7
Officers British Dining Staff British/International		Cabins: Software	9.0	8.6	7.8
Total Cabins	936	Food: Dining Room/Cuisine	9.3	7.6	6.6
Size Range (sq ft/m)	107-785/10.0-73.0	Food: Buffets/Informal Dining	8.3	8.3	8.3
Outside Cabins 665 Inside Cabins	271	Food: Quality of Ingredients	9.3	8.2	7.0
Single Cabins 116 Supplement 75-100%		Service: Dining Room	9.0	7.2	6.6
Balcony Cabins 33 Wheelchair Cabins 4		Service: Bars	8.8	8.5	8.0
Cabin Current	110/220 AC	Service: Cabins	9.1	8.5	7.0
Refrigerator	All Grill-Class cabins	Cruise: Entertainment	8.3	8.4	8.5
Cabin TV All cabins VCR All Grill-Class cabins		Cruise: Activities Program	8.6	8.4	8.6
Dining Rooms 5 Sittings 1 (2 in Mauretania)		Cruise: Hospitality Standard	9.2	8.1	6.6
Elevators	13	OVERALL RATING	134.4	124.8	114.8

+ QE2 is the only regularly scheduled transatlantic liner still in service, and the fastest, as well as the most integrated cruise ship in the world. Excellent range of joint travel programs are integrated into the marketing of this ship.

— Expect lines for embarkation, disembarkation, shore tenders, and, at peak times, buffets. Has two sittings in the Mauretania Restaurant. Baggage delivery could be improved. There is no forward observation lounge. Following the latest refurbishment, there are no small, intimate hideaway bars. Sadly, there is no forward lookout bar. Passenger flow from 4 Deck and 5 Deck cabins to the Caronia Restaurant is awkward. One cannot have just a sauna without paying a $10 charge for a "Spa Experience" package; this is absurd.

Dining There are, at present, five restaurants (which include many tables for two), assigned according to the grade of suite or cabin booked. The menus are always varied and well balanced.

Other Comments She is a world-renowned dual-purpose superliner that performs a regular schedule of two dozen or so transatlantic crossings as well as several cruises each year, together with an annual round-the-world cruise from January to April.

Originally constructed as a steam turbine ship, she underwent a $160 million refit in Bremen, Germany, in 1986. Her old steam turbines were extracted and exchanged for a diesel-electric propulsion system, resulting in greater speed, better economy and more reliability. A new, fatter funnel was constructed, designed to better keep any soot off her expansive open decks. In Nov/Dec 1994, the ship underwent a dramatic $45 million interior refurbishment which included numerous structural changes, designed to facilitate better passenger flow and even more dining and other choices. Her interiors were changed to provide a more cohesive and coordinated color scheme, with the use of beautiful wood paneling and more traditional furnishings reminiscent of the ocean liners of yesteryear. This is exactly what passengers expect of this ship.

All cabin bathrooms were entirely replaced. They now sport marble fixtures and bright new art deco-style toiletries cabinets. Several new suites were added, as well as an enlarged library, with multimedia CD-Rom center and a fine new, enlarged memorabilia/bookshop, and dedicated florist. The Club Lido magrodome-covered pool was replaced with a new informal buffet bistro-like dining area (The Lido) complete with its own galley and bar. The present Mauretania (Premium Class) was moved from Upper Deck to where the Columbia Restaurant was formerly located on Quarter Deck, and a new Captain's Dining Area was added. Meanwhile, the Columbia Restaurant (Deluxe Class) was moved upstairs to become the Caronia Restaurant. The three Grill Rooms remain (with the former Princess Grill Starboard now renamed Britannia Grill), but the Queens Grill had banquette seating replaced by individual chairs.

The balcony of the showlounge (formerly the Grand Lounge) was blocked off, and the room became a more dedicated showlounge. The shops themselves remain in their present position, as does the Theatre. A new Golden Lion Pub now occupies replaced the former Theatre Bar, and became an instant success.

The former Midships Bar was expanded and renamed The Chart Room (it contains a piano from the Queen Mary). The Yacht Club was greatly enlarged and a new night club created from space created from an aft deck extension. The new enhancements have provided grace, pace and space.

Other Comments: *Transatlantic Crossings* She is the fastest cruise ship presently in service, but even at speeds over 30 knots there's almost no vibration at the stern. Features the most extensive facilities of any passenger ship afloat. Also carries up to 40 cars. She is a city at sea, and, like any city, there are several parts of town. There are three distinct classes: Grill Class (424 beds), Deluxe Class (558 beds) and Premium Class (910 beds). Grill Class accommodations consist of penthouse suites (with butler service) and "luxury" outside cabins, with dining in one of three grill rooms: Queens Grill, Britannia Grill and Princess Grill (5-stars). Deluxe Class accommodations consist of outside double cabins, and inside and outside single cabins, with dining in the Caronia Restaurant (4-stars). Premium Class accommodations feature lower-priced cabin grades, with two-sitting dining in the Mauretania Restaurant (3-stars). All other restaurants feature one sitting dining with flexible dining hours. All passengers enjoy the use of all public rooms, except the Queens Grill Lounge, reserved exclusively for Grill Class passengers. The Queens Grill has its own separate galley, the best waiters and service, a formal atmosphere, and food that is extremely good when ordered off-menu. The Britannia Grill, Princess Grill and Caronia Restaurant share the same galley, but service in the intimate Britannia Grill and Princess Grill is superior. The Mauretania Restaurant has a fine menu but food is served by the least experienced waiters. Grill Class and Deluxe Class passengers have a separate deck space and assigned chairs (for an extra fee), but must sit with all other passengers for major shows, other entertainment events, and social functions. Grill Class is an elegant way to cross the Atlantic; Deluxe Class (formerly first class) isn't quite what it used to be; Premium Class (formerly transatlantic class) is mass-market transportation, albeit in a fine, price-sensitive setting. In the final analysis, this is the last of the transatlantic liners and a wonderful experience, and there are still many people who do not like to fly who enjoy the grace of this ship, and the enormous amount of personal luggage one is allowed – good for relocating between continents.

Other Comments: *Cruises* After an extensive refit in December 1994, the public rooms and passenger facilities have been changed and color-coordinated for the better. The Penthouse Suites are truly superb. Heritage Trail, a ship-wide display of ocean liner history that ship buffs everywhere will find fascinating, includes wonderful ship models of former Cunarders (including a stunning 16-foot illuminated model of the 1907 *Mauretania* outside the restaurant of the same name), and a great abundance of memorabilia items (some of which are for sale in the fine new memorabilia bookshop/library). The Grand Lounge is now a dedicated showlounge with thrust stage, has three seating tiers and a new high-tech sound system. A new Tour and Travel Center was added. Shopping concourse features brand name merchandise at European prices. The extended, expansive, aft-facing Yacht Club is a delightfully nautical, practical and popular room that becomes a good nightclub (afternoon classical concerts here are a delight). Extensive safety deposit center and passenger accounts office, and an automated telephone system. The Queens Room, now used as a ballroom for dancing to a big band, is more stately than before, with comfortable chairs. The Midships Lobby, the ship's embarkation point, has a distinctive, true ocean liner image and feel, with its fine birds-eye maple woodwork and wrap-around murals of the former and present Cunard Queens. Beauty Salons, and all five restaurants remain, but two restaurants have been repositioned, three have been renamed and one redecorated. The large computer center is a real bonus. There is a dedicated florist and greenery (flower dispensary). Has a large self-service launderette (no charge). The Lido, a large, informal bistro dining area (with 24-hour hot beverage dispense stations), is a real bonus on cruises. The elegant Chart Room Bar (formerly the Midships Bar) is better than before. There's also a large balconied theater. The Golden Lion Pub is a roaring success, with its Victorian decor, and selection of 20 beers (both bottled and draught). Superb Library (houses over 6,000 books in five languages, together with the video library and memorabilia bookshop) has been doubled in size, and features two professional librarians (the only ship to do so). Player's Club Casino features fitting art deco and blond wood decor. The health spa is extensive, and its treatment programs (at extra cost) are varied. Synagogue. British officers and seamanship, but hotel staff has changed to an international mix, quite attentive and service-oriented, though many don't speak English well. Consistently good quality entertainment and outstanding lecture programs. One class only for cruises. Dining room assigned according to accommodations chosen. Open or one sitting in all dining rooms except Mauretania. Luncheon and midnight buffets are improved. Cashless cruising. Excellent laundry and dry-cleaning facilities. English nannies and childrens' facilities. This ship offers refined living at sea for those in upper-grade accommodations, otherwise it's just a big ship, albeit with some superb facilities. *Queen Elizabeth 2* is certainly the most perfectly integrated ship afloat, and she's fast. Tender ports should be avoided whenever possible, however, although the new double deck shore tenders are superb additions.

MORE ABOUT *QE2* Physically challenged passengers will appreciate four new cabins specially equipped for wheelchair-bound passengers. They were created using the newly introduced guidelines of the American Disabled Association (ADA). The cabin door is wide enough for a wheelchair to pass through easily (no "lip"). The bathroom door slides open electronically at the touch of a button (located at wheelchair height), and there is no "lip" into the bathroom. The full bath has special assist handles, and the toilet has grab bars in the right places. Closets have hanging rails that have a hydraulically balanced long lever that lowers the rail towards the outside of the closet, down to the height you need. There's an intercom, alarm, and remote-control of lighting, curtains, and doors. These cabins are also good for the hearing-impaired, as there are three brightly colored lighted signs on the cabin bulkhead, as well as a telephone system for the deaf. While these cabins are specially designed for the physically challenged, their ingenious design would not upset a regular passenger.

The Cunard/British Airways Concorde program is most definitely worth saving for. Combining a *QE2* transatlantic crossing with a one-way British Airways Concorde flight is, without doubt, the ultimate way to go. Five days one way, and three hours, fifteen minutes the other is one of the great travel experiences available today. And, with the special, Cunard-subsidized fares, there's no excuse for not indulging, at least once in your life.

ms Queen Odyssey ★★★★★

OPERATES

7 TO 14-DAY CRUISES WORLDWIDE

Cruise Line	Royal Cruise Line
Former Names	Royal Viking Queen
Gross Tonnage	9,975
Builder	Schichau Seebeckwerft (Germany)
Original Cost	$87 million
Christened By	Mrs Inger Kloster
Entered Service	Mar 25, 1992/Jan 14, 1995
Interior Design	Yran & Storbraaten
Country of Registry	Bahamas (C6KO6)
Tel No 130-5227 Fax No 130-5232	
Length (ft/m)	439.9/134.10
Beam (ft/m) 62.9/19.20 Draft (ft/m) 16.7/5.10	
Propulsion	diesel (7,280kW)
Propellers	2 (CP)
Decks 6 Crew 145	
Pass. Capacity (basis 2) 212 (all berths) 212	
Pass. Space Ratio (basis 2) 47.0 (all berths) 47.0	
Officers Greek Dining Staff European	
Total Cabins	106
Size Range (sq ft/m)	277-590/25.7-54.8
Outside Cabins 106 Inside Cabins 0	
Single Cabins 0 Supplement 60-100%	
Balcony Cabins 6 Wheelchair Cabins 4	
Cabin Current	110/220 AC
Refrigerator	All cabins
Cabin TV Yes VCR Yes	
Dining Rooms 1 Sittings Open	
Elevators	3

Casino	Yes	Slot Machines	Yes
Swimming Pools (outside) 1		(inside)	0
Whirlpools	3	Gymnasium	Yes
Sauna/Steam Room Yes/Yes		Massage	Yes
Self-Service Launderette			Yes
Movie Theater/Seats	No	Library	Yes
Children's Facilities			No
Watersports Facilities Aft platform with marina			
pool, windsurfers, waterski, 2 Zodiacs			
Classification Society		Det Norske Veritas	

RATINGS	SCORE
Ship: Condition/Cleanliness	9.2
Ship: Space/Flow/Comfort	9.3
Ship: Facilities	9.0
Ship: Decor/Furnishings	9.3
Ship: Fitness/Watersports	8.7
Cabins: Comfort/Facilities	9.4
Cabins: Software	9.1
Food: Dining Room/Cuisine	9.1
Food: Buffets/Informal Dining	8.5
Food: Quality of Ingredients	8.4
Service: Dining Room	9.0
Service: Bars	8.9
Service: Cabins	9.0
Cruise: Entertainment/Lecture Program	8.4
Cruise: Hospitality Standard	9.0
OVERALL RATING	134.3

+ Strikingly sleek ship with a handsome profile, almost identical in looks to *Seabourn Pride* and *Seabourn Spirit*, but with streamline bars along the upper superstructure side. Has two fine mahogany water taxis. Also features an aft watersports platform and marina, which is used in suitably calm warm water areas. Inviting, sumptuous public areas have warm colors. Has wide central passageway throughout the accommodation areas. Finest quality interior fixtures, fittings and fabrics combine to present an outstanding, elegant decor, with warm color combinations and artwork. Wonderful, 360 degree mural in the reception lobby (the ship's interior designer is painted into the mural). Quite relaxed, informal dress code applies. All suites are comfortably large, and beautifully equipped with everything, including large walk-in closet, 100% cotton towels and bathrobes, personalized stationery, and leather ticket wallet. Nutrogena cabin amenities are now standard. Non-smoking cabins are available. For the ultimate in privacy the two Owner's Suites (001/002), located forward on Deck 6 offer a superbly private living environment at sea. Each has a walk-in closet, second closet, one full bathroom and a second room with toilet and washbasin (for guests). There's also a forward-facing balcony, complete with sun lounge chairs and wooden drinks table. These are secluded, and good for nude sunbathing. The living area has ample bookshelf space (included is a complete edition of Encyclopedia Britannica), refrigerator and drinks cabinet, television and VCR (there's a second television in the bedroom). All windows as well as the door to the

balcony have electric blinds, and a complete blackout is possible in both bedroom and living room. On the Christmas cruise, each Owner's suite has its own decorated and illuminated Christmas tree.

— The Norwegian officers have been supplanted by Greek officers, who are warmer, but decidedly more casual. There's no wrap-around outdoor promenade deck. All beverages should be included in the cruise fare, as on the Sea Goddess and Silversea Cruises ships, but then the cruise fare would have to rise accordingly. Plastic chairs on deck are incorrect for this type of ship.

Dining In-suite, course-by-course dining available at any time. Very elegant decor in the formal dining room (arguably nicer than the Seabourns). Fine, very creative cuisine is well presented, with most items cooked to order. The menu is not repeated, no matter how long the voyage. Special orders are available whenever you want them, and caviar is always available on request. Good choice of exotic fruits and cheeses. The wine list is extensive, but prices are rather high. Hand-picked European dining room staff provide impeccable service.

General Comments You pay for all bar and in-suite drinks. This ship will provide discerning passengers with a fine level of personal service and an outstanding cruise experience. Sadly, the product delivery is not as good as when she was under the Royal Viking Line banner with Norwegian officers, but, although more casual, is still extremely good nonetheless. The brochure suggests $12 per person per day in gratuities, pooled for staff due to its open-sitting dining operation.

ssc Radisson Diamond ★★★★★

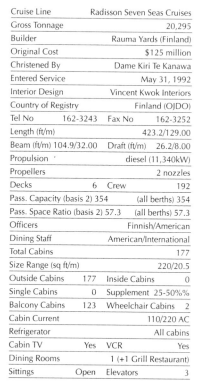

OPERATES

4, 5 AND 7-DAY CARIBBEAN AND MEDITERRANEAN CRUISES

Cruise Line	Radisson Seven Seas Cruises
Gross Tonnage	20,295
Builder	Rauma Yards (Finland)
Original Cost	$125 million
Christened By	Dame Kiri Te Kanawa
Entered Service	May 31, 1992
Interior Design	Vincent Kwok Interiors
Country of Registry	Finland (OJDO)
Tel No 162-3243	Fax No 162-3252
Length (ft/m)	423.2/129.00
Beam (ft/m) 104.9/32.00	Draft (ft/m) 26.2/8.00
Propulsion ·	diesel (11,340kW)
Propellers	2 nozzles
Decks 6	Crew 192
Pass. Capacity (basis 2) 354	(all berths) 354
Pass. Space Ratio (basis 2) 57.3	(all berths) 57.3
Officers	Finnish/American
Dining Staff	American/International
Total Cabins	177
Size Range (sq ft/m)	220/20.5
Outside Cabins 177	Inside Cabins 0
Single Cabins 0	Supplement 25-50%%
Balcony Cabins 123	Wheelchair Cabins 2
Cabin Current	110/220 AC
Refrigerator	All cabins
Cabin TV Yes	VCR Yes
Dining Rooms	1 (+1 Grill Restaurant)
Sittings Open	Elevators 3

Casino	Yes	Slot Machines	Yes
Swimming Pools (outside) 1		(inside)	0
Whirlpools	1	Gymnasium	Yes
Sauna/Steam Room Yes/Yes		Massage	Yes
Self-Service Launderette			No
Movie Theater/Seats No		Library	Yes
Children's Facilities			No
Watersports Facilities		Retractable aft marina, jet-ski, water-ski	
Classification Society		Det Norske Veritas	

RATINGS	SCORE
Ship: Condition/Cleanliness	9.0
Ship: Space/Flow/Comfort	8.6
Ship: Decor/Furnishings	8.4
Ship: Fitness Facilities	6.8
Cabins: Comfort/Facilities	9.2
Cabins: Software	8.7
Food: Dining Room/Cuisine	9.1
Food: Buffets/Informal Dining	9.0
Food: Quality of Ingredients	9.0
Service: Dining Room	8.7
Service: Bars	8.2
Service: Cabins	9.2
Cruise: Entertainment	7.3
Cruise: Activities Program	6.7
Cruise: Hospitality Standard	8.2
OVERALL RATING	126.1

+ This ship features an innovative design. She is stable, with four stabilizing fins (two on the inner side of each pontoon) so motion is really minimal. The wide beam design provides outstanding passenger space, although the public rooms are stacked vertically. Casino has gaming tables on one side of the passageway, slot machines on the other.
A five-deck-high atrium has glass-enclosed elevators. There is also a little-used underwater viewing area (actually two portholes). Has an outdoor jogging track.
Nicely designed, spacious and well-equipped all-outside cabins, most with private balconies (they even have lights), are all furnished in blond woods, with marble bathroom vanities and tiny bathtub. There are bay windows in 47 suites.
All cabins are the same size, with the exception of two VIP master suites with private balconies. Each cabin is an outside, and features a spacious sitting area with sofa and chairs, dressing table with hairdryer, minibar and refrigerator, telephone, color remote-control TV with integral VCR player, twin beds which convert to a queen sized unit, two good strong, adjustable reading lamps that are bright, a personal safe (somewhat hidden and difficult for older passengers to reach and operate), full-length mirror, and excellent, usable drawer space. Closet space, however, is very small, but adequate for short cruises. It is, however, tight for two even on a 7-day cruise, worse for longer cruises.

The mini-bar is stocked with beer and soft drinks, while half-liter bottles of four liquors are provided. Bottled mineral water carries the name and logo of the ship. The only glasses provided are two champagne flutes and two small glasses for mixed cocktails.

Has a sophisticated business center and facilities that are ideal for small groups and conventions. For groups and meetings, the high-tech audio and video conference facilities, and a high-tech security system that uses approximately 50 cameras to monitor just about everywhere, provide a good feeling of exclusivity.

— The design means that many public rooms are inside, with little or no connection with the sea. Flowers, and more flowers, would help a lot. Has a maximum speed of 12.5 knots, which means leisurely cruising, but slow going on longer itineraries. Awkward one-way (contra-flow) interior staircase is frustrating. The spaciousness of the ship, while providing flexibility of the several individual public rooms, actually detracts from the overall flow. Multi-level entertainment room is awkward. Has excellent health spa facilities, but they can't be reached by elevator. Still has those uncomfortable chairs in the main dining room. Meet and greet service inconsistent. Cabin bathrooms have tiny tubs (they are not bathtubs, but shower tubs).

Dining The two-deck-high dining room is quite elegant, and has a 270 degree view over the stern, and open seating. Cuisine quality and food presentation are European in style, and quite outstanding in both quality, choice and presentation. Also features health foods and dietary specials. The waitresses are quite charming, supervised superbly by experienced Italian headwaiters. Although basic whites and reds are included for lunch and dinner, a wine list is available for those who appreciate better wines (at extra cost).

The Grill is an alternative casual indoor/outdoor dining spot (at no extra charge). Run like a real restaurant ashore (make reservations early), this casual dining spot features superb home-made pasta dishes daily, fine menu, cream sauces and exotic garnishes. Each day is different, and food is presented, in small portions, course by course. It is lovingly prepared and exquisite to taste, although somewhat rich. Seating is at sturdy, practical glass-topped wooden tables for two, four, or six. Table-side dessert flambeaus are often featured. Dining is a pleasure on this ship, and it is the vessel's strongest point.

Other Comments This semi-submersible twin hulled cruise vessel, which looks like a white-caped "Batman" from the stern, certainly has distinctive looks, although its design has not been as successful as hoped. This ship will appeal to those seeking extremely high standards of service in sophisticated and personable, yet somewhat bland surroundings. Gratuities are included.

ms Regal Empress ★★+

OPERATES

2 TO 7-DAY BERMUDA AND CARIBBEAN CRUISES

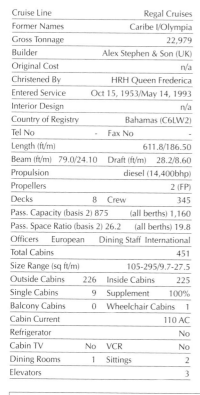

Cruise Line	Regal Cruises	Casino	Yes	Slot Machines	Yes
Former Names	Caribe I/Olympia	Swimming Pools (outside) 1	(inside)	0
Gross Tonnage	22,979	Whirlpools	2	Gymnasium	Yes
Builder	Alex Stephen & Son (UK)	Sauna/Steam Room	No/No	Massage	No
Original Cost	n/a	Self-Service Launderette		No
Christened By	HRH Queen Frederica	Movie Theater/Seats		Yes/166
Entered Service	Oct 15, 1953/May 14, 1993	Library		Yes
Interior Design	n/a	Children's Facilities		Yes
Country of Registry	Bahamas (C6LW2)	Watersports Facilities		None
Tel No	- Fax No -	Classification Society		Lloyd's Register

Length (ft/m)	611.8/186.50
Beam (ft/m) 79.0/24.10 Draft (ft/m)	28.2/8.60
Propulsion	diesel (14,400bhp)
Propellers	2 (FP)
Decks 8 Crew	345
Pass. Capacity (basis 2) 875 (all berths)	1,160
Pass. Space Ratio (basis 2) 26.2 (all berths)	19.8
Officers European Dining Staff	International
Total Cabins	451
Size Range (sq ft/m)	105-295/9.7-27.5
Outside Cabins 226 Inside Cabins	225
Single Cabins 9 Supplement	100%
Balcony Cabins 0 Wheelchair Cabins	1
Cabin Current	110 AC
Refrigerator	No
Cabin TV No VCR	No
Dining Rooms 1 Sittings	2
Elevators	3

RATINGS	SCORE
Ship: Condition/Cleanliness	5.7
Ship: Space/Flow/Comfort	5.9
Ship: Decor/Furnishings	6.3
Ship: Fitness Facilities	5.0
Cabins: Comfort/Facilities	6.5
Cabins: Software	6.3
Food: Dining Room/Cuisine	6.1
Food: Buffets/Informal Dining	5.6
Food: Quality of Ingredients	5.4
Service: Dining Room	6.0
Service: Bars	6.1
Service: Cabins	6.4
Cruise: Entertainment	6.0
Cruise: Activities Program	5.8
Cruise: Hospitality Standard	6.4
OVERALL RATING	89.5

+ This 40-year-old ship has a traditional ocean liner profile. Good open deck space for sun-lovers, although very crowded when the ship is full. Polished teak decking. Enclosed promenade decks are popular with strollers. Satin woods and brass on staircases. Superb library with original paneling. There is a wide range of cabin sizes and configurations. Most are quite roomy, with good closet and reasonable drawer space, and heavy-duty fittings.

— Steep, narrow gangway in some ports. Expect lines for embarkation, disembarkation and buffets. Has an awkward layout; many passageways are dead ends.

Dining Lovely old-world dining room is a step back in time, with its original oil paintings on burnished wood paneling, ornate lighting fixtures, etched glass panels, and original murals depicting New York and Rio. Most tables are for six or more, with a few tables for four. Smoking and non-smoking sections are provided on the starboard and port sides respectively. Food is plentiful, but the buffets are awful.

Other Comments Large casino sees lively, noisy action. This ship will provide you with a cruise in adequate surroundings, at a modest price, but the ship is old and service is perfunctory, at best.

mv Regal Princess ★★★★+

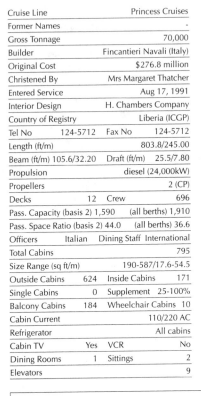

OPERATES

7-DAY ALASKA AND CARIBBEAN CRUISES

Cruise Line	Princess Cruises		
Former Names	-		
Gross Tonnage	70,000		
Builder	Fincantieri Navali (Italy)		
Original Cost	$276.8 million		
Christened By	Mrs Margaret Thatcher		
Entered Service	Aug 17, 1991		
Interior Design	H. Chambers Company		
Country of Registry	Liberia (ICGP)		
Tel No 124-5712	Fax No 124-5712		
Length (ft/m)	803.8/245.00		
Beam (ft/m) 105.6/32.20	Draft (ft/m) 25.5/7.80		
Propulsion	diesel (24,000kW)		
Propellers	2 (CP)		
Decks 12	Crew 696		
Pass. Capacity (basis 2) 1,590	(all berths) 1,910		
Pass. Space Ratio (basis 2) 44.0	(all berths) 36.6		
Officers Italian	Dining Staff International		
Total Cabins	795		
Size Range (sq ft/m)	190-587/17.6-54.5		
Outside Cabins 624	Inside Cabins 171		
Single Cabins 0	Supplement 25-100%		
Balcony Cabins 184	Wheelchair Cabins 10		
Cabin Current	110/220 AC		
Refrigerator	All cabins		
Cabin TV Yes	VCR No		
Dining Rooms 1	Sittings 2		
Elevators	9		

Casino	Yes	Slot Machines	Yes
Swimming Pools (outside) 2		(inside)	0
Whirlpools	4	Gymnasium	Yes
Sauna/Steam Room Yes/No		Massage	Yes
Self-Service Launderette			Yes
Movie Theater/Seats			Yes/169
Library			Yes
Children's Facilities			No
Watersports Facilities			None
Classification Society			Lloyd's Register

RATINGS	SCORE
Ship: Condition/Cleanliness	8.0
Ship: Space/Flow/Comfort	7.8
Ship: Decor/Furnishings	8.1
Ship: Fitness Facilities	8.0
Cabins: Comfort/Facilities	8.1
Cabins: Software	8.2
Food: Dining Room/Cuisine	7.4
Food: Buffets/Informal Dining	7.2
Food: Quality of Ingredients	7.0
Service: Dining Room	7.5
Service: Bars	7.7
Service: Cabins	7.9
Cruise: Entertainment	8.1
Cruise: Activities Program	7.8
Cruise: Hospitality Standard	7.6
OVERALL RATING	116.4

+ Innovative styling mixed with traditional features. Has twin pools. Dolphin-shaped observation dome is huge, and houses the casino, but it doesn't work as a nightclub. Elegant three-deck-high atrium is spacious and well designed. Well-coordinated colors and carpeting. Flowers and lovely artwork help create a more intimate atmosphere. Plenty of public rooms, but most have pillars obstructing flow and sightlines. Excellent drinks from extensive list in Characters Bar. Well-designed accommodations, with ample drawer and hanging space, and spacious, marble-walled bathrooms. Prompt, attentive room service.

— Crowded outdoor sunning space when the ship is full. Disjointed layout. No wrap-around outdoor promenade deck. Galley fumes seem to waft constantly over the aft open decks. Suites and mini-suites suffer from poor ceiling insulation and noise from lido deck above. Expect lines for embarkation, disembarkation, shore tenders, and buffets.

Dining Has a quieter dining hall than on the *Crown*, but it's still noisy (though non-smoking), and there are no tables for two. Unfortunately, the food quality not as good as one would expect from this company, although it is improving. Poor bread and fruits.

Other Comments This is the sister ship to the *Crown Princess*. Ideal for those who want a big ship around them, with well-proven service, but there's little contact with the outside.

mv Regent Calypso ★★★

OPERATES
*7- AND 14-DAY EUROPE AND
SOUTH-EAST ASIA CRUISES*

Cruise Line	Regency Cruises/		
	Transocean Cruise Lines		
Former Names	Sun Fiesta/Canguro Verde, Durr		
Gross Tonnage		8,000	
Builder		Fincantieri (Italy)	
Original Cost	n/a	Christened By	n/a
Entered Service		1968/Jun 26, 1994	
Interior Design		A&M Katzourakis	
Country of Registry		Bahamas (C6JK4)	
Tel No	130-6564	Fax No	130-6565
Length (ft/m)		425.0 ft/129.5	
Beam (ft/m)	63.0/19.2	Draft (ft/m)	17.7/5.4
Propulsion		diesel (7,790kW)	
Propellers		2 (CP)	
Decks	8	Crew	240
Pass. Capacity (basis 2) 502		(all berths) 618	
Pass. Space Ratio (basis 2) 15.9		(all berths) 12.9	
Officers		Greek/European	
Dining Staff		European/International	
Total Cabins		251	
Size Range (sq ft/m)		135-244/12.5-22.6	
Outside Cabins	158	Inside Cabins	93
Single Cabins	0	Supplement	50-100%
Balcony Cabins	0	Wheelchair Cabins	2
Cabin Current	110 AC	Refrigerator	No
Cabin TV	Yes	VCR	No
Dining Rooms	1	Sittings	2
Elevators		2	

Casino	Yes	Slot Machines	Yes
Swimming Pools (outside) 1		(inside)	0
Whirlpools	1	Gymnasium	Yes
Sauna/Steam Room No/No		Massage	Yes
Self-Service Launderette			No
Movie Theater/Seats			No
Library			Yes
Children's Facilities			No
Watersports Facilities			None
Classification Society		Lloyd's Register	

RATINGS	SCORE
Ship: Condition/Cleanliness	6.4
Ship: Space/Flow/Comfort	6.2
Ship: Decor/Furnishings	6.9
Ship: Fitness Facilities	5.5
Cabins: Comfort/Facilities	6.8
Cabins: Software	7.2
Food: Dining Room/Cuisine	7.3
Food: Buffets/Informal Dining	6.6
Food: Quality of Ingredients	6.8
Service: Dining Room	6.7
Service: Bars	6.4
Service: Cabins	6.9
Cruise: Entertainment	6.1
Cruise: Activities Program	5.8
Cruise: Hospitality Standard	6.4
OVERALL RATING	98.0

+ This ship was recently reconstructed, and features an enclosed promenade deck. Has a good number and range of public rooms for the size of the ship. The mostly outside cabins are quite attractive, with pastel colors, but the fabrics and soft furnishings could be of better quality. Cabin bathrooms have showers. No cabins have bathtubs. Some 66 cabins have double beds, while others are twins, with many featuring third and fourth berths.

— This high-density ship means it's really crowded when it's full, so expect long lines for embarkation, disembarkation, shore excursions and buffets. Expect a large number of smokers. Cabins are quite small, and barely adequate.

Dining The same comments apply as per other Regency Cruises ships with regard to food and service. Has poor selection of fruit in cabins, and limited room service menu, but these are due to the low price per passenger the company pays for its food concession.

Other Comments This former Strintzis Line ferry was reconstructed in Greece, but her profile is not an attractive one. Regency Cruises has such a diverse fleet that it's hard to find consistency. This ship is under a five-year bareboat charter to Transocean Cruise Lines, so it carries a predominantly German-speaking clientele who strictly seek to travel to interesting and somewhat off-beat destinations in modest surroundings, at a low price.

tss Regent Isle ★★★

OPERATES

ALASKA AND TRANS-CANAL CRUISES

Cruise Line	Regency Cruises	Elevators		3
Former Names	Fair Princess/Fairsea/	Casino	Yes	Slot Machines	Yes
	Fairland/Carinthia	Swimming Pools (outside) 3	(inside)	0
Gross Tonnage	24,724	Whirlpools	0	Gymnasium	Yes
Builder	John Brown & Co. (UK)	Sauna/Steam Room Yes/No	Massage	Yes
Original Cost	n/a	Self-Service Launderette		No
Christened By	HRH Princess Margaret	Movie Theater/Seats	Yes (with balcony)/330
Entered Service	Jun 27, 1956/Oct 14, 1995	Library	Yes	Children's Facilities	Yes
Interior Design	Barbara Dorn (1984 redesign)	Watersports Facilities		None
Country of Registry	Bahamas	Classification Society	Lloyd's Register

Tel No	n/a	Fax No	n/a
Length (ft/m)			608.2/185.40
Beam (ft/m) 80.3/24.49	Draft (ft/m)	28.5/8.71
Propulsion	steam turbine (18,300kW)
Propellers			2 (FP)
Decks	11	Crew	450
Pass. Capacity (basis 2) 890	(all berths) 1,100
Pass. Space Ratio (basis 2) 27.7	(all berths) 22.4
Officers	Italian	Dining Staff	European
Total Cabins			464
Size Range (sq ft/m)		90-241/8.3-22.3
Outside Cabins	230	Inside Cabins	234
Single Cabins	0	Supplement	40-100%
Balcony Cabins	0	Wheelchair Cabins	0
Cabin Current			110 AC
Refrigerator		Category A only
Cabin TV	Yes	VCR	No
Dining Rooms	2	Sittings	2

RATINGS	SCORE
Ship: Condition/Cleanliness	6.4
Ship: Space/Flow/Comfort	6.2
Ship: Decor/Furnishings	6.6
Ship: Fitness Facilities	5.0
Cabins: Comfort/Facilities	6.4
Cabins: Software	6.7
Food: Dining Room/Cuisine	6.8
Food: Buffets/Informal Dining	6.6
Food: Quality of Ingredients	6.7
Service: Dining Room	6.8
Service: Bars	7.0
Service: Cabins	7.2
Cruise: Entertainment	7.4
Cruise: Activities Program	6.6
Cruise: Hospitality Standard	7.0
OVERALL RATING	99.4

+ This solidly constructed former ocean liner has classic, but now dated, lines and profile. The open deck and sunning space is quite good, unless the ship is full. Has a jogging track. Inside, the art deco interiors on Promenade Deck are quite elegant. Decent old-style library. Good facilities for families with children. Cabins are generally quite spacious, with heavy-duty furnishings and fittings.

— Very crowded when full. Expect lines for embarkation, disembarkation, and shore tenders. Mundane interior decor and colors. Not much sophistication anywhere. Public rooms are reasonably comfortable, but barely adequate for the number of passengers carried, and it's difficult to get away from smokers. Cabin bathrooms are now antiquated, with much exposed plumbing. There are too many announcements.

Dining The dining rooms, although crowded and noisy, have plenty of tables for two. The cuisine is low-budget banquet food, and quantity not quality. Fairly attentive, but tired, staff. There is an excellent Pizzeria.

Other Comments This high-density ship is good value if you don't expect much, but she is now old and tired. The ship was taken over by Regency Cruises in October 1995. Her early itineraries include several two-day party cruises.

ss Regent Rainbow ★★★

OPERATES

4 AND 5-DAY MEXICAN
CARIBBEAN CRUISES

Cruise Line	Regency Cruises	Elevators	3
Former Names	Diamond Island/Santa Rosa/	Casino	Yes	Slot Machines	Yes
	Samos Sky	Swimming Pools (outside) 1	(inside)	0
Gross Tonnage	24,851	Whirlpools	2	Gymnasium	Yes (tiny)
Builder	Newport News Shipbuilding (USA)	Sauna/Steam Room Yes/No	Massage	Yes
Original Cost	$25 million	Self-Service Launderette	No
Christened By	Mrs J. Peter Grace	Movie Theater/Seats	No	Library	Yes
Entered Service	Jun 12, 1958/Jan 22, 1993	Children's Facilities	Yes
Interior Design	Polly Pahyanni	Classification Society	American Bureau
Country of Registry	Bahamas (C6HX6)		of Shipping
Tel No 130-5570 Fax No 130-5573			

Length (ft/m)	599.0/182.57
Beam (ft/m) 84.0/25.6 Draft (ft/m) 27.5/8.38	
Propulsion	steam turbine (16,400kW)
Propellers	2 (FP)
Decks 10 Crew 420 Total Cabins 484	
Pass. Capacity (basis 2) 956 (all berths) 1,168	
Pass. Space Ratio (basis 2) 2,5.8 (all berths) 21.4	
Officers	Greek/European
Dining Staff	International
Size Range (sq ft/m) 125-305/11.6-28.3	
Outside Cabins 329 Inside Cabins 155	
Single Cabins 12 Supplement 50-100%	
Balcony Cabins 0 Wheelchair Cabins 2	
Cabin Current	110/220 AC
Refrigerator	Suites only
Cabin TV Yes VCR No	
Dining Rooms 1 Sittings 2	

RATINGS	SCORE
Ship: Condition/Cleanliness	6.4
Ship: Space/Flow/Comfort	6.3
Ship: Decor/Furnishings	6.8
Ship: Fitness Facilities	4.0
Cabins: Comfort/Facilities	6.3
Cabins: Software	6.6
Food: Dining Room/Cuisine	7.4
Food: Buffets/Informal Dining	6.8
Food: Quality of Ingredients	6.9
Service: Dining Room	7.0
Service: Bars	7.0
Service: Cabins	6.2
Cruise: Entertainment	5.6
Cruise: Activities Program	6.0
Cruise: Hospitality Standard	6.0
OVERALL RATING	95.3

+ Has wrap-around outdoor promenade. Has very pleasant, surprisingly comfortable and warm interior decor that is contemporary without being brash, but the artwork is cheap. Original cabins are quite spacious, with good closet and drawer space.

— She's high sided, with a narrow beam, and rolls in poor weather. With new upper decks added, her new profile is not handsome. Very poor open deck and sunning space. High density ship means little room to move about in when full. Newly added cabins are smaller and have very poor insulation. Large casino with high ceiling, and adjacent poker room, are very lively.

Dining The dining room has large picture windows and a neat orchestra balcony (with an awful piano). Food quality and presentation are good for the budget provided. Service is friendly yet somewhat perfunctory.

Other Comments Former American-built liner has had a great amount of reconstruction ($72 million) in 1992 in Greece, after being laid up for over ten years. Squat funnel is awkward, although the conversion itself was a practical one. Low-budget entertainment is generally of poor quality. For short cruises, however, the ship provides a range of public spaces that, in turn, promotes a good party ambiance.

mv Regent Sea ★★★

OPERATES

7-DAY ALASKA AND CARIBBEAN CRUISES

Cruise Line	Regency Cruises		
Former Names	Samantha/San Paolo/		
	Navarino/Gripsholm		
Gross Tonnage	22,785		
Builder	Ansaldo Sestri-Ponente (Italy)		
Original Cost	UK£7,000,000		
Christened By	Princess Margarethe/Robert Stack		
Entered Service	May 14, 1957/Nov 17, 1985		
Interior Design	Patricia Hayes & Associates		
Country of Registry	Bahamas (C6117)		
Tel No	110-3126	Fax No	110-3257
Length (ft/m)		631.2/192.41	
Beam (ft/m)	81.8/24.95	Draft (ft/m)	27.8/8.49
Propulsion		diesel (11,916kW)	
Propellers		2	
Decks	8	Crew	365
Pass. Capacity (basis 2) 714		(all berths) 760	
Pass. Space Ratio (basis 2) 31.9		(all berths) 29.9	
Officers	European	Dining Staff International	
Total Cabins		357	
Size Range (sq ft/m)		172-280/16.0-26.0	
Outside Cabins	337	Inside Cabins	20
Single Cabins	0	Supplement	40-100%
Balcony Cabins	0	Wheelchair Cabins	3
Cabin Current	110 AC	Refrigerator	Suites only
Cabin TV	No	VCR	No
Dining Rooms	2 (1 smoking, 1 non-smoking)		
Sittings		2	

Elevators			4
Casino	Yes	Slot Machines	Yes
Swimming Pools (outside) 1		(inside)	0
Whirlpools	2	Gymnasium	Yes
Sauna/Steam Room Yes/No		Massage	Yes
Self-Service Launderette			No
Movie Theater/Seats			Yes/218
Library	Yes	Children's Facilities	No
Watersports Facilities			None
Classification Society		Lloyd's Register	

RATINGS	SCORE
Ship: Condition/Cleanliness	6.0
Ship: Space/Flow/Comfort	7.1
Ship: Decor/Furnishings	6.4
Ship: Fitness Facilities	5.3
Cabins: Comfort/Facilities	5.8
Cabins: Software	6.7
Food: Dining Room/Cuisine	7.4
Food: Buffets/Informal Dining	6.8
Food: Quality of Ingredients	6.9
Service: Dining Room	7.0
Service: Bars	7.1
Service: Cabins	6.4
Cruise: Entertainment	5.6
Cruise: Activities Program	6.0
Cruise: Hospitality Standard	6.2
OVERALL RATING	96.7

+ Well-constructed former ocean liner has classic lines and styling, and is one of only a handful of two-funnel ships. Generous open deck and sunning space, with good teakwood decking. Has a glass-enclosed promenade deck. Wide array of public rooms, which are quite spacious and well appointed, with high ceilings and lots of wood accents. The ship has indoor whirlpools and adjacent spa facilities. Distinct European flair is evident in the decor, furnishings, and colors. Richly paneled library. The mostly outside cabins, in wide variety of configurations, are of generous proportions, with spacious closets and ample drawer space; most beds parallel the ship's axis. Friendly, comfortable ambiance throughout.

— The ship looks well worn and tired and is in need of more investment in maintenance. Awkward layout and flow, due to conversion from former two-class liner. Stale cigarette smoke odor everywhere, particularly in soft furnishings. Most Sun Deck cabins have lifeboat-obstructed views. Poor book selection in the library. Long lines for buffets and shore tenders.

Dining Bright, cheerful dining room is split into three sections. Open seating for breakfast and lunch. The company only provides a low budget for food, and it shows.

Other Comments Go for the destinations and this ship will provide cruising in a good style reminiscent of bygone days, and at a modest price.

mv Regent Spirit ★★★

OPERATES

CARIBBEAN AND MEDITERRANEAN CRUISES

Cruise Line	Regency Cruises		
Former Names	Constellation/Danaos/Anna Nery		
Gross Tonnage	12,433		
Builder	Brod Uljanik (Yugoslavia)		
Original Cost	n/a	Christened By	n/a
Entered Service	Aug 27, 1962/Nov 20, 1993		
Interior Design	A&M Katzourakis		
Country of Registry	Bahamas (C6DP8)		
Tel No	130-5421	Fax No	130-5422
Length (ft/m)	492.1/150.00		
Beam (ft/m) 62.3/19.00	Draft (ft/m) 18.3/5.60		
Propulsion	diesel (5,958kW)		
Propellers	2		
Decks 8	Crew	230	
Pass. Capacity (basis 2) 422	(all berths) 532		
Pass. Space Ratio (basis 2) 29.4	(all berths) 23.3		
Officers	Greek/European		
Dining Staff	Greek/International		
Total Cabins	211		
Size Range (sq ft/m)	145-230/13.5-21.3		
Outside Cabins 211	Inside Cabins 0		
Single Cabins 0	Supplement 40-100%		
Balcony Cabins 0	Wheelchair Cabins 5		
Cabin Current	110/220 AC		
Refrigerator	No		
Cabin TV No	VCR No		
Dining Rooms 1	Sittings 2		
Elevators	2		

Casino	Yes	Slot Machines	Yes
Swimming Pools (outside) 1	(inside)	0	
Whirlpools	0	Gymnasium	Yes
Sauna/Steam Room Yes/No	Massage	Yes	
Self-Service Launderette			No
Movie Theater/Seats			No
Library			Yes
Children's Facilities			No
Watersports Facilities			None
Classification Society		Lloyd's Register	

RATINGS	SCORE
Ship: Condition/Cleanliness	6.3
Ship: Space/Flow/Comfort	5.7
Ship: Decor/Furnishings	6.8
Ship: Fitness Facilities	4.0
Cabins: Comfort/Facilities	6.3
Cabins: Software	6.6
Food: Dining Room/Cuisine	7.4
Food: Buffets/Informal Dining	6.8
Food: Quality of Ingredients	6.9
Service: Dining Room	7.0
Service: Bars	7.0
Service: Cabins	6.2
Cruise: Entertainment	5.6
Cruise: Activities Program	6.0
Cruise: Hospitality Standard	6.1
OVERALL RATING	94.7

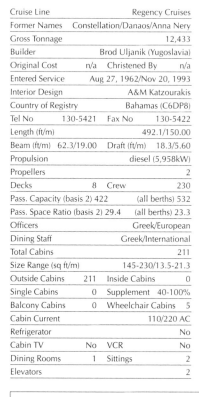

+ This smart looking ship with a squat funnel was converted into a well-balanced cruise ship in 1982. Has good enclosed promenade deck and outdoor wrap-around promenade deck. Features all-outside, "minimum-decor" cabins that are comfortable, though soft furnishings could be improved. The bathrooms are very small in all except the ten suites.

— Reasonable open deck and sunning space, but the swimming pool is very small. There are few public rooms. Cabins have little closet and drawer space, particularly as most cabins accommodate a third (and some a fourth) person.

Dining The same comments for other Regency Cruises ships also apply here. The menu descriptions make the food appear better than it is, although there is a reasonable choice of items. However, there is a limited selection of fruits and vegetables, breads and garnishes. Put quite simply, you get what you pay for.

Other Comments There are few public rooms, but one of them is now an enlarged casino. Regency Cruises keeps changing the deployment of its ships, so do check the latest brochure. The ship is pleasant, but it is not a luxury ship, or product, by any means, so don't let the brochure fool you.

mv Regent Star ★★★

OPERATES

7-DAY ALASKA AND CARIBBEAN CRUISES

Cruise Line	Regency Cruises		
Former Names	Statendam/Rhapsody		
Gross Tonnage	24,413		
Builder	Wilton-Fijenoord (Holland)		
Original Cost	n/a		
Christened By	HRH Crown Princess Beatrix		
Entered Service	Feb 6, 1957/Jul 26, 1987		
Interior Design	Patricia Hayes & Associates		
Country of Registry	Bahamas (C6DY)		
Tel No 110-4137	Fax No	110-3646	
Length (ft/m)	642.3/195.80		
Beam (ft/m) 81.0/24.70	Draft (ft/m)	27.5/8.40	
Propulsion	diesel (16,400kW)		
Propellers	2 (FP)		
Decks 9	Crew	450	
Pass. Capacity (basis 2) 944	(all berths) 1,000		
Pass. Space Ratio (basis 2) 25.8	(all berths) 24.4		
Officers	European/Greek		
Dining Staff	International		
Total Cabins	474		
Size Range (sq ft/m)	86-260/8.0-24.0		
Outside Cabins 291	Inside Cabins	183	
Single Cabins 2	Supplement	40-100%	
Balcony Cabins 0	Wheelchair Cabins	0	
Cabin Current 110 AC	Refrigerator	No	
Cabin TV No	VCR	No	
Dining Rooms 1	Sittings	2	
Elevators	2		

Casino	Yes	Slot Machines	Yes
Swimming Pools (outside) 1		(inside)	1
Whirlpools	2	Gymnasium	Yes
Sauna/Steam Room Yes/No		Massage	Yes
Self-Service Launderette			No
Movie Theater/Seats			Yes/294
Library			Yes
Children's Facilities			No
Watersports Facilities			None
Classification Society			Lloyd's Register

RATINGS	SCORE
Ship: Condition/Cleanliness	5.7
Ship: Space/Flow/Comfort	6.4
Ship: Decor/Furnishings	6.2
Ship: Fitness Facilities	5.3
Cabins: Comfort/Facilities	5.8
Cabins: Software	6.7
Food: Dining Room/Cuisine	7.4
Food: Buffets/Informal Dining	6.8
Food: Quality of Ingredients	6.9
Service: Dining Room	7.0
Service: Bars	7.0
Service: Cabins	6.2
Cruise: Entertainment	5.6
Cruise: Activities Program	6.0
Cruise: Hospitality Standard	6.0
OVERALL RATING	95.0

+ Well-constructed older vessel with classic former ocean liner profile. Now looking tired, however. Exterior maintenance is very shoddy, but a recent refurbishment has cosmetically upgraded interior spaces and public rooms. Reasonable amount of open deck and sunning space. Good array of public rooms, with tasteful decor and colors. Useful indoor fitness center. Quite roomy and nicely furnished outside cabins, many of which feature a full bathtub, and have good closet and drawer space.

— Bridge Deck cabins have lifeboat-obstructed views. Lines for buffets, shore tenders. Awful stale smoke odor everywhere. Same size as *Regent Sea* but carries many more passengers, so always feels crowded. Inside cabins are very small.

Dining Low-cost food quality and choice could be improved, although most passengers seem satisfied.

Other Comments European-style service and continental cuisine. The ship does, however, provide a reasonably good cruise experience at modest, always discounted rates, in reasonably comfortable surroundings, with a friendly staff, but increased competition provides a much greater choice of alternative, and cleaner, ships.

ss Regent Sun ★★★+

OPERATES

*7-DAY CARIBBEAN AND
CANADA-NEW ENGLAND CRUISES*

Cruise Line	Regency Cruises
Former Names	Royal Odyssey, Doric,
	Hanseatic, Shalom
Gross Tonnage	25,500
Builder	Chantiers de l'Atlantique (France)
Original Cost	UK£7,500,000
Christened By	Mrs Paula Ben Gurion
Entered Service	Apr 17, 1964/Dec 9, 1988
Interior Design	A&M Katzourakis
Country of Registry	Bahamas (C6HB3)
Tel No 110-3762 Fax No	110-3763
Length (ft/m)	628.9/191.70
Beam (ft/m) 81.5/24.85 Draft (ft/m)	27.3/8.33
Propulsion	steam turbine (18,650kW)
Propellers	2 (FP)
Decks 9 Crew	410
Pass. Capacity (basis 2) 842 (all berths)	930
Pass. Space Ratio (basis 2) 30.2 (all berths)	27.4
Officers	Greek/European
Dining Staff	International
Total Cabins	420
Size Range (sq ft/m)	140-294/13.0-27.3
Outside Cabins 346 Inside Cabins	76
Single Cabins 2 Supplement	50-100%
Balcony Cabins 0 Wheelchair Cabins	2
Cabin Current 110 AC Refrigerator	No
Cabin TV No VCR	No
Dining Rooms 1 Sittings	2

Elevators	5
Casino Yes Slot Machines	Yes
Swimming Pools (outside) 1 (inside)	1
Whirlpools 0 Gymnasium	Yes
Sauna/Steam Room Yes/No Massage	Yes
Self-Service Launderette	No
Movie Theater/Seats	Yes/263
Library Yes Children's Facilities	No
Classification Society	American Bureau
	of Shipping

RATINGS	SCORE
Ship: Condition/Cleanliness	6.8
Ship: Space/Flow/Comfort	6.9
Ship: Decor/Furnishings	6.9
Ship: Fitness Facilities	5.5
Cabins: Comfort/Facilities	6.6
Cabins: Software	6.8
Food: Dining Room/Cuisine	7.4
Food: Buffets/Informal Dining	6.8
Food: Quality of Ingredients	6.9
Service: Dining Room	7.5
Service: Bars	7.3
Service: Cabins	6.8
Cruise: Entertainment	5.9
Cruise: Activities Program	6.0
Cruise: Hospitality Standard	6.2
OVERALL RATING	100.3

+ Good-looking ship with classic profile and pleasing lines. Good, contemporary yet elegant, decor and colors. Spacious, well equipped and nicely furnished cabins have good amount of closet, drawer and storage space. Spacious interior features two enclosed promenades and a good array of public rooms.

— Maintenance is shoddy and needs more attention and supervision. The odor of stale cigarette smoke throughout the ship is overbearing, and the poor air-conditioning doesn't help. Long lines for lido buffets, and the seats are very low. Officers rarely socialize. The casino is constantly full of smokers.

Dining Features Continental cuisine. Limited selection of vegetables. Dining room service is poor and uncoordinated.

Other Comments Cabins on top deck have lifeboat-obstructed views. Attractive dining room and seating. This ship is the nicest of the fleet of Regency's ships, and will cruise you in reasonably comfortable style and at a modest price, but those added cabins mean crowded spaces at times. Staff are reasonably friendly, but there's no real finesse.

ms Renaissance One/Two/ Three/Four ★★★★

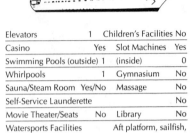

OPERATES

7-DAY CRUISES WORLDWIDE

Cruise Line		Renaissance Cruises	
Former Names	n/a	Gross Tonnage	3,990
Builder		Cantieri Navale Ferrari (Italy)	
Original Cost		$20 million each	
Christened By	Ms C Astrup (1); Mrs G Reggio (2);		
	Mrs Papagitos (3)	Mrs F Paoletti (4)	
Entered Service	Dec 30, 1989 (1) Apr 21, 1990 (2)		
	Aug 18, 1990 (3) Jan 7, 1991 (4)		
Interior Design	Bertelotti/Yran & Storbraaten		
Country of Registry	Liberia ELGI7 (1); ELGI8 (2);		
	ELGI9 (3); ELGI2 (4)		
Tel/Fax No	(1) 115-0510/115-0565;		
(2) 125-0164/125-0165; (3) 125-0166/125-0167;			
(4) 125-0171/125-0172			
Length (ft/m)		289.6/88.30	
Beam (ft/m) 50.1/15.30		Draft (ft/m)	11.9/3.65
Propulsion/Propellers		diesel (3,514kW)/2 (CP)	
Decks	5 Crew 72	Total Cabins	50
Pass. Capacity (basis 2) 100		(all berths) 111	
Pass. Space Ratio (basis 2) 39.9		(all berths) 35.9	
Officers Italian	Dining Staff European/Filipino		
Size Range (sq ft/m)		231-282/21.5-26.2	
Outside Cabins	50	Inside Cabins	0
Single Cabins	0	Supplement	30-65%
Balcony Cabins	4	Wheelchair Cabins	0
Cabin Current	110 AC	Refrigerator	All cabins
Cabin TV	Yes	VCR	Yes
Dining Rooms	1	Sittings	1

Elevators	1	Children's Facilities	No
Casino	Yes	Slot Machines	Yes
Swimming Pools (outside) 1		(inside)	0
Whirlpools	1	Gymnasium	No
Sauna/Steam Room Yes/No		Massage	No
Self-Service Launderette			No
Movie Theater/Seats	No	Library	No
Watersports Facilities		Aft platform, sailfish,	
		snorkel equipment, zodiacs	
Classification Society			RINA

RATINGS	SCORE
Ship: Condition/Cleanliness	7.2
Ship: Space/Flow/Comfort	7.3
Ship: Decor/Furnishings	8.0
Ship: Fitness Facilities	7.5
Cabins: Comfort/Facilities	8.0
Cabins: Software	8.0
Food: Dining Room/Cuisine	7.6
Food: Buffets/Informal Dining	7.1
Food: Quality of Ingredients	7.6
Service: Dining Room	8.0
Service: Bars	7.8
Service: Cabins	8.0
Cruise: Entertainment	6.0
Cruise: Activities Program	6.3
Cruise: Hospitality Standard	7.6
OVERALL RATING	112.0

+ Contemporary private yacht look, with twin flared funnels and handsome styling throughout. Redesigned layout (Renaissance Five–Eight) makes the second set of four vessels superior to the first four in the series, especially for stability and comfort. All have exquisite all-outside suites, which combine highly polished imitation rosewood paneling with lots of mirrors, handcrafted Italian furniture, wet bar (pre-stocked when you book, at extra cost). Wooden outside promenade deck. Refined and attractive interior decor. Accommodations are located forward, with public rooms aft. Cabins have queen-sized bed, a sitting area, and feature most things you need. Bathrooms have showers with fold-down seat, real teakwood floors and marble vanities.

— Renaissance One–Four don't sail well in inclement weather, being smaller and less stable than Renaissance Five–Eight. Tiny "dip" pool is not a swimming pool. Open deck and sunning space is quite cramped. Plastic woods instead of real woods everywhere (looks too perfect). Small library is attractive, but book selection is poor. Cabins have small closets. Space for luggage is tight, and there is not much drawer space. Bathrooms are very compact and none have bathtubs.

Dining The dining room, which has open seating, is small and elegant. It is on lowest deck and has portholes (a requirement of the construction regulations), although it is quite cozy

ms Renaissance Five/Six/ Seven/Eight ★★★★

OPERATES
7-DAY CRUISES WORLDWIDE

Cruise Line	Renaissance Cruises	Elevators	1 Children's Facilities No
Former Names	n/a Gross Tonnage 4,280	Casino	Yes Slot Machines Yes
Builder	Nuovi Cantieri Apuania (Italy)	Swimming Pools (outside) 1 (inside) 0	
Original Cost	$25 million each	Whirlpools	1 Gymnasium No
Christened By	Mrs Lyng-Olsen (5);	Sauna/Steam Room Yes/No Massage Yes	
Blessed by shipyard priest (6); n/a (7); n/a (8)		Self-Service Launderette	No
Entered Service Mar 24, 1991 (5); Oct 5, 1991 (6);		Movie Theater/Seats No Library Yes	
Dec 21, 1991 (7); May 30, 1992 (8)		Watersports Facilities Aft platform, sailfish,	
Interior Design	Bertelotti/Yran & Storbraaten	snorkel equipment, Zodiacs	
Country of Registry	Liberia ELGI3 (5); ELGI4 (6)	Classification Society	RINA
ELGI5 (7); ELGI6 (8)			
Tel/Fax No	(5) 125-0135/ 125-0134;	**RATINGS**	**SCORE**
(6) 125-0142/125-0141; (7) 115-1322/125-0146;		Ship: Condition/Cleanliness	8.0
(8) 115-1375/125-0145		Ship: Space/Flow/Comfort	7.8
Length (ft/m)	297.2/90.60	Ship: Decor/Furnishings	8.2
Beam (ft/m) 50.1/15.30 Draft (ft/m) 12.9/3.95		Ship: Fitness Facilities	7.8
Propulsion/Propellers	diesel (5,000kW)/2 (CP)	Cabins: Comfort/Facilities	8.1
Decks 5 Crew 72 Total Cabins 50		Cabins: Software	8.0
Pass. Capacity (basis 2) 114 (all berths) 114		Food: Dining Room/Cuisine	7.7
Pass. Space Ratio (basis 2) 37.5 (all berths) 37.5		Food: Buffets/Informal Dining	7.1
Officers Italian Dining Staff European/Filipino		Food: Quality of Ingredients	7.4
Size Range (sq ft/m) 215-312/20.0-29.0		Service: Dining Room	7.8
Outside Cabins 50 Inside Cabins 0		Service: Bars	7.7
Single Cabins 0 Supplement 30-65%		Service: Cabins	7.8
Balcony Cabins 4 Wheelchair Cabins 0		Cruise: Entertainment	6.6
Cabin Current 110 AC Refrigerator All cabins		Cruise: Activities Program	6.4
Cabin TV Yes VCR Yes		Cruise: Hospitality Standard	7.7
Dining Rooms 1 Sittings 1		OVERALL RATING	114.1

and welcoming, and there are tables for two, four, six, and even eight. Sit where you like, with whom you like, and at what time you like. Meals are self-service buffet-style cold foods for breakfast and lunch, with hot foods chosen from a table menu and served properly. The dining room operation works well. Food quality, choice and presentation are all fairly decent, but not at all memorable. While the food is reasonably presented, it is quite limited in choice, particularly the entrees. An "800 Calorie" menu is good for those wanting small portions. Service is fair to good, depending on ship and crew.

Other Comments This is a fleet of eight small, intimate cruise vessels, out of a fleet of eight (Nos 1 and 2 on Singapore-based charter). Similar in concept to the *Sea Goddess* ships, though less formal, and less expensive. These vessels are comfortable and inviting, but have been poorly maintained since new. Not the equal of other small luxury ships, but neither is the price. These ships will provide a destination-intensive, refined, quiet and very relaxed cruise experience for passengers who don't like crowds, dressing up, scheduled activities, or entertainment. While not up to the standard of Sea Goddess or Seabourn, these small ships can still provide a pleasant cruise experience, for a moderate sum of money.

mv Rhapsody ★★★+

OPERATES

7 TO 14-DAY MEDITERRANEAN CRUISES

Cruise Line	StarLauro Cruises	Casino	Yes	Slot Machines	Yes
Former Names	Cunard Princess/Cunard Conquest	Swimming Pools (outside) 1	(inside)	0
Gross Tonnage	17,495	Whirlpools	2	Gymnasium	Yes
Builder	Burmeister & Wein (Denmark)	Sauna/Steam Room Yes/No	Massage	No
Original Cost	UK£12 million	Self-Service Launderette	No
Christened By	HRH Princess Grace of Monaco	Movie Theater/Seats	Yes/130
Entered Service	Mar 15, 1977/May 17, 1995	Library	Yes
Interior Design	McNeece Design	Children's Facilities	No
Country of Registry	Bahamas (CPCG)	Watersports Facilities	None
Tel No 110-4111 Fax No 110-4111	Classification Society	Lloyd's Register
Length (ft/m)	536.6/163.56		

RATINGS	SCORE
Beam (ft/m) 74.9/22.84 Draft (ft/m) 19.0/5.82	Ship: Condition/Cleanliness	6.8
Propulsion	diesel (15,670kW)	Ship: Space/Flow/Comfort	6.3
Propellers	2 (CP)	Ship: Decor/Furnishings	6.6
Decks 8 Crew 350	Ship: Fitness Facilities	6.7
Pass. Capacity (basis 2) 804 (all berths) 959	Cabins: Comfort/Facilities	5.8
Pass. Space Ratio (basis 2) 21.7 (all berths) 18.1	Cabins: Software	7.7
Officers British Dining Staff International	Food: Dining Room/Cuisine	6.6
Total Cabins 402	Food: Buffets/Informal Dining	6.1
Size Range (sq ft/m) 88-265/8.1-24.6	Food: Quality of Ingredients	6.2
Outside Cabins 266 Inside Cabins 136	Service: Dining Room	7.0
Single Cabins 1 Supplement 50%	Service: Bars	6.8
Balcony Cabins 0 Wheelchair Cabins 0	Service: Cabins	7.2
Cabin Current 110/220 AC	Cruise: Entertainment	7.3
Refrigerator Category 1/2 only	Cruise: Activities Program	7.1
Cabin TV No VCR No	Cruise: Hospitality Standard	7.6
Dining Rooms 1 Sittings 2	OVERALL RATING	101.8
Elevators 2		

+ Has a good amount of open deck space for sun-worshippers. Fine selection of public rooms with attractive decor, in light, bright colors, including an observation lounge above the bridge overlooking the bow. Has an excellent indoor-outdoor entertainment nightclub, which incorporates the occasional use of an aft open deck area. The cabins have pleasant soft furnishings, and closet and drawer space is reasonable.

— Cabins are small and compact, with tinny metal fixtures, and very thin walls that provide extremely poor cabin insulation. There's no outdoor wrap-around outdoor promenade deck.

Dining Pleasant dining room has sea views from big picture windows. Reasonable banquet food standard tailored to Italian passengers, with typical Italian food, including lots of pasta dishes. Service is bubbly, cheerful, and attentive, and comes with a smile, but lacks finesse. Limited selection of breads and fruits. Poor cabin service menu.

Other Comments Almost identical sister ship to *Cunard Countess*, with the same contemporary profile and good balanced looks. Acquired in 1995 by StarLauro Cruises, as a replacement for the *Achille Lauro*. This ship will provide a very comfortable first cruise experience in a pleasing, very informal environment, at an excellent price, to some well-chosen destinations. This ship is now marketed almost exclusively to Italian passengers.

mv Romantica ★

OPERATES
3- AND 4-DAY EGYPT/ISRAEL CRUISES

Cruise Line	Travelwise Cruises	Casino	No	Slot Machines	Yes
Former Names	Romanza/Aurelia/	Swimming Pools (outside) 1		(inside)	0
	Beaverbrae/Huscaran	Whirlpools	0	Gymnasium	No
Gross Tonnage	7,537	Sauna/Steam Room No/No		Massage	No
Builder	Blohm & Voss (Germany)	Self-Service Launderette			No
Original Cost	n/a	Movie Theater/Seats			Yes/204
Christened By	n/a	Library			No
Entered Service	Apr 1939/1991	Children's Facilities			No
Interior Design	n/a	Watersports Facilities			None
Country of Registry	Cyprus (P3DW4)	Classification Society		Lloyd's Register	

Tel No	110-1113	Fax No	110-1113
Length (ft/m)			487.5/148.60
Beam (ft/m) 60.3/18.39	Draft (ft/m)	21.9/6.70	
Propulsion	diesel-electric (5,958kW)		
Propellers			1 (FP)
Decks	7	Crew	190
Pass. Capacity (basis 2) 568		(all berths) 727	
Pass. Space Ratio (basis 2) 13.2		(all berths) 10.3	
Officers	Greek	Dining Staff	International
Total Cabins			293
Size Range (sq ft/m)			n/a
Outside Cabins	152	Inside Cabins	141
Single Cabins	8	Supplement	100%
Balcony Cabins	0	Wheelchair Cabins	0
Cabin Current	220 AC	Refrigerator	No
Cabin TV	No	VCR	No
Dining Rooms	1	Sittings	2
Elevators			0

RATINGS	SCORE
Ship: Condition/Cleanliness	4.3
Ship: Space/Flow/Comfort	4.5
Ship: Decor/Furnishings	5.1
Ship: Fitness Facilities	3.6
Cabins: Comfort/Facilities	5.2
Cabins: Software	5.4
Food: Dining Room/Cuisine	5.6
Food: Buffets/Informal Dining	5.0
Food: Quality of Ingredients	5.4
Service: Dining Room	5.8
Service: Bars	5.7
Service: Cabins	6.2
Cruise: Entertainment	5.0
Cruise: Activities Program	5.1
Cruise: Hospitality Standard	5.8
OVERALL RATING	77.7

+ Well-constructed ship of real vintage years; despite her age, she has been quite well maintained and is still going strong. The interior decor is typically Mediterranean. Service is quite friendly. Reasonable public rooms, but they have low ceilings.

— The open deck and sunning space is very limited, and is crowded when full. Steep, narrow gangway in most ports. Very narrow interior passageways and steep stairways with short steps. Cabins are very small indeed, and there's virtually no closet and storage space, except under the beds. The bathrooms are tiny and have been patched considerably to keep them operating. There are too many annoying announcements.

Dining Has quite a charming old style dining room. Barely adequate food seldom arrives hot, and buffet meals are totally uninspiring and unattractive. The selection of breads, fruits and cheeses is poor, and service, while friendly, is totally without finesse.

Other Comments This high-density vessel is marketed specifically to residents of and visitors to Cyprus. This ship is suggested only for those wanting to cruise in the most basic of surroundings and comfort, at a modest price. However, the ship should really be retired from service and is operated with only the most basic standards.

ss Rotterdam ★★★+

OPERATES
ALASKA AND CARIBBEAN CRUISES

Cruise Line	Holland America Line
Former Names	-
Gross Tonnage	38,645
Builder	Rotterdamsche Dry Dock (Holland)
Original Cost	$30 million
Christened By	HRH Queen Juliana
Entered Service	Sep 3, 1959
Interior Design	Kym Anton/Julie Stanley
Country of Registry	Netherlands Antilles (PJSU)
Tel No 175-0101	Fax No 175-0124
Length (ft/m)	748.6/228.20
Beam (ft/m) 94.1/28.71	Draft (ft/m) 29.6/9.04
Propulsion	steam turbine (28,700kW)
Propellers	2 (FP)
Decks 10	Crew 603
Pass. Capacity (basis 2) 1,114	(all berths) 1,250
Pass. Space Ratio (basis 2) 34.6	(all berths) 30.9
Officers	Dutch
Dining Staff	Filipino/Indonesian
Total Cabins	575
Size Range (sq ft/m)	112-370/10.5-34.3
Outside Cabins 307	Inside Cabins 268
Single Cabins 32	Supplement 50-100%
Balcony Cabins	0
Wheelchair Cabins	0 (ramps available)
Cabin Current	110 AC
Refrigerator	Category A only
Cabin TV No	VCR No

Dining Rooms	2	Sittings	2
Elevators			7
Casino	Yes	Slot Machines	Yes
Swimming Pools (outside) 1		(inside)	1
Whirlpools	0	Gymnasium	Yes
Sauna/Steam Room	Yes/No	Massage	Yes
Self-Service Launderette			Yes
Movie Theater/Seats			Yes/620
Library	Yes	Children's Facilities	No
Classification Society			Lloyd's Register

RATINGS	SCORE
Ship: Condition/Cleanliness	6.9
Ship: Space/Flow/Comfort	7.0
Ship: Decor/Furnishings	6.6
Ship: Fitness Facilities	6.3
Cabins: Comfort/Facilities	6.3
Cabins: Software	7.5
Food: Dining Room/Cuisine	6.3
Food: Buffets/Informal Dining	6.0
Food: Quality of Ingredients	6.6
Service: Dining Room	6.7
Service: Bars	7.4
Service: Cabins	7.5
Cruise: Entertainment	6.4
Cruise: Activities Program	6.7
Cruise: Hospitality Standard	7.6
OVERALL RATING	101.8

+ Sturdily built ship has beautiful rounded lines; this grand dame is lovely—and well loved. Gracious and graceful, she has been well maintained. Expansive open deck and sunning space, with real wooden deck lounge chairs. Gorgeous flower displays offset otherwise drab interior. Beautiful wood paneling and wood trim. Two-level art deco Ritz Carlton is most elegant. Wide choice of cabin sizes and configurations, all comfortably equipped. Lots of cabins for single cruisers. Lovely balconied theater.

— No wrap-around outdoor promenade deck. Numerous public rooms, but poor color combinations. Smokers and non-smokers are poorly separated. Many cabin bathrooms have exposed plumbing. Has poor entertainment. Expect lines for embarkation, disembarkation, buffets, and shore tenders. Many cabin bathrooms have exposed plumbing.

Dining Two high-ceilinged dining rooms. Reasonable food, though robotic service. Open sitting for breakfast and lunch; two sittings for dinner. Food is attractively presented, but meals are not memorable, and standards have declined. Poor selection of breads, cheeses, and fruit.

Other Comments A cruise on this stately ship fits comfortably—like a well-worn shoe—and the price is agreeable, too. However, remember that she is old, and cannot compete with the latest high-tech contemporary ships. Perhaps it's time for her retirement.

ms Royal Majesty ★★★★

OPERATES

*3- AND 4-DAY BAHAMAS AND
7-DAY BERMUDA CRUISES*

Cruise Line	Majesty Cruise Line	Casino Yes	Slot Machines Yes
Former Names	-	Swimming Pools (outside) 1	(inside) 0
Gross Tonnage	32,396	Whirlpools 2	Gymnasium Yes
Builder	Kvaerner Masa Yards (Finland)	Sauna/Steam Room Yes/No	Massage Yes
Original Cost	$229 million	Self-Service Launderette	No
Christened By	Ms Liza Minelli	Movie Theater/Seats	Yes/100
Entered Service	Sep 18, 1992	Library	Yes
Interior Design	A&M Katzourakis	Children's Facilities	Yes (also children's pool)
Country of Registry	Panama (3ETG9)	Watersports Facilities	none
Tel No 133-6557 Fax No	133-6563	Classification Society	Lloyd's Register
Length (ft/m)	567.9/173.10		

RATINGS	SCORE
Ship: Condition/Cleanliness	8.7
Ship: Space/Flow/Comfort	8.6
Ship: Decor/Furnishings	8.7
Ship: Fitness Facilities	7.6
Cabins: Comfort/Facilities	8.0
Cabins: Software	8.1
Food: Dining Room/Cuisine	7.7
Food: Buffets/Informal Dining	6.8
Food: Quality of Ingredients	7.0
Service: Dining Room	6.7
Service: Bars	7.0
Service: Cabins	7.4
Cruise: Entertainment	7.6
Cruise: Activities Program	6.7
Cruise: Hospitality Standard	7.2
OVERALL RATING	113.8

Beam (ft/m) 90.5/27.60	Draft (ft/m) 20.3/6.20
Propulsion	diesel (21,120kW)
Propellers	2 (CP)
Decks 9	Crew 525
Pass. Capacity (basis 2) 1,056	(all berths) 1,501
Pass. Space Ratio (basis 2) 31.3	(all berths) 21.5
Officers Greek	Dining Staff International
Total Cabins	528 (132 no-smoking)
Size Range (sq ft/m)	118-375/11.0-34.8
Outside Cabins 343	Inside Cabins 185
Single Cabins 0	Supplement 50%
Balcony Cabins 0	Wheelchair Cabins 4
Cabin Current	110/220 AC
Refrigerator	Suites only
Cabin TV Yes	VCR Suites only
Dining Rooms 1	Sittings 2
Elevators	4

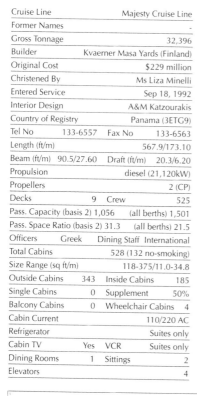

+ Smart contemporary ship has a good profile and is a well-conceived vessel. Tastefully appointed, with lots of teak and brass accents, discreet lighting, soothing colors and no glitz. Wide passageways. Circular lobby is bright and classical in appearance. Suites feature butler service, and are well equipped, though not really large. Most other cabins are on the small side, but comfortable, with excellent bathroom showers. There are many cabins designated for non-smokers. All cabins have ironing boards. Bathrobes are provided.

− Open deck and sunning space is cramped. No cushioned pads for deck chairs. Many cabins on Queen's Deck have obstructed views. Showroom is poorly designed, with obstructed sightlines, and production shows are weak. Too many announcements. Expect lines for shore excursions, buffets and pizza.

Dining The dining room is attractive, though very noisy, and the tables are close together. The food, menu, creativity, and service are basically sound, but bread rolls, cheese, and fruits could be better. Service is too fast, consistently poor, and seems to be getting worse, however.

Other Comments In the Royal Observatory, models and plans of 19th-century sailing ships provide a nautical ambiance. This ship will provide you with a very comfortable short cruise experience in warm, elegant surroundings, with a modicum of hospitality.

ms Royal Odyssey ★★★★

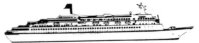

OPERATES
VARIOUS EUROPE AND SOUTH PACIFIC CRUISES

Cruise Line	Royal Cruise Line
Former Names	Royal Viking Sea
Gross Tonnage	28,078
Builder	Wartsila (Finland)
Original Cost	$22.5 million
Christened By Mrs Ulla Klaveness/Mrs Eva Golteus	
Entered Service	Nov 25, 1973/Dec 21, 1991
Interior Design	A&M Katzourakis
Country of Registry	Bahamas (C6CN4)
Tel No 110-4504 Fax No 110-4511	
Length (ft/m)	674.2/205.50
Beam (ft/m) 83.6/25.50 Draft (ft/m) 23.6/7.20	
Propulsion	diesel (13,400kW)
Propellers	2 (CP)
Decks 8 Crew	435
Pass. Capacity (basis 2) 765 (all berths) 820	
Pass. Space Ratio (basis 2) 36.7 (all berths) 34.2	
Officers European Dining Staff International	
Total Cabins	410
Size Range (sq ft/m)	136-580/12.6-53.8
Outside Cabins 357 Inside Cabins 53	
Single Cabins 55 Supplement 100%	
Balcony Cabins 9 Wheelchair Cabins 0	
Cabin Current	110/220 AC
Refrigerator	Category A/B only
Cabin TV Yes VCR No	
Dining Rooms 1 Sittings 1	
Elevators	5

Casino	Yes	Slot Machines	Yes
Swimming Pools (outside) 1		(inside)	0
Whirlpools	3	Gymnasium	Yes
Sauna/Steam Room Yes/No		Massage	Yes
Self-Service Launderette			No
Movie Theater/Seats			Yes/156
Library			Yes
Children's Facilities			No
Watersports Facilities			None
Classification Society		Det Norske Veritas	

RATINGS	SCORE
Ship: Condition/Cleanliness	7.8
Ship: Space/Flow/Comfort	8.5
Ship: Decor/Furnishings	8.1
Ship: Fitness Facilities	8.1
Cabins: Comfort/Facilities	7.6
Cabins: Software	7.8
Food: Dining Room/Cuisine	7.3
Food: Buffets/Informal Dining	7.2
Food: Quality of Ingredients	6.9
Service: Dining Room	7.7
Service: Bars	7.8
Service: Cabins	7.7
Cruise: Entertainment	7.1
Cruise: Activities Program	7.0
Cruise: Hospitality Standard	7.7
OVERALL RATING	114.3

+ Has a contemporary profile, with well-balanced lines and sharply raked bow. Well maintained, with good open deck, sunning and sports areas. Public rooms are quite elegant and have high ceilings. Good spa and fitness facilities. Nine penthouse suites are named after destinations (one has lifeboat-obstructed views). All other cabins are well appointed with good closet, drawer, and storage space, but some bathrooms have awkward access. Non-smoking cabins available. Gentleman "host" program ideal for older single female passengers.

— Cabin numbering system reversed from the seagoing norm. Generally good service. Tinny drawers in cabins.

Dining Food is Continental in style, with emphasis on meat, chicken and prawn dishes, overcooked and highly salted. Health-conscious cruisers can choose from the "Dine to Your Heart's Content" program. Reduced salt, fat, cholesterol and calories meals available. Wine selection quite reasonable. Dining is in a single seating, with assigned tables for two, four, six or eight. Poor bread rolls and fruits. Hot food choice reasonable, but presentation is lacking.

Other Comments Stretched in 1983. Attention to detail is apparent in most areas. Poor destination information. This ship will, however, provide RCL's repeat passengers with a fine cruise experience and refined lifestyle at an appropriate price.

mv Royal Princess ★★★★+

OPERATES

VARIOUS CRUISES WORLDWIDE

Cruise Line	Princess Cruises		
Former Names	-		
Gross Tonnage	44,348		
Builder	Wartsila (Finland)		
Original Cost	$165 million		
Christened By	HRH Princess Diana of Wales		
Entered Service	Nov 19, 1984		
Interior Design	Njal Eide		
Country of Registry	Great Britain (GBRP)		
Tel No	144-0211	Fax No	144-0215
Length (ft/m)	754.5/230.00		
Beam (ft/m)	95.8/29.20	Draft (ft/m)	25.5/7.80
Propulsion	diesel (29,160kW)		
Propellers	2 (CP)		
Decks	9	Crew	520
Pass. Capacity (basis 2) 1,200	(all berths) 1,275		
Pass. Space Ratio (basis 2) 36.9	(all berths) 34.7		
Officers	British	Dining Staff	International
Total Cabins	600		
Size Range (sq ft/m)	68-806/6.3-74.8		
Outside Cabins	600	Inside Cabins	0
Single Cabins	0	Supplement	25-100%
Balcony Cabins	150	Wheelchair Cabins	10
Cabin Current	110/220 AC		
Refrigerator	All cabins		
Cabin TV	Yes	VCR	No
Dining Rooms	1	Sittings	2
Elevators	6		

Casino	Yes	Slot Machines	Yes
Swimming Pools (outside)		2 (+2 splash pools)	
Swimming Pools (inside)			0
Whirlpools	2	Gymnasium	Yes
Sauna/Steam Room	Yes/No	Massage	Yes
Self-Service Launderette			Yes
Movie Theater/Seats			Yes/150
Library	Yes	Children's Facilities	No
Watersports Facilities			None
Classification Society			Lloyd's Register

RATINGS	SCORE
Ship: Condition/Cleanliness	8.7
Ship: Space/Flow/Comfort	8.8
Ship: Decor/Furnishings	8.8
Ship: Fitness Facilities	7.8
Cabins: Comfort/Facilities	8.6
Cabins: Software	8.2
Food: Dining Room/Cuisine	7.7
Food: Buffets/Informal Dining	7.2
Food: Quality of Ingredients	7.0
Service: Dining Room	7.5
Service: Bars	7.7
Service: Cabins	7.8
Cruise: Entertainment	8.2
Cruise: Activities Program	8.0
Cruise: Hospitality Standard	8.3
OVERALL RATING	120.3

+ Contemporary outer styling, with short, well raked bow. Quality construction. Excellent outdoor deck and sunning space, and wrap-around outdoor promenade deck. Good, though unconventional, interior layout and passenger flow has passenger cabins above public room decks. Spacious passageways and delightful staircases. Contemporary but not garish, the decor reflects the feeling of space, openness, and light. All-outside cabins are well appointed and comfortable. Suites are gorgeous and feature upgraded amenities. All cabins have full bathtub and shower, and three-sided mirrors. Prompt, attentive room service. Large, beautifully appointed public rooms. Bathrobes are provided for all passengers.

— Lacks small, intimate public rooms, although public rooms are spacious. Some cabins on Baja and Caribe decks have lifeboat-obstructed views. Cabin numbering system is illogical. Signs throughout the ship are adequate, but most are hard to read.

Dining The elegant dining room is set low down, adjacent to the lobby. Food and service are moderately good, having been improved recently. There is always a pasta dish on the menu, and table captains are willing to make something special for you. Portions are generous.

Other Comments This ship, will provide a fine cruise experience in spacious, elegant surroundings, at the appropriate price, although attention to the small details is missing.

mv Royal Star ★★★

OPERATES

*VARIOUS SOUTH INDIAN
OCEAN CRUISES*

Cruise Line	Star Line Cruises	Casino	Yes	Slot Machines Yes
Former Names	Ocean Islander/San Giorgio/	Swimming Pools (outside) 1		(inside) 0
	City of Andros	Whirlpools	0	Gymnasium Yes
Gross Tonnage	5,360	Sauna/Steam Room Yes/No		Massage Yes
Builder	Cantieri Riuniti dell' Adriatico (Italy)	Self-Service Launderette		No
Original Cost	n/a	Movie Theater/Seats No		Library Yes
Christened By	Mrs Sandra Ruedin	Children's Facilities		No
Entered Service	1956/Dec 15, 1990	Watersports Facilities		None
Interior Design	A&M Katzourakis	Classification Society		American Bureau
Country of Registry	Bahamas (C6CF4)			of Shipping

Tel No 110-4407 Fax No 110-3460	
Length (ft/m) 367.4/112.00	
Beam (ft/m) 51.0/15.55 Draft (ft/m) 18.2/5.56	
Propulsion/Propellers diesel (4,817kW)/2 (FP)	
Decks 5 Crew 120	
Pass. Capacity (basis 2) 222 (all berths) 255	
Pass. Space Ratio (basis 2) 24.1 (all berths) 21.0	
Officers Greek Dining Staff European	
Total Cabins 111	
Size Range (sq ft/m) 107-398/10.0-37.0	
Outside Cabins 97 Inside Cabins 14	
Single Cabins 0 Supplement Set rates	
Balcony Cabins 1 Wheelchair Cabins 0	
Cabin Current 110/220 AC	
Refrigerator Superior suites only	
Cabin TV No VCR Superior suites only	
Dining Rooms 1 Sittings 2	
Elevators 1	

RATINGS	SCORE
Ship: Condition/Cleanliness	6.7
Ship: Space/Flow/Comfort	6.8
Ship: Decor/Furnishings	7.1
Ship: Fitness Facilities	4.3
Cabins: Comfort/Facilities	6.4
Cabins: Software	6.7
Food: Dining Room/Cuisine	7.0
Food: Buffets/Informal Dining	6.6
Food: Quality of Ingredients	6.8
Service: Dining Room	7.2
Service: Bars	7.3
Service: Cabins	7.4
Cruise: Entertainment	5.2
Cruise: Activities Program	4.8
Cruise: Hospitality Standard	6.7
OVERALL RATING	97.0

+ Charming little vessel, with well-balanced profile. Best suited for cruising in sheltered areas. Clean and tidy throughout. Warm, intimate and highly personable ambiance. Ample open deck space for sunning. Attractive contemporary Scandinavian interior decor. The cabins, although not large, are pleasantly decorated with good-quality furnishings and ample closet and drawer space.

— Has a steep, narrow gangway in some ports. Cabin bathrooms are tiny.

Dining Charming dining room, with good service and international cuisine, although standards are variable. Table wines are included with meals. Limited selection of breads, cheeses and fruits. Limited cabin service menu. Poor afternoon tea.

Other Comments Well packaged and operated by the African Safari Club group of hotels, this ship will provide a most enjoyable cruise and safari experience in very comfortable, small-ship surroundings, at an extremely realistic price.

ms Royal Venture ★★★

OPERATES
7-DAY MEXIBBEAN CRUISES

Cruise Line	Royal Venture Cruise Line	Casino	Yes	Slot Machines	Yes
Former Names	Gruziya	Swimming Pools (outside) 1	(inside)	0
Gross Tonnage	15,402	Whirlpools	0	Gymnasium	Yes
Builder	Wartsila (Finland)	Sauna/Steam Room Yes/No	Massage	Yes
Original Cost	$25 million	Self-Service Launderette		Yes
Christened By	n/a	Movie Theater/Seats		Yes/143
Entered Service	Jun 30, 1975/Jan 1996	Library		Yes
Interior Design	n/a	Children's Facilities		No
Country of Registry	Ukraine (UUFC)	Watersports Facilities		None
Tel No 140-0162 Fax No	140-0162	Classification Society		RS
Length (ft/m)	512.6/156.27			

Beam (ft/m) 72.3/22.05	Draft (ft/m)	19.4/5.92	
Propulsion	diesel (13,430kW)	**RATINGS**	**SCORE**
Propellers	2 (CP)	Ship: Condition/Cleanliness	6.4
Decks 8	Crew 250	Ship: Space/Flow/Comfort	6.2
Pass. Capacity (basis 2) 432	(all berths) 640	Ship: Decor/Furnishings	6.1
Pass. Space Ratio (basis 2) 35.6	(all berths) 24.0	Ship: Fitness Facilities	4.7
Officers Ukrainian	Dining Staff Ukrainian	Cabins: Comfort/Facilities	6.1
Total Cabins	226	Cabins: Software	6.3
Size Range (sq ft/m)	150-428/14.0-39.7	Food: Dining Room/Cuisine	5.7
Outside Cabins 116	Inside Cabins 110	Food: Buffets/Informal Dining	5.2
Single Cabins 0	Supplement 50%	Food: Quality of Ingredients	5.5
Balcony Cabins 0	Wheelchair Cabins 0	Service: Dining Room	6.5
Cabin Current	220 AC	Service: Bars	7.1
Refrigerator	No	Service: Cabins	7.2
Cabin TV No	VCR No	Cruise: Entertainment	4.7
Dining Rooms 2	Sittings 1	Cruise: Activities Program	5.7
Elevators	2	Cruise: Hospitality Standard	6.8
		OVERALL RATING	90.2

+ This ship has a smart-looking contemporary profile with swept-back squarish funnel. An extensive refurbishment program has added a new nightclub, high-ceiling cinema, and new cabins. The tiered aft decks provide well-protected outdoor seating. An unusually deep swimming pool is a welcome change from those on most ships, even though the pool is small. Smart interior decor, but uninteresting ceilings. The top-grade suites are very spacious and welcoming. Other cabins are compact, yet quite comfortable, but more color would provide a more homely ambiance.

— Open deck and sunning space crowded when ship is full. Fresh flowers are needed to provide a more welcoming ambiance.

Dining The two dining rooms (one is no-smoking), although plain, have light decor, big picture windows and comfortable seating. The food is quite attractive, but the choice is rather limited and could be upgraded. Family-style service is reasonable, but it lacks any kind of finesse, and, although the hotel staff are now more eager to please, language and communication is sometimes frustrating.

Other Comments This ship was rated while under its former name, *Gruziya*.

ms Royal Viking Sun ★★★★★+

OPERATES

VARIOUS CRUISES WORLDWIDE

Cruise Line	Cunard Royal Viking	Casino	Yes	Slot Machines	Yes
Former Names	-	Swimming Pools (outside) 2	(inside)	0
Gross Tonnage	37,845	Whirlpools	2	Gymnasium	Yes
Builder	Wartsila (Finland)	Sauna/Steam Room Yes/Yes	Massage	Yes
Original Cost	$125 million	Self-Service Launderette	Yes
Christened By	Mr James Stewart	Movie Theater/Seats	Yes/101
Entered Service	Dec 16, 1988	Library	Yes
Interior Design	Njal Eide	Children's Facilities	No
Country of Registry	Bahamas (C6DM3)	Watersports Facilities	None
Tel No 110-4517 Fax No 110-4514	Classification Society	Det Norske Veritas
Length (ft/m)	674.2/205.50	
Beam (ft/m) 91.8/28.00 Draft (ft/m) 23.6/7.20		

RATINGS	SCORE
Ship: Condition/Cleanliness	9.2
Ship: Space/Flow/Comfort	9.5
Ship: Decor/Furnishings	9.5
Ship: Fitness Facilities	9.3
Cabins: Comfort/Facilities	9.2
Cabins: Software	9.1
Food: Dining Room/Cuisine	9.0
Food: Buffets/Informal Dining	9.0
Food: Quality of Ingredients	8.7
Service: Dining Room	9.2
Service: Bars	9.1
Service: Cabins	9.4
Cruise: Entertainment	8.6
Cruise: Activities Program	8.6
Cruise: Hospitality Standard	9.4
OVERALL RATING	136.8

Propulsion	diesel (21,120kW)
Propellers	2 (CP)
Decks	8	Crew	460
Pass. Capacity (basis 2) 740	(all berths) 814
Pass. Space Ratio (basis 2) 51.1	(all berths) 46.4
Officers	Norwegian
Dining Staff	European
Total Cabins	370
Size Range (sq ft/m)	138-724/12.8-67.2
Outside Cabins	350	Inside Cabins	20
Single Cabins	2	Supplement	60-100%
Balcony Cabins	145	Wheelchair Cabins	4
Cabin Current	110 AC	Refrigerator	All cabins
Cabin TV	Yes	VCR	Yes
Dining Rooms	1	Sittings	1
Elevators	4		

+ This contemporary, well-designed ship has sleek, flowing lines, a sharply raked bow and well-rounded profile, with lots of floor-to-ceiling glass. The ship's tenders are thoughtfully air-conditioned and even have radar, and a toilet. Maintenance of the ship is excellent. Wide outdoor teakwood decks provide excellent walking areas, including a wrap-around promenade deck (even the ship's bridge has a wooden floor). There are two glass-walled elevators. Separate baggage elevators mean passengers never have to wait for luggage. Has an incredibly spacious interior layout. Impressive public rooms and tasteful decor reign throughout. Two handrails, one wooden, one chrome, are provided on all stairways, a thoughtful extra touch. The Stella Polaris Lounge, the ship's forward observation lounge, is simply lovely, and one of the most elegant lounges at sea. Pebble Beach is the name of the ship's own golf club, complete with wet bar and electronic golf simulator. The Dickens Library is now a well organized center. Distinguished male guest hosts are provided on all cruises. The Owner's Suite, at 723 sq ft (67.2m^2), is delightful, and features two bathrooms, one of which has a large whirlpool bathtub with ocean views. Fine penthouse suites have large balconies, and gracious butler service. Most cabins are of generous proportions, and are well appointed, with just about everything you would need. Some 38 percent of all cabins have a private balcony.

All cabins have walk-in closets, lockable drawers, full-length mirrors, hairdryers, and fluffy cotton bathrobes. Fine Scandinavian stewardesses provide excellent, unobtrusive service. Four well equipped, L-shaped cabins for the handicapped are well designed, quite large, and feature special wheel-in bathroom with shower facilities, and closet. First class air is provided to all passengers on long, exotic voyages. Cunard seems committed to keeping up the standards aboard this ship, and that's good for passengers.

— More maintenance needed on the balconies. There's no way to get from the uppermost pool, which has a swim-up (sit-in) bar, to the second pool, located adjacent to the health spa and gymnasium, without first going inside the vessel. The carpeting quality in some areas is poor, however, with too many strips and joins, typical of shipyard subcontractors. The Oak Room features a marble fireplace, although it can't be used due to United States Coast Guard regulations.

Dining Excellent cuisine and fine European service are provided in an unhurried, caring atmosphere, with a menu that is never repeated, no matter how long the voyage. The food is creative and well presented, with good use of garnishes. There is a delightful, well-chosen wine list from distinguished vintners from around the world. There is also a separate, but somewhat under-used wine bar.
In the dining room, mineral water, which should be included at these prices, should be served for all meals, instead of the chlorinated water provided. There's also an excellent and well utilized indoor-outdoor lido buffet area. A separate Grill Room is an elegant alternative dining spot with a great view. Although the wine list is extensive, wine prices are quite high.

Other Comments Presently the highest rated ship in the world (but by a narrow margin), this delightful vessel operates mainly long-distance cruises (including an annual complete world cruise) in great comfort. Her beauty is the result of three designers – Njal R. Eide, ship design); Finn G. Nilsson (accommodations); and Frank Mingis (Owner's Suite and Penthouse Suites, who also assisted in selecting the interior color scheme, china, glass and silverware). There are two outdoor swimming pools. The gymnasium and spa facilities are excellent.
Whether by intention or not, the ship has created a two class feeling, with passengers in "upstairs" penthouse suites and "A" grade staterooms gravitating to the somewhat quieter Stella Polaris lounge, while other passengers (the participants) go to the main entertainment deck.
This ship has a wide range of facilities, including a concierge, self-service launderettes, guest lecture program, 24-hour information office, and true 24-hour cabin service, for the discriminating passenger who demands the very finest in personal surroundings, food and service, regardless of price. Absolutely first class, this Sun is set to shine for a long time. Committed to the pursuit of gracious living at sea, she is one of the finest breed of grand floating hotels, with a warm ambiance, ably commanded by a well-loved and very proud Captain Ola Harsheim. The ship's direct competitors are the *Crystal Harmony/Crystal Symphony* (arguably more elegant ships, with larger suites, but with two sittings for dinner) and the outstanding Europa (principally for German-speaking passengers). While this ship is not perfect (the perfect ship has not yet been delivered), the few design flaws that are evident (for example: poorly designed bar service counters; odd signage in the elevators), Royal Viking Line has a long tradition of excellence. This will, without doubt, be maintained and even improved by Cunard Royal Viking, who purchased the vessel along with the brand name Royal Viking in 1994. A long cruise aboard Royal Viking Sun is arguably one of the world's finest travel experiences. Port taxes and all gratuities are included. Finally, the ship's greatest asset is her outstanding, friendly and personable, mostly European crew.

ms Ryndam ★★★★

OPERATES

7-DAY CARIBBEAN AND
EUROPE CRUISES

Cruise Line	Holland America Line	Casino	Yes	Slot Machines	Yes
Former Names	-
Gross Tonnage	55,451
Builder	Fincantieri (Italy)
Original Cost	$215 million
Christened By	Mrs Madeleine Arison
Entered Service	Nov 9, 1994
Interior Design	VFD Interiors/Joe Farcus
Country of Registry	Bahamas (C6MM2)
Tel No	130-6562 Fax No 130-6562
Length (ft/m)	719.3/219.30
Beam (ft/m) 101.0/30.80 Draft (ft/m) 24.6/7.50
Propulsion	diesel-electric (34,560kW)
Propellers	2 (CP)
Decks	10 Crew 588
Pass. Capacity (basis 2) 1,264 (all berths) 1,627
Pass. Space Ratio (basis 2) 43.8 (all berths) 34.0
Officers Dutch Dining Staff Filipino/Indonesian
Total Cabins	632
Size Range (sq ft/m) 187-1,126/17.3-104.5
Outside Cabins 501 Inside Cabins 131
Single Cabins 0 Supplement 50-100%
Balcony Cabins 150 Wheelchair Cabins 6
Cabin Current	110/220 AC
Refrigerator	Category PS/S/A/B only
Cabin TV Yes VCR No
Dining Rooms 1 Sittings 2
Elevators	12

Casino Yes Slot Machines Yes
Swimming Pools (outside) 1
Swimming Pools (inside) 1 (magrodome)
Whirlpools 2 Gymnasium Yes
Sauna/Steam Room Yes/No Massage Yes
Self-Service Launderette Yes
Movie Theater/Seats Yes/249
Library Yes Children's Facilities No
Watersports Facilities None
Classification Society Lloyd's Register

RATINGS	SCORE
Ship: Condition/Cleanliness	8.8
Ship: Space/Flow/Comfort	8.4
Ship: Decor/Furnishings	8.5
Ship: Fitness Facilities	7.7
Cabins: Comfort/Facilities	8.1
Cabins: Software	8.2
Food: Dining Room/Cuisine	6.8
Food: Buffets/Informal Dining	6.6
Food: Quality of Ingredients	6.7
Service: Dining Room	6.1
Service: Bars	7.2
Service: Cabins	8.0
Cruise: Entertainment	7.1
Cruise: Activities Program	7.7
Cruise: Hospitality Standard	8.3
OVERALL RATING	114.2

+ Sister ship to *Maasdam* and *Statendam*. Excellent teakwood decking. Asymmetrical layout breaks up her interiors and reduces bottlenecks. Stunning three-deck-high atrium foyer. Magrodome roof covers indoor-outdoor pool and central lido area. Fine Dutch antiques and art collection. Subdued and tasteful interior decor. Flowers everywhere. Cabins are spacious, tastefully decorated and well laid out, although some are a little cramped for two.

— Two-deck-high showroom is well thought out, but the ceiling is low and sightlines are not good in the upper level. Expect lines at embarkation, disembarkation, for the buffet, and shore tenders. Communication with staff, particularly at the Purser's Office, is often frustrating. Self-service launderette incurs an extra charge for both washers and dryers. Very noisy waiter stations in dining room. No bell-push outside the suites.

Dining Elegant two-deck-high dining room with dramatic grand staircase at stern. Food and service are of typical HAL standards (disappointing and non-memorable), with much use of fine china. In-suite dining can be done in 28 suites, each of which can accommodate four.

Other Comments Well-built ship, the third in a series of four. The ship continues the company's strong maritime traditions, but the food and service components let the rest of the ship and cruise experience down badly at present.

RMS St. Helena

OPERATES

*ENGLAND-ST. HELENA/SOUTH
AFRICA CRUISES*

Cruise Line	Curnow Shipping/St. Helena Line	Casino	No	Slot Machines	Yes (3)
Former Names	-	Swimming Pools (outside) 1	(inside)	0
Gross Tonnage	6,767	Whirlpools	0	Gymnasium	No
Builder	A&P Appledore (Scotland)	Sauna/Steam Room No/No	Massage	No
Original Cost	UK£32 million	Self-Service Launderette	Yes
Christened By	HRH The Prince Andrew	Movie Theater/Seats	No
Entered Service	Oct 1990	Library	Yes
Interior Design	Ron Baxter	Children's Facilities/Playroom	Yes
Country of Registry	England (MMHE5)	Watersports Facilities	none
Tel No 144-1730 Fax No 144-1731		Classification Society	Lloyd's Register

Length (ft/m)	344.4/105.00
Beam (ft/m) 62.9/19.20 Draft (ft/m) 19.6/6.00	
Propulsion	diesel (6,534kW)
Propellers	2 (CP)
Decks 4 Crew	53
Pass. Capacity (basis 2) 96 (all berths) 128	
Pass. Space Ratio (basis 2) 70.4 (all berths) 52.8	
Officers	British/St. Helenian
Dining Staff	British/St. Helenian
Total Cabins	49
Size Range (sq ft/m)	51-202/4.8-18.7
Outside Cabins 37 Inside Cabins 12	
Single Cabins 0 Supplement 30%	
Balcony Cabins 0 Wheelchair Cabins 1	
Cabin Current 220 AC Refrigerator No	
Cabin TV No VCR No	
Dining Rooms 1 Sittings 2	
Elevators 1	

RATINGS	SCORE
Ship: Condition/Cleanliness	NYR
Ship: Space/Flow/Comfort	NYR
Ship: Decor/Furnishings	NYR
Ship: Fitness Facilities	NYR
Cabins: Comfort/Facilities	NYR
Cabins: Software	NYR
Food: Dining Room/Cuisine	NYR
Food: Buffets/Informal Dining	NYR
Food: Quality of Ingredients	NYR
Service: Dining Room	NYR
Service: Bars	NYR
Service: Cabins	NYR
Cruise: Entertainment	NYR
Cruise: Activities Program	NYR
Cruise: Hospitality Standard	NYR
OVERALL RATING	

+ Has all modern conveniences, including stabilizers and air-conditioning. Passengers can even take their pets. Operates just like a full-size cruise vessel, and has a n open bridge policy. Pleasant library/reading lounge. There is a free self-service laundry. Accommodations are in two-, three-, or four-berth cabins, which are simply furnished, yet quite comfortable. The brochure states that landing at Ascension is at times "a hazardous process" owing to slippery and steep wharf steps—now that's telling it like it is. The staff are warm, welcoming, eager to see you enjoying the journey and delightful to sail with.

— Two-sitting dining on such a small ship is rather disruptive. There are nine cabins that do not have private facilities. The swimming pool is really a "dip" pool only, and is tiny.

Dining The dining room is totally non-smoking. The food is very British, with hearty breakfasts and a relatively simple menu, but the food is attractively presented on fine china. Afternoon tea, complete with freshly baked cakes, is a must.

Other Comments This amazing little combination cargo-passenger ship operates a regular Cardiff-Tenerife-St. Helena-Ascension Island-Tristan Da Cunha-Capetown line service which is like a mini-cruise, or long voyage, with lots of days at sea. There are six round-trip sailings a year.

ms Sagafjord ★★★★★

OPERATES
VARIOUS CRUISES WORLDWIDE

Cruise Line	Cunard
Former Names	-
Gross Tonnage	24,474
Builder	Forges et Chantiers de la Mediteranee (France)
Original Cost	$30 million
Christened By	Mrs Leif Hoegh
Entered Service	Oct 2, 1965/1983
Interior Design	Platou Design
Country of Registry	Bahamas (C6ZU)
Tel No 110-4115 Fax No	110-3564
Length (ft/m)	619.6/188.88
Beam (ft/m) 80.3/24.49 Draft (ft/m)	27.0/8.25
Propulsion	diesel (20,150kW)
Propellers	2 (FP)
Decks 7 Crew	350
Pass. Capacity (basis 2) 589 (all berths)	620
Pass. Space Ratio (basis 2) 41.5 (all berths)	39.4
Officers Norwegian Dining Staff	European
Total Cabins	321
Size Range (sq ft/m)	97-387/9.0-36.0
Outside Cabins 298 Inside Cabins	23
Single Cabins 43 Supplement	75%
Balcony Cabins 26 Wheelchair Cabins	13
Cabin Current	110 AC
Refrigerator	Category I/II only
Cabin TV Yes VCR	No
Dining Rooms 1 Sittings	1

Elevators			4
Casino	Yes	Slot Machines	Yes
Swimming Pools (outside) 1		(inside)	1
Whirlpools	1	Gymnasium	Yes
Sauna/Steam Room Yes/No		Massage	Yes
Self-Service Launderette			Yes
Movie Theater/Seats			Yes/181
Library	Yes	Children's Facilities	No
Watersports Facilities			None
Classification Society			Lloyd's Register

RATINGS	SCORE
Ship: Condition/Cleanliness	8.0
Ship: Space/Flow/Comfort	9.1
Ship: Decor/Furnishings	8.6
Ship: Fitness Facilities	8.6
Cabins: Comfort/Facilities	9.1
Cabins: Software	8.9
Food: Dining Room/Cuisine	9.2
Food: Buffets/Informal Dining	8.3
Food: Quality of Ingredients	9.1
Service: Dining Room	9.0
Service: Bars	8.8
Service: Cabins	9.1
Cruise: Entertainment	8.6
Cruise: Activities Program	8.6
Cruise: Hospitality Standard	9.1
OVERALL RATING	132.1

+ One of the most beautifully proportioned ships afloat, with a sweeping profile, graceful lines, and funnel amidships. Like an aging Bentley, she won't go out of style. Built for long-distance cruising, she has a very spacious interior, high-ceilinged public rooms and tasteful decor. Quiet as a fine watch, this classic ship provides a refined life at sea for discriminating passenger. Wide, open decks. Fine quality furnishings and fittings, including hardwoods, brass and stainless steel (it's difficult to find any plastic in her). Large, classic movie theater. Main lounge is among the best afloat for cocktail parties, with furniture that can be moved for almost any configuration. Has large, fairly spacious suites and cabins, with superb appointments, all with excellent insulation. Generous drawer, underbed storage and lighted closet space. Gracious service is provided by Scandinavian stewardesses.

— Now in need of a serious refit and refurbishment, as she looks tired and worn.

Dining Sumptuous dining room with its high central ceiling and grand entrance staircase is both a rarity and a real classic among ships today. High-quality food and service (see comments for *Vistafjord*).

Other Comments This ship fits like an old shoe—so comfortable you don't want to discard it. Although still a fine ship and cruise experience, she is in need of some tender loving care.

ss Sapphire Seas ★★

OPERATES

3- AND 4-DAY EGYPT/ISRAEL CRUISES

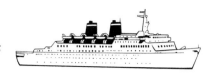

Cruise Line	Discovery Cruises	Casino Yes	Slot Machines Yes
Former Names Emerald Seas, Atlantis, President Roosevelt, Leilani, LaGuardia, General Richardson		Swimming Pools (outside) 1	(inside) 0
		Whirlpools 0	Gymnasium No
Gross Registered Tonnage:	24,458	Sauna/Steam Room No/No	Massage No
Builder	Federal Shipbuilding (USA)	Self-Service Launderette	No
Original Cost	n/a	Movie Theater/Seats	Yes/158
Christened By	n/a	Library	No
Entered Service	Dec 10, 1944/Apr 8, 1993	Children's Facilities/Playroom	No
Interior Design	n/a	Watersports Facilities	none
Country of Registry	Liberia (3FCV)	Classification Society	American Bureau
Tel No n/a Fax No	n/a		

Length (ft/m)	622.6/189.77
Beam (ft/m) 75.5/23.04 Draft (ft/m)	26.5/8.10
Propulsion	steam turbine (14,000kW)
Propellers	2 (FP)
Decks 9 Crew	425
Pass. Capacity (basis 2) 800 (all berths)	1,050
Pass. Space Ratio (basis 2) 30.5 (all berths)	23.2
Officers Greek Dining Staff	International
Total Cabins	396
Size Range (sq ft/m)	176-440/16.3-40.8
Outside Cabins 278 Inside Cabins	118
Single Cabins 0 Supplement	100%
Balcony Cabins 0 Wheelchair Cabins	0
Cabin Current 110 AC Refrigerator	No
Cabin TV No VCR	
Dining Rooms 1 Sittings	2
Elevators	3

RATINGS	SCORE
Ship: Condition/Cleanliness	5.8
Ship: Space/Flow/Comfort	6.3
Ship: Decor/Furnishings	5.7
Ship: Fitness Facilities	3.6
Cabins: Comfort/Facilities	5.7
Cabins: Software	6.0
Food: Dining Room/Cuisine	5.6
Food: Buffets/Informal Dining	4.8
Food: Quality of Ingredients	5.0
Service: Dining Room	5.7
Service: Bars	6.0
Service: Cabins	6.1
Cruise: Entertainment	5.0
Cruise: Activities Program	4.8
Cruise: Hospitality Standard	5.8
OVERALL RATING	81.9

+ Classic old liner styling. Extremely strong hull built to quality specifications has a sponson stern. This is one of only a handful of two-funnel ships still in service, albeit now on short cruises based on Limassol, Cyprus. Quite well maintained. Has a good amount of open deck and sunning space. There are several good sized public rooms, most with high ceilings. Most cabins are of a generous size, and some have large bathrooms. Good program of lecturers.

— She's an old ship, and cannot compete with more contemporary vessels.

Dining The dining room has nostalgic old-world decor that is moderately cheerful. The cuisine is definitely not a strong point, with food best described as marginally acceptable, but lacking in quality, variety, and presentation.

Other Comments The interior decor is very conservative, a little heavy, and now quite worn. This ship will provide only a moderately fair short cruise experience, without any of the finesse one would like to see aboard ship. Cruisegoers should not expect much from this ship. Operated seasonally only as this book was going to press, but the ship is getting old and tired and should be retired completely.

mv Sea Goddess I ★★★★★+

OPERATES

*VARIOUS CARIBBEAN AND
EUROPE CRUISES*

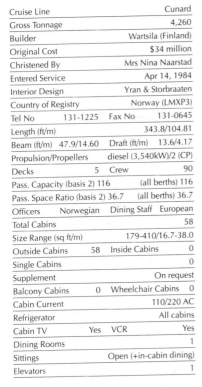

Cruise Line	Cunard		
Gross Tonnage	4,260		
Builder	Wartsila (Finland)		
Original Cost	$34 million		
Christened By	Mrs Nina Naarstad		
Entered Service	Apr 14, 1984		
Interior Design	Yran & Storbraaten		
Country of Registry	Norway (LMXP3)		
Tel No 131-1225	Fax No 131-0645		
Length (ft/m)	343.8/104.81		
Beam (ft/m) 47.9/14.60	Draft (ft/m) 13.6/4.17		
Propulsion/Propellers	diesel (3,540kW)/2 (CP)		
Decks 5	Crew 90		
Pass. Capacity (basis 2) 116	(all berths) 116		
Pass. Space Ratio (basis 2) 36.7	(all berths) 36.7		
Officers Norwegian	Dining Staff European		
Total Cabins	58		
Size Range (sq ft/m)	179-410/16.7-38.0		
Outside Cabins 58	Inside Cabins 0		
Single Cabins	0		
Supplement	On request		
Balcony Cabins 0	Wheelchair Cabins 0		
Cabin Current	110/220 AC		
Refrigerator	All cabins		
Cabin TV Yes	VCR Yes		
Dining Rooms	1		
Sittings	Open (+in-cabin dining)		
Elevators	1		

Casino	Yes	Slot Machines	Yes
Swimming Pools (outside) 1		(inside)	0
Whirlpools	1	Gymnasium	Yes
Sauna/Steam Room Yes/No		Massage	Yes
Self-Service Launderette			No
Movie Theater/Seats	No	Library	Yes
Children's Facilities			No
Watersports Facilities Aft platform, scuba, snorkel, waterski, windsurf, zodiacs (2)			
Classification Society		Lloyd's Register	

RATINGS	SCORE
Ship: Condition/Cleanliness	9.0
Ship: Space/Flow/Comfort	8.8
Ship: Facilities	9.1
Ship: Decor/Furnishings	9.1
Ship: Fitness/Watersports Facilities	9.1
Cabins: Comfort/Facilities	9.0
Cabins: Software	9.0
Food: Dining Room/Cuisine	9.5
Food: Buffets/Informal Dining	9.3
Food: Quality of Ingredients	9.2
Service: Dining Room	9.2
Service: Bars	9.2
Service: Cabins	9.1
Cruise: Entertainment/Lecture Program	8.6
Cruise: Hospitality Standard	9.3
OVERALL RATING	136.5

+ *Sea Goddess I* and *Sea Goddess II* are two lovely vessels that have a sleek, contemporary, handsome profile and private club ambiance. Shallow draft allows access to small ports that mainstream ships cannot enter. Meticulously maintained. They have an aft platform with watersports facilities at no extra charge. Elegant, chic public rooms and decor. Beautiful flower displays and green plants everywhere, giving the ships a warm connection with nature. Cute gymnasium and spa (classes are by Golden Door of California). Oriental rugs in lobby. Fine quality furnishings and fabrics throughout, with marble and blond wood accents. Charming all-outside cabins, although small, come fully equipped with everything you'll need. The bedroom is next to the window, unlike on the *Seabourn* ships, so you can entertain in the living area without going past the sleeping area, as one must on the Seabourns. Everything, including all beverages, wines, and caviar, is included. Hospitality and anticipation are art forms practiced to the highest degree by staff.

— Bathroom doors open inward. Pleasant waterfall at outdoor café, but it doesn't belong on a ship.

Dining Dining is what the *Sea Goddess* experience is all about—the height of *haute cuisine* at sea. Elegant, warm, cozy, inviting dining salons have leather-bound menus, beautiful crystalware and supremely attentive, impeccable personalized European service. Plenty of

mv Sea Goddess II ★★★★★+

OPERATES
VARIOUS EUROPE AND ORIENT CRUISES

Cruise Line		Cunard		
Former Names	-	Gross Tonnage	4,260	
Builder			Wartsila (Finland)	
Original Cost			$34 million	
Christened By	HRH Princess Caroline of Monaco			
Entered Service			May 11, 1985	
Interior Design			Yran & Storbraaten	
Country of Registry			Norway (LNQX3)	
Tel No	131-1235	Fax No	131-0644	
Length (ft/m)			343.8/104.81	
Beam (ft/m)	47.9/14.60	Draft (ft/m)	13.6/4.17	
Propulsion/Propellers		diesel (3,540kW)/2 (CP)		
Decks	5	Crew	90	
Pass. Capacity (basis 2) 115		(all berths) 115		
Pass. Space Ratio (basis 2) 36.7		(all berths) 36.7		
Officers	Norwegian	Dining Staff	Scandinavian	
Total Cabins			58	
Size Range (sq ft/m)		179-410/16.7-38.0		
Outside Cabins	58	Inside Cabins	0	
Single Cabins			1	
Supplement			On request	
Balcony Cabins	0	Wheelchair Cabins	0	
Cabin Current			110/220 AC	
Refrigerator			All cabins	
Cabin TV	Yes	VCR	Yes	
Dining Rooms			1	
Sittings		Open (+in-cabin dining)		
Elevators			1	

Casino	Yes	Slot Machines	Yes
Swimming Pools (outside) 1		(inside)	0
Whirlpools		1 Gymnasium	Yes
Sauna/Steam Room Yes/No		Massage	Yes
Self-Service Launderette			No
Movie Theater/Seats	No	Library	Yes
Children's Facilities			No
Watersports Facilities		Aft platform, banana boat,	
scuba, snorkel, waterski, windsurf, zodiacs (2)			
Classification Society			Lloyd's Register

RATINGS	SCORE
Ship: Condition/Cleanliness	9.0
Ship: Space/Flow/Comfort	8.8
Ship: Facilities	9.1
Ship: Decor/Furnishings	9.1
Ship: Fitness/Watersports Facilities	9.1
Cabins: Comfort/Facilities	9.0
Cabins: Software	9.0
Food: Dining Room/Cuisine	9.5
Food: Buffets/Informal Dining	9.3
Food: Quality of Ingredients	9.2
Service: Dining Room	9.2
Service: Bars	9.2
Service: Cabins	9.1
Cruise: Entertainment/Lecture Program	8.6
Cruise: Hospitality Standard	9.3
OVERALL RATING	136.5

space around each table for fine service, and a floating culinary celebration. Tables for two, four, six, or eight are immaculately laid with settings of real silver base plates, pristine white table linen, and always fresh flowers. Hutschenreuther, Villeroy and Boch, and Tiffany are the appointments. Open seating means you dine wherever, whenever, and with whomever you want. Exquisite cuisine, and everything is prepared individually to order. Only the freshest and finest ingredients are used. You can, naturally, dine in-suite at any time, course by course. You can also eat à la carte 24 hours a day if you wish. Has excellent outdoor buffets, and you never have to get your own food. There's plenty of caviar, at any time of the day or night. And never a hint of baked Alaska! A selection of fine wines accompanies each meal, while connoisseurs will appreciate the availability of an extra-cost wine list, of special vintages and premier crus.

Other Comments For the discriminating person requiring a very private environment in which to be pampered in an unstructured setting. Highly recommended for those who do not like cruise ships (particularly the large ships with their platoons of people). Daytime dress code is resort casual, dressy at night. The staff is simply wonderful, and it's hard for them to say "no" to any request. Port taxes and insurance are extra, but all shore excursions and gratuities are included, and no further tipping is allowed. The ship was well refurbished in 1995.

ms Sea Prince ★★★

OPERATES

7-DAY MEDITERRANEAN CRUISES

Cruise Line	Sunshine Cruise Line		
Former Names	Ocean Princess/Italia/		
	Princess Italia		
Gross Tonnage	11,125		
Builder	Cantieri Navale Felszegi (Italy)		
Original Cost	n/a	Christened By	n/a
Entered Service	Aug 17, 1967/Apr 14, 1995		
Interior Design	A&M Katzourakis		
Country of Registry	Greece (EFUG4)		
Tel No	n/a	Fax No	n/a
Length (ft/m)	491.7/149.80		
Beam (ft/m) 70.9/21.50	Draft (ft/m)	21.6/6.60	
Propulsion	diesel (11,050kW)		
Propellers	2 (CP)		
Decks	8	Crew	225
Pass. Capacity (basis 2) 500	(all berths) 539		
Pass. Space Ratio (basis 2) 22.5	(all berths) 20.6		
Officers	Greek		
Dining Staff	European/Filipino		
Total Cabins	250		
Size (sq ft/m.):	75.3-226.0/7-21		
Outside Cabins	125	Inside Cabins	125
Single Cabins	0	Supplement	50%
Balcony Cabins	0	Wheelchair Cabins	0
Cabin Current	110 AC		
Refrigerator	No		
Cabin TV	No	VCR	No
Dining Rooms	1	Sittings	2

Elevators			5
Casino	Yes	Slot Machines	Yes
Swimming Pools (outside) 1	(inside)		0
Whirlpools	0	Gymnasium	Yes
Sauna/Steam Room Yes/No	Massage		Yes
Self-service Launderette			No
Cinema/Theatre:			Yes/170
Library			Yes
Children's Facilities/Playroom:			No
Classification Society			RINA

RATINGS	SCORE
Ship: Condition/Cleanliness	6.5
Ship: Space/Flow/Comfort	7.1
Ship: Decor/Furnishings	7.2
Ship: Fitness Facilities	5.8
Cabins: Comfort/Facilities	6.6
Cabins: Software	6.8
Food: Dining Room/Cuisine	6.3
Food: Buffets/Informal Dining	6.1
Food: Quality of Ingredients	6.0
Service: Dining Room	6.6
Service: Bars	6.5
Service: Cabins	7.0
Cruise: Entertainment	5.8
Cruise: Activities Program	6.0
Cruise: Hospitality Standard	6.3
OVERALL RATING	96.6

+ Long, low, handsome lines and swept-back aft-placed funnel provide a very attractive profile for this small ship. Has inboard lifeboats. Has good open deck and sunning space, but the heated outdoor pool is small. Contemporary interior decor with attractive colors add warm decor in public rooms. Reasonable sized cabins have pleasing, though plain, decor, furnishings and fittings. All have tiled bathrooms, but they are small.

— Cabin closet and drawer space is very limited. The sauna is really tiny (big enough for one). Some public rooms have a fairly low ceiling height. Steep gangway in some ports.

Dining Charming dining room has an art deco feel, has raised center ceiling and lovely etched glass dividers, but it is noisy. Reasonably attentive service from a willing, though somewhat distant staff. Good general standard of international cuisine.

Other Comments After running aground in the Amazon River in 1989, the ship was taken to Greece and refurbished. The ship now operates under new ownership. This ship will take its mainly European passengers to some decent destinations in good general style and relaxed comfort, and the realistic price of this product is a real plus.

ms Seabourn Pride ★★★★★+

OPERATES

*7- AND 14-DAY EUROPE AND
SOUTH PACIFIC CRUISES*

Cruise Line		Seabourn Cruise Line
Gross Tonnage		9,975
Builder		Seebeckwerft (Germany)
Original Cost		$50 million
Christened By		Mrs Shirley Temple Black
Entered Service		Dec 4, 1988
Interior Design		Yran & Storbraaten
Country of Registry		Norway (LALT2)
Tel No 131-1351	Fax No	131-1352
Length (ft/m)		439.9/134.10
Beam (ft/m) 62.9/19.20	Draft (ft/m)	16.8/5.15
Propulsion/Propellers		diesel (5,355kW)/2 (CP)
Decks 6	Crew	140
Pass. Capacity (basis 2) 204		(all berths) 204
Pass. Space Ratio (basis 2) 48.8		(all berths) 48.8
Officers Norwegian	Dining Staff	European
Total Cabins		106
Size Range (sq ft/m)		277-575/25.7-53.4
Outside Cabins 106	Inside Cabins	0
Single Cabins 0	Supplement	10-100%
Balcony Cabins 6	Wheelchair Cabins	4
Cabin Current		110/220 AC
Refrigerator		All cabins
Cabin TV Yes	VCR	Yes
Dining Rooms		1
Sittings		Open (+in-cabin dining)
Elevators		3
Casino Yes	Slot Machines	Yes

Swimming Pools (outside)		1 (+ 1 aft marina-pool)
(inside)			0
Whirlpools	3	Gymnasium	Yes
Sauna/Steam Room Yes/Yes		Massage	Yes
Self-Service Launderette			Yes
Movie Theater/Seats	No	Library	Yes
Watersports Facilities		Aft platform, enclosed
		marina pool, banana boat, pedalos,
		scuba, snorkel, windsurf, waterski
Classification Society		Det Norske Veritas

RATINGS	SCORE
Ship: Condition/Cleanliness	9.2
Ship: Space/Flow/Comfort	9.3
Ship: Facilities	9.0
Ship: Decor/Furnishings	8.9
Ship: Fitness/Watersports Facilities	9.2
Cabins: Comfort/Facilities	9.4
Cabins: Software	9.0
Food: Dining Room/Cuisine	9.0
Food: Buffets/Informal Dining	9.0
Food: Quality of Ingredients	9.2
Service: Dining Room	8.7
Service: Bars	9.0
Service: Cabins	9.2
Cruise: Entertainment/Lecture Program	9.0
Cruise: Hospitality Standard	9.1
OVERALL RATING	136.2

+ *Seabourn Pride* and *Seabourn Spirit* are strikingly sleek ships with a handsome profile and swept-back, rounded lines. They each have two fine mahogany water taxis. They also feature an aft watersports platform and marina, used in suitably calm warm water areas. There is a wide central passageway throughout the accommodation areas. Inviting, sumptuous public areas have warm colors. Fine quality interior fixtures, fittings and fabrics combine to present an outstanding, elegant decor, color combinations and artwork. All-outside cabins (Seabourn calls them suites) are comfortably large, and beautifully equipped with everything, including refrigerator, personal safe, personalized stationery, and large walk-in illuminated closet with wooden hangers. Beautiful blond wood cabinetry has softly rounded edges. Cabin doors are neatly angled away from passageway. Large, marble bathrooms have two washbasins, decent-sized bathtub, plenty of storage areas, 100% cotton towels and bathrobe.

For ultimate privacy the two Owner's Suites (001/002) offer a superbly private living environment. Each has a walk-in closet plus a second closet, one full bathroom and a second room with toilet and washbasin (for guests), and butler service. There's also a forward-facing balcony, complete with sun lounge chairs and wooden drinks table. These are secluded (good for nude sunbathing). The living area has ample bookshelf space (included is a complete edition of *Encyclopedia Britannica*), refrigerator and drinks cabinet, television and VCR (there's a second television in the bedroom), four-person dining table, and large circular glass

ms Seabourn Spirit ★★★★★+

Cruise Line	Seabourn Cruise Line		Swimming Pools (outside)	1 (+ aft marina-pool)	
Gross Tonnage	9,975		(inside)		0
Builder	Seebeckwerft (Germany)		Whirlpools	3 Gymnasium	Yes
Original Cost	$50 million		Sauna/Steam Room Yes/Yes	Massage	Yes
Christened By	Mrs Audun Brynestad		Self-Service Launderette		Yes
Entered Service	Nov 10, 1989		Movie Theater/Seats No	Library	Yes
Interior Design	Yran & Storbraaten		Watersports Facilities	Aft platform, enclosed	
Country of Registry	Norway (LAOW2)			marina pool, banana boat, pedalos,	
Tel No 131-0464 Fax No	131-0527			cuba, snorkel, windsurf, waterski	
Length (ft/m)	439.9/134.10		Classification Society	Det Norske Veritas	
Beam (ft/m) 62.9/19.20 Draft (ft/m)	16.8/5.15				
Propulsion/Propellers	diesel (5,355kW)/2 (CP)		**RATINGS**		**SCORE**
Decks 6 Crew	140		Ship: Condition/Cleanliness		9.2
Pass. Capacity (basis 2) 204	(all berths) 204		Ship: Space/Flow/Comfort		9.3
Pass. Space Ratio (basis 2) 48.8	(all berths) 48.8		Ship: Facilities		9.0
Officers Norwegian Dining Staff	European		Ship: Decor/Furnishings		8.9
Total Cabins	106		Ship: Fitness/Watersports Facilities		9.2
Size Range (sq ft/m)	277-575/25.7-53.4		Cabins: Comfort/Facilities		9.4
Outside Cabins 106 Inside Cabins	0		Cabins: Software		9.0
Single Cabins 0 Supplement	10-100%		Food: Dining Room/Cuisine		9.0
Balcony Cabins 6 Wheelchair Cabins	4		Food: Buffets/Informal Dining		9.0
Cabin Current	110/220 AC		Food: Quality of Ingredients		9.2
Refrigerator	All cabins		Service: Dining Room		8.7
Cabin TV Yes VCR	Yes		Service: Bars		9.0
Dining Rooms	1		Service: Cabins		9.2
Sittings	Open (+in-cabin dining)		Cruise: Entertainment/Lecture Program		9.0
Elevators	3		Cruise: Hospitality Standard		9.1
Casino Yes Slot Machines	Yes		OVERALL RATING		136.2

coffee table. All windows as well as the door to the balcony have electric blinds, and a complete blackout is possible in both bedroom and living room. However, the telephone system to call the butler is archaic and difficult to master.

— There's no wrap-around outdoor promenade deck. Deck lounge chairs are plastic. Deck beverage service is spotty (obtaining champagne in the Jacuzzi, for example, has proved an impossible task in the past). There are no seat cushions on the wooden chairs at the indoor/outdoor café. There's only one dryer in the self-service launderette. Ceilings are very plain. Drinks are extra (except at beginning of the cruise, when your refrigerator is stocked gratis), but they are low-priced.

Dining Marble and carpet dining room features portholes and elegant decor, but is not as intimate as on the Sea Goddesses. Culinary excellence prevails, however, and both food quality and presentation are outstanding. Menus are not repeated, even on long cruises. Special orders are most welcome, and caviar is always available. Service is near impeccable.

Other Comments Not for the budget-minded, these ships are for those desiring the utmost in supremely elegant, stylish, small-ship surroundings (they are too small for long voyages in open waters, however). Utterly civilized cruising. Gratuities are included, and no further tipping is allowed.

ss SeaBreeze I ★★★

OPERATES

7-DAY CARIBBEAN CRUISES
(YEAR-ROUND)

Cruise Line	Dolphin Cruise Line	Casino	Yes	Slot Machines Yes
Former Names	Federico "C"/Royale	Swimming Pools (outside) 1	(inside)	0
Gross Tonnage	21,900	Whirlpools	3	Gymnasium Yes
Builder	Ansaldo Sestri-Ponente (Italy)	Sauna/Steam Room No/No	Massage	Yes
Original Cost	n/a	Self-Service Launderette		No
Christened By	n/a	Movie Theater/Seats		Yes/110
Entered Service	Mar 22, 1958/Mar 5, 1989	Library		No
Interior Design	A&M Katzourakis	Children's Facilities		Yes
Country of Registry	Bahamas (3FGV)	Watersports Facilities		None
Tel No 133-6354 Fax No 133-6354		Classification Society		Lloyd's Register

Length (ft/m)	605.6/184.61
Beam (ft/m) 78.9/24.06 Draft (ft/m)	29.0/8.84
Propulsion	steam turbine (21,350kW)
Propellers	2 (FP)
Decks 8 Crew	410
Pass. Capacity (basis 2) 842 (all berths)	1,250
Pass. Space Ratio (basis 2) 26.0 (all berths)	17.5
Officers Greek Dining Staff	International
Total Cabins	421
Size Range (sq ft/m)	65-258/6.0-24.0
Outside Cabins 263 Inside Cabins	158
Single Cabins 2 Supplement	50%
Balcony Cabins 0 Wheelchair Cabins	0
Cabin Current	110/220 AC
Refrigerator	No
Cabin TV No VCR	No
Dining Rooms 1 Sittings	2
Elevators	4

RATINGS	SCORE
Ship: Condition/Cleanliness	6.1
Ship: Space/Flow/Comfort	5.8
Ship: Decor/Furnishings	6.3
Ship: Fitness Facilities	4.3
Cabins: Comfort/Facilities	6.3
Cabins: Software	6.5
Food: Dining Room/Cuisine	7.1
Food: Buffets/Informal Dining	6.7
Food: Quality of Ingredients	6.5
Service: Dining Room	6.8
Service: Bars	6.9
Service: Cabins	7.1
Cruise: Entertainment	6.2
Cruise: Activities Program	6.6
Cruise: Hospitality Standard	6.7
OVERALL RATING	95.9

+ Classic old former ocean liner styling still looks decent, and has a forthright white profile and sea-wave stripes in the center of her hull. Sports a neat sail-cloth canopy over aft outdoor area. The public rooms are bright and cheerful, and tastefully decorated, although there are lots of mirrored and chromed surfaces. There is a wide variety of cabins and many different configurations to choose from. Many cabins can accommodate five—ideal for families with children. Drawer space is limited but closet space is good. There's no real finesse, but the staff are very willing to please, and they're quite attentive, for a budget operation.

— Open deck and sunning space on this high density ship is quite limited, and thus extremely crowded when full. Has an awkward layout, a carry-over from her former three-class ocean liner nights, hinders passenger flow. Steep passenger gangway in some ports. She's getting too old and should be retired.

Dining The dining room has bright decor, but tables are much too close together for serving comfort. There are, however, several tables for two. Both food and service are very good for the price paid.

Other Comments This ship has plenty of life and atmosphere, is quite comfortable, caters well to families and remains very good value for a first cruise experience, but she is getting old.

ms Sea Venture ★★★

OPERATES

*CARIBBEAN, MEDITERRANEAN AND
SOUTH AMERICA CRUISES*

Cruise Line	Royal Venture Cruise Line	Casino	Yes	Slot Machines	Yes
Former Names	Ukraine/Kazakhstan	Swimming Pools (outside) 1	(inside)	0
Gross Tonnage	15,410	Whirlpools	0	Gymnasium	Yes
Builder	Wartsila (Finland)	Sauna/Steam Room Yes/No	Massage	Yes
Original Cost	$25 million	Self-Service Launderette		Yes
Christened By	n/a	Movie Theater/Seats		Yes/140
Entered Service	Jul 1, 1975/Mar 22, 1996	Library		Yes
Interior Design	n/a	Children's Facilities		No
Country of Registry	Ukraine (ULSB)	Watersports Facilities		None
Tel No 140-0772 Fax No	140-0772	Classification Society Ukraine Register of Shipping

Length (ft/m)	512.6/156.27
Beam (ft/m) 72.3/22.05 Draft (ft/m)	19.4/5.92
Propulsion	diesel (13,430kW)
Propellers	2 (CP)
Decks 7 Crew	250
Pass. Capacity (basis 2) 470	(all berths) 640
Pass. Space Ratio (basis 2) 32.7	(all berths) 24.0
Officers	Russian/Ukrainian
Dining Staff	Russian/Ukrainian
Total Cabins	235
Size Range (sq ft/m)	90-492/8.4-45.7
Outside Cabins 117 Inside Cabins	118
Single Cabins 0 Supplement	Set rates
Balcony Cabins 0 Wheelchair Cabins	0
Cabin Current 220 AC Refrigerator	No
Cabin TV No VCR	No
Dining Rooms 2 Sittings	1
Elevators	1

RATINGS	SCORE
Ship: Condition/Cleanliness	6.7
Ship: Space/Flow/Comfort	6.4
Ship: Decor/Furnishings	6.4
Ship: Fitness Facilities	4.8
Cabins: Comfort/Facilities	6.0
Cabins: Software	6.2
Food. Dining Room/Cuisine	6.0
Food: Buffets/Informal Dining	5.5
Food: Quality of Ingredients	5.7
Service: Dining Room	6.7
Service: Bars	7.0
Service: Cabins	7.3
Cruise: Entertainment	4.5
Cruise: Activities Program	5.6
Cruise: Hospitality Standard	6.7
OVERALL RATING	91.5

+ Fairly sleek-looking ship with contemporary profile and smart, square funnel. Has a good outdoor promenade area. Recent refurbishment added a movie theater, new nightclub, foyer, Crimea Bar and more cabins. Eight suites on Boat Deck are quite spacious, have full bathtubs, good closet and drawer space and artwork. Other cabins are small and sparingly furnished, but quite adequate.

— Most cabins have little drawer space, and the insulation is poor. Communication with staff is frustrating even though the staff are friendly. There are no cushioned pads for the deck chairs.

Dining There are two dining rooms, both of which are nicely decorated, and are quite comfortable. One is for smokers, the other for non-smokers, but there are no tables for two. One wall features a multi-color, multi-image contemporary glass mural.

Other Comments The service is somewhat perfunctory, but the staff do try hard. The ship itself provides a good cruise experience at a modest price, but there's little finesse. Rated while under charter to a German operator as the *Ukraine*.

ms Seaward ★★★★

OPERATES

*7-DAY CARIBBEAN CRUISES
(YEAR-ROUND)*

Cruise Line	Norwegian Cruise Line
Former Names	-
Gross Tonnage	42,276
Builder	Wartsila (Finland)
Original Cost	$120 million
Christened By	Ms Greta Weiss
Entered Service	Jun 12, 1988
Interior Design	Robert Tillberg
Country of Registry	Bahamas (C6DM2)
Tel No 110-4601 Fax No 110-4602	
Length (ft/m)	708.6/216.00
Beam (ft/m) 95.1/29.00 Draft (ft/m) 22.9/7.00	
Propulsion	diesel (21,120kW)
Propellers	2 (CP)
Decks 9 Crew	630
Pass. Capacity (basis 2) 1,534 (all berths) 1,798	
Pass. Space Ratio (basis 2) 27.5 (all berths) 23.5	
Officers Norwegian Dining Staff International	
Total Cabins	767
Size Range (sq ft/m)	110-270/10.2-25.0
Outside Cabins 486 Inside Cabins 281	
Single Cabins 0 Supplement 50-100%	
Balcony Cabins 0 Wheelchair Cabins 4	
Cabin Current	110 AC
Refrigerator	Category 1/2/3 only
Cabin TV Yes VCR No	
Dining Rooms 2 Sittings 2	
Elevators	6

Casino	Yes	Slot Machines	Yes
Swimming Pools (outside) 2		(inside)	0
Whirlpools	2	Gymnasium	Yes
Sauna/Steam Room Yes/No		Massage	Yes
Self-Service Launderette			No
Movie Theater/Seats			No
Library			No
Children's Facilities			No
Watersports Facilities			None
Classification Society		Det Norske Veritas	

RATINGS	SCORE
Ship: Condition/Cleanliness	8.0
Ship: Space/Flow/Comfort	7.9
Ship: Decor/Furnishings	7.8
Ship: Fitness Facilities	7.8
Cabins: Comfort/Facilities	7.6
Cabins: Software	6.2
Food: Dining Room/Cuisine	7.5
Food: Buffets/Informal Dining	7.1
Food: Quality of Ingredients	6.3
Service: Dining Room	7.4
Service: Bars	7.5
Service: Cabins	7.2
Cruise: Entertainment	8.0
Cruise: Activities Program	7.1
Cruise: Hospitality Standard	7.5
OVERALL RATING	110.9

+ Fine teakwood outdoor wrap-around promenade deck. The interior decor is designed to remind you of sea and sky: coral, blue and mauve are the predominant colors. There is an excellent gymnasium/fitness center. Striking two-deck-high lobby has a crystal and water sculpture. Has two glass-walled stairways. Lovely Crystal Court two-deck-high lobby. Fine theater-showroom provides large-scale dazzle shows. The most intimate place is the mahogany-paneled Oscar's Lounge. The cabins are of an average size for a 7-day cruise ship, tastefully appointed, and quite comfortable. Hairdryers are included in bathroom.

— Has tinny steps on stairways. There are too many unnecessary announcements.

Dining The two main dining rooms are quite homely, with pastel decor. The cuisine, for a mass-market ship, ranges from adequate to quite good, no more, although it has been improved. The emphasis is on meat dishes, with heavy sauces, and overcooked vegetables. However, fish and fowl are good. Nothing arrives hot at tableside. The service is, on the whole, adequate. The selection of wines is good, but breakfast and luncheon buffets are not.

Other Comments This angular, yet attractive ship with contemporary European cruise-ferry profile has a well-raked bow, and sleek mast and funnel. This ship is well designed, with good passenger flow. It provides a good first-cruise experience, but there's little finesse.

tss Seawind Crown ★★★★

OPERATES

7- AND 14-DAY SOUTHERN CARIBBEAN CRUISES (YEAR-ROUND)

Cruise Line	Seawind Cruise Line	Casino	Yes	Slot Machines Yes
Former Names	Vasco da Gama/	Swimming Pools (outside) 2		(inside) 0
	Infante Dom Henrique	Whirlpools	0	Gymnasium Yes
Gross Tonnage	24,568	Sauna/Steam Room Yes/No		Massage Yes
Builder	Cockerill-Ougree (Belgium)	Self-Service Launderette		No
Original Cost	n/a	Movie Theater/Seats		Yes/208
Christened By	n/a	Library		Yes
Entered Service	Sep 25, 1961/Oct 6, 1991	Children's Facilities		Yes
Interior Design	Kohnemann/Schindler	Watersports Facilities		None
Country of Registry	Panama (3EIY6)	Classification Society		Lloyd's Register
Tel No 133-1251 Fax No 133-1252				
Length (ft/m)	641.6/195.59	**RATINGS**		**SCORE**
Beam (ft/m) 84.4/25.73 Draft (ft/m) 26.9/8.20		Ship: Condition/Cleanliness		6.7
Propulsion	steam turbine (16,180kW)	Ship: Space/Flow/Comfort		7.8
Propellers	2 (FP)	Ship: Decor/Furnishings		7.6
Decks 8 Crew	311	Ship: Fitness Facilities		6.2
Pass. Capacity (basis 2) 728 (all berths) 823		Cabins: Comfort/Facilities		6.8
Pass. Space Ratio (basis 2) 33.4 (all berths) 29.8		Cabins: Software		7.3
Officers Greek Dining Staff European		Food: Dining Room/Cuisine		7.5
Total Cabins	367	Food: Buffets/Informal Dining		7.2
Size Range (sq ft/m) 118-560/11.0-52.0		Food: Quality of Ingredients		7.0
Outside Cabins 246 Inside Cabins 121		Service: Dining Room		6.7
Single Cabins 6 Supplement 0-100%		Service: Bars		6.5
Balcony Cabins 2 Wheelchair Cabins 2		Service: Cabins		7.0
Cabin Current 220 AC Refrigerator Yes		Cruise: Entertainment		6.6
Cabin TV Yes VCR No		Cruise: Activities Program		6.0
Dining Rooms 2 Sittings 2		Cruise: Hospitality Standard		7.3
Elevators	4	OVERALL RATING		104.2

+ Handsome profile for this former long-distance line. Extensively refurbished. Has a long foredeck, rakish bow, and teak promenade decks (one outdoor, one covered). Surprisingly spacious, classic vessel. Mix of old-world elegance and contemporary features. Host of public rooms feature tasteful decor and pastel tones. Has a chapel and well-equipped hospital. Fine wood paneling and trim. Spacious foyers. Bavarian-style taverna. Wide assortment of cabins; some with queen-, double- or twin beds, some with upper/lower berths. All cabins have excellent closet and drawer space, refrigerator, hairdryer, cotton bathrobes and towels. The suites (they really are suites) are huge. Sports facilities include indoor squash courts.

— Emergency drill conducted in six languages. Smokers are everywhere. Pleasant movie theater, but seats should be staggered. Announcements in several languages are irritating. Poor library.

Dining The two dining rooms are quite comfortable, and both food and service are good considering the cruise fare charged. There are few tables for two. Food budget is quite low. Limited selection of breads, cheeses and fruits.

Other Comments The ship has two names: *Seawind Crown* and *Vasco da Gama*. There is a multi-national passenger mix on each cruise.

ms Seawing ★★★

OPERATES

*6 AND 13-DAY MEDITERRANEAN
CRUISES*

Cruise Line	Airtours Cruises		
Former Names	Southward		
Gross Tonnage	16,607		
Builder	Cantieri Navale Del Tirreno		
	et Riuniti (Italy)		
Original Cost	n/a	Christened By	n/a
Entered Service	Nov 16, 1971/Mar 25, 1995		
Interior Design	Tage Wandborg		
Country of Registry	Bahamas (C6CM6)		
Tel No 110-4165	Fax No	110-4165	
Length (ft/m)	535.7/163.30		
Beam (ft/m) 74.7/22.79	Draft (ft/m)	21.3/6.50	
Propulsion	diesel (13,400kW)		
Propellers	2 (CP)		
Decks 7	Crew	320	
Pass. Capacity (basis 2) 754	(all berths) 976		
Pass. Space Ratio (basis 2) 22.0	(all berths) 17.0		
Officers Norwegian	Dining Staff International		
Total Cabins	377		
Size Range (sq ft/m)	90-256/8.3-23.7		
Outside Cabins 262	Inside Cabins	115	
Single Cabins 0	Supplement	50-100%	
Balcony Cabins 0	Wheelchair Cabins	0	
Cabin Current	110 AC		
Refrigerator	Category 1/2 only		
Cabin TV No	VCR	No	
Dining Rooms 1	Sittings	2	
Elevators	4		

Casino	Yes	Slot Machines	Yes
Swimming Pools (outside) 1		(inside)	0
Whirlpools	0	Gymnasium	Yes
Sauna/Steam Room Yes/No		Massage	Yes
Self-Service Launderette			No
Movie Theater/Seats			Yes/198
Library			Yes
Children's Facilities			No
Watersports Facilities			None
Classification Society		Det Norske Veritas	

RATINGS	SCORE
Ship: Condition/Cleanliness	6.7
Ship: Space/Flow/Comfort	6.6
Ship: Decor/Furnishings	7.0
Ship: Fitness Facilities	5.6
Cabins: Comfort/Facilities	6.2
Cabins: Software	6.7
Food: Dining Room/Cuisine	6.6
Food: Buffets/Informal Dining	6.2
Food: Quality of Ingredients	6.1
Service: Dining Room	7.1
Service: Bars	7.0
Service: Cabins	7.1
Cruise: Entertainment	6.5
Cruise: Activities Program	6.7
Cruise: Hospitality Standard	6.8
OVERALL RATING	98.9

+ Has a good selection of comfortable public rooms with bright, contemporary decor. Perhaps the favorite is the nightclub, set high atop the forward mast. Also has a balconied theater. Families with children will find lots to do. Ten suites are quite spacious, and well-equipped, and have full bathtubs; other cabins are compact but clean and tidy, with adequate closet space for these one-week cruises, but not for longer. Airtours provides good value for money with these cruises designed for the young at heart.

— Cabins are not assigned until embarkation. High-density ship means crowds and lines for buffets, embarkation, and disembarkation. Open deck and sunning space limited. Sightlines in the showroom are poor. Too many repetitive announcements. Rowdy ship with lots of children running around during holiday sailings. "Blue coats" provide the entertainment.

Dining Dining room is charming, with warm colors. The food is adequate (for the price), but basic fare. Bread and fruit selections are poor. Service and ambiance are both informal. Extra charge for room service menu items. The wine list is decent, and so are the prices.

Other Comments This ship provides all the right ingredients for an active, fun-filled short cruise vacation for sun-loving couples and families at the right price, tailored specifically to the UK family cruise market (on-board currency is UK£ Sterling).

ms Sensation ★★★★

OPERATES

*7-DAY CARIBBEAN CRUISES
(YEAR-ROUND)*

Cruise Line		Carnival Cruise Lines
Former Names	n/a	Gross Tonnage 70,367
Builder		Kvaerner Masa-Yards (Finland)
Original Cost		$300 million
Christened By		Geri Donnelly, Vicki Freed,
		Roberta Jacoby, Cheri Weinstein
Entered Service		Nov 21, 1993
Interior Design		Joe Farcus
Country of Registry		Liberia (3ESE9)
Tel No	134-1372 Fax No	134-1373
Length (ft/m)		855.0/260.60
Beam (ft/m) 104.0/31.40	Draft (ft/m)	25.9/7.90
Propulsion		diesel-electric (42,240kW)
Propellers		2 (CP)
Decks	10 Crew	920
Pass. Capacity (basis 2) 2,040	(all berths) 2,594
Pass. Space Ratio (basis 2) 34.4	(all berths) 26.7
Officers	Italian Dining Staff	International
Total Cabins		1,020
Size Range (sq ft/m)		185-421/17.0-39.0
Outside Cabins	620 Inside Cabins	402
Single Cabins		0
Supplement	50% (cat. 1-3)/100% (cat. 4-12)
Balcony Cabins	54 Wheelchair Cabins	20
Cabin Current		110 AC
Refrigerator		Category 11/12 only
Cabin TV	Yes VCR	No
Dining Rooms	2 Sittings	2

Elevators			14
Casino	Yes	Slot Machines	Yes
Swimming Pools (outside) 3		(inside)	0
Whirlpools	6	Gymnasium	Yes
Sauna/Steam Room Yes/Yes		Massage	Yes
Self-Service Launderette			Yes
Movie Theater/Seats	No	Library	Yes
Children's Facilities			Yes
Watersports Facilities			None
Classification Society			Lloyd's Register

RATINGS	SCORE
Ship: Condition/Cleanliness	9.0
Ship: Space/Flow/Comfort	8.1
Ship: Decor/Furnishings	8.2
Ship: Fitness Facilities	7.8
Cabins: Comfort/Facilities	7.6
Cabins: Software	7.4
Food: Dining Room/Cuisine	6.7
Food: Buffets/Informal Dining	6.4
Food: Quality of Ingredients	5.3
Service: Dining Room	7.0
Service: Bars	7.2
Service: Cabins	6.4
Cruise: Entertainment	8.2
Cruise: Activities Program	7.8
Cruise: Hospitality Standard	6.3
OVERALL RATING	109.4

+ Has a dramatic six-deck-high atrium, topped by a large colored-glass dome and an artistic centerpiece. Expansive open deck areas and an excellent health spa including a large gymnasium with the latest high-tech muscle machines. Public entertainment lounges, bars and clubs galore, with something for everyone. Dazzling colors and design themes in handsome public rooms connected by wide indoor boulevards. $1 million art collection, much of it bright and vocal. The library is a lovely room, but few books. The Michelangelo Lounge is a creative thinker's delight, while Fingers Lounge is sheer sensory travel. Lavish multi-tiered showroom and high-energy razzle-dazzle shows. Dramatic three-deck-high glass-enclosed health spa. Huge casino has non-stop action. 28 outside suites have whirlpool tubs. Standard cabins are of a decent size and have ample closet and drawer space.

— Sensory overkill. Large shop, poor merchandise. Too many announcements. Expect long lines for embarkation, disembarkation, buffets, and shore tenders. Aggressive hustling for drinks by bar waiters is irritating, as are drinks in plastic glasses.

Dining Two large dining rooms are noisy. Programmed service and so-so food.

Other Comments This ship will entertain you well, with sensory overkill, like a video game parlor. (See also comments for *Imagination* and other Carnival ships.)

ms Shota Rustaveli ★★+

OPERATES

VARIOUS EUROPE CRUISES

Cruise Line	Black Sea Shipping
Former Names	-
Gross Tonnage	20,499
Builder	VEB Mathias Thesen (Germany)
Original Cost	n/a
Christened By	n/a
Entered Service	Jun 30, 1968
Interior Design	Shipyard
Country of Registry	Ukraine (UUGF)
Tel No	140-0253 Fax No 140-0253
Length (ft/m)	576.6/175.77
Beam (ft/m) 77.4/23.60 Draft (ft/m) 26.5/8.09	
Propulsion	diesel (15,700kW)
Propellers	2 (CP)
Decks	8 Crew 350
Pass. Capacity (basis 2) 493 (all berths) 602	
Pass. Space Ratio (basis 2) 41.4 (all berths) 34.0	
Officers	Russian/Ukrainian
Dining Staff	Russian/Ukrainian
Total Cabins	249
Size Range (sq ft/m)	n/a
Outside Cabins 244 Inside Cabins 5	
Single Cabins 0 Supplement 100%	
Balcony Cabins 0 Wheelchair Cabins 0	
Cabin Current 220 AC Refrigerator No	
Cabin TV No VCR No	
Dining Rooms 3 Sittings 2	
Elevators	3

Casino	No	Slot Machines	No
Swimming Pools (outside) 2		(inside)	0
Whirlpools	0	Gymnasium	Yes
Sauna/Steam Room Yes/No		Massage	Yes
Self-Service Launderette			Yes
Movie Theater/Seats			Yes/130
Library			Yes
Children's Facilities			Yes
Watersports Facilities			None
Classification Society			RS

RATINGS	SCORE
Ship: Condition/Cleanliness	6.0
Ship: Space/Flow/Comfort	6.5
Ship: Decor/Furnishings	6.1
Ship: Fitness Facilities	5.1
Cabins: Comfort/Facilities	6.1
Cabins: Software	6.2
Food: Dining Room/Cuisine	5.7
Food: Buffets/Informal Dining	5.4
Food: Quality of Ingredients	5.6
Service: Dining Room	6.1
Service: Bars	6.6
Service: Cabins	7.3
Cruise: Entertainment	5.5
Cruise: Activities Program	5.4
Cruise: Hospitality Standard	6.1
OVERALL RATING	89.7

+ Good-looking, well-built traditional ship styling. Good teakwood decks and wrap-around open promenade. Good open deck space for sunning, with real wooden deck chairs. Nice inside swimming pool. Spacious interior with quite pleasing decor, although colors are a little dour. Lots of wood paneling and trim. Apart from some de-luxe cabins with private balconies, this ship has small but very comfortable all-outside cabins, with attractive wood accents, solid fixtures, and pleasing decor. Many portholes actually open—unusual in today's air-conditioned world of ships.

— Has a steep, narrow gangway in some ports. Spartan, dated decor. Expect lines for embarkation, disembarkation, buffets, and shore tenders.

Dining The dining room is quite comfortable. The food is quite good (though stodgy), but there is little choice. Limited selection of breads and fruits. Free carafes of wine for lunch and dinner. Service is attentive but somewhat inflexible.

Other Comments This ship, one of a group of five, was nicely renovated in 1991, and is often chartered to a European cruise-tour company. European cruise staff cater well to principally French- and Italian-speaking passengers. Good for the passenger on a low budget who doesn't expect any degree of luxury or finesse.

ms Silver Cloud ★★★★★

OPERATES
VARIOUS CRUISES WORLDWIDE

Cruise Line		Silversea Cruises
Former Names	n/a	Gross Tonnage 16,800
Builder		SEC/T. Mariotti (Italy)
Original Cost		$125 million
Christened By		Mrs Eugenia Beck Lefebvre
Entered Service		Apr 2, 1994
Interior Design		Yran & Storbraaten
Country of Registry		Bahamas (C6MQ5)
Tel No 130-6601	Fax No	130-6602
Length (ft/m)		514.4/155.80
Beam (ft/m) 70.62/21.40	Draft (ft/m)	17.3/5.30
Propulsion		diesel (11,700kW)
Propellers		2 (CP)
Decks	8	Crew 198
Pass. Capacity (basis 2) 306		(all berths) 325
Pass. Space Ratio (basis 2) 54.9		(all berths) 51.6
Officers	Italian	Dining Staff European
Total Cabins		153
Size Range (sq ft/m)		240-1,085/22.2-100.7
Outside Cabins	153	Inside Cabins 0
Single Cabins		0
Supplement		10–100%
Balcony Cabins	119	Wheelchair Cabins 0
Cabin Current		110/220 AC
Refrigerator		All cabins
Cabin TV Yes	VCR	Yes
Dining Rooms	1 (open seating+in-cabin dining)
Elevators		4

Casino	Yes	Slot Machines	Yes
Swimming Pools (outside) 1		(inside)	0
Whirlpools		2	Gymnasium Yes
Sauna/Steam Room Yes/Yes		Massage	Yes
Self-Service Launderette			Yes
Movie Theater/Seats			Yes/306
Library	Yes	Children's Facilities No
Watersports Facilities		side platform, kayaks,
Zodiacs, sailfish, snorkel, windsurf, waterski boats
Classification Society			RINA

RATINGS	SCORE
Ship: Condition/Cleanliness	9.3
Ship: Space/Flow/Comfort	9.7
Ship: Decor/Furnishings	9.2
Ship: Fitness Facilities	8.5
Cabins: Comfort/Facilities	9.1
Cabins: Software	9.2
Food: Dining Room/Cuisine	8.6
Food: Buffets/Informal Dining	8.6
Food: Quality of Ingredients	8.6
Service: Dining Room	8.8
Service: Bars	8.5
Service: Cabins	9.2
Cruise: Entertainment	9.0
Cruise: Activities Program	8.5
Cruise: Hospitality Standard	8.7
OVERALL RATING	133.5

+ Sleek, handsome profile, rather like a small version of *Crystal Harmony*, or larger version of the Seabourn ships (*Silver Wind* has better fit and finish than *Silver Cloud*). Vertical stacking of public rooms aft and accommodations forward ensures quiet cabins. There is a teakwood wrap-around outdoor promenade deck, and an excellent, spacious outdoor pool deck. The interiors are well planned, with elegant decor and fine quality soft furnishings, accented by a gentle use of brass and fine woods and creative ceilings. Useful business center as well as a CD-ROM and hardback book library. Excellent two-level showroom with tiered seating.

All outside suites (75% of which have private teakwood balconies) have convertible queen-to-twin beds and are beautifully fitted out with just about everything, including huge floor-to-ceiling windows, large walk-in closets, dressing table, writing desk, stocked mini-bar, and fresh flowers. Marble-floored bathrooms have bathtub and plenty of towels. Personalized stationery, bathrobes and good amenities kit in all cabins. Top suites also have CD-players.

Good watersports facilities for use in warm weather areas. There is an outstanding amount of space per passenger, and no hint of a line anywhere. Excellent documentation is provided.

— Walk-in closets don't provide much hanging space (particularly for full-length items), and doors should open outward instead of inward. While cabin insulation above and below each

ms Silver Wind ★★★★★

OPERATES
VARIOUS CRUISES WORLDWIDE

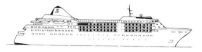

Cruise Line			Silversea Cruises
Former Names	n/a	Gross Tonnage	16,800
Builder		Societa Esercizio Cantieri (Italy)	
Original Cost			$125 million
Christened By			Mrs Patricia Lefebvre
Entered Service			Jan 29, 1995
Interior Design			Yran & Storbraaten
Country of Registry			Italy (IBEW)
Tel No	115-2245	Fax No	115-2250
Length (ft/m)			514.4/155.80
Beam (ft/m) 70.62/21.40		Draft (ft/m)	17.3/5.30
Propulsion			diesel (11,700kW)
Propellers			2 (CP)
Decks	6	Crew	197
Pass. Capacity (basis 2) 306		(all berths) 325	
Pass. Space Ratio (basis 2) 54.9		(all berths) 51.6	
Officers	Italian	Dining Staff	European
Total Cabins			153
Size Range (sq ft/m)		240-1,085/22.2-100.7	
Outside Cabins	153	Inside Cabins	0
Single Cabins			0
Supplement			10–100%
Balcony Cabins	119	Wheelchair Cabins	2
Cabin Current			110/220 AC
Refrigerator			All cabins
Cabin TV	Yes	VCR	Yes
Dining Rooms		1 (open seating+in-cabin dining)	
Elevators			4

Casino	Yes	Slot Machines	Yes
Swimming Pools (outside) 1		(inside)	0
Whirlpools	2	Gymnasium	Yes
Sauna/Steam Room Yes/Yes		Massage	Yes
Self-Service Launderette			Yes
Movie Theater/Seats			Yes/306
Library	Yes	Children's Facilities	No
Watersports Facilities		side platform, kayaks,	
Zodiacs, sailfish, snorkel, windsurf, waterski boats			
Classification Society			RINA

RATINGS   SCORE

RATINGS	SCORE
Ship: Condition/Cleanliness	9.4
Ship: Space/Flow/Comfort	9.7
Ship: Decor/Furnishings	9.4
Ship: Fitness Facilities	8.6
Cabins: Comfort/Facilities	9.2
Cabins: Software	9.2
Food: Dining Room/Cuisine	8.7
Food: Buffets/Informal Dining	8.6
Food: Quality of Ingredients	8.6
Service: Dining Room	8.7
Service: Bars	8.5
Service: Cabins	9.2
Cruise: Entertainment	8.6
Cruise: Activities Program	8.5
Cruise: Hospitality Standard	8.7
OVERALL RATING	133.6

cabin is good, insulation between cabins could be improved, and a privacy curtain should be installed. Spa areas need improvement, and the tiled decor is bland and uninviting. The shorter itineraries are too busy, with not enough days at sea. The self-service launderette is poor and simply not large enough for longer cruises.

Dining Lovely dining room has an arched gazebo center ceiling. Set with fine Limoges china and well-balanced flatware, under a stunning, wavy ceiling. Features 24-hour in-suite dining service, but the balcony tables are too low for outdoor dining. Good dining throughout the ship, with choice of formal and informal areas, although the cuisine and presentation are simply not up to the standards of products like Sea Goddess or Seabourn. Wines are included for lunch and dinner, a special connoisseur's list is available (at extra charge) for those who enjoy good wines. There is also 24-hour in-cabin dining service (full course by course dinners are available).

Other Comments Managed and operated by "V" Ships, the company that created Sitmar Cruises some years ago. With no pressure, no hype, and a good staff to pamper you, it's a pleasure to cruise on these two ships. Port taxes and insurance are extra, but gratuities are included, and, refreshingly, no further tipping, anywhere on board, is allowed.

tss Sky Princess ★★★★+

OPERATES

7-DAY ALASKA AND CARIBBEAN CRUISES

Cruise Line	Princess Cruises	Casino	Yes
Former Names	Fairsky	Swimming Pools (outside)	3
Gross Tonnage	46,314	Whirlpools	1
Builder	C.N.I.M. (France)	Sauna/Steam Room Yes/No	
Original Cost	$156 million	Self-Service Launderette	
Christened By	Mrs Jenny Ueberroth	Movie Theater/Seats	
Entered Service	May 5, 1984	Library	
Interior Design	Giacomo Mortola	Children's Facilities	
Country of Registry	Great Britain (GYYP)	Watersports Facilities	
Tel No 144-2264 Fax No	144-2266	Classification Society	

Casino	Yes
Swimming Pools (outside)	3
Whirlpools	1
Sauna/Steam Room Yes/No	
Self-Service Launderette	
Movie Theater/Seats	
Library	
Children's Facilities	
Watersports Facilities	
Classification Society	

Casino	Yes	Slot Machines	Yes
Swimming Pools (outside)	3	(inside)	0
Whirlpools	1	Gymnasium	Yes
Sauna/Steam Room	Yes/No	Massage	Yes
Self-Service Launderette			Yes
Movie Theater/Seats			Yes/237
Library			Yes
Children's Facilities			Yes
Watersports Facilities			None
Classification Society			Lloyd's Register

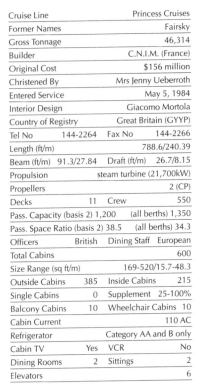

Length (ft/m)			788.6/240.39
Beam (ft/m) 91.3/27.84	Draft (ft/m)		26.7/8.15
Propulsion	steam turbine (21,700kW)		
Propellers			2 (CP)
Decks 11	Crew		550
Pass. Capacity (basis 2) 1,200	(all berths)		1,350
Pass. Space Ratio (basis 2) 38.5	(all berths)		34.3
Officers British	Dining Staff		European
Total Cabins			600
Size Range (sq ft/m)		169-520/15.7-48.3	
Outside Cabins 385	Inside Cabins		215
Single Cabins 0	Supplement		25-100%
Balcony Cabins 10	Wheelchair Cabins		10
Cabin Current			110 AC
Refrigerator		Category AA and B only	
Cabin TV Yes	VCR		No
Dining Rooms 2	Sittings		2
Elevators			6

RATINGS	SCORE
Ship: Condition/Cleanliness	8.1
Ship: Space/Flow/Comfort	8.0
Ship: Decor/Furnishings	8.1
Ship: Fitness Facilities	7.7
Cabins: Comfort/Facilities	8.2
Cabins: Software	8.2
Food: Dining Room/Cuisine	7.6
Food: Buffets/Informal Dining	7.2
Food: Quality of Ingredients	7.0
Service: Dining Room	7.6
Service: Bars	7.7
Service: Cabins	7.8
Cruise: Entertainment	8.1
Cruise: Activities Program	7.7
Cruise: Hospitality Standard	7.9
OVERALL RATING	116.9

+ Well-designed contemporary vessel has short, sharply raked bow and swept-back funnel. First cruise ship to have steam turbine machinery since the *QE2* debuted in 1969. Comfortable, easy layout. Has a good enclosed promenade deck. Fine array of public rooms, including expansive shops. Improved showroom. Horizon Lounge restful at night. Popular Pizzeria. Split casino configuration. Good health spa. Has spacious and very comfortable, well-appointed cabins, with all the essentials, and good-sized showers. Outstanding are the large Lido Deck suites. Cabins have bathrobes for all passengers.

— No wrap-around outdoor promenade deck. Clean, bland, clinical minimalist interior decor lacks warmth. Veranda Café, a popular outdoor buffet area, is poorly designed. Long lines for embarkation, disembarkation, buffets, and shore tenders.

Dining Two dining rooms (both non-smoking) are brightly lit, and there are no tables for two, although decor is pleasant. Pasta dishes are good, but other food lacks quality, flair and presentation. The service, while quite attentive, is somewhat impersonal and superficial.

Other Comments This well-designed ship provides a well-balanced, pleasing cruise experience for the mature passenger, with plenty of space and little crowding.

ms Song of America ★★★★

OPERATES

7-DAY BERMUDA AND
CARIBBEAN CRUISES

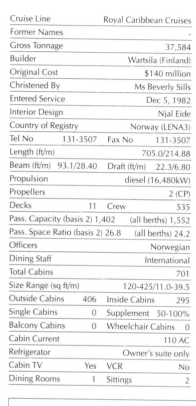

Cruise Line	Royal Caribbean Cruises
Former Names	-
Gross Tonnage	37,584
Builder	Wartsila (Finland)
Original Cost	$140 million
Christened By	Ms Beverly Sills
Entered Service	Dec 5, 1982
Interior Design	Njal Eide
Country of Registry	Norway (LENA3)

Tel No	131-3507	Fax No	131-3507
Length (ft/m)			705.0/214.88
Beam (ft/m)	93.1/28.40	Draft (ft/m)	22.3/6.80
Propulsion			diesel (16,480kW)
Propellers			2 (CP)
Decks	11	Crew	535
Pass. Capacity (basis 2) 1,402		(all berths) 1,552	
Pass. Space Ratio (basis 2) 26.8		(all berths) 24.2	
Officers			Norwegian
Dining Staff			International
Total Cabins			701
Size Range (sq ft/m)		120-425/11.0-39.5	
Outside Cabins	406	Inside Cabins	295
Single Cabins	0	Supplement	50-100%
Balcony Cabins	0	Wheelchair Cabins	0
Cabin Current			110 AC
Refrigerator			Owner's suite only
Cabin TV	Yes	VCR	No
Dining Rooms	1	Sittings	2

Elevators			7
Casino	Yes	Slot Machines	Yes
Swimming Pools (outside) 2		(inside)	0
Whirlpools	0	Gymnasium	Yes
Sauna/Steam Room	Yes/No	Massage	Yes
Self-Service Launderette			No
Movie Theater/Seats	No	Library	Yes
Children's Facilities			No
Watersports Facilities			None
Classification Society		Det Norske Veritas	

RATINGS	SCORE
Ship: Condition/Cleanliness	8.2
Ship: Space/Flow/Comfort	7.9
Ship: Decor/Furnishings	8.2
Ship: Fitness Facilities	7.8
Cabins: Comfort/Facilities	5.8
Cabins: Software	7.7
Food: Dining Room/Cuisine	6.8
Food: Buffets/Informal Dining	6.6
Food: Quality of Ingredients	7.1
Service: Dining Room	6.7
Service: Bars	6.5
Service: Cabins	6.1
Cruise: Entertainment	7.8
Cruise: Activities Program	7.6
Cruise: Hospitality Standard	7.4
OVERALL RATING	108.2

+ Contemporary ship has rounded lines and sharply raked bow. Striking Viking Crown Lounge wrapped around funnel is the line's trademark, and incorporates a bar. Good open deck and sunning space. Beautifully polished wooden decks and rails. Has a good array of public rooms with musical-themed decor. Has conference center for meetings and group business. Better shopping center and casino. The Veranda Café has good flow. Attentive, polished service throughout.

— Dining room is large, but the low ceiling creates a high level of ambient noise. The cabins, and particularly the bathrooms, with their wrap-around shower curtains, are very, very small, yet most passengers seem happy with them. There are many irritating announcements.

Dining Madame Butterfly Dining Room has tables for four to eight (no tables for two). Service is consistently good and the dining operation efficient. French, Italian, Oriental, Caribbean or American themes each night. Food is of a generally high quality and portions are reasonable. Bottled water (extra cost) is pushed heavily; drinking water is not provided *unless requested*.

Other Comments In typical Royal Caribbean Cruises fashion, the ship caters superbly to passengers in the public entertainment rooms. Recommended for both first-time and repeat passengers and provides a consistently good product in very comfortable surroundings.

ms Song of Flower ★★★★★

OPERATES
VARIOUS CRUISES WORLDWIDE

Cruise Line	Radisson Seven Seas Cruises
Former Names	Explorer Starship
Gross Tonnage	8,282
Builder	Kmv (Norway)/Lloyd Werft (Germany)
Original Cost	n/a
Christened By	Ms Mamiko Matsunari
Entered Service	1986/Feb 11, 1990
Interior Design	Yran & Storbraaten
Country of Registry	Norway (LATY2)
Tel No 131-0152	Fax No 131-0153
Length (ft/m)	407.4/124.20
Beam (ft/m) 52.4/16.00	Draft (ft/m) 16.0/4.90
Propulsion	diesel (5,500kW)
Propellers	2 (CP)
Decks 6	Crew 144
Pass. Capacity (basis 2) 214	(all berths) 214
Pass. Space Ratio (basis 2) 38.7	(all berths) 38.7
Officers	Norwegian
Dining Staff	European/Filipino
Total Cabins	107
Size Range (sq ft/m)	183-398/17.0-37.0
Outside Cabins 107	Inside Cabins 0
Single Cabins 0	Supplement 25%
Balcony Cabins 10	Wheelchair Cabins 0
Cabin Current 220 AC	Refrigerator All cabins
Cabin TV Yes	VCR Yes
Dining Rooms 1	Sittings Open
Elevators	2

Casino	Yes	Slot Machines	Yes
Swimming Pools (outside) 1		(inside)	0
Whirlpools		1	Gymnasium	Yes
Sauna/Steam Room Yes/No		Massage	Yes
Self-Service Launderette			No
Movie Theater/Seats No		Library	Yes
Children's Facilities			No
Watersports Facilities	jet skis, snorkel equipment,
	waterski boat, windsurfers
Classification Society	Det Norske Veritas

RATINGS	SCORE
Ship: Condition/Cleanliness	9.0
Ship: Space/Flow/Comfort	9.2
Ship: Facilities	9.0
Ship: Decor/Furnishings	8.9
Ship: Fitness/Watersports Facilities	8.7
Cabins: Comfort/Facilities	9.0
Cabins: Software	9.0
Food: Dining Room/Cuisine	9.1
Food: Buffets/Informal Dining	9.0
Food: Quality of Ingredients	8.6
Service: Dining Room	8.6
Service: Bars	8.8
Service: Cabins	8.8
Cruise: Entertainment/Lecture Program	8.7
Cruise: Hospitality Standard	9.4
OVERALL RATING	133.8

+ Excellent small cruise ship, with tall, twin funnels that give a somewhat squat profile. Well maintained and cared for, and spotlessly clean. Good sheltered open deck and sunning space. Elegant interior, with warm decor and colors. Fine furnishings and fabrics throughout. Has a compact health spa. Excellent tiered showroom is very comfortable, with good sightlines. Ten suites are really elegant; ten are strictly no-smoking cabins; all others are well equipped. Superb closet and drawer space. Many have (very tiny) bathtubs. Passengers with disabilities should choose a cabin with a shower instead of a bath. Has a wonderful, warm, caring staff who really do anticipate your every need. Totally understated.

— The bow should be a little longer to give a sleeker appearance! Sadly, there are no in-cabin dining facilities for dinner.

Dining Charming dining room has warm colors and ambiance. Very creative food and presentation, with small portions. All alcoholic and non-alcoholic beverages included with the exception of some premium wines. Outstanding personal service from a warm, highly attentive staff. There are several tables for two, and plenty of space around each table.

Other Comments Outstanding, destination-intensive, yet relaxing cruise experience, delivered with style. Gratuities included, no further tipping allowed, but port charges extra.

ms Song of Norway ★★★+

OPERATES

*ALASKA AND MEXICAN
RIVIERA CRUISES*

Cruise Line	Royal Caribbean Cruises		
Former Names	-		
Gross Tonnage	23,005		
Builder	Wartsila (Finland)		
Original Cost	$13.5 million		
Christened By	Mrs Magnhild Borten		
Entered Service	Nov 7, 1970		
Interior Design	Njal Eide		
Country of Registry	Norway (LNVP3)		
Tel No 131-0562	Fax No 131-0562		
Length (ft/m)	637.5/194.32		
Beam (ft/m) 78.8/24.03	Draft (ft/m) 21.9/6.70		
Propulsion	diesel (13,400kW)		
Propellers	2 (CP)		
Decks 8	Crew 423		
Pass. Capacity (basis 2) 1,004	(all berths) 1,138		
Pass. Space Ratio (basis 2) 22.5	(all berths) 20.2		
Officers Norwegian	Dining Staff International		
Total Cabins	502		
Size Range (sq ft/m)	120-266/11.0-24.7		
Outside Cabins 325	Inside Cabins 177		
Single Cabins 0	Supplement 50-100%		
Balcony Cabins 0	Wheelchair Cabins 0		
Cabin Current	110 AC		
Refrigerator	Owner's suite only		
Cabin TV No	VCR No		
Dining Rooms 1	Sittings 2		
Elevators	4		

Casino	Yes	Slot Machines	Yes
Swimming Pools (outside) 1		(inside)	0
Whirlpools	0	Gymnasium	Yes
Sauna/Steam Room No/No		Massage	No
Self-Service Launderette			No
Movie Theater/Seats			No
Library			No
Children's Facilities			No
Watersports Facilities			None
Classification Society		Det Norske Veritas	

RATINGS	SCORE
Ship: Condition/Cleanliness	7.4
Ship: Space/Flow/Comfort	6.7
Ship: Decor/Furnishings	7.0
Ship: Fitness Facilities	6.6
Cabins: Comfort/Facilities	5.8
Cabins: Software	7.7
Food: Dining Room/Cuisine	6.8
Food: Buffets/Informal Dining	6.6
Food: Quality of Ingredients	7.1
Service: Dining Room	6.7
Service: Bars	6.5
Service: Cabins	6.1
Cruise: Entertainment	7.8
Cruise: Activities Program	7.6
Cruise: Hospitality Standard	7.4
OVERALL RATING	103.8

+ Contemporary, but now dated seventies look with sleek lines, sharply raked bow and distinctive cantilevered Viking Crown Lounge high up around the ship's funnel. Has a polished wrap-around outdoor wood deck. Has a good, but now dated interior layout that has been well maintained. The Scandinavian decor is clean and bright. There is a good amount of open deck space, but it does get crowded when the ship is full, which is always. Good wood trim in passageways.

— This is a high-density ship with expansive open deck and sunning space that becomes cramped when full—OK in the seventies, but not today. Beautifully polished, though slippery, wooden decks. Narrow passageways. The cabins, which need refurbishing, are very small, and have very limited closet and drawer space. There are too many announcements.

Dining Attractive, but very noisy dining room. It is a good operation, but the food, while consistent, is not memorable. Service is generally good, but very robotic.

Other Comments Stretched in 1978. This ship caters to novice and repeat passengers with well-programmed flair, and consistently provides a fine-tuned cruise product in comfortable, but very crowded surroundings. For the same or similar cruise price, perhaps one should consider one of the company's newer megaships, where there is more space.

mv Southern Cross ★★★+

Cruise Line	CTC Cruise Lines		
Former Names	Star/Ship Majestic, Sun Princess,		
	Spirit of London		
Gross Tonnage	17,270		
Builder	Cantieri Navale Del Tirreno		
	& Riuniti (Italy)		
Original Cost	n/a		
Christened By	Mrs Beatrice Marriott		
Entered Service	Nov 11, 1972/Mar 8, 1995		
Interior Design	A&M Katzourakis		
Country of Registry	Bahamas (C6HK9)		
Tel No	110-4553	Fax No	110-4553
Length (ft/m)			536.0/163.40
Beam (ft/m)	81.4/24.82	Draft (ft/m)	21.3/6.52
Propulsion			diesel (13,450kW)
Propellers			2 (CP)
Decks	7	Crew	270
Pass. Capacity (basis 2)	720	(all berths)	982
Pass. Space Ratio (basis 2)	23.9	(all berths)	17.5
Officers			Ukrainian/European
Dining Staff			Ukrainian/European
Total Cabins			377
Size Range (sq ft/m)			99-237/9.0-22.0
Outside Cabins	255	Inside Cabins	122
Single Cabins	29	Supplement	0–50%
Balcony Cabins	0	Wheelchair Cabins	2
Cabin Current	220/110 AC	Refrigerator	No
Cabin TV	Yes	VCR	No

Dining Rooms	1	Sittings	2
Elevators			4
Casino	Yes	Slot Machines	Yes
Swimming Pools (outside)		1 (+children's pool)	
Whirlpools	0	Gymnasium	Yes
Sauna/Steam Room	No/No	Massage	Yes
Self-Service Launderette			No
Movie Theater/Seats			Yes/186
Library	Yes	Children's Facilities	Yes
Classification Society			Lloyd's Register

RATINGS	SCORE
Ship: Condition/Cleanliness	7.1
Ship: Space/Flow/Comfort	6.6
Ship: Decor/Furnishings	7.2
Ship: Fitness Facilities	5.0
Cabins: Comfort/Facilities	6.6
Cabins: Software	7.0
Food: Dining Room/Cuisine	7.6
Food: Buffets/Informal Dining	7.1
Food: Quality of Ingredients	6.8
Service: Dining Room	7.5
Service: Bars	7.4
Service: Cabins	7.4
Cruise: Entertainment	6.7
Cruise: Activities Program	6.5
Cruise: Hospitality Standard	6.8
OVERALL RATING	103.3

+ Reasonable amount of open deck and sunning space for ship size, but is cramped when full. Interior decor features tasteful earth tones mixed with extensive use of reflective surfaces. Has comfortable public rooms, with pleasant, attractive decor and soft furnishings. The deluxe suites are quite spacious; other cabins are on the small side, but quite well equipped. Well-designed itineraries include plenty of sea days on longer voyages.

— Loud announcements are irritating. No cushion pads for deck lounge chairs. Antiquated cabin telephone system. The cabin walls are very thin, and there's little drawer space.

Dining Charming dining room with high ceiling has a light and airy feel, but is extremely noisy and tables are so close together. Better service than on CTC's other ships, due to increased standards of a catering concession. Although it's all done to a price, the quality of food and presentation is reasonably good. Limited choice of breads, cheeses and fruits. Buffets are good and presented well.

Other Comments The ship has a smart contemporary profile with rakish superstructure, and an unmistakable scarlet red hull. She will provide a comfortable cruise experience that's good value for money, in very informal, relaxed surroundings.

ms Sovereign of the Seas ★★★★+

Cruise Line	Royal Caribbean Cruises
Former Names	-
Gross Tonnage	73,192
Builder	Chantiers de l'Atlantique (France)
Original Cost	$183.5 million
Christened By	Mrs Roslyn Carter
Entered Service	Jan 16, 1988
Interior Design	Njal Eide
Country of Registry	Norway (LAEB2)
Tel No 131-0711 Fax No 131-0711	
Length (ft/m)	873.6/266.30
Beam (ft/m) 105.6/32.20 Draft (ft/m) 24.7/7.55	
Propulsion	diesel (21,844kW)
Propellers	2 (CP)
Decks 12 Crew	808
Pass. Capacity (basis 2) 2,276 (all berths) 2,524	
Pass. Space Ratio (basis 2) 32.1 (all berths) 28.9	
Officers Norwegian Dining Staff International	
Total Cabins	1,138
Size Range (sq ft/m)	120-446/11.0-41.5
Outside Cabins 722 Inside Cabins 416	
Single Cabins 0 Supplement 50-100%	
Balcony Cabins 0 Wheelchair Cabins 10	
Cabin Current	110 AC
Refrigerator	Category R/A only
Cabin TV Yes VCR No	
Dining Rooms 2 Sittings 2	
Elevators	18

Casino	Yes	Slot Machines	Yes
Swimming Pools (outside) 2		(inside)	0
Whirlpools	1	Gymnasium	Yes
Sauna/Steam Room Yes/No		Massage	Yes
Self-Service Launderette			No
Movie Theater/Seats		Yes-2/146 each	
Library			Yes
Children's Facilities			Yes
Watersports Facilities			None
Classification Society		Det Norske Veritas	

RATINGS	SCORE
Ship: Condition/Cleanliness	8.0
Ship: Space/Flow/Comfort	8.0
Ship: Decor/Furnishings	7.9
Ship: Fitness Facilities	7.6
Cabins: Comfort/Facilities	7.6
Cabins: Software	7.7
Food: Dining Room/Cuisine	7.9
Food: Buffets/Informal Dining	7.6
Food: Quality of Ingredients	7.1
Service: Dining Room	7.7
Service: Bars	7.6
Service: Cabins	7.6
Cruise: Entertainment	8.2
Cruise: Activities Program	7.9
Cruise: Hospitality Standard	8.0
OVERALL RATING	116.4

+ Handsome megaship has well-balanced profile, nicely rounded lines and high superstructure. Viking Crown Lounge wrapped around funnel has superb views. Has wrap-around outdoor polished wood deck. Impressive array of spacious and elegant public rooms. Stunning five-deck-high Centrum lobby, with cascading stairways and two glass-walled elevators. Good two-level showroom and fine array of shops. Twelve suites on Bridge Deck are quite large and nicely furnished; other cabins are very small, but an arched window treatment gives illusion of greater space (almost all cabins convert to double-bed configuration). Good childrens' and teens' programs and counselors. The dress code is casual.

— Open deck space is adequate, no more. Awkward layout. Congested passenger flow in some areas. Cabins have little closet and drawer space (you'll need some "luggage engineering"). Too many announcements.

Dining Two dining rooms feature well-presented food and service, but there are no tables for two. Poor breads, rolls and fruit, but a good selection of light meals for the calorie-conscious, and a vegetarian menu is available. Decent wine list and prices. Staff are overly friendly.

Other Comments This floating resort provides a well-tuned yet somewhat impersonal cruise experience for upwards of 2,000 fellow passengers.

ms Splendour of the Seas

OPERATES

*12-DAY CARIBBEAN AND
EUROPE CRUISES*

Cruise Line	Royal Caribbean Cruise Line
Former Names	-
Gross Tonnage	70,000
Builder	Chantiers de l'Atlantique (France)
Original Cost	$325 million
Christened By	n/a
Entered Service	Mar 26, 1996
Interior Design	Njal Eide
Country of Registry	Norway
Tel No	n/a	Fax No	n/a
Length (ft/m)	867.0/264.20
Beam (ft/m) 105.0/32.00	Draft (ft/m)	24.5/7.46
Propulsion	diesel (40,200kW)
Propellers	2 (CP)
Decks	11	Crew	732
Pass. Capacity (basis 2) 1,804	(all berths) 2,064
Pass. Space Ratio (basis 2) 38.8	(all berths) 33.9
Officers Norwegian	Dining Staff International
Total Cabins	902
Size Range (sq ft/m)	138-1,148/12.8-106.6
Outside Cabins	575	Inside Cabins	327
Single Cabins	0	Supplement	50%
Balcony Cabins	231	Wheelchair Cabins	17
Cabin Current	110/220 AC
Refrigerator	
Cabin TV	Yes	VCR	Suites only
Dining Rooms	1	Sittings	2
Elevators	11

Casino	Yes	Slot Machines	Yes
Swimming Pools (outside)		2 (1 with sliding roof)
Swimming Pools (inside)			0
Whirlpools	4	Gymnasium	Yes
Sauna/Steam Room Yes/Yes	Massage	Yes
Self-Service Launderette	
Movie Theater/Seats	No	Library	Yes
Children's Facilities			Yes
Watersports Facilities			None
Classification Society		Det Norske Veritas

RATINGS	SCORE
Ship: Condition/Cleanliness	NYR
Ship: Space/Flow/Comfort	NYR
Ship: Decor/Furnishings	NYR
Ship: Fitness Facilities	NYR
Cabins: Comfort/Facilities	NYR
Cabins: Software	NYR
Food: Dining Room/Cuisine	NYR
Food: Buffets/Informal Dining	NYR
Food: Quality of Ingredients	NYR
Service: Dining Room	NYR
Service: Bars	NYR
Service: Cabins	NYR
Cruise: Entertainment	NYR
Cruise: Activities Program	NYR
Cruise: Hospitality Standard	NYR
OVERALL RATING	

+ Good passenger flow. Pool deck overhangs the hull, to provide a very wide deck, yet still allows the ship to navigate the Panama Canal. Outside light is brought into the inside in many places, and there's a lot of glass area, which provides contact with sea and air. Features an innovative single-level sliding glass roof (not a magrodome) over a more formal setting of one of two swimming pools, thus providing a multi-activity all-weather indoor-outdoor area called the Solarium. The health spa is excellent. Tiered and balconied showlounge has excellent sightlines. The cabins are larger than on previous Royal Caribbean Cruises ships, and include some outstanding large suites.

— As with any large ship, you can expect lines for embarkation, disembarkation, buffets, and shore excursions.

Dining Two-deck-high dining room has dramatic double-deck-high glass side walls. Cavernous indoor-outdoor café and sizeable snack area adds to choices for informal eating. Royal Caribbean's upgraded food and service provides a better than ever experience.

Other Comments This ship is built for longer itineraries. Few other details for this ship were available at press time, but this promises to be an outstanding cruise vessel for Royal Caribbean Cruises passengers. Also see comments for sister ship *Legend of the Seas*.

ms Star Odyssey ★★★★

OPERATES

*VARIOUS ALASKA AND
NEW ENGLAND CRUISES*

Cruise Line	Royal Cruise Line	Casino	Yes
Former Names	Westward/Royal Viking Star	Swimming Pools (outside) 2	
Gross Tonnage	28,492	Whirlpools	2
Builder	Wartsila (Finland)	Sauna/Steam Room Yes/Yes	
Original Cost	$22.5 million	Self-Service Launderette	
Christened By	Mrs Thor Heyerdahl	Movie Theater/Seats	
Entered Service	Jun 26, 1972/May 9, 1994	Library	
Interior Design	Njal Eide	Children's Facilities	
Country of Registry	Bahamas (C6CN2)	Watersports Facilities	
Tel No 110-4507 Fax No	110-4554	Classification Society	

Casino	Yes	Slot Machines	Yes
Swimming Pools (outside)	2	(inside)	0
Whirlpools	2	Gymnasium	Yes
Sauna/Steam Room	Yes/Yes	Massage	Yes
Self-Service Launderette			Yes
Movie Theater/Seats			Yes/156
Library			No
Children's Facilities			Yes
Watersports Facilities			None
Classification Society		Det Norske Veritas	

Length (ft/m)		674.1/205.47		
Beam (ft/m) 82.6/25.20	Draft (ft/m)	24.7/7.55		
Propulsion		diesel (13,400kW)		
Propellers			2 (CP)	
Decks	8	Crew		325
Pass. Capacity (basis 2) 790		(all berths) 790		
Pass. Space Ratio (basis 2) 36.0		(all berths) 36.0		
Officers European	Dining Staff		International	
Total Cabins				404
Size Range (sq ft/m)		136-580/12.6-53.8		
Outside Cabins	356	Inside Cabins		48
Single Cabins	33	Supplement	50-100%	
Balcony Cabins	9	Wheelchair Cabins		0
Cabin Current			110/220 AC	
Refrigerator		Category 1-6 only		
Cabin TV	Yes	VCR		No
Dining Rooms	1	Sittings		1
Elevators				5

RATINGS	SCORE
Ship: Condition/Cleanliness	7.8
Ship: Space/Flow/Comfort	8.5
Ship: Decor/Furnishings	8.1
Ship: Fitness Facilities	8.1
Cabins: Comfort/Facilities	7.6
Cabins: Software	7.8
Food: Dining Room/Cuisine	7.3
Food: Buffets/Informal Dining	7.2
Food: Quality of Ingredients	6.9
Service: Dining Room	7.7
Service: Bars	7.8
Service: Cabins	7.7
Cruise: Entertainment	6.8
Cruise: Activities Program	7.0
Cruise: Hospitality Standard	7.7
OVERALL RATING	114.0

+ This handsome ship has a sharply raked bow and distinctive lines. Excellent open deck and sunning space, and a fine health-fitness spa high atop ship. Interior decor is restful, having been made more attractive in a 1994 refit. Good materials, fabrics and soft furnishings add to a pleasant ambiance and warmth. Spacious public rooms have high ceilings. There is a good movie theater with steeply tiered floor. The observation lounge high atop ship has commanding views and is very comfortable. A wide range of cabins provides something for everyone, from spacious suites to small inside cabins. All are nicely equipped, and have good closet, drawer and storage space. Non-smoking cabins are also available.

– Cabin numbering system is reversed from the seagoing norm. Some cabin bathrooms have awkward access, and the cabin drawers are tinny and noisy. The insulation between cabins is also poor. Very poor library needs upgrading, and some up-to-date reference books added.

Dining Spacious dining room with high ceiling features good cuisine and relaxed operation. Continental-style food, but inconsistent quality and presentation. Overly friendly waiter service. Poor selection of breads, cheeses and fruits. Varied wine list, but poor vintages.

Other Comments Stretched in 1981. This ship provides a reasonable cruise experience at a decent price.

mv Star Pisces ★★★★+

OPERATES

2 AND 3-DAY SOUTH-EAST ASIA CRUISES (YEAR-ROUND)

Cruise Line	Star Cruise	Casino Yes	Slot Machines Yes
Former Names	Kalypso	Swimming Pools (outside) 1	(inside) 1
Gross Tonnage	40,012	Whirlpools 3	Gymnasium Yes
Builder	Wartsila (Finland)	Sauna/Steam Room Yes/Yes	Massage Yes
Original Cost	SEK650 million	Self-Service Launderette	No
Christened By	Ms Marianne Myrsten	Movie Theater/Seats	Yes (2)/210 each
Entered Service	May 1, 1990/May, 1994	Library	Yes
Interior Design	Robert Tillberg/PM design	Children's Facilities	Yes
Country of Registry	Panama (3FWP3)	Watersports Facilities	None
Tel No 635-286122 Fax No	635-286111	Classification Society	Det Norske Veritas
Length (ft/m)	579.3/176.6		
Beam (ft/m) 97.1/29.6 Draft (ft/m)	20.3/6.2	**RATINGS**	**SCORE**
Propulsion	diesel (23,760kW)	Ship: Condition/Cleanliness	8.3
Propellers	2 (CP)	Ship: Space/Flow/Comfort	7.7
Decks 12 Crew	750	Ship: Decor/Furnishings	8.4
Pass. Capacity (basis 2) 1,530 (all berths)	1,900	Ship: Fitness Facilities	8.2
Pass. Space Ratio (basis 2) 26.1 (all berths)	21.0	Cabins: Comfort/Facilities	6.0
Officers Scandinavian Dining Staff	Filipino	Cabins: Software	7.6
Total Cabins	598	Food: Dining Room/Cuisine	8.2
Size Range (sq ft/m)	67-145/6.3-13.5	Food: Buffets/Informal Dining	7.7
Outside Cabins 258 Inside Cabins	340	Food: Quality of Ingredients	8.0
Single Cabins 0 Supplement	Set rates	Service: Dining Room	7.8
Balcony Cabins 0 Wheelchair Cabins	0	Service: Bars	7.3
Cabin Current 220 AC Refrigerator	No	Service: Cabins	7.2
Cabin TV Yes VCR	No	Cruise: Entertainment	7.5
Dining Rooms	3 (+2 cafes)	Cruise: Activities Program	7.0
Sittings	1	Cruise: Hospitality Standard	8.6
Elevators	5	OVERALL RATING	115.5

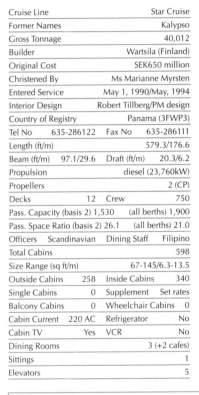

+ Scandinavian design combined with a touch of the Orient. Also has a helipad. Huge duty-free shopping center and supermarket. Regal casino for VIPs is large and has a high, detailed ceiling (there's also a second casino for general use). Except for some very imperial suites, cabins are very small, and come with just basic facilities. Has a superb health club for men. There are many meeting rooms, conference auditoria and a business center. Children's facilities are extensive and include computers and educational rooms as well as play areas and huge video machine section. Free ice cream for kids. Excellent Asian hospitality.

— High-density ship means crowded public rooms, and long lines for shore visits, buffets, embarkation, and disembarkation. Cabin insulation is poor, and bathrooms are very small. Poor open deck space, but enough for the Asian market.

Dining Seven restaurants provide a wide choice of cuisine and dining styles, and all feature very attentive service. This ship has a real Chinese Restaurant (Cantonese and Sichuan) with a Hong Kong chef; Japanese, including a sushi bar and private tatami rooms; Italian; Spice Island buffet restaurant for laksa, satay and hawker delights; and three other snack cafés.

Other Comments Skilfully converted into a cruise vessel specifically for the Asian family market. Has a low ticket price, but everything costs extra. Gratuities are prohibited.

ms Star Princess ★★★★+

OPERATES

VARIOUS ALASKA AND
CARIBBEAN CRUISES

Cruise Line	Princess Cruises	Casino	Yes	Slot Machines Yes
Former Names	FairMajesty	Swimming Pools (outside) 3		(inside) 0
Gross Tonnage	63,564	Whirlpools	4	Gymnasium Yes
Builder	Chantiers de L'Atlantique (France)	Sauna/Steam Room Yes/No		Massage Yes
Original Cost	$200 million	Self-Service Launderette		Yes
Christened By	Ms Audrey Hepburn	Movie Theater/Seats		Yes/205
Entered Service	Mar 24, 1989	Library		Yes
Interior Design	Ellerbe Becket	Children's Facilities		Yes
Country of Registry	Liberia (ELIR8)	Watersports Facilities		None
Tel No 124-0247 Fax No	124-0236	Classification Society		Lloyd's Register
Length (ft/m)	805.7/245.60			
Beam (ft/m) 105.6/32.20 Draft (ft/m)	25.0/7.62	**RATINGS**		**SCORE**
Propulsion	diesel-electric (39,000kW)	Ship: Condition/Cleanliness		8.1
Propellers	2 (CP)	Ship: Space/Flow/Comfort		8.3
Decks 12 Crew	600	Ship: Decor/Furnishings		8.1
Pass. Capacity (basis 2) 1,470 (all berths) 1,620		Ship: Fitness Facilities		7.7
Pass. Space Ratio (basis 2) 43.2 (all berths) 39.2		Cabins: Comfort/Facilities		8.2
Officers Italian Dining Staff European		Cabins: Software		8.2
Total Cabins	735	Food: Dining Room/Cuisine		7.6
Size Range (sq ft/m)	180-530/16.7-49.2	Food: Buffets/Informal Dining		7.2
Outside Cabins 570 Inside Cabins	165	Food: Quality of Ingredients		7.0
Single Cabins 0 Supplement 25-100%		Service: Dining Room		7.6
Balcony Cabins 50 Wheelchair Cabins 10		Service: Bars		7.7
Cabin Current	110/220 AC	Service: Cabins		8.0
Refrigerator	All cabins	Cruise: Entertainment		8.1
Cabin TV Yes VCR	No	Cruise: Activities Program		7.7
Dining Rooms 1 Sittings	2	Cruise: Hospitality Standard		7.9
Elevators	9	OVERALL RATING		117.4

+ Innovative styling mixed with traditional shipboard features. Spacious public rooms have tasteful decor, and an excellent selection of artwork provides some warmth to what would otherwise be a clinical interior. Horseshoe-shaped balconied showroom. Three-deck-high foyer highlighted by kinetic sculpture. Neat wine bar and pizzeria. Characters Bar serves colorful drinks in jazzy glasses. In-pool bar. Multi-tiered main restaurant has two-deck-high center ceiling. Spacious, well-equipped cabins have large, modular bathrooms and plenty of closet, drawer and storage space. Bathrobes provided, as well as better amenities kits.

— No wrap-around outdoor promenade deck. Domed observation lounge is out of traffic flow. Poor outdoor promenade area. Expect lines for embarkation, disembarkation, shore tenders, and buffets. Poor sound insulation between cabins.

Dining Multi-tiered dining room has high center ceiling, but is noisy, and there are no tables for two. Food is adequate, but presentation is lacking. Good pasta dishes. Service is so-so, but could be much improved. Indoor-outdoor buffet restaurant is too small.

Other Comments Provides a traditional approach to cruising for repeat passengers who like a large ship, families, and some degree of anonymity.

Star/Ship Atlantic ★★★★

Cruise Line	Premier Cruise Lines	Casino	Yes
Former Names	Atlantic	Swimming Pools (outside) 1	(inside) 1
Gross Tonnage	35,143	Whirlpools 3	Gymnasium Yes
Builder	C.N.I.M. (France)	Sauna/Steam Room Yes/No	Massage Yes
Original Cost	$100 million	Self-Service Launderette	No
Christened By	n/a	Movie Theater/Seats	Yes/251
Entered Service	Apr 17, 1982/Jan 13, 1989	Library Yes	Children's Facilities Yes
Interior Design	A&M Katzourakis	Watersports Facilities	None
Country of Registry	Liberia (ELAJ4)	Classification Society	American Bureau
Tel No - Fax No	-		of Shipping

Length (ft/m)		671.9/204.81
Beam (ft/m) 89.7/27.36	Draft (ft/m)	25.5/7.80
Propulsion		diesel (22,070kW)
Propellers		2 (CP)
Decks 9	Crew	535
Pass. Capacity (basis 2) 972	(all berths)	1,600
Pass. Space Ratio (basis 2) 36.1	(all berths)	21.9
Officers		Greek
Dining Staff		International
Total Cabins		549
Size Range (sq ft/m)		137-427/12.7-39.5
Outside Cabins 380	Inside Cabins	169
Single Cabins 0	Supplement	75%
Balcony Cabins 0	Wheelchair Cabins	Yes
Cabin Current 110 AC	Refrigerator	No
Cabin TV No	VCR	No
Dining Rooms 1	Sittings	2
Elevators		4

RATINGS	SCORE
Ship: Condition/Cleanliness	8.0
Ship: Space/Flow/Comfort	8.0
Ship: Decor/Furnishings	8.1
Ship: Fitness Facilities	7.6
Cabins: Comfort/Facilities	7.8
Cabins: Software	8.1
Food: Dining Room/Cuisine	7.6
Food: Buffets/Informal Dining	7.1
Food: Quality of Ingredients	6.7
Service: Dining Room	7.3
Service: Bars	7.2
Service: Cabins	7.4
Cruise: Entertainment	6.6
Cruise: Activities Program	6.7
Cruise: Hospitality Standard	6.8
OVERALL RATING	111.0

+ This ship has a short, stubby bow and squat funnel, coupled with a distinctive scarlet red hull. Has an excellent amount of outdoor deck space, although when the ship is full, with lots of children, it can be extremely noisy. The interior is quite spacious, with plenty of public rooms and high ceilings. There is a good indoor-outdoor pool area. Good duty-free shopping. Spacious cabins are generously equipped and very comfortable.

— The decor is somewhat garish in places, but there's a generous amount of stainless steel and teak wood trim. Good observation lounge. No cushioned pads are provided for deck lounge chairs. The cabin insulation is very poor. Hundreds of kids mean it's difficult to find a quiet place anywhere. There are too many add-on charges in the Orlando cruise-and-stay programs.

Dining The dining room (non-smoking for both sittings), located on a lower deck, is attractive, but the tables are too close together, so noise level is high. The food quality generally is very good. Good basic service provided by an attentive multi-national staff.

Other Comments Plenty of children's and teens' counselors. This ship will provide a good cruise experience for families with children at the right price, in typical Premier Cruise Lines style.

Star/Ship Oceanic ★★★★

OPERATES

3- AND 4-DAY BAHAMAS CRUISES (YEAR-ROUND)

Cruise Line	Premier Cruise Lines	Casino	Yes	Slot Machines	Yes
Former Names	Oceanic	Swimming Pools (outside) 2	(inside)	0
Gross Tonnage	38,772	Whirlpools	3	Gymnasium	Yes
Builder	Cantieri Riuniti dell' Adriatico (Italy)	Sauna/Steam Room No/No	Massage	Yes
Original Cost	$40 million	Self-Service Launderette	No
Christened By	Ms Minnie Mouse	Movie Theater/Seats	Yes/420
Entered Service	Apr 3,1965/Apr 25, 1986	Library	No	Children's Facilities Yes
Interior Design	A&M Katzourakis	Watersports Facilities	None
Country of Registry	Bahamas (C62F7)	Classification Society	American Bureau
Tel No	112-0520	Fax No	112-0520		of Shipping

Length (ft/m)	782.1/238.40
Beam (ft/m) 96.5/29.44	Draft (ft/m)	28.2/8.60
Propulsion	steam turbine (45,100kW)
Propellers	2 (FP)
Decks 10	Crew	565
Pass. Capacity (basis 2) 1,180	(all berths) 1,500
Pass. Space Ratio (basis 2) 32.8	(all berths) 25.8
Officers	Greek
Dining Staff	International
Total Cabins	590
Size Range (sq ft/m)	139-455/13.0-42.2
Outside Cabins 261	Inside Cabins	329
Single Cabins 0	Supplement	75%
Balcony Cabins 8	Wheelchair Cabins	0
Cabin Current 110 AC	Refrigerator	No
Cabin TV No	VCR	No
Dining Rooms 1	Sittings	2
Elevators	5

RATINGS	SCORE
Ship: Condition/Cleanliness	7.7
Ship: Space/Flow/Comfort	7.9
Ship: Decor/Furnishings	7.6
Ship: Fitness Facilities	6.6
Cabins: Comfort/Facilities	6.8
Cabins: Software	7.1
Food: Dining Room/Cuisine	7.6
Food: Buffets/Informal Dining	7.3
Food: Quality of Ingredients	6.8
Service: Dining Room	7.3
Service: Bars	7.2
Service: Cabins	7.5
Cruise: Entertainment	6.6
Cruise: Activities Program	6.7
Cruise: Hospitality Standard	6.8
OVERALL RATING	107.5

+ Expansive open deck space for sunning. Swimming pool atop ship has magrodome roof for inclement weather. Contemporary interior decor and cheerful, bright colors. Delightful enclosed promenades. Balconied Sun Deck suites are superb and so spacious. Wide choice of other cabin grades, sizes and shapes. All cabins have heavy-duty furniture and are well equipped, although some need refurbishing. Many cabins feature double beds. This ship does a wonderful job for families with children, with well-trained counselors. Cruise-and-stay packages are well designed.

— Long lines for embarkation, disembarkation, buffets, and shore tenders to out-island. Constant repetitive announcements. No cushioned pads are provided for deck lounge chairs. The interiors need more attention to furnishing detail. There are simply too many add-on charges in the Orlando cruise-and-stay programs.

Dining The dining room (non-smoking for both sittings) is cheerful, but noisy when full. Good food and service considering the cruise fare, but a limited selection of breads, cheeses and fruits. First sitting is non-smoking.

Other Comments Distinctive scarlet red hull. An excellent, family-oriented, fun-filled cruise at an attractive price. More like a summer camp at sea.

ms Statendam ★★★★

OPERATES

VARIOUS CARIBBEAN AND
EUROPE CRUISES

Cruise Line	Holland America Line	Casino	Yes	Slot Machines	Yes
Former Names	- Gross Tonnage 55,451	Swimming Pools (outside)		1
Builder	Fincantieri (Italy)	Swimming Pools (inside)		1 (magrodome)
Original Cost	$215 million	Whirlpools	2	Gymnasium	Yes
Christened By	Lin Arison	Sauna/Steam Room Yes/No	Massage	Yes
Entered Service	Jan 25, 1993	Self-Service Launderette		Yes
Interior Design	VFD Interiors/Joe Farcus	Movie Theater/Seats		Yes/249
Country of Registry	Bahamas (C6TV)	Library	Yes	Children's Facilities No
Tel No 130-5566 Fax No	130-5567	Watersports Facilities		None
Length (ft/m)	719.4/219.30	Classification Society	Lloyd's Register

Beam (ft/m) 101.0/30.80	Draft (ft/m) 24.6/7.50		
Propulsion	diesel-electric (34,560kW)	**RATINGS**	**SCORE**
Propellers	2 (CP)	Ship: Condition/Cleanliness	8.7
Decks 10	Crew 588	Ship: Space/Flow/Comfort	8.4
Pass. Capacity (basis 2) 1,264	(all berths) 1,627	Ship: Decor/Furnishings	8.3
Pass. Space Ratio (basis 2) 43.8	(all berths) 34.0	Ship: Fitness Facilities	7.7
Officers	Dutch	Cabins: Comfort/Facilities	8.1
Dining Staff	Filipino/Indonesian	Cabins: Software	8.2
Total Cabins	632	Food: Dining Room/Cuisine	6.8
Size Range (sq ft/m)	187-1,126/17.3-104.5	Food: Buffets/Informal Dining	6.6
Outside Cabins 501	Inside Cabins 131	Food: Quality of Ingredients	6.7
Single Cabins 0	Supplement 50-100%	Service: Dining Room	6.1
Balcony Cabins 150	Wheelchair Cabins 6	Service: Bars	7.2
Cabin Current	110/220 AC	Service: Cabins	8.0
Refrigerator	Category PS/S/A/B only	Cruise: Entertainment	7.1
Cabin TV Yes	VCR No	Cruise: Activities Program	7.7
Dining Rooms 1	Sittings 2	Cruise: Hospitality Standard	8.3
Elevators	12	OVERALL RATING	113.9

+ Has teakwood outdoor decks and a traditional wrap-around promenade deck.
Magrodome roof covers indoor-outdoor pool, whirlpools and central lido area, whose focal
point is a huge dolphin sculpture. Elegant, yet eclectic interior design and decor features
traditional styling and use of classic materials—woods and ceramics, providing a restrained
approach to interior styling, and little glitz. Three-deck-high atrium foyer with statue is lovely,
but space is tight. Good reference library and card room. Art collection adds much color.
Suites (each of which can accommodate four) feature an in-suite dining alternative, and free
laundry/dry-cleaning. Other cabins are spacious, tastefully decorated and well laid out, and
most feature daytime sitting area. Excellent large flower displays throughout.

— Expect long lines for embarkation, disembarkation, shore tenders and buffets. Crows Nest
lounge has awful decor. Standard cabins have little closet space for long cruises. Showroom
has glitzy decor but poor sightlines. Entertainment is poor. Extra charge for use of the self-
service launderette is petty.

Dining Two-level dining room has grand staircase and music balcony. Fine china and
silverware. Food and service standards declining. Tasteless food (particularly in the Lido).

Other Comments Really unmemorable cruising that could be better.

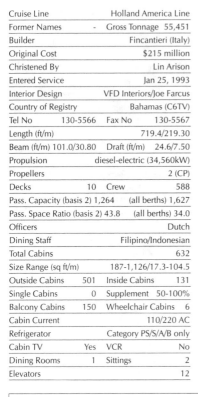

ms Stella Maris ★★★

OPERATES

7-DAY AEGEAN/
MEDITERRANEAN CRUISES

Cruise Line	Sun Line Cruises		
Former Names	Bremerhaven		
Gross Tonnage	4,000		
Builder	Alder Werft (Germany)		
Original Cost	n/a		
Christened By	Mrs Daniela Caneli		
Entered Service	1960/1965		
Interior Design	Mrs Isabella Kousseoglou		
Country of Registry	Greece (SZPS)		
Tel No	113-0322	Fax No	113-0323
Length (ft/m)	289.4/88.22		
Beam (ft/m) 45.9/14.00	Draft (ft/m)	14.4/4.40	
Propulsion	diesel (6,220kW)		
Propellers	2 (FP)		
Decks	4	Crew	110
Pass. Capacity (basis 2) 180	(all berths) 180		
Pass. Space Ratio (basis 2) 22.2	(all berths) 22.2		
Officers	Greek	Dining Staff	Greek
Total Cabins	93		
Size Range (sq ft/m)	96-151/9.0-14.0		
Outside Cabins	80	Inside Cabins	13
Single Cabins	0	Supplement	0-50%
Balcony Cabins	0	Wheelchair Cabins	0
Cabin Current	220 AC		
Refrigerator	No		
Cabin TV	No	VCR	No
Dining Rooms	1	Sittings	1
Elevators	0		

Casino	No	Slot Machines	No
Swimming Pools (outside) 1	(inside)	0	
Whirlpools	0	Gymnasium	No
Sauna/Steam Room No/No	Massage	No	
Self-Service Launderette	No		
Movie Theater/Seats	No		
Library	Yes		
Children's Facilities	No		
Watersports Facilities	None		
Classification Society	Lloyd's Register		

RATINGS	SCORE
Ship: Condition/Cleanliness	6.7
Ship: Space/Flow/Comfort	6.0
Ship: Decor/Furnishings	7.1
Ship: Fitness Facilities	3.0
Cabins: Comfort/Facilities	6.7
Cabins: Software	7.4
Food: Dining Room/Cuisine	7.3
Food: Buffets/Informal Dining	7.0
Food: Quality of Ingredients	6.4
Service: Dining Room	7.6
Service: Bars	7.4
Service: Cabins	7.6
Cruise: Entertainment	5.3
Cruise: Activities Program	5.7
Cruise: Hospitality Standard	7.7
OVERALL RATING	98.9

+ Charming little ship has an intimate, yacht-like atmosphere. Well maintained and spotlessly clean, neat and tidy. Fresh flower arrangements throughout add a splash of color. Excellent service from attentive, considerate staff who are pleased to serve with a smile. Cabins are quite spacious for ship size, and tastefully appointed, but there is not much drawer space. Very warm and intimate ambiance. Good for close-in destination cruising among the Greek islands and Turkey, which Sun Line does well.

— There are limited public rooms and open spaces, and the swimming pool is tiny— it's really just a "dip" pool. Cabins bathrooms are small. Being a small ship, she does not sail well in open waters.

Dining Charming dining room, decorated in sunshine yellow and brown. The food is quite good, though loaded with oil and olives. Nice wine list. Limited selection of breads, fruits and cheeses.

Other Comments This ship will provide you with very comfortable surroundings, and the line's personal attention to detail makes for a personable experience.

ms Stella Oceanis ★★★

OPERATES

3- AND 4-DAY AEGEAN/
MEDITERRANEAN CRUISES

Cruise Line	Sun Line Cruises	Casino	No	Slot Machines	No
Former Names	Aphrodite	Swimming Pools (outside) 1	(inside)	0
Gross Tonnage	6,000	Whirlpools	0	Gymnasium	No
Builder	Cantieri Riuniti dell' Adriatico (Italy)	Sauna/Steam Room No/No	Massage	No
Original Cost	n/a	Self-Service Launderette	No
Christened By	Mrs Isabella Kousseoglou	Movie Theater/Seats	No
Entered Service	1965/1967	Library	Yes
Interior Design	Mrs Isabella Kousseoglou	Children's Facilities	No
Country of Registry	Greece (SZLX)	Watersports Facilities	None
Tel No	113-0471	Fax No	113-0471	Classification Society	Lloyd's Register
Length (ft/m)	344.9/105.14		
Beam (ft/m) 55.5/16.92	Draft (ft/m)	14.9/4.56	**RATINGS**	**SCORE**
Propulsion	diesel (8,090kW)	Ship: Condition/Cleanliness	6.5
Propellers	1 (CP)	Ship: Space/Flow/Comfort	6.0
Decks	6	Crew	140	Ship: Decor/Furnishings	7.0
Pass. Capacity (basis 2) 300	(all berths) 369	Ship: Fitness Facilities	3.0
Pass. Space Ratio (basis 2) 20.0	(all berths) 16.2	Cabins: Comfort/Facilities	6.5
Officers Greek	Dining Staff	Greek	Cabins: Software	7.2
Total Cabins	159	Food: Dining Room/Cuisine	7.3
Size Range (sq ft/m)	96-208/9.0-19.3	Food: Buffets/Informal Dining	7.0
Outside Cabins 113	Inside Cabins	46	Food: Quality of Ingredients	6.4
Single Cabins 0	Supplement	50-100%	Service: Dining Room	7.5
Balcony Cabins 0	Wheelchair Cabins	0	Service: Bars	7.4
Cabin Current	220 AC	Service: Cabins	7.6
Refrigerator	No	Cruise: Entertainment	5.2
Cabin TV No	VCR	No	Cruise: Activities Program	5.5
Dining Rooms 1	Sittings	2	Cruise: Hospitality Standard	7.6
Elevators	1	OVERALL RATING	97.7

+ Tidy-looking, well-maintained ship with clean, rounded lines. Intimate atmosphere. Public rooms limited, but nicely decorated; a favorite is the Plaka Taverna, decorated in rich woods. The cabins (eight categories) are small, and plainer than on the smaller sister, and have limited closet and drawer space, but those on Lido and Stella decks have interconnecting doors. Some have full bathtub, while others have shower only, but all have private bathrooms.

— Has few public rooms and not much open deck and sunning space. Has a narrow, steep gangway.

Dining Tastefully decorated, charming dining room. Good food, but little choice.

Other Comments This ship lacks the sophistication of the other ships in the fleet, but is nonetheless quite charming. Sun Line provides a fine destination-intensive cruise experience, made better by the charming, friendly officers and staff.

ss Stella Solaris ★★★★

OPERATES

CARIBBEAN, EUROPE AND
SOUTH AMERICA CRUISES

Cruise Line	Sun Line Cruises	Casino	Yes	Slot Machines	Yes
Former Names	Stella V/Camboge	Swimming Pools (outside)	1	(inside)	0
Gross Tonnage	17,832	Whirlpools	0	Gymnasium	Yes
Builder	Ateliers et Chantiers de France (France)	Sauna/Steam Room	Yes/No	Massage	Yes
Original Cost	n/a	Self-Service Launderette			No
Christened By	Mrs Isabella Kousseoglou	Movie Theater/Seats			Yes/275
Entered Service	Jul 31, 1953/Jun 25, 1973	Library			Yes
Interior Design	Mrs Isabella Kousseoglou	Children's Facilities			No
Country of Registry	Greece (SYWT)	Watersports Facilities			None
Tel No 113-0403 Fax No	113-0403	Classification Society		Lloyd's Register	
Length (ft/m)	545.1/166.15				

Beam (ft/m) 72.4/22.08	Draft (ft/m)	25.8/7.88	
Propulsion	steam turbine (17,900kW)		
Propellers	2 (FP)		
Decks 8	Crew	330	
Pass. Capacity (basis 2) 620	(all berths) 700		
Pass. Space Ratio (basis 2) 28.7	(all berths) 25.4		
Officers Greek	Dining Staff	Greek	
Total Cabins	329		
Size Range (sq ft/m)	96-225/9.0-21.0		
Outside Cabins 250	Inside Cabins	79	
Single Cabins 0	Supplement	50-100%	
Balcony Cabins 0	Wheelchair Cabins	0	
Cabin Current	110/220 AC		
Refrigerator	No		
Cabin TV Yes	VCR	No	
Dining Rooms 1	Sittings	2	
Elevators	3		

RATINGS	SCORE
Ship: Condition/Cleanliness	7.7
Ship: Space/Flow/Comfort	7.0
Ship: Decor/Furnishings	7.8
Ship: Fitness Facilities	5.1
Cabins: Comfort/Facilities	7.1
Cabins: Software	7.8
Food: Dining Room/Cuisine	7.4
Food: Buffets/Informal Dining	7.0
Food: Quality of Ingredients	6.6
Service: Dining Room	7.8
Service: Bars	7.7
Service: Cabins	7.7
Cruise: Entertainment	6.1
Cruise: Activities Program	5.7
Cruise: Hospitality Standard	7.8
OVERALL RATING	106.3

+ Traditional ship profile, with attractive funnel amidships. Clean and well maintained throughout. Well-planned itineraries. Expansive open deck space, including an outdoor wrap-around promenade deck. Attractive twin pools and sunning area. Elegant public rooms have quality furniture and fixtures. Nice feeling of space and grace. Fresh flowers everywhere add warmth. Cabins are spacious and well appointed – many have full bathtub. Lido Deck suites are delightful. The decor has recently been updated, with brighter fabrics and colors.

— There's no forward observation lounge. Cabins located on Sapphire Deck and midships on Emerald Deck are subject to engine noise.

Dining Delightful dining room features good food, some good wines and old-world European service.

Other Comments This ship is for the older passenger who seeks a relaxed, unhurried and gracious cruise experience in fine surroundings, at reasonable cost, with friendly all-Greek service, but without the hype of the more contemporary ships.

ms Sun Princess

OPERATES

*7-DAY ALASKA AND
CARIBBEAN CRUISES*

Cruise Line	Princess Cruises	Elevators	11
Former Names	-	Casino	Yes	Slot Machines	Yes
Gross Tonnage	77,000	Swimming Pools (outside) 3	(inside)	0
Builder	Fincantieri (Italy)	Whirlpools	5	Gymnasium	Yes
Original Cost	$300 million	Sauna/Steam Room	Yes	Massage	Yes
Christened By	n/a	Self-Service Launderette		Yes
Entered Service	Dec 16, 1995	Movie Theater/Seats	Yes	Library	Yes
Interior Design	Njal R. Eide/Giacomo Mortola	Children's Facilities		Yes
Country of Registry	Italy	Watersports Facilities		None
Tel No	n/a	Fax No	n/a	Classification Society	Lloyd's Register
Length (ft/m)	856.2/261.0		

Beam (ft/m) 105.8/32.25	Draft (ft/m) 26.0/7.95
Propulsion	diesel-electric (28,000kW)
Propellers	2 (FP)
Decks	14	Crew	900
Pass. Capacity (basis 2) 1,950	(all berths) 2,322
Pass. Space Ratio (basis 2) 39.4	(all berths) 33.1
Officers	Italian	Dining Staff	International
Total Cabins	1,050
Size Range (sq ft/m)	159-611/14.7-56.7
Outside Cabins	652	Inside Cabins	398
Single Cabins	0	Supplement	25-100%
Balcony Cabins	446	Wheelchair Cabins	19
Cabin Current	110/220 AC
Refrigerator	Yes
Cabin TV	Yes	VCR	Suites only
Dining Rooms	2 main/3 others
Sittings	2 (main dining rooms)

RATINGS	SCORE
Ship: Condition/Cleanliness	NYR
Ship: Space/Flow/Comfort	NYR
Ship: Decor/Furnishings	NYR
Ship: Fitness Facilities	NYR
Cabins: Comfort/Facilities	NYR
Cabins: Software	NYR
Food: Dining Room/Cuisine	NYR
Food: Buffets/Informal Dining	NYR
Food: Quality of Ingredients	NYR
Service: Dining Room	NYR
Service: Bars	NYR
Service: Cabins	NYR
Cruise: Entertainment	NYR
Cruise: Activities Program	NYR
Cruise: Hospitality Standard	NYR
OVERALL RATING	

+ Wide teakwood outdoor wrap-around promenade deck. Great amount of glass area on the upper decks provides plenty of light. Wide range of public rooms. Huge forward-view observation lounge. Tasteful decor throughout. There are two four-deck-high atrium lobbies, one with panoramic glass-walled elevators. The main public rooms are located underneath three decks of accommodations. There's plenty of space, and passenger flow is good. Health spa complex surrounds a swimming pool suspended between two decks (there are two other pools). Conference center for up to 300. Excellent collection of artwork. Cabins are well designed and extremely functional; many outside cabins have private balconies (more than any other Princess ship to date), and all are quite well soundproofed.

— There are too many inside cabins. As on any large ship expect lines for embarkation, disembarkation, buffets, shore tenders and shore excursions.

Dining There are two main dining rooms; each has its own galley, and each is split into multi-tier sections. Indoor-outdoor food court-style dining includes a Patisserie, Wine/Caviar bar, and Pizzeria.

Other Comments This ship is presently the largest in the cruise industry, until September 1996, when Carnival's 100,000-grt vessel debuts.

ms Sun Viking ★★★+

OPERATES

SOUTHEAST ASIA, CHINA
AND JAPAN CRUISES

Cruise Line		Royal Caribbean Cruises
Former Names		-
Gross Tonnage		18,556
Builder		Wartsila (Finland)
Original Cost		$17.5 million
Christened By		Mrs Sigurd Skaugen
Entered Service		Dec 9, 1972
Interior Design		Njal Eide
Country of Registry		Norway (LIZA3)
Tel No 131-2151	Fax No	131-2151
Length (ft/m)		563.2/171.69
Beam (ft/m) 78.8/24.03	Draft (ft/m)	20.6/6.30
Propulsion		diesel (13,400kW)
Propellers		2 (CP)
Decks 8	Crew	341
Pass. Capacity (basis 2) 714		(all berths) 818
Pass. Space Ratio (basis 2) 25.9		(all berths) 22.6
Officers		Norwegian
Dining Staff		International
Total Cabins		357
Size Range (sq ft/m)		120-237/11.0-22.0
Outside Cabins 240	Inside Cabins	117
Single Cabins 0	Supplement	50-100%
Balcony Cabins 0	Wheelchair Cabins	0
Cabin Current		110 AC
Refrigerator		Owner's suite only
Cabin TV No	VCR	No
Dining Rooms 1	Sittings	2

Elevators			4
Casino	Yes	Slot Machines	Yes
Swimming Pools (outside) 1		(inside)	0
Whirlpools	0	Gymnasium	Yes
Sauna/Steam Room Yes/No		Massage	Yes
Self-Service Launderette			No
Movie Theater/Seats No		Library	Yes
Children's Facilities			No
Watersports Facilities			None
Classification Society		Det Norske Veritas	

RATINGS	SCORE
Ship: Condition/Cleanliness	7.4
Ship: Space/Flow/Comfort	6.3
Ship: Decor/Furnishings	6.9
Ship: Fitness Facilities	5.6
Cabins: Comfort/Facilities	5.8
Cabins: Software	7.7
Food: Dining Room/Cuisine	6.8
Food: Buffets/Informal Dining	6.6
Food: Quality of Ingredients	7.1
Service: Dining Room	6.7
Service: Bars	6.5
Service: Cabins	6.1
Cruise: Entertainment	7.2
Cruise: Activities Program	6.7
Cruise: Hospitality Standard	7.4
OVERALL RATING	100.8

+ Well-proportioned ship with contemporary styling. Cantilevered Viking Crown lounge set atop funnel housing provides an impressive view. Smallest and most intimate ship in the Royal Caribbean Cruises fleet, a real gem. Good open deck and sunning space, with wrap-around outdoor polished wood deck. Public rooms decorated in modern Scandinavian style and colors, and named after musicals. Charming, friendly ambiance throughout.

— High-density ship means public rooms are always busy. Long wait for elevator, buffet line, disembarkation. Small and moderately comfortable cabins have little closet, drawer and storage space.

Dining Pleasant, attractive dining room with large picture windows has tables for four, six or eight (no tables for two). Consistently good food and service, although there's little flexibility. Poor breads, rolls and fruit selection. Good wine list but limited vintages.

Other Comments This company wants its passengers out and about the public rooms, not in their small cabins, and caters to passengers wanting a more intimate cruise, with all the Royal Caribbean Cruises trimmings at a fair price.

ms SuperStar Gemini ★★★★

OPERATES

2 AND 5-DAY SOUTH-EAST ASIA CRUISES (YEAR-ROUND)

Cruise Line	Star Cruise
Former Names	Crown Jewel
Gross Tonnage	19,046
Builder	Union Navale de Levante (Spain)
Original Cost	$100 million
Christened By	Isabel Cebrian de Viguerra
Entered Service	Aug 10, 1992/1995
Interior Design	Yran & Storbraaten
Country of Registry	Panama (3EW9)
Tel No 133-6652 Fax No 133-6653	
Length (ft/m)	537.4/163.81
Beam (ft/m) 73.8/22.50 Draft (ft/m) 17.7/5.40	
Propulsion	diesel (13,200kW)
Propellers	2 (CP)
Decks 7 Crew	330
Pass. Capacity (basis 2) 820 (all berths) 900	
Pass. Space Ratio (basis 2) 23.2 (all berths) 21.1	
Officers Scandinavian Dining Staff International	
Total Cabins	410
Size Range (sq ft/m)	140-350/13.0-32.5
Outside Cabins 285 Inside Cabins 125	
Single Cabins 0 Supplement 50-100%	
Balcony Cabins 10 Wheelchair Cabins 4	
Cabin Current	110/220 AC
Refrigerator	Category 1 only
Cabin TV Yes VCR	No
Dining Rooms	1
Sittings	2 (open seating breakfast/lunch)

Elevators			4
Casino	Yes	Slot Machines	Yes
Swimming Pools (outside) 1		(inside)	0
Whirlpools	3	Gymnasium	Yes
Sauna/Steam Room Yes/No		Massage	Yes
Self-Service Launderette			No
Movie Theater/Seats No		Library	No
Children's Facilities			No
Watersports Facilities			None
Classification Society		Det Norske Veritas	

RATINGS	SCORE
Ship: Condition/Cleanliness	8.0
Ship: Space/Flow/Comfort	7.8
Ship: Decor/Furnishings	8.1
Ship: Fitness Facilities	8.0
Cabins: Comfort/Facilities	7.7
Cabins: Software	7.9
Food: Dining Room/Cuisine	7.5
Food: Buffets/Informal Dining	6.8
Food: Quality of Ingredients	6.5
Service: Dining Room	7.6
Service: Bars	7.5
Service: Cabins	7.0
Cruise: Entertainment	7.8
Cruise: Activities Program	4.8
Cruise: Hospitality Standard	7.2
OVERALL RATING	110.2

+ Traditional layout with reasonable horizontal passenger flow features picture windows in almost all public rooms, providing a connection with sea and light. Good open deck and sunning space. Attractive decor, with upbeat color combinations. Nicely furnished cabins all feature large picture windows. Although not large, they are very comfortable, with wood-trimmed accents and colorful soft furnishings. Bathrooms are pleasing, and feature a large toiletries cabinet, but they have a small shower area.

— Fit and finish was poor when built. The artwork is not aesthetically pleasing. Poor cabin soundproofing.

Dining Attractive but cramped dining room has charming ambiance, but there are no tables for two. Cuisine is international with an Oriental touch. Food rarely arrives hot.

Other Comments Handsome mid-sized cruise ship with smart exterior styling is the largest ever built in Spain. Features a five-deck-high glass-walled atrium. This ship is a welcome addition and refreshing change for the Asian market. It is a sound product, and, with more tweaking and fine-tuning in the hotel service areas, will prove an admirable success story for Star Cruise.

ts Symphony ★★★

OPERATES

6 TO 11-DAY EUROPE CRUISES

Cruise Line	StarLauro Cruises		
Former Names	EnricoCosta/Enrico "C"/Provence		
Gross Tonnage	16,495		
Builder	Swan, Hunter (UK)		
Original Cost	n/a		
Christened By	n/a		
Entered Service	Mar 30, 1951/1995		
Interior Design	Architects Falletti/De Jorio		
Country of Registry	Italy (ICEI)		
Tel No 115-0561	Fax No 115-0561		
Length (ft/m)	579.0/176.49		
Beam (ft/m) 73.1/22.31	Draft (ft/m) 24.6/7.52		
Propulsion	diesel (11,768kW)		
Propellers	2 (FP)		
Decks 7	Crew 330		
Pass. Capacity (basis 2) 664	(all berths) 845		
Pass. Space Ratio (basis 2) 24.8	(all berths) 19.5		
Officers	Italian		
Dining Staff	Italian/International		
Total Cabins	332		
Size Range (sq ft/m)	86-216/8.0-20.1		
Outside Cabins 159	Inside Cabins 173		
Single Cabins 0	Supplement 50%		
Balcony Cabins 0	Wheelchair Cabins 0		
Cabin Current 220 DC	Refrigerator No		
Cabin TV No	VCR No		
Dining Rooms 1	Sittings 2		
Elevators	2		

Casino	No	Slot Machines	No
Swimming Pools (outside)	3	(inside)	0
Whirlpools	0	Gymnasium	No
Sauna/Steam Room	No/No	Massage	No
Self-Service Launderette			Yes
Movie Theater/Seats			Yes/85
Library			No
Children's Facilities			Yes
Watersports Facilities			None
Classification Society			RINA

RATINGS	SCORE
Ship: Condition/Cleanliness	6.4
Ship: Space/Flow/Comfort	6.1
Ship: Decor/Furnishings	7.2
Ship: Fitness Facilities	4.6
Cabins: Comfort/Facilities	6.4
Cabins: Software	6.8
Food: Dining Room/Cuisine	6.7
Food: Buffets/Informal Dining	6.3
Food: Quality of Ingredients	6.7
Service: Dining Room	7.1
Service: Bars	7.2
Service: Cabins	7.4
Cruise: Entertainment	6.4
Cruise: Activities Program	6.3
Cruise: Hospitality Standard	7.2
OVERALL RATING	98.8

+ This solidly built vessel recently received an extensive refurbishment. Has a deep draft, and so is reasonably stable at sea. Good open deck promenade areas. The newer facilities are fine, while others have been much upgraded. The public rooms feature "Belle Epoque" decor and are very smart, but crowded when full. Cabins are compact but comfortable, with tasteful pastel decor and soft furnishings to match.

— Has steep gangway. Does not have stabilizers. Ceilings are very plain and uninteresting. The entertainment is loud and of very poor quality. There are too many loud, unnecessary and repetitious announcements.

Dining The dining room is comfortable, though rather noisy. Good bubbly Italian service and food, with excellent pasta, but other dishes lack quality.

Other Comments Traditional ocean liner styling, reconstructed from her former life as a cargo-passenger liner. Has a large, single yellow funnel. Some 75 cabins are still without private facilities. Beautiful wood paneling and brass trim throughout the ship adds warmth and old-world elegance lacking in many new ships. This ship, which was acquired in 1995 by StarLauro Cruises, caters primarily to budget-minded European passengers looking for a Mediterranean cruise without the trimmings, with mainly Italian passengers.

ms Taras Shevchenko ★★★

OPERATES

*VARIOUS BLACK SEA AND
MEDITERRANEAN CRUISES*

Cruise Line	Primexpress Cruise Lines
Former Names	-
Gross Tonnage	20,027
Builder	VEB Mathias Thesen (Germany)
Original Cost	n/a
Christened By	n/a
Entered Service	Apr 26, 1967/1994
Interior Design	Shipyard team
Country of Registry	Ukraine (UTVT)
Tel No 140-0266 Fax No	140-0266
Length (ft/m)	577.4/176.00
Beam (ft/m) 77.4/23.60 Draft (ft/m)	26.7/8.16
Propulsion	diesel (15,700kW)
Propellers	2 (CP)
Decks 8 Crew	370
Pass. Capacity (basis 2) 574 (all berths)	712
Pass. Space Ratio (basis 2) 34.8 (all berths)	28.1
Officers	Russian/Ukrainian
Dining Staff	East European
Total Cabins	287
Size Range (sq ft/m)	n/a
Outside Cabins 287 Inside Cabins	0
Single Cabins 0 Supplement	100%
Balcony Cabins 0 Wheelchair Cabins	0
Cabin Current 220 AC Refrigerator	No
Cabin TV No VCR	No
Dining Rooms 3 Sittings	1
Elevators	3

Casino	Yes	Slot Machines	Yes
Swimming Pools (outside) 2		(inside)	1
Whirlpools	1	Gymnasium	Yes
Sauna/Steam Room Yes/No		Massage	No
Self-Service Launderette			Yes
Movie Theater/Seats			Yes/130
Library			Yes
Children's Facilities			Yes
Watersports Facilities			None
Classification Society			RS

RATINGS	SCORE
Ship: Condition/Cleanliness	6.1
Ship: Space/Flow/Comfort	6.5
Ship: Decor/Furnishings	6.1
Ship: Fitness Facilities	5.2
Cabins: Comfort/Facilities	6.1
Cabins: Software	6.2
Food: Dining Room/Cuisine	6.1
Food: Buffets/Informal Dining	5.8
Food: Quality of Ingredients	6.1
Service: Dining Room	6.2
Service: Bars	6.7
Service: Cabins	6.7
Cruise: Entertainment	6.0
Cruise: Activities Program	5.4
Cruise: Hospitality Standard	6.2
OVERALL RATING	91.4

+ Solidly constructed vessel has nicely rounded lines and a classic profile, with an all-white, ice-hardened hull. Good open deck and sunning space. Has wrap-around outdoor promenade deck. Has pleasant, but very plain interior decor that could do with more tropical greenery to enhance it. Recent substantial refurbishment has upgraded the vessel considerably and added more color. Spacious music salon. Has all-outside cabins that are very comfortable, each with private facilities. 10 suites are very spacious, and tastefully appointed.

— Has very plain ceilings throughout, as well as spartan decor that is quite dated. Has a narrow, steep gangway in most ports. No cushioned pads on deck chairs.

Dining Single seating dining room is functional, nothing more, and needs upgrading. The food is adequate, but there's little menu choice. Service is attentively provided by attractive Ukrainian waitresses. Poor selection of bread rolls, cheeses and fruits.

Other Comments While this ship is not yet up to western standards, it was renovated in 1988 and will provide a reasonable cruise experience at a modest rate, for a mostly French and Italian clientele. Often operates under charter, but there's no finesse.

mv The Azur ★★★+

OPERATES

VARIOUS SOUTHERN EUROPE CRUISES

Cruise Line	Festival Cruises
Former Names	Eagle/Azur
Gross Tonnage	14,717
Builder	Dubigeon-Normandie (France)
Original Cost	n/a
Christened By	n/a
Entered Service	May 18, 1971/Apr 23, 1994
Interior Design	A&M Katzourakis
Country of Registry	Panama (3EPR5)
Tel No 133-2515 Fax No 133-2515	
Length (ft/m)	465.8/142.00
Beam (ft/m) 71.8/21.90 Draft (ft/m) 18.7/5.73	
Propulsion	diesel (16,300kW)
Propellers	2 (CP)
Decks 7 Crew 340	
Pass. Capacity (basis 2) 665 (all berths) 750	
Pass. Space Ratio (basis 2) 22.1 (all berths) 19.6	
Officers	Greek
Dining Staff	International
Total Cabins	335
Size Range (sq ft/m)	n/a
Outside Cabins 152 Inside Cabins 183	
Single Cabins 10 Supplement 50%	
Balcony Cabins 0 Wheelchair Cabins 2	
Cabin Current 220 AC Refrigerator No	
Cabin TV No VCR No	
Dining Rooms 1 Sittings 2	
Elevators	3

Casino	Yes	Slot Machines	Yes
Swimming Pools (outside) 2		(inside)	0
Whirlpools	0	Gymnasium	Yes
Sauna/Steam Room No/No		Massage	No
Self-Service Launderette			No
Movie Theater/Seats			Yes/175
Library			Yes
Children's Facilities			Yes
Watersports Facilities			none
Classification Society			Bureau Veritas

RATINGS	SCORE
Ship: Condition/Cleanliness	7.6
Ship: Space/Flow/Comfort	6.6
Ship: Decor/Furnishings	7.6
Ship: Fitness Facilities	7.7
Cabins: Comfort/Facilities	6.4
Cabins: Software	7.0
Food: Dining Room/Cuisine	7.1
Food: Buffets/Informal Dining	6.5
Food: Quality of Ingredients	6.4
Service: Dining Room	7.2
Service: Bars	7.0
Service: Cabins	7.3
Cruise: Entertainment	6.3
Cruise: Activities Program	6.2
Cruise: Hospitality Standard	6.9
OVERALL RATING	103.8

+ Generous open deck space for sunning, but crowded when full. Good selection of public rooms and numerous bars, with light, well-chosen contemporary decor and many mirrored surfaces. Two-level movie theater. Most cabins are plain, but nicely furnished, and decorated in earth tones. Has two outside cabins for the physically challenged. Lively action in the casino. Excellent sports facilities include an indoor squash and volleyball court.

— Small swimming pools. Showroom has poor sightlines and low ceiling (but is good for meetings). Has many inside cabins. Constant announcements in several languages are irritating, but typical of European operations that try to cater for everyone.

Dining Charming low-ceilinged dining room has ocean-view windows on three sides, but uncomfortable chairs. Typically decent food, but presentation lacks flair. Limited selection of breads, fruits and cheeses. Courteous staff and service.

Other Comments Smart, though stubby-looking ship has a short bow, and twin tall funnels set well aft. This ship will appeal to the young, active set looking for a good first cruise experience to a host of destinations, at a very reasonable price, as well as to those seeking a venue for meetings and incentive cruises. The ship operates successfully in several languages for its multi-national European-based passenger mix. Currency aboard: Lire.

ms Triton ★★★+

OPERATES

3, 4 AND 7-DAY AEGEAN AND MEDITERRANEAN CRUISES

Cruise Line	Epirotiki Cruise Line	Casino	Yes	Slot Machines	Yes
Former Names	Cunard Adventurer/Sunward II	Swimming Pools (outside) 1	(inside)	0
Gross Tonnage	14,155	Whirlpools	0	Gymnasium	Yes
Builder	Rotterdamsche Dry Dock (Holland)	Sauna/Steam Room Yes/No	Massage	Yes
Original Cost	n/a	Self-Service Launderette	No
Christened By	n/a	Movie Theater/Seats	Yes/96
Entered Service	Oct 9, 1971/May 10, 1992	Library	Yes
Interior Design	Arminio Lozzi	Children's Facilities	Yes
Country of Registry	Greece (SVKR)	Watersports Facilities	None
Tel No 113-1266 Fax No 113-1266		Classification Society	Lloyd's Register
Length (ft/m)	491.1/149.70		
Beam (ft/m) 70.5/21.50 Draft (ft/m) 19.22/5.86		**RATINGS**	**SCORE**
Propulsion	diesel (19,860kW)	Ship: Condition/Cleanliness	7.5
Propellers	2 (CP)	Ship: Space/Flow/Comfort	6.5
Decks 7 Crew 265		Ship: Decor/Furnishings	7.4
Pass. Capacity (basis 2) 756 (all berths) 945		Ship: Fitness Facilities	5.2
Pass. Space Ratio (basis 2) 18.7 (all berths) 14.9		Cabins: Comfort/Facilities	6.6
Officers Greek Dining Staff Greek		Cabins: Software	7.9
Total Cabins	378	Food: Dining Room/Cuisine	7.1
Size Range (sq ft/m)	118-132/11.0-12.2	Food: Buffets/Informal Dining	6.1
Outside Cabins 236 Inside Cabins 142		Food: Quality of Ingredients	6.2
Single Cabins 0 Supplement 50%		Service: Dining Room	7.2
Balcony Cabins 0 Wheelchair Cabins 0		Service: Bars	6.8
Cabin Current	110/220 AC	Service: Cabins	7.1
Refrigerator	No	Cruise: Entertainment	6.2
Cabin TV No VCR No		Cruise: Activities Program	6.1
Dining Rooms 1 Sittings 2		Cruise: Hospitality Standard	7.7
Elevators	2	OVERALL RATING	101.6

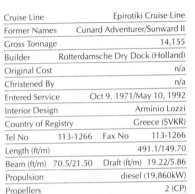

+ Has a handsome, sleek profile, deep clipper bow and is the most contemporary ship in the Epirotiki fleet. Inside, there is good layout and passenger flow, with ample public rooms and delightful, contemporary interior decor, with some interesting regional artwork. Excellent destination-intensive itineraries are good for those who want to see more places in a short time. Has wrap-around outdoor promenade deck. Fine nightclub with forward observation views. Good open deck space for sunning. Well-appointed cabins for ship size, even though they are rather small. Friendly staff and ambiance.

— High-density ship means crowded public areas. Small cabins and bathrooms. Long lines for buffets. Too many announcements for tours, when in ports of call. Cabin bathrooms have very small shower units.

Dining While the dining room is quite attractive and has contemporary colors and ambiance, it is also very noisy. The cuisine is Continental, which means much use of oils. Choice is adequate, but presentation is inconsistent. Poor bread rolls and fruits. Service is attentive but hurried.

Other Comments Well maintained, although now showing its age. Excellent ship for short cruises. This ship provides excellent value for money, and features a well delivered product.

ms Tropicale ★★★+

OPERATES

7-DAY ALASKA AND CARIBBEAN CRUISES

Cruise Line	Carnival Cruise Lines
Former Names	-
Gross Tonnage	36,674
Builder	Aalborg Vaerft (Denmark)
Original Cost	$100 million
Christened By	Mrs Madeleine Arison
Entered Service	Jan 16, 1982
Interior Design	Joe Farcus
Country of Registry	Liberia (ELBM9)
Tel No 124-0561	Fax No 124-0561
Length (ft/m)	671.7/204.76
Beam (ft/m) 86.7/26.45	Draft (ft/m) 23.3/7.11
Propulsion	diesel (19,566kW)
Propellers	2 (CP)
Decks 10	Crew 550
Pass. Capacity (basis 2) 1,022	(all berths) 1,400
Pass. Space Ratio (basis 2) 35.8	(all berths) 26.1
Officers Italian	Dining Staff International
Total Cabins	511
Size Range (sq ft/m)	180/9.2
Outside Cabins 324	Inside Cabins 187
Single Cabins	0
Supplement	50% (cat.1-3)/100% (cat. 4-12)
Balcony Cabins 12	Wheelchair Cabins 11
Cabin Current	110 AC
Refrigerator	(Suites only)
Cabin TV Yes	VCR No
Dining Rooms 1	Sittings 2

Elevators			8
Casino	Yes	Slot Machines	Yes
Swimming Pools (outside) 3		(inside)	0
Whirlpools	0	Gymnasium	Yes
Sauna/Steam Room Yes/No		Massage	Yes
Self-Service Launderette			Yes
Movie Theater/Seats	No	Library	Yes
Children's Facilities			Yes
Watersports Facilities			None
Classification Society			Lloyd's Register

RATINGS	SCORE
Ship: Condition/Cleanliness	7.7
Ship: Space/Flow/Comfort	7.0
Ship: Decor/Furnishings	6.8
Ship: Fitness Facilities	7.8
Cabins: Comfort/Facilities	7.5
Cabins: Software	7.4
Food: Dining Room/Cuisine	6.7
Food: Buffets/Informal Dining	6.1
Food: Quality of Ingredients	5.3
Service: Dining Room	6.9
Service: Bars	7.0
Service: Cabins	6.4
Cruise: Entertainment	7.5
Cruise: Activities Program	7.6
Cruise: Hospitality Standard	6.6
OVERALL RATING	104.3

+ Distinctive contemporary look, with large, wing-tipped funnel. Well-laid-out interior design, with good passenger flow. Well maintained. Public rooms are decorated in stimulating colors. Always lively casino action. Most cabins are of the standard cookie-cutter variety, with little imaginative decor, and just enough closet and drawer space to manage for a week. Good ship for families with children, as Carnival goes out of its way to entertain young cruisers as well as their parents.

— Noisy, cramped dining room. Long lines for embarkation, disembarkation, shore tenders and buffets. Too many repetitive announcements. Aggressive hustling for drinks.

Dining The dining room is located on a lower deck. It is colorful, cheerful, brightly lit, but noisy, and there are no tables for two. Typical Americana, with quantity, not quality (consistently uninspiring). Poor selection of bread rolls, fresh fruits, cheeses and pastry items. Service is hurried and inflexible, but cheerful. Lunch buffets are poor.

Other Comments This ship will provide novice cruisers with a well-proven product that is attractively packaged, at a reasonable price, but it is not a luxury cruise by any means, nor does it pretend to be. But you'll have fun and lots of hoop-la. This ship will be Carnival's first in the 1996 Alaska summer cruise season.

ss Universe ★★★

OPERATES

14-DAY ALASKA CRUISES

Cruise Line	World Explorer Cruises		
Former Names	Atlantic Universe Campus/		
	Badger Mariner		
Gross Tonnage	18,100		
Builder	Sun Shipbuilding (USA)		
Original Cost	n/a	Christened By	n/a
Entered Service	Nov 1953/1976		
Interior Design	Ocean Craft Interiors		
Country of Registry	Liberia (5LGK)		
Tel No	124-0713	Fax No	124-0713
Length (ft/m)	563.6/171.81		
Beam (ft/m) 76.3/23.27	Draft (ft/m)	28.6/8.72	
Propulsion	steam turbine (14,160kW)		
Propellers	1 (FP)		
Decks	7	Crew	200
Pass. Capacity (basis 2) 542	(all berths) 833		
Pass. Space Ratio (basis 2) 33.5	(all berths) 21.7		
Officers	Chinese		
Dining Staff	Chinese/Filipino		
Total Cabins	314		
Size Range (sq ft/m)	63-180/5.8-16.7		
Outside Cabins	138	Inside Cabins	176
Single Cabins	25	Supplement	None
Balcony Cabins	0	Wheelchair Cabins	0
Cabin Current	110 AC	Refrigerator	No
Cabin TV	No	VCR	No
Dining Rooms	1	Sittings	2
Elevators	1		

Casino	No	Slot Machines	No
Swimming Pools (outside) 1	(inside)		0
Whirlpools	0	Gymnasium	Yes
Sauna/Steam Room	No/No	Massage	Yes
Self-Service Launderette			Yes
Movie Theater/Seats			Yes/200
Library	Yes	Children's Facilities	No
Watersports Facilities			None
Classification Society		American Bureau	
		of Shipping	

RATINGS	SCORE
Ship: Condition/Cleanliness	5.9
Ship: Space/Flow/Comfort	5.7
Ship: Decor/Furnishings	6.8
Ship: Fitness Facilities	4.6
Cabins: Comfort/Facilities	5.9
Cabins: Software	6.4
Food: Dining Room/Cuisine	6.3
Food: Buffets/Informal Dining	5.6
Food: Quality of Ingredients	5.8
Service: Dining Room	6.5
Service: Bars	6.2
Service: Cabins	6.8
Cruise: Entertainment	5.2
Cruise: Activities Program	6.1
Cruise: Hospitality Standard	6.5
OVERALL RATING	90.3

+ Solidly constructed ship with cargo-liner profile. Part floating campus (fall/winter) and part cruise ship (spends summers in Alaska). Onboard life and ambiance is very casual and unpretentious. Good lecture and life-enrichment programs. Has spacious public rooms that feature conservative (no frills) decor. Excellent library and reference center contains over 13,000 books. Cultured, tasteful entertainment consists of lecturers and semi-classical music. Goes to more ports of call than any other cruise line going to Alaska. Culture without any hint of glitz. Best cabins are on Boat Deck. Also has gentleman "hosts" on selected sailings.

— Most cabins have three or four berths, but decor is spartan, and bathrooms are utilitarian. Has limited number of public rooms and open deck space. Lifeboats/tenders are old and well worn. Has a narrow, steep gangway in most ports.

Dining Informal dining room is cozy and quite comfortable. Cuisine is Asian-American, but there's little choice of breads, cheeses and fruits. Staff provide attentive service with a smile.

Other Comments Originally built for U.S. Maritime Commission. Presently owned by Orient Overseas Line and operated by World Explorer Cruises. Caters particularly well to passengers of wisdom years who are seeking a leisurely two-week destination-intensive Alaska cruise in comfortable, unpretentious and non-glamorous surroundings, at an attractive price.

ms Veendam

OPERATES

*7-DAY CARIBBEAN AND
EUROPE CRUISES*

Cruise Line	Holland America Line	Casino Yes	Slot Machines Yes
Former Names	-	Swimming Pools (outside)	1
Gross Tonnage	55,451	Swimming Pools (inside)	1 (magrodome)
Builder	Fincantieri (Italy)	Whirlpools 2	Gymnasium Yes
Original Cost	$215 million	Sauna/Steam Room Yes/No	Massage Yes
Christened By	n/a	Self-Service Launderette	Yes
Entered Service	May 21, 1996	Movie Theater/Seats	Yes/249
Interior Design	VFD Interiors/Joe Farcus	Library Yes	Children's Facilities No
Country of Registry	Bahamas	Watersports Facilities	none
Tel No n/a Fax No	n/a	Classification Society	Lloyd's Register
Length (ft/m)	719.3/219.30		

Beam (ft/m) 101.0/30.80 Draft (ft/m) 24.6/7.50	**RATINGS**	**SCORE**
Propulsion diesel-electric (34,560kW)	Ship: Condition/Cleanliness	NYR
Propellers 2 (CP)	Ship: Space/Flow/Comfort	NYR
Decks 10 Crew 588	Ship: Decor/Furnishings	NYR
Pass. Capacity (basis 2) 1,264 (all berths) 1,627	Ship: Fitness Facilities	NYR
Pass. Space Ratio (basis 2) 43.8 (all berths) 34.0	Cabins: Comfort/Facilities	NYR
Officers Dutch Dining Staff Filipino/Indonesian	Cabins: Software	NYR
Total Cabins 632	Food: Dining Room/Cuisine	NYR
Size Range (sq ft/m) 187-1,126/17.3-104.5	Food: Buffets/Informal Dining	NYR
Outside Cabins 501 Inside Cabins 131	Food: Quality of Ingredients	NYR
Single Cabins 0 Supplement 50-100%	Service: Dining Room	NYR
Balcony Cabins 150 Wheelchair Cabins 6	Service: Bars	NYR
Cabin Current 110/220 AC	Service: Cabins	NYR
Refrigerator Category PS/S/A/B only	Cruise: Entertainment	NYR
Cabin TV Yes VCR No	Cruise: Activities Program	NYR
Dining Rooms 1 Sittings 2	Cruise: Hospitality Standard	NYR
Elevators 12	OVERALL RATING	

+ Has lots of teakwood decking and no sign of astroturf anywhere. Three-deck-high atrium foyer has a sculpture in its center that dominates it. Magrodome roof covers the always popular indoor-outdoor pool and central lido area. There is good passenger flow throughout the main entertainment deck, and lots of nooks and crannies. The library is lovely. There is a wide range of cabins and suites to choose from, many with private balconies. Most cabins use their space well, are tastefully decorated and well laid out, but, although drawer space is good, closet space is very tight, particularly for long cruises.

— Two-deck-high showroom is good, but the ceiling is low and sightlines are not good from the upper level. Expect lines for embarkation, disembarkation, buffet, and shore tenders.

Dining Two-deck-high dining room (located at the stern) has dramatic grand staircase, is quite elegant (lower level has windows on three sides). 28 suites feature an in-suite dining alternative. Food and service expected to be typical of HAL standards of late, and completely non-memorable.

Other Comments This well-built ship will carry HAL passengers in fine comfort and style. Expect the rating to be similar to that of her sister ships *Maasdam*, *Ryndam* and *Statendam*.

mv Victoria ★★★★

OPERATES

*14-DAY CARIBBEAN AND
EUROPE CRUISES*

Cruise Line			P&O Cruises
Former Names		Sea Princess/Kungsholm	
Gross Tonnage			28,891
Builder		John Brown & Co. (UK)	
Original Cost			$22 million
Christened By		Mrs Dan Axel-Brostron	
Entered Service		Apr 22, 1966/Feb 16, 1979	
Interior Design			Robert Tillberg
Country of Registry		Great Britain (GBBA)	
Tel No	144-0320	Fax No	144-0320
Length (ft/m)			660.2/201.23
Beam (ft/m) 87.1/26.57		Draft (ft/m)	28.0/8.56
Propulsion		diesel (18,800kW)	
Propellers			2 (CP)
Decks	8	Crew	380
Pass. Capacity (basis 2) 714		(all berths) 743	
Pass. Space Ratio (basis 2) 40.4		(all berths) 38.8	
Officers	British	Dining Staff	British/Goan
Total Cabins			365
Size Range (sq ft/m)			138-467/12.8-43.3
Outside Cabins	295	Inside Cabins	70
Single Cabins	22	Supplement	Set rates
Balcony Cabins	0	Wheelchair Cabins	10
Cabin Current			220 AC
Refrigerator		Category AA/BA/BD only	
Cabin TV		Yes (higher grade cabins only)	
VCR			No
Dining Rooms	1	Sittings	2

Elevators			4
Casino	Yes	Slot Machines	Yes
Swimming Pools (outside) 2		(inside)	1
Whirlpools	1	Gymnasium	Yes
Sauna/Steam Room Yes/No		Massage	Yes
Self-Service Launderette			Yes
Movie Theater/Seats			Yes/289
Library	Yes	Children's Facilities	Yes
Watersports Facilities			None
Classification Society		Lloyd's Register	

RATINGS	SCORE
Ship: Condition/Cleanliness	7.4
Ship: Space/Flow/Comfort	7.6
Ship: Decor/Furnishings	7.5
Ship: Fitness Facilities	6.8
Cabins: Comfort/Facilities	7.4
Cabins: Software	7.6
Food: Dining Room/Cuisine	7.4
Food: Buffets/Informal Dining	6.2
Food: Quality of Ingredients	6.5
Service: Dining Room	7.4
Service: Bars	7.6
Service: Cabins	7.6
Cruise: Entertainment	7.4
Cruise: Activities Program	6.3
Cruise: Hospitality Standard	7.6
OVERALL RATING	107.4

+ Solidly built ex-ocean liner has flowing, rounded lines and well-balanced profile. Nicely refurbished and well maintained. Open deck and sunning space is good. There are numerous spacious public rooms with fine quality furnishings and fabrics, and trimmed with fine woods. Generally good British entertainment. Wide range of cabins to choose from. Most are quite roomy, nicely refurbished, and have excellent closet and drawer space, with fine wood-paneled walls. Generous-sized bathrooms have solid fixtures and storage space for toiletries.

— Some cabins have upper and lower berths. The wine list is quite limited. Plastic chairs at the lido buffet should have cushions. Bathroom towels are small.

Dining Tiered European-style dining room is elegant, with old-world traditions and charm, and display of 18th-century Chinese porcelain. Good general food and selection tailored for British tastes, and excellent service from the Goanese staff. The buffets are very basic, and disappointing in both display and food quality, as is the selection of breads and fruits.

Other Comments You should have an enjoyable cruise experience on this ship, which provides some attention to detail, and European finesse, at an appropriate price. Has mainly British passengers. While an excellent ship for long voyages, at 30 years old, she is now looking a little tired. Port taxes and insurance are included for British passengers.

ms Viking Serenade ★★★★

OPERATES

*3- AND 4-DAY BAJA MEXICO CRUISES
(YEAR-ROUND)*

Cruise Line	Royal Caribbean Cruises
Former Names	Stardancer/Scandinavia
Gross Tonnage	40,132
Builder	Dubigeon-Normandie (France)
Original Cost	$100 million
Christened By	Ms Liv Ullmann/
	Ms Whoopi Goldberg
Entered Service	Oct 2, 1982/Jan 27, 1990
Interior Design	Njal Eide/Petter Yran
Country of Registry	Bahamas (C6CP)
Tel No 110-3132 Fax No	110-3132
Length (ft/m)	623.0/189.89
Beam (ft/m) 88.6/27.01 Draft (ft/m)	22.6/6.90
Propulsion	diesel (19,800kW)
Propellers	2 (CP)
Decks 7 Crew	612
Pass. Capacity (basis 2) 1,512 (all berths)	1,863
Pass. Space Ratio (basis 2) 26.5 (all berths)	21.5
Officers International Dining Staff	International
Total Cabins	756
Size Range (sq ft/m)	144-400/13.3-37.0
Outside Cabins 478 Inside Cabins	278
Single Cabins 0 Supplement	50-100%
Balcony Cabins 5 Wheelchair Cabins	4
Cabin Current	110 AC
Refrigerator	Category R/A only
Cabin TV Yes VCR	No
Dining Rooms 2 Sittings	2

Elevators			5
Casino Yes	Slot Machines		Yes
Swimming Pools (outside)		1 (magrodome)
(inside)			0
Whirlpools 0	Gymnasium		Yes
Sauna/Steam Room Yes/No	Massage		Yes
Self-Service Launderette			No
Movie Theater/Seats No	Library		Yes
Children's Facilities			Yes
Classification Society		Det Norske Veritas

RATINGS	SCORE
Ship: Condition/Cleanliness	7.9
Ship: Space/Flow/Comfort	6.4
Ship: Decor/Furnishings	7.2
Ship: Fitness Facilities	7.5
Cabins: Comfort/Facilities	6.3
Cabins: Software	7.7
Food: Dining Room/Cuisine	6.8
Food: Buffets/Informal Dining	6.6
Food: Quality of Ingredients	7.1
Service: Dining Room	6.7
Service: Bars	6.5
Service: Cabins	6.1
Cruise: Entertainment	7.8
Cruise: Activities Program	7.6
Cruise: Hospitality Standard	7.4
OVERALL RATING	105.6

+ Has good open deck and sunning space, and a magrodome-covered pool for inclement weather. Wide array of public rooms and facilities, including a conference center and Viking Crown lounge cantilevered around the funnel. Public rooms have contemporary decor, tasteful colors and good quality furnishings. Compact cabins are well appointed, and have reasonable closet space for short cruises. Fine health spa facilities. Attentive service from Caribbean staff. Good for families with children.

— So many inside cabins, and drawer space is poor. Tiny cabin bathrooms. Expect lines for embarkation, disembarkation, shore tenders and buffets. Too many announcements.

Dining Two large, attractive dining rooms are well laid out, but there are no tables for two. Typical standard hotel banquet food, perfectly portioned, with robotic presentation, and everything seems to taste the same. Poor bread rolls and fruits.

Other Comments This medium-density ship, which underwent a $75 million reconstruction in 1991, provides a well-programmed cruise experience in upbeat surroundings, at a decent cruise rate.

mts Vinland Star ★★

OPERATES

3- AND 4-DAY AEGEAN CRUISES

Cruise Line	Vinland Cruises	Casino	No	Slot Machines	No
Former Names	City of Mykonos/San Marco	Swimming Pools (outside) 1	(inside)	0
Gross Tonnage	4,755	Whirlpools	0	Gymnasium	No
Builder	Cantieri Riuniti dell' Adriatico (Italy)	Sauna/Steam Room No/No	Massage	No
Original Cost	n/a	Self-service Launderette		No
Christened By	n/a	Cinema/Theatre:		No
Entered Service	1956/1995	Cabin TV		No
Interior Design	-	Library		Yes
Country of Registry	Greece (SVYW)	Children's Facilities/Playroom:		No
Tel No - Fax No	-	Classification Society	American Bureau
Length (ft/m)	367.4/111.99		

Beam (ft/m) 51.0/15.55 Draft (ft/m) 17.5/5.34	
Propulsion	diesel (4,119kW)
Propellers	2 (FP)
Decks 4 Crew	90
Pass. Capacity (basis 2) 276 (all berths) 370	
Pass. Space Ratio (basis 2) 17.2 (all berths) 12.8	
Officers Greek Dining Staff Greek	
Total Cabins	138
Size (sq ft/m.):	107-398/10.0-37.0
Outside Cabins 117 Inside Cabins 21	
Single Cabins	0
Single Supplement	200%
Balcony Cabins 0 Wheelchair Cabins 0	
Cabin Current	220 AC
Refrigerator	No
Dining Rooms 1 Sittings	2
Elevators	0

RATINGS	SCORE
Ship: Condition/Cleanliness	5.7
Ship: Space/Flow/Comfort	5.5
Ship: Decor/Furnishings	6.1
Ship: Fitness Facilities	3.0
Cabins: Comfort/Facilities	5.7
Cabins: Software	6.0
Food: Dining Room/Cuisine	5.6
Food: Buffets/Informal Dining	5.1
Food: Quality of Ingredients	5.5
Service: Dining Room	6.2
Service: Bars	6.4
Service: Cabins	6.5
Cruise: Entertainment	4.2
Cruise: Activities Program	4.6
Cruise: Hospitality Standard	6.0
OVERALL RATING	82.1

+ Small, quite handsome and intimate ship, with pleasing shape and nice lines. She is the twin sister *Royal Star*, yet quite different in terms of operation and standards. Upgraded interior decor and colors are slightly better now, but materials used are of low quality. The cabins are mostly quite small, but adequate for short cruises, although there is little closet and drawer space.

— The ship is quite cramped when full. Very limited public room and open deck space. Cabin bathrooms are very small, and hard to maneuver in. Has a steep gangway in some ports of call.

Dining The dining room is intimate and almost charming, but it is extremely noisy, particularly adjacent to the waiter stations. The overcooked food is typically Mediterranean in style, choice is limited, and the quality could be improved, particularly the presentation. The staff are reasonably attentive, but not overly friendly.

Other Comments This ship offers Aegean cruising in adequate surroundings, operated by a company new to cruising, Vinland Cruises, and featuring Greek staff, food and service, but don't expect very much.

ms Vistafjord ★★★★★+

OPERATES

VARIOUS CRUISES WORLDWIDE

Cruise Line	Cunard	Elevators	6
Former Names	-	Casino Yes	Slot Machines Yes
Gross Tonnage	24,492	Swimming Pools (outside) 1	(inside) 1
Builder	Swan, Hunter (UK)	Whirlpools 2	Gymnasium Yes
Original Cost	$35 million	Sauna/Steam Room Yes/No	Massage Yes
Christened By	Mrs Agnes Cecille Henrikson	Self-Service Launderette	Yes
Entered Service	May 22, 1973/May 1984	Movie Theater/Seats	Yes/190
Interior Design	Platou Design	Library Yes	Children's Facilities No
Country of Registry	Bahamas (C6ZV)	Watersports Facilities	None
Tel No 110-4114	Fax No 130-5630	Classification Society	Lloyd's Register
Length (ft/m)	626.9/191.09		

Beam (ft/m) 82.1/25.05	Draft (ft/m) 27.0/8.23
Propulsion	diesel (17,900kW)
Propellers	2 (FP)
Decks 9	Crew 379
Pass. Capacity (basis 2) 677	(all berths) 732
Pass. Space Ratio (basis 2) 36.1	(all berths) 33.4
Officers Norwegian	Dining Staff European/Asean
Total Cabins	376
Size Range (sq ft/m)	67-325/6.2-30.0
Outside Cabins 324	Inside Cabins 52
Single Cabins	73
Supplement	75% (for double cabins)
Balcony Cabins 25	Wheelchair Cabins 4
Cabin Current	110/220 AC
Refrigerator	Category I/II
Cabin TV Yes	VCR No
Dining Rooms 1	Sittings 1

RATINGS	SCORE
Ship: Condition/Cleanliness	9.2
Ship: Space/Flow/Comfort	9.1
Ship: Decor/Furnishings	9.1
Ship: Fitness Facilities	8.8
Cabins: Comfort/Facilities	9.0
Cabins: Software	9.2
Food: Dining Room/Cuisine	9.3
Food: Buffets/Informal Dining	9.0
Food: Quality of Ingredients	9.2
Service: Dining Room	9.2
Service: Bars	8.8
Service: Cabins	8.8
Cruise: Entertainment	8.7
Cruise: Activities Program	8.6
Cruise: Hospitality Standard	9.1
OVERALL RATING	135.1

+ Very well maintained and extremely clean. At sea she is stable, smooth and quiet as a swan. Has expansive open decks and ample sunning space. Built with the finest quality materials throughout. Features a teakwood outdoor wrap-around promenade deck, and deck lounge chairs have cushioned pads. Spacious and elegant public rooms with high ceilings. Has tasteful decor throughout, and improved in the latest refit. Thick cotton bathrobes provided for all. Excellent Scandinavian stewardesses. Conservative, sophisticated, classically oriented entertainment. Wide interior stairwells. Suites with balconies are superbly equipped, but all cabins are extremely well appointed and tastefully redecorated, although smaller than on *Sagafjord* (all cabins benefitted from brand new bathrooms, installed in the 1994 refit). All have excellent closet and drawer space and lighted closets. Excellent range of cabins for single travelers.

Really outstanding are two new duplex suites; the lower level contains a bedroom and bathroom with Jacuzzi bathtub; the upper level has an expansive living room, with Bang & Olufsen sound system, treadmill, private bar, another bathroom (with Jacuzzi bathtub), and separate private sauna, while outdoors is a private balcony with whirlpool. Refreshingly few announcements and interruptions.

Few international ships can compete with *Vistafjord* for her relaxing ambiance and service from a well-organized and happy crew.

— Operates in two languages: English and German, which may be negative for some. Some Sun Deck and Promenade Deck suites have obstructed views. Tub chairs in North Cape Bar are uncomfortable.

Dining The dining room is a grand, elegant room, recently expanded, for single-sitting dining. There are tables for two, four, six or eight (there are more tables for two aboard both *Sagafjord* and *Vistafjord* than any other ship afloat). Senior officers host tables for dinner each evening. Features single-waiter service in the best European tradition. The tables are a little closer together than on sister ship *Sagafjord*, making it somewhat difficult for waiters to serve in some areas.

Has international cuisine featuring the highest quality and variety of ingredients (outstanding variety of breads and cheeses at every meal, which are particularly appreciated by the ship's 40% German-speaking clientele). At all dining room meals, a cold table is set for such things as breads and cheeses at lunchtime, and passengers can either help themselves (German passengers in particular like to do this), or be served by a waiter. Salad items, salad dressings (10 varieties), juices (9 varieties), and cheeses (a fine selection of more than two dozen international cheeses) are always set on the cold table.

A mixture of silver-service (where entrees and vegetables are brought to the table on large silver platters and served individually), and plate-service (where vegetables and entrees are set artistically on the main course plate) is featured. Extra vegetables can be obtained at any time. Waiters are well trained through a sophisticated management structure on board.

Table-side flambeaus cannot be done at individual tables, but they are done in two or three central locations, and the waiters collect the finished product to take to their respective tables. Although the chef has his favorites, the menus are never repeated, even on the longest voyages. Also, one of the good points about this and other ships in her class (five-stars-plus) is that, while the menus are incredibly creative, you can order "off-menu" at any time, and create your own delightful cuisine. Little touches in presentation, such as paper doilies under teacups, soup bowls, and towel-wrapped water jugs, make a difference in product delivery. Apart from the regular menu (four appetizers, three soups, sorbet, five entrees, two salads, several desserts, and a superb selection of at least ten different international cheeses at every dinner meal), there is always a Golden Door Spa menu, a vegetarian menu, and diabetic dessert every day.

Different color tablecloths and napkins are featured daily for luncheon and dinner. There is an extensive wine list, with prices ranging from $13 to almost $400. Cappuccino and espresso coffees are available at any time in the dining room, without charge. There's an outstanding fruit selection.

Tivoli, a new, completely separate 40-seat Italian à la carte restaurant (an alternative dining spot added in the 1994 refit), is intimate and very elegant, and the food is outstanding, from a varied menu that features many special dishes daily.

The Lido Deck Café is an informal dining area that is extremely popular, but the traffic flow would be improved by a centrally located steam table.

Other Comments This ship has classic liner styling and profile. She is a finely proportioned ship with beautiful, rounded, flowing lines and classic, sleek profile from any angle. Grandly refurbished in late 1994, this ship caters especially well to discerning passengers in an elegant, refined, yet friendly style and supremely comfortable surroundings. Although not shiny and new, but well refurbished, the ship provides one of the world's most pleasant and civilized travel experiences. Gratuities are included.

ms Vistamar ★★★+

OPERATES

MEDITERRANEAN AND
SOUTH AMERICA CRUISES

Cruise Line	Mar Line	Casino	No	Slot Machines	Yes

Cruise Line	Mar Line
Former Names	-
Gross Tonnage	7,478
Builder	Union Navale de Levante (Spain)
Original Cost	$45 million
Christened By	n/a
Entered Service	Sep 1989
Interior Design	Oliver Design
Country of Registry	Liberia (3EKG7)
Tel No 133-2275	Fax No 133-2275
Length (ft/m)	385.1/117.40
Beam (ft/m) 55.1/16.82	Draft (ft/m) 14.9/4.55
Propulsion	diesel (3,900kW)
Propellers	2 (CP)
Decks 6	Crew 100
Pass. Capacity (basis 2) 295	(all berths) 340
Pass. Space Ratio (basis 2) 25.3	(all berths) 21.9
Officers Spanish	Dining Staff European
Total Cabins	150
Size Range (sq ft/m)	n/a
Outside Cabins 126	Inside Cabins 24
Single Cabins 5	Supplement Set rates
Balcony Cabins 0	Wheelchair Cabins 0
Cabin Current	220 AC
Refrigerator	No
Cabin TV Yes	VCR No
Dining Rooms 1	Sittings 1
Elevators	3

Casino	No	Slot Machines	Yes
Swimming Pools (outside)	1	(inside)	0
Whirlpools	0	Gymnasium	Yes
Sauna/Steam Room Yes/No		Massage	Yes
Self-Service Launderette			No
Movie Theater/Seats			No
Library			Yes
Children's Facilities			No
Watersports Facilities			None
Classification Society		Det Norske Veritas	

RATINGS	SCORE
Ship: Condition/Cleanliness	8.0
Ship: Space/Flow/Comfort	7.8
Ship: Decor/Furnishings	7.6
Ship: Fitness Facilities	5.7
Cabins: Comfort/Facilities	7.6
Cabins: Software	7.7
Food: Dining Room/Cuisine	6.3
Food: Buffets/Informal Dining	6.0
Food: Quality of Ingredients	6.0
Service: Dining Room	6.6
Service: Bars	6.7
Service: Cabins	7.0
Cruise: Entertainment	6.2
Cruise: Activities Program	6.4
Cruise: Hospitality Standard	7.1
OVERALL RATING	102.7

+ Small, rather smart but squat ship profile. Has a single, central staircase. All passenger accommodations are forward, public rooms aft, which means minimal noise in cabins. Wood-trimmed interior decor is attractive and warm, but mirrored ceilings are irritating. Outdoor pool has splash surround and neat water fountain. A very jazzy nightclub/disco, with acres of glass, is set around funnel base. Contemporary four-deck-high atrium with "skydome" has a glass-walled elevator and wrap-around staircase. Cabins are extremely comfortable and come well equipped, although the bathrooms are small.

— Has a narrow, steep gangway in some ports of call. The cabin closet and drawer space is limited.

Dining The single sitting dining is attractive, with warm, contemporary colors and decor. The food is moderate, but the selection of breads, cheeses and fruits is limited.

Other Comments Spanish-speaking passengers should enjoy this intimate ship, which features very attractively priced cruises that have comfort, style and flair. Sailings have, however, been somewhat sporadic recently.

ms Westerdam ★★★★

OPERATES

7-DAY CARIBBEAN CRUISES

Cruise Line	Holland America Line
Former Names	Homeric
Gross Tonnage	53,872
Builder	Meyer Werft (Germany)
Original Cost	$150 million
Christened By	n/a
Entered Service	May 31, 1986/Nov 12, 1988
Interior Design	Robert Tillberg/VFD Interiors
Country of Registry	Bahamas (C6HE2)
Tel No 110-4521 Fax No	110-4520
Length (ft/m)	797.9/243.23
Beam (ft/m) 95.1/29.00 Draft (ft/m)	23.6/7.20
Propulsion	diesel (23,830kW)
Propellers	2 (CP)
Decks 9 Crew	642
Pass. Capacity (basis 2) 1,494	(all berths) 1,773
Pass. Space Ratio (basis 2) 36.0	(all berths) 30.3
Officers Dutch Dining Staff	Filipino/Indonesian
Total Cabins	747
Size Range (sq ft/m)	131-425/12.0-39.5
Outside Cabins 495 Inside Cabins	252
Single Cabins 0 Supplement	50-100%
Balcony Cabins 0 Wheelchair Cabins	4
Cabin Current 110 AC Refrigerator	No
Cabin TV Yes VCR	No
Dining Rooms 1 Sittings	2
Elevators	7
Casino Yes Slot Machines	Yes

Swimming Pools (outside)	2 (1 with magrodome)
Swimming Pools (inside)	0
Whirlpools 2 Gymnasium	Yes
Sauna/Steam Room Yes/No Massage	Yes
Self-Service Launderette	Yes-5
Movie Theater/Seats	Yes/237
Library	Yes
Children's Facilities	Yes
Watersports Facilities	None
Classification Society	Lloyd's Register

RATINGS	SCORE
Ship: Condition/Cleanliness	8.0
Ship: Space/Flow/Comfort	8.0
Ship: Decor/Furnishings	7.7
Ship: Fitness Facilities	6.8
Cabins: Comfort/Facilities	7.7
Cabins: Software	7.8
Food: Dining Room/Cuisine	6.6
Food: Buffets/Informal Dining	6.5
Food: Quality of Ingredients	6.7
Service: Dining Room	6.1
Service: Bars	7.2
Service: Cabins	7.9
Cruise: Entertainment	7.0
Cruise: Activities Program	7.4
Cruise: Hospitality Standard	8.0
OVERALL RATING	109.4

✛ Has teakwood outdoor decks and a wrap-around promenade deck. Good open deck and sunning space. Elegant, functional interior, with restful public rooms decorated in pastel tones, though some decor looks dated. Absorbs passengers well and has good layout. High-quality furnishings and fabrics throughout. Good open deck space for sunning. Fine health and fitness center. Cabins are generously proportioned, well appointed and equipped with everything, including ample closet, drawer and storage space, and generous-sized bathrooms.

▬ Too many inside cabins. Long lines for embarkation, disembarkation, buffets, and shore tenders. Magrodome-covered swimming pool deck is too small for number of passengers carried. The entertainment is disappointing.

Dining Traditional dining room has a raised center dome and portholes, highlighted at night by special lighting. The food, while attractively presented, is virtually tasteless. Poor selection of breads, cheeses and fresh fruits. Service is reasonable, though communication is frustrating (smiles can only do so much).

Other Comments This well-built, contemporary ship, which underwent a $84 million stretch in 1990, is fine to cruise on, and provides a fairly refined, comfortable setting, but carries too many passengers, although fortunately, there's never a feeling of being crowded.

ms Windward ★★★★

OPERATES

7-DAY ALASKA AND
CARIBBEAN CRUISES

Cruise Line	Norwegian Cruise Line		
Former Names	- Gross Tonnage 39,217		
Builder	Chantiers de l'Atlantique (France)		
Original Cost	$240 million		
Christened By	Mrs Barbara Bush		
Entered Service	May 23, 1993		
Interior Design	Yran & Storbraaten		
Country of Registry	Bahamas (C6LG6)		
Tel No	130-5713/130-5715		
Fax No	130-5714/130-5716		
Length (ft/m)	623.3/190.00		
Beam (ft/m) 93.5/28.50	Draft (ft/m) 22.3/6.80		
Propulsion	diesel (18,480kW)		
Propellers	2 (CP)		
Decks 11	Crew 483		
Pass. Capacity (basis 2) 1,246	(all berths) 1,450		
Pass. Space Ratio (basis 2) 32.9	(all berths) 28.2		
Officers Norwegian	Dining Staff International		
Total Cabins	623		
Size Range (sq ft/m)	140-350/13.0-32.5		
Outside Cabins 531	Inside Cabins 92		
Single Cabins 0	Supplement 50-100%		
Balcony Cabins	48		
Wheelchair Cabins	6 (+ 30 for hearing impaired)		
Cabin Current	110 AC		
Refrigerator	Category 1/2/3 only		
Cabin TV Yes	VCR No		
Dining Rooms 2	Sittings 2		

Elevators			7
Casino	Yes	Slot Machines	Yes
Swimming Pools (outside) 2		(inside)	0
Whirlpools	2	Gymnasium	Yes
Sauna/Steam Room Yes/No		Massage	Yes
Self-Service Launderette			No
Movie Theater/Seats No		Library	Yes
Children's Facilities			Yes
Watersports Facilities			None
Classification Society		Det Norske Veritas	

RATINGS	SCORE
Ship: Condition/Cleanliness	8.6
Ship: Space/Flow/Comfort	7.9
Ship: Decor/Furnishings	8.2
Ship: Fitness Facilities	8.1
Cabins: Comfort/Facilities	7.8
Cabins: Software	8.0
Food: Dining Room/Cuisine	7.2
Food: Buffets/Informal Dining	6.3
Food: Quality of Ingredients	6.4
Service: Dining Room	7.6
Service: Bars	7.5
Service: Cabins	7.4
Cruise: Entertainment	8.3
Cruise: Activities Program	7.8
Cruise: Hospitality Standard	7.6
OVERALL RATING	114.7

+ Excellent exterior design, protected aft decks and sun terraces overlooking a swimming pool. Good public rooms, and spacious, open lobby area. Soothing interior decor and colors. Good showlounge and colorful, jazzy shows. Cabins are warm and cozy, with soft colors and wood trim. This mid-size ship feels large, and provides plenty of space inside so that crowding shouldn't happen.

— There really is no entrance foyer. Cabins have almost no drawer or storage space. Long lines for buffets. Poor room service.

Dining Three dining rooms: Sun Terrace, The Terraces (which is the nicest), and Four Seasons (all have the same menu and food), plus The Bistro (for casual dining) and ultra-casual Sports Bar. Cuisine is family diner food, with thick sauces. Quantity is present, but not quality. Perfunctory service by waiters whose English is poor. Nice wine list, and well put together. Sports Bar has large selection of beers. Afternoon tea is not served anywhere.

Other Comments Has squat funnel housing, and inboard lifeboats. Upper, tiered outdoor pool deck is always busy, but fun. Fairly good interior layout and passenger flow. Special cabins for the hearing impaired—a first for any large ship. Together with *Dreamward*, she's pricier than NCL's other ships, but worth it for first-time cruisegoers not seeking fine cuisine.

ms World Discoverer ★★★★+

OPERATES

*WORLDWIDE EXPEDITION CRUISES
(INCLUDING ANTARCTICA)*

Cruise Line			Society Expeditions
Former Names			Bewa Discoverer
Gross Tonnage			3,153
Builder		Schichau Unterweser (Germany)	
Original Cost	n/a	Christened By	n/a
Entered Service			Apr 7, 1977
Interior Design			Carleton Varney
Country of Registry			Liberia (ELDU3)
Tel No	124-2744	Fax No	124-2744
Length (ft/m)			287.1/87.51
Beam (ft/m) 49.6/15.12		Draft (ft/m)	14.6/4.46
Propulsion/Propellers		diesel (3,530kW)/1 (CP)	
Decks	4	Crew	75
Pass. Capacity (basis 2) 138		(all berths) 138	
Pass. Space Ratio (basis 2) 22.8		(all berths) 22.8	
Officers			European
Dining Staff			European/Filipino
Total Cabins			71
Size Range (sq ft/m)			89-218/8.2-20.2
Outside Cabins	71	Inside Cabins	0
Single Cabins	0	Supplement	Set rates
Balcony Cabins	0	Wheelchair Cabins	0
Cabin Current			110/220 AC
Refrigerator			No
Cabin TV	No	VCR	No
Dining Rooms			1 (open seating)
Elevators			1
Casino	No	Slot Machines	No

Swimming Pools (outside) 1		(inside)	0
Whirlpools	0	Gymnasium	Yes
Sauna/Steam Room No/No		Massage	Yes
Self-Service Launderette			No
Lecture Room/Theater	No	Library	Yes
Zodiacs:	Yes	Helicopter Pad: No	
Watersports Facilities		Scuba diving, snorkeling,	
	fishing, waterski and windsurf equipment		
Classification Society		American Bureau	
			of Shipping

RATINGS	SCORE
Ship: Condition/Cleanliness	8.0
Ship: Space/Flow/Comfort	7.8
Ship: Expedition Equipment	7.9
Ship: Decor/Furnishings	8.0
Cabins: Comfort/Facilities	7.7
Cabins: Software	7.8
Food: Dining Room/Cuisine	7.8
Food: Buffets/Informal Dining	7.2
Food: Quality of Ingredients	7.1
Service: Dining Room	7.7
Service: Bars	7.5
Service: Cabins	7.8
Cruise: Itineraries/Operations	8.0
Cruise: Lecture Program	7.6
Cruise: Hospitality Standard	7.8
OVERALL RATING	115.7

+ Features ice-hardened hull and is extremely maneuverable. Well maintained. Well-equipped for in-depth expedition cruising in comfort. Elegant and impressive public rooms and interior decor. Cabins are of good proportions, are comfortable, and very tastefully furnished. Naturalists and expert lecturers and nature specialists escort every expedition. One of the best expedition cruise vessels of its type in service today.

— Has steep passenger gangway. Closet space is limited in cabins.

Dining Has a very attractive, cozy dining room (some tables for two). Big picture windows and comfortable chairs make for an elegant setting. Excellent cuisine and service, although it relies heavily on dairy products. Limited selection of breads and fruits.

Other Comments Sophisticated, small, but very comfortable vessel built expressly for adventure cruising has sleek, well-proportioned profile with contemporary swept-back funnel. This ship provides a fine setting for expedition cruising to some of the most remote destinations in the world. It's quite expensive, but worth it for discerning, well-traveled passengers yearning for a sense of adventure and who enjoy learning about the world around us and its fascinating peoples. Gratuities are not included.

ms World Renaissance ★★★+

OPERATES
MEDITERRANEAN AND RED SEA CRUISES

Cruise Line	Epirotiki Cruise Line	Casino	Yes	Slot Machines Yes
Former Names Renaissance/Homeric Renaissance		Swimming Pools (outside) 2		(inside) 0
Gross Tonnage	11,724	Whirlpools	0	Gymnasium Yes
Builder Chantiers de l'Atlantique (France)		Sauna/Steam Room Yes/No		Massage Yes
Original Cost	n/a	Self-Service Launderette		No
Christened By	n/a	Movie Theater/Seats		Yes/110
Entered Service	May 10, 1966/1978	Library		Yes
Interior Design	n/a	Children's Facilities		No
Country of Registry	Greece (SYXQ)	Watersports Facilities		None
Tel No 113-0440 Fax No 113-0440		Classification Society		Lloyd's Register

Length (ft/m)	492.1/150.02
Beam (ft/m) 69.0/21.06 Draft (ft/m) 22.9/7.00	
Propulsion	diesel (10,060kW)
Propellers	2 (FP)
Decks 8 Crew	204
Pass. Capacity (basis 2) 527	(all berths) 599
Pass. Space Ratio (basis 2) 22.2	(all berths) 19.5
Officers Greek Dining Staff	Greek
Total Cabins	266
Size Range (sq ft/m)	110-270/10.2-25.0
Outside Cabins 188 Inside Cabins	80
Single Cabins 5 Supplement	50%
Balcony Cabins 0 Wheelchair Cabins	0
Cabin Current	110 AC
Refrigerator	No
Cabin TV No VCR	No
Dining Rooms 1 Sittings	2
Elevators	2

RATINGS	SCORE
Ship: Condition/Cleanliness	6.8
Ship: Space/Flow/Comfort	6.4
Ship: Decor/Furnishings	6.9
Ship: Fitness Facilities	6.4
Cabins: Comfort/Facilities	7.0
Cabins: Software	8.1
Food: Dining Room/Cuisine	7.1
Food: Buffets/Informal Dining	6.7
Food: Quality of Ingredients	6.2
Service: Dining Room	7.2
Service: Bars	7.4
Service: Cabins	7.3
Cruise: Entertainment	7.0
Cruise: Activities Program	6.3
Cruise: Hospitality Standard	7.0
OVERALL RATING	103.8

+ Charming vessel has yacht-like intimacy and ambiance. Generous open deck and sunning space. Beautiful wood paneling in cabins, which are homely and quite spacious for ship size, though not luxurious. Bathrooms are tiled. The library-quiet room is restful. Friendly staff and ambiance.

— Has a steep passenger gangway. There's no wrap-around outdoor promenade deck.

Dining The dining room is quite pleasant, but there are no tables for two. Continental cuisine is predominantly Mediterranean, with an overabundance of oils used. Limited selection of breads, pastry, fruit and cheeses. Good basic service throughout, but there's no finesse.

Other Comments This ship has traditional sixties styling and profile topped by a slender funnel. Public rooms are few, but main lounge is very comfortable. Xenia Tavern is colonial in style and decor, and functions as setting for both intimate classical concerts as well as ship's disco. This ship will cruise you in comfortable surroundings, at a very fair price.

ib Yamal ★★★+

OPERATES
ANTARCTICA/TRANSPOLAR EXPEDITION CRUISES

Cruise Line	Murmansk Shipping/ Quark Expeditions		
Former Names	- Gross Tonnage 20,646		
Builder	Baltic Shipyard, Murmansk (Russia)		
Original Cost	$150 million		
Christened By	n/a Interior Design n/a		
Entered Service	Dec 1989		
Country of Registry	Russia		
Tel No	n/a Fax No n/a		
Length (ft/m)	492.1/150.00		
Beam (ft/m) 98.4/30.00	Draft (ft/m) 36.0/11.00		
Propulsion	nuclear-powered turbo-elec (75,000shp)		
Propellers	3		
Decks	4 Crew 130		
Pass. Capacity (basis 2) 100	(all berths) 100		
Pass. Space Ratio (basis 2) 206.4	(all berths) 206.4		
Officers	Russian/Ukrainian		
Dining Staff	European/Ukrainian		
Total Cabins	50		
Size Range (sq ft/m)	130-300/14.3-27.8		
Outside Cabins 50	Inside Cabins 0		
Single Cabins 0	Supplement 80%		
Balcony Cabins 0	Wheelchair Cabins 0		
Cabin Current 220 AC	Refrigerator All cabins		
Cabin TV Yes	VCR Yes		
Dining Rooms 1	Sittings open seating		
Elevators	0		

Casino	No	Slot Machines	No
Swimming Pools (inside) 1			
Whirlpools	0	Gymnasium	Yes
Sauna/Steam Room			Yes-2/No
Massage			No
Self-Service Launderette			Yes
Lecture/Film Room		Yes (seats 100)	
Library	Yes	Zodiacs	4
Helicopter Pad	2 helicopters for passenger use		
Classification Society			RS

RATINGS	SCORE
Ship: Condition/Cleanliness	7.6
Ship: Space/Flow/Comfort	6.0
Ship: Expedition Equipment	9.0
Ship: Decor/Furnishings	5.8
Cabins: Comfort/Facilities	5.7
Cabins: Software	6.0
Food: Dining Room/Cuisine	6.8
Food: Buffets/Informal Dining	6.4
Food: Quality of Ingredients	7.0
Service: Dining Room	6.6
Service: Bars	6.6
Service: Cabins	6.6
Cruise: Itineraries/Operations	7.8
Cruise: Lecture Program	7.7
Cruise: Hospitality Standard	7.6
OVERALL RATING	103.2

+ The ultimate in technology accompanies this special ship, one of a fleet of the world's most powerful ice-breakers. Has Zodiacs for shore landings, plus two helicopters for reconnaissance and passenger sightseeing use. Rugged, yet surprisingly comfortable surroundings. Tiered lecture theater with stage is the setting for a team of biologists, scientists, geologists and other lecturers. Has two lounges. Heated indoor pool. All cabins are generously sized, and are outside, all with private facilities. Attentive and friendly Russian service. Passengers are allowed on the bridge at all times.

— Limited closet and drawer space in most cabins. Bathrooms are small and utilitarian. Limited number of public rooms.

Dining Nicely appointed dining room. The catering, supervised by Swedish company, is surprisingly hearty, with plenty of meat and potato dishes, but little fruit and cheese. Remember, this is not gourmet cuisine.

Other Comments This is an incredible vessel, with a three-inch-thick reinforced bow for negotiating tough ice conditions. Has enough fuel for four years without refueling! Try the incredible Transpolar voyage via the North Pole. This is one of the most unusual, exciting expedition cruise experiences available today.

mv Yorktown Clipper ★★★

OPERATES

*VARIOUS U.S. COAST AND
CARIBBEAN CRUISES*

Cruise Line		Clipper Cruise Line
Former Names		-
Gross Tonnage		2,354
Builder	First Coast Shipbuilding (USA)	
Original Cost		$12 million
Christened By		Mrs Richard Wilson
Entered Service		Apr 30, 1988
Interior Design		Christner Partnership
Country of Registry		USA (WTA4768)
Tel No	none	Fax No none
Length (ft/m)		257.0/78.30
Beam (ft/m) 43.0/13.10	Draft (ft/m)	8.0/2.43
Propulsion		diesel (1,400shp)
Propellers		2 (FP)
Decks	4	Crew 37
Pass. Capacity (basis 2) 138		(all berths) 149
Pass. Space Ratio (basis 2) 17.0		(all berths) 15.7
Officers		American
Dining Staff		American
Total Cabins		69
Size Range (sq ft/m)		121-138/11.2-12.8
Outside Cabins	69	Inside Cabins 0
Single Cabins	0	Supplement Set rates
Balcony Cabins	0	Wheelchair Cabins 0
Cabin Current	110 AC	Refrigerator No
Cabin TV	No	VCR No
Dining Rooms	1	Sittings 1
Elevators		0

Casino	No	Slot Machines	No
Swimming Pools (outside) 0		(inside)	0
Whirlpools	0	Gymnasium	No
Sauna/Steam Room No/No		Massage	No
Self-Service Launderette			No
Movie Theater/Seats			No
Library	Yes	Children's Facilities No	
Watersports Facilities			None
Classification Society		American Bureau	
		of Shipping	

RATINGS	SCORE
Ship: Condition/Cleanliness	7.3
Ship: Space/Flow/Comfort	4.0
Ship: Decor/Furnishings	7.2
Ship: Fitness Facilities	3.0
Cabins: Comfort/Facilities	6.1
Cabins: Software	6.5
Food: Dining Room/Cuisine	7.1
Food: Buffets/Informal Dining	6.2
Food: Quality of Ingredients	7.0
Service: Dining Room	7.1
Service: Bars	7.0
Service: Cabins	7.3
Cruise: Entertainment	4.0
Cruise: Activities Program	5.6
Cruise: Hospitality Standard	7.4
OVERALL RATING	92.8

+ This small vessel is built for coastal and inland cruises. Has shallow draft and good maneuverability. Well maintained. Teakwood outdoor sun deck. Has rubber Zodiac craft for close-in excursions. Glass-walled observation lounge. The all-outside cabins are small, but, with lots of wood-accented trim and restful colors, are quite comfortable and tastefully furnished. "Americana" experience for those seeking to learn more about the coastal ports around the USA. Casual, unregimented lifestyle, rather like a small, congenial country club.

— This is a high-density ship with only two public rooms: a dining room and a lounge. High engine and generator noise when underway.

Dining Warm, inviting dining room has large picture windows, but no tables for two. Friendly service is provided by young, all-American mid-western college types. The food is of good quality, and made from locally purchased fresh ingredients, although there is little choice. Limited selection of breads and fruits.

Other Comments This ship cannot be compared with big ship ocean cruising. The per diem price is high for what you get, and air fare is extra, but it does appeal to the older American passenger who doesn't want to be on the megaships.

mv Zenith ★★★★★

OPERATES

7-DAY BERMUDA AND CARIBBEAN CRUISES

Cruise Line	Celebrity Cruises		
Former Names	-		
Gross Tonnage	47,255		
Builder	Meyer Werft (Germany)		
Original Cost	$210 million		
Christened By	Mrs Antony Chandris		
Entered Service	Apr 4, 1992		
Interior Design	Katzourakis/McNeece		
Country of Registry	Liberia (ELOU5)		
Tel No 124-5564	Fax No 124-5567		
Length (ft/m)	681.0/207.59		
Beam (ft/m) 95.1/29.00	Draft (ft/m) 23.6/7.20		
Propulsion	diesel (19,960kW)		
Propellers	2 (CP)		
Decks 9	Crew 628		
Pass. Capacity (basis 2) 1,374	(all berths) 1,796		
Pass. Space Ratio (basis 2) 34.3	(all berths) 26.3		
Officers	Greek		
Dining Staff	International		
Total Cabins	687		
Size Range (sq ft/m)	185-334/17.0-31.0		
Outside Cabins 541	Inside Cabins 146		
Single Cabins 0	Supplement Set rates		
Balcony Cabins 0	Wheelchair Cabins 4		
Cabin Current 110 AC	Refrigerator No		
Cabin TV Yes	VCR No		
Dining Rooms 1	Sittings 2		
Elevators	7		

Casino	Yes	Slot Machines	Yes
Swimming Pools (outside)	2	(inside)	0
Whirlpools	3	Gymnasium	Yes
Sauna/Steam Room	Yes/No	Massage	Yes
Self-Service Launderette			No
Movie Theater/Seats			Yes/850
Library			Yes
Children's Facilities			Yes
Watersports Facilities			None
Classification Society			Lloyd's Register

RATINGS	SCORE
Ship: Condition/Cleanliness	9.1
Ship: Space/Flow/Comfort	8.7
Ship: Decor/Furnishings	9.0
Ship: Fitness Facilities	8.2
Cabins: Comfort/Facilities	8.1
Cabins: Software	8.1
Food: Dining Room/Cuisine	8.5
Food: Buffets/Informal Dining	8.2
Food: Quality of Ingredients	8.1
Service: Dining Room	8.4
Service: Bars	8.1
Service: Cabins	8.2
Cruise: Entertainment	8.8
Cruise: Activities Program	8.2
Cruise: Hospitality Standard	8.3
OVERALL RATING	126.0

+ Smart, contemporary profile. Similar interior layout and elegant decor to sister ship *Horizon*. Enlarged and enhanced forward observation lounge. Double-wide indoor promenade. Fine artwork throughout. Art deco hotel-like lobby, with two-deck-high ceiling. Soothing pastel colors and high-quality furnishings. Good library. Well-insulated cabins are nicely appointed, and have good closet and drawer space. Bathrooms are practical, with large shower areas. Suites are very tasteful, and have butler service. Excellent showlounge. Good seasonal, unobtrusive children's program. Children's playroom has a neat puppet theater.

— Expect lines for embarkation, disembarkation, shore excursions and buffets. Heavy doors to restrooms and outdoor decks. Most outside cabins on Bermuda Deck have lifeboat-obstructed views. No cushioned pads for deck lounge chairs.

Dining Good quality food, presentation and service. Large, elegant dining room has several tables for two. Chairs do not have armrests. Separate vegetarian and children's menu. Improved cabin service menu. Windsurf Café features good breakfast and luncheon buffets. The Grill serves fast-food items.

Other Comments For superb, value-for-money cruising in the Caribbean, this ship provides the benchmark for mainstream cruises and will almost certainly exceed your expectations.

SAIL SHIPS

mys Club Med I ★★★★+

OPERATES

*7-DAY CARIBBEAN AND
EUROPE CRUISES*

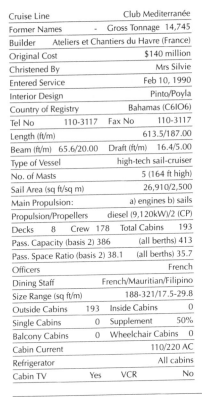

Cruise Line	Club Mediterranée
Former Names	-
Gross Tonnage	14,745
Builder	Ateliers et Chantiers du Havre (France)
Original Cost	$140 million
Christened By	Mrs Silvie
Entered Service	Feb 10, 1990
Interior Design	Pinto/Poyla
Country of Registry	Bahamas (C6IO6)
Tel No 110-3117 Fax No	110-3117
Length (ft/m)	613.5/187.00
Beam (ft/m) 65.6/20.00 Draft (ft/m)	16.4/5.00
Type of Vessel	high-tech sail-cruiser
No. of Masts	5 (164 ft high)
Sail Area (sq ft/sq m)	26,910/2,500
Main Propulsion:	a) engines b) sails
Propulsion/Propellers	diesel (9,120kW)/2 (CP)
Decks 8 Crew 178 Total Cabins	193
Pass. Capacity (basis 2) 386	(all berths) 413
Pass. Space Ratio (basis 2) 38.1	(all berths) 35.7
Officers	French
Dining Staff	French/Mauritian/Filipino
Size Range (sq ft/m)	188-321/17.5-29.8
Outside Cabins 193 Inside Cabins	0
Single Cabins 0 Supplement	50%
Balcony Cabins 0 Wheelchair Cabins	0
Cabin Current	110/220 AC
Refrigerator	All cabins
Cabin TV Yes VCR	No

Dining Rooms 2 (open seating) Elevators 2
Casino Yes Slot Machines Yes
Swimming Pools (outside) 2
Whirlpools 0 Gymnasium Yes
Sauna/Steam Room Yes/No Massage Yes
Self-Service Launderette No Library Yes
Watersports Facilities Aft platform, 12 windsurfers,
3 sailboats, 2 water-ski boats, 20 single scuba
tanks, snorkels, 4 motorized watersport boats
Classification Society Bureau Veritas

RATINGS	SCORE
Ship: Condition/Cleanliness	8.2
Ship: Space/Flow/Comfort	8.0
Ship: Decor/Furnishings	8.6
Ship: Watersports Facilities	9.0
Cabins: Comfort/Facilities	8.4
Cabins: Software	8.0
Food: Dining Room/Cuisine	8.2
Food: Buffets/Informal Dining	7.6
Food: Quality of Ingredients	7.7
Service: Dining Room	7.6
Service: Bars	7.7
Service: Cabins	8.2
Cruise: Sail-Cruise Experience	7.2
Cruise: Entertainment/Activities	6.1
Cruise: Hospitality Standard	7.3
OVERALL RATING	117.8

+ Extensive watersports facilities and fine aft marina platform. Computer workshop. Golf simulator (provided instead of a gymnasium) incurs extra charge. Good public rooms. Cabins very well equipped, with plenty of storage space and 24-hour room service (but you pay for food). Six four-person cabins. Some 35 doubles are fitted with an extra pullman berth.

— Programmed activities under the direction of a large team of young, energetic GOs (Gentils Organisateurs), who have full run of the ship, are rather clown-like and amateurish.

Dining Two lovely dining rooms have tables for one, two or more. Open seating for all meals. The Odyssey Restaurant has a charming open terrace for informal meals. Afternoon tea is a delight. Open-air dining terrace. Cuisine is mainly French and Continental, but presentation needs improving. Beer and standard wines are included for lunch and dinner.

Other Comments One of a pair of the world's largest sail-cruisers is part cruise ship, part yacht. Larger version of the Windstar Cruises vessels. Five huge masts provide seven computer-controlled sails with a total area of 2,500 sq m. Superb for more upscale active singles and couples who might prefer casual elegance to the wilder vacation experience at some Club Med resorts. Cruise can be combined with a Club Med Village Vacation (Bora Bora and Moorea). No gratuities are expected or accepted, as at all Club Med resorts.

mys Club Med II ★★★★+

OPERATES

TAHITI AND SOUTH PACIFIC CRUISES

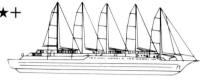

Cruise Line	Club Mediterranée	Dining Rooms 2 (open seating)	Elevators 2
Former Names - Gross Tonnage 14,745		Casino Yes Slot Machines Yes	
Builder Ateliers et Chantiers du Havre (France)		Swimming Pools (outside) 2	
Original Cost $145 million		Whirlpools 0 Gymnasium No	
Christened By n/a		Sauna/Steam Room Yes/No Massage Yes	
Entered Service Dec 15, 1992		Self-Service Launderette No Library Yes	
Interior Design Pinto/Poyla		Watersports Facilities Aft platform, 12 windsurfers,	
Country of Registry Wallis & Fortuna (FNIR)		3 sailboats, 2 water-ski boats, 20 single scuba	
Tel No 110-2173 Fax No 110-2173		tanks, snorkels, 4 motorized watersport boats	
Length (ft/m) 613.5/187.00		Classification Society Bureau Veritas	
Beam (ft/m) 65.6/20.00 Draft (ft/m) 16.4/5.00			
Type of Vessel high-tech sail-cruiser		**RATINGS** **SCORE**	
No. of Masts 5 (164 ft high)		Ship: Condition/Cleanliness 8.2	
Sail Area (sq ft/sq m) 26,910/2,500		Ship: Space/Flow/Comfort 8.0	
Main Propulsion a) engines b) sails		Ship: Decor/Furnishings 8.6	
Propulsion/Propellers diesel (9,120kW)/2 (CP)		Ship: Watersports Facilities 9.0	
Decks 8 Crew 181 Total Cabins 196		Cabins: Comfort/Facilities 8.4	
Pass. Capacity (basis 2) 392 (all berths) 419		Cabins: Software 8.0	
Pass. Space Ratio (basis 2) 37.6 (all berths) 35.1		Food: Dining Room/Cuisine 8.2	
Officers French		Food: Buffets/Informal Dining 7.7	
Dining Staff French/Mauritian/Filipino		Food: Quality of Ingredients 7.7	
Size Range (sq ft/m) 188-321/17.5-29.8		Service: Dining Room 7.6	
Outside Cabins 196 Inside Cabins 0		Service: Bars 7.7	
Single Cabins 0 Supplement 50%		Service: Cabins 8.2	
Balcony Cabins 0 Wheelchair Cabins 0		Cruise: Sail-Cruise Experience 7.2	
Cabin Current 110/220 AC		Cruise: Entertainment/Activities 6.1	
Refrigerator All cabins		Cruise: Hospitality Standard 7.3	
Cabin TV Yes VCR No		OVERALL RATING 117.9	

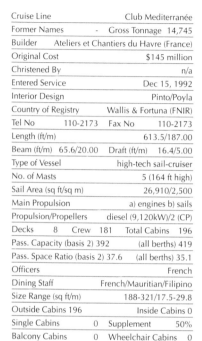

+ Extensive watersports facilities and fine aft marina platform. Computer workshop. Golf simulator (provided instead of a gymnasium) incurs extra charge. Good public rooms. Cabins very well equipped, with plenty of storage space and 24-hour room service (but you pay for food). Six four-person cabins. Some 35 doubles are fitted with an extra pullman berth.

— Programmed activities under the direction of a large team of young, energetic GOs (Gentils Organisateurs), who have full run of the ship, are rather clown-like and amateurish.

Dining Two lovely dining rooms have tables for one, two or more. Open seating for all meals. The Odyssey Restaurant has a charming open terrace for informal meals. Afternoon tea is a delight. Open-air dining terrace. Cuisine is mainly French and Continental, but presentation needs improving. Beer and standard wines are included for lunch and dinner.

Other Comments One of a pair of the world's largest sail-cruisers is part cruise ship, part yacht. Larger version of the Windstar Cruises vessels. Five huge masts provide seven computer-controlled sails with a total area of 2,500 sq m. Superb for more upscale active singles and couples who might prefer casual elegance to the wilder vacation experience at some Club Med resorts. Cruise can be combined with a Club Med Village Vacation (Bora Bora and Moorea). No gratuities are expected or accepted, as at all Club Med resorts.

mys Le Ponant ★★★★+

OPERATES

*VARIOUS CARIBBEAN AND
MEDITERRANEAN CRUISES*

Cruise Line	Compagnie des Isles du Ponant	
Former Names	- Gross Tonnage	1,489
Builder	SFCN (France)	
Original Cost	n/a Christened By	n/a
Entered Service	1991	
Interior Design	Sterling Design	
Country of Registry	France (FGZZ)	
Tel No 111-1406	Fax No 111-1406	
Length (ft/m)	288.7/88.00	
Beam (ft/m) 39.3/12.00	Draft (ft/m) 13.1/4.00	
Type of Vessel	high tech sail-cruiser	
No. of Masts	3	
Sail Area (sq ft/sq m)	16,150/1,500	
Main Propulsion	a) engine b) sails	
Propulsion	diesel/sail power	
Propellers	1 (CP)	
Decks 3	Crew	30
Pass. Capacity (basis 2) 56	(all berths) 67	
Pass. Space Ratio (basis 2) 26.5	(all berths) 22.2	
Officers French	Dining Staff	French
Total Cabins	32	
Size Range (sq ft/m)	140/13.0	
Outside Cabins 32	Inside Cabins	0
Single Cabins 0	Supplement	50%
Balcony Cabins 0	Wheelchair Cabins	0
Cabin Current 220 AC	Refrigerator All cabins	
Cabin TV No	VCR	No
Dining Rooms	1 (open seating)	

Elevators			No
Casino	No	Slot Machines	No
Swimming Pools (outside)			0
Whirlpools	0	Gymnasium	Yes
Sauna/Steam Room	No/No	Massage	No
Self-Service Launderette			No
Library			Yes
Watersports Facilities			Aft marina platform,
		windsurf, water-ski boat, scuba, snorkel	
Classification Society			Lloyd's Register

RATINGS	SCORE
Ship: Condition/Cleanliness	8.8
Ship: Space/Flow/Comfort	7.4
Ship: Decor/Furnishings	9.0
Ship: Watersports Facilities	8.8
Cabins: Comfort/Facilities	8.7
Cabins: Software	8.1
Food: Dining Room/Cuisine	8.5
Food: Buffets/Informal Dining	8.1
Food: Quality of Ingredients	8.0
Service: Dining Room	8.0
Service: Bars	7.7
Service: Cabins	8.0
Cruise: Sail-Cruise Experience	7.7
Cruise: Activities Program	7.6
Cruise: Hospitality Standard	8.0
OVERALL RATING	122.4

+ This captivating ship has plenty of room on her open decks for sunbathing. Features a watersports platform at the stern. Very elegant, no glitz interior design is clean, stylish and functional, and ultra-high-tech throughout. Three public lounges have pastel decor, soft colors and great European flair. Crisp, clean blond woods and pristine white cabins feature double or twin beds, mini-bar, personal safe, and private bathroom. All cabins feature portholes and crisp artwork.

— Cabin bathrooms are quite small. Cabins have limited storage space, and few drawers.

Dining The lovely Karukera dining room features complimentary wines and good food. There is fresh fish every day, and meals are true *affaires gastronomiques*. Charming outdoor café under canvas sail-cloth awning.

Other Comments Ultra-sleek, very efficient, this latest generation of sail-cruise ship has three masts that rise 54.8 ft (16.7 m) above the water line. One price fits all. Marketed mainly to young, sophisticated French-speaking passengers who love yachting and the sea. *Très* French, *très* chic. Gratuities are not "required," but they are expected.

sy Lili Marleen

OPERATES

CARIBBEAN AND BALTIC CRUISES

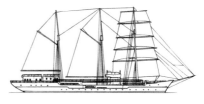

Cruise Line		Peter Deilmann Reederei	
Former Names	-	Gross Tonnage	750
Builder		Elsflether Werft (Germany)	
Original Cost		DM16 million	
Christened By	n/a	Interior Design	-
Entered Service		July 30, 1994	
Country of Registry		Germany	
Tel No	513-9278	Fax No	112-3466
Length (ft/m)		249.3/76.0	
Beam (ft/m)	31.6/9.5	Draft (ft/m)	12.7/3.9
Type of Vessel		barkentine schooner	
No. of Masts		3/16 manually furled sails	
Sail Area (sq ft/sq m)		12,917/1,200	
Main Propulsion		sail power	
Propulsion		diesel (660kW)	
Propellers		1 (CP)	
Decks	3	Crew	30
Pass. Capacity (basis 2) 50		(all berths) 50	
Pass. Space Ratio (basis 2) 15.0		(all berths) 15.0	
Officers	German	Dining Staff	European
Total Cabins			25
Size Range (sq ft/m)			n/a
Outside Cabins	25	Inside Cabins	0
Single Cabins	0	Supplement	50%
Balcony Cabins	0	Wheelchair Cabins	0
Cabin Current	220 AC	Refrigerator	No
Cabin TV	Yes	VCR	No
Dining Rooms	1	Sittings	Open

Elevators			0
Casino	No	Slot Machines	No
Swimming Pools (outside) 0		(inside)	0
Whirlpools	0	Gymnasium	No
Sauna/Steam Room	No	Massage	No
Self-Service Launderette			No
Movie Theater/Seats	No	Library	Yes
Children's Facilities/Playroom			No
Watersports Facilities			None
Classification Society		Germanischer Lloyd	

RATINGS	SCORE
Ship: Condition/Cleanliness	NYR
Ship: Space/Flow/Comfort	NYR
Ship: Decor/Furnishings	NYR
Ship: Fitness Facilities	NYR
Cabins: Comfort/Facilities	NYR
Cabins: Software	NYR
Food: Dining Room/Cuisine	NYR
Food: Buffets/Informal Dining	NYR
Food: Quality of Ingredients	NYR
Service: Dining Room	NYR
Service: Bars	NYR
Service: Cabins	NYR
Cruise: Sail-Cruise Experience	NYR
Cruise: Activities Program	NYR
Cruise: Hospitality Standard	NYR
OVERALL RATING	

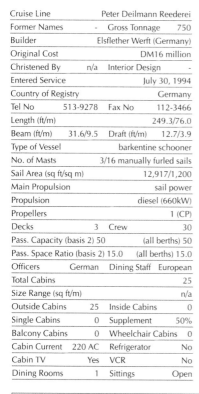

+ This is a beautiful three-masted barkentine (one square-rigged and two gaff- or schooner-rigged masts), one of which is a 236-ft-high (71-m) mast. Timeless design that relies on the power of Nature most of the time. You can certainly take an active part with the sails, and even go up the rigging (at the captain's discretion). Oneness with the elements is exhilarating. Twin and double cabins are very comfortable. Bathrobes are provided for all passengers (on request). Has good amenities for passenger comfort.

— None known at press time.

Dining Has a really charming dining room, and on many evenings dinner is often candlelit. Finest quality china and silverware. International cuisine with regional specialties, with much emphasis on hearty German cuisine.

Other Comments Only casual clothing is needed on this kind of cruise, which is a really relaxing way to travel. Currency is the Deutschmark. Gratuities and insurance not included.

sy Sea Cloud ★★★★★

OPERATES

*7-DAY CARIBBEAN AND
EUROPE CRUISES*

Cruise Line		Sea Cloud Cruises/Deilmann Reederei
Former Names		Antaria/Patria/Angelita/Hussar
Gross Tonnage		2,532
Builder		Krupp Werft (Germany)
Christened By		Mrs Marjorie Merriweather-Post
Entered Service		1931/1978 (restored)
Interior Design		Marjorie Merriweather-Post
Country of Registry		Malta (9HOM2)
Tel No 125-6105	Fax No	125-6173
Length		315.9/96.30m
Beam 49.0/14.94m	Draft	16.8/5.13m
Type of Vessel		4-masted barque
No. of Masts		4 (17.7 m)/(30 sails)
Sail Area (sq ft/sq m)		32,292/3,000
Main Propulsion		sail power
Propulsion diesel	Propellers	1 (FP)
Decks 3 Crew 60	Total Cabins	34
Pass. Capacity (basis 2) 69		(all berths) 69
Pass. Space Ratio (basis 2) 37.2		(all berths) 37.2
Officers European	Dining Staff	European
Size Range (sq ft/m)		143/13.2
Outside Cabins 34	Inside Cabins	0
Single Cabins		0
Supplement		Fixed rates
Balcony Cabins 0	Wheelchair Cabins	0
Cabin Current		110/220 AC
Refrigerator		No
Cabin TV No	VCR	No

Dining Rooms			1 (open seating)
Elevators			0
Casino	No	Slot Machines	No
Swimming Pools (outside)			0
Whirlpools	0	Gymnasium	No
Sauna/Steam Room	No/No	Massage	No
Self-Service Launderette	No	Library	Yes
Watersports Facilities		Snorkeling, water-skiing, windsurfing	
Classification Society		Germanischer Lloyd	

RATINGS	SCORE
Ship: Condition/Cleanliness	8.8
Ship: Space/Flow/Comfort	8.2
Ship: Decor/Furnishings	8.8
Ship: Watersports Facilities	7.6
Cabins: Comfort/Facilities	8.1
Cabins: Software	8.5
Food: Dining Room/Cuisine	8.6
Food: Buffets/Informal Dining	8.1
Food: Quality of Ingredients	8.4
Service: Dining Room	8.3
Service: Bars	8.1
Service: Cabins	8.2
Cruise: Sail-Cruise Experience	9.2
Cruise: Activities Program	7.8
Cruise: Hospitality Standard	8.4
OVERALL RATING	125.1

+ Has plenty of deck space under the expanse of sail. Incredibly fine handcrafted interior, with antique furniture, original oil paintings, gorgeous carved oak paneling everywhere. Two owner's suites are lavish, with Chippendale furniture, gilt detailing, a real fireplace, and Italian marble bathrooms.

— Steep interior staircase, as on most sailing vessels.

Dining Elegant dining room (which is also the ship's library) has wood-paneled walls and a wood beam ceiling. Ample space at each table. Excellent Continental food and presentation, although choice limited. Good breakfast and lunch buffets. Wines included with lunch and dinner.

Other Comments The oldest and most beautiful tall ship sailing, and the largest private yacht ever built, constructed of the best materials. Her masts reach as high as a 20-floor building. Originally built for Marjorie Merriweather Post (the American cereal heiress), this lovely working sailing ship is now owned by a consortium of German yachtsmen and chartered to various operators. It is, in a single word, exhilarating. A special ship like no other, for the discerning few to relish the comfort and elegance of a bygone era. This is one of the world's most delightful travel and vacation experiences. I cannot recommend it highly enough.

sy Sir Francis Drake ★★

OPERATES

3 TO 7-DAY UK/US VIRGIN ISLANDS AND CARIBBEAN CRUISES

Cruise Line		Tall Ship Adventures
Former Names		Godewind/Landkirchen
Gross Tonnage		450 DWT
Builder		(Germany)
Original Cost	n/a	Christened By n/a
Entered Service		1917
Interior Design		n/a
Country of Registry		Honduras
Tel No		809-496-0914 (cellular)
Fax No		-
Length (ft/m)		162.4/49.50
Beam (ft/m)	22.9/7.00	Draft (ft/m) 9.1/2.80
Type of Vessel		topsail schooner
No. of Masts		3 (9 manually furled sails)
Sail Area (sq ft/sq m)		1,968/600
Main Propulsion		sail power
Propulsion	diesel	Propellers 1 (FP)
Decks	2	Crew 14
Pass. Capacity (basis 2) 28		(all berths) 30
Pass. Space Ratio (basis 2) 16.0		(all berths) 15.0
Officers	British	Dining Staff International
Total Cabins		14
Size Range (sq ft/m)		n/a
Outside Cabins	14	Inside Cabins 0
Single Cabins	0	Supplement 100%
Balcony Cabins	0	Wheelchair Cabins 0
Cabin Current		110/220 AC
Refrigerator		No

Cabin TV	No	VCR	No
Dining Rooms		1 (open seating)	
Casino	No	Slot Machines	No
Swimming Pools (outside)			0
Whirlpools	0	Gymnasium	No
Sauna/Steam Room	No/No	Massage	No
Self-Service Launderette			No
Library			No
Watersports Facilities			None
Classification Society		Germanischer Lloyd	

RATINGS	SCORE
Ship: Condition/Cleanliness	6.6
Ship: Space/Flow/Comfort	4.6
Ship: Decor/Furnishings	6.1
Ship: Watersports Facilities	3.8
Cabins: Comfort/Facilities	4.4
Cabins: Software	4.7
Food: Dining Room/Cuisine	5.5
Food: Buffets/Informal Dining	5.1
Food: Quality of Ingredients	5.8
Service: Dining Room	6.0
Service: Bars	6.0
Service: Cabins	6.2
Cruise: Sail-Cruise Experience	6.8
Cruise: Activities Program	5.6
Cruise: Hospitality Standard	6.2
OVERALL RATING	83.4

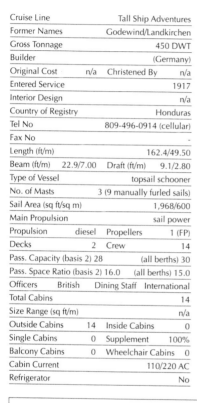

+ Authentic topsail schooner, restored to her original condition, and well appointed. Cozy chairs and benches on deck. More than a windjammer, this tall ship is a treasure for those who don't expect the service finesse offered aboard more contemporary ships. There is much wood paneling, brass fittings, and solid furniture. Cabins have various configurations, and a mixture of beds and upper bunks that are comfortable (for a sailing vessel). Carries snorkeling equipment. Passengers can, and often do, participate in hoisting the sails, but otherwise, there's little to do but relax, and her crew will help you unwind totally.

— Has steep interior stairways, as on most true sailing vessels. Constant music on deck is irritating.

Dining Charming dark-wood paneled dining room with wood-trimmed chairs and picture windows. Cuisine is decidedly casual Americana fare. Little choice for non-meat eaters, although the chef will try to accommodate requests. Food quality is barely adequate, although most passengers seem happy with it.

Other Comments You'll have a relaxing, unhurried vacation, in fairly comfortable but basic surroundings, aboard one of the last tall ships. This is for people who really like sailing ships and the hands-on experience this kind of vessel can provide.

sv Star Clipper ★★★★

OPERATES

*7- AND 14-DAY CARIBBEAN CRUISES
(YEAR-ROUND)*

Cruise Line	Star Clippers
Former Names	- Gross Tonnage 3,025
Builder	Scheepswerven van
	Langerbrugge (Belgium)
Original Cost	$30 million
Christened By	Ms Maria Krafft
Entered Service	May 16, 1992
Interior Design	Struik & Hammerslag
Country of Registry	Luxembourg (LXST)
Tel No 125-3210	Fax No 125-3206
Length (ft/m)	366.1/111.60
Beam (ft/m) 49.2/15.00	Draft (ft/m) 17.7/5.60
Type of Vessel	barkentine schooner
No. of Masts	4 (208 ft)/16 manually furled sails
Sail Area (sq ft/sq m)	36,221/3,365
Main Propulsion	sail power
Propulsion/Propellers	diesel (1,030kW)/1 (CP)
Decks 4 Crew 72	Total Cabins 79
Pass. Capacity (basis 2) 170	(all berths) 182
Pass. Space Ratio (basis 2) 17.7	(all berths) 16.6
Officers European	Dining Staff International
Size Range (sq ft/m)	95-150/8.8-14.0
Outside Cabins 85	Inside Cabins 6
Single Cabins 0	Supplement 50%
Balcony Cabins 0	Wheelchair Cabins 0
Cabin Current	110 AC
Refrigerator	Category 1 cabins only
Cabin TV Yes	VCR No

Dining Rooms		1 (open seating)	
Elevators			0
Casino	No	Slot Machines	No
Swimming Pools (outside)			2
Whirlpools	0	Gymnasium	No
Sauna/Steam Room	No/No	Massage	No
Self-Service Launderette	No	Library	Yes
Watersports Facilities		Waterski boat, sunfish,	
		scuba, snorkel, 8 Zodiacs	
Classification Society		Lloyd's Register	

RATINGS	SCORE
Ship: Condition/Cleanliness	7.3
Ship: Space/Flow/Comfort	7.6
Ship: Decor/Furnishings	7.7
Ship: Watersports Facilities	6.6
Cabins: Comfort/Facilities	7.8
Cabins: Software	7.8
Food: Dining Room/Cuisine	6.3
Food: Buffets/Informal Dining	6.2
Food: Quality of Ingredients	6.4
Service: Dining Room	7.2
Service: Bars	7.1
Service: Cabins	7.2
Cruise: Sail-Cruise Experience	9.1
Cruise: Activities Program	6.8
Cruise: Hospitality Standard	7.3
OVERALL RATING	108.4

+ These true sailing ships with cruise accommodations evoke memories of the 19th-century clipper sailing ships. Accurate four-masted barkentine-rigged vessels have graceful lines, a superbly shaped hull and 63-ft-high (19.3-m) masts and 36,221 sq ft (3,365 m²) of sail. Absolutely breathtaking! Good for watersports lovers, these vessels have excellent sea manners. Sports directors provide basic dive instruction, albeit for a fee. Classic Edwardian nautical decor throughout is clean, warm, intimate and inviting. Paneled library has a fireplace, and chairs that are supremely comfortable. Well-equipped, comfortable, contemporary cabins. No lines. No hassle. "Sailing a Square Rigger" classes are now part of every cruise.

— These ships are not for the physically impaired, nor children. The internal stairs are steep, as in most sailing vessels. There is no room service. Pooled tipping system needs modification.

Dining Charming dining room is used for rather unimaginative buffet breakfasts and luncheons, and a mix of buffet and à la carte dinners. Poor seating arrangement. Cuisine is not gourmet, but is quite creative given the incredibly small galley space.

sv Star Flyer ★★★★

OPERATES

7-DAY EUROPE AND SOUTHEAST ASIA CRUISES

Cruise Line	Star Clippers
Former Names	- Gross Tonnage 3,025
Builder	Sheepswerven van
	Langerbrugge (Belgium)
Original Cost	$25 million
Christened By	Mrs Ann Krafft
Entered Service	Jul 7, 1991
Interior Design	Struik & Hammerslag
Country of Registry	Luxembourg (LXSF)
Tel No 154-6232 Fax No	154-6231
Length (ft/m)	366.1/111.60
Beam (ft/m) 49.2/15.00 Draft (ft/m)	17.7/5.60
Type of Vessel	barkentine schooner
No. of Masts	4 (208 ft)/16 manually furled sails
Sail Area (sq ft/sq m)	36,221/3,365
Main Propulsion	sail power
Propulsion/Propellers	diesel (1,030kW)/1 (CP)
Decks 4 Crew	72
Pass. Capacity (basis 2) 170 (all berths)	182
Pass. Space Ratio (basis 2) 17.7 (all berths)	16.6
Officers European Dining Staff	International
Total Cabins	85
Size Range (sq ft/m)	95-150/8.8-14.0
Outside Cabins 79 Inside Cabins	6
Single Cabins 0 Supplement	50%
Balcony Cabins 0 Wheelchair Cabins	0
Cabin Current 110 AC Refrigerator	All cabins
Cabin TV Yes VCR	No

Dining Rooms	1 (open seating)
Elevators	0
Casino No Slot Machines	No
Swimming Pools (outside)	2
Whirlpools 0 Gymnasium	No
Sauna/Steam Room No/No Massage	No
Self-Service Launderette No Library	Yes
Watersports Facilities Waterski boat, sunfish,	
scuba, snorkel, 8 Zodiacs	
Classification Society	Lloyd's Register

RATINGS	SCORE
Ship: Condition/Cleanliness	7.3
Ship: Space/Flow/Comfort	7.6
Ship: Decor/Furnishings	7.7
Ship: Watersports Facilities	6.6
Cabins: Comfort/Facilities	7.8
Cabins: Software	7.8
Food: Dining Room/Cuisine	6.3
Food: Buffets/Informal Dining	6.2
Food: Quality of Ingredients	6.4
Service: Dining Room	7.2
Service: Bars	7.1
Service: Cabins	7.2
Cruise: Sail-Cruise Experience	9.1
Cruise: Activities Program	6.8
Cruise: Hospitality Standard	7.3
OVERALL RATING	108.4

It would have made more sense to have fewer passenger cabins and more room in the galley to provide a better dining experience than the present arrangement, which makes it very trying for any chef, even if provided with ingredients of a good standard. Dinner is à la carte, with a choice of just two entrees. A pasta dish would be a welcome, and simple, addition. Poor bread rolls, pastry items and fruits.

Tea and coffee should be, but is not, available 24 hours a day, particularly in view of the fact that there is no cabin food service at all. When it is available, only paper cups are provided (they should be real china).

Other Comments The staff are very casual, and often mix in areas that should be reserved for passengers. This is a carefree sailing cruise experience in a totally unstructured setting at a modest price. Take only casual clothes, as you won't need jackets, ties, high-heeled shoes, cocktail dresses, or the slightest hint of formal wear. *Star Clipper* and *Star Flyer* promote total informality. This is recommended for those that don't require much entertainment other than wind and sea.

mys Wind Song ★★★★+

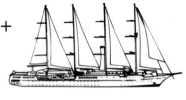

OPERATES

7-DAY FRENCH POLYNESIA CRUISES
(YEAR-ROUND)

Cruise Line	Windstar Cruises
Former Names	- Gross Tonnage 5,703
Builder	Ateliers et Chantiers du Havre (France)
Original Cost	$34.2 million
Christened By	Mrs Nadia Stolt-Nielsen
Entered Service	Jul 24, 1987
Interior Design	Archiform Design/Marc Held
Country of Registry	Bahamas (C6CB2)
Tel No 110-4270	Fax No 110-4271
Length (ft/m)	440.2/134.20
Beam (ft/m) 51.8/15.80	Draft (ft/m) 13.4/4.10
Type of Vessel	computer-controlled sail-cruiser
No. of Masts	4 (204 ft)/6 self-furling sails
Sail Area (sq ft/sq m):	21,489/1,996.4
Main Propulsion	a) engines b) sails
Propulsion	diesel-electric (1,400kW)
Propellers	1 (CP)
Decks 5	Crew 91
Pass. Capacity (basis 2) 148	(all berths) 159
Pass. Space Ratio (basis 2) 38.5	(all berths) 34.1
Officers British	Dining Staff Indonesian/Filipino
Total Cabins	74
Size Range (sq ft/m)	185-220/17.0-20.5
Outside Cabins 74	Inside Cabins 0
Single Cabins 0	Supplement 50-100%
Balcony Cabins 0	Wheelchair Cabins 0
Cabin Current 110 AC	Refrigerator All cabins
Cabin TV Yes	VCR Yes

Dining Rooms			1 (open seating)
Casino	Yes	Slot Machines	Yes
Swimming Pools (outside)			1 (dip pool)
Whirlpools	1	Gymnasium	Yes
Sauna/Steam Room Yes/No		Massage	Yes
Self-Service Launderette No		Library	Yes
Watersports Facilities			Aft marina platform,
kayaks (2), sunfish sailboats (2), windsurf boards,			
waterski boat, scuba, snorkel, Zodiacs (4)			
Classification Society			Bureau Veritas

RATINGS	SCORE
Ship: Condition/Cleanliness	8.2
Ship: Space/Flow/Comfort	7.8
Ship: Decor/Furnishings	8.3
Ship: Watersports Facilities	8.0
Cabins: Comfort/Facilities	8.2
Cabins: Software	8.3
Food: Dining Room/Cuisine	7.4
Food: Buffets/Informal Dining	7.0
Food: Quality of Ingredients	7.2
Service: Dining Room	7.6
Service: Bars	7.7
Service: Cabins	7.8
Cruise: Sail-Cruise Experience	8.1
Cruise: Activities Program	7.4
Cruise: Hospitality Standard	8.1
OVERALL RATING	117.1

+ Beautifully crafted interior with fine, blond woods, together with soft, complementary colors. Adequate open deck and sunning space. Cabins are all-outside one-price suites and come completely equipped. Bathrooms are a neat figure-of-eight shape. Watersports platform at stern. No scheduled activities make this a real relaxing vacation.

— Not much deck space, owing to the complex sail machinery. Constant whine from the ship's engine audible in most cabins. No bathtubs. Tiny dip pool. Ambiance could be warmer. Communication with the crew sometimes proves frustrating. Drinks prices are high.

Dining Charming, elegant dining room, with ocean views from large, picture windows. Creative and attractively presented *nouvelle cuisine*, but not up to the standard of the small luxury ships. Quality of ingredients needs upgrading. Attentive, friendly service throughout, but communication proves frustrating at times. Poor pastry items, breads and fruits.

Other Comments Long, sleek-looking craft that is part yacht, part cruise ship, with four giant masts and computer-controlled sails. One of three identical vessels (the fourth, *Wind Saga*, was never built). It will provide a relaxing, unstructured cruise experience that's just right for seven idyllic nights in sheltered areas. You'd be under sail about 40% of the time (conditions permitting). Gratuities "not required," but they are expected.

mys Wind Spirit ★★★★+

OPERATES

7-DAY CARIBBEAN AND MEDITERRANEAN CRUISES

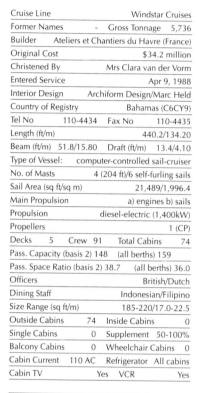

Cruise Line	Windstar Cruises
Former Names - Gross Tonnage	5,736
Builder	Ateliers et Chantiers du Havre (France)
Original Cost	$34.2 million
Christened By	Mrs Clara van der Vorm
Entered Service	Apr 9, 1988
Interior Design	Archiform Design/Marc Held
Country of Registry	Bahamas (C6CY9)
Tel No 110-4434 Fax No	110-4435
Length (ft/m)	440.2/134.20
Beam (ft/m) 51.8/15.80 Draft (ft/m)	13.4/4.10
Type of Vessel:	computer-controlled sail-cruiser
No. of Masts	4 (204 ft)/6 self-furling sails
Sail Area (sq ft/sq m)	21,489/1,996.4
Main Propulsion	a) engines b) sails
Propulsion	diesel-electric (1,400kW)
Propellers	1 (CP)
Decks 5 Crew 91 Total Cabins	74
Pass. Capacity (basis 2) 148 (all berths)	159
Pass. Space Ratio (basis 2) 38.7 (all berths)	36.0
Officers	British/Dutch
Dining Staff	Indonesian/Filipino
Size Range (sq ft/m)	185-220/17.0-22.5
Outside Cabins 74 Inside Cabins	0
Single Cabins 0 Supplement	50-100%
Balcony Cabins 0 Wheelchair Cabins	0
Cabin Current 110 AC Refrigerator	All cabins
Cabin TV Yes VCR	Yes

Dining Rooms		1 (open seating)	
Casino Yes	Slot Machines	Yes	
Swimming Pools (outside)		1 (dip pool)	
Whirlpools 1	Gymnasium	Yes	
Sauna/Steam Room Yes/No	Massage	Yes	
Self-Service Launderette No	Library	Yes	
Watersports Facilities	Aft marina platform,		
kayaks (2), windsurf boards (2), sunfish sailboats			
(2), water ski boat, scuba, snorkel, zodiacs (4)			
Classification Society	Bureau Veritas		

RATINGS	SCORE
Ship: Condition/Cleanliness	8.2
Ship: Space/Flow/Comfort	7.8
Ship: Decor/Furnishings	8.3
Ship: Watersports Facilities	8.0
Cabins: Comfort/Facilities	8.2
Cabins: Software	8.3
Food: Dining Room/Cuisine	7.4
Food: Buffets/Informal Dining	7.0
Food: Quality of Ingredients	7.2
Service: Dining Room	7.6
Service: Bars	7.7
Service: Cabins	7.8
Cruise: Sail-Cruise Experience	8.1
Cruise: Activities Program	7.4
Cruise: Hospitality Standard	8.1
OVERALL RATING	117.1

+ Nicely crafted, elegant nautical-themed interior. Light woods used throughout. No lines, no hassle. Outdoor deck space quite good unless full. All-outside suites are one price, well appointed, with a CD player and two portholes. Elegant main lounge, with crisp, stark colors. Good indoor-outdoor eatery. Recommended for watersports fans. Unstructured living at sea.

— Constant whine from the ship's generator audible in most cabins. Not much deck space, owing to the complex sail machinery. No bathtubs in cabins. Tiny "dip" pool. Interior colors a little cold. Communication with Indonesian crew sometimes frustrating. High drinks prices.

Dining Charming, elegant dining room, with ocean views from large, picture windows. Creative and attractively presented *nouvelle cuisine*, but not up to the standard of the small luxury ships. Quality of ingredients needs upgrading. Attentive, friendly service throughout, but communication proves frustrating at times. Poor pastry items.

Other Comments Sister to *Wind Song/Wind Spirit*. Part yacht, part cruise ship, with four giant masts and computer-controlled sails. While novel, it is definitely not *Sea Goddess*. The staff are very casual. This sail-cruise ship will provide you with relaxed, fairly refined surroundings, and cocoon you with seven nights of unstructured living, but only partly under sail. Gratuities are "not required," but they are expected.

mys Wind Star ★★★★+

OPERATES

*7-DAY CARIBBEAN AND
EUROPE CRUISES*

Cruise Line		Windstar Cruises	
Former Names	-	Gross Tonnage	5,703
Builder	Ateliers et Chantiers du Havre (France)		
Original Cost		$34.2 million	
Christened By		Mrs Louise Andren	
Entered Service		Dec 13, 1986	
Interior Design		Archiform Design/Marc Held	
Country of Registry		Bahamas (C6CA9)	
Tel No	110-4266	Fax No	110-4267
Length (ft/m)		440.2/134.20	
Beam (ft/m) 51.8/15.80	Draft (ft/m)	13.4/4.10	
Type of Vessel	computer-controlled sail-cruiser		
No. of Masts	4 (204 ft)/6 self-furling sails		
Sail Area (sq ft/sq m)		21,489/1,996.4	
Main Propulsion		a) engines b) sails	
Propulsion	diesel-electric (1,400kW)		
Propellers		1 (CP)	
Decks	5	Crew	91
Pass. Capacity (basis 2) 148		(all berths) 167	
Pass. Space Ratio (basis 2) 38.5		(all berths) 34.1	
Officers British	Dining Staff Indonesian/Filipino		
Total Cabins		74	
Size Range (sq ft/m)		185-220/17.0-22.5	
Outside Cabins	74	Inside Cabins	0
Single Cabins	0	Supplement	50-100%
Balcony Cabins	0	Wheelchair Cabins	0
Cabin Current	110 AC	Refrigerator	All cabins
Cabin TV	Yes	VCR	Yes

Dining Rooms		1 (open seating)	
Casino	Yes	Slot Machines	Yes
Swimming Pools (outside)		1 (dip pool)	
Whirlpools	1	Gymnasium	Yes
Sauna/Steam Room Yes/No		Massage	Yes
Self-Service Launderette No		Library	Yes
Watersports Facilities		Aft marina platform,	
kayaks (2), windsurf boards (2), sunfish sailboats			
(2), water ski boat, scuba, snorkel, Zodiacs (4)			
Classification Society		Bureau Veritas	

RATINGS	SCORE
Ship: Condition/Cleanliness	8.2
Ship: Space/Flow/Comfort	7.8
Ship: Decor/Furnishings	8.3
Ship: Watersports Facilities	8.0
Cabins: Comfort/Facilities	8.2
Cabins: Software	8.3
Food: Dining Room/Cuisine	7.4
Food: Buffets/Informal Dining	7.0
Food: Quality of Ingredients	7.2
Service: Dining Room	7.6
Service: Bars	7.7
Service: Cabins	7.8
Cruise: Sail-Cruise Experience	8.1
Cruise: Activities Program	7.4
Cruise: Hospitality Standard	8.1
OVERALL RATING	117.1

+ Elegant, high-quality interior is beautifully crafted. Light woods used extensively. No lines, no hassle. Outdoor deck space quite good. All-outside suites are one price, well appointed and finished, with two portholes and even a CD player. Lots of wood trim everywhere. Elegant main lounge, with crisp, but stark colors. Recommended for watersports fans.

— Constant whine from the ship's engine audible in most cabins. No bathtubs in cabins. There's not much deck space, owing to complex sail machinery. Tiny pool. Interior colors a little cold. Communication with Indonesian crew often frustrating. High beverage prices.

Dining Charming, elegant dining room, with ocean views from large, picture windows. Creative and attractively presented *nouvelle cuisine*, but not up to the standard of the small luxury ships. The quality of ingredients should be upgraded. Attentive, friendly service throughout, but communication often proves frustrating. Poor pastry items, breads and fruits.

Other Comments One of three identical sisters that is part yacht, part cruise ship, this high-tech vessel has four tall masts with computer-controlled sails. She's a very comfortable ship throughout, and, with emphasis on refined privacy, will provide you with a very relaxing, casual cruise experience, but only partly under sail. Gratuities are "not required," but they are expected.

APPENDIXES

The Cruise Industry: Milestones (1960–1996)

1960

◤ Passenger shipping directories listed more than 30 ships operating transatlantic voyages for the better part of each year. Many ships were laid up in the ten-year period 1960–1970, and most were sold for a fraction of their value (or building cost). Most passenger lines simply went out of business or tried to survive by mixing transatlantic crossings with voyages south in search of the sun, which proved difficult for those without sufficient air-conditioning systems.

1961

◤ Sun Line Cruises was founded by the late Charalambos A. Keusseouglou, who began his career at Home Lines, the immigrant carrier. He died in 1984, aged 64, after a 37-year cruise industry career.

1962

◤ The Compagnie Générale Transatlantique's ss *France*, at 1,035 feet the world's longest passenger ship ever built, entered service between Le Havre and New York, in spite of the growing competition from the airlines.

1963

◤ Cunard Line's *RMS Queen Elizabeth* made an experimental cruise from New York to the West Indies, which met with great success. This led to her being fitted with full air conditioning in a 1965/66 refit, as well as to more extensive cruising activities.

1965

◤ P&O obtained the remaining shares of the Orient Steam Navigation Company. The new company became known as the Peninsular & Oriental Steam Navigation Company.

◤ Princess Cruises was founded by Seattle entrepreneur and industrialist Stanley B. McDonald.

◤ Sitmar Cruises started cruise operations from Sydney, Australia.

1966

◤ The Norwegian company, Klosters Reederei, formed a partnership with Miami businessman Ted Arison to market Caribbean cruises from Miami. Kloster provided the ship and Arison provided the passengers.

◤ Commodore Cruise Line was founded by Sanford Chobol, and a single ship, *Boheme* (now *Freewinds*).

1967

◤ Cunard announced the imminent withdrawal of both *Queen Mary* and *Queen Elizabeth*. *Queen Mary* was withdrawn from service on September 26 after completing 1,001 transatlantic crossings. She was sold to the City of Long Beach, California. She left Southampton on October 31, 1967 and has been in Long Beach been ever since she arrived.

1968

🛥 Cunard's *Queen Elizabeth* (at 83,673-grt, the world's largest ever passenger ship) was withdrawn from service in October. She had steamed a total of 3,472,672 miles and carried a total of 2,311,324 passengers (1,500,000 in peacetime, 811,324 in wartime) during her career.

🛥 Cunard Line refused delivery of the new *Queen Elizabeth 2* from her builders, John Brown, in December, owing to unacceptable turbine vibration levels. Repairs led to a five-month delay on her maiden transatlantic sailing to New York.

🛥 Boise Cascade bought Princess Cruises from its founder, Stanley B. McDonald, who re-purchased the line two years later.

1969

🛥 Lars-Eric Lindblad's *Lindblad Explorer* was launched expressly for close-in expedition cruising.

🛥 Royal Caribbean Cruise Line was founded January 31 by a consortium of Norwegian shipping companies, Gotaas-Larsen (actually it was American-owned), I.M. Skaugen, and Anders Wilhelmsen, and formally incorporated as Royal Caribbean Cruise Line A/S in Oslo. Edwin Stephan, who provided the initial concept and wisdom, was made President, and set up the Miami marketing arm of the company, which, at the end of 1968, ordered two new sister ships for delivery in 1970 and 1971.

🛥 The liner *United States* was laid up in November following a strike against the ship by the militant seamen's union, and the fact that the U.S. Government no longer wanted to subsidize the loss-making ship (which cost $118.8 million between 1955 and 1969).

1970

🛥 Royal Viking Line was founded by a consortium of three partners (Bergen Line, A.F. Klaveness, and Nordenfjeldske) who each contributed one ship (*Royal Viking Sea, Royal Viking Sky, Royal Viking Star*).

🛥 Germany's Norddeutscher Lloyd and Hapag (Hamburg American Line) merged on September 1. They chose the new name of Hapag-Lloyd.

1971

🛥 Cunard Line was sold to Trafalgar House Investments.

1972

🛥 Carnival Cruise Lines was formed by Ted Arison, following a disagreement with Knut Kloster, when both worked for Kloster's Norwegian Cruise Lines. After unsuccessfully trying to purchase Cunard's *Carmania* and *Franconia*, he learned of the availability of the *Empress of Canada*. The new company, funded by and operated as a subsidiary of the Boston-based American International Travel Service, Inc. (AITS). The company thus started with just one ship, the *Mardi Gras* (ex-*Empress of Canada*). After a poor start (*Mardi Gras* ran aground on its first voyage, and competing company's ships even named a drink after her, called "Mardi Gras on the Rocks"), the company went from strength to strength, under Arison's aggressive direction, and went on to become the biggest success story of the contemporary cruise industry.

1973

🚢 Holland America Line withdrew sister ships *Veendam* and *Volendam* from service and laid them up, owing to the abundance of other cruise ships, high operating costs, a fall in the value of the U.S. Dollar, and a dramatic rise in fuel costs. The ships were placed under charter to Monarch Cruise Lines in 1976 for the sum of $5,000 each per day (*Veendam* became *Monarch Star*, *Volendam* became *Monarch Sun*). The Dutch-flag ships were re-registered in Panama and staffed by a multinational crew.

🚢 Sitmar Cruises began operations from the Port of Sydney, Australia, with a single ship, the *Fairstar*, a converted troop carrier formerly operated by Bibby Line.

🚢 Deutsche Atlantik Line suspended operations, following financial difficulty. The company's *Hanseatic*, in service for only four years, was laid-up at Hamburg. In December, the intended sale of the ship to Ryutsu Kaiun KK of Japan for $25 million failed to materialize. She was instead sold to Robin International Corporation, New York, acting as buyers for the Black Sea Shipping Company of Odessa. The ship was renamed *Maxim Gorkiy* and is still in service for Phoenix Seereisen, catering to German-speaking passengers.

1974

🚢 P&O purchased Princess Cruises from its founder, Stanley B. McDonald, during the summer.

🚢 In July, the Compagnie Générale Transatlantique announced that after only 12 years of service, the ss *France* was to be withdrawn from

service with effect from October 25. The reason was that she was losing money, and was being subsidized by the French government to the tune of $12 million a year. As the ship was about to berth in Le Havre on September 12, angry French trade unionists took over the ship from its officers and anchored her in the entrance channel, in protest to the impending loss of jobs. Passengers disembarked by tender. The ship was able to dock on October 9 and was laid-up.

🚢 Royal Cruise Lines' first ship, *Golden Odyssey*, purpose-built to accommodate the equivalent passenger load of a Boeing 747 aircraft (425 passengers) was introduced. The company, which was founded by Pericles S. Panagopoulos in 1971, attracted a loyal U.S. west coast following, gained mainly by direct marketing methods.

1975

🚢 Princess Cruises' *Island Princess* and *Pacific Princess* become the "stars" in the American television show *The Love Boat*.

1977

🚢 World Explorer Cruises was founded and entered the cruise industry with one ship, the *Universe*.

🚢 Princess Grace of Monaco christened the *Cunard Princess* at the Passenger Ship Terminal in March, the first time a passenger ship christening had taken place in the Port of New York.

🚢 Union-Castle/Safmarine, the South Africa-based shipping company, ceased passenger operations when its last vessel, the *S.A. Vaal*, was sold to Carnival Cruise Lines in April.

Holland America Line announced it would take over the entire operation of Monarch Cruise Lines Inc. The two Monarch ships were handed back to Holland America Line in January, 1978.

1978

United States Cruises was formed by Mr Richard Hadley, who paid $5 million for the liner *United States*.

After an unsuccessful June 30 cruise from New York for new owners Venture Cruise Lines (also called America Cruise Lines), the *America* (ex-*Australis*) was arrested for debt and auctioned on August 28. Her previous owners, the Chandris Group, re-purchased the ship and renamed her *Italis*.

Royal Caribbean Cruise Line's *Song of Norway* was lengthened at the Wartsila shipyard in Helsinki. The *Nordic Prince* was lengthened at the same shipyard (March-June, 1980).

1979

American Hawaii Cruises was formed. Jimmy Carter, then President of the United States, signed a bill re-documenting the *Independence* under the U.S.-flag. The new company began cruise operations on June 21, 1980, with the *Independence*, joined by sister ship *Constitution* in 1982.

Special Expeditions founded by Sven-Olof Lindblad, son of Lars-Eric Lindblad, to provide expedition cruise vacations to little-visited destinations.

Society Expeditions formed by a group of German investors under sole stockholder T.C. Schwartz, to manage and operate the adventure/expedition cruises of *World Discoverer*.

The *France* was purchased by Lauritz Kloster in June. The ship was taken to Bremerhaven and rebuilt for the Caribbean cruise trade by Hapag-Lloyd at Bremerhaven. She was renamed *Norway*, and transferred to the ownership of Norwegian Caribbean Lines in September, 1984.

1980

Sea Goddess Cruises was founded by Helge Naarstad. The first of two twin vessels, *Sea Goddess I* was delivered four years later, in 1984.

Denmark's DFDS (United Steamship Company) founded Scandinavian World Cruises to operate one-day cruises from Miami (the company subsequently became SeaEscape).

The International Organization of Masters, Mates and Pilots formed a joint venture company with Aloha Pacific Cruises. The company purchased the *Monterey* (the last U.S.-flag ship that qualified under the Jones Act to operate between American ports) for intended cruise service in Tahiti. The purchase went through in 1981. The union poured $5.7 million into the ship, for upkeep alone, between 1981 and 1986.

After a planned merger with Royal Viking Line failed in May, Norwegian America Cruises (formerly Norwegian America Line) was formed to manage *Sagafjord* and *Vistafjord*.

1981

Astor Cruises was formed in the UK, and began operations with a single ship, the *Astor* (now *Arkona*).

Royal Viking Star lengthened in the A.G. Weser shipyard in Bremerhaven, Germany. Sister ships *Sky* and

Sea were lengthened by the same shipyard (in 1982 and 1983 respectively).

1982

The British government chartered Cunard's *Queen Elizabeth 2* for use as a troop carrier for the famous Ghurka Regiment, among others, during the Falklands War between Argentina and Britain, at a rate of $225,000 per day. The ship eluded an Argentinean submarine sent to destroy it, due to the submarine's ineffectiveness in the icebergs close to the Falklands, and the speed of the *QE2*. The government also chartered P&O Cruises' *Canberra* for use as a troopship (sailed from Southampton April 9, returned to Southampton July 11, and returned to passenger service in September), as well as B&I Line's *Uganda*, used as a hospital ship. All three ships performed well.

Lindblad Travel, the company founded by Lars-Eric Lindblad in 1969, sold its *Lindblad Explorer*, and the rights to the Lindblad name, to Salen-Lindblad Cruising.

1983

Clipper Cruise Line (a completely American cruise company) was founded by Barney Ebsworth, in St. Louis.

Holland America Line ceased operating its lucrative New York-Bermuda sailings. The company moved its headquarters from New York to Seattle.

Ocean Cruise Lines was founded by British entrepreneur Gerry Herrod, as an offshoot of Travellers, Europe's largest tour operator for Americans abroad.

P&O appointed Jeffrey Sterling as chairman in order to fend off a takeover bid by Trafalgar House Investments, owners of Cunard Line.

Premier Cruise Lines was co-founded by Bruce Nierenburg and Bjornar Hermansen, both former executives of Norwegian Cruise Lines.

The B&I's *Uganda* was taken over by the British Ministry of Defence in January for two years for service between Ascension and the Falkland Islands. This marked the end of passenger service for the British and India Steam Navigation Company.

Cunard's parent company, Trafalgar House, purchased Norwegian America Cruises (NAC) in May, together with *Sagafjord* and *Vistafjord*.

Salen-Lindblad Cruising's *Lindblad Explorer* became the first passenger ship to successfully navigate the Northwest Passage (in September), sailing 4,790 miles from Saint John's, Newfoundland to Point Barrow, Alaska. The 41-day cruise, begun on August 20, finished in Yokohama, Japan, on September 29. When the ship reached Point Barrow, the champagne flowed, and beards were shaved off (the crew had all vowed not to shave until that point). Lars Wikander provided the idea and planning.

1984

Sundance Cruises, founded by Stanley B. McDonald, entered the industry with a single ship, *Sundancer*.

Carnival Cruise Line launched a $10 million television advertising campaign—the largest ever in the cruise industry. Two different 30-second spots were aired a total of 133 times in the U.S.A.

474

An American investor group headed by J.H. Whitney & Company signed an agreement in principle in May for the purchase of Royal Viking Line and its three ships for $240 million. The sale did not go through, and Royal Viking Line was purchased by Kloster Cruise Limited, Oslo.

Regency Cruises was founded by William Schanz and Fred Mayer. The new company completed its initial public stock offering in June 1985, and commenced operations with a single ship, *Regent Sea*, in November.

Windstar Sail Cruises was founded in December by Karl Andren and Jacob Stolt-Nielsen to build and operate a fleet of three sail-cruise ships originally designed by Kai Levander, then of Wartsila shipyard in Helsinki, Finland. Andren intended to re-launch the age of commercial sail.

Dolphin Cruise Line was founded by Peter Bulgarides and Paris Katsoufis (but actually owned by Ulysses Shipping, Piraeus).

Premier Cruise Lines, owned by the Greyhound-Dial Corporation, entered the industry with its first ship.

1985

The Chandris Group of Companies acquired Fantasy Cruises from GoGo Tours. Fantasy Cruises became known as Chandris Fantasy Cruises in the U.S.A., and Chandris Cruises in the U.K.

The first sailing ship designed for crewing by physically disabled passengers was launched at Wivenhoe, Essex on October 15. The sts *Lord Nelson*, owned by the Jubilee Sailing Trust, was named at Southampton, England, on May 9, 1986.

1986

Signet Cruise Line was founded in Norway by an investment group headed by Atle Brynestad. Owing to a lawsuit brought by an American who claimed the right to the name Signet, the company changed its name to Seabourn Cruise Line. The company's first ship, *Seabourn Pride*, entered service in December, 1988.

Eastern Cruise Lines, Western Cruise Lines, and Sundance Cruises were merged into one unit, called Admiral Cruises.

Diamond Cruise Ltd. was founded in Helsinki, Finland, by Captain Offe Nyblin and his partner Christian Aspegren. They were to take delivery of *Radisson Diamond*, a semi-submersible twin-hulled vessel.

Cunard acquired Sea Goddess Cruises, together with the *Sea Goddess I* and *Sea Goddess II*, through a complex financial and management package negotiated with Norske Cruise A/S, whose 138 shareholders provided the funding for the construction and introduction of the new luxury yacht-ship concept.

1987

Carnival Cruise Lines made its first public stock offering.

Cunard's *QE2* was converted from steam turbine to diesel-electric power. It was the largest ever conversion in maritime history.

Society Expeditions purchased by German businessman Heiko Klein, chairman of Discoverer Reederei, which owns the vessels marketed and operated by Society Expeditions.

Kockums, the Swedish shipyard, ceased shipbuilding operations

after the delivery of twin cruise ships for Carnival Cruise Lines, *Celebration* (1987) and *Jubilee* (1986).

🚢 Bahama Cruise Line changed its name to Bermuda Star Line.

🚢 Ocean Cruise Lines merged with Pearl Cruises.

🚢 The United States Public Health Service (USPH) resumed ship inspections January 1 (after being halted in May, 1986).

🚢 Holland America Line acquired a 50% share in Windstar Sail Cruises, in March.

🚢 Norwegian Caribbean Lines changed its name and logo (though not its initials: NCL) to Norwegian Cruise Line.

1988

🚢 Commodore Cruise Lines sold its *Boheme* to the Church of Scientology. The ship was renamed *Freewinds*.

🚢 Crystal Cruises was formed as a wholly-owned company of Nippon Yusen Kaisha (NYK) of Japan, the world's largest shipping company. The company's first ship, *Crystal Harmony* entered service in July, 1990.

🚢 The three owning partners of Royal Caribbean Cruise Line (Gotaas-Larsen, I.M. Skaugen, Anders Wilhelmsen) decided, in March, to merge RCCL with the Gataas-Larsen-dominated Admiral Cruises (the Swedish company Axel Johnson group and the Finnish EFFOA group held 49%). Named Royal Admiral Cruises (later renamed Royal Caribbean Cruises) the new group was owned 36% by Gotaas-Larsen, and 28% each by Skaugen and Wilhelmsen, while Johnson/EFFOA held the remaining 8% of stock.

🚢 Home Lines ceased operations in April. Its two ships, A*tlantic* (1984) and *Homeric* (1986) were purchased by Holland America Line. The *Atlantic* was subsequently placed under long-term charter to Premier Cruise Lines.

🚢 Effjohn International purchased Bermuda Star Line in May for $17 million. Included in the deal were the *Bermuda Star, Queen of Bermuda* and *Veracruz I*. The company was renamed BSL Cruises, Inc.

🚢 Sitmar Cruises (Societa Italiana Trasporti Marittimi), founded in 1938 by Alexandre Vlasov, was purchased by Princess Cruises (part of the P&O Group) for $210 million.

🚢 Carnival Cruise Lines' negotiations with Gotaas-Larsen to purchase its share in Royal Caribbean Cruise Line for $260 million came to light in August, following RCCL's administration moved from Oslo to Miami. At first, I.M. Skaugen and Wilhelmsen tried to pre-empt the Carnival offer. Later, Skaugen accepted a similar offer from Carnival. Wilhelmsen, the remaining partner in RCCL (28 per cent), pre-empted the Carnival offer of $567 million by going 50/50 with the Hyatt Hotel group of companies, owned by the Pritzker family of Chicago. The new joint owners paid the agreed amount five days before the deadline date of October 5th.

🚢 Holland America Line completed the purchase of Windstar Sail Cruises in March. Carnival Cruise Lines acquired Holland America Line in November, including its land-based hotel/transport operations, and Windstar Cruises, for $625 million, plus liabilities that pushed the purchase price effectively to $900 million.

1989

Ⓐ The Chandris Group of Companies announced the creation of a new company, Celebrity Cruises, which promptly set about ordering two new cruise ships, to be named *Horizon* and *Zenith*, from Meyer Werft shipyard in Papenburg, Germany. The company also announced plans for the conversion of the *Galileo* into the *Meridian*, at the Lloyd Werft shipyard in Bremerhaven, Germany.

Ⓐ Meyer Werft, Papenburg, Germany, became the first shipyard to conduct a "chop and stretch" operation on a major cruise vessel in drydock when the *Westerdam* (ex-*Homeric*) was lengthened in the same building shed as the *Horizon*, under construction for Celebrity Cruises.

Ⓐ Renaissance Cruises was formed by Fearnley & Eger, the 120-year-old, Oslo-based shipping concern.

Ⓐ Showa Line entered the cruise passenger market in Japan for the first time in 60 years with the introduction of its *Oceanic Grace*.

Ⓐ Mitsui OSK Line entered the cruise market in Japan for the first time in 50 years with its 23,340-grt, 600-passenger *Fuji Maru*.

Ⓐ The Panama Canal is now 75 years old.

Ⓐ Aloha Pacific Cruises went into bankruptcy just six months after start-up. The company's single ship, the *Monterey*, was put up for sale.

Ⓐ Wartsila Industries, Helsinki, Finland, one of the most famous and prestigious builders of cruise ships, collapsed in a tangle of financial problems. It was re-organized as Masa-Yards and is presently owned by Kvaerner of Norway.

1990

Ⓐ Ocean Cruise Lines was acquired by Croisières Paquet, itself owned by the French giant Accor leisure company.

Ⓐ Japan Cruise Line entered the cruise passenger market in Japan with its newbuild 21,906-grt, 606-passenger *Orient Venus*.

Ⓐ Aloha Pacific Cruises' *Monterey* was purchased by the Mediterranean Shipping Company, who chartered same to StarLauro Cruises.

Ⓐ Chandris Cruises introduced its new premium grade Celebrity Cruises product in April with the debut of the reconstructed *Meridian* and the brand new *Horizon*.

Ⓐ Delfin Cruises, established only one year earlier, ceased operations.

Ⓐ At the start of the Persian Gulf War, the U.S. Government chartered the *Cunard Princess* for six months as a rest and relaxation center for U.S. service personnel. The ship was docked in Bahrain for the $31 million charter.

1991

Ⓐ EffJohn International, parent company of Commodore Cruise Lines, purchased Bermuda Star Line, together with its two ships, *Enchanted Isle* and *Enchanted Seas*.

Ⓐ Carnival Cruise Lines acquired a 25% stake in Seabourn Cruise Line.

Ⓐ The Soviet cruise fleet was divided into its constituent parts: Baltic Shipping Company (Russia), Black Sea Shipping Company (Ukraine), Estonian Shipping Company (Estonia), Far East Shipping Company (Russia).

Ⓐ In March, Fearnley & Eger, owner of Renaissance Cruises,

announced voluntary liquidation and protection from its creditors under Chapter 11 of the U.S. Bankruptcy Code. Renaissance Cruises was sold to a new investment group consisting of the Cameli Group, controlled by Sebastiano Cameli (Italy), and Luxury Liners, Ltd., a holding company involving Norwegian shipowner Jorgen Jahre, and controlled by Edward B. Rudner in the U.S.A.

Effjohn International purchased the rights to the name Crown Cruise Line.

Seawind Cruise Line commenced cruise operations with its single ship, the *Seawind Crown* (ex-*Vasco da Gama*), following a 70%/30% interest purchase in the company by Swedish concern Nordisk, and Arcalia Shipping, Lisbon.

Nippon Yusen Kaisha (NYK) purchased the expedition cruise company Salen Lindblad Cruising.

Nippon Yusen Kaisha (NYK) Cruises introduced the *Asuka*, the first cruise vessel to have been specifically designed for Japanese passengers.

New York-based Overseas Shipholding Group agreed to lend Kloster Cruise $175 million in exchange for a 50% stake in the company. The offer was later withdrawn.

1992

Society Expeditions ceased operation. Its two expedition vessels, *Society Explorer* and *World Discoverer* were placed on the sale/charter books.

Costa Cruise Lines introduced its new Euro-Luxe cruise concept with the debut of the *CostaClassica*.

Admiral Cruises ceased operations. The company's two vessels,

Azure Seas and *Emerald Seas* were sold to other interests (Dolphin Cruise Line, SunFest Cruises, respectively), at $3.9 million for both.

Some 16 cruise ships were chartered for use as accommodation vessels in Barcelona for the 1992 Olympic Games (July 24-August 9). The ships: *Berlin, Club Med I, Crown Jewel, Crystal Harmony, Cunard Princess, Daphne, Golden Odyssey, Royal Majesty, Royal Viking Sun, Sally Albatross, Sea Cloud, Sea Goddess II, Seabourn Spirit, Star Clipper, Star Flyer, Vistafjord.*

Hurricane Andrew hit the south Miami area. Carnival Cruise Lines, with 600 of its staff made homeless, deployed the *Mardi Gras* for use as an accommodation ship.

The cruise division of The Chandris Group of Companies and Overseas Shipholding Group (OSG) signed an agreement on October 21 to form a joint venture company, to be called Celebrity Cruise Lines, Inc. The deal involved Chandris supplying the three ships of Celebrity Cruises, plus the three ships of Fantasy Cruises, while OSG put up $220 million cash, with Chandris holding a 51% interest.

Chargeurs and Accor, the French property and leisure industries group that own Paquet Cruises and Ocean Cruise Lines, purchased a 23 per cent stake in Costa Crociere, the parent company of Costa Cruises, through a rights issue worth Lire 80 billion ($60 million). The Costa family's stake in Costa Crociere was reduced from 40 to 31 per cent.

1993

In January, Carnival Cruise Lines announced a new subsidiary,

FiestaMarina Cruises, specifically for the Spanish-speaking Latin American marketplace. The company's ship, *FiestaMarina* (ex-*Carnivale*), would commence operations October 22 from San Juan.

Cunard and Effjohn announced a joint venture, good for 10 years, and created Cunard Crown Cruises.

American Family Cruises was announced by Bruce Nierenberg. The new company would initially use two Costa ships (*CostaRiviera* and *Eugenio-Costa*). Only the *CostaRiviera* was converted into the *American Adventure*.

In May, Rainbow Cruises purchased all the stock of Regency Cruises. Both companies were merged under the name Regency Cruises.

American Hawaii Cruises' secured lenders forced the line into involuntary bankruptcy in federal court in Honolulu. The company was subsequently purchased by the Delta Queen Steamboat Company.

Festival Cruises was founded by George Poulides and George Zoros, who re-acquired *The Azur*, on charter to Chandris Fantasy Cruises.

Kloster Cruise Ltd. signed a letter of intent to sell Royal Cruise Line and Royal Viking Line to ASA Investors, Inc. The purchase price for the two lines was to be $565 million. Royal Cruise Line ships: *Crown Odyssey*, *Royal Odyssey* and *Star Odyssey* (the *Golden Odyssey* was not included in the deal). Royal Viking Line ships: *Royal Viking Queen* and *Royal Viking Sun*. The deal was expected to be finalized in the spring of 1994, but did not go through, the investment group concluding that there was not enough profit potential.

1994

Delta Queen Steamboat Company changed its corporate name to American Classic Voyages Company. The company owns American Hawaii Cruises and the Delta Queen Steamboat Company.

Festival Cruises started operations with one ship.

Trafalgar House, Cunard's parent company, signed an agreement to purchase, for $170 million, the rights to the name Royal Viking Line, together with the *Royal Viking Sun*. The *Royal Viking Queen*, not part of the agreement, would go to Royal Cruise Line, to be renamed *Queen Odyssey*, on 1 January 1995.

In September, American Family Cruises ceased operations. The company's single ship, the *American Adventure*, was returned to the Costa Cruises fleet, to be renamed *CostaRiviera*.

In September, FiestaMarina Cruises, a division of the Carnival Corporation, ceased operations.

Cycladic Cruises, based in Greece, ceased operations.

1995

British company Airtours Cruises purchased the Southward from (Norwegian Cruise Line) and the *Nordic Prince* (Royal Caribbean Cruises) late last year, and commenced operations in March, 1995.

Commodore Cruise Line was sold to International Cruise Finance Ltd., and renamed New Commodore Cruise Line.

Royal Venture Cruise Line was formed. The company would be using the *Gruziya* (now *Royal Venture*) and *Ukraine* (now *Sea Venture*).

479

NEW OCEAN-GOING SHIPS TO DEBUT: 1996/1997/1998

Debut Date	Cruise Line	Name of Ship	Tonnage	Cost ($m)	Length (ft)	Cabins	Builder
March 1996	Carnival Cruise Line	Inspiration	70,367	270	864.80	1,020	Kvaerner-Masa Yards (Finland)
March 1996	Royal Caribbean Cruises	Splendour of the Seas	70,950	325	867.00	902	Chantiers de l'Atlantique (France)
May 1996	Costa Cruises	CostaVictoria	74,000	350	817.50	975	Bremer Vulkan Werft (Germany)
May 1996	Holland America Line	Veendam	55,451	225	715.20	625	Fincantieri (Italy)
June 1996	Deutsche Seereederei	Aida I	38,600	180	633.20	594	Kvaerner Masa-Yards (Finland)
August 1996	Carnival Cruise Lines	Carnival Destiny	100,000	400	882.60	1,321	Fincantieri (Italy)
November 1996	Celebrity Cruises	Galaxy	73,850	320	852.00	900	Meyer Werft (Germany)
November 1996	Royal Caribbean Cruises	Grandeur of the Seas	73,600	300	915.20	977	Kvaerner-Masa Yards (Finland)
Winter 1996	Regency Cruises	Regent Sky	50,000	170	726.70	700	Avlis Shipyards (Greece)
February 1997	Deutsche Seereederei	Aida II	38,600	180	633.20	594	Kvaerner Masa-Yards (Finland)
April 1997	Royal Caribbean Cruises	Rhapsody of the Seas	75,000	275	834.00	1,000	Chantiers de l'Atlantique (France)
May 1997	Princess Cruises	Dawn Princess	77,000	300	856.00	1,050	Fincantieri (Italy)
June 1997	Costa Cruises	n/a	78,000	350	837.50	1,050	Bremer Vulkan (Germany)
September 1997	Holland America Line	Rotterdam	62,000	300		660	Fincantieri (Italy)
September 1997	Royal Caribbean Cruises	Enchantment of the Seas	73,600	300	915.20	977	Kvaerner-Masa Yards (Finland)
October 1997	Princess Cruises	Grand Princess	104,000	385	935.00	1,300	Fincantieri (Italy)
November 1997	Celebrity Cruises	Constellation	73,850	320	852.00	900	Meyer Werft (Germany)
December 1997	Carnival Cruise Lines	n/a	70,367	300	864.80	1,020	Kvaerner-Masa Yards (Finland)
January 1998	Disney Cruise Lines	n/a	85,000	325	718.50	1,200	Fincantieri (Italy)
February 1998	Carnival Cruise Lines	n/a	70,367	300	864.80	1,020	Kvaerner Masa-Yards (Finland)
April 1998	Royal Caribbean Cruises	Vision of the Seas	75,000	275	915.20	1,000	Chantiers de l'Atlantique (France)
November 1998	Carnival Cruise Lines	n/a	70,367	300	864.80	1,020	Kvaerner Masa-Yards (Finland)